The
Nature
and
Conditions
of
Learning

THE
NATURE
AND
CONDITIONS
OF
LEARNING

third edition

Ralph Garry

The Ontario Institute for Studies in Education

Howard L. Kingsley

Prentice-Hall, Inc.
Englewood Cliffs, New Jersey

PRENTICE-HALL INTERNATIONAL, INC.
London
PRENTICE-HALL OF AUSTRALIA, PTY. LTD.
Sydney
PRENTICE-HALL OF CANADA, LTD.
Toronto
PRENTICE-HALL OF INDIA PRIVATE LTD.
New Delhi
PRENTICE-HALL OF JAPAN, INC.
Tokyo

Current printing (last .digit):

10 9 8 7 6 5 4 3 2 1

13-610683-8

Library of Congress Catalog Card Number: 70-93478

Printed in the United States of America

Preface

My acquaintance with Howard Kingsley comes from his writings and from the affectionate reports of his students, for I succeeded him at Boston University following his death. My surmise is that his intention in the original edition of *The Nature and Conditions of Learning* was to present students with a broad range of experimental and empirical information about learning without adhering to a given theoretical view. His position is one with which I sympathize and have followed in the subsequent revisions. This is not to say that these editions are without bias. The range of information about learning, both animal and human, is so extensive that the necessary act of selection is certain to produce some bias. Our critics will undoubtedly be more aware of this than we have been.

The attempt to bridge the fields of psychology and education presents problems. Although psychologists have long regarded education in general and the school in particular as their natural arena, it is only in recent years that they have made serious efforts to shift their research from laboratory to classroom. This schism finds its reflection in the organization of the text, with the first two parts devoted more to the theoretical aspects and the psychological data regarding the variables affecting learning. The third part attempts to relate these data to instruction. As a result, considerable latitude is available to the instructor in determining the order in which he wishes to discuss or present various topics.

The primary responsibility for the organization and content of this revision, whatever its strengths or weaknesses, is mine. Most authors of texts are translators and transmitters of the research developed by others, which creates a special obligation. We acknowledge our indebtedness to all the psychologists whose work makes this text possible, and to the publishers who generously gave permission to quote or use materials from their publications. Helen Harris deserves special credit for successfully nurturing a crude manuscript into a published text.

Preparing a preface produces an extraordinary awareness of the continued support and direct assistance of those close to me, in particular my wife Mimi, and my daughter Pam. To all who have provided intellectual and personal sustenance, my heartfelt thanks.

RALPH GARRY

TORONTO, 1969

Contents

Part Three
Learning in Behavioral Areas 293

one

THE
STUDY
OF
LEARNING

1

The Nature of Learning

Reading	*Prayers*	*Mothering*
Bird recognition	*Stripteasing*	*Safecracking*
Cheating	*Self-understanding*	*Neuroticism*
Foreign languages	*Walrus hunting*	*Caressing*
Fighting	*School songs*	*Anti-Semitism*
Pearl diving	*Eel eating*	*Knitting*
Nervous tics	*Deciphering*	*Movie-making*
Politics	*Tooth brushing*	

Learning is a fundamental process of life. Every individual learns and through learning develops modes of behavior by which he lives. All human activity and achievement manifest the results of learning. Whether we look at life in terms of culture, the community, or the individual, we are confronted on every side by the pervasive effects of learning. Through the centuries, each generation has been able to profit by learning from the experiences and discoveries of the generations that have preceded it, and in turn, has added its contribution to the ever-growing fund of human knowledge and skills. Customs, laws, religions, languages, and social institutions have been developed and maintained as a result of man's ability to learn.

We see the products of learning in the skilled performances of the builder, the engineer, the craftsman, the surgeon, and the artist. They are evident in the spectacular discoveries and inventions of modern science, in the thought of the philosopher, and in the decisions of the statesman. The everyday behavior of common people, their beliefs, their fears, and their adherence to tradition are determined largely by tendencies and predispositions acquired through learning. We "live and learn." We may live better or worse for it, yet we are sure to live according to what we learn.

When we consider all the skills, interests, attitudes, and information acquired both outside and inside the school and the relation of these to conduct, personality, and manner of living, we find learning to be a momentous and continuous feature of life, an activity which engages a major portion of every individual's life. Learning is a process so important to the successful survival of human beings that the institution of education and the school has been devised as a procedure for making learning more efficient. The tasks to be learned are so complex and so important that they cannot be left to chance. Nor can it be said that the tasks which human beings are called upon to learn are "normal" to human development and growth, for adding, multiplying, reading, using tooth-brushes, lacing shoes, operating typewriters, and a host of other skills to be acquired are not activities that normally would be learned. In fact, most of the routines to be learned are those which do not come naturally.

Experience has long been called the best teacher. Yet that phrase is meaningless for experience may be said to be the only teacher. Learning cannot be defined as merely experiencing. The problem is to understand the ways in which different experiences bring about changes in response and behavior in human beings and to perceive what experiences cause what learning under what circumstances.

If we are to understand the behavior and actions, the interests and attitudes, the ideals and beliefs, the skills and knowledge which characterize any human being, we have to understand the learning process because it and maturation comprise the two major influences affecting human behavior. The fact that learning is subject to environmental manipulation and control makes it essential that we not only understand the process, account for it, and explain it, but also that we develop skill in effective manipulation of the environmental variables which influence learning.

VARIED NATURE OF LEARNING

We shall approach our discussion of the nature of learning by way of a few examples drawn from everyday life and representing different forms of learning. Despite their diversity, the cases have certain features in common. The isolation of these common features is the first step in formulating a working concept of learning.

An Infant Learns. A baby cries because he is hungry. He is taken up, petted, and fed. He enjoys the attention as well as being fed. Soon he cries when he wants to be taken up even when he is not hungry.

An Animal Learns. A dog wants to leave the house but he finds his way blocked by a screen door. He pushes against the door with his nose and then with a front foot; he paws at the lower part of the door, but it does not open. He whines and moves about in an agitated manner. Finally, he rears on his hind legs, planting his forefeet high up on the door. As he moves about, one paw by chance strikes the latch. The dog's weight against the door causes it to swing open, and out he dashes. With a few repetitions of this situation, the behavior of the dog changes. He soon singles out the latch, and when he wants to leave the house, he approaches the door, rises immediately on his hind legs, releases the latch with a direct thrust of a forepaw, and goes out. His procedure is now calm and direct. The useless reactions that were so pronounced a feature of his first performance have disappeared. He has learned how to open the door.

Acquiring a Motor Skill. A boy of eight years has just received a pair of skates for Christmas. He is anxious to try them out. He has never had skates on his feet before, but he assumes skating must be easy from observing how swiftly and smoothly the other fellows skim around the pond. With effort he finally gets the skates on his feet. He stands up on the ice. Ankles wobble. He teeters forward. One foot starts off by itself, quite out of control. Hands fly up, but there is nothing to grasp; so down he goes with a bump. Undismayed, he tries again. On his feet, he tries to go ahead. Cautiously, body tense, he pushes one foot forward a bit. He teeters. Unsteadily, he draws the other foot up. He is using, or attempting to use, the movements which have served him well in walking. In this awkward and hesitating manner he creeps forward a few feet. It is fun even if he does fall down frequently. As he contnues, we see him improve. He discovers how to turn his foot outward to push forward on the other foot. Coördination of movements and balance develop. Soon he is skimming over the ice, making rapid turns, playing hockey with the other fellows in what appears an utter forgetfulness of his feet. They just seem to take him around wherever he wants to go as faithful, obedient, efficient, unquestioning servants.

Memorizing a Poem. A girl in the eighth grade has been asked to memorize a poem. Book open to the poem, she reads the first two lines three or four times, looks up, and tries to say them without looking at the book. At the end of the first line she cannot recall how the second one begins. She glances at the first word of this line. That starts her off. She completes the line without reading. The next time she gets through both lines without looking at the book. She repeats them aloud three or four times just to be sure she has them mastered. She goes on to the next lines and continues reading, reciting to herself, prompting herself when she cannot remember, and repeating until she is able to recite unhesitatingly four stanzas without the book.

Acquiring Information.   In his home room in high school, a boy is preparing his American history lesson. He is bent over his book, reading, eyes moving back and forth from line to line. His lips move a bit. Occasionally he makes a few notes. Later in class, in response to a question about the reconstruction period in the South the boy tells about the carpetbaggers, though he knew nothing about them before he studied this lesson.

Developing Understanding.   A college student, listening to a lecture on genetics, hears the word *mitosis* for the first time. She writes it down in her notebook and follows the professor's explanations attentively. She copies his blackboard sketches. A point is not clear. She asks the instructor to explain it. She understands the explanation, and as she leaves the room, she has many ideas related to the term *mitosis* that make clear to her the nature of the process of cell division. Asked later, in the examination, for an explanation of *mitosis* she is able to write a passable answer to the question.

Acquiring and Reducing a Fear.   A 9-year-old boy, running home from the grocery store with a bottle of milk in his hand, trips and falls; he smashes the milk bottle, cuts a deep and jagged gash in his wrist, and severs a tendon. Hospitalization and surgery are necessary to repair the injury. One result of the entire experience is that the boy becomes afraid of glass. When he returns home from the hospital, he refuses to touch any object made of glass. The suddenness of the fall, fright, and associated pain have produced a newly acquired fear of a material which had previously been looked upon in a matter-of-fact way: the youngster has learned to fear glass. He has adopted a response which will insure his protection from future similar injury, but which is maladaptive in light of the extensive use of glass in his environment.

Two different approaches are utilized in efforts to readapt the child's behavior. The child's mother attempts to ease the situation by using plastic glasses for drinking water and milk, hoping that the fear will gradually subside and that the youngster will outgrow his alarm if no issue is made of it. The boy's teacher first becomes aware of the fear when he refuses to handle the jars and glasses in which the class is collecting science specimens. The teacher assists the boy on the first occasion or two but is tempted to insist that the boy put the bottles on the shelf himself, believing it unhealthy to concede to his fear. Both teacher and pupil find it difficult to modify their established reaction patterns in the situation. Receiving assurance that attempts to reduce the fear and encourage the youngster to discover alternate responses to the situation do not constitute concession to the fear, the teacher proceeds to induce the youngster to modify his fear response. Her first attempt is to assign the boy with another pupil to collect the bottles. The boy avoids the tasks by having the other pupil pick up the bottles and place them in the crate which he then carries, thus solving the problem of executing a task required by the teacher, while simultaneously satisfying his fear. In the course of the next two or three weeks, the teacher observes the boy on an occasion or two standing in front of the aquarium in the classroom, attracted by the fish and perhaps propelled by his fear, gingerly reaching out to touch the glass and then quickly withdrawing his fingers. The teacher asks the boy if he would like an aquarium on his desk. Prompted by his delighted response, she places a small fish in some water in a bottle and puts it on the corner of his desk. For several days, the boy makes the same gingerly touching response to the glass, gradually gaining more assurance until finally he can be seen rubbing his fingers on the bottle, poking his finger down in the water at the fish, and then engaging in a variety of such actions which involve touching and handling the bottle. Taking advantage of this development one afternoon when she has the children cleaning their desks for some repair work that is to be done during vacation by the carpenter, the teacher casually asks the boy to take the bottle containing the fish to her desk. Unthinkingly, he grasps the bottle and carries it to her desk. As he is placing it on the desk, she calls his attention to what he has just done—taking hold of a glass bottle and carrying it. Thus, a fear response which had been learned is gradually being unlearned under the guidance of the teacher.

COMMON FEATURES OF LEARNING

The foregoing examples represent some different kinds of learning, although not all of the varieties that we shall have occasion to consider are among them. There are several features common to all of them. *First,* the learning took place during some type of activity in which the organism was engaged with a purpose. *Second,* the organism attempted various responses in an effort to reach a solution. *Third,* hitting upon a correct response, whether by accident or by forethought, produced either a new kind of performance or a change from previous performance in that the organism adopted this response as a habitual one. The sequential steps in learning have these three common features. Some purpose or motivation directed toward a goal results in varied responses in connection with certain aspects of the environment ultimately leading to the stabilization of a particular response or response pattern. Learning, then, is the process by which an organism, in satisfying its motivations, adapts or adjusts its behavior in order to reach a goal.

DEFINITION OF LEARNING

We shall soon see that this definition is incomplete and must be qualified. In each of the foregoing illustrations, the behavior described was definitely and permanently changed as a result of learning. The dog opening a door, the child memorizing a poem, the boys skating, the college students writing during their examinations, the boy eliminating his fear—all are examples of new or modified forms of behavior resulting from learning. It is evident, too, that the learning took many different forms: conditioning, trial and error, motor skill, verbal fluency, conceptual development and emotional change.

Process Versus Product. To make the definition more meaningful, certain modifications and distinctions must be made. One of these distinctions to be made in clarifying the definition of learning is that learning is a process, not a product. Human beings learn many things—attitudes, fears, gestures, motor skills, language skills, and so on—all of which represent changes of performance in some area of human behavior. From the lay point of view, the end product—the particular performance change—is

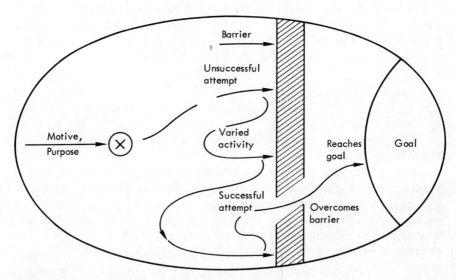

Fig. 1.1 Elements in a learning situation: *purpose, varied responses, selection of successful response, and ultimate stabilization of response.*

frequently seen as learning. For the psychologist, however, learning is the process by which the changes in performance were brought about.

Learning as Improvement. Another common misconception is that learning always results in improvement of performance. This is, of course, a common conception when one is thinking of the learning that takes place in the classroom according to the wishes and intent of the teacher or when one engages in learning for a definite purpose. But even here changes occur which result in bad habits, the fixation of error, and undesirable attitudes; these are quite definitely learned and such learning is scarcely improvement. The child learns many things in the classroom that do not fall within the range of the teacher's objectives. He may learn habits of idleness and disrespect for authority. He may learn to write more poorly or he may acquire habits of poor reading. Any definition of learning has to be broad enough to include the undesirable and inefficient.

Learning as Adjustment. Learning has been described as a process of progressive adjustment to the ever-changing conditions which one encounters. To *adjust* means to bring into proper relation. When the individual is out of adjustment with the conditions of life, he is disturbed, dissatisfied, and unhappy.

Yet children and adults frequently adopt modes of behavior that are definitely maladjustive. One acquires emotional habits detrimental to mental health, habits of conduct that cause trouble with the authorities of the school or state, and attitudes that cause failure on schoolwork or job. In school one may learn to aspire to unattainable goals. If a domestic science course teaches a girl to buy and cook in a manner not suited to the budget within which she must operate, the outcome is more likely to be maladjustment than adjustment. There is not much consolation in saying that her learning constitutes an adjustment to the school requirement.

Learning Versus Maturation. Two further aspects of the definition of learning require clarification. The first is the distinction between learning and maturation. Learning is not the only process by which behavior is modified. A second important process producing behavior changes is maturation, the process whereby behavior is modified as a result of growth and development of physical structures. It is most easily illustrated by the fact that until a child is ready to walk or talk, i.e., has the neuromuscular development for such activities, no amount of training can bring about these particular changes in performance. Similarly, many higher thought processes are not available to immature humans, e.g., utilization of symbolic notation or algebraic operations. Although such illustrations can be made to clarify the distinction between learning and maturation, it is not as easy to make the distinction in actual practice because learning and maturation are interrelated.

Learning and Proficiency.   Another distinction to be made is between changes in performance produced by work decrements and those produced by learning. For example, practice can produce both increases and decreases in proficiency at the same time—a decrease resulting from fatigue and an increase resulting from learning. Both can occur simultaneously, and both are inferred from changes observed in performance; e.g., one effect of a rest period on learning is to produce a loss in proficiency of performance due to the occurrence of forgetting, whereas performance is *more* efficient after a rest period in which fatigue dissipates. Boredom, illness, and intoxicaticn are other factors producing work decrements.

Giving consideration to the foregoing qualifications, our definition now stands: *Learning is the process by which behavior (in the broad sense) is originated or changed through practice or training.* (After Hunter, 1934; Hilgard, 1948.)

Learning and Education.   At this point, it is worth-while to distinguish between learning and education. From our discussion, we are aware that learning includes the changes in behavior, both favorable and unfavorable, which result from experience, whether in school or out, whether intentional or accidental. Much learning is intentional: when a child studies his multiplication tables in order to be able to recite them, when a college student reviews his lecture notes for an examination, when a golfer drives two hundred golf balls on a driving range in order to improve his golf score. Much learning is unintentional or incidental to another purpose: boys playing a game of football or baseball for the enjoyment of the game can incidentally improve their passing, kicking, or tackling ability. Children and adults also without a conscious desire unintentionally learn advertising slogans seen on billboards or television.

Education in the formal sense of the word refers to the systematically organized programs designed to produce certain knowledge, skills, understanding, attitudes, and behavior patterns in members of a given social group. Schools are established and maintained for the purpose of securing desired learning outcomes. In a general way, it may be said that organized education seeks to perpetuate the good features of the social order, to secure the continuance of certain social institutions, and to combat the evils that threaten the society by producing the so-called "educated man" whose behavior theoretically epitomizes the society's best.

Along with this, we seek through education to secure and safeguard the individual's welfare and security in a complex society. These long-range objectives can be achieved only by developing appropriate forms of behavior in the individual members of the social group. This requires that educational goals be envisaged in terms of individual learning outcomes. Our success in accomplishing the purposes of organized education depends primarily upon the learning that takes place in the classroom under the direction of the teacher.

It is possible to forecast certain types of situations that the individual is likely to encounter. We know with some degree of assurance what kinds of abilities and what forms of behavior will serve the individual to advantage in these situations and at the same time be socially acceptable or desirable. These include certain *skills,* such as writing, reading, and arithmetical computations; certain *habits* of personal hygiene, emotional stability, and social behavior; and a variety of *verbal responses.* They represent forms of functioning which we are quite certain will be useful or necessary. Since we can foresee the need for them, it becomes our task to develop these talents so that they will be ready when the occasion demands.

It is apparent, however, that we cannot foresee all the situations a child will be called upon to face during his life. We cannot supply him with ready-made habits, skills, and memorized materials that will serve all his future needs. The futility of such a desire is increasingly clear in an age in which the revelation and discovery of new knowledge and technological changes proceed at such a rate that what one learns in school is certain to be outmoded before death. In addition, unpredictable demands and questions are certain to arise. Each of us must therefore be equipped with *knowledge, understanding,* and some *training* in the *art of problem solving* and of *learning how to learn* so that we can devise for ourselves appropriate answers and suitable modes of behavior for unexpected situations.

Finally, it is essential that the individual be disposed to conduct himself so that his own well-being and the interests of his associates will be safeguarded and preserved. *Attitudes, ideals, and values* are the learning outcomes that meet this need.

These four types of learning outcomes are the educational objectives toward which the work of the teacher is directed: first, skills and habits; second, knowledge and understanding; third, problem solving and learning skill; and fourth, attitudes, ideals, and values.

That which does, or should, constitute the formal education of members of any group is a philosophical question dependent upon the values and beliefs held by that particular group. Our particular concern is less with educational objectives than with the process by which changes in human behavior are produced and with the variables which contribute to these changes, regardless of the source of the training or practice.

VARIABLES INFLUENCING LEARNING

In the descriptions of the learning process, several aspects were identified: an organism with its motivation, which directs it toward a given goal; a period of varied responses as the organism attempts to reach the goal; and the discovery of the appropriate response followed by stabilization and fixation, retention, and generalization of the response. In the study of learning, we are interested in the many factors which influence behavior in these episodes: (1) how the motives and the goals capable of satisfying the motives are determined, (2) what factors influence the variability of responses, (3) which factors affect the speed of discovery, fixation, and retention of the correct response and what the conditions are under which they operate, and (4) what the conditions or circumstances are under which the learned response is utilized or transferred to new and different situations.

The many variables which affect these different aspects of the learning process may be grouped under three headings: (1) variables associated with the individual, (2) variables associated with the task to be performed, and (3) environmental variables. Although separate chapters will be devoted to each group, they will be briefly identified now.

Individual Variables. Maturation, readiness, capacity, motivation, and personality traits are variables—associated with the individual learner—which affect the outcome of learning. The level of maturation of the individual learner plays a significant role in the amount of material, the kind of knowledge acquired, the rate of learning, and the amount of retention. Generally speaking, the more mature the individual, the greater the learning; however, such a generalization does not hold throughout life, e.g., the difficulty of teaching old dogs new tricks. Individuals also differ in their capacity for learning given tasks. Differences in capacity may be either physical or intellectual; such differences may be outgrowths of variations in experience. Individual readiness at any given period is a function of both maturation and prior experience and signifies the degree to which any individual is prepared for learning a particular task.

It need scarcely be said that the more highly motivated the individual, the greater the learning. Personality factors such as perseverance, curiosity, self-confidence, level of aspiration, aggressiveness, and so on are closely allied to motivation in their effect upon learning. Each of these variables may be isolated for experimental purposes in order to measure their separate contribution or effect upon learning under certain circumstances; nevertheless, they operate simultaneously and multifariously in any actual learning situation.

Task Variables. The meaningfulness of the task to be learned, its difficulty, its similarity to previously performed tasks, its pleasantness or unpleasantness, and the manner in which it is organized or presented are variables which affect the speed of learning and the amount of retention obtained.

The more meaningful the task, the more readily it is learned. The more an individual understands the task, the more readily he can select the appropriate response for the particular situation. The degree of meaningfulness is one of the variables which is associated with tasks and affects learning outcomes. Second, the difficulty of the task affects learning outcomes, and although difficulty tends to vary with the degree of meaningfulness, it is not identical inasmuch as difficulty varies with the length of material as well as with complexity.

Tasks vary in their degree of similarity and hence, in the amount of transfer of learning which may occur from one task to another. Meaningfulness is in part a function of the degree of transfer, i.e., the extent to which previous learning makes the immediate task easier. Some tasks are pleasant, some are unpleasant, and many are neutral. The affective reaction of an individual influences the learning situation.

Environmental Variables.   In addition to individual variables and task variables, a number of environmental variables influence the learning process. The frequency with which a response is practiced affects the speed with which the response is acquired and fixed and the length of time it is retained. Closely associated with practice are overlearning and drill. To overlearn is to practice a response beyond the first perfect performance, as one frequently does with many motor skills such as swimming, skiing, dancing. Knowledge of results is another variable which aids the individual in selecting the correct response from the sequence of varied responses attempted in any learning situation. The incentives in play in a given situation have a marked influence on the learning process. Reward, punishment, competition, cöoperation, praise, blame, grades, honor rolls, and so forth —all have their influence upon learning. The degree of influence may be great or slight depending upon the relationship between the incentives and the motives characterizing the individual learner. In the classroom as distinguished from the laboratory, factors of a social nature have to be considered, such as group attitudes and values, motivation of other individuals in the situation, including the teacher, and the social restraints in operation.

Interaction of Variables.   It is possible in an experimental situation to reduce the number of variables that are operating freely at any given time, but such is rarely the case in the learning situations that occur in home or school. In any situation, several of these variables are operating simultaneously and interrelatedly. To give a simple illustration: an individual's efforts will vary greatly depending upon whether he is alone or in a group situation. Our problem is to understand not only how the many factors operate individually, but more important, how their combined operations in the classroom interact with each other.

ORGANIZATION OF THE TEXT

This text is organized in three main sections. The initial section concerns itself with a study of learning, first attempting to define learning, describing how learning is measured both in experiments and in school settings, and describing the effect of error upon such measures.

Although experimental evidence and observation provide facts about learning, it is necessary to explain, account for, or organize these facts into some overall scheme or theory of learning. As a matter of fact, each instructional procedure used by a teacher implies some theory of how learning occurs, however unsystematic or inconsistently organized the procedure may be. The chapter on learning theory traces certain of the mainstreams of theoretical development in the psychology of learning, since no single theory is as yet able to explain all aspects of learning; it then describes the current issues. Two additional chapters—one on research methods which identifies typical experimental methods used in the study of learning, the second on techniques and problems of measurement—complete the first part of the text.

The second section of the book is concerned with those variables operating in learning which have been already identified—individual variables, task variables, and method variables—and the interaction between them. Experimental evidence related to each of the many variables will be presented in order to illustrate and specify the relationship of each variable to learning. By the end of Part Two, the student should have identified the many factors to be considered and established some general answers to these important questions: what is the relationship of capacity to learning; how does capacity change with age; do individual differences affect learning and vice-versa; what influence does learning have upon individual differences; how do motivation and incentives operate in learning; how do such factors as reward and punishment, cooperation and competition, success and failure operate; what are the differences between massed and distributed practice; what is the relationship of each question to various kinds of learning and to retention?

Part Three is intended to relate the many variables affecting learning to the kind of learning tasks with which children are confronted in growing to maturity. It is possible to classify learning in any one of several ways; e.g., learning tasks may be classified according to the kind of experimental situation typically utilized, such as classical conditioning, instrumental conditioning, discrimination learning, and problem solving. Teachers often utilize instructional outcomes such as skills, knowledge, attitudes, and behavior in a particular subject as a basis for classifying learning. From a psychological viewpoint, there is no value in attempting to distinguish between verbal learning in science versus that in art or any other subject. Instead, the value lies in discovering general principles about verbal learning which hold for all subjects.

In this text, the classification scheme adopted distinguishes between motor skills, perception, rote learning, comprehension, problem solving, motives, and attitudes. This scheme is adopted, not because learning is intrinsically divided into such categories, but because such a classification seems convenient for the study of learning as it relates to schools. These may be considered the main types of learning fostered in our schools in all of the various subject matter areas. The final chapter considers the ultimate problem of the transfer of learning from school to life situations.

Experimental and Empirical Knowledge. In acquiring our understanding of the learning process, two main sources of information are available: (1) the results of experimental studies (those which are carried out both in laboratory and in life situations), and (2) the empirical judgments of skilled teachers and observers. It would be desirable, even though it is well nigh impossible, to have conclusive experimental evidence upon which to base our knowledge of the many influences which operate in all learning situations so that we could be most proficient in manipulating these experiences to produce maximum learning with a minimum of effort. In situations where we lack direct experimental evidence, we are forced to make inferences from related experiments, particularly those involving animal learning, or depend upon empirical judgment based upon experience. In the pages that follow, the student will find both types of information; nevertheless, we shall try to maintain the distinction between the two and utilize experimental evidence as far as possible as a basis for judgment.

At the end of each chapter a set of selected references will be provided, using three main divisions. First, some general source will be listed in which a brief overview of the topic can be obtained. This is intended to provide a general map of the terrain. Second, several selected references will be provided, usually single volumes providing an in-depth treatment of different aspects of the chapter subject. Finally, some original investigations will be identified which illustrate the nature of specialized research in the field. The references provided for this chapter are necessarily general.

SUMMARY

Learning is a fundamental process of life engaging much of our waking hours and affecting all forms of human behavior—skills, knowledge, attitudes, personality, motivations, fears, mannerisms, and others. Learning is defined as the process by which behavior is originated or changed through practice. Learning and maturation are the two main processes through which changes in behavior occur.

Learning may occur intentionally or unintentionally, through organized or unorganized activity. Education is the formal procedure through which the attempt is made to develop in individuals certain socially sanctioned behavioral patterns. The study of learning includes not only formal training but all factors producing behavior changes.

The variables which influence learning may be grouped under three headings: (1) individual variables, such as capacity and motivation, (2) task variables, such as meaningfulness and difficulty, and (3) environmental variables, such as practice and knowledge of results.

A consideration of the measurement of learning, research procedures, and theories of learning will be found in the first section of the text, and the variables affecting learning will be reviewed in the second section. The third section is concerned with learning in different areas of behavior: motor learning, perception, memory, comprehension, problem solving, emotions, and motivation. The final chapter deals with problems related to transfer of training.

Two main sources of information are utilized: experimental evidence and empirical observation.

FURTHER READING

Overview

ESTES, W. K. Learning. In C. W. Harris (ed.). 1960. *Encyclopedia of Educational Research.* New York: Macmillan. (The Encyclopedia provides summary statements of a wide range of topics, educational as well as psychological, including school practices.) Third edition published in 1969.

Selected References

BLAIR, GLENN, R. S. JONES, and R. H. SIMPSON. 1968. *Educational Psychology.* New York: Macmillan.

GAGNÉ, R. M. 1965. *The conditions of learning.* New York: Holt, Rinehart, Winston.

HOVLAND, C. I. Human learning and retention. In S. S. Stevens (ed.). 1951. *Handbook of experimental psychology.* New York: Wiley.

KIMBLE, G. A. 1961. *Hilgard and Marquis' conditioning and learning.* New York: Appleton-Century-Crofts.

MELTON, A. W. 1964. *Categories of human learning.* New York: Academic Press.

TRAVERS, R. (chrmn.). 1967. Committee on Growth, Development, and Learning, American Educational Research Association. Growth, development, and learning. *Rev. of Educ. Research,* 37, #5.

Original Investigations

BARKER, R. G., TAMARA DEMBO, and K. LEWIN. 1941. Frustration and regression: studies in topological and vector psychology, II. *Univ. of Iowa Stud. Child Welfare,* 18, #1.

DUNCAN, C. P. 1959. Recent research on human problem-solving. *Psychol. Bul.,* 56: 397-429.

HARLOW, H. F. 1949. The formation of learning sets. *Psychol. Rev.,* 56: 51-65.

MILLER, N. E. 1948. Studies of fear as an acquirable drive, I. Fear as motivation and fear reduction as reinforcement in learning of new responses. *J. Exp. Psychol.,* 38: 89-101.

A comprehensive index to psychological research is provided by the journal, *Psychological Abstracts,* which provides single paragraph summaries of research reports with the source of the original investigation identified.

2

Research Methods

Although the systematic, experimental study of learning is scarcely more than a lifetime old, man's concern and interest in learning is undoubtedly as old as man himself, for there has always been the problem of teaching children the most rudimentary knowledge for survival and self-care. We may never know exactly when the interest in making learning efficient began, but it is as old as recorded history. In the written records are many shrewd observations regarding factors that influence learning and numerous procedures suggested for making learning more effective. But until experimental confirmation and investigation of the circumstances were made to determine when the judgments held true and when they did not, they remained no more or less than judgments of uncertain validity and application.

EXPERIMENTING AND EXPERIMENTS

We can observe many of these judgments as they operate in daily life. The parent telling the 5-year-old who wants to try his older brother's bicycle that he isn't old enough or big enough to ride the bicycle is expressing the conviction that with increased age comes increased capacity or readiness for learning a complex motor skill, and that there is a factor, call it maturation or something else, that makes learning to ride the bicycle either easier or more rapid. Similarly, the parent who teaches his child to use a knife or fork, to keep his fingers out of his food, or to read while still in nursery school makes a number of assumptions about learning: that the child is capable of learning the particular task, that he is desirous of learning, that he has had the necessary prior training, that the parent's procedure for explaining or illustrating the skill is intelligible to the child, that the length of the training period is suited to the task at hand, and that a number of other conditions are being met. If the child learns, both parent and child may be pleased; but if the child fails to learn, the parent is unable to specify which of the several conditions is not being properly manipulated—whether the child lacks sufficient maturity, interest, or motivation, whether the child is capable of learning but the parental demonstration is confusing or meaningless, or whether the practice period is overly long. The parent may attempt to analyze the situation and by trial and error, modify procedures until success is achieved or failure appears inevitable. This occurred in the following situation. A father was attempting to teach his 5-year-old son the first steps in swimming (the term "first steps" implies that a preferable sequence of steps exists, in contradiction to the throw-them-into-deep-water school of thought). Following an accepted procedure, the father had the boy put his face into the water, then followed this with instructions to grasp his knees and pull them up to his body so that he would float "like a jellyfish." Repeatedly and unsuccessfully he gave varied instructions on the same theme to the boy. Finally, he abandoned his instructional procedure and attempted alternate ways of demonstrating body buoyancy in water. Taking the boy into very shallow water, he pointed at some painted circles on the bottom of the pool and asked the boy if he could touch his nose on a circle. Attempting this, the boy had to take his feet off the bottom of the pool in order to submerge his head. In doing this and prompted by questions from his father, he suddenly became aware of the way in which the water held him up and made submerging difficult.

In this situation, the father was experimenting with the variables affecting his son's learning—experimenting crudely, but in this instance, effectively. The psychologist is engaged in a similar activity but with somewhat different purposes and with many more restrictions and refinements. Where the father was interested primarily in the results, the psychologist is interested in the events contributing to the results, particularly in the extent to which manipulating the events produces differences in the results. Second, the father was utilizing a crude empiricism, more or less randomly varying his procedure in accordance with the dictates of his analysis. In contrast, the psychologist is especially concerned with systematically studying the effects of different variables, singly and in combination. In doing so, he must utilize a number of procedures for controlling or holding constant the many variables which affect learning, e.g., age of subject, amount of previous training, amount of practice during the experiment, motivation, and instructions to subject, while the psychologist systematically investigates the influence of any one of the variables or combinations thereof. Third, while both father and psychologist were using a performance score as a measure of learning (the father was aware of roughly the number of unsuccessful trials or unsuccessful attempts), the psychologist strives to utilize performance scores that are more refined, more subject to precision of measurement, and more clearly related to the learning variable being manipulated. Thus, the psychologist is interested in the systematic, experimental study of learning for the sake of understanding what happens when an organism learns.

The Experimental Study of Learning.   Systematic experimenting with learning began in the latter part of the nineteenth century and rapidly expanded during the present century. One of the earliest experimenters in the study of learning was Hermann Ebbinghaus. In studying conditions affecting memorizing, Ebbinghaus was confronted with a type of problem which psychologists must meet and overcome in their experimental study of learning. It is obvious that certain kinds of material, such as poetry, are more readily memorized than others, such as series of numbers, because of the meaningfulness or familiarity of the material. To secure units of equal difficulty, it is necessary to use learning material as free as possible from meaning or previously formed associations. Ebbinghaus met this requirement by inventing the nonsense syllable, a meaningless combination of three letters consisting of two consonants joined by a vowel, e.g., keb, ruk, meg, cej. With this type of material, Ebbinghaus investigated problems of memory, retention, and recall. For example, he studied the number of repetitions required for learning series of different lengths. He studied the relation of the number of repetitions to the retention of the series. Since his time, Ebbinghaus' pioneering work has been supplemented by the work of many other investigators, but his methods of measuring memory are still standard experimental procedures, and the results of his experiments are regarded as an important contribution to our knowledge of learning and forgetting.

Thorndike and Pavlov.   At the beginning of the present century, two more chains of experimental studies were begun by Edward L. Thorndike and Ivan Pavlov. Thorndike began a series of experiments on animal learning by placing a hungry cat in a puzzle box from which the cat could escape by operating a latch string in order to obtain food placed outside the box. From the results, Thorndike formulated his theories regarding learning and his concept of learning by trial and error. He saw the need and the possibility of applying experimental methods to the study of learning in the schools and devoted himself to this task.

Pavlov, a physiologist, began a series of experiments utilizing the conditioning of reflex responses to various stimuli and studied the conditions under which conditioned responses were established and maintained. His procedures and hypotheses about the nature of learning have stimulated extensive experimentation and have been significant contributions to both procedures for studying learning and theories for explaining learning.

Scientific Method and Theory.   The divorce of psychology from philosophy began when psychological questions were put to experimental test instead of depending upon logical deduction. Psychology thus shifted from a speculative system to a scientific system.

Between the simplicity of the scientific method and the stringency of its application of experimental methods in order to answer psychological questions lie many bewildering details. The logic of the scientific method is fairly simple. One starts with a question. For instance, one may question whether the whole-method is more effective than the part-method in the memorization of poetry. Having established a question which is usually quite specifically limited in its scope, one undertakes an investigation. This may be in the form of controlled field observation or in the form of an experiment utilizing rigid controls in which an effort is made to study the several variables which can influence results. The useful results are those which contribute to, confirm, or refute a scientific theory or explanation. More often, the main result of an experiment is further questions rather than answers. An important condition of the scientific method is that results are verifiable by other investigators. The value of this condition is that it makes the results independent of the experimenter.

Subsequently, generalizations are made upon the basis of groups of related studies. Finally, theories are proposed in order to account for or explain the data and the generalizations. Usually, several theories are proposed in different attempts to explain the same data. The theory which stands in the face of the facts will survive; the others are discarded. Sound theories permit deductions which can be tested by scientific experiments to support or refute the theory. The validity of a theory rests upon the kind and extent of predictions that can be made in utilizing the theory. When the prediction fails or the theory fails to coincide with the observed facts, the theory is altered or discarded. Thus, the scientific method produces a body of verified knowledge from which inferences, generalizations, and explanations are made in an effort to organize existing knowledge into consistent systems.

The problems of using the scientific method in the study of human behavior are not logical but methodological. The fact that human behavior is the complex product of numerous factors acting simultaneously makes it extremely difficult to adequately control these factors influencing experimental results in such a way that the relationships between any single variable in behavior can be systematically investigated. Moreover, the fact that behavior results from the interaction of many variables rather than the singular action of one variable imposes a limitation upon the extent to which generalizations can be established on the basis of laboratory experiments. For these and other reasons, the body of knowledge that has been accumulated in efforts to explain human learning includes data from not only experimental but also nonexperimental sources.

NONEXPERIMENTAL METHODS

Systematic observation of behavior has been and will continue to be a fruitful source of information and deductions regarding human behavior, particularly in supplying clues to relationships which exist between different variables. In nonexperimental methods, little or no attempt is made to control or manipulate the situation. Rather, the purpose is to bring to light the factors, conditions, or relationships present and essentially to provide a description of the world of behavior.

Differential Psychology. Nonexperimental methods may be subdivided into two main categories called differential psychology and clinical psychology, the former being the study of differences between individuals and groups and the latter the study of individual adjustment. Two studies serve to illustrate the type of investigation undertaken in the area of differential psychology. A longitudinal study of intelligence was completed by Honzik, Macfarlane, and Allen (1948), who administered intelligence tests to a group of children each year from infancy to age 18 in order to determine the stability of intelligence as measured by standard tests and the predictive value of early tests for terminal intelligence scores. In another type of study Anastasi and Cordoba (1953) administered Spanish and English forms of the Cattell Culture-Free Intelligence Tests to Puerto Rican children of both sexes in New York. Half the children received the tests in the Spanish-English sequence with an interval of two weeks between tests, and the other half received the tests in the reverse order. The investigators were able to compare the influence of such variables as sex, language, and test sequence on obtained scores. These studies illustrate two procedures extensively used in differential psychology: the longitudinal or genetic study and the cross-sectional study. Norms of physical growth and intellectual development have been established by studying groups of children at different age levels and comparing them with respect to such given characteristics as height, weight, mental age, and so forth and establishing norms on the basis of results. Cross-sectional methods are continually used in public opinion polls to appraise reactions of differing groups. Interests,

fears, preferences, social development are only a few of the many characteristics which have been studied using this approach. The longitudinal
method as illustrated by the Honzik-Macfarlane-Allen study is more intensive, for it involves a series of planned and systematic observations
of children's behavior over a considerable period of time to discover the
nature of their development. Physical and mental tests and examinations
are frequently used in addition to observation.

Clinical Methods. If a child presents a behavior problem or is malad-
justed educationally, socially, or emotionally, adequate treatment calls for
an understanding of the factors that have contributed to his particular difficulty. The clinical method provides a diagnosis of the underlying causes
of misbehavior or maladjustment. It rests on the conviction that treatment
should be concerned with *causes* rather than *symptoms*.

When a child is taken to a psychological clinic, he is given various
tests to determine his physical, intellectual, and educational status. The
record prepared usually constitutes a case history, with information about
development and varied aspects of his behavior obtained from a variety of
sources: parents, school, play observations, and others.

Although the treatment of individual difficulties is the primary purpose
of this method, the data from clinical tests and case histories have thrown
much light on many general problems of psychology. Here are revealed
the concrete workings of the complex tangle of conditions that determine
human behavior.

Studies of the effectiveness of clinical procedures depend upon a be-
fore-and-after comparison in order to compare changes in behavior. Many
difficulties beset such studies attempting to measure the outcomes of clinical
procedures. First, it is difficult to determine what general population any
particular group of patients represents or how typical the group is of emotionally disturbed persons. Second, it is difficult to identify explicitly the
procedure, and even more so, to isolate its effects from the host of other
influences affecting any individual's life. The frequent dependence upon
the verbal report of the subject as to how he feels or has improved injects
additional uncertainty into the validity of findings. Finally, no control
comparison with untreated persons or those treated by another method is
available. Yet in spite of flaws, such studies will be made and used until
more effective procedures are devised. Recent years have seen increased
efforts to introduce more rigorous controls into the clinical studies of personality dynamics, in order to improve the validity of conclusions. This
means establishing sound experimental procedures which basically require
a definition of the population (in order to substantiate subsequent generalizations), an explicit statement of procedures (to permit replication),
and most important a control group in order that a comparison of changes
can be made.

Figure 2.1 identifies the methods used for obtaining descriptive information in differential and clinical psychology. These methods are subdivided into two main classifications: test procedures including both objective and projective tests, and non-test procedures including observation and report. In general, differential psychology relies more heavily upon test and statistical procedures, whereas clinical psychology uses non-test procedures such as the case study. Nevertheless, a job analysis of the work performed by the clinical psychologist shows that he not only engages in clinical interviews, counseling, and preparation of case histories but also utilizes a wide variety of testing instruments—particularly projective tests—in performing his work.

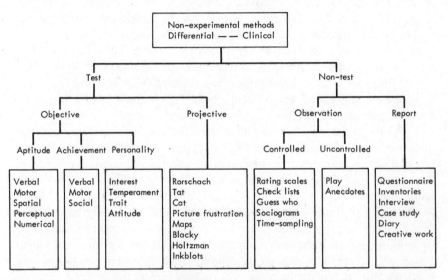

Fig. 2.1   Non-experimental methods for obtaining descriptive information.

Tests.   There are several ways of subdividing tests: pencil-and-paper versus performance, individual versus group, objective versus projective tests. In Figure 2.1 the objective-projective categories are used as a primary distinction in types of tests. Objective tests are so-called because they employ standardized procedures of administration and scoring which produce scores or results that are highly consistent and not dependent upon the examiner's interpretation. Furthermore, the range of response to the items in the test is usually restricted by using such items as multiple-choice, true-false, and short-answer items. Intelligence and achievement tests are usually objective in format. Projective tests are so named because the test situation permits the person being tested to project himself into the situation. The person taking the test is presumed to interpret the situation in a way characteristic to his personality structure with the result that his responses may be interpreted to provide further understanding of the dynamics of his personality. Obviously, the effective use of projective tests is dependent upon the clinical skill and understanding of the psychologist administering the test. Widely used projective tests are the Rorschach Test, which consists of a series of ink blots, and the Murray Thematic Apperception Test, which is a series of pictures of people and situations. The examinee describes what the ink blot or situation means to him. This report is then scored and interpreted by the psychologist.

Objective tests in particular have been useful in descriptive research as well as in controlled studies of learning, particularly when statistical methods are utilized in conjunction with the tests. Statistical methods make it possible to reduce large numbers of scores or data to a few simple expressions which are meaningful to the observer.

Statistics.   The statistics used in describing groups provide three kinds of information. They describe: (1) the central tendency or mid-point of the group, such as mean, median, and mode, (2) the dispersion or variability of the group, such as range or standard deviation, and (3) the relationship between traits or characteristics, such as a correlation coefficient. These statistics make it possible to draw conclusions regarding differences in the characteristics of one or more groups. Figure 2.2 illustrates two groups which differ in their mid-point—one group being considerably below the other, even though both groups have approximately the same range of scores. Such distributions could be obtained if one were to compare the scores of third with sixth grade children on an achievement test of arithmetic or spelling. Figure 2.3 illustrates two groups which differ considerably in their range of scores: Group A is more variable than Group B, even though both groups have the same mid-points or averages. Such a distribution of scores could be obtained if one were comparing the scores of a sixth grade class in reading comprehension with the scores obtained by all twelve grades in the school system. The standard deviation

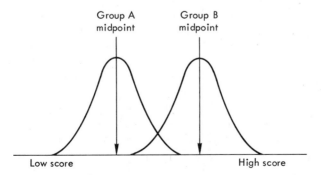

Fig. 2.2   Central tendency differences of two groups.

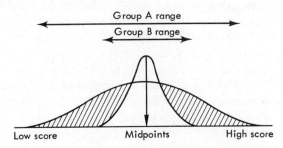

Fig. 2.3 Variability differences of two groups.

(represented by the symbol σ) is a commonly used statistic for describing the variability of groups. It is a statistic which portrays the extent to which all individuals in a group vary from all other individuals.

A third statistic commonly used is the correlation coefficient (represented by the symbol r) which is used to describe the strength of relationship between two variables. If a comparison were made between the intelligence test scores of a group of pupils and their achievement test scores, a diagram like Figure 2.4 would be the likely result. In this figure intelligence test scores range from low to high along the horizontal axis, and the paired achievement test scores range from low to high up the vertical axis. If the correlation between intelligence and achievement were perfect (r = 1.00), i.e., if the highest in intelligence was highest in achievement, and second in intelligence was second in achievement, and so on, the scores would fall along a diagonal line running from lower left to upper right. If there was no correlation (r = 0.00) between intelligence and achievement, the scores would be scattered over the entire grid as shown in Figure 2.5. Inasmuch as the correlation between achievement and intelligence is approximately r = .50, the scores would fall in an egg-shaped distribution as

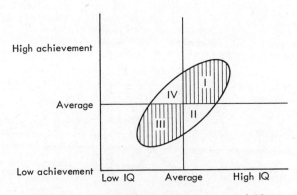

Fig. 2.4 Correlation between two variables.

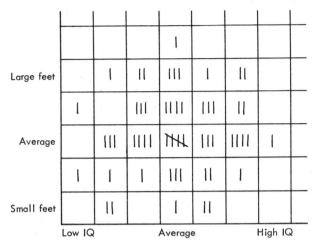

Fig. 2.5 Two variables having zero correlation.

shown in Figure 2.4. In general, it can be seen that the higher the intelligence score, the higher the achievement score is likely to be; but that the relationship is not perfect can be seen by observing scores in quadrants II and IV, in which those persons of high intelligence have low achievement scores, and those of low intelligence are high in achievement.

Figure 2.4 also illustrates one of the difficulties in making predictions on the basis of correlation coefficients. If a prediction were made that persons of above average intelligence would succeed in a given program and those below average would not succeed, then the successful predictions are represented by quadrants I and III, the errors in prediction by quadrants II and IV. Granted, the predictions as far as the several groups are concerned are more successful than would occur by chance or by interview; nevertheless, very high correlation coefficients (.90 to 1.00) are needed to be confident of the success of predictions in *individual* cases.

Thus, correlation coefficients can range from 0.00, as might be expected if one attempted to correlate shoe size and intelligence, to 1.00 if the correlation were perfect. Correlation may be either positive (r.50) or negative (r − .80). The closer to 1.00, whether positive or negative, the higher the degree of correlation.

Near perfect correlation can be obtained if an intelligence test is administered twice within a short time to the same group and the scores on the first administration correlated with scores on the second. Such a correlation coefficient is referred to as a reliability coefficient, for in effect one obtains an estimate of the consistency of test scores from one testing to the next. One would expect little change from one test to the next; hence, the test is reliable, i.e., has a high r (.90 to .99) between the two sets of scores.

Correlation coefficients may also be used to describe the relationship between different combinations of variables. It may be between two variables within the same group as in Figure 2.4, or it may describe the relationship on a single variable between two groups, such as the correlation between intelligence scores of brothers or of identical twins. When one of the sets of scores is used for predicting performance on another variable, e.g., predicting achievement on the basis of an intelligence test as in Figure 2.4, the resulting correlation coefficient is referred to as a validity coefficient. Thus, the intelligence test is valid (to the degree shown by the correlation coefficient) for estimating academic achievement. Because most aspects of human performance are influenced by many variables, validity coefficients tend to be lower, ranging from r.10 to r.50. For example, many conditions affect scholastic achievement—intelligence, prior achievement, motivation, study habits, and so forth; hence, no single one can be expected to account for even half, much less all, of the achievement results. It is also possible to describe relationships between a number of variables simultaneously. Such a coefficient is known as a multiple correlation coefficient (R).

Observation. This method is valuable because it permits study of kinds of behavior for which no tests are available. It should be performed systematically, however, if it is to be of value. Rating scales and check lists direct observation toward certain aspects of behavior and generally require some discrimination or judgment on the part of the observer. The guess-who procedure and sociograms are devices for obtaining information from members of a group about their feelings and attitudes toward each other. In the guess-who procedure, children are given a list of descriptive phrases such as "the person who is most helpful" and are asked to indicate the classmate who is best fitted by the phrase. A sociogram is a device for plotting the pattern of choices and rejections between members in a group. Each of these procedures provides systematic information about intra-group attitudes and status. Time sampling is a method for making observations at given time intervals and for given lengths of time, thus insuring the observer of a well balanced behavior sample of the person being observed, rather than merely recording that which happened to attract the viewer's attention. Accidental observations by teachers are not unlike dripping faucets and squeaking wheels. We tend to see what we are conscious of and looking for and overlook that which does not attract our attention. As a result, we develop distorted—or at least highly selective—pictures of a child's behavior.

Reports and Questionnaires. Verbal reports, both written and oral, are used extensively in the clinical method of obtaining information. Questionnaires, inventories, and interviews are used to develop case studies and make available intensive background information for understanding the individual. The use of these procedures is not restricted to individual case studies but may be used also in inventories of interests, vocational preference, samplings of public opinion and attitudes, and market research. These procedures have to be used with skill and discretion if the results are to have any validity.

McNemar (1946) provides a detailed analysis of the difficulties besetting the questionnaire method, which, because of its inherent weaknesses, is not considered a first-rate scientific procedure. In addition to vexing problems in formulating good questions, there is danger that the data will be unreliable because the subjects misinterpret questions, answer inaccurately on account of ignorance, or answer untruthfully through desire to make a good impression. Responses of individuals will vary with the status of the person to whom they are reporting. Furthermore, the interviewer may exert influence on the forthcoming response by such means as the following: making negative statements of the question, attempting to balance positive statements, loading by introducing emotionally charged words or phrases, presenting contingent or conditional ideas, juxtaposing questions, inserting suggestive elements, using alternate wording, introducing prestige elements, personalizing the question, stereotyping, and using technical or biased words. Thus, many hazards beset the investigator who uses the questionnaire for obtaining data, for the way in which the questions are framed will cause variations in the answers obtained. Another major flaw which frequently results is that of biased returns. In all research, it is essential that a representative sample be obtained if results are to be meaningful. Questionnaire methods are particularly susceptible to biased or unrepresentative samples.

In spite of such difficulties, the questionnaire has its place when used with discretion. It has been fruitful in making surveys of opinions and interests and has been the means of collecting valuable data when no other method was available. It is widely used in public opinion polling with reasonable accuracy when sample and questions are carefully drawn, although major errors still occur, as in the 1948 presidential election in which pollsters erred in their prediction. They are less likely to do so today because of increasing methodological sophistication.

Diaries and creative work—finger painting, clay modeling, story writing, or poetry—provide material which in the hands of trained psychologists may be interpreted in a manner similar to the projective tests, and probably are most useful in providing clues or leads for further study or investigation by other methods.

EXPERIMENTAL METHODS

The more exact and refined methods of research are to be found in the scientific experiment which differs from the non-experimental procedures largely in the extent to which rigid controls are introduced in order to determine the relationships between independent and dependent variables. The investigator is primarily interested in functional relationships—the extent to which alteration in an independent variable is associated with or produces variations in the dependent variable. For example, how do variations in amount of practice facilitate or hamper the learning of a given motor skill?

A variety of procedures has been devised for studying learning—both animal and human—under different circumstances. Conditioning experiments, puzzle boxes, discrimination problems, mazes, detour problems, reasoning tasks, and social learning situations have been utilized in both animal and human learning experiments, while the learning of verbal materials, motor skills, concepts, and the solving of problems has been used extensively with human subjects. Usually a particular procedure has been associated with certain types of learning questions.

Laboratory Experiments.   In considering the various experimental procedures utilized, it is convenient to distinguish between laboratory and field situations. The laboratory provides an enormous advantage in the degree of control that can be exerted on conditions influencing experimental results and the restrictions which the experimenter can introduce on the number of variables in operation. However, the restrictions imposed in obtaining experimental rigor also often limit the generalizations that can be made to life situations. Several basic types of experimental situations are widely used.

Classical Conditioning.   The study of conditioning originated with Pavlov, who perceived that the salivation which occurs in response to food can also be elicited by a different stimulus, such as a bell, if the ringing of the bell precedes or accompanies the presentation of the food for a number of trials. He called these responses to the substitute stimuli conditioned reflexes; in present usage, the term applied is *conditioned response*. A wide variety of responses such as salivation, muscular contraction, eye wink, leg flexion, and others can be conditioned to substitute stimuli in both animal and human subjects. The essential characteristic of classical conditioning is that a previously unassociated stimulus comes to substitute for the original unconditioned stimulus in eliciting a particular response.

Pavlov chose salivating as the particular response to be studied, not only because he was a physiologist but also because it was easily obtained and observed and the amount of salivation readily measured. As Pavlov (1927) wrote:

> . . . if the intake of food by the animal takes place simultaneously with the action of a neutral stimulus which has been hitherto in no way related to the food, the neutral stimulus readily acquires the property of eliciting

the same reaction in the animal as would the food itself. This was the case with the dog employed in our experiment with the metronome . . . . after several repetitions of the combined stimulation, the sounds of the metronome had acquired the property of stimulating salivary secretion and of evoking the motor reactions characteristic of the alimentary reflex.

The critical relationship in the experiment was the time relation between the original stimulus (*Unconditioned*) and the neutral (*Conditioned* *Stimulus*). The two had to occur close together in time with the CS occurring ahead of the US. The conventional diagram for this type of conditional learning is:

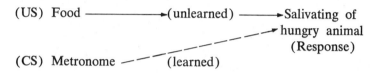

(US) Food ─────────→(unlearned) ─────→Salivating of
                                          hungry animal
                                          (Response)
(CS) Metronome ─ ─ ─ ─ (learned)

The natural response of salivating in the presence of food is referred to as the *Unconditioned Response*. When this response comes to be given to the metronome in the absence of food, it is referred to as a *Conditioned Response*.

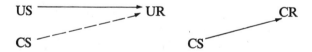

US ─────────→ UR   CR
CS ─ ─ ─ ─   CS ─

An essential feature of the experimental design is the link between the US and the UR. The original response follows the presentation of the US. We shall see that this distinction is important when we look at instrumental learning where the reverse occurs, food following the response. It is important to recall that Pavlov chose to study salivation. This was not the only response conditioned during the experiment, merely the response observed by the experimenter. It follows that other reactions of the animal were being simultaneously conditioned. For example, if the animal pressed forward as well as salivated, that too was subject to the same conditioning. Note also that salivation is only a fraction of the total set of responses made by an animal to food. It makes various muscular and postural movements as well. To a greater or lesser degree, some conditioning occurs between the range of stimuli and the set of responses occurring contemporaneously with the presentation of the food. In Pavlov's experiments, primary reinforcement was given by design to the association between the sound and salivation.

Is the association between the conditioned stimulus and the conditioned response permanent? The answer to this question is obtained by presenting the conditioned stimulus repeatedly without the presence of the food. When this is done, the salivation gradually decreases and ultimately disappears. This procedure is known as *extinction*. After a rest interval, the association shows a *spontaneous recovery,* indicating that it had not been exhausted but *inhibited*. However, over a repeated series of extinction trials, the point is reached where the conditioned response is completely extinguished. Some periodic reinforcement (presentation of food in conjunction with the conditioned stimulus) is needed to maintain the strength of the association. Thus, the conditioning of the response to the sound and its preservation depend upon the repetition of the reinforcement provided by the food.

Reinforcement plays a vital role in learning. In many respects, the initial learning situation of the newborn infant parallels that of Pavlov's dogs. Each time the hungry infant is fed, a range of stimuli (being held, mother's face, mother's voice, various smells, and so on) occurs contemporaneously with the primary reinforcer, the milk, and consequently the milk and the stimuli become combined in the infant's experience. The critical questions are: (1) what sorts of stimuli function as reinforcers, (2) how do they function, and (3) are they essential? Put another way: can learning occur in the absence of any reinforcement?

Trial and Error Learning. It was pointed out that an essential feature of the classical conditioning experiment was the fact that the response was contingent upon the occurrence of the reinforcer. Until the food was presented, salivation did not occur and could not be conditioned to the sound of the metronome. This situation is reversed in trial and error learning; the response to the conditioned stimulus *must* be made before reinforcement can occur. Parents and principals frequently dictate that participation in athletics is forbidden without passing grades. Without arguing its validity, the assumption is that whatever behavior is required to get passing grades will be strengthened. It can be demonstrated in many less complicated learning situations that this is a fact, not an assumption.

Thorndike studied the character of trial and error learning in a number of experiments with cats. A favorite device was the puzzle box, essentially a cage with a door operated by some type of release mechanism such as a string, lever, or pole as shown in Figure 2.6. In order to escape from the box and obtain a reward, such as food placed outside the box, the animal must operate the release mechanism.

On each trial, the cat was placed in the box and the door was shut. A dish of salmon was placed on the floor outside the box near the door but beyond the cat's reach. The cat was given 100 trials, ten each morning and each afternoon for five days. He was fed at the end of each experimental period and then was given nothing more to eat until after the next session. If, after opening the door in any trial, he went immediately to the food, he

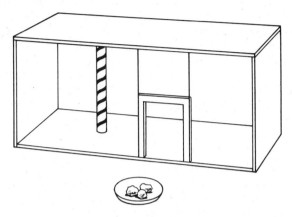

Fig. 2.6 Cage with pole releasing mechanism. *Used in puzzle-box experiments.*

was allowed a small taste. A complete record was made of the cat's behavior during each trial.

The outstanding points revealed by the results were:

1. In the early stages there was *a great variety of activity,* and the tripping of the lever which opened the door was just part of the great mass of activity that was taking place. This activity included looking around, turning, walking about, sticking paws through the opening at the side of the door, poking and scratching the door inside and out, sitting down, biting the levers in the cage, reaching for the food with paws, mewing, clawing at a peg by the door, backing around, and so on.

2. *The situation was problematic.* The cat wanted to get out. He was hungry and the only way to get to the food was to escape from the box. He did not know how to get out. All he could do was to keep trying with all the means available. He had to experiment, and he experimented by doing just about everything a cat could do in such a situation.

3. *The successes in the early trials were accidental* in the sense that the cat saw no relation between pressing the lever and the opening of the door. In some cases he did not even notice that the door had opened for several seconds after he had released the fastener.

4. There was *a gradual elimination of useless activity* as the cat was called on to repeat his performance in successive trials. It is significant, moreover, that elimination took place of actions that had been repeated dozens of times—an example of the fact that repetition alone does not serve to "stamp in" a mode of response.

5. After the cat had opened the door several times in the early part of the experiment by awkwardly backing onto the lever, sitting on it, or

stumbling over it when backing from the door, he apparently *related his backing up with escape.* The record shows that as soon as he backed into the lever he turned to look at the door. He followed the backing procedure for many trials. At this stage in the development of his knowledge, he doubtless would have argued stoutly with his feline companions that he knew walking backward caused the door to open. That he had not yet grasped the relation between pushing down the lever and the opening of the door is shown by the several instances in which he stepped completely over the lever while backing. When he did this, he continued walking backward all the way around the cage.

6. As the trials went on, there was *a gradual discovery of the relation between pushing on the lever and the opening of the door.* This discovery, indicated by the cat's looking toward the door as he pressed the lever, gave new significance to the lever and the reaction to it.

7. There was a gradual *differentiation* and *consolidation* of the movements appropriate for the quickest and most direct solution of the situation. The behavior became effectively organized with respect to the goal.

8. Throughout the 100 trials of this experiment, *the cat's behavior was not a response to an isolated stimulus* but to a whole constellation of factors making up the entire problem situation. The food was a stimulus-object, but the cat acted as he did because the food was outside the box, beyond his reach, and he was inside and hungry.

The elements present were: (1) motivation, (2) varied activity, (3) progressive elimination of unsuccessful responses, and (4) discovery and stabilization of the correct response. Central to the entire process was what Thorndike dubbed "The Law of Effect," which states, essentially, that learning results as an effect of motivation being satisfied. Thus began one of the major streams of experimental psychology in America and one of the most significant for education, that of prescribing the role of reward (reinforcement) in learning.

Thorndike was a prodigious worker and as concerned with the practical matters of learning as with the theoretical. He started inquiries into the study of rewards and punishments which are only today coming to fruition as Skinner's work on operant conditioning is being translated into behavioral modification techniques.

Operant Conditioning. B. F. Skinner and his associates have intensively studied trial and error learning and successive approximation, naming it operant conditioning. As an example of operant conditioning (see Figure 2.7): a pigeon is placed in a Skinner Box with the intention of having it learn a right-turning response. Obviously, the response selected has to be within the capacity of the organism. The box is rigged so that when the bird makes an appropriate response, a buzzer sounds and feed drops into the food tray. To begin with, each time the bird begins to move to the right he is rewarded with feed in the food tray. In order to con-

Fig. 2.7 Skinner Box showing food trough in which
pigeon receives reward when he gives desired pecking
response at black disc.

tinue to receive food, he has to turn farther and farther. Responses other
than right-turning are not rewarded. Gradually, the bird swings in longer
and longer arcs, being rewarded as he does so, until he ultimately swings
past the mid-point of the turn. With successive reinforcement, the turning
becomes more proficient as extraneous moves are dropped. Diagrammatically, the behavior is seen as follows:

Turning Response ⟶ Food ⟶ Eating

Operant behavior ⟶ Reinforcing ⟶ Unconditioned
                   Stimulus   Response

Skinner refers to the training sequence just described as *response
differentiation*. The appropriate response is singled out from others. Similarly, operant conditioning can be applied to *stimulus discrimination*. A
white disc can be presented to the pigeon on the wall above the food tray.
By receiving a reward for every move towards the disc and no reward for
other moves, the pigeon can be trained to peck the disc to obtain food. He
gradually gets closer and closer and ultimately pecks at the disc. Once the
pecking response is stabilized, the pigeon can learn not to peck at a black
disc by being given a reward for every peck at the white and no reward
for a peck at the black. This behavior may be diagrammed as follows:

White disc ⟶ Pecking Behavior ⟶ Food ⟶ Eating

Conditioned ⟶ Operant Behavior ⟶ Reinforcing ⟶ Unconditioned
Stimulus   (Conditioned   Stimulus   Response
               Response)

The essential difference between this pattern and that of classical
conditioning should be clear. In classical conditioning, the CS is presented

in conjunction with the US (reinforcer), which elicits the UR. After repeated presentations, the CS acquires the capacity to elicit the CR, which differs in degree from the UR. In operant conditioning, the pigeon operates on the environment, offering a response to the particular stimulus arrangement. When the response is appropriate (satisfies the experimenter—or the teacher), reinforcement is provided; i.e., food appears and is eaten.

In discrimination learning experiments, the organism, animal or human, is presented with the problem of differentiating between two stimuli, one of which requires a positive response, the other requiring either no response or a different one. The situation is analogous to that of the aviation gunner who must identify an approaching plane as friend or foe before deciding whether or not to fire. The situation requires that the gunner be able to recognize small differences in shape or silhouette of various aircraft and respond accordingly. Considering aircraft speed, which makes a decision necessary within a short time, the similarity of aircraft shapes, and the variety of airplanes involved, the discrimination required is a difficult one.

Escape Learning. Thus far the reinforcers described have been positive stimuli in that they provide a satisfying end state. Avoidance of or escape from painful or noxious stimuli can also be reinforcing (as teachers and parents, with their either-or conditions, well know). Figure 2.8 shows a training apparatus used by Miller (1948) in the study of learned drives. It contains two compartments, the left painted white, the right painted black. The floor of the white compartment contains an electric grid by means of which a rat can be shocked. Animals placed in the white compartment and shocked on ten successive trials quickly learned to escape the shock by running into the other compartment. Prior to this experience, the animals exhibited no preference for either side; subsequently, they were motivated to avoid the white side even though a shock did not occur on subsequent trials. That the animals had learned to fear (had acquired a fear drive through learning) the white side was seen by the fact that a drive state existed which produced further learning. If the exitway was blocked by a door which opened by the turning of a wheel, the animals learned to operate the wheel to escape. On first encountering this barrier, they exhibited symptoms of fear (tenseness, crouching, defecating), but they also engaged in varied actions which ultimately led to opening the door. Much as in trial and error learning, proficiency at wheel turning progressed rapidly. The escape learning can be diagrammed as follows:

Fear ⟶	Avoidance of Shock ⟶	Wheel-turning ⟶	Escape and fear reduction
(Conditioned Stimulus)	(Uncond. Response)	(Conditioned Response Operant behavior)	(Reinforcement)

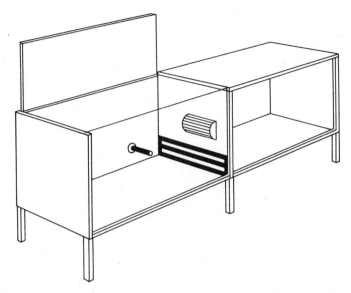

Fig. 2.8 Box used by Miller to study acquired fear in rats. *Left side of box was white, right side was black. In conditioning series of trials, animal was shocked in white box, door in center dropped, permitting animal to escape to black side. In subsequent trials, fear functioned as a drive, the animal learning to operate lever or wheel to drop door and escape the white compartment, even though no further shocks were administered.*

Taken as a group, trial and error learning, operant conditioning, and escape learning are referred to as *instrumental learning* to distinguish them from classical conditioning. The term instrumental implies that some act or response of the animal is instrumental in producing reinforcement, in contrast with classical conditioning where the reinforcement elicits the response.

Verbal Learning.   A type of material used extensively with human subjects is verbal material, both meaningful and nonsense. As previously described, Ebbinghaus invented the nonsense syllable for study of the learning of verbal materials in order to control variation in meaningfulness. However, these so-called nonsense syllables vary in meaningfulness, as-sociations being more easily established with syllables such as JAN, KEN, MEX than with GUQ, SIJ, YUS. Material can be varied from that which is completely meaningless to the more meaningful words found in lan-guage. Nonsense syllables, word lists, foreign words, prose, poetry, and so on, have all been used in experiments studying the learning and reten-tion of verbal materials.

Of the several procedures available for studying the influence of practice on the learning of verbal materials, two procedures are most frequently used. The first is called the *anticipation method* in which a list of words, either nonsense or meaningful, is presented for a standard period of time at a uniform rate to the subject. The latter's task is to associate each word with the subsequent one so that he can anticipate its occurrence on subsequent trials by naming it prior to its appearance. The subject is expected to announce his anticipation. Each word serves as the cue for the following word, and the subject's anticipation is confirmed or corrected when the following word appears. A typical example from everyday experience is memorizing prose or poetry, or remembering directions.

A second procedure is the *paired associates method* in which the words are presented in discrete pairs to the subject, whose task is to recall the second after seeing the first. The order of the pairs of words is usually varied from trial to trial in order to prevent the subjects from using serial anticipation learning of the second words in each pair, rather than associating them with the stimulus word, the first word of the pair. The pairs may consist of two words, a word and a number, two nonsense syllables, or items of other kinds of material. The score consists of the number of appropriate responses given when the stimulus items are presented in the test. To illustrate, the learning series could be: house–62, leaf–96, dog–35, and so forth. After training, the words would be presented one at a time, and the subject would be expected to give the number paired with each. The total number of correct responses is the score. The paired associates method is similar in form to several common learning tasks. Pairing state capitals with their respective states, foreign vocabulary words with their English equivalents, or learning multiplication tables are all everyday uses of the paired associates method.

Problem Solving. Several different types of experiments may be grouped under the heading of problem solving. Delayed reaction experiments are those in which a stimulus such as food is placed in a container and then hidden from view for a short period of time by interposing a screen, thus forcing a delay in the response of the animal. Particularly in long delays, some kind of learning has to mediate between the presentation of the stimulus and the making of the correct response. Experiments of this type have been used for comparing differences in capacity of organisms to make correct responses after varying delays.

So-called reasoning problems, which require the organism to achieve a novel solution either on the first trial or after repeated failures, differ from the conditioning and trial and error learning tasks: the solution is abruptly made, rather than gradually in the manner characteristic of conditioning and trial and error. An illustration may be given from an experiment by Maier (1945) in which two strings were suspended from the ceiling far enough apart so that they could not both be reached simultaneously. The subject was instructed to tie the ends together. Solving such a problem requires recombining previous experiences into new combinations.

Detour problems, which require a subject to move away from the goal in order to finally reach it, have been used particularly with children. The situation ordinarily involves a desired goal-object to which access is blocked by a barrier. The goal can be obtained only by moving away from the goal in order to get around the barrier. For example, candy may be placed within view on the opposite side of the screen from a child who may try to reach through the screen unsuccessfully. To obtain the candy, the child must overcome the immediate appeal of the goal-object—the candy—and move to one end of the screen in order to get past it and obtain the candy.

Field Experiments.   Applied psychology depends on experiments performed under natural conditions as well as the results of laboratory experiments. Field studies may come from an attempt to extend laboratory findings; they may represent a preliminary exploration aimed at identifying relevant variables operational in a given area; and they may consist of empirical effort to increase functional effectiveness in a given learning situation. In the laboratory experiment, the objective is more likely an attempt to isolate or demonstrate the effects of a single variable. In the field situation, the experimenter's task is essentially to establish a procedure which permits him to identify or control the effects or influences which determine the outcomes of the experiment. Generally, three sources of influence have to be controlled in an experiment. They are: (1) those associated with the population used, (2) those derived from the experimental procedure followed, and (3) external influences, including the experimenter.

Establishing adequate controls in a complex learning experiment is difficult. An investigator wishes to determine whether teaching arithmetic by drill or understanding is the more satisfactory method. The question is broad, too broad for a single experiment, and must be delimited: (1) what arithmetic: addition, multiplication, fractions, and so on; (2) at which grade level; and (3) what specifically is meant by "drill or understanding?"

Controlling Population Variables.   With respect to the population to be utilized in such a study, there are several factors which could influence the results that would be obtained in the experiment. Age, intelligence, previous experience, motivation, and education are factors associated with population and could produce variations in the results obtained; they must therefore be controlled in some fashion.

It is quite apparent that learning varies with the age of the subject and with differences in intelligence. The amount of arithmetic learned by either method could easily vary with differences in previous experience or education. If some students were more highly motivated than others, they would be likely to learn more. Native characteristics and previous experience can affect experimental results, therefore procedures which do two things have been adopted: (1) identify variations in experimental outcomes associated with individual differences by systematically varying the differences, and (2) distribute the effects of individual variation as uniformly as possible by randomly assigning individuals to experimental groups. In experimental terminology, "random" does not mean haphazard but rather unbiased variation.

In the arithmetic groups, the influence of certain individual differences could be ascertained. Within the experimental groups, it would be possible to identify sub-groups of superior, average, and inferior ability, or sub-groups whose prior training had been by drill or understanding methods, or even combinations of these categories. Attitudes and motivation would be more difficult to control by systematic variation. A most important consideration is the selection of representative samples from the stipulated populations. The experimenter must first define the population to be utilized in his experiment and then, being unable to experiment on all such subjects, randomly select a sample of that population for the experiment. If the sample is biased, it is impossible to know if the results hold true for the total population.

Unfortunately, there are often deviations which occur in actual practice and produce unspecified effects. Many learning experiments are performed upon volunteer groups of college students. Considering the variations in student bodies from college to college and even the differences between students in one college curriculum compared with those in another, it can scarcely be claimed that samples used in these studies are representative of human beings in general or college students in particular. In the arithmetic experiment being discussed, it would not be uncommon to use entire classes; for example, three entire classes may be selected to provide a sample of 100 fourth grade pupils, instead of taking a random sample of all fourth grade pupils in the community, mainly because it is easier to work with intact classes than to use a few students from each class. Such a procedure violates the requirement for having *representative, randomly selected samples.*

A third step in controlling errors resulting from differences in the population samples is the use of large enough numbers to insure some reliability and stability of results. The smaller the sample, the greater is the possibility that it is not representative. Large numbers offset this type of error. Unfortunately, large numbers do not offset errors resulting from biased sampling.

Controlling Experimental Variables. Another set of variables arising from the experimental procedure must be controlled. In the case being discussed, the amount of practice, the distribution of practice, the subject matter content for various lessons, the measures used to establish gains, the total time period over which the lessons extend, and other details of organization would have to be regulated. It well could be that a drill method would show greater results over a short time period, or that it would show greater gains by the end of the teaching period but greater losses than the understanding method over a longer period of time. Conversely the understanding method could easily show smaller initial gains but less forgetting over an extended period of time. The subject material would have to be equally susceptible to teaching by either method. Another important consideration would be the criterion established for measuring gains. For instance, if the measure used was speed of multiplication or addition, the drill group would likely be superior, whereas if the solving of unfamiliar problems involving multiplication and addition were the test, the understanding group would probably be favored. Utilizing several measures is a safeguard against such errors.

Two methods are utilized for controlling the effects of practice. The control group method is a procedure whereby two groups are selected as representative samples from the same population. One of the groups is exposed to the experimental procedure, a second is used as a control group. In the present experiment, it would be necessary to have two experimental groups, one for drill and one for understanding, and a control group. The effects of practice are established by determining the net differences between the scores of the experimental and control groups at the beginning and end of the experiment. Thus, the amount by which the drill group exceeded the control group would be compared to the like gain of the understanding group.

Statistical procedures have been developed for comparing scores of groups, thus making it possible to tell whether the differences in scores of two groups are sufficiently great to be real differences or whether they are only chance fluctuations. If the dart throwing scores of an individual or group of individuals were recorded over several trials, they would have some variation, even though the skill of the throwers remained constant. If many scores for each individual were available, it would be possible to use an average score. But in experiments such as have been described, the experimenter ordinarily has only a single score for each person, with no way of knowing whether that score happens to be typical or a chance low score or a chance high score. In order to make sound conclusions regarding the usefulness of one method over another, the experimenter has to know whether the differences obtained between experimental and control groups are greater than could be anticipated on the basis of chance fluctuations in scores. The experimenter starts by making the assumption that there is basically no difference (the *null hypothesis*) and that observed differences are merely chance fluctuations. Only when the observed differences become so great that it is improbable to attribute them to chance, does the investigator reject the null hypothesis and accept the difference as real; i.e., one method is more effective than the other.

The problems of control of method are essentially to reduce errors which arise from differences in the way groups are treated. This is in contrast to the problems discussed in the section on controlling population variables in which the errors arose from biased or faulty sampling of individuals. Statistical procedures which permit an estimate of chance fluctuations make it possible for the experimenter to say that a difference between two methods is greater than can be anticipated on the basis of chance; i.e., it is statistically significant. Where chance fluctuations are small, or large numbers of subjects are used, a modest difference will often prove statistically significant, i.e., have a low probability (P.05, .01, .001) of occurring by chance. Where sampling fluctuations are large, or the number of subjects small, a difference will have to be proportionately greater to be significant.

When differences are small and statistically non-significant, one has no way of knowing whether they are chance fluctuations or real differences.

Controlling External Influences. Finally, external influences have to be controlled; the physical and social environment can influence outcomes. Extraneous noise or poor acoustics which interferes with attention or hearing must be avoided. The questions of teacher proficiency and personality and how to control them are difficult even if several instructors are used. If only two teachers are used, one for each method, they can easily vary in their skill or preference for a given method. Several instructors can be used, but still a problem of assignment exists—of guaranteeing that both methods are taught at equivalent levels of proficiency by equally motivated instructors. It is implicit in the scientific method that an experiment should yield the same results if repeated. However effectively the population and method variables may be controlled, a third set of errors derives from unequal characteristics allied with external conditions of the experiment.

Experimental Design. No mention has been made of the effects of interaction between the many variables, but it should be evident that no one variable operates singly in human learning, that several or perhaps all are operating simultaneously and in conjunction with each other, and that they are likely to produce different results in different combinations.

As we see, an experiment is a procedure for finding answers to research questions by introducing controls which reduce or eliminate variation in scores due to sources other than the variables associated with the research question—namely, errors in sampling, faults in procedure, or extraneous influences. The essential purpose of the experiment is to expose a relationship between variables and/or permit a comparison of the degree of influence of experimental variables.

In both laboratory and field, the experiment is designed and conducted to provide maximum contrast between the selected variables. In both, every effort is made to minimize error variance. In the field, it is more difficult to avoid or control extraneous factors which systematically affect results. For example, a study of two procedures for teaching science, using one hour of the school week, has no way of knowing or controlling the amounts of learning which result from other sources, e.g., television programs, reading, hobbies, and others.

Several procedures are available to the researcher in attempting to control the influence of extraneous factors. Again, the most important of these is *randomization.* In the true experiment, the researcher has the power to randomly select and assign subjects to groups, and then to randomly assign the groups to experimental treatments. This is sometimes true in the laboratory, rarely in the field. For example, a psychology instructor asks for volunteers for an experiment. He has no way of knowing what the volunteers represent by way of population. Obviously, they differ from students in general because of greater interest, at least in a willingness to volunteer. Thus the experimenter has lost control over selection. An even greater fault is that mentioned earlier regarding most studies in school settings, assigning entire classes to a given experimental condition. Ideally, the experimenter should randomly select and assign the pupils, but because it is administratively awkward to break up classes for purposes of an experiment, this rarely happens. And when the experimenter assigns one class from school A to the experimental group, and another from school B as a control group, he knowingly violates the principle of randomization because the two classes are most likely not equivalent.

A second procedure for controlling extraneous influences is *homogenization.* For example, in the science experiment mentioned above, it would be possible to eliminate sex differences as a factor affecting result by using boys only or girls only, knowing that boys and girls differ in their interests in science and that this difference could affect results. Thus, the experimenter might choose to perform his experiment in boys' schools. Another extraneous factor could be teacher enthusiasm and skill in teaching science. The presence of such teachers in the experimental group but not in the control group could easily produce superior results which would lead the experimenter to think it was the instructional materials which were superior. In one study, this factor of teacher ability was controlled by using teachers of only average ability (as measured by class achievement in science in a previous experiment). Thus, the teachers were relatively homogeneous.

A third procedure for controlling an extraneous factor is to *make it an experimental variable.* Should the experimenter decide to use private boys' schools in his science study, he is controlling the sex variable but introducing a socioeconomic factor. Whatever his experimental outcomes, the experimenter does not know if they apply to boys in general. One possible solution is to use boys in a school serving a less advantaged population, perhaps a parochial school in a poorer neighborhood. (Once more, the student would see another factor being introduced in the attempt to exercise control over the socioeconomic variable.)

A final procedure available to the experimenter is that of *matching* subjects. He could select pairs of students matched for intelligence, sex and socioeconomic background, then randomly assign them to experimental or control conditions. For example, if he is studying the effects of different environments upon the development of intelligence or temperament, the use of identical twins (matched genetically) would control the factor of native ability. In practice, it is difficult to effectively match on more than one or two variables, which creates a problem where several are operative. Thus, the most difficult task facing the person experimenting with human learning is establishing experimental conditions which take into account the simultaneous operation of multiple variables producing multiple effects.

An exposition on the variety of research designs available requires a volume in its own right. Several are suggested in the bibliography at the end of the chapter. Certain important distinctions between faulty and good experimental design emerge from the discussion thus far. Faulty designs usually fail to provide for randomized selection and assignment of subjects, and for the provision of suitable control groups with which comparison of results can be made. Thus, the retrospective case study approach fails on both counts. One need only observe the multiple and conflicting explanations offered to account for crime and delinquency to understand the problem. Looking back through the life history of individuals or looking at existing conditions may offer possible clues but fails to provide dependable explanation. The sampling is selective, control over variables non-existent, and the data haphazard, to mention only the most obvious faults. Not quite so bad a design is the single-group study in which the group is tested before and after some specified experimental treatment. Many experiments in teaching follow such a pattern, experiments in which an instructor evaluates the effectiveness of a given procedure by testing before and afterward and noting gains made. Aside from the dubiousness of generalizing from the results due to the accidental nature of the grouping, the basic shortcoming is the lack of a control group in order to make a comparison. Occasionally, an effort is made to include a control group by using a second group or class which happens to be available; but if the experimenter lacks knowledge of the equivalence of the groups, any comparisons he may make are invalid. Thus, it is essential that the experimental subjects be randomly assigned to experimental treatments, even if they cannot be randomly selected. Second, pre- and post-tests or measures are needed to determine the changes resulting from experimental conditions. Third, a control group (again randomly assigned) is needed for a basis of comparison. Ideally, the experiment will include more than one experimental group in order that one set of experimental conditions can be compared with another—something versus something—and more than one control group will be used. It has been demonstrated with both animals and men that merely being subjected to an experiment can produce effects. For example, taking a pre-test can produce learning with the result that post-test scores may be higher. Thus, one control group can be pre- and post-tested, providing testing experience comparable to the experimental groups, whereas the second control group is post-tested only to check the effects of participating in the experiment.

The student may marvel that experiments are ever attempted in view of the difficulties involved. Actually, there is no shortage of experiments. Unfortunately, the results of many experiments are of dubious value because of experimental naïveté. With carefully performed experiments, comparisons are difficult because of variations in procedure or population. Nevertheless, in spite of these difficulties, an extensive body of experimental research has been established which today resembles a partly finished jig-saw puzzle.

There are many areas in psychology and learning in which research is limited. Our knowledge of creative thinking, imagination, forgetting, development of attitudes, and emotional responses is rudimentary. Many of our teaching practices are based upon conjecture, logic, and limited experience. To a great extent, our teaching practices are based upon *experimenting* rather than on *experiments*. The results of such empirical judgments can be excellent; nevertheless, we do not know the *how* and *why* of what occurs, only the *what*. Controlled experiments are needed to learn the *how* and *why*.

SUMMARY

An experimental approach to problem solving and adjustment to new situations can be found in much of our behavior. Usually, the approach is unsystematic even though based on guesses with respect to solutions. Scientific experiments differ in their provision for systematic procedures for gathering information and testing hypotheses under controlled conditions. Scientific theory results from attempts to generalize regarding a range of experimental data and to explain those data. Further experiments refute, confirm, or force modification of theory. Psychology became a science when an experimental approach was adopted.

Both experimental and non-experimental methods are fruitfully used. Tests, statistics, observations, and verbal reports are used in differential psychology and clinical psychology in surveys, descriptive studies, and investigations of individual and group behavior.

The purpose of experimental studies is to discover the relationships functioning between variables. Controls are essential to eliminate or hold constant the influence from factors other than the variables being investigated. Such influences arise from population sources, experimental procedures, and external influences. Sampling procedures, matched groups, control groups, counterbalanced presentation, statistical methods, standardized experimental procedures, and reporting of procedures and results are methods used in the effort to control variables and carry on experimental investigations. In the laboratory, several experimental prototypes are regularly used in studying classical conditioning, instrumental learning, verbal learning, and problem solving.

FURTHER READING

Overview

HILGARD, E. R. Methods and procedures in the study of learning. In S. S. Stevens (ed.). 1951. *Handbook of Experimental Psychology*. New York: Wiley.

Selected References

ANASTASI, ANNE and J. P. FOLEY. 1950. *Differential Psychology*. New York: Macmillan.

CAMPBELL, D. T. and J. C. STANLEY. Experimental and quasi-experimental designs for research in teaching. In N. L. Gage (ed.). 1963. *Handbook of Research on Teaching*. Chicago: Rand-McNally.

GAGE, N. L. Paradigms for research on teaching. In N. L. Gage (ed.). 1963. *Handbook of Research on Teaching*. Chicago: Rand-McNally.

HYMAN, R. 1963. *The Nature of Psychological Inquiry*. Englewood Cliffs, N. J.: Prentice-Hall.

KERLINGER, F. N. 1964. *Foundations of Behavioral Research*. New York: Holt, Rinehart, Winston.

LINDQUIST, E. G. 1953. *Design and Analysis of Experiments in Psychology and Education*. Boston: Houghton Mifflin.

OSGOOD, C. E. 1953. *Method and Theory in Experimental Psychology*. New York: Oxford Univ. Press.

Original Investigations

CAMPBELL, D. T. 1957. Factors relevant to the validity of experiments in social settings. *Psychol. Bull.*, 54: 297-312.

CHANDLER, R. E. 1957. The statistical concepts of confidence and significance. *Psychol. Bull.*, 54: 429-30.

SIEGEL, L. and LILA SIEGEL. 1967. A multivariate paradigm for educational research. *Psychol. Bull.*, 68: 306-26.

SITGREAVES, ROSEDITH and H. SOLOMON. 1957. Research methods: status studies and sample surveys. *R. Educ. Res.*, 27: 460-70.

STANLEY, J. C. 1957. Research methods: experimental design. *Rev. Educ. Res.*, 27: 449-59.

3

The Measurement
of Learning

In the investigation of learning in the psychological laboratory, the early experimenters studied forms of learning which were easily observable and measurable, such as typewriting or rote memorizing of nonsense materials. In these situations, it was easy to plot the rate of learning or forgetting in terms of such scores as the number of items learned, the number of items retained, or the number of errors made in a series of trials. Initially, there was a tendency to underestimate the complexity of learning; the result was that overgeneralizations were made from the experimental results. An experimental fact with which many students in college are familiar is the rapidity of forgetting; forgetting is greatest immediately after learning, then gradually slows.

This generalization, which was experimentally established in Ebbinghaus's studies of retention, is frequently presumed to apply to all situations and all materials, overlooking the fact that the generalization is limited to situations in which the conditions and the materials are similar to those in the experiment.

As psychological experimentation in learning expanded during the last half century, much effort was devoted to determining the circumstances under which particular generalizations regarding learning applied. More important, psychologists strove to develop theories which could reconcile or account for the many divergent facts and generalizations which were obtained in experiments under different conditions, and to develop experimental procedures and measures which would permit more refined observation and more sophisticated conclusions regarding the effect of different variables upon learning.

Essentially the measurement of learning consists of obtaining a dependable set of observations of performance during a series of practice trials. Complications are introduced by the fact that the same types of measures are not applicable to all kinds of learning. Perceptual-motor learning ordinarily involves observation of the speed, accuracy, or volume of work or skill demonstrated; verbal learning, the recognition or recall of symbolic materials; and problem solving, the ability to achieve a solution. Moreover, in describing verbal and motor learning, a distinction must be made between the acquisition of the material or skill and its retention. In actual experience, both learning and retention are occurring simultaneously and are interacting with each other. For instance, a child learning to spell words ending in "ought," such as fought or bought, may begin misspelling words which he had previously learned, such as caught and taught. If learning occurred on a single trial, then subsequent measures of the event would be of retention. But where learning requires repeated trials, an individual's performance on any trial after the first includes that which he has retained from previous trials plus that which he has learned during the most recent trial. In practice, it is customary to describe the acquisition of a skill or behavior up to a specified point or degree of mastery as learning, and naming subsequent measures as retention.

Response Frequency, Latency, and Amplitude.   The frequency with which a response occurs, the length of time elapsing between presentation of a stimulus and the occurrence of the response (latency), and the amplitude or strength of the response are commonly used measures of simple learning, particularly in conditioning experiments, both classical and instrumental. The strength of a habit is commonly gauged by the number of responses which will be given without reinforcement during a series of extinction trials. As we shall see in the discussion of theories of learning, Skinner uses frequency of responses, either per unit of time or per number of reinforcements, as a measure of the efficacy of different reinforcement schedules. The speed with which a response can be given provides a natural index of learning, particularly in the discrimination learning of both animal and human subjects. In simplest form, the task may require no more than speed of recognition of a size, shape, or color difference. At a more complex level, it may involve coding and decoding, a task in which a continuous sequence of stimuli are experienced and translated. The situation may involve Morse Code or more complicated simultaneous translation of a foreign language. In either case, speed of response provides a measure of degree of learning. Latency measures tend to be somewhat less reliable than response frequency, in part because of oscillations in the response set of the organism. Amplitude of response is more likely to involve a physiological measure, e.g., amount of salivation to conditioned stimuli or strength of galvanic skin response in studies of emotional reactivity.

Work, Time, and Error Scores. The most frequently used measures in the study of the learning of motor skills are work scores (quantity of work accomplished within a given unit of time), time scores (the time required to complete a trial or unit of work), and error scores (the number of errors within a given trial or series of trials). With time held constant, the more skillful will complete a greater amount of work. With work held constant, the more skillful will complete it more rapidly or with fewer errors.

Problem solving commonly involves a unitary task for which the appropriate and often only measure is the speed with which a solution is achieved. One of the limitations of speed or time scores is seen in such instances. Those persons failing to achieve a solution receive no score, although their attack on the problem may have been more systematic or more logical than some who succeeded. In such a case, the scoring system does not differentiate between those who demonstrated some skill in attacking the problem and those demonstrating none, even though both failed at solving the problem. All methods of measurement have limitations, but work scores have the general advantage over time scores in that even the poorest learner obtains some score, perhaps no more than zero; but more important, as learning progresses, improvement is shown by a rising curve and a divergence of scores late in practice. Nevertheless, time scores are appropriate to certain tasks such as speed of reading or typing or time required to run or swim given distances in sports events.

The plotting of number of errors is applicable to a wide variety of learning situations ranging from instrumental learning in mazes to problem solving tasks. Progress in learning is reflected in a descending curve reflecting a decreasing number of errors until perfect performance (zero errors) is attained. Certainly in school situations, the tally of errors is most common. However the form of the learning curve, particularly with verbal learning, will vary with regard to certain characteristics of the type of item employed. Five commonly employed types of items used in the measurement of the retention of learning are recognition, reconstruction, aided recall, reproduction, and relearning.

The Recognition Method. The ability to recognize an object depends upon previous experience with it. Therefore, we are measuring the persistence of the results of learning when we ascertain the extent of a subject's ability to recognize items previously experienced. The characteristic features of the recognition method of measuring retention are: (1) the presentation (one or more times) of a series of items for learning, (2) a subsequent test in which the same items are again presented but mixed with a number of other similar items, and (3) a response as to whether each item appeared in the original list or not. Scoring is in terms of the number of items correctly recognized. For example, if we let letters represent the items used, we might present for learning M Z D G X B J Y and for the test series K U G Z O N D T J M P X Q Y B F. The subject would be asked to state if each item in the second group appeared in the first one.

Recognition is a commonly used measure, particularly in achievement tests. Many true–false test items, though not all, and many multiple choice test items are essentially recognition tests requiring *selection* of the correct response. Higher retention scores generally occur with recognition testing than with recall methods which require one to *supply* the correct response. It is probably true that this indicates that recognition is easier than recall; in recognition, the subject actually has before him the identical stimulus pattern previously observed. Nevertheless, simple recognition is of value in distinguishing minimal amounts of learning from no learning, and the relative difficulty of recognition items can be increased at will. The material to be recognized may be imbedded in other materials; the similarity of the foil items may be increased making discrimination more difficult; or the time allowed for responding may be shortened. The comparable ease or difficulty is less significant than the validity of the type of measure being used with respect to the learning involved. Certainly stimulus recognition is vital in many aspects of life—traffic indicators and signs, facial expressions and gestures, topographical features, and others.

The Reconstruction Method.   In testing retention by this method, the experimenter first presents a group of items in a certain order or pattern. He then breaks up the arrangement and turns the materials over to the subject who tries to arrange them in the former order or pattern. The unique feature of this method is that it calls for the reproduction, not of the items, but of the order or arrangement in which they are originally presented. It may be used not only for verbal materials but also for colors, odors, and objects of various sorts. When this method is used to measure learning, the score is usually based on the number of trials or time required to learn the arrangement well enough to reproduce it exactly. When using it to secure a measure of retention over an interval following learning, the degree to which the reconstructed order coincides with the presented order may be taken as the basis for scoring.

A number of practical adaptations of this method may be made. For example, in the domestic science course the teacher may test her students' mastery of the lesson on the proper arrangement of the dishes and utensils on the dinner table by having them set the table. After the members of a class in general science have been shown an electric bell correctly connected with batteries and switch, a good reconstruction test of the knowledge gained would be to separate the parts of the assemblage and have the pupils attempt to put them together again. In any case where the proper assembling or arrangement of materials or parts is the aim of teaching, this method with suitable adaptations may be used to determine the extent to which the aim has been achieved.

Aided Recall.   Reproduction may be unaided, as described below, or cues may be given to aid the recall. The latter procedure is followed in the serial anticipation method of presenting verbal materials, where each word serves as a cue to prompt the recall of the following word which has become associated with it. The completion type of question in which a word or phrase is omitted from a question and the student is asked to fill in the correct answer is another illustration of the aided recall method. Similarly, the short answer question in which the response is a phrase or sentence, or perhaps a diagram, is another illustration. Many workbook tasks for elementary school children depend upon recall as a measure of learning.

Reproduction.   This method employs recall except that no cues are given, e.g., the typical essay question in examinations. More than any of the previous methods, this form of measurement is dependent on learning being carried to a sufficiently high level of acquisition, often to one or more perfect trials. Quite obviously, it is easier to recognize than to recall with help, and easier to recall than to reproduce, hence the need for a higher level of original learning. Given such a criterion, the material reproduced tends to be accurate but incomplete, whereas aided recall provides more complete coverage but more frequent errors because of guessing or prompting provided.

One of the values of this method of measurement lies in its similarity to many life situations in which knowledge must be readily accessible without the assistance of extensive prompting. As a measure of learning, it suffers from the fact that the student may possess more knowledge than he reproduces. Evidence of this can be obtained through testing with others of the methods being described. As typically used in school situations, in essay questions for example, another defect occurs. The time involved in responding to a single question limits the number of questions which can be asked. This in turn introduces serious problems of sampling of achievement; the questions may tap only a limited aspect of the information available, hence not provide a valid measure. A further difficulty occurs in scoring, for objective scoring with recalled material is much harder to obtain than with any of the other procedures described.

The Relearning, or Saving, Method.   Devised by Ebbinghaus, this method has one advantage over all the other methods, and that is: It can be used to measure the degree of retention after forgetting has proceeded to the point of being unable to recall or recognize. In the usual procedure one learns a list of items to the point of one or sometimes two perfect recitals. Since the material is not overlearned, some is soon forgotten so that its recall is impossible. After an interval, the subject relearns the same list to the same criterion of mastery. Ordinarily, it takes less time to relearn than was required for the original learning. The time saved (that is, the difference between the time required for learning and for relearning) is taken as the measure of retention existing at the time relearning was undertaken. It is commonly stated in terms of the percentage of the original learning time. Thus, if it takes a person ten minutes to learn a list of words to the point of one perfect recital, and four minutes to relearn it after five hours, the time saved for relearning as a result of having previously learned the list would be six minutes. This would indicate a saving or retention of 60 percent, and a loss of 40 percent for the five-hour interval. The difference between the number of trials required for learning and for relearning may also be used as an index of the amount of retention when this method is employed.

The length of the time interval that elapses between the initial learning and the subsequent relearning introduces another variable which must be controlled in order to avoid spurious retention scores. Again using the illustration of the person who relearned the list of words in four minutes after a lapse of five hours, it is obvious that only if the person required the original time of ten minutes (approximately) to learn a new list of equally difficult words can it be safely concluded that the saving in time results from having previously learned the original material. If he learns a new list in four minutes, then apparently something has occurred whereby he has become able to learn such lists of words faster, rather than having retained a residue from the original list.

In 1922 Luh identified five methods of measuring retention in conjunction with verbal materials which he designated as recall, reproduction, recognition, relearning, and reconstruction. Figure 3.1 shows the percent of retention obtained by Luh when he had subjects learn lists of twelve nonsense syllables to a criterion of one perfect recitation and subsequently measured their retention at four intervals by the different procedures of measurement described. It can be seen readily that the impression one obtains of the amount of material learned and retained will vary with the kind of measure utilized. This fact suggests that some sophistication on the part of teachers is necessary to interpret the meaning of scores obtained on any measure of learning; particularly they must recognize that performance is not absolute but relative to the measure used. To illustrate, unaided recall is more difficult than aided recall because no cues are present to suggest or stimulate response. Similarly, recognition measures vary in difficulty. A learned list of adjectives buried in a set of numbers would be immediately identified; but the same adjectives included

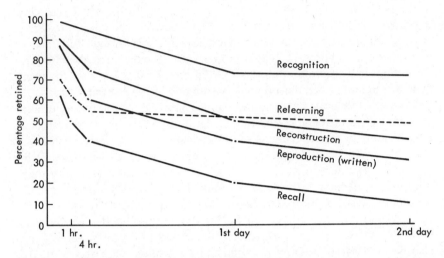

Fig. 3.1 Rentention curves obtained by five different methods of measuring retention (after Luh, 1922).

in a list of words would be more difficult to recognize. Bahrich (1964) has demonstrated that the greater the similarity the more difficult recognition, with the result that the level and slope of recognition curves can parallel recall curves under conditions where high similarity exists.

APPLICATION IN SCHOOL SITUATIONS

The learning of verbal materials and motor skills and, to a lesser degree, discrimination learning and problem solving are typical of most school situations. Children are learning to read and spell. They acquire information about the area and the world in which they live and about natural science. They are learning to move their eyes in prescribed fashion and to discriminate small differences in the reading of verbal symbols. They are learning to manipulate a pencil in certain designs in order to print and write letters and words. They are learning procedures and sometimes understanding the principles involved in arithmetical computations. Simultaneously, the teacher is engaged in manipulating the variables of motivation, practice, transfer, and so on in a variety of procedures just as the psychologist does in his learning experiments, although with a different purpose and without the stringent experimental controls found in the laboratory. Like the psychologist, the teacher is using similar measures of performance in order to appraise learning. The five measures previously described—recall, reproduction, recognition, reconstruction, and relearning —are commonly utilized by the teacher.

The true-false and matching questions utilized in the achievement tests, both standardized and teacher-made, depend upon pupil recognition. The essay question is an illustration of unaided reproduction, whereas the short answer, in which a preliminary cue is given by presenting the stem of a sentence with the answer omitted, is a recall question. Scrambled sentences which the student has to rearrange are based upon the reconstruction method of measurement. Relearning is used less frequently as a measure of learning, although teachers are aware of summer loss in achievement in certain school subjects such as arithmetic and spelling. Were it not for the gains possible through relearning in a shorter period of time, this loss would produce a very slow rate of learning in such subjects.

Although recall and recognition are the two most widely used measures in the classroom and in achievement tests, they have their limitations as measures of retention, for important concomitant learnings such as development of attitudes, problem solving ability, and concept development are overlooked.

Another word of caution regarding the interpretation and use of learning scores by teachers is advisable. Aside from the variation by type of measure, all measurements in general and psychological measures in particular are subject to error. This is to say that any single measure or score is at best an approximation rather than a true score. If repeated measures of exactly the same object are taken by a number of persons, they will show variation which may be small or great according to the precision of the measuring instrument being used. Any *single* measure, it follows, is incorrect by some amount; this variation in scores or measures is termed unreliability. Thus, when a teacher has a performance or achievement score of a pupil, it is at best an approximation of the pupil's true score. If the same pupil were to be given an identical test immediately thereafter (and if it could be assumed that having taken the first test would in no way affect his score on the second test), in all probability the second score would vary from the first.

In the psychological experiments, it is possible to introduce rigid controls in order to insure moderate to high reliability of scores; unfortunately, in the classroom such circumstances are less possible for the teacher. His best protection is to understand the limitation of the scores being used in order to avoid making faulty judgments.

LIMITATIONS OF PSYCHOLOGICAL AND EDUCATIONAL SCALES

One source of inaccurate measurement arises from the nature of psychological measures themselves. We are accustomed to using instruments which measure such physical phenomena as distance, area, and weight; also familiar is a second type of measuring scale, e.g., thermometers for such phenomena as temperature. These two classes of scales have advantages which are denied to psychological measures. Both have equal units of measurement; that is to say, the distance from 2 centimeters to 6 centimeters is the same as from 10 centimeters to 14 centimeters, or the temperature increase from 80° to 82° Fahrenheit represents the same increase in heat as the increase from 105° to 107° Fahrenheit. Thus, any unit at any point on the scale is equal to any unit at any other point. In addition, measures of height, weight, distance, and area have an additional advantage in that the scales have a true zero, i.e., zero pounds of weight or zero inches in height. Having a true zero makes comparative measures possible. Thus, it is possible to say that a person weighing 150 pounds is twice as heavy as a person weighing 75 pounds, or that a person 6 feet tall is twice as tall as a person 3 feet tall. Such comparisons are not possible unless the scale has a true zero. By comparison, 50° Fahrenheit is not twice as hot as 25° Fahrenheit. It would be true if 0° on the Fahrenheit scale were a *true zero,* i.e., complete absence of heat. One need only to convert the temperatures to a centigrade scale to realize that such a comparison does not hold.

The two types of comparisons that are possible with the physical scales, one with a true zero and equal units of measurements, the second having only the equal units of measurement, are not possible with psychological measures.

In general, psychological measures provide only a rank ordering of individuals or items from high to low in standing. The most widely used of all psychological measures, intelligence tests, provide scores called intelligence quotients, which range from approximately 40 to 160. Such scores make it possible to rank a group of individuals from most intelligent to least intelligent, but no more. The units along the scale are not of equal size, which means that the intellectual gaps between individuals at different points on the scale may not be proportional to the score differences. And because psychological tests lack a true zero, it is not possible to say that a person with an IQ of 100 is twice as intelligent as a person with an IQ of 50. All that can be said is that he is considerably more intelligent.

Unreliability of Scores.   Aside from the limitation of scores, there are other sources of unreliability. Different types of tests have differing reliability. For instance, standardized achievement tests usually possess much higher reliability than do teacher-made tests owing to the more careful selection of test questions. A series of environmental factors can contribute to errors in measurement and produce scores which are either too low or too high. The person administering the test may inadvertently give cues as to the correct answers, or the person seated in the front of the room may hear questions more readily if the test is given orally or see them more clearly if it is written on a blackboard. Extraneous noise or interruptions can affect the scores obtained. Scores can be affected by the mere factor of administering a test in a different setting from that to which the subjects are accustomed. Variations in motivations, fatigue, and misunderstanding of instructions are but a few more of the factors which may affect individual performance and produce a degree of error or unreliability in scores. The limitations introduced by unreliability do not make tests valueless but merely suggest caution in interpreting test scores.

Validity of Measures.   A second major source of error in psychological measures centers around the question of validity. This is the quality or characteristic of a test which makes possible judgment or prediction regarding the performance of the subject. For instance, an individual's speed in running the 100 yard dash provides little information upon which to base a prediction regarding his swimming ability; the running scores have little validity as far as estimating swimming ability. In contrast, an intelligence test is valid to a degree for estimating school achievement because it apparently measures some of the components that contribute to school achievement; it has, however, little validity for estimating success in salesmanship.

Figure 3.2 provides an illustration of a situation in which there is high reliability but no validity. From time to time, it has been claimed without considerable success that it is possible to predict criminals on the basis of their physical characteristics. Let us assume that an individual believes all persons with bushy eyebrows, broken noses, and thin lips are criminal types, and that he proceeds to classify a group of people on the basis of his belief. As is shown in Figure 3.2, it would be possible for him on two successive trials to put the same individual into identical categories; that is to say, on each trial he would put all individuals with bushy eyebrows, broken noses, and thin lips in the criminal category—the square box in the figure—and all other persons in the non-criminal category—the circles in the figure. Thus, his measures have high reliability; they are consistent. But do they have validity? Is he distinguishing between criminals and non-criminals on better than a chance basis, i.e., is he more successful than if he sorted them blindfolded? One criterion of how to validate the measure would be to check the police records. As is shown in the illustration, the distribution of criminals and non-criminals is no better than could be anticipated on the basis of chance; hence, the procedure is invalid.

Ignoring the scientific findings for the purpose of illustrating simultaneous reliability and validity, let us assume that the people were sorted as in Figure 3.3 and their criminal records checked. In this instance, although the reliability is not perfect, it is high; the classifier is consistent in getting nearly all individuals in the same category on each trial. On both trials, criminals C_3, C_4, C_5, and C_6 are placed in the criminal category while C_1

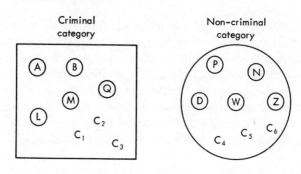

Trial 1

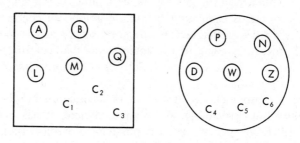

Trial 2

Fig. 3.2 Perfect reliability without validity. *On each trial, subjects are consistently placed in the same category; however, criminals are not predicted better than chance (o_1 to o_6 are criminals; (A) to (Z) are non-criminals).*

and C_2 are interchanged on the second trial. Nevertheless, the proportion of criminals in each category remains the same. Similarly, the non-criminals are each placed in the same category on both trials with the exception of W and A, who as a result of inconsistency are interchanged on the second trial. In this illustration, the sorting shows both high reliability—consistency of measurement—and high validity—dependable prediction based on an outside criterion (the police records).

One factor contributing to the problem of validity stems from the distinction between performance and learning. In any learning situation, the observed and scored behavior is a variation in performance resulting from the experimental or classroom procedures. The learning itself is always an inference derived from this change in performance; it cannot be assumed that the performance change is a direct measure of the learning

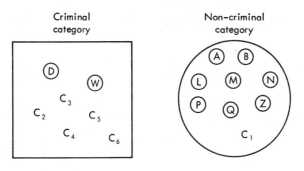

Trial 1

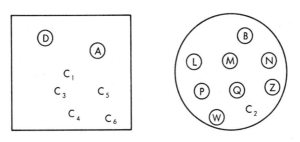

Trial 2

Fig. 3.3 High reliability and validity. *On each trial, nearly all subjects are placed in the same category; the criminals are separated (although not perfectly) on the basis of the measure used.*

obtained. A ready illustration of this fact is found in the extent to which changes in motivation influence performance scores. Figure 3.4 is a schematic illustration taken from studies performed by Tolman and Honzik (1930) on latent learning. Three groups of animals were used in the maze experiment. Two of the groups served as control groups, one being fed each day in the maze while the second group received no food. The experimental group was not fed until the eleventh trial, yet on the twelfth day, this group which had previously been unrewarded performed as well or better than the control group which had been consistently rewarded. This fact suggests that the performance of the experimental group up to the eleventh day was not a true measure of what had been learned. It is quite tempting to equate performance and learning. The broken line in Figure 3.4 shows how erroneous such a conclusion can be. Judging by performance scores up until the eleventh day, one would conclude that less learning had

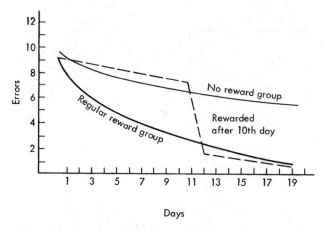

Fig. 3.4 Latent learning in a maze; schematic graph (after Tolman and Honzik, 1930).

occurred in the no-reward group. Yet changing incentives produced an abrupt shift in performance, suggesting that learning had been going on which had not been revealed in performance. Although conclusions about the learning process depend upon demonstrated performance, the lack of performance does not prove lack of learning, any more than the high school drop-out who spent hours every day in the public library reading about art was an illiterate because, as his teachers reported, he couldn't (wouldn't) read in school.

LEARNING CURVES

When several trials are given in an experiment and measures of learning or of retention are obtained, these measures may be plotted in the graphic form known as a learning curve, a graph which affords a comparison of the performance on each trial with a performance on other trials. It is customary to plot the independent variable on the horizontal axis, the abscissa, and the dependent variable on the vertical axis, the ordinate. The dependent variable is the variable which undergoes changes as a result of the experimenter's manipulations. Scores on the dependent variable are dependent upon or are a function of the experimental factor and are usually some form of a learning score—errors made, number of words learned, time consumed, and so on. In constructing a curve, a scale for the dependent variable is marked off on the vertical axis and numbered with units suitable to the size of the scores. The units of the scale must be equal and the range great enough to cover the largest score. Because scores are usually arbitrarily defined and because they vary greatly in magnitude for different measures, the number of score points represented by a given section of the vertical line is a matter of convenience to be determined by the size and range of the scores and the desired shape of the graph. The units of the scale are numbered from the bottom upward. The successive trials are indicated by numbers along the base line at equal intervals from left to right. Next, a point is located directly above each trial number. The distance of each point from the base line is equivalent to that of the point on the vertical scale which corresponds to the score for that trial. Then, these points are connected by straight lines. The lines connecting the points constitute the curve of learning. It shows at a glance how the learner has progressed from trial to trial.

An example of a learning curve so constructed is shown in Figure 3.5. The scores are taken from an experiment in which the subject was required to learn the English equivalents of ten Hebrew words to a criterion of three successive perfect performances. The scores (words correct) for the fifteen trials were as follows:

Trial: 1 2 3 4 5 6 7 8 9 10 11 12 13 14 15
Score: 0 1 3 2 2 4⁻ 4 4 5   5   7   9 10 10 10

As the highest score was ten, the scale is made up of ten equal units numbered from bottom to top. Each unit of the scale represents one score point. The fifteen trials are represented from left to right on the base line. The height of the curve above the trial points indicates the score for each trial.

Fig. 3.5 Learning curve showing improvement in ability to reproduce the English equivalents of Hebrew words.

Figure 3.6 shows an arrangement of the scale to represent larger scores, and in this graph three curves are presented. A and B are curves of two individuals; the middle curve represents the average scores for twenty-three students. The scores of A and B are included in the averages used to construct the group curve. It is possible to compare here the progress of the two individuals with each other and with the average of the whole group. We see that A was faster than the group average on the first trial and that she gained more with the same amount of practice. We see also that she did not fall back on trial 5 as did most of the group. The lower curve shows that B started off more slowly than the average, and although she gained at about the same rate, she was approximately as far behind after six practice periods as at the end of the first period.

The Rate of Improvement.   One of the things a learning curve reveals is the rate of improvement and the changes in this rate. A uniform rate of improvement is indicated by graphs of the type shown in Figure 3.7. Here progress is indicated by a straight line. Such a graph means that the increment of gain is the same for each successive trial. When the rate of improvement is constant, we have what is known as *zero acceleration.*

Most curves of learning show variations in the rate of improvement. Curves for motor learning usually show the fastest rate of gain at the

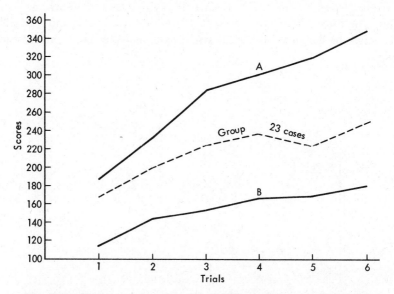

Fig. 3.6 Curves of learning in a digit-symbol experiment. *The subjects were given a sheet containing the digits and were instructed to write as rapidly as possible a symbol under each digit, as indicated by a key. The scores are the number of symbols written during a practice period of five minutes.*

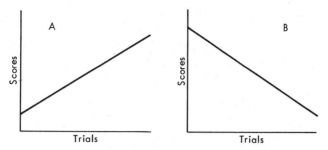

Fig. 3.7   Theoretical learning curves showing zero acceleration, or a uniform rate of improvement. *In A improvement is shown by an increase in scores. B depicts those learning situations wherein decreasing scores indicate improvement, such as fewer errors.*

beginning and a slowing up as practice continues. Such a change in rate is called *negative acceleration*. It should not be confused with a loss of skill. It refers to those cases wherein improvement is still being made, but the increment of gain is smaller on each successive trial. Theoretical curves for negative acceleration are presented in Figure 3.8.

In the cases in which the scores grow smaller (time scores or error scores on successive trials) as performance improves, negative acceleration is indicated by a downward concave curve. Negatively accelerated curves are most frequently obtained in situations in which: (1) the learning task is relatively simple, (2) the subjects are of average or above average ability (either well practiced or bright), (3) there is positive transfer from previous learning, or (4) the tests are given toward the end of a series of trials.

Sometimes there is very slow progress at the start, with an increase in the increments of improvement as practice is continued. This increase in the rate of improvement is called *positive acceleration* (Figure 3.9).

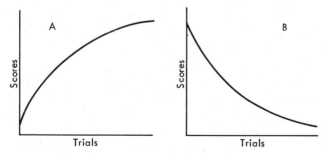

Fig. 3.8   Theoretical curves of negative acceleration showing a decrease in the rate of gain.

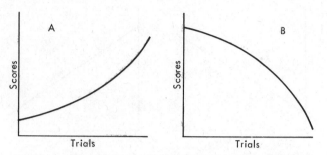

Fig. 3.9 Two theoretical curves of positive acceleration. *In both, the rate of improvement is faster in the
second half of the learning period than in the first part.*

Curves of positive acceleration are frequently found: (1) in motor
learning, (2) in tests with very young children or children of less than
average ability, (3) early in the learning of material that is difficult or
meaningless, such as nonsense syllables, or (4) where previous learning
interferes with the new learning. An example of positive acceleration is
found in the increase of children's vocabularies during the second year. In
an investigation by Smith (1926), the average number of words in children's vocabularies at 1 year was found to be three words. Vocabulary increased slowly to twenty-two words at eighteen months, then it increased
rapidly to reach 272 words at age 2. These findings are presented graphically in Figure 3.10.

It is clear that positive acceleration cannot continue indefinitely, for
sooner or later the learner reaches complete mastery, or the curve levels
off as he approaches the limit of his ability to improve. Which of these two
possibilities takes place will depend upon the nature of the learning task and
the manner of scoring the performance. In many cases, a rate of learning
that is positively accelerated at first changes to negative acceleration as it
continues. This provides an S-shaped curve, examples of which are shown
in Figure 3.11, which illustrates several variations in rate of improvement;
its general form indicates rapid improvement in the first few trials, followed
by a slowing up.

It is likely that if we were able to plot a complete learning curve
from zero to the absolute limit of improvement for any single performance,
we should find the S-shaped curve with relatively slow progress at first followed by increasing increments of gain and leveling off with decreasing
gains as the limit was approached (Culler, 1928). It may be presumed that
a very rapid initial rise in a learning curve is due to the fact that the learning task is not altogether new to the learner and that he therefore does not
begin at a zero point. Initial ability may make some aspects of the total
performance easier to master than others. If these easier steps have a direct

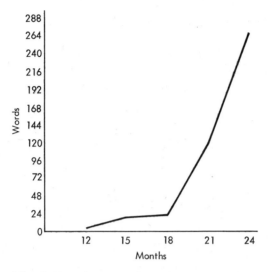

Fig. 3.10   The increase in the average number of words in children's vocabulary during the second year. *The curve for this period is positively accelerated. (Constructed from data by Smith.)*

effect on the score, there naturally will be rapid improvement as indicated by the method of scoring. The harder steps are not mastered so quickly; therefore, the apparent progress becomes slow after the easier initial gains have been accomplished.

The increase in the rate of improvement, or positive acceleration, may be due to the fact that the results of practice are cumulative in their effect on the score. Much of the early practice may be a kind of preparation that makes possible the more rapid advance later. Various aspects of the total performance may be undergoing improvement with comparatively little effect on the score; then, when they are being integrated and consolidated, the curve rises more rapidly. Faster progress may also come with new insight or with mastery of tools of learning. In a first course in science, progress may be slow at the beginning when the student is becoming accustomed to the terminology of the new field, to new points of view, and to new methods of study. Once he becomes oriented, learning goes ahead at a faster pace.

The slowing down of the rate of improvement may be caused by several factors such as reaching the limit of improvement, fatigue, loss of interest, a sense of sufficiency, lack of desire for further advancement, and the needless repetition or overlearning of parts of the performance mastered in the early steps of learning. A learning curve seldom rises smoothly from

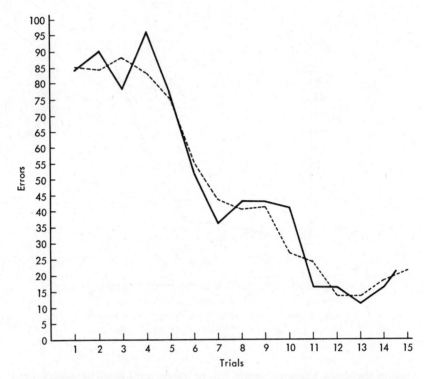

Fig. 3.11 Learning curves showing positive acceleration in the early stages and negative acceleration near the end. *The scores for one subject represent errors made in tracing a star outline while looking at its image in a mirror. The solid line is the actual curve; the dotted line is the same curve smoothed by the method of averages.*

trial to trial. While the general trend may be upward (or downward), there is frequently a great deal of zigzagging (see Figure 3.11).

Plateaus. Frequently one finds a level stretch in a learning curve in which the scores remain very nearly the same through several trials. It appears from the scores that no advancement is being made even though practice is going on as usual. Such level stretches of the learning curve in which there is no apparent progress are known as *plateaus.* Investigators have pointed out that since plateaus are more likely to occur in complex performances than in simple ones, they may be due to the fact that the learner concentrates on one part at a time. It is suggested, therefore, that if the learner attacks the whole performance as a unit, he is more likely to make steady and continuous progress (Kao, 1937). In a performance measured for both speed and accuracy, we may get a plateau in the reduction of errors when the subject sets himself to improve his speed. If he suddenly decides to concentrate on accuracy, his curve of speed may show a plateau.

In general, it may be concluded that plateaus are caused by several different factors. They may be due to: concentration on one part of a complex performance; the fact that the learner is doing as well as he can for the method he is using; imperfectly established elementary habits; poor physical condition, or aspects of attitude or set of the learner, such as loss of interest, discouragement, or divided attention. Because most investigators are inclined to believe that the plateaus are not a necessary feature of learning progress, the teacher should be on the alert to detect any slumps in classroom learning. When they occur, an attempt should be made to discover the cause and help the learner to resume his progress.

Composite Curves.   The progress of a group of subjects may be indicated by a curve based on the average scores for the various trials. In Figure 3.12 the individual curves for six subjects based on their scores in a letter-digit substitution experiment are shown. The individual curves appear in dotted and broken lines. The heavy solid line is the curve for the averages of the group. The composite curve is usually much smoother than

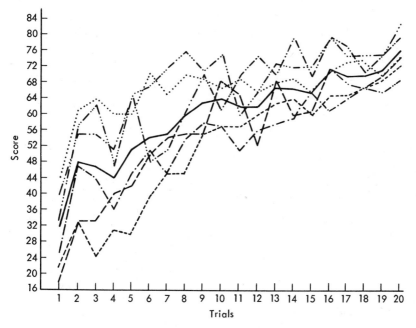

Fig. 3.12 Composite curve; individual curves for six subjects in a letter-digit substitution experiment. *The scores represent the number of digits written in one minute practice periods. The dotted and broken lines are the curves for individual subjects; the heavy solid line represents the mean scores of the group for the various trials.*

the individual curves because the fluctuations for the various trials tend to cancel out. A drop in one case is offset by a spurt made by another subject. The composite scores are useful in indicating the general course of improvement of a group taken as a whole. Any pronounced dip or sudden rise in a curve based on them reflects a potent factor common to the group rather than an individual peculiarity.

INDIVIDUAL DIFFERENCES IN RATE OF IMPROVEMENT

The improvement or gain resulting from a given amount of practice in a performance varies for different individuals. A child of six may not be expected to gain so much proficiency in typewriting with 100 hours of practice as a high school student. Even in a group of the same age we find that some advance faster and farther than others with an equal amount of practice. In Figure 3.13 appear the smoothed curves for the performance

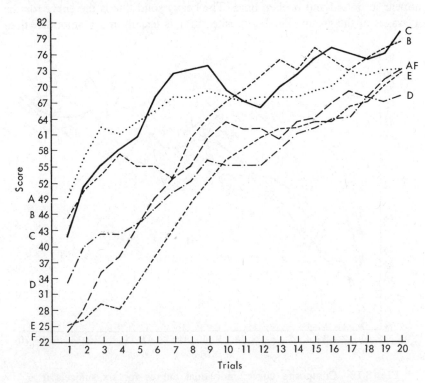

Fig. 3.13 Smoothed individual curves. *These curves, made by averaging the individual scores for each three successive trials for the individual curves appearing in Fig. 3.12, show individual differences in rate of improvement and gain over the initial score.*

of six subjects whose individual curves are shown in Figure 3.12. These curves indicate a similar negatively accelerated trend for all six subjects, but they also show that there are differences in the rate of improvement and the amount of gain over the initial score, e.g., A starts with the highest initial score but in the last trial is tied with F, who was the lowest initially.

If practice in any function is carried on long enough, the learner sooner or later reaches the limit of his ability to improve under the conditions operating at the time. Different kinds of limits are distinguished on the basis of the conditions which make further progress impossible.

Physiological Limits. All activity involves physiological mechanisms, and although the functioning of these mechanisms is subject to great improvement, there are limits inherent in them beyond which any amount of practice cannot produce a faster or more perfect performance. It takes a certain amount of time for the arousal of sense receptors and transmission of the nerve impulse over the fibrous pathways of the nervous system to the effectors. It takes a measurable unit of time for the muscle to contract after the impulse has reached it. Practice can reduce simple reaction times to something like one tenth of a second, but that seems to be about the minimum time required for the simple voluntary motor response. It is a limit for such a performance. Motor performances also may be limited by the capacity of the nervous system for developing coördination of movement, by the strength of the muscles, or by the amount of energy the body is able to supply. Just as no amount of practice would enable a six-week-old baby to walk, so no amount of practice would enable a college student to make a broad jump to fifty feet or run a mile in one minute, simply because such levels of performance are beyond the possibilities of the normal neuromuscular equipment.

The physiological limit is probably rarely reached. To reach it requires a high degree of motivation. It is more easily reached in a simple performance such as flexing the finger as quickly as possible in response to a signal, than it is in the case of complex performances like typewriting or violin playing. In fact, so many factors are involved in the improvement of the more complex performances that it is practically impossible to know when one has reached his physiological limit. There is need for caution in assigning the cause for a final plateau to the physiological limit. This is indicated by cases of further improvement with a change to more favorable conditions when the limit of one's ability was supposed to have been reached. We cannot consider that the individual is approaching his physiological limit until he has discovered and adopted all possible short cuts, eliminated all useless movements, adopted the best possible methods, and is working at maximum motivation.

Practical Limits. The absolute limit of efficiency in any function and the degree of excellence which is good enough for all practical purposes are usually quite different. It is usually much lower than the absolute limit of improvement. Workers in industrial establishments, clerks, stenographers, and others tend to strike a level of proficiency good enough to get them by and then go on year after year without making any improvement in their work. That this level is much below their possible achievement is shown by the fact that under the incentive of demands for a better grade of work as the price for retaining their position or under the stimulus of competition with other workers for a coveted promotion, they immediately increase their output.

Students in college courses probably never do their absolute best. They are usually satisfied with a good grade and sometimes with a mediocre grade that gives them credits toward a degree. More time and more effort would enable them to accomplish a greater degree of mastery of any subject, but their time is divided between studies and other activities.

The child might be able to learn to spell all the words in the dictionary, but the cost of such an achievement would be entirely incompatible with its practical value. It is a waste of a child's time to require him to learn the spelling of more than two thousand of the most commonly used words. The same could be said for much of history, science, and other subjects. The practical limits of training in any school subject must be determined by a consideration of individual and social needs in relation to the values the subject offers. To require a child to learn useless material is to waste his time and deprive him of more essential experience.

Motivational Limits.   Closely related to the limits imposed by practical considerations are motivational limits. A person has reached his *motivation limit* of improvement when he is content with his present achievement and is not interested in doing better. Much poor work in school is due, not to lack of ability, but to lack of application of effort because of insufficient motivation.

Incentives determine in a large measure how far a person advances his skill and knowledge. A comparatively few persons in every field of endeavor rise above the level of mediocrity. To become great requires energy, ability, opportunity, and effort. There is probably no case more difficult for a counselor to work with than the talented student who does not care whether he makes anything of himself or not; arousing motivation is often difficult. Teachers are often quite casual in using the cliché: You could do better if you tried harder. They ignore the fact that the statement holds true for practically everyone all of the time, including the teacher. The trick lies in knowing how to spur motivation.

As we have seen, learning curves provide a graphic record of the course of learning. They reveal the fluctuations in progress, stages of rapid advancement, periods of slowing down, and the plateaus where no apparent improvement is being made even when practice is continued. The teacher may use them for her own enlightenment and as an impressive means for informing pupils of their progress. Learning graphs based on scores derived from standardized tests may indicate whether satisfactory advancement is or is not being made by the pupils individually or as a class. Plateaus in those curves will serve as a warning that all is not going well. They may indicate the intrusion of some detrimental factor, the need for a change in teaching methods, or the desirability of some new form of incentive.

In Figure 3.14 are presented curves showing the progress in five school subjects of a pupil of average intelligence over a period of two years. They are based on grade equivalents of scores which the pupil made on the Metropolitan Achievement Tests given at the mid-year period near the end of January and at the close of the school year near the end of May. This sample record was selected at random from the school's test files.

The standing of the pupil in the five subjects is indicated by solid line curves. The dotted line shows the grade norm for the pupil's attained age. An examination of this graph reveals many things concerning this pupil's accomplishments. First, we see a marked difference between his achievement in the five subjects as indicated by his performance on these standardized tests. His literature curve is consistently much higher than the

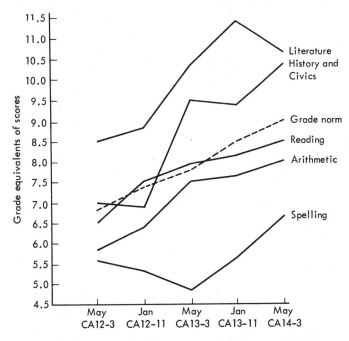

Fig. 3.14   A two-year record of the progress in five school subjects made by a pupil of average intelligence.

grade norm. The curve for history and civics begins near the grade norm but rises considerably above it during the two years. Reading keeps close to the grade norm throughout but falls off slightly in the second year. Arithmetic is down but is slightly nearer the norm at the end of the two years than at the start. Before seeing this graph, the child's teacher had not realized that he was so much below his grade norm in arithmetic. The curve for spelling shows a marked deficiency in that subject. It reveals that while this child was 1.2 grades below where he should have been in spelling at the beginning of this period, after the two years he was 2.2 grades below the standard for his age. During these two years he made but one year's advance in this subject. The graph reveals the areas in which the child has and has not been making satisfactory progress. It indicates the need for discovering and correcting the causes of his deficiencies in arithmetic and spelling.

Graphic presentation of learning curves of groups of children over time are useful in plotting rates of progress in different subjects and for detecting common difficulties or lags in progress. Figure 3.15 shows the achievement year by year of an elementary school class. The heavy horizontal bar indicates grade norm for the achievement test at the time administered. The distribution of scores above and below the norm is observable, as well as rate of progress including spurts and lags in different subjects. The class shown lived in a small, stable community so that class membership was fairly stable from year to year permitting a plot of the same children over a period of years. Such graphs would not be useful where populations were highly mobile.

SUMMARY

The measurement of learning requires dependable observations of performance during a series of practice trials. No single type of measure is applicable to all kinds of learning. Commonly used measures of simple learning are response frequency, latency, and amplitude. Work and time scores are frequently used measures of perceptual motor learning, recognition or recall with verbal learning. Error scores can be plotted for a wide variety of learning situations ranging from simple learning to problem solving.

Five commonly employed types of items used in the measurement of retention are recognition, reconstruction, aided recall, reproduction, and relearning. The first four are regularly used in teacher-made and standardized achievement tests.

Achievement measurements have limitations inherent in the nature of psychological and educational scales. The lack of equal units and of a true zero makes quantitative relational statements invalid. Psychological

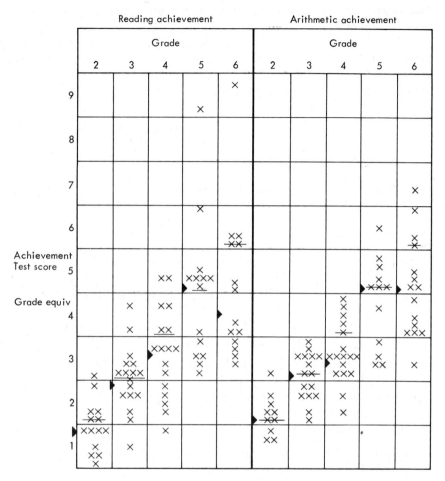

Fig. 3.15 Achievement test scores in successive years for the same group of children. *Horizontal line indicates expected achievement if class were at grade level. Arrow indicates median achievement attained by class on test. Note that in both reading and arithmetic the class made limited progress between 3-4 and 5-6, but more than a year's gain in 4-5. Note narrower range of scores in arithmetic.*

scales provide a rank ordering which permits a man-to-man comparison or a comparison relative to some arbitrary standard such as grade level. Conclusions based on test scores are limited to the kinds of validation data available.

Learning curves can be plotted which reflect rates of progress of individuals and groups over a series of trials or a period of time. The slope of such curves will show variations in rate of acceleration caused by numerous factors such as difficulty of materials, individual differences, amount of transfer, and others.

The absolute limit of performance is rarely reached. In most instances, practical limits and motivational limits are the determinant factors. Learning curves are useful for diagnostic purposes, for knowledge of rate of progress, and as incentives to progress.

FURTHER READING

Overview

STEVENS, S. S. 1951. Mathematics, measurement, and psychophysics. *Handbook of experimental psychology*. New York: Wiley.

Selected References

BUROS, E. K., JR. (ed.). 1941-1965. Mental Measurements Yearbooks, Editions 1-6. Highland Park, N. J.: Gryphon Press.

MCGEOCH, J. A. and A. L. IRION. 1952. *The Psychology of Human Learning* (rev.). New York: Longmans, Green.

THORNDIKE, R. L. and ELIZABETH HAGEN. 1955. *Measurement and Evaluation in Psychology and Education*. New York: Wiley.

TYLER, LEONA. 1963. *Tests and Measurements*. Englewood Cliffs, N. J.: Prentice-Hall.

WOOD, DOROTHY ADKIN. 1961. *Test Construction*. Columbus, Ohio: Merrill.

Original Investigations

BAHRICK, H. P. 1964. Retention curves: facts or artifacts? *Psychol. Bul.*, 61: 188-94.

FLANAGAN, J. C. Units, scores, and norms. In E. F. Lindquist (ed.). 1951. *Educational measurements*. Washington, D. C.: Amer. Council on Education.

LOEVINGER, JANE. 1947. A systematic approach to the construction and evaluation of tests of ability. *Psychol. Monogr.*, No. 4: 61.

POSTMAN, L. and L. RAU. 1957. Retention as a function of the method of measurement. *Univ. Calif. Publ. Psychol.*, 8: 217-70.

SCATES, D. E. 1947. Fifty years of measurement and research in education. *J. Ed. Res.*, 41: 241-64.

4

Theories of Learning

The word "theory" conveys a sense of intangibility which is forbidding to some students. To others, theory is associated with a sense of impracticality and unrealism which prompts a negative initial reaction. Yet nearly every one, whether teacher, parent, employer, or college student, has and believes in his private theory of learning, however unsystematic it may be. Whether explicitly stated or not, each person's behavior in attacking learning problems, whether learning himself or teaching others, is based upon personal judgment as to how people learn and retain learning once acquired. The school principal who states, "We don't teach arithmetic by drill anymore," infers his acceptance of a cognitive theory giving precedence to understanding as opposed to association. The opposite is true of the teacher who whole-heartedly believes that only by repeated drill of basic number combinations can children acquire arithmetic fundamentals. The teaching of typing by letter combinations implies a different assumption about the nature of learning than does teaching typing by phrase and sentence groups. Parents who admonish their children with, "Why don't you pay attention?"

or "Didn't you hear me?" are expressing assumptions regarding the importance of attention or set for performance. Requiring a youngster who is learning to play the piano to practice an hour each day implies particular assumptions regarding the relationship of amount of practice to speed of learning.

In practice, the usual parent is likely to espouse a dual theory inasmuch as he is likely to believe that his child should have immediate insight whenever the parent is giving an explanation, while simultaneously supporting the value of drill in habit formation. For all practical purposes, it is not important that either parent or teacher have explicitly explained theories of learning or that they adopt a single point of view. But it is important that teachers have some understanding of learning theory in order to be aware of the premises upon which their own teaching methods are based. More important, it may help them obtain a critical attitude with respect to the merits of differing teaching procedures. In view of the extent to which theories of learning have affected educational practice and vice versa, understanding of the main views of learning is important.

ASSOCIATION THEORIES VERSUS COGNITIVE THEORIES

Theories of learning fall into two main groups, those classified as *cognitive* theories and those classified as *association* theories. The former stress changes in cognition and the learner's perception as crucial to learning, whereas in the association theories it is the response of the learner, the association of the response with particular stimuli, and the changes within the learner himself that receive greatest emphasis. The sharp distinctions which once existed between the various schools of learning have disappeared as research on learning has become more sophisticated, with consequent need to revise the simple explanations vouchsafed in early theory making. These modifications have brought various theories into juxtaposition as well as extending lines of inquiry in new directions.

Association Theory. The concept of association has had a long history and an important influence in psychology. Aristotle formulated certain laws of association and distinguished association by similarity, by contrast, and by contiguity. The English psychologists of the eighteenth and early nineteenth centuries regarded association as the key to the secrets of mental life. They used it to explain memory, perception, and reasoning. According to this doctrine, when mental processes occur together, they become linked so that if at some later time one of them is aroused, it in turn tends to arouse the others. If, for example, a person sees a boy standing on a bridge, the mental processes meaning boy and bridge become associated so that later sight of the boy calls up the idea of the bridge; or if someone in conversation mentions this particular bridge, the person in whom this association is established is inclined to think of the boy. The sequence of ideas was believed to be governed by the associations formed by previous experiences. The qualities from which these associations arise, according to Hume (1711-1776), were three: resemblance, contiguity in time or place, and cause and effect.

Experimental psychologists of the late nineteenth century found this doctrine of association of ideas unsatisfactory. They rejected the notion that ideas are discrete mental entities with a mysterious link binding them together and causing them to be recalled together. The qualities of resemblance, contiguity, and cause and effect were observed to belong to the objects themselves rather than to the mental processes. The belief in a link between ideas as such was supplanted by the belief that the sequence of mental events was due to associative tendencies established in the nervous system as a result of previous activity. A new form of associationism appeared based on associations between stimuli and responses.

The *stimulus-response* psychology of learning built around this concept sees in any activity first, a *situation* which influences or affects the individual, second, a *response* which the individual makes to the situation, and third, a *connection* between the situation and the response by means of which the former is enabled to produce the latter. This connection was called the S-R bond. The term signifies a tendency or predisposition to respond in a particular manner to a given stimulus. In terms of observed behavior, it refers to a degree of probability that a certain kind of response will be made to certain stimuli. The bond of association is said to be strong when this probability is great and weak when the probability is small.

According to this connectionist point of view, knowledge, behavior, and personality are systems of bonds, each S-R connection being a unit part of the total. Learning is regarded as a process of building new bonds and organizing them into systems. This conception of learning involves the point of view that wholes are developed by compounding parts. Learning is a process of putting together units to form total experiences and complex forms of behavior.

Thorndike's Laws of Learning.   Modern association theories spring from the work of Pavlov and, in particular, Thorndike, whose experiments on trial and error learning have been described in Chapter 2. From such experiments, Thorndike proposed a set of principles to account for the changes he observed in the process of learning. The major principles were his laws of *readiness, exercise,* and *effect.* By readiness, he meant that when an animal or a human is prepared to respond or act, giving the response is satisfying and being prevented from doing so is annoying. Second, Thorndike believed that repeated exercising of a response strengthened its connection with the stimulus and that disuse of a response weakened it. He subsequently revised this assumption to make the strengthening or weakening of a connection during exercise dependent upon the satisfying or annoying effect derived from making the response. The most important of Thorndike's principles was his *law of effect,* which stated in essence that when a connection is accompanied by a satisfying state of affairs, its strength is increased; by this, Thorndike meant that the probability of its recurrence is greater. Inversely, when the connection is accompanied by an annoying state of affairs, its strength is reduced or weakened. Thorndike's primary law rests upon his conviction that an organism tends to repeat that which has previously been satisfying and avoid that which has been dissatisfying. Thus, favorable outcomes strengthen connections between responses and stimuli.

In addition, Thorndike had several subsidiary principles which are evidenced in the preceding descriptions of behavior in the experimental situations. The first maxim is that an individual *varies his responses* in a novel situation, using different responses until he hits upon a correct solution. Second, an individual's previous experiences, beliefs, and attitudes cause certain *sets* or *predispositions* which determine what goals the individual will seek and what will satisfy or annoy him. For instance, many Chinese candies are not palatable to occidental taste, accustomed to cream-filled chocolates. Third, Thorndike believed that individuals have the capacity to select the important from the irrelevant elements of a situation in order to *determine the appropriate response* to make. Fourth, he held that one's responses to a new situation are determined by the extent to which that situation is similar to or identical with a previously experienced situation, the result being that one responds as in the previous similar situations. Finally, Thorndike believed that any responses of which an organism is capable can be connected with any situation to which he is sensitive, terming this characteristic *associative shifting.* Thorndike subsequently added the concept of *belongingness,* which in effect said that a response is more easily learned if it fits the situation or belongs to it. Thus the Spanish word "Sabado" for Saturday would be more readily learned by English-speaking person than "Viernes" for Friday because there appears to be a relationship between the former pair.

Thorndike's theory of connectionism has proved important to learning for three reasons. Most important, in his law of effect he called attention to the importance of motivation and reinforcement in learning, heretofore largely neglected. Second, the specificity of his theory contributed to the ready identification of the acts or responses to be learned and their gradation from simple to complex for most efficient learning. Third, he placed much emphasis upon experimental verification.

Cognitive Theory. Differing from the associationist point of view, the field theories place emphasis upon the concept that learning is a process of discovering and understanding relationships, and of organizing and find-ing significance in the sensory experiences aroused by the external situation. It has frequently been observed in learning experiments that an animal, child, or adult human subject hits rather suddenly upon the correct solu-tion. This sometimes appears in marked contrast to the slow, often clumsy process of trial and error. When a conspicuous change in a learner's method of attack upon a problem occurs in a single trial and leads directly to the solution of the problem, the learner is said to have manifested *insight*.

Although the word *insight* was occasionally used by writers before the time of Köhler's experiments with chimpanzees (1913-1917), it is to his work and his use of the term that we owe most of the present emphasis on it in the literature on learning. To Köhler, it appeared that the trial and error feature of animal learning was due to complexity of the problem and that a better type of problem solving procedure might be found in animals if suitable problem situations were arranged for them. He arranged and con-ducted many experiments in which the animals showed a rather direct ap-proach to the solution and in which insightful behavior was attributed to the subjects. He regarded behavior as insightful when, in the face of barriers blocking any self-evident course, it leads by a roundabout path to an im-mediate solution. If, for example, a dog placed before a fence between a building and a short wall, sees food through the fence and runs directly back around the wall to the food instead of merely running back and forth along the fence or lunging against it, his behavior would be regarded as indicating insight.

As an example of the type of problem used by Köhler (1929), we shall describe one in which a box was used as an implement in reaching the objective. Six young chimpanzees were placed in a room, on the ceiling of which a banana was fastened. The banana served as a lure. On the floor some distance from the banana was a wooden box. In their eagerness to secure the banana, all six chimpanzees jumped repeatedly toward it but could not grasp it because it was too high. Now there are individual dif-ferences in learning aptitudes among anthropoids as well as among human beings, and one of these chimpanzees, whose name was Sultan, seemed more apt than the others in solving problems of this type. Sultan at first tried leaping toward the banana as did the others. Soon, however, he ceased his jumping and paced back and forth across the room. Then, he stopped for a moment in front of the box. Quickly he moved it over under the banana, climbed onto the box, and then jumped from this point of vantage to secure the fruit. Sultan seemed to grasp the situation in such a way as to bring the box into relation with the banana. From the moment of his hesita-tion before the box, his behavior showed unified and continuous action adapted to securing the banana.

In the case of experiments with animals and children, the term *insight* should be understood as referring to the character of the behavior employed in reaching the goal or solving the problem. It is commonly contrasted with trial and error behavior. Insightful behavior is marked by an attentive survey of the problem situation. Sometimes the animal halts his precipitous and miscellaneous assault and, after deliberately sizing up the situation, proceeds directly to the goal or to the solution by a well ordered series of appropriate responses. During the course of insightful behavior, the attention is persistently or recurrently fixed on the objective. Once the problem is successfully solved by the aid of insight, the adaptive behavior is readily repeated. In the case of crude trial and error learning, the situation is not mastered when the successful reaction is first accomplished. The succeeding trials are still full of trial and error. The successful reactions are differentiated only gradually, and mastery comes only when and insofar as the learner discovers the relation of the successful responses to the solution of the problem. Insight implies that the animal grasps this relationship at once or at least in a comparatively few trials.

The writer observed a 5-year-old child trying to get his coin bank from a plate rail high up on the dining room wall. The child climbed into a chair and reached for the bank, but it was about six inches beyond the tips of his fingers. He paused a moment, ran into the living room, picked up a small hassock. He brought this back, placed it on the chair, mounted the chair, and then climbed onto the hassock. From there he seized the bank and descended with it in his hand. This case resembles in many respects the box problem used with apes mentioned above. There is one important difference. The child showed insight more quickly than the best of the apes. He was able to bring the hassock into relation with his objective even when it was not within the range of his vision. He remembered or thought of the hassock, and the idea of it was incorporated into the total situation. In the case of human learners, at least, insight may be achieved through memory or imagination. In very young children and animals, the ideational element is presumably meager or entirely lacking, and the relations which provide insight are apparently those found in the organization of the perceptual field.

Differences Between the Theories.   The differences evident in the preceding illustrations contrast the two main sets of theories—association and cognition. The issues around which the differences in cognitive and association theories may be grouped have been identified by Hilgard and Bower in their *Theories of Learning* (1965) in which they describe in greater detail than is possible here the basic positions and workings of the individual theories. They identifies the issues as: (1) acquisition of habits versus acquisition of cognitive structures, (2) peripheral versus central intermediaries, and (3) trial and error versus insight in problem solving.

In Hilgard and Bower's view, the associationists emphasize the role of prior learning and experience, and they conceive of the whole as being no more or less than the sum of the parts; this means that a complex habit is merely the combination of simple habits which add together to equal the whole. The associationist stresses the significance of the responses or reactions that an organism makes and the association of the responses with the external stimuli, and minimizes the notion that mediating ideas or perceptions may intervene between the stimuli and the responses. The associationist, endorsing an historical viewpoint, sees responses and response patterns being built up gradually through the accumulation of many trials. In problem situations, he sees the learner vary his responses by trial-and-error until he achieves a solution.

In principle, the cognitive theorist's views on these issues would be diametrically opposed to that of the associationist. The cognitive theorist believes the whole to be greater than the sum of the parts, just as the melody of a song is more than the musical notes of which it is made. He sees the whole as preceding the parts, and the latter being derived by degrees from the whole. He places stress upon cognition and insight, and on the development of perceptions and the understanding of relationships between stimuli in the environment. This leads the cognitivist to stress contemporary causation and to place emphasis upon the present components of the field.

It will soon be evident that even within these major divisions of learning theory there is considerable disagreement and difference with respect to how learning occurs. In part, this is because psychology is still in the process of searching for and describing the variables which determine and account for learning. The behavioral sciences have not progressed as far as the physical sciences in formulating the inter-relationships between the known variables into an integrated theory.

Limitations in Theory Making.   It is possible to compare the situation of theory making in psychology to the situation which existed during the early exploration of the Western Hemisphere. Anyone who has looked at a series of maps which reflect educated man's idea of the shape and extent of the Western Hemisphere would find that the early maps contained sharp misconceptions regarding the outlines and extent of the New World and certain disproportions in size between different areas. As explorations progressed, these early misconceptions were gradually eliminated until the cartographers were in essential agreement regarding most particulars. The work of the early explorers tended to be associated with a given area; for instance, most of Columbus' voyages centered around the Caribbean, while the Cabots' explorations were associated with the North Atlantic. It was no accident that being the first voyager to a given area led one on subsequent voyages to extend previously obtained knowledge and information in the same area, e.g., as Columbus did in his remaining voyages. It is also worth noting that, although the explorations were rapidly pushed forward and the early misconceptions were eliminated with general agreement being achieved, nevertheless today, nearly five centuries later, detailed exploration and mapping still continue.

It will probably be some time before a complete theory of learning is developed, for the situation with respect to theories of learning is much the same as the exploration of the New World five centuries ago. Early experimental explorations have been pushed by a number of experimenters who, upon obtaining some fruitful results, have extended their work in a given area while simultaneously attempting to explain their previous results. Thus, we have rough maps of certain areas of human learning with many areas which scarcely have been explored. It has only been in the last twenty years that the explorations have been pushed into common territory.

In order to understand this more fully it might be well to take a brief look at a few of the theories that represent the two groups—association and cognitive theories—in order to obtain some understanding of them.

SIGNIFICANCE OF LEARNING THEORY
FOR EDUCATION

The classroom teacher, faced with the daily task of working with thirty active children, is typically a practical person. Given such a bent, theory making often appears quite remote from her needs and experience, a luxury which professors can better afford than she. Yet, her very empiricism should lead her to question many of her wasted motions. For example, teachers almost unanimously espouse the dictum that *practice makes perfect*. They should, considering the endless drills they give children. Yet this dictum as stated is one that learning theorists would almost unanimously reject—even though for different reasons. Most associationists espousing the *law of effect* would argue with good evidence that for practice to be effective, *reinforcement* is essential. The experiments of Skinner described earlier center on the effects that variations in reinforcement schedules have in shaping behavior. Cognitive theorists would disagree that reinforcement was crucial. They would see as aimless and useless practice which did not contribute to understanding and insight. Naturally, teachers starting with an assumption that their drills are useful seldom question the efficacy of their procedures. Learning theory stems from such questioning and as a result has relevance to education practice.

Few learning theories have had as marked an effect upon educational practice as Thorndike's, and much of this was due to his prodigious volume of writing. He devoted his attention not only to theoretical aspects of learning, but more to the applied aspects and classroom situations. The specificity of his theory contributed much to its applicability in classroom situations. Thorndike recognized in the learner an individual ready to make certain responses, capable of varying his responses, and trying to respond to the aspects of a stimulus situation which appeared familiar with a response previously successful in a similar situation. He believed that in order to develop these potentials efficiently, it was essential for the teacher to identify the specific elements of the learning task: to determine the particular responses desired to the given stimulus, to gradate the parts of the task from simple to complex, and to present the elements in a way providing the most favorable opportunity for eliciting the correct response, which could then be rewarded. Repetition and rewarding of the correct response would stamp in the desired response and gradually eliminate the inappropriate responses. Although Thorndike did not deny that insightful learning occurred, he believed it to be a less frequent form of learning.

It is interesting to pause for a moment and consider the educational program that follows from a literal application of Thorndike's theory of learning. One essential aspect of the program would be knowing the responses the individual is capable of making. The other would be identifying the tasks to be done—tasks within the capability of the individual—and subdividing these tasks into their elemental component parts in order that they may be arranged in a sequence which progresses from simple to complex. The latter point may be illustrated in relation to language development. Thorndike, in order to determine which words should be taught earliest, made a frequency count in order to determine the words most often used in the English language. These high frequency words he considered the more important—the words which should be taught first. Thorndike established these two component parts for the learning situation: a task to be presented with the least confusion, making certain that the significant stimulus would clearly precede it to increase the probability of the appropriate response; and upon occurrence, the correct response would be rewarded, the reward being either the intrinsic satisfaction derived from making the correct response or an extrinsic incentive such as praise. In either event, the learner would know that he had made a correct response. The situation would be repeated under motivating circumstances in order that the response would be firmly connected with the given stimulus.

The traditional method of teaching arithmetic closely follows such a scheme. The prime numbers are the first to be taught. Then, the combining of these basic numbers through simple addition and subtraction follows. The more difficult addition and subtraction are followed by multiplication and division. In each process, the learning task begins with the simple so-called basic addition facts and proceeds to the complex. In each response the child makes, the problem is followed by confirmation as to the correctness of the answer. There is little effort spent in developing meaning or understanding, for instance, of the "place" concept; rather, the emphasis is on specific steps, with the assumption being made that mastery of the simple component parts ultimately provides the essential understanding of the whole.

It would be a mistake to confuse these events with rote learning; it would be more accurate to see them as segmented learning. School should be made as interesting as possible, the learning child's enthusiasm and interest should be cultivated, and the tasks should be presented in as stimulating a fashion as possible. Nevertheless, the task proceeds from the part to the whole, rather than vice versa. Regardless of the limitations of Thorndike's theory with respect to explaining learning, it nevertheless has advantages in actual operation within the classroom, for its very specificity permits a direct attack upon learning problems. The teacher may identify errors and directly proceed to their elimination. Here, diagnosis of errors leads directly to suggestions for correction. Thorndike's theory is utilitarian in the sense that one teaches what is most useful as determined from actual practice. The curriculum does not consist of subjects such as Latin, Greek, or other subjects presumed to be valid of themselves or because of their effect on mental faculties such as memory or reasoning. Instead, subject matter has to be justified because of what it does for the child. On the other hand, it has a serious limitation in its lack of concern regarding understanding. Thorndike did not consider understanding unimportant but merely assumed that it would follow as a natural result of well organized learning. He believed that insightful learning, though it did occur, was infrequent.

The position which cognitive theorists espouse is inferred above. In teaching arithmetic, the important emphasis would not be on association between number facts but on number concepts and relationships. For example, many children learn the mechanics of borrowing in subtraction problems without ever understanding the significance of the "1" they borrow, i.e., why it becomes a "10" in the adjacent column—actually a 10, 100, or 1000 as the column may indicate. Thus, the teacher's task is to help the child see significant relations and to manage the instructional situation so that the child will be able to organize his experiences into effectual functional patterns. The teacher does not organize the child's experiences, nor does she establish relations for him any more than she learns the child's lessons for him. But in verbal explanations, showing pictures, putting words on the blackboard, presenting reading matter, and in many other teaching activities, she is arranging and providing stimulating situations. Now, since the stimulus pattern may and often does determine the character of the experiential configuration, it follows that the arrangement of the subject matter and materials of instruction and the order in which they are presented will affect greatly the child's observations, his comprehension, and, in general, his learning.

For this reason, careful lesson planning with due regard for suitable arrangement and orderly presentation is essential for good teaching. Practices conducive to the establishment of appropriate relations and organization include starting with the familiar, basing each step on those already taken, putting together facts which belong together, grouping items according to their natural connections, placing sub-topics under the topic to which they belong, using illustrations based on the learner's experience, giving major emphasis to essentials, centering supporting details around the main points, and avoiding irrelevant details.

Furthermore, effectual classroom learning requires the integration of all the divisions and topics of each subject. Previews, outlines, and reviews reveal relations between the various parts of a subject and promote the organization of a subject as a whole. When a reader begins a new book, an examination of the table of contents will often provide a degree of orientation which facilitates comprehension because it helps him to see each part in relation to the whole.

Just as the material of each subject should be organized into a coherent whole, so also all the various subjects of a course of study should be integrated. As reading should be tied to spelling, arithmetic, and the social studies, so every subject should be related to all the others. Projects or activity units which call for the use of reading, writing, spelling, arithmetic, geography, and oral expression in a single undertaking provide excellent opportunities for binding together the substance of different subjects.

Given these general views, specific theories can be considered: Guthrie and Hull with associationists' views, Lewin and Tolman with cognitive views, followed by recent developments in learning theory.

GUTHRIE'S S-R CONTIGUITY THEORY

"A combination of stimuli which has accompanied a movement will, on its recurrence, tend to be followed by that movement." Upon this statement rests Guthrie's contiguity theory of learning, an association theory based upon the connection of stimuli and responses but differing radically from Thorndike's connectionism in that the Law of Effect is rejected. Guthrie's statement could be paraphrased to read, "We repeat what we learn and we learn what we do." Moreover, according to Guthrie, the full associative strength—the pairing of the stimulus and the response—is established on a single trial.

The Stimulus-Response Bond. In Chapter 3 a brief description was given of Pavlov's conditioned response experiment: the response, the dog's salivation, becomes associated with the conditioned stimulus, a bell or buzzer, when the conditioned stimulus is presented simultaneously with the original stimulus, the food, which elicited the response. Using puzzle box experiments similar to Thorndike's, Guthrie takes the model of the substitution of one stimulus for another as the basis for his theory of learning, when he contends that the responses given in any situation will be reproduced or repeated on any occasion on which the same situation is presented. Thus, if a youngster copying the multiplication table of 9's from the blackboard mistakenly inverts $6 \times 9 = 45$, he will tend to respond 45 on the next occasion on which he is presented with the stimulus 6×9. Guthrie's argument is based first upon the principle of substitution and second upon the contiguity in time, i.e., the simultaneous occurrence of stimulus and response. According to this view, any stimulus-response situation—any learning situation—is composed of a variety of stimuli and responses. Some of the stimuli are external to the organism, others are internal. For example, in the preceding instance of the boy learning the multiplication table, the various attracting and distracting visual stimuli in the room, sounds occurring at the instant (the teacher's voice or his own repeating the problem), the movements of his fingers and hands as he writes the problems and answers on the paper, and all the other various stimuli that are impinging upon his sense organs are being associated with all the movements and responses which he is making. All responses the boy makes have the effect of altering or modifying the situation; some furnish cues for further action (getting pencil and paper ready), others sustain action (looking up at the blackboard at the illustration), while others terminate the stimulus situation (getting the answer to the problem written on the paper). In any situation, particularly a complex one, many responses are being associated with many stimuli. Some may be the correct associations, others may be erroneous or faulty associations. Guthrie contends that learning is complete on each trial and that all the responses are associated with some stimuli and will be repeated on repetition of the stimuli. In other words, the strength of the association will not gain through repetition, for it attains full strength on the first occurrence. Improvement is brought about not by strengthening the association or the connection of any single stimulus and response, but rather by building up the number of correct associations in the total stimulus-response situation. To give another illustration which will illustrate the application of this idea to a complex learning situation, picture a boy learning to shoot a basketball. According to Guthrie, the act of shooting the ball through the hoop incorporates within it a large number of movements which become associated with all the stimuli present at the moment: the balance of the body, the position of the feet, the feel of the ball, the position of the hands, the visual stimuli being received from all sources such as the reflections of the backboard, the distance and angle from the hoop, and the different sounds occurring. All become associated. On the next trial, the same stimuli will elicit identical responses, but unfortunately some of the associations made on the previous trials interfere with a perfect performance: for example, the boy may have sighted for the front of the hoop, he may have been standing on the wrong foot as he released the shot. Some of the responses will have been correctly associated with the stimuli, for instance, the feel of the ball in the hands, the amount of force, and the trajectory of the ball in making the shot. Improvement comes on subsequent trials not because the correct responses were strengthened but because new learning occurs to replace the erroneous fraction of the response —improper stance and improper sighting—with the result that total performance shows improvement.

In any situation, then, there are many cues and many responses. That which occurs on each trial, the particular combination of cues and responses, is that which is learned. Perfect performance comes from ultimately associating all the correct responses with the appropriate cues. It follows from this also that forgetting occurs, not from disuse or lack of practice but because of the interference resulting from subsequent learning. In other words, what we learn today tends to interfere with that which we have previously learned.

The essentials of Guthrie's position have been specified by Voek (1950), one of his students. In order for a response to be associated with a stimulus, it must immediately follow the stimulus. Where two incompatible responses occur contiguously with a stimulus, only the more recent one is associated. The greater the number of associated stimuli to which the response is conditioned, the greater the likelihood of the occurrence of the response. Finally, the learning situation is fluid, being affected both by variations internal to the organism and by variations in environmental conditions. Thus, variations are unavoidable because no two learning trials are identical, even when immediately following each other.

The appeal of Guthrie's theory lies in its simplicity. Motivation, repetition, and reward are discounted as relatively unimportant to learning; drive and motivation merely arouse the individual and cause him to act and to vary responses. In addition, motives serve to maintain stimuli, induce activity and keep it going. Furthermore, behavior gets organized into sequences because of the development of anticipatory behaviors or actions which have become associated with maintaining stimuli during previous learning. In direct contradiction of Thorndike and the Law of Effect, which holds that rewarded responses tend to be repeated, Guthrie contends that reward as such does not enter into the learning (association) process. Rather, he holds that reward brings about a finale by disrupting the sequence, and as a result, on a repetition of the situation, the response preceding the reward is likely to occur because it was the last response made.

Significance for Education. The teacher in Guthrie's classroom would behave in a different manner from the one in Thorndike's classroom. To begin with, Guthrie's program would involve activity in an experience curriculum with the child learning that which he is to do in the way in which he is expected to do it. The teacher would not be concerned with motivation, as such, other than that he would want children to be active and engaged in work. In no sense would he be interested in the use of reward or punishment for the purpose of establishing the correct responses. In any learning situation, it would be important that extraneous stimuli be reduced to a minimum and that the widest association of correct responses with appropriate stimuli be established. This would necessitate rote learning and frequent drill; learning necessitates doing. In Guthrie's view, habit formation is produced by the association of the greatest number of correct responses with stimuli and the progressive elimination of faulty responses. Drill is justified not to *develop* habits but to prevent new associations from occurring. Higher mental processes involve either the conditioning of a complex stimuli and responses or the association of the particular responses within a possible range.

Guthrie would have several suggestions to make regarding the appropriate manner for handling faulty or negative learning, e.g., when a boy having difficulty in learning to read develops a dislike for reading and attempts to avoid the task, Guthrie would suggest that the reading be presented: (1) in a form that was too faint to arouse the negative response, i.e., small doses, (2) when the negative response was fatigued, or (3) in combination with other stimuli which produced desired responses. To be specific, one would: (1) present reading that was so simple the boy could easily read it, (2) force the boy to persist in the task in spite of all his protests, or (3) present reading material of such inherent interest that the boy would want to read it in spite of the difficulty.

HULL'S REINFORCEMENT THEORY

In the introductory chapter, learning was described as the process by which an activity was originated or changed as a result of practice. In this chapter, we have been considering different theories which attempt to account for what occurs in the process of learning. The two theories we have considered thus far, those of Thorndike and Guthrie, together with that which we will now consider, Hull's reinforcement theory, are classified as association theories. Yet Thorndike and Guthrie could scarcely lay claim to having accounted for the learning process; rather, they defined what they considered to be the essential conditions upon which learning is dependent. Guthrie, espousing a substitution theory of learning, stressed the importance of contiguity in time of the stimulus and the response as an essential condition to learning. Thorndike gave priority to motivation and reward as the important essentials for learning. But naming a condition is not explaining its operation. In contrast, Hull has systematically and explicitly attempted to define the nature of the process we call learning. His theory is a conceptual descendent of Thorndike's inasmuch as he adopts reinforcement as an essential characteristic of learning. On the basis of the experimental variables that have been shown to play a role in conditioning experiments, Hull formulated a series of postulates or laws by which he defined the intervening variables essential to learning. As suggestive of the explicitness and precision with which Hull attempted to define the intervening variables upon which learning is dependent, consider his fourth postulate:

> Whenever an effector activity and a receptor activity occur in close temporal contiguity, and this is closely and consistently associated with the diminution of a need or with a stimulus which has been closely and consistently associated with the diminution of a need, there will result an increment or a tendency for that afferent impulse on later occasions to evoke that reaction. The increments from successive reinforcements summate in a manner which yields a combined habit strength which is a simple positive growth function of the number of reinforcements.

Hull's Basic Postulates.   Paraphrasing Hull's postulates, it may be said that the strengthening or the establishment of connection between responses of an organism and particular stimulating conditions is dependent upon two events: first, the close proximity in time of the stimulus and the response, and second, reinforcement, a rewarding state of affairs which produces reduction of drive or need.

As originally conceived, the essential conditions of learning could be diagrammed:

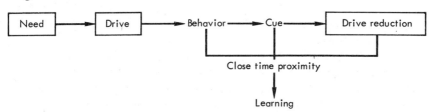

Hull's basic postulate as originally proposed contained an inherent conflict, for it stipulated that learning occurred when drive reduction closely followed responses given in the presence of certain stimuli. It is true that when a hungry rat runs down a maze and obtains food at the end, his running responses and turns lead to and occur shortly before reaching the food. However, getting to and eating food is not drive reduction. Some time passes before the food is digested and the physiological needs are actually satisfied (!), certainly more than the half-second which Hull specifies as the critical time period. Furthermore, the diagram does not account for the circumstances that occur when reward apparently enhances rather than diminishes drive, as anyone who has stuffed himself at a Thanksgiving feast knows well. Whatever the limitations which may ultimately be found with Hull's theory, he faced facts as they came, seeking to integrate theory with evidence. As a result, he repeatedly elaborated his theory. Perhaps Hull is like Columbus, who was forced by facts to change his views of having found the Indies. Where Guthrie was content to rest his case on a main generalization, Hull labored for specificity and congruence between theory and fact.

As a result, over the years in which he pursued his research, Hull incorporated several important changes into his theory. One was that a drive produced internal responses which serve as stimuli. Learning occurs when such drive-produced stimuli are reduced (reinforced) in the presence of cues in the environment. Thus, the basic diagram has to be modified to incorporate these internal stimulus conditions between drive and behavior and in conjunction with environmental cues.

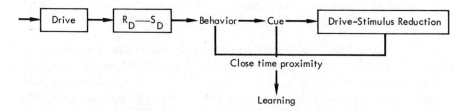

In his original design, Hull conceived of learning being related to the *amount* of drive reduction and this in primary drives such as hunger, sex, thirst, and so on. As modified, the amount of learning is viewed as a function of the *number* of reinforcements associated with reduction of drive stimuli. A third important change occurs in his acceptance of what is known as secondary reinforcement.

Reinforcement may be primary, associated with relief of basic tissue needs of the organism (hunger, thirst, sex, and so on), or secondary, derived from once neutral stimuli which have acquired reinforcement strength by having been repeatedly associated with primary reinforcement. Hull saw needs as the states or conditions within the organism which result when external conditions deviate from the optimal conditions necessary for survival. Deprivation of water or deprivation of food in the external environment gives rise to physiological changes which produce a state of hunger or thirst and the need for food or water. These needs give rise to certain drive states which arouse the organism. At birth, each organism has the capacity of making certain responses which are capable of satisfying needs and drives. These responses become associated with certain stimuli as the result of their occurring in proximity to need reduction. Moreover, other stimuli which are present at the time of need reduction tend to acquire the capacity to reinforce, i.e., to provide need reduction. For example, the appearance of the mother or the sound of her approaching footsteps frequently has the effect of soothing a crying infant, although initially it was either the feeding or the direct soothing of the baby by holding it that had the desired effect. However, in time, the stimuli preceding the event have acquired the capacity of reinforcement.

Secondary reinforcement has the effect of expanding the number and kind of once neutral cues which are capable of acting as reinforcers. Although it introduces great flexibility into the system, it also makes definitive tests difficult because secondary reinforcers are much more difficult to specify than primary ones. Further flexibility was achieved through the concept of fractional goal responses occurring during a sequence of actions. The restrictions imposed by the need for contiguity of response and cue in time if learning is to occur are avoided by accepting anticipatory goal responses occurring at any point in a sequence of actions leading to the goal. Thus, a chaining of responses and stimuli occurs leading up to the culminating event.

Other Variables.   In addition to his construct of habit strength and its relation to reinforcement, Hull introduced several more intervening variables which, in terms of experimental conditions, have been shown to affect the strength of conditioned responses. One is that habit strength and drive strength interact in a multiplicative manner to produce a reaction potential which governs the strength of response. The strength of response at any given moment is a function of the reaction potential, derived from habit strength and drive strength in relation to certain inhibitory factors. The first of these inhibitory factors is reactive inhibition, a term for describing the fact that once we perform an act, we are somewhat reluctant to repeat it immediately Second, the greater the amount of work involved in the act or the more frequent the number of performances of the act within a given period of time, the greater the reluctance, or as Hull describes it, the greater the reactive inhibition. This inhibition subsides with the passage of time, the so-called spontaneous recovery of conditioned response experiments. Furthermore, Hull adds that organisms vary from moment to moment, showing an oscillation in their capacity to respond, which Hull believes distributes itself according to the normal probability function. At any given moment, an organism's effective reaction potential is controlled by the sum of reaction potential and inhibitory influences.

The essence of Hull's theory is seen in the following diagram, although a full understanding requires reference at least to Estes (*et al.,* 1954), Hilgard and Bower (1965), and preferably Hull's own writing (1943, 1951, 1952).

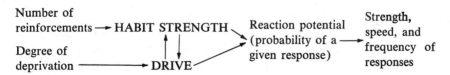

Number of reinforcements → HABIT STRENGTH ⟍ Reaction potential (probability of a given response) → Strength, speed, and frequency of responses

Degree of deprivation ⟶ DRIVE

Limitations.   Although Hull's theory is the most rigorous that has yet been devised and is the model for association theory, and although his use of intervening variables holds the promise of a shift in psychological theory making from those that are purely descriptive to those that are explanatory, nevertheless certain marked limitations exist which are of critical importance to the survival of his theory. One is the restrictive experimental base upon which the theory is built. His experimental verification with human subjects is limited. More important, having placed reinforcement as the central consideration in his system and having held that strength of habit is a direct function of the number of reinforcements, Hull's theory is challenged by experimental findings which do not support these assumptions. Two kinds of experiments have been carried out which do just this: the experiments on latent learning (Figure 3.4) suggest that under some circumstances reinforcement is not an essential condition of learning, and second, the experiments on partial reinforcement (50 percent instead of 100 percent of the trials are reinforced) produce conditioned responses which are more resistant to extinction than those resulting from 100 percent reinforcement. These two sets of experiments, raising certain questions regarding the place of reinforcement and the force of reinforcement in learning, will be discussed later in this chapter.

At the same time, these weaknesses represent a strength as far as psychology is concerned, for the theory is sufficiently explicit to permit fairly precise experimental verification. Although the ultimate effect of such tests may be the refutation of Hull's theory, the subsequent theory will be the more complete for the precision with which Hull labored to explicate his views. One needs only to review the fruitful efforts of Hull and his colleagues, Miller, Dollard, Doob, Sears, Mowrer, *et al.,* to link Hull's theory and psychoanalytic principles to realize the theory's significance for psychological theorizing.

Significance for Education. Systematic order and arrangement would characterize the classroom patterned after Hull's theory. The development of habits and skills would proceed from the simple to the complex with a clear understanding of the stimuli and responses to be associated. The program would have to be dynamic and stimulating in view of the central position that reinforcement holds, inasmuch as aroused drives which can be reduced by satisfying outcomes are an essential condition of learning. In the early stages of learning, few artificial incentives would be used with young children, but gradually such incentives would be developed for the values to be derived from secondary reinforcement. Practice would be presented for the purpose of building the desired habits and maintaining them but would not proceed to the point at which the increase in inhibition from repeating the same response would make the child reluctant to respond. The teacher's role would consist of selecting the most suitable education materials, i.e., establishing appropriate stimulus conditions, assisting the child to discriminate appropriate response, and regulating rewards so that such responses would be reinforced as they occurred. Close attention to the overt responses of the child would be necessary in order to make reinforcement effective.

In spite of the differences that exist between the theories of Thorndike, Guthrie, and Hull, the similarities far outweigh the differences. The structure of learning which they visualize is like a brick wall, put together brick by brick until the total structure is complete, with the upper courses of bricks resting and dependent upon the foundation courses. For these theorists, learning proceeds in much the same manner, with the responses of the organism becoming associated with the stimuli in the environment, bond by bond, until the entire complex structure of human learning is erected. The process proceeds automatically and mechanically with little, if any, need for thought, insight, or cognition on the part of the learner. Both Thorndike and Hull give motivation a central place in their theories, implying not that the learner has conscious purposes, but rather that he has needs and seeks their satisfaction, thus creating situations which make reinforcement possible. The desired satisfaction of the learner's motives leads him to repeat responses which previously have been need satisfying in the presence of particular stimuli. All three men stress the importance of contiguity of stimulus and response, and their proximity in time. In fact, Guthrie gives contiguity the central position in his theory, denying the primary importance of motivation.

The difference between the association theorist and the cognitive theorist is readily apparent, for the latter adopts a diametrically opposed view on many of the basic issues. He believes that the characteristic form of learning is one involving sudden solutions of problems—insight, as it is called. He disagrees with the concept that learning consists of the gradual association of connections—of stimulus and response—but rather, believes it depends upon insight into the relationships existing in any given situation. The whole is more than simply the sum of its parts: it is a unique organization in itself.

LEWIN'S TOPOLOGICAL THEORY

A derivative from Gestalt psychology is seen in Kurt Lewin's topological psychology, which like Gestalt theory contends that the total pattern or field of events determines learning but differs in the greater emphasis that is placed upon motivation. Lewin saw each person as existing within a field of forces. The field of forces to which the individual is responding or reacting is called his "life space." The life space includes features of the environment to which the individual is reacting—the people he meets, the material objects he encounters and manipulates, and his private thoughts, fantasies, and imaginings. In addition to the external aspects of his environment of which he is aware, each individual is responding to certain internal tensions, some of which are the basic physiological drives for food, water, and so forth, and others the tension systems of a psychological nature which cause the individual to seek certain goals, objects, and situations in the external environment.

Life Space. The concept of life space can be illustrated by a United States weather map, which is a diagram representing the dynamic interplay of high and low pressure areas across the continent; shown is the resultant field of weather forces—cold fronts, occluded fronts, sun, wind, and rain being experienced in different areas as the result of the interplay of the high and low pressure areas, which in turn are the outgrowth of still greater forces within the solar system. Like the weather in any one spot, an individual is caught up in vast networks of forces. At the moment of this writing, it is cold in the midwest, unseasonably warm in the southeast, and snowing and sleeting in the middle Atlantic and the New England states. Yet each individual is reacting to only a fraction of this and all of the other physical characteristics which constitute his total physical environment. For instance, yesterday, aside from a few moments of clearing snow from the steps and sidewalk, I was relatively oblivious to the physical presence of snow which began about midday. Today, however, is a different matter, inasmuch as a twenty-mile trip to the university is necessary even though the weather is considerably worse. Today the snow and sleet are very much a part of my life space, in contrast with their small significance to me yesterday.

The forces acting in a person are considered as psychological, not physical, forces. Lewin's system sees behavior as resulting from the interplay of forces, both those from tension systems within the individual and those external to the individual. He placed considerable emphasis upon the present, insisting that past events do not exist now and therefore cannot have effects now. Instead, for Lewin, individuals possess different degrees of organizational complexity and personality differentiation as outgrowths of past experiences, and it is these differences of complexity and differentiation which contribute to behavior differences in the present field.

According to Lewin, learning occurs as a result of a change in cognitive structures, which is to say that one develops a more highly differentiated life space. These changes in cognitive structure result from two types of forces, one from the structure of the cognitive field itself and the other from the internal needs or motivation of the individual. Changes in the cognitive structure may occur suddenly or they may require repetition if the structure is to be changed; however, there is not such a one-to-one relationship between repetitions and performance as we observed in the association theories. The repetition may produce either a change in the cognitive structure (a more highly differentiated knowledge of the relationships between facts in the environment) or a change in needs (the tension system). Attractive goals may lose their attractiveness as a result of repetition. For instance, one who works in a candy store gradually becomes much less enthusiastic about candy. Second, unattractive goals may become attractive through repetition, as in the proverbial "learning to like avocados," or through a change in meaning, as is observed frequently in the previously disheveled adolescent when he begins "going steady" for the first time.

Motivation.   Perhaps as a result of his emphasis upon the immediate field of forces, Lewin was much more sensitive to the factors affecting motivation and involved in motivation than any of the theorists we have been considering. Motivation involves more than mere reward, irrespective of whether it is need reducing or situation terminating. Lewin recognized that it is the individual who is motivated and who possesses the tension systems which give rise to his responses. These motives are related to specific goals which are established by what the individual learner is trying to do or wants to do, and the satisfaction of the motive is determined by changing the goal or achieving it. Such a success is different from reward, for it is defined not by what is given by such an external authority as the teacher, but by what the learner seeks. Closely related to success and failure is the individual's level of aspiration; this is the temporary goal established as a result of an estimate of his own capabilities in the present situation.

Significance for Education.   Much of what has previously been said regarding the implications of cognitive theory for educational practice holds for Lewin as well, particularly with respect to the process of increasing differentiation of life space. Lewin would go further to point out the importance of recognizing the forces in play in any individual's life space and to emphasize that the teacher must effectively understand the relationships between the learner, his environment, and his behavior. Particularly important is the distinction between goals and incentives and between success and reward. Success consists of reaching goals, which in turn depend upon individual motives. The teacher's task consists of aiding the learner to establish attainable goals and then assisting in his attaining them by reducing or helping overcome the barriers that block achievement. Particularly, the teacher should be sensitive enough not to interpose unnecessary barriers by overmanaging the environment or by arbitrarily establishing or creating unattainable or artificial goals through the use of such incentives as rewards or praise.

Lewin casts the teacher into a profoundly different role. From an associationist viewpoint, her primary concern would be with the order of presentation of stimuli so as to elicit the desired response or responses with a minimum of error. For Thorndike and Hull, providing immediate reinforcement would be crucial, and Skinner would admonish her to consider well her frequency and rate of reinforcement.

In contrast to the associationists, Lewin would occupy the teacher with: (1) the learner's motives, and (2) the learner's perceptions of his world. Thus, the teacher would have to begin with the learner's motives, rather than her incentives, hopefully channeling the motives into available activities and paying close heed to the effect of events on motivation. Second, her task would be to modify and expand the learner's perception to incorporate a wider life space. Although the overlap between individuals may be great, an essential degree of uniqueness is inherent in the concept. In contrast to Lewin's position, the associationists endorse an environmentalist view with objective reality and truth posited, with which all learners are expected to come into correspondence.

TOLMAN'S SIGN-GESTALT-EXPECTATION THEORY

If the Gestalt psychologists' formulations apply mainly to perception, and Lewin's topological psychology to behavior, Edward Tolman's theory of sign learning applies primarily to learning. Although Tolman may be grouped with the Gestaltists as a field theorist, he nevertheless proposes that more than one kind of learning may occur and that these different kinds of learning may be temporarily best explained by a particular theory. This view results from his recognition that psychological theory making is still in swaddling clothes, and that the ultimate theory or theories, while derived from current points of view, will probably, if not certainly, be more complexly organized. Yet, of the cognitive theories of learning, Tolman's is the most highly developed.

Response Learning.   Fundamentally, Tolman rejects the ideas that a person learns to do something and that learning is the association of responses to particular stimuli. From the associationist viewpoint, it is the response or sequence of responses resulting in reward which is learned. In contrast, Tolman believes it is the route to the goal which is learned. The animal or human, seeking to satisfy needs, learns to recognize certain cues or signs and the relationship of these signs to particular goals. In other words, he learns *what leads to what*. Compare this with the associationist viewpoint, which sees needs as leading to arousal of activity in the organism, permitting performance to be stamped in by repeated rewards.

Tolman conceives of behavior as being purposive in nature, directed toward goals capable of satisfying needs. He thinks that organisms, at their respective levels of ability, are capable of recognizing and learning the relationships between signs and desired goals; in short, they perceive the significance of the signs. This perception permits behavior that is purposeful and which gets to goals with the least effort. Learning consists of recognizing the signs and understanding their meaning in relationship to goals—in short, the forming of cognitions.

The sequence of events resulting in learning is sign-behavior-significate. The organism's perception of a stimulus, a sign, is followed by behavior which results in the reaching of particular goals; Tolman refers to these goals as significates in the memory of the organism. The result of this sequence is the learning of a means-end relationship, so that on a repetition of the same situation the organism responds with expectations of what leads to what. In Tolman's words:

> The process of learning any specific maze is thus the building-up of, or rather a refinement and correction in, the expectations of such specific (sign, significate, and signified means-end relations) wholes, or, as we may hereafter call them, sign-gestalts.

Tolman's theory is referred to as a sign-Gestalt-expectancy theory because of his supposition that the organism forms maps or Gestalts of the relationships between signs and goals, and that the organism's behavior is directed by expectations of how to get to a particular goal.

One of the crucial points of difference between Tolman's sign-Gestalt theory and the association theories is concerned with the role of reinforcement in learning. As we have seen in both Thorndike's and Hull's theories, reinforcement holds the key position. Learning is directly dependent upon the reinforcement of responses; this stand is consistent with their concept of learning as the association of response (performance) with stimulus. To understand Tolman's position, one must distinguish between the roles that reinforcement plays in relation to performance and in relation to the acquisition of cognitions. Rewards and punishment are related directly to performance. Hungry animals seek food. The performance of the animal is regulated by the need for obtaining food to satisfy its motivating conditions. Under these circumstances, learning is *used* to satisfy needs, but the acquisition of learning is not dependent on need satisfaction. And if, as Tolman contends, learning consists of acquiring a knowledge of means-ends relationships, then it is not the satisfying of hunger by reward that is important, but the effect of the reward upon the map or cognition of means-end relationship. Tolman contends that the extent to which pleasant or unpleasant experiences (rewards or punishments) accelerate learning is dependent upon how they emphasize or make vivid the relationships between signs and goal objects and confirm or refute the expectation held. In this setting, reward or punishment is not essential to learning, although either can contribute to learning. The essential condition is whether or not either confirms expectancies.

Experimentation.   To support this distinction, Tolman relied upon three types of experiments: latent learning, place learning, and intermittent reinforcement experiments. Reference to the latent learning experiments has already been made in Figure 3.4, in which a group of rats was run in a multiple T maze for ten days without receiving food at the end of the maze. Food was introduced on the eleventh day. The performance on the twelfth day and thereafter was as good as that of a group which had been fed each day from the beginning, suggesting that in spite of the absence of reward, learning had occurred, being demonstrated in the immediate improvement on the twelfth day. Under a reinforcement theory, improvement should have been gradual from this point forward, paralleling the rewarded group.

In a series of experiments in which place learning was opposed to response learning, Tolman and his associates further attempted to demonstrate that the learning of cognitions was demonstrable and took precedence over the learning of responses. The first experiment (Tolman, Ritchie, and Kalish, 1946, 1947) utilized an elevated maze, shaped like a cross.

Rats were started at either the north or south end of the cross and fed at either the east or west end. Both the place learning group and the response learning group were randomly alternated in starts between north and south. The response learning group always had to make a right turn to get food. Thus, if they started at the north end, food was to be found in the west wing of the maze. When they were started at the south end, the food was located at the end of the east wing of the maze. A particular response, a right turn, was always required to get to the food. For the place learning group, the food was always at the same place, irrespective of whether they started at the north or south ends. They had to learn to go right or left, depending upon the end at which they had started, in order to reach the food which was constantly in the same wing of the maze. The results of the experiment confirmed Tolman's position. All eight rats in the place learning group learned within eight trials, but none of the response learning group learned as quickly, and several were unable to learn the response.

The second experiment utilized a maze consisting of three paths to a goal. The first was a straight run to the goal which passed a choice point at which the animal could turn left into the second path or right into the third path. Both the second and third paths were longer than the first; the second path returned to the first approximately half-way to the food box, while the third and longest path returned to the first at the food box. The arrangement of the pathways made it possible to block the direct run to the food box (by inserting the block between the choice point and the reentry of the second path) in such a way that the second way was the best alternate (shorter) route to the goal. In a second arrangement, the direct run could be blocked by inserting the block beyond the reentry of the second route in such a way that both the direct run and the second route were closed with the result that the third route, the longest of all three, was the only route open.

In preliminary trials, a preferential hierarchy for the differing routes was established. With all paths open, the animals preferred the direct route.

With that blocked, they preferred the second, and only when both the first and second were blocked did they choose the longest of the routes, the third. In establishing the preference hierarchy, the block had been placed between the choice point and the reentry of the second route, so that the rat had to back out of the direct path, then turn left into the second route.

Having established the preference order for the different routes, the test consisted of placing the block in the direct run beyond the reentry of the second path, so that the longest and least preferred route was the only one open. The question was whether the rats could perceive that both the first and second routes were closed, or whether they would perform in order of their preference. The rats most frequently rejected the second pathway and chose the longest but open route. Apparently they had formed a cognition which permitted the selection of appropriate pathways, rather than being habituated to a given sequence of responses.

The third set of experiments which supports Tolman's position includes the experiments in which intermittent instead of 100 percent reinforcement is used in the conditioning of given responses (human eyelid conditioning). Humphreys (1939) showed that random alternation during conditioning led to as rapid conditioning as did 100 percent reinforcement, and further that the response established showed greater resistance to extinction. The results, according to Humphreys, support a preparatory set or expectancy hypothesis; this is to say that it is not the frequency of reinforcement that is responsible for the learning that occurs or its resistance to extinction, but the effect that the reinforcement has in confirming or refuting the expectations of the learner.

In conjunction with his position, Tolman, like Hull, attempts to explain what is happening when learning occurs. To do this, he defines a series of intervening variables which are operative in learning. Unlike Hull, no attempt is made by Tolman to describe rigorously the quantitative relationships between the variables, because he believes such action would be premature.

To begin with, Tolman recognizes three sets of factors which are operative in learning: those of individual differences in the capacity of the organism, those related to variations in the nature of the material or learning task, and those related to variations in the manner of presentation. These are the factors that are known to affect learning outcomes. To account for their influence, Tolman conceives of two kinds of determinants or intervening variables: cognitive variables and demand variables. The cognitive variables relate to the perceptual organization of stimuli by the organism, and operate under Gestalt laws. The demand variables refer to the motivational states existing, such as sex, hunger, thirst, and so on. The interaction of these variables leads to certain expectations in the organism with respect to the goal-objects or significates which produce the observed behavior.

Although both Hull and Tolman hypothesized the presence of intervening variables to explain the learning process, Hull was more explicit in definition and in his attempt to specify the quantitative relationships. Simultaneously, he restricted the type of learning situations which he attempted to apply experimentally to verify his hypothetical constructs. Attempts at extending the theory to cover all forms of learning were usually by logical analogy. Tolman doesn't restrict himself to a single type of learning; instead, he suggests that several different kinds of learning probably exist and need different theoretical approaches to explain them. Similarly, he does not attempt to define and explain the various ramifications which are implicit in this theory; rather, he is content to treat learning on a broad basis.

Significance for Education. The fact that Tolman accepts different forms of learning makes it more difficult to infer how an educational program which followed his theory literally would operate. Among the different kinds of learning which Tolman (1949) presumes to exist are what he terms: cathexes and equivalence beliefs, field expectancies and field cognition modes, drive discrimination, and motor patterns. A cathexis is the attachment of a specific goal object, such as the preference for a particular food, to a basic drive, such as hunger. All organisms have the basic drives of hunger, thirst, fright, and so on, and they learn that certain objects, in either a positive or negative manner, satisfy them. They also learn that they can obtain equivalent satisfactions from various sub-goals. Tolman gives the illustration of how the obtaining of A grades may provide the equivalent of parental approbation, provided the individual did not directly continue to seek the approval of the parent; in the latter case, the A grade is a means to an end, not an end in itself, and thus is not an equivalence belief. Tolman expresses the thought that cathexes and equivalence beliefs are best explained by a reinforcement doctrine.

The suggestion for education would be that parents and teachers clearly define the type of goal-objects they desire children to seek in the satisfaction of their motives, utilizing reward and punishment to establish them. Tolman would probably go further and suggest that an analysis be made to determine whether the goal objects which are being established by children, consciously or unconsciously, are those desired by parents and teachers, particularly because he believes these are not subject to the usual forgetting as are field-expectancies and field-cognition modes. It is with the latter that the teacher's task is primarily concerned—the creating of stimulus conditions which make it possible for the learner to perceive clearly what leads to what, and to understand the different means by which a given goal can be reached. Emphasis would be placed upon making vivid the relationships between the parts and the whole, thus following Gestalt principles. Because of variations in capacity with age, previous experience, and so on, it would be necessary to select learning tasks which can be perceived as wholes. Field-cognition-modes is the term by which Tolman describes the established memory-perception-inference patterns which play an important, but undefined, part in the expectancies or perceptual set of the organism in any situation, particularly a novel one. If in each new learning situation the field-expectancies had been clearly established so that a minimum of ambiguity in the sign-Gestalt existed, then the probability of appropriate memory, perception, and inference in a new situation would be at a maximum. Ambiguities or confusion would reduce the probability of appropriate memories or inferences being made.

Drives.   Tolman has little to say about drive discriminations. By inference, however, it would appear that any way in which an individual can learn to discriminate between his own needs as they operate and to demand certain actions would make possible more satisfaction, particularly where a choice exists between different equivalences, many of which are arbitrarily attached to basic drives. Much of psychotherapy or reeducation would consist of helping individuals make such discriminations, for instance in the breaking of compulsive-obsessive behavior. Another aspect of drive discrimination would be the importance of the teacher's recognizing high drive states and the extent to which they may interfere with the desired learning. A crude illustration would be the case of attempting to teach a child a given arithmetic skill at a time when he was extremely hungry. The demands of his high drive state would make it difficult for him to learn a task involving a lesser drive—that of maintaining teacher approbation. In view of the relatively neutral aspect of much learning, particularly as children became older, the recognition and prior satisfaction of such high drive states would be important.

BASIC CONFLICTS IN THEORY

The learning theories which have been described by no means exhaust the available supply, but they do provide an overview of first efforts at theory building in the all important area of learning, animal and human. Further, they present sharp conceptual differences regarding the learning process.

Guthrie, for example, argues with some evidence that learning is an all-or-none affair achieved on a single trial and that the only essential condition is contiguity of stimulus and response in time. The apparent gradual nature of learning is because of the complexity, the number of S-R associations involved in the act. Hull, too, argues for association of stimulus and response but makes reinforcement and consequent drive stimulus reduction the sine qua non of learning. Tolman in his stead does not dismiss associations; instead, he contends the association is between a sign for an event and a significate, a cognition of how to achieve a goal.

Each theory is plausible, but plausibility is not the test of successful theory. Instead, how well can it account for the known facts. Once consideration is given to the wide range of behavior changes which are incorporated under the heading of learning—motor perceptual skills, symbolic processes, attitudes, problem solving, acquired motives—it becomes obvious that no single theory seriously attempts to explain all. Rather, all are vigorous efforts to penetrate the territory, beginning at some important aspect, much like the explorations of the Antarctic during the Geodetic Year saw several nations pushing their research from isolated points on the polar icecap. Even Hull's theory, the most painstakingly developed and conscientiously tested, has undergone repeated changes over the years and as yet does not come to grips with all aspects of learning. One has only to reconsider the reference experiments—the cat in the puzzle box, barpressing in a Skinner box, maze-running by rats, problem solving by chimp or child—to recognize the inherent limitations in current theory making.

Yet without these theories, these rudimentary efforts to create basic explanatory principles, we would be like ancient man looking at the heavens. Although there haven't been as many experiments as there are stars, they number many thousands, each experiment producing one or more factual findings, however related or remote to the others. Researchers can pile up any number of experimental observations at various levels in applied and pure research. But without some method of relating these facts, confusion results, like the confusion among the stars in a night sky. Man's first astronomical efforts lay in identifying distinguishing features such as constellations and planets; then in identifying functional relationships such as solar systems and nebulae; then in explaining separate phenomena; and finally in formulating cosmologies attempting to provide a comprehensive explanation. Psychology is engaged in a similar sequence. One product of theory making is dissension, because not only does any theory fail to account for the known facts, but it stimulates dissenters to generate new evidence refuting it and supporters to defend it by refuting or accommodating to socalled crucial tests. Once a theoretical principle has been proposed, e.g., that reinforcement is essential to learning, subsequent if–then statements are generated: if reinforcement is crucial, then any demonstration of learning in the absence of reinforcement refutes the proposed principle.

This has been the effect of early theory making—to identify basic conflicts in the several positions proposed, resulting in further experimentation designed to resolve the questions.

The Role of Reinforcement in Learning.   The systematic rigor and explicitness with which Hull formulated his model made it a central redoubt to be challenged by all comers. Reinforcement was the keystone, and if it could be cracked, Hull's position was untenable. Hull originally defined reinforcement as the reduction of a drive state, and the amount of learning was related to the amount of drive reduction. But it has already been pointed out that too much time elapses between the consumption of food or water and the actual chemical transformations which satisfy the tissue needs which give rise to these drives. More critical evidence was produced by Sheffield and Roby (1950), who demonstrated that saccharin, which has no nutritive value, served satisfactorily as reinforcement with hungry rats. Further doubts were raised by analogous experiments in which food was used but prevented from reaching the stomach and hence from reducing drive. From his experiments with acquired motives, particularly fear and fear reduction (see the section on escape learning in Chapter 2), Miller came to the conclusion that drives, whether primary or acquired, gave rise to internal stimuli and that it was the reduction of these stimuli that was reinforcing.[1]

The result of such research was that Hull modified his theory, accepting the idea that reinforcement involved drive stimulus reduction rather than direct need reduction, that learning was a function of the number of reinforcements rather than the amount of drive reduction, and giving a greater credence to acquired drives and secondary reinforcement. Such change is illustrative of the process of theory making. However, the satisfactions provided by consummatory actions do not possess exclusive powers of reinforcements. More recent work by Chambers (1956) and Miller, Sampliner, and Woodrow (1957) indicate that direct need reduction of primary drive is important as well as the secondary reinforcement produced by consummatory actions such as eating.

Tolman and his colleagues were mounting the attack against reinforcement from another sector, that of latent learning. As we saw in Figure 3.4, Tolman and Honzik (1930) demonstrated that hungry rats apparently learned a maze, even though they were not rewarded, for once food was introduced they performed as well as the animals which had been fed every trial. Several different experimental procedures have been utilized besides the preceding one of unrewarded trials followed by subsequent rewarded trials. One modification is free exploration in the absence of drive with subsequent runs when motivated. These have provided evidence of latent learning. At first presentation, the experiments on latent learning, place versus response learning, and partial reinforcement appeared to be critical refutations of the reinforcement theory. They were responded to as such by those favoring an S-R position, using the converse procedure of running the animal under strong drive conditions (hunger) but in the course of the trial exposing him to an irrelevant incentive (such as water).

---

[1] A common oversimplification of the terms stimulus and response is to assume that both are external and observable, that stimuli are objective environmental events and that responses are instrumental motor acts. The environment may be internal as well as external, i.e., we may respond to internal stimuli such as hunger, pain, and emotional feeling as much as to lights, sounds, or smells. Furthermore, reactions given to some stimuli set off their own chain of stimuli, e.g., as we reach for a glass, we are aware of the sensations arising in arm and shoulder and use this feedback to guide or correct the action.

Tolman would predict that a *subsequently* thirsty animal would go to the water faster than a control group with no experience. Under these circumstances (strong drive conditions), the evidence has tended to go against the Tolman position. Several experiments (Kendler, 1947; Kendler and Mencher, 1949; Walker, 1948; MacCorquodale and Meehl, 1949; Walker, Knotter, and DeValois, 1950) show that latent learning occurs only under restricted conditions. Animals operating under strong drive conditions, e.g., hunger, but exposed freely or forcibly to the presence of water during their seeking of food, fail to demonstrate any latent learning regarding the whereabouts of water, as evidenced by their subsequent behavior under thirst motivation. Apparently, conditions of satiated drive favor latent learning, whereas strong drive conditions interfere with it. Nevertheless, the sum total of the evidence indicates that latent or perhaps better termed hidden learning does occur, at least under mild drive conditions. As a result, Tolman contends that reinforcement is relevant to performance, but not crucial to learning.

Movements Versus Cognitions. Another set of experiments initiated by Tolman and his colleagues were the place learning experiments. Using an elevated maze shaped like a + sign, animals trained to run from the south to find food in the east would learn a sequence of instrumental responses involving a right turn, all of which would be reinforced by the reward. According to association theory, these animals when started at the north would then follow their habit pattern of making a right turn, ending in the west, the wrong place for food. If during the training runs, however, the animals acquire a knowledge of "what-leads-to-where," a cognitive map of the terrain, they will still go to the east for food, even though it involves a novel (unlearned) movement response. When a light is used as an orientation stimulus in conjunction with the food box in the east, the animals associate the sign, the light, with the significate, the goal box, and when started in the north do not follow their movement habit but reverse directions and go to the food box in the east. Thus, they have learned their way around, rather than acquired a habit pattern of movements. Another variant of place learning experiments is the use of alternate routes to a goal when the learned route is blocked. Will the animal resort to trial and error learning or does his subsequent performance indicate an awareness of the location of the goal and the best substitute route to it? One thing such experimentation has proved is that rats can learn both movements and spatially determined stimuli; place learning, as the circumstances require for these apparently crucial tests of theory, did not end in clean cut, absolute results. Perhaps it was naïve to hope for such results. Anyone who has learned to tie a bow-tie in a mirror knows that visual cues and reverse place learning are involved in the early stages but that as skill mounts, the entire action can be run off automatically. Yet, blind persons can learn to tie a bow-tie or lace a shoe largely as a sequence of movements without benefit of spatial cues.

The Discontinuity Issue.   A third line of test experiments involved the question of whether learning was continuous or discontinuous. According to association theory, discrimination learning is a cumulative process based on the strength of the association that is built up between cues and reinforced responses. Thus, an animal that was being taught to make a discrimination involving a large circle and a small triangle (where initially size was the relevant cue, the large one being rewarded, the small one not) would experience greater difficulty when the relevant cues were changed to shape (and size ignored) than would an animal trained to discriminate shape from the beginning. Association theory would hold that learning is continuous, i.e., that a greater number of trials would be required to learn the new discrimination because circles had been associated as positive cues during training trials. In other words, all stimuli present were being reinforced positively or negatively, shape as well as size. Cognitive theory would be supported if the new learning took no longer, i.e., was discontinuous, arguing that shape had been an irrelevant and unattended cue during the first training series.

Although early experimentation favored a continuity hypothesis, particularly where trials were spaced and discriminations simple, the opposite appears true under massed conditions and difficult discriminations. Work by Lawrence (1949, 1950, 1955) indicates that the results are a function of the distinctiveness of the cues acquired during training and that a simplified continuity theory is inadequate, leading Lawrence to suggest a mediation hypothesis.

EFFECTS ON THEORY

What began as crucial tests of theoretical positions (Is learning essentially a change in perceptual organization or a change in stimulus-response connections? and, Is reinforcement an essential condition for the occurrence of learning?) have ended less in victory than in variation as theories were modified in the light of experimental findings.

For some students, the total results of such controversy is confusion and dissatisfaction, for none of the results are final and neither side wins the argument; characteristically, we find it difficult to tolerate uncertainty. It should be noted, however, that each set of controversial experiments produces new knowledge regarding different conditions and variables affecting learning and forces modification and extension of alternate theories to account for the observed facts. A theory which cannot account for the experimental facts must either deny them or discount them as unimportant or else must cease to exist as theory. The pathways of all sciences are littered with discarded theories, and psychology does not differ in this respect.

The changes in Hull's theory are illustrative: Originally postulating reinforcement as essential to learning, Hull defined reinforcement in terms of reduction of primary drives such as hunger, thirst, and sex. Two important changes have been the shift in definition of reinforcement from need reduction to drive stimulus reduction (described earlier) and the acceptance of the principle of secondary reinforcement in attempting to account for learning in the absence of primary drive reduction, e.g., latent learning under satiated conditions of primary drive and learning involving acquired drives such as fear and anxiety. Primary reinforcement occurs when there is a reduction in drive level, e.g., attaining food when hungry. Hull further postulated that neutral stimuli which regularly occur in conjunction with primary reinforcement acquire reinforcing powers in their own right. This has been termed secondary reinforcement. How else explain the importance that money acquires as an incentive in our lives? It can't be eaten. Through the use of secondary reinforcement, Hull can maintain a reinforcement theory in circumstances when primary reinforcement can be shown to be absent. Unfortunately, it makes clear tests for theoretical differences more difficult, for the absence of secondary reinforcement is much more difficult to demonstrate than the absence of primary reinforcement. Nevertheless, it is an inevitable development, if learning theory is to account for much human learning and human behavior, for in man it is his acquired drives, his desire for recognition, social approval, and mastery, as well as his anxiety, which stimulate his actions much more than simple hunger or thirst.

Another development in Hull's position was the use made of so-called *fractional anticipatory goal responses.* Any goal response consists of a set of responses which are being reinforced. Eating consists not only of the actual ingesting of the food, but salivating, picking up food in the hands or with a fork, pursing the lips, positioning the body to eat, moving hands to mouth, smelling the odor, and so forth. And the stimulus situation consists of a set of stimuli, not merely the actual taste of the food. When we enter the house in the evening and smell the dinner, we often give fractional parts of the total goal response, smacking our lips in anticipation of actually eating. We may even anticipate the enjoyment several hours in advance on contemplating the coming meal.

This capacity to step up parts of the goal response in time, coupled with the principle of secondary reinforcement (formerly neutral stimuli can acquire reinforcing capacity) provides a simple association theory with enormous flexibility in accounting for complex behavior patterns. For instance, certain aspects of the stimulus situation are bound to the object— the actual taste of the food, for example—but others are not. We hear a popular tune which is associated with a fiancée and turn to telephone her. The music as a sign produced self-stimulation, leading to a sequence of reactions culminating in a reinforcing event, the satisfaction of the telephone conversation. Through the use of the *fractional anticipatory goal response,* association theory can explain the functioning of percepts and concepts and other apparently pure stimulus actions in learning—the self-stimulation so commonplace in everyday experience.

For one illustration of the functioning of these fractional responses, the ($r_g \longrightarrow s_g$) stimulus act, consider two professional football teams at the point of running a play in a game. The twenty-two men are there with all their individual and team skills acquired as an outgrowth of whatever drives, primary and secondary, motivated them to play football—physical activity, aggressiveness, acquisitiveness, social recognition, and so on. As the offensive team sets itself, the defensive captain notices the blocking back shift his weight to the right and anticipating a play on that side, calls his defensive formation accordingly. He subsequently notices that the halfback makes this fractional goal response in anticipation of running or passing plays to the right but not to plays into the line, and he uses the information to adjust the defense accordingly. While the illustration is quite complex in the actions involved, so too is much of social behavior when compared with the typical association learning experiments, and the availability of such explanatory mechanisms provides association theory with the potency for dealing with such learning and behavior.

Cognitive theory has to account for the same experimental facts, so that it is not surprising that developments and changes occur on its side of the fence. The most ambitious effort to develop such a theory has been made by MacCorquodale and Meehl (1953, 1954) in the postulates they propose for an expectancy theory. One of their key tasks is to explain the development of percepts and their role in behavior. They define expectancy as consisting of three elements ($S_1R_1S_2$). The S signs represent environmental events, the R, a response. For example, the child sitting at the dinner table might think to herself, "If I ask father for more dessert he will say 'no'; if I ask mother for more dessert, maybe she will say 'yes.' " Both propositions represent expectancies. In both, the *eliciting* (to use the M-M terminology) stimulus object (S_1) is the dessert; the response (R_1) of asking father or (R_2) of asking mother; and the consequence of these responses is (S_2 or S_2). Using this, MacCorquodale and Meehl have developed a set of twelve postulates, half of which describe the acquisition, extinction, and generalization of expectancies, the remainder, the interplay of motivation and expectancies. The acquisition of expectancies is dependent on contiguity. The more frequent the occurrence of a given sequence, the greater the strength of the expectancy (SRS). Reinforcement enters the theory, not only through the role played by drive conditions, but also because both the elicitor (S_1) and the consequence of the response (S_2) acquire reinforcing capacities, much in the way of neutral stimuli with respect to secondary reinforcement.

The possible rapprochement between association and cognitive theories is readily seen when a comparison is made of the fractional anticipatory goal response ($r_g \longrightarrow s_g$) and the expectancy (srs). Both are internal events mediating between external stimulus conditions and response to them. Both are linked to observables. Both involve lawful relationships with respect to motivation and reinforcement, discrimination, and generalization. Yet both are consistent with different theoretical viewpoints, for the (r_g — s_g) sequence involves fractions of observable responses serving as stimuli and subject to laws of conditioning, while the (SRS) represents a hypothesis or expectancy of what will occur as a consequence of a given action.

These developments in association and cognitive theory represent efforts to develop a single theory to account for all types of learning—a comprehensive theory. Under such circumstances, the clear line which once distinguished one theoretical position from another inevitably disappears in much the same way that the sharp boundaries which once distinguished one geographic area from another in the United States are disappearing in the face of increased communication and population mobility. Some theorists doubt that a single theory can encompass all forms of learning, at least at this time. In 1949, Tolman proposed that on the surface at least, several different types of learning appeared to occur; among them: expectancies which are acquired as Tolman proposed in his theory, sensori-motor learning which was acquired by contiguity alone as Guthrie argued, and acquired drives obtained through the effects of reinforcement. Whether or not these various types could ultimately be reduced to a single theoretical model remained to be seen. Mowrer (1960) doubts the feasibility of this, proposing that there are essentially two different kinds of learning, one involving emotions, attitudes, and cognitions ("sign learning" in Mowrer's terms) which are acquired by simple conditioning; the other involving instrumental learning ("solution learning") which is dependent on reinforcement. He argues that the voluntary responses which are under the control of the central nervous system—overt responses involving skeletal muscles—function differently than do the involuntary responses involving the autonomic nervous system—fear or other emotional responses.

A somewhat different current line of theory making has been the development of mathematical models of learning. Responding to developments in probability theory, information theory, and the application of the theory of games to human behavior, several psychologists have attempted to develop mathematical models of learning. In part, these models represent efforts to develop equations based upon assumptions regarding the applicability of different branches of mathematics to behavior, equations which (1) predict known empirical curves of learning, and (2) do so involving the least number of variables.

Another glance at various learning curves presented in the preceding chapter shows again the various shapes which learning curves can take, both as an outgrowth of the units of measurement used and the kind of learning and experimental variables involved. The variation in the curves is seemingly endless. A first measure of the usefulness of mathematical models is their ability to produce equations which provide accurate fits to known data, permitting a reconciliation of seemingly different data; the second is the extent to which the variables can be expressed and quantified in terms of specified functional relationships. The two most prominent mathematical models are those of Estes (1959) and Bush and Mosteller (1955), the former being based on a contiguity theory of association, the latter adopting principles of learning utilizing reinforcement.

The student and particularly the teacher may find the present state of affairs frustrating for several reasons—the seeming hair splitting, the lack of immediate empirical application, and other reasons. It is clear, however, that the earlier theoretical differences have resulted in considerable research. The volume of the research is not the important element, but rather the feedback between research and theory. Experiments designed to verify or refute theoretical predictions have the advantage of theoretical relevance. Too much research, in the field of education especially, lacks this reference and lacking it, is of limited value to theoretician or practitioner alike. Second, the consequent research has shown clearly that simple explanations fail to explain all learning. Yet, many teachers find themselves operating on the basis of just such over-simplified assumptions: repeat drill to produce learning; reward success, punish failure, and so on. If questions regarding the soundness of certain theories of learning arise from the laboratory, where experimental conditions are far simpler than in the classroom, surely the teacher should have some questions regarding his procedures.

POINTS OF AGREEMENT

Finally, in regarding the differences between various theoretical positions, many points of agreement, however general, are easily overlooked.

1. Association and cognitive theorists alike agree on the complexity of stimulus-response relationships. Learning requires identification of the relevant stimuli in a complex field. Where these lack the prominence provided by field-ground relationships or natural groupings, steps to heighten the relevant stimuli are needed.

2. Individual organisms differ in their capacity to recognize or discriminate relevant stimuli. These differences stem from innate organic differences and from previous experiences. Regardless of the course of the differences, the task has to be appropriate to and within the range of competence of the individual.

3. Individual organisms differ in their capacity for making the required responses. Whatever the individual response repertoire, stimulus conditions must be arranged to increase the probability of the occurrence of the desired response relative to other possible responses.

4. Motivation initiates and directs behavior and leads to particular re-

sponses organized for the attainment of a particular end, which, if resulting in satisfaction of motives, are more likely to recur. Motives may be organic or acquired, general or specific. Motives may serve to heighten sensitivity to specific stimuli (food or fear), or to provide general arousal (anxiety). Excessive motivation disrupts the complex of stimulus-response relationships by producing a narrowing of stimulus sensitivity and concomitant emotional response. Acquired motives are subject to principles of learning.

5. The crux of learning lies in the learner's recognizing the appropriateness of his response and modifying future tries in the light of previous experience. This action is dependent upon the ability of the organism to discriminate betweeen differences and generalize between similarities. Direct knowledge of results may suffice. The less the capacity of the organism and the more complex the stimulus-response relationship, the more dependent success will be on the manipulation of rewards and punishment.

SUMMARY

The essential characteristics of several learning theorists have been described: Guthrie and Hull representing the association or stimulus-response theories and Lewin and Tolman representing the cognitive or field theories. Guthrie's contiguity theory and Hull's reinforcement theories are similar in their emphasis upon the effects of the environment, the development of the whole from the parts, the importance of previous learning upon present behavior, and particularly the association of responses with stimuli. In contrast, the cognitive theorists, placing emphasis upon perception and cognition, believe that learning consists of discovering what leads to what, that the whole is greater than the sum of its parts, and that insight into the relationships between the parts is vital.

No single theory has proved adequate to account for all forms of learning. The key issues between the two sets of theories center on whether learning is a change in perceptual organization or a change in stimulus-response connections, and whether or not reinforcement is an essential condition for the occurrence of learning. The basic conflicts have stimulated experiments designed to specify the exact role of reinforcement in learning —if it is essential or not, if its effect is on performance rather than learning, or if it merely changes stimulus conditions. Other lines of investigation have been directed at the question of perceptual organization versus response learning in the place learning experiments, to the question of continuity versus discontinuity in discrimination experiments. The effect of such research has been to erase the once clear differences between theoretical positions. As each theoretist attempts to accommodate to new experimental findings, theories become both more sophisticated yet less complete. The modifications bring existing theories closer together; their incompleteness leads to efforts to develop new positions or expand old ones; this is seen in the developments of multi-factor theories and mathematical models of learning.

FURTHER READING

Overview

SPENCE, K. W. 1951. "Theoretical interpretations of learning." In S. S. Stevens (ed.), *Handbook of Experimental Psychology*. New York: Wiley, pp. 690-729.

Selected References

ESTES, W. K., S. KOCH, K. MAC CORQUODALE, P. E. MEEHL, C. G. MUELLER, JR., W. N. SCHOENFELD, and W. S. VERPLANCK. 1954. *Modern Learning Theory*. New York: Appleton-Century-Crofts.

HILGARD, E. R. and G. H. BOWER. 1965. *Theories of Learning*, 2nd ed. New York: Appleton-Century-Crofts.

KIMBLE, G. A. 1961. *Hilgard & Marquis's Conditioning and Learning*. New York: Appleton-Century-Crofts.

KOCH, S. 1959. *Psychology: A Study of Science:* Vol. II, General systematic formulations, learning, and special processes. New York: McGraw-Hill.

MOWRER, O. H. 1960. *Learning Theory and Behavior*. New York: Wiley.

OSGOOD, C. E. 1954. *Method and Theory in Experimental Psychology*. New York: Oxford.

STAATS, A. W. and CAROLYN STAATS. 1963. *Complex Human Behavior*. New York: Holt, Rinehart, Winston.

Original Investigations

ESTES, W. K. 1962. Learning theory. In P. R. Farnsworth (ed.), *Annual Review of Psychology*. Palo Alto, Calif.: Annual Reviews, 13: 107-44.

LAWRENCE, D. H. 1950. Acquired distinctiveness of cues: II, Selective association in a constant stimulus situation. *J. Exp. Psychol.*, 40: 175-88.

SPENCE, K. W. 1960. *Behavior Theory and Learning*. Englewood Cliffs, N. J.: Prentice-Hall.

STOLUROW, L. M. 1953. *Readings in Learning*. Englewood Cliffs, N. J.: Prentice-Hall.

two

VARIABLES
INFLUENCING
LEARNING

5

Individual Variables

Any learning experiment involves a choice of some end behavior to be achieved, an experimental methodology appropriate to the study of such behavior which permits control of the conditions influencing outcomes, the choice of subjects to be exposed, and the manipulation of experimental conditions in such a manner as to provide an adequate test of the chosen conditions.

The task confronting the teacher is analogous, if not parallel, even to the uncertainty of the outcomes. A curriculum represents a set of end behaviors to be achieved, a lesson plan represents a set of specific end behaviors chosen by the teacher. Teaching methodology consists of techniques designed to produce the desired outcomes through control and manipulation of the conditions affecting learning; little choice of subjects is permitted under compulsory school laws, but the age and capacity of the pupils affects the content and procedure of instruction. Finally, through a given set of environmental manipulations the hoped-for educational outcomes are achieved and evaluated.

The main difference between the experimenter's and the teacher's position lies in the explicit identification of the hypothetical relationship between environmental manipulation and outcome, in the rigor of control over extraneous influences, and in the tests applied to the evaluation of results. Basically, however, the endeavors of teachers and educational psychologists are quite similar. In both situations there are three general sources of variation in conditions which affect the outcomes: the subject variables, the task variables, and the method variables. The following diagram identifies some of the more significant variables and places them in context with the learning process, the expected behavioral outcomes, and learning theory and measurement as seen in Part I. Variables in bold face type are of major importance.

←———————— EXPERIMENTAL METHODOLOGY AND MEASUREMENT ————————→

←————————————— PSYCHOLOGICAL THEORY ——————————————→

VARIABLES INFLUENCING LEARNING	PROCESS	OUTCOMES
Subject variables	*Learning*	*Perceptual-motor skills*
Capacities	Changes in behavior re-	
Motivation	sulting from training and	
Age, sex	practice	*Verbal-information*
Prior experience		*learning*
Task variables	Acquisition	
Length		*Cognitive learning*
Difficulty	Retention	Concept formation
Meaningfulness		Thinking
Interference	Utilization and transfer	Problem solving
Method variables	*Maturation*	*Affective learning*
Practice	Changes in behavior as-	Emotions
Overlearning	sociated with physical	Attitudes
Knowledge of results	growth and development	Values
Incentives		
Sensory modality		
Guidance		

At the right of the diagram, one sees the various outcomes possible. Typically, the expected outcome of an experiment will be a limited aspect of any one of the categories listed. In contrast, teachers will concern themselves with all aspects as they apply to certain subject matters. For example, in developing a lesson plan, teachers will customarily consider the skills, knowledge, attitudes, and behavior to be acquired regarding a given subject such as science, foreign language, English, or mathematics.

On the left side of the diagram is a partial listing of the subject, task, and method variables to be taken into account in understanding learning. Connecting the two extremes are the processes by which the change is achieved. Learning was defined earlier as the process by which an activity is initiated or modified as a result of training, practice, or experience. The experience may be systematically organized as in learning to read, or accidental as with some prejudice. A relatively permanent change is implied, involving the acquisition, retention and presumably the utilization of the responses in different situations.

Learning is not the only process by which changes in behavior occur. Maturation is a second. Further, any injury which permanently damages the organism can result in disabilities affecting capacity to learn. Temporary decrements in performance regularly result from fatigue, boredom, illness, and intoxication.

Having identified learning as a process through which certain behavioral changes are brought about, we are concerned with the factors and conditions which affect the learning process. In school situations, three primary sets of variables enter into the equation: those associated with the learner, the task to be mastered, and the teacher. Learners vary in their capacity, readiness, and previous experience; tasks vary in difficulty and complexity; teachers vary in the kinds of incentives they provide and the amount of practice and drill they employ. Each of these variables must be studied and understood, for each, singly and together, affects the learning process.

Learning is not going to occur without learner or task, but it can occur without a teacher. Many of our most important learnings—personal, emotional, attitudinal—are learned informally through contacts with family and friends. Sometimes it appears that the main function of teachers, at least as far as factual learning is concerned, is to tell us where to look and provide us a schedule for looking. However, as our knowledge of learning progresses and educational technology grows more sophisticated, the role of the teacher is slowly changing from the time-honored routine of assign, recite, test, to that of a concert master bringing the many parts into accord. Experimental methodology, measurement, and theory are shown in the diagram as bearing on all aspects of the process. The generalizations which can be made about learning are only as good as the confidence we have in the measures upon which they are based and only as meaningful as the theoretical formulations which we can evolve. In Part I, we have looked briefly at research design, measurement, and theory. In this Part, the variables affecting learning will be discussed, a chapter being devoted to each set and followed by consideration of their relationship to educational practice.

ASPECTS OF LEARNING

Acquisition and Retention.   In common usage, little distinction may be made between acquisition and retention in discussions of learning. Especially in schools, learning is frequently thought to be synonymous with the amount of information or skill acquired, overlooking the generally known fact that the amount retained does not equal the amount learned. All of us recognize areas of former proficiency in which, for lack of practice or other reasons, we have lost our former skill. Acquisition of new knowledge, skill, or information is not the only measure of proficiency in learning. For all practical purposes retention is by far the more important.

Transfer of Training.   This term is used to identify and describe the process by which a mental or motor function shows improvement without direct practice but as a result of practice at some other related activity. A person with some skill in tennis should adapt to the game of squash more quickly than would a person with commensurate skill in volleyball, and he would more quickly acquire skill at squash even though it is quite different from tennis. Having learned tennis facilitates learning squash, just as Latin shows a greater transfer of training to the learning of Spanish than to the study of Swahili. Fundamentally, our entire arrangement for education of children in schools is based on transfer of training. Presumably the skills, knowledge, information, and behaviors obtained in school are directly transferable to out-of-school life to such a degree that one's life outside of the school is the better for the education. Were transfer of training non-existent, each person would have to have direct training in every activity in which he would participate during his life. As simple an act as getting on a bus or a subway in a strange city would require separate training if the arrangements for paying fares, and so on, were different from those with which one was acquainted. The absence of transfer of training would impose tremendous restrictions upon our lives. A third index of proficiency in learning, then, is the amount and kind of transfer of training that occur as the results of different variables operating in learning.

In describing the functioning of the variables and reporting their effect upon the learning process, consideration must be given to their effect upon acquisition, retention, and transfer of training. Because verbal and motor learning have been more exhaustively investigated than many aspects of learning such as thinking, problem solving, and attitude development, the discussions to follow will reflect these biases.

Individual Differences.   It takes a rare degree of tunnel-vision to overlook the variations in ability, achievement, family backgrounds, personality, and behavior present in any group of school children. Yet, our concern with the subject matter we teach, aided by the similarity of the garb and grooming of children and abetted by their docile acceptance of school routines, encourages us to overlook their wide individual variation. To provide some idea of the range of differences, consider a typical fifth grade class. Ages are likely to range from 9.5 to 12 or 13 years of age, and heights from 48 to 66 inches, with some girls among the tallest members of the class because of the advent of the adolescent growth spurt and attendant sexual maturation. Weights may range from 55 to 125 pounds with physical coördination and athletic skills as greatly different. And these are only the grossest physical attributes. Vision, hearing, energy output, metabolism, and nutrition will show differences as great. IQ scores from the most frequently used and misused measures of learning ability, intelligence tests, will range from 70 to 150, relatively meaningless numbers unless one converts them to mental ages. Based on ten as an average age, the mental ages in this class would range from 7 to 15, in many respects a staggering difference. In various aptitudes, which is to say the potential for development in specific areas—verbal, numerical, mechanical, musical and artistic—the range is as great as in mental ages.

The achievements of the children, whether scholastic or non-academic, will be no less diversified. Reading achievement is likely to range from second to ninth grade levels. Fortunately for the teacher, two thirds or three quarters will probably be between fourth and sixth grade level, with approximately a tenth above and below this middle range. Achievement in other school subjects may be nearly as great, depending upon the amount of practice or experience that the children have out of school as well as in. In special accomplishments—sports, music, crafts, and hobbies—the children will range from almost complete inexperience to considerable skill (see Figure 5.1).

Family background, as identified by such factors as occupational dif-

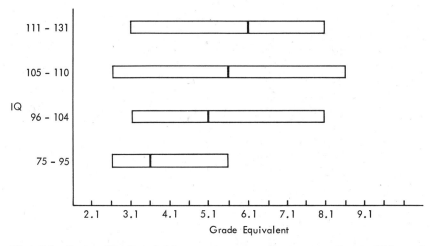

Fig. 5.1 Spring Reading Achievement scores prior to promotion to fifth grade of 120 children randomly selected from twelve classes. *Although each successively higher IQ group shows a progressively higher average grade score, the overlap between different groups is great. Thus, any assumption that achievement will parallel IQ score in individual cases is invalid, even though the expected differences in performance hold for mean scores of groups. The range of scores of the three higher IQ groups is roughly equivalent, ranging from third to eighth grade level.* (After Tilton, 1949.)

ferences of parents, ethnic characteristics, social attitudes, travel experiences, number and variety of books, tools, equipment or other objects in the home, number and ages of children and adults, or any other index, will be as heterogeneous as the other variables. Sometimes the fact that the children within a school come from a fairly restricted geographic area which is somewhat homogeneous as far as economic or welfare level will make for less divergence socio-economically. But in spite of this, the gamut of the out-of-school experiences of the children will be great. The goals, the values, the attitudes, and the personalities will be as manifold as the more measurable attributes listed in the preceding paragraphs.

The following list identifies a number of such differences:

PHYSICAL	CAPACITY
Age	Intelligence
Height	Aptitudes
Weight	Language
Sex	Mathematics
Vision	Science
Hearing	Art
Motor ability	Music
Coördination	Athletic
Physical handicaps	Social
Energy	
Stamina	

PERSONALITY	ACHIEVEMENT
Character traits	School achievement
Motivational needs	Reading
Interests	Arithmetic
Attitudes	Science
Affective reactions	Art
Adjustment problems	Music
Self-concept	Sports
	Social studies

SOCIAL	OUT-OF-SCHOOL
Socio-economic status	
Religious background	Hobbies
Ethnic background	Art
Family relationships	Music
Peer group relationships	Sports

Although the differences between children may sometimes be overlooked, they cannot be ignored if one would have children learn. Whether one is confronted with a group of children or a single child, the concern with individual differences in learning is ever present. Our tendency to label a given child as bright or dull has behind it the erroneous and unfortunate assumption that *all* the aptitudes and achievements of a given child are highly correlated. Again, it would be a convenience for teachers if children who were capable in a given way such as reading or arithmetic were equally capable in all other matters—music, social studies, sociability, motor skills, and others. One has only to recall how few decathlon champions are found, much less individuals who are also highly skilled simultaneously in golf, cricket, archery, basketball, football, lacrosse, and swimming, to be aware of the fact that the range of abilities within an individual is nearly as great as that between the individuals in a classroom. This is readily seen in Figure 5.2, which presents the test profile of scores of a 16-year-old girl in three areas, aptitude, achievement (measured by vocabulary), and interest. Although the variation in level of interest is not surprising, the range of differences in both aptitude and achievement is considerable.

The work of the teacher, then, is to select tasks of suitable difficulty and to organize and present them in ways which make it possible for children of different abilities to acquire and retain the necessary skill and understanding.

We think of maturation as the process of attaining full development of all abilities and capacities; emotional maturity, social maturity, sexual maturity, physical maturity are terms descriptive of certain states of human development. In each, the term maturity has a different meaning. A glance at Table 5.1 will illustrate the difference in the meaning of these terms in common usage. Social and emotional maturity describes an idealized concept of behavior which is almost completely dependent upon learning. Sexual maturity can be used in either of two ways, with reference to the attainment of physical capacity for reproduction or as regards the learned ability for effectively relating to members of the opposite sex. Physical maturity describes the attainment of a condition of full physical growth and development. Sexual maturity occurs in mid-adolescence, while physical maturity is attained five to ten years later. Emotional and social maturity are achieved no earlier than physical maturity and are frequently delayed much longer. The size of the prison and state hospital population permits the conclusion that many never attain emotional or social maturity.

In distinguishing between the two processes of learning and maturation, the latter is used in the restricted sense associated with physical maturation. Changes in behavior resulting from physical growth and development are attributed to maturation. The actual course of human development shows a continuous process of change over the entire span of life from conception to death. One does not suddenly become an adult and is no longer a child. Within the gradual sequence of changes that occur are many trends both in rate and direction, trends which vary with different aspects of human development.

Differentiation of Development. One characteristic of maturation based on experimental evidence is *differentiation.* Gross movement precedes specific movement; simple movement precedes complex movement. Differentiation begins in the germinal stages following the fertilization of the ovum. In

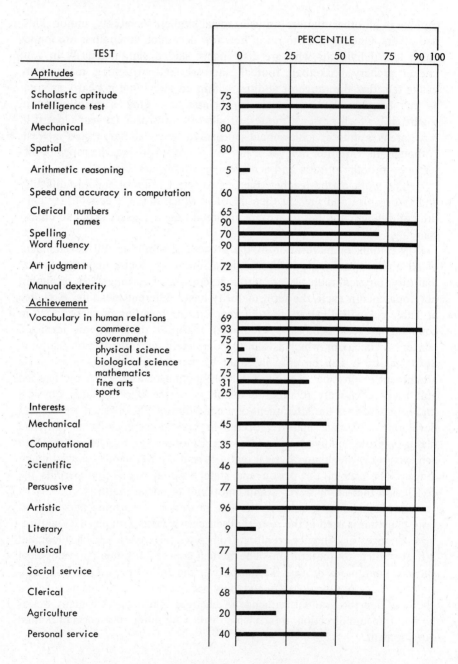

Fig. 5.2 Test profile of high school girl, senior, age 16.

TABLE 5.1.

	IMMATURITY	MATURITY
Emotional	Impulsive, uninhibited, easily upset, cries easily, fearful, anxious Gives full expression of all feeling, easily angered, sensitive, inconsistent, easily hurt by criticism	Able to control impulses and work toward deferred goals Avoids unnecessary worry Able to express wholesome feelings without embarrassment Consistent in responses toward others; can take constructive criticism
Social	Shy, withdrawn, isolated from groups Self-centered Unable to co-operate with others Acts solely to satisfy personal needs Prejudiced or disdainful towards some social groups Forces others to comply with wishes or refuses to participate in groups Extremely docile or submissive in groups	Understands and accepts group goals and values Able to work effectively with groups Able to maintain status and individuality in group without infringing on others Accepts responsibility
Sexual	Unable to reproduce species Antagonistic toward opposite sex Promiscuous in love-making activities Prudish, disgusted regarding sex Body build characteristic of childhood	Capable of reproduction Able to establish friendly relationships with opposite sex Romantic interest with single person Accepts sexual role without embarrassment Body build with primary and secondary sex characteristics associated with adulthood
Physical	Lack of bladder or bowel control Incomplete skeletal development Unable to learn complex motor skills Partial intellectual development	Control of body functions Complete dentition Neuromuscular development Peak intellectual development

the early fetal stages, growth takes place rapidly by an increase in the number of cells through cell division; in the later stages, growth is accomplished almost entirely through enlargement of the cells.

When the baby is born, his receptor-neuromuscular system is developed sufficiently to provide for a great many essential activities, such as breathing, feeding, crying, digestion, and elimination. He yawns, hiccoughs, sneezes, pulls his hand away from painful stimuli, grasps a small rod placed in his hand, and turns his big toe upward when the sole of his foot is stimulated. Besides these comparatively specific reflexes, there is a great amount of mass activity in the form of wriggling, twisting, waving of arms, and kicking of legs.

Longitudinal studies of growth and development show that a strikingly uniform sequence of behavioral changes occur. In infancy and childhood, development is characterized by rapid change, both in size and complexity of function, with increasing stability and gradual decrement in function occurring with advancing age. But regardless of the rate, the sequence of changes follows fairly constant patterns from conception to maturity. This differentiation occurs not only in physical development but also in social, emotional, and intellectual development.

Although the process of differentiation of responses is clear, the evidence for specific learned changes during the prenatal period is inconclusive and equivocal. Learning probably has limited influence due to the relaitvely constant environment of the fetus in the uterus, wherein the range of stimuli to which the fetus is exposed is at best restricted. Furthermore, if learning is dependent upon cortical functioning which in turn depends upon myelination, then learning is not possible until after birth.

That gross changes in environment before and after birth alter development is shown by studies by Sontag (1935), Corner (1944), and Spitz (1945). Marked deficiencies in maternal diet, infectious diseases such as measles at given stages of pregnancy, and gross deprivation of human contact after birth contribute to marked deficiencies in development. Spitz's studies of children in foundling homes showed that infants deprived of the stimulation of human contact were slower to develop physically, socially, and emotionally and were subject to a higher incidence of death and infant diarrhea.

In general, it appears that the younger the child, the greater the influence of maturation upon ability to modify behavior; inversely, the greater the age, the greater the influence of environmental stimuli.

Individual Differences in Maturation.   Studies by Shirley (1931) and those of Gesell (1924, 1934) and Bayley (1935), as well as the review of research prepared by Bayley and Espenschade (1941), demonstrate not only the sequential development of behavior but also the wide individual differences between children in rate of growth and development. No two children grow alike. Not only do children differ in the age at which they pass through different stages of development and in their native talent for various skills, but apparently they also differ in their activity levels and their willingness to spontaneously participate in different activity. These longitudinal studies have been useful in setting up norms for various ages. Against these norms we are able to compare a child with others of his own age, but we cannot be certain that his status at any subsequent time will be constant. Children vary in the way in which they progress toward maturity with wide differences in timing. Some children maintain a fairly constant status, while others are highly variable. The growth of some functions is closely correlated so that certain predictions are possible; others are not. Youngsters who score high in verbal aptitude are likely to be above average in mathematical aptitude. Prediction of art or musical or motor aptitude from verbal aptitude is little better than chance. Rate of development and level of development in early childhood is of limited value in predicting later status. This is due mainly to the fact that observations and tests of infant ability are largely sensori-motor in character and have low positive to negative correlation with later intelligence tests which are highly verbal in content.

Such variations in growth suggest two important cautions: (1) It is hazardous to make predictions with respect to individual progress, especially with young children. Low correlations indicate that only limited predictions can be made for short runs of time, and (2) individual differences in growth rate make it desirable to chart each child's development in concrete terms (see Figure 5.3) in order to appraise actual and estimate probable progress in individual growth trends. For example, quarterly grades are useless because they are (a) too far apart, and (b) vague. They merely report high or low status according to some teacher judgment. Better measures would be reading speed, vocabulary size, pronunciation faults, and many others.

Maturation and Sensori-Motor Skills.   The acquisition of sensori-motor skills is of primary importance to children, particularly during preschool years. Acquiring skill in managing the body and manipulating objects in the environment are major aspects of early development. Crawling, walking, running, and manipulating objects by hand develop out of the child's untutored activity and appear to result mainly from maturational changes rather than from formal training. In fact, one of the chief occasions in the first two years in which formal training is undertaken—toilet training—indicates the relative ineffectiveness of formal training, especially if it is begun before an appropriate level of neuro-muscular maturation has been reached. Early studies on maturation have confirmed these observations. In fact, observation (Amanda, 1965) indicates that even in as rudimentary a habit as toilet training, cognitive and volitional aspects occur. The habit depends not only on the muscular control but on an awareness of what is desired plus a willingness to comply.

Hilgard (1932) gave a group of ten children 24 to 36 months old practice in buttoning, climbing, and cutting with scissors for a period of twelve weeks. A control group, equated for chronological age, mental age, sex, and initial abilities, was also tested in these skills at the end of this twelve week period. The performances of the trained group were superior in all tests at the end of the practice period. But after one week of practice, the performances of the control group were as good as those of the practice group after its twelve weeks of training. The fact that the control group gained more rapidly was believed to be due to factors of maturation and general practice in related activity.

More recently Gesell, Ames, and Ilg (1946, 1948, 1951) have col-

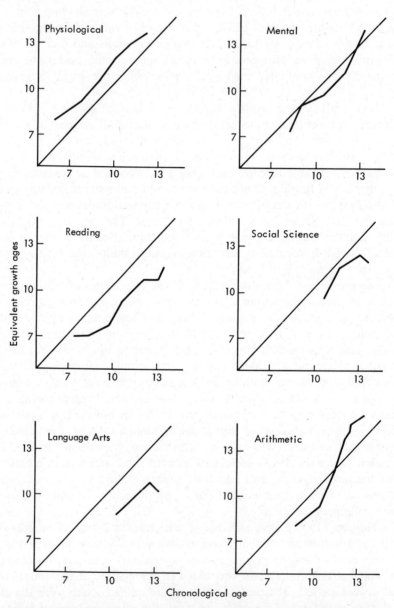

Fig. 5.3 Variations in growth curves of an individual child. *(Uniform growth in each area would follow the diagonal line.)*

Source: C. V. Millard and J. W. M. Rothney, *The Elementary School Child* (New York: The Dryden Press, 1957).

laborated in several studies of developmental trends in handwriting and associated behavior, such as posture and directionality of writing. By obtaining repeated samplings of writing and drawings of given figures of small groups of children at six month intervals, and by taking samples of writing of children of different age levels and comparing the production at various age levels for amount, accuracy, size, slant of letters, and direction of movement, fairly consistent developmental trends were observed. Not only can children write more letters, figures, and words more accurately with increase in age, but also they tend to form their figures in characteristic ways at a given age, e.g., making circles counterclockwise at age three and clockwise at age three and a half. The authors attribute these sequential trends to maturation occurring in spite of the difference in environments and instruction experienced by the children.

Without minimizing the importance of maturation, the early studies in this area tend to overgeneralize from the results obtained in stressing the significance of maturation. The lack of control groups, the failure to include complex tasks, the overlooking of variability in performance, and the use of selected samples of children, usually from more favored socio-economic levels, limit the certainty with which all early acquisition and retention of motor skills can be attributed to maturation.

Rarick and McKee (1949) administered a test of motor skills, including running, jumping, balance, agility, catching, and throwing, to 172 children, and selected the twenty boys and girls with highest and lowest scores and investigated their previous histories. The superior group came from a more homogeneous family educational background, had more and better play facilities, and had showed an earlier preference for large muscle activity, for more active games, and for companionship of older children. While it may be argued that such earlier preferences may suggest earlier maturation, the reverse effect of varied stimulation upon maturation cannot be rejected. It suggests that extrinsic factors have to be considered.

A more conclusive study of the relationship between learning, maturation, and complexity of task is Mattson's (1933) in which an experimentally trained group and a control group were tested on rolling ball mazes of differing complexity. Simple, intermediate, and complex maze patterns were used. Fifty boys and girls, of average IQ, ranging from 58 to 72 months in age, were divided into experimental and control groups, matched for age, sex, IQ, and maze scores after four days of training. Following the initial four day training experience, the experimental group received nine trials per day for 26 days. All three mazes were used in training in equal proportion and in counter-balanced order. At the end of the 26 days' training, both groups were tested on each of eight days with progress being measured in time and error scores. After an interval of 60 days, both groups were again tested for eight days for retention. Thus, the control groups had a total of 20 days experience in the three test periods, in addition to which the experimental group had the 26 day training experience. The performance of the trained group was superior to the control group on error and time scores both at the end of the training and after the retention period, and the differences were statistically significant on all but two retest error scores on the two simpler mazes. Most striking was the fact that the greater the complexity of the task, the greater the difference in favor of the experimental group. This study suggests that the simpler the task (and this would apply to many of the earlier studies of the relationship between maturation and motor skills), the greater the likelihood that the gains from maturation, and possibly from incidental practice, will be as great as from specific practice. However, the more complex the skill, the more persistent the advantage derived from training.

Maturation and Intellectual Functions.   In general, the data concerning the influence of maturation upon various intellectual functions are limited. Much more attention has been given to the relationship between maturation and motor skills because motor skills are more easily observed and experimentally controlled and are not plagued with the problem of definition or validation—a difficulty with measures of intellectual function. The distinction between environmental and maturational influences is more difficult to discern in intellectual functions, largely because both are inextricably interwoven in the functioning of intelligence. In recent years, the research trends in child psychology in this country have shifted markedly to studies of personality dynamics and development, with less than 20 percent devoted to intellectual functioning and few of these to the influence of maturation, provided that the Children's Bureau Bulletin reviewing research is a representative sampling (1953).

The exact nature of the mental growth curve is not precisely established, but the evidence points to rapid growth in early childhood with annual increments which are fairly uniform, followed by a gradual slowing. The increments from year to year in mental growth are sufficiently great in childhood that reliable measures can be made. From mid-adolescence on, the annual gains are small, making reliable measurement more difficult. Exact point of termination of mental growth is uncertain, being estimated to occur between ages 14 and 20, perhaps later. One of the difficulties is that gains in test scores occurring during this period may reflect growth in information and knowledge rather than growth in mental capacity, inasmuch as greater gains occur in areas in which greater training occurs, e.g., vocabulary and language ability. A second difficulty centers on the nature of intelligence test scores. They represent a composite of a number of specific abilities—verbal, numerical, spatial, perceptual—intermixed in varying proportions in different tests. Even where the test components are constant, the contributions of the separate abilities to total score varies at different ages because of differential growth rates for the separate abilities. Several studies, of which Bayley's (1935) is one, show the correlations between scores of children tested in infancy and in childhood to be negative, thus suggesting either marked reversals in rate of intellectual maturation or different abilities being tested at different levels. The latter interpretation is the favored one, infant tests being largely sensori-motor tests whereas later tests incorporate more and more tasks of mental functioning.

The concept of mental age is the criterion ordinarily utilized in gauging intellectual development. *Mental age* is defined in terms of the average performance of children of a given chronological age. Any child, irrespective of chronological age, whose responses in an intelligence test situation correspond to those of the average ten year old, is assigned a mental age of 10. If at the time he is tested his chronological age is 8, he is intellectually advanced for his age. This advancement is indicated by the intelligence quotient which indicates *rate of intellectual growth to chronological age.*

$$\frac{\text{Mental Age}}{\text{Chronological Age}} = \text{Intelligence quotient}$$

$$\frac{10}{8} = 1.25$$

The quotient is reported as a whole number—125 in this case—as a convenience (obtained by multiplying by 100). If a child with the mental age of 10 had a chronological age of 15 his IQ would be 67, suggesting that his rate of intellectual growth is approximately two thirds of normal.

Early studies showed that children who scored below a mental age of 6.5 on admission to the first grade showed a higher frequency of reading failure in the first grade than did children who scored above this mental age. From such studies, the conclusion was made that intellectual maturation equivalent to mental age of 6.5 was required for success in reading. Subsequent investigations have shown that success in reading is more dependent upon the presence of given skills in visual and auditory discrimination than upon mental age, and that training designed to produce the visual and auditory discrimination necessary to word recognition reduces the failure rate. Such investigations have resulted in a shift of emphasis from the search for the given level of maturation necessary for acquiring given skills to consideration of the hierarchy of skills essential to the acquisition of proficiency in complex skills such as reading, which involves visual and auditory discrimination, eye movements, perceptual speed, persistence, experiential backgrounds, and so forth (Durrell and Harrington, 1960).

Maturation and Readiness.   Readiness is the educational concept associated with maturation. Prior to introducing a learner to a task, a judgment has to be made as to whether or not he is ready to learn the task. The concept of readiness involves the two different meanings of maturation described earlier. With young children, readiness involves the question of whether or not the child has matured physiologically to the point where he can undertake the task: is his neuromuscular and intellectual development sufficient? As the child grows older, the question becomes less one of whether or not he is physically ready and more one of whether or not he has had (in addition to the required aptitude) the experiences prerequisite to learning the task. In order to learn skills such as typing, shorthand, and algebra, one must have not only a sufficient degree of motor or intellectual ability but also skill in language and mathematics.

Important as the question of readiness is, there is only limited tangible evidence available upon which to base determination, especially in complex tasks. For simple motor skills, training is likely to be of little value if a child lacks the minimal strength or motor control needed to perform the task, and training may even contribute to the acquisition of faulty procedures that will subsequently interfere with learning. The same applies to certain cognitive tasks. Children taught number computation without sufficient opportunity to develop understanding of the meaning of numbers develop errors which subsequently hinder their work. The types of errors occurring most frequently on college entrance examinations in mathematics are application of the incorrect formula for a solution of a problem and inability to remember the complete formula. Lacking sufficient understanding of mathematics, students are unable to reconstruct a formula or analyze its suitability, probably as a result of over-emphasis on the mechanical aspects of arithmetic and insufficient attention to conceptual development. Basic to the Montessorri materials for preschool children and the several "modern math" curricula for elementary and secondary students is the focus on concept development rather than rote learning.

Generally, a determination of readiness is made by introducing a task or a sample of it and checking rate of learning during early practice sessions. A slow rate of gain and low degree of retention indicates either lack of readiness or excessively difficult materials or both. Accelerated rate of gain and high retention indicate material suitable to learning capacity. When learning tasks are appropriately suited to readiness level, retention will be equivalent for different ability levels (Klausmeier and Feldhusen, 1959). The difficulty lies in determining what constitutes appropriate experiences. One step is to base the decision on difficulty level, a second on selection of essential sub-skills. An important diagnostic skill that teachers bring to instruction is the analysis of particular individual difficulties and selection of appropriate instruction steps to overcome them.

If the adage "You can't teach an old dog new tricks" were true, this section could be concluded with that sentence. Unfortunately, the adage applies only to certain dogs, and perhaps recalcitrant rather than incapable dogs; facts suggest that even with the decline in certain abilities found with advancing age, learning of many varieties of tasks is quite possible. An interesting example of this is seen in Thales of Miletus, an enterprising olive oil tycoon on the coast of Asia Minor before the time of Christ. Upon retirement, Thales turned his efforts to mathematics and is credited with having developed the basic propositions which became the foundations of abstract geometry. Thus the real question is: What tricks can old dogs learn?

Knowledge of the relationship between age and different kinds of learning abilities is important in determining which tasks shall be assigned to which age-grade levels of instruction. What differences in learning ability exist between young and old, and are the differences of degree or of kind? Are they qualitative or quantitative differences?

Although a distinction between perceptual motor learning and skills of the symbolic conceptual type is necessary, certain generalizations can be made. The majority of studies shows that older children and adolescents exceed younger children in superiority of performance. The older child is stronger, has more endurance, is willing to persist longer at given tasks, is able to direct his energy and attention more effectively and for longer periods of time, and has better motor coördination, work habits, and memory. He can follow verbal instructions, explore more methodically, and generalize more effectively. The younger child tires easily, makes more errors, has less motivation, poorer work habits, and poorer motor coordination. The advantages of the younger child lie in being less cautious, more responsive to stimulation, and more active. (This generalizaiton regarding youth and age will hold throughout life.) In general, studies comparing children at different ages with adults show similar results on both motor and ideational learning with regard to the form of the learning curve, trials for relearning, spacing of practice, interference between learning tasks, and transfer of training. Adults and older children have an advantage in initial attack upon problems, in the ability to generalize, and in the ability to synthesize isolated experiences in obtaining solutions to problems. Presumably, these advantages are associated with greater intelligence, broader experience, and greater verbal facility.

Age and Motor Learning. At first glance it would appear reasonable to assume that ability to acquire motor skills improves with age up to maturity. The young child is limited by lack of maturation. As he grows older, his coördination, control, and steadiness of movement improve, he becomes more resistant to fatigue, and he is more capable of sustained attention and interest. In comparison with a 5-year-old, an average child of 7 years of age can run faster, throw a ball farther and more accurately, kick harder, and jump farther (Jenkins, 1930). A young child's reaction time is considerably slower than an adolescent's or a college student's (Goodenough, 1935).

When children of different ages are compared with each other or with adults in ability to master an experimental task in motor learning, the older individuals are found almost invariably to be superior in the degree of skill attained under similar conditions of practice. Cron and Pronko (1957) report a progressive improvement with age in sense of balance in both boys and girls from age 4 up to age 12 at which point it levels off. Similarly, the Ammons and Alprin report (1955), testing age and sex differences in ability to keep a metal stylus on a continuous rotary pursuit (an off-center disc on a turntable like a record player), shows a marked overall increase in proficiency associated with age between 3 and 12 years. Humphries and Shephard (1959) and Henry and Nelson (1956) corroborate these results with perceptual motor, gross motor, and discrimination tasks.

A more careful analysis of the facts discloses that the differences that occur between younger and older children are the result of initially higher starting scores in the older children rather than the result of more rapid learning. Munn (1954) has thoroughly reviewed the evidence and concluded that there is no clear evidence that the same amount of practice produces greater improvement in performance with older than with younger children. McGinnis's (1929) experiment with 3-, 4-, and 5-year-old children may be cited as an illustration. Twenty children at each age level of both sexes were given 50 trials at pushing a stylus through a slot maze. Error and time scores were recorded. At both beginning and end, each older age group was superior to the younger groups, but the gains made by all 3 groups during the 50 trials were equivalent. Thus, the youngest group gained as much as each of the older groups during the same number of trials. Most noticeable was the difference in variability. Variation was greater on initial than on final scores, and the older groups showed the greater decrease in variability by the end of the 50 trials. An unanswered question is whether or not the mazes had sufficient progression in difficulty to permit the better learners to increase their scores.

Several studies done with elementary and secondary school children corroborate the foregoing conclusions with respect to the relationship of age to learning. Seels (1951) investigated the relationship of height, weight, age, and skeletal maturity (determined by X-rays of the bones of the wrist) to large muscle motor skills involved in running, jumping, throwing, balancing, agility, striking, and catching. The highest correlation coefficients (between .40 and .50) were obtained between skeletal maturity and performance. Height, weight, and age showed low coefficients. McCloy (1935) in cross-sectional studies and Jones (1949) and Espenschade (1942) in longitudinal studies of adolescent children came to the conclusion that strength, rather than chronological age, appeared to be an important determinant of degree of motor ability.

In comparing infants and school children in their acquisition and retention of motor skills, the inferiority of the younger children resulting from their neuromuscular immaturity is strikingly evident. In comparing school children at different ages with adults in the learning of motor skills, it appears that the differences are not so much those of neuro-muscular immaturity as differences in strength, experience, and motivation. Age in itself is not the crucial factor, inasmuch as marked differences in learning rates of motor skills do not appear with difference in age. Beyond the early years, practically all differences—especially the higher initial starting scores—may be attributed to the greater *range of experience accumulated and to differences in motivation.* The older person has greater ability to sustain attention, follow instructions, and maintain a given set, especially in delayed reaction type problems. Where gross motor skills involving the large muscles are involved in the task, the lesser strength of the younger subjects handicaps their performance. It should be apparent that it is difficult to devise tasks which are comparable in difficulty, sufficiently motivating, and equally novel for a wide age range. As tasks become more complex, they tend to incorporate abilities other than motor skill, e.g., remembering instruction and perceptual or symbolic skills. In some instances, the previous learning of the older subjects may interfere with the new learning. Foreign language instruction provides a good example. Younger children can learn to pronounce a foreign language more rapidly because they have less interference resulting from the much practiced, familiar sounds of one's native language, but the total advantage goes to the older subject because his greater understanding and knowledge of language offsets the advantage in pronounciation held by young children. Similarly, in typewriting, a motor skill which incorporates perceptual and symbolic skills, e.g., spelling, grammar, vocabulary, and so on, we cannot expect a child of 10 years to improve as fast with the same amount of practice as a student of 16 or 18 years of age.

The illustrations just given disclose the difficulty in making generalizations with reference to age differences in learning without taking into account the level and type of learning task. Unless one stops to consider the differences between the tasks presented in the laboratory and the greater complexity of the learning tasks in and out of school, there is danger of overgeneralizing from the results of experimental studies.

Age and Verbal Learning.   The available evidence on the relationship between age and verbal learning or problem solving shows a progressive improvement in learning with increase in age. Yet there is the same limitation as posed above: is it improved learning ability or difference in experience and motivation?

Memory span for digits (Terman-Merrill, 1937) and objects (McGeoch, 1928), nonsense syllables and poetry (Stroud and Maul, 1933), problem solving ability (Harter, 1930; Gellerman, 1931), reasoning ability (Maier, 1936), ability to generalize (Heidbreder, 1927, 1928), and ability to learn school subject matter (Thorndike, 1928) shows progressive improvement with age.

The rather popular notion that childhood is the golden age for memorizing is contrary to the findings of systematic investigations of age differences in ability to learn. Evidence from many studies shows that the ability to memorize increases from its earliest manifestation in the young child to the late teens or early twenties.

When children of various ages are given the same learning tasks, the older ones learn in fewer trials and retain better than the younger ones, but the critical determinant is the difference in mental age, not chronological age. Thorndike is credited with the classic investigation of the relationship between age and learning (1928). Working with over two thousand persons between the ages of 20 and 60, he investigated their performance on code learning, motor tasks, paired associations, addition, and school subjects. Generalizing from his findings, Thorndike concluded that the curve showing the relationship between learning and age shows a steep rise through adolescence, attains a peak in the twenties, then gradually declines. Commenting on the argument that childhood is the ideal time for education because of the greater plasticity of the child's mind, Thorndike wrote:

> . . . . . If there were nothing in favor of early schooling save the greater mental plasticity of the youth, in the sense of youth's ability to learn, we might better replace "Childhood is the time for learning" by "The time for learning anything is the time when you need it." For there are great advantages which occur when learning satisfies some real need, benefits some cherished purpose, and is made use of at once and so kept alive and healthy for further use.

Some thirty years later, Bayley (1955) came to the same conclusion in a review of studies of intellectual development, contradicting the popularly held misconception that mental maturity reached a peak at age 14 and declined thereafter. Table 5.2 collates some of the findings from diverse sources regarding the rise and fall of various abilities.

No single generalization can be made for all abilities. Like the several tissues, differential rates of maturation and degeneration occur with different mental abilities. For example, tonal memory matures early (age 10) and shows no decline until hearing is impaired, whereas perceptual speed reaches its peak between 12 and 14 years and shows a progressive decline with age, especially after 50. In comparison, intellectual ability as measured by information and vocabulary shows little decline. Further, and often overlooked, certain of the changes which occur are qualitative such as lan-

TABLE 5.2   RELATIONSHIP OF AGE TO VARIOUS ABILITIES

No decline or rise with increased age in	Sensori-motor ability until age 50 Memory for simple materials Rote memory until age 70 or more Reasoning by analogy until age 30 Tonal memory Vocabulary General information Reasoning by analogy until age 60 in high ability groups
Some progressive decline in	School subjects Typewriting Addition and arithmetic Analogous reasoning after age 30 Imaginative thinking Perceptual speed Motor speed Object assembly, block design Similarities and comprehension sub-tests Wechsler Intelligence Scale Reasoning by analogy in average ability groups
Greatest or rapid decline in	Recall of new materials Sensori-motor ability after age 50 Rote memory after age 70 Code learning Associating numbers with nonsense syllables Reasoning by analogy in low ability groups after age 30

guage usage in adolescence (Feifel and Lorge, 1950) and strategies used in concept attainment (Yudin and Kates, 1963). In general, it can be said that

1. There is a gradual decline in all types of measurable ability setting in after 30, but not becoming marked until well after 50.
2. Decline in learning ability varies with the type of material to be learned. The more meaningful and familiar the material, the less the decline.
3. Sensory and perceptual abilities decline most and earliest. Motor abilities hold up well until late middle age.
4. Wide individual differences occur so that in any age group individuals occur who are superior to the average of much younger groups. Differences within groups are far greater than differences in averages of groups.
5. Differential decline is related to the occupational activities of adults.

Research on the symbolic processes such as thinking, problem solving, and imagination is less conclusive, but the available data supports the generalization of increase with age. Using ten subjects at each of four age levels (3, 4, 6 to 10, and adult), Heidbreder (1928) presented them with three discrimination problems of increasing difficulty involving the selection of a doll in a box which could be the left or right, near or far, plain or marked, or combinations of these. Scores were in terms of the number of persons in each age group solving the problem and the number of trials necessary. Not before age 6 did all subjects of a group solve all problems, and progressively fewer trials were needed by older subjects. Adequate verbal explanation of the solution was not found under 6 years of age.

In a study of reasoning ability in children, Maier (1936) utilized a swastika-shaped maze with a booth at the end of each arm in which children ranging in ages from approximately 4 to 9 years were first allowed to explore for a brief period. After being taken out of the maze, each child was walked by a devious route around the maze to another of the four booths in which he was shown a toy house which played a tune when a penny was inserted. For the second time, the child was taken out of the maze, ostensibly to go find another penny to play another tune but actually to disorient the child. Having found the penny, the child entered the maze. The problem was to find the correct booth which could be identified by the size of the chair and the position of the light within it. A solution could be obtained only if the child were able to synthesize his two past experiences to solve the problem, which process Maier believes to be the basis of reasoning. On an accidental basis, a child could get to the correct goal once in three trials. Only when the proportion of correct solutions for repeated trials was significantly greater than one in three could reasoning be attributed to the children. It was not until age 6 that the proportion of correct trials went far above chance (59 percent).

Such data is in agreement with observation of the development of space and time concepts in children, whose understanding of temporal and spatial relationships does not approach adult concepts until well along in elementary school. Similarly, children are inferior to adults in both range and reliability of reports on what they have seen and heard. This is due to the child's more limited experience, immature judgment, imperfect understanding, and greater suggestibility. As he grows older, the range of his report increases faster than its accuracy. The reports of very young children in picture tests are usually mere enumerations of objects. Later, the ability to describe in terms of relationships develops, and at the age of 10 or 12, children are usually able to evaluate and interpret. Through adolescence, there is growth in the ability to analyze and organize experiences.

A study which incorporates the least disparity in task and motivation for different age levels is that of Holaday and Stoddard (1933), who tested the retention of items recalled at different intervals after viewing a motion picture. The percentage of items retained by different age groups at three intervals after viewing are as follows:

| Age group | 1 day | Percent of items recalled at stated intervals after viewing of motion picture | |
		6½ weeks	12 weeks
Adult	88	72	73
15-16	81	71	65
11-12	66	59	56
8-9	52	47	48

The evidence offered in this section on the relationship of age and learning indicates that there is a progressive increase in learning of complex skills with advancing age, and although there do not appear to be learning rate differences in motor skills at different ages, the performances of the older person will begin and end at a higher level. The inability of younger children to perform more difficult tasks only emphasizes the necessity of grading tasks to children's level of readiness—sensori-motor, intellectual, experiential, and motivational. Variations in instruction and motivation may make it possible for children to learn given tasks at earlier ages than customary, but in general, if ease and rapidity are the standards for determining age-grade level of instruction, much of the instruction offered at given grade levels, such as reading, arithmetic, geography, and others, could well be deferred. However, usefulness—not ease or rapidity of learning—is the standard for determining level of instruction. Even though the illiterate adult can learn to read more quickly than the illiterate 6-year-old, both individuals profit from earlier instruction. Neither the adult or child is likely to be asked, "How rapidly do you read?" or, "How long did it take you to learn to read?" but rather, "Can you read"? The earlier the skill is obtained, the more valuable it is, provided it is of sufficient use to be maintained through incidental practice (which recalls Thorndike's words that the time for learning something is when you need it and can use it). Undoubtedly, some differences between experimental and control groups which disappear in time and as a result are attributed to maturation would continue to exist with continued equal amounts of practice. The earlier a skill can be acquired, the greater an asset it becomes, provided it serves some useful purpose, some increase in the child's life space or in his control over his environment.

SEX DIFFERENCES

There are few readers of this section who do not already have definite and frequently strong convictions about differences between the sexes with respect to many skills, attitudes, interests, temperament, aptitudes, and behavior patterns, and not a few are equally convinced that such differences are innately derived from the difference in sex. It would be pleasant, at least for those who favor the status quo, to confirm such beliefs, but fortunately or unfortunately, the evidence prevents it. This is not to deny that there is a physiological sex difference nor to contradict the fact that there are associated differences in attitude, interest, and occupation. But this is to deny the fallacious deduction that the relationship establishes the physiological difference as the cause and the difference in attitudes and so on as the effect. Enough evidence has been accumulated from anthropological studies of different societies to show that the ways of behaving which are called masculine or feminine in any society are the result of cultural customs and conventions which evolve over a considerable period of time. Margaret Mead's (1935) study of three New Guinea tribes of the same racial stock showed that in one tribe both men and women tended to be gentle, submissive, and coöperative; in the second, both were aggressive, competitive, and antagonistic; and in the third, the women were aggressive and performed the tasks usually thought of as masculine and the men behaved in a manner which would be called feminine in the Western World, engaging in the arts, performing the dances, being easily offended or slighted, and becoming emotionally upset quite easily. It was evident that the manner in which men or women acted was the result of traditions that evolved over a long period of time rather than the result of innate sex differences. Again, this is not to deny that differences in attitude between the sexes in interests and in occupations are observable, but to caution against attributing the cause to physiological differences. The contribution of physical structure, basal metabolism, pulse, strength, and so on to attitudes, interest, and others is little known, but from the available evidence, it appears that most differences are learned behavior patterns resulting from social tradition.

Sex and Motor Learning.   There is no clear cut evidence of significant differences between the sexes in motor learning ability. Some reports favor men whereas others indicate a slight superiority of women. It is commonly supposed that motor activities involving great endurance or muscular strength can be handled better by men, and that women are likely to excel in skills requiring close coördination of small muscles and strict attention to detail. It is doubtful, however, whether there are any innate differences other than possibly that of muscular strength. Watchmaking, surgery, and violin playing are examples of skills requiring delicate coördination of small muscles and close attention to detail, and in these it cannot be said that women surpass men. Moreover, there are comparatively few skills depending so much upon brawn that women may not become as competent in them as men.

The same results are obtained with children. Of the studies which have been done with motor learning by children, no consistent difference favoring either sex has been found. Occasionally, the boys will be found to have higher starting scores; nevertheless, the amount of gain made by both sexes as a result of specified amounts of training has been equivalent. Presumably, the difference in initial scores may result from differences in previous experience.

Sex and Verbal Learning. It is frequently stated that girls surpass boys in ability to memorize; Jordan (1942), for example, writes that only 40 percent of the boys do as well as or better than the median for girls in memory for words. On the other hand, Stroud (1935) cites a study in which no sex differences were found for memorizing nonsense syllables and poetry. For reproduction after one presentation of a list of nonsense syllables, fifteen unrelated monosyllabic words and fifteen related words, the writer obtained the following averages for five groups of students making up a total of 106 men and 161 women:

	Nonsense syllables	Unrelated words	Related words
106 men	4.36	9.94	13.63
161 women	4.34	10.09	13.08

It will be noted that there is practically no difference between the scores for the men and women. These data are based on one impression, and the learning is incomplete; they do not speak for complete mastery or for learning under other conditions.

If such a difference exists, it is small in comparison with the differences likely to occur with variation in interest and familiarity with material to be memorized. Again, in evaluating sex differences in learning, caution must be exercised in distinguishing between that which is associated with a given sex by social custom and training and that which is sex-linked by birth. Earlier students of the problem fell into the same trap. Comparing famous men in history to famous women, one finds the men outnumbering the women on roughly a 10 to 1 ratio. From such data, a conclusion could be (and was) made that men are innately more capable than women, if the matter of equality of opportunity or differences in training derived from social tradition is overlooked. The fact of the matter is that no primary sex difference in average intelligence exists. A number of studies have been completed which give a slight advantage one way or the other, apparently depending upon the particular test being used. The two most thorough samplings have been Scottish Mental Surveys (1933) and MacMeeken (1939). In the first, a verbal group test was given to all children (87,000) born in a given year; and in the second, all children born on a given day were given the 1916 Stanford-Binet individual intelligence test. In both studies, the means for boys and girls were almost identical.

Where aptitude tests based upon factor analyses have been used so that single relatively pure tests of a given aptitude are available (in contrast to the general intelligence test which is a mixture of items—vocabulary, numbers, analogies, and so on—in different proportions in different tests), specific sex differences are observed. Hobson (1947) administered the Thurstone Primary Mental Abilities Tests which measure six factors— number, verbal, spatial, word fluency, reasoning, and rote memory—to approximately 2400 eighth and ninth grade boys and girls. Although some bias in sampling occurred because of students leaving the public school either to drop out of school or transfer to private schools, the particular community utilized has a very high proportion of its students in public schools. The girls showed significantly higher mean scores in word fluency, reasoning, and rote memory. The boys were higher on the spatial and verbal meanings tests. Interestingly enough, the boys were not higher than the girls on the number factor, which would be anticipated from obtained differences in school achievement.

In vocational aptitude tests and scholastic achievement tests, boys obtain superior scores on mechanical aptitude and in science and mathematics, while girls obtain superior scores in clerical aptitude and all kinds of language skills (Stroud and Lindquist, 1942; Edgerton and Britt, 1944; Burt, 1941).

With respect to these differences, it is important to note that they are usually not great enough to be statistically significant with preschool and primary grade children (Bergen, 1943; Buckingham and MacLatchy, 1930). It is possible that the tests may be insufficiently sensitive at the earlier ages, but it is more probable that experience and interest—which become progressively self-generating—contribute to the sizeable differences. Some confirmation of this is found in two studies by Milton (1957, 1959). In the first, he assumed that problem solving ability was a set of learned behaviors associated with the male sex role in our culture. If this were true, then a positive relationship should exist between problem solving ability and masculine identification, and controlling for the latter should reduce the sex-differential in problem solving achievement. Using the Terman-Miles Masculinity-Femininity Score as an index of masculine identification and adjusting for this factor with mathematical and verbal aptitudes held constant, Milton found that the sex difference was no longer significant. Going further, he adapted a set of problems so that they were less male oriented to discover again that the sex differences in problem solving skill diminished. A general summary of differences associated with sex is provided in Table 5.3.

PREVIOUS EXPERIENCE

Our basic interest in the previous experience of a learner stems from a need to determine what he is ready to learn and capable of learning. But it is a short step to the recognition that today's experience yields tomor-

TABLE 5.3 SUMMARY OF SEX DIFFERENCES

Characteristic	Tending to be higher in		
	Males	Females	No Difference
Physical			
Body Size	X		
Endurance		X	
Strength	X		
Rate of maturation		X	
Mortality rate	X		
Stability of physical functioning	X		
Visual acuity			X
Color discrimination		X	
Hearing			X
Intelligence			X
Aptitudes			
Word fluency		X	
Numerical reasoning	X		
Computation			X
Spatial visualization	X		
Perceptual detail		X	
Memory		X	
Motor coordination (fine)		X	
Motor coordination (gross)	X		
School Achievement			
English		X	
Speech		X	
Art		X	
History, geography	X		
Science	X		
Mathematics	X		
General information	X		
Interests			
Theoretical	X		
Scientific	X		
Mechanical	X		
Computational	X		
Persuasive	X		
Exploit–adventure	X		
Vigorous activity	X		
Sedentary activity		X	
Aesthetic		X	
Literary		X	
Social service		X	
Domestic		X	
Temperament			
Aggressiveness	X		
Dominance	X		
Self-confidence	X		
Emotionality		X	
Sociability		X	
Social adjustment		X	
Ambitiousness	X		
Independence	X		

row's readiness and, conversely, to ponder the nature of the early experiences which provided today's capacities, and to wonder if they could have been different.

The Nature–Nurture Controversy.   Three decades ago a major concern of a number of investigators was to discover whether heredity or environment played the greater role in the determination of intelligence. Head Start programs are a contemporary version of the question: Are individual differences in mental ability due to hereditary or to environmental influences? Are those differences susceptible to modification through change in environment? Are there genetically superior racial stocks? The questions cannot be answered with any finality for three reasons: first and most important is the fact that hereditary and environmental influences are constantly interacting with each other to produce a human organism which, at any stage of development, is the product of this interaction. The two forces are inseparable. Second, it is impossible to achieve complete experimental control of either the hereditary or environmental variables affecting human behavior. Third, most of the studies have used the intelligence test score as the dependent variable; this score is susceptible in an uncontrolled manner to variation from other influences as well, making it difficult to determine which change in intelligence test score is associated with which factor. Perhaps the dilemma of attempting to resolve the controversy is best illustrated in *Twins, A Study of Heredity and Environment* (1937) by Newman, a biologist, Freeman, a psychologist, and Holzinger, a statistician. Discussing the same data, the biologist thought the influences of heredity were well demonstrated; the psychologist thought the same for environment; and the statistician agreed with both.

The early studies on the heredity-environment question attempted to establish situations in which one or the other was held constant. If environment could be held constant, then it was reasonable to attribute observed differences in intelligence to heredity factors. Unfortunately, it was an easy leap to the conclusion that observed differences in intelligence *were* hereditary, overlooking that identical environments rarely, if ever, occur. Even where the physical evironment is the same, individuals perceive it differently and respond differently because of their genetic makeup, providing the unique interaction between each individual and his environment at all levels, cellular to social. A rash of early studies purporting to show the intellectual superiority of one ethnic or immigrant group over another, or of civilians over criminals, completely overlooked the effects of language and cultural differences on performance on intelligence tests.

Over the thousands of centuries since man first put in an appearance on this earth, intelligence has slowly evolved, imperceptibly within any generation but sufficiently over time if one compares the differences in skills. During the greatest part of this time, 99 percent or more, evolution was dependent on survival, and with it natural selection, making genetic factors determinant in the process. Our environmental control over natural predators such as disease introduces a change in the scheme that alters the balance in natural forces. For example, we are presently grappling with the results of one such control in terms of overpopulation; we have achieved a high degree of death control but not birth control. What the course of future evolution of talents will be is unforeseen,[1] but it is immediately apparent that survival in today's technological environment is dependent upon developed talent. This fact, coupled with our goal of permitting each man equal opportunity for development, contributes to the massive undertaking to create environmental shifts in underprivileged areas. Behind these efforts is the assumption that intelligence is *not fixed by heredity* but is *variable relative to environment*. Thus, intelligence is a product of events as well as a determinant of accomplishment. In effect, the IQ becomes a measure of learning.

An investigation of the content of most intelligence tests will show that they measure performance in skills or information in which an individual has had direct or indirect (transfer of training) experience, but only if the previous experience of those being tested is equivalent (which it rarely is) can the tests be said to measure differences in native ability. Instead, they may be said to measure those differences in capacity which result from whatever combinations of nature and nurture are useful in predicting performance on some tasks, particularly school subjects. As a result, they may be useful in evaluating the results of environmental changes.

Circumstances Contributing to Variation of Test Scores.   Certain precautions are required in making judgments about such effects based on scores on intelligence tests. Rarely will any person obtain the same score twice on two testings or on two tests because of fluctuations due to error and those due to real changes. Thus a distinction is required between those changes resulting from the testing per se, and those changes in score produced by environmental changes, differences in rate of maturation, or other factors. A review of these factors is pertinent at this point, prior to consideration of the available data.

Test Suitability.   When intelligence tests are administered to different nationalities or to bilingual persons, it is obvious that the scores on verbal tests will vary according to the similarities between the languages and with the language achievement levels of the persons being tested. Any degree of language handicap tends to invalidate the results. (We shall soon see an interesting extension of this concept regarding children from underprivileged economic areas, where the environment handicaps a person in his native language.) An illustration of this is found in a study of Mead's

---

[1] At hand is the possibility of determining the sex of the child you will have. And not far off is the possibility of selecting by artificial means your child's probable size, IQ, hair coloring, and so on.

(1927) in which United States children of Italian parents were divided into four groups based on the amount of English spoken at home—Italian only, Italian plus some English, English plus some Italian, and English only. As the amount of English increased, so did the average intelligence score. Further complicating the picture are personality factors. Anastasi and Cordova (1953) administered intelligence tests in English and Spanish form to Puerto Rican boys and girls in New York City. The girls scored higher on the Spanish form, the boys on the English.

Test Composition.   IQ scores may differ if two different tests are used, the variance resulting from differences in content in the two tests. Even where the same test is used, but at different age levels, the content may differ noticeably. This disparity is particularly true between items suited for infants and older children.

Instability of Early IQ's.   Intelligence test scores of children under four have generally negative correlation with later test scores, thus suggesting possible changes in the functions being measured or differential growth rates effecting changes in variability. To a large extent, this instability reflects the inadequacy of the tests designed to measure intellectual functions of infants and young children.

Errors in Norms.   Because one's IQ is determined by comparison to the performance of the group of children selected for standardization of the test, any failures to obtain a representative sample of children at a given age will produce apparent changes in IQ even though one's performance has not changed.

Motivation.   Attitudes of the person taking intelligence tests can have a detrimental effect upon score, particularly with younger children. Mayer (1935) reports the number of negativistic responses from preschool children ranging from 4 to 7 being tested by highly trained examiners. The extent to which negativism can influence scores was shown by Rust (1931), who repeated on successive days the items which 100 children had refused to perform until they passed or failed them. A quarter of the group gained 15 or more points; two thirds of the total group showed some gain.

Administration of Test.   Intentionally or unintentionally, the attitude and skill of the examiner in administering the test can and does produce differences in scores. Goodenough (1940) reports a correlation of .40 between ratings of personal attractiveness of children and number and direction of errors made by teachers in scoring spelling papers. Under conditions in which teachers were attempting not to make errors, their errors were in favor of those children they rated as attractive and opposed to those rated unattractive.

In another illustration taken from one of the studies on the effect of nursery school attendance upon intelligence, on the second test the examiner administered only the items which the child had previously failed. Obviously, the scores could go nowhere but up.

Statistical Regression.   When groups being studied are selected from either the high or low ends of the distribution of intelligence test scores, the second test score tends to regress closer to the mean, showing a loss for the above average groups and a gain for the below average groups which is due not to changes in intelligence but to fluctuations in error factors inherent in mental tests.

Practice Effects.   Depending upon the test, age, education, and test-wiseness of the subjects, small to great differences in test scores result merely from taking the same test twice in succession. Terman and Merrill report an average gain of 2 to 4 points on successive administration of the same test or of a comparable form of the Stanford-Binet (1937 revision). Dearborn and Rothney (1941), in the Harvard Growth Study, report gains in median IQ of 11 points on successive tests which dropped when a different test was substituted. However, other data are available which show that gains occur not only on the same tests but on different tests. Generally in tests in which a principle can be learned, e.g., maze problems, the greater gains are shown, whereas the more specific the test in terms of information or speed required, the smaller the gains.

Practice effects, while representing a limitation of tests, nevertheless constitute an illustration of valid learning. The greater gains are obtained in those areas which tend to be most susceptible to practice in daily life. In general, the greatest gain in score occurs on the second trial. The gains, of course, may result from a difference in speed of taking the test, in different work methods in attacking the test problems, or in memory or insight into the solution. Particularly in test-wiseness and its effect upon gains between first and second trials, the practice effects are not unlike the results obtained by Harlow in his experiment related to "learning how to learn," to be discussed in the chapter on transfer of training.

Keeping the foregoing limitations of test results in mind, we can divide the studies providing information about the effects of previous experience into two types: those dealing with variations in family background such as parent education and social class status and those dealing with the effects of schooling.

Social Status and Family Background.   That differences in the environment in which the family lives can produce differences in intelligence test scores is seen in the numerous comparisons of children living in rural and urban environments both in this country and Europe. The rural children consistently attain lower scores on both intelligence and achievement tests. Some of the variation in the results of particular tests is a function of vocabulary content, which favors urban children and is partly due to the tendency of rural children to be slower and more deliberate in their work methods. Nevertheless, some of the differences are probably associated with marked variations in the range of stimulation available in the environment, e.g., libraries, museums, and the like; in the lesser educational opportunity for the rural areas in terms of books, school facilities, training of teachers, and length of school term; in the kinds of recreational activities pursued; and in the kind and extent of social stimulation. Typical of a series of studies which show a progressive retardation in intellectual development are one by Baldwin (1930) and others in which children in four rural Iowa communities were compared with urban children. Scores of rural infants were comparable to urban infants, but beginning with 5 to 6 year olds the intellectual retardation became progressively greater and was more noticeable in those children attending one room schools.

Three explanations have been offered for the differences: (1) the depressing effect of poor homes on intellectual development, (2) selective migration and resultant differences in hereditary strains, and (3) test unsuitability. Jones and Conrad (1932) compared the responses of urban and rural New England children (ages 4 to 14) to different test items and identified differences in responses to specific items which could be associated with cultural differences. They estimated that about half of the point difference between rural and urban children could be attributed to social and economic factors. Several studies have shown also that selective migration of the more intelligent from rural to urban areas occurs in areas adjacent to cities and in badly depressed areas but that it is not uniform for all rural areas. Undoubtedly, the explanations differ according to the particular area.

Another distinction besides the rural-urban which is commonplace is between "working-class," or "blue-collar," and "white-collar." Sometimes the terms "lower class" and "upper class" are used. They identify recognized distinctions in attitude, behavior, privilege, and status between members of the same community. Early studies by the Lynds (1929) and Warner (1945) stimulated a series of investigations of these phenomena in modern communities. Nearly any community of any size will have its preferred residential sections with their greater exclusiveness. Furthermore, there will exist second best and third best and the "wrong side of the tracks" areas. Ask the residents in these areas who their friends are, with whom they participate in different activities, and with whom they hold beliefs in common; you will observe distinct groupings. Ask the members of these groups whom they look up to and whom they look down on; differences in the status of the various groups and in the amount of prestige they command in the community will be noticeable. Having identified these groups, check on such characteristics as property owned, occupations held, education obtained, church and club membership, amount of income, attitude on unionization, and so on; definite differences will be observed.

Warner found he could subdivide the community into three major groupings which he called upper, middle, and lower class on the basis of their prestige or social status and which included approximately 3, 38, and 59 percent of the community respectively. These three social strata could be subdivided again into upper and lower fractions. These six strata are identifiable ranging from upper-upper to lower-lower. Of special interest is the fact that people who are members of a given social class differ from the other classes in intelligence, educational achievement, home life, recreational pursuits, occupations, religious observance, child rearing practices, sexual behavior, personality, and attitudes (Warner, 1945; Kinsey, 1948; Davis and Havighurst, 1946; Maddy, 1943).

Nearly all of the studies of social class have been conducted in a single community, and their findings about social class, while true to the community, may be at some variance from other communities. Davis points out that three systems of social rank (to be distinguished from social class) exist in the United States. These are: (1) social classes, (2) ethnic or foreign born groups, and (3) color castes. The three may overlap. In one community, blacks (color caste) and poor whites (social class) may occupy the bottom rung; in another, it may be Orientals. The number of social classes will vary according to the age, the size, economic complexity, ethnic composition, and nature of the community. It is less important to determine the number of levels than the differences they create in learning environments for children.

When a comparison is made of the mean IQ's of children classified according to their father's occupation as in Table 5.4, higher mean IQ's are found to correspond to higher occupational status.

A difference of nearly 20 IQ points is noted between children of professional workers and children of day laborers in this study in which painstaking efforts were made to obtain a large and representative sample of

TABLE 5.4   MEAN STANFORD-BINET IQ's OF 2757 CHILDREN
CLASSIFIED ACCORDING TO PATERNAL OCCUPATION*

Father's Occupation	Chronological age of child			
	2-5½	*6-9*	*10-14*	*15-18*
Professional	114.8	114.9	117.5	116.4
Semi-professional and managerial	112.4	107.3	112.2	116.7
Clerical, skilled trades, and retail business	108.8	104.9	107.4	109.6
Semi-skilled, minor clerical, and minor businesses	104.3	104.6	103.4	106.7
Rural owners	97.8	94.6	92.4	94.3
Slightly skilled	97.2	100.0	100.6	96.2
Day labor, rural, and urban	93.8	96.0	97.2	97.6

*From McNemar (1942), p. 38.

American children for the standardization of the 1937 Revision of the Stanford-Binet Intelligence Test. It is interesting to note—and this has been confirmed by other investigations—that the differences are observable as early as age 2½ to 4.

Correlation coefficients between social status and scores on the Thurstone Tests of Primary Mental Abilities ranging between .21 and .42 were obtained by Havighurst (1947) in a study of the relationships with 10- to 16-year-old children, confirming the preceding results obtained by McNemar. Highest coefficient (.42) was that between verbal comprehension and social status. Words, test content, and social status go together. Number ability and word fluency were .32 and .30 respectively, while spatial, reasoning, and memory abilities were all in the low .20s. Mechanical aptitude tests show the least correlation with social class. It is possible that the foregoing relationships may be the outgrowth of different environments in which the children living in the most favored environment, e.g., professional homes, show greater development, particularly in verbal areas, than do children living at poorer socio-economic levels. It is also possible, as Allison Davis (1951) points out, that the tests are loaded in favor of upper socio-economic levels. In other words, the items contained in the test pertain to vocabulary, objects, and experiences which are characteristically obtained in middle class families, and thus children from lower social classes are at a disadvantage in taking such tests and are penalized as a result.

Davis contends that such tests underestimate the learning ability of children from lower social classes. He is very likely correct. He argues that the obtained differences are the result of faulty tests rather than being due to genetic differences in social classes. The opposing argument, of course, is that by a selective process in operation in the selecting and qualifying for different occupations, the more capable people rise in the social scale.

There is no question that Davis is correct in his contention that intelligence tests discriminate against lower socio-economic classes. Three studies of many that could be cited show that infant test scores (given their limitations) show few differences, but that the differences become greater with age, until a correlation of .40 between social status and IQ score is reached. Both Hess (1955) and Noll (1960) have demonstrated that tests can be developed which reduce or avoid these cultural differences by eliminating items regarding which middle class children would be knowledgeable but not lower class children. For example, where the Otis Intelligence Test (a popular group pencil-and-paper test) correlates .21 to .49 with social class, the Davis-Eells test scores .04 to .19. Unfortunately, the Davis-Eells test correlates only .27 to .38 with measured achievement, where the Otis correlates .80 or higher. It may be true, as Davis argues, that such correlation merely demonstrates the narrow, rigid, and culturally biased nature of the average classroom. Nevertheless, the basic purpose of any test is to discriminate, not in terms of race, social class, or creed, but in terms of a given criterion. The best test is that which is most valid, namely the one which correlates most highly with a given criterion. And it is here that the culture free tests fail, for they are less valid as far as what we call academic achievement is concerned, and alternate (possibly more socially desirable) validities have not been specified. Radical changes in the school curriculum could reverse the situation, invalidating current tests.

It might be advisable at this point to consider some of the data regarding the mutability of intelligence as a function of environmental conditions. Twins provide an opportunity to make two kinds of comparisons: between individuals of identical hereditary makeup (identical or monozygotic twins) reared in the same and in different environments and between individuals of non-identical heredity born at the same time (fraternal twins) and reared in the same and different environments. In the study mentioned earlier, Newman, Holzinger, and Freeman (1937) tested 50 pairs of identical twins reared together and 50 pairs of fraternal twins reared together. In addition, they were able to test 19 pairs of identical twins reared apart. All but two had been separated prior to the age of 2 years. Table 5.5 provides a comparison of identical and fraternal twins on height, weight, and intelligence test score.

Inspection of Table 5.5 reveals the high correlation on all characteristics occurring when the identical twins are reared together. These children have the same heredity and similar, although not necessarily identical, environments. The correlation between fraternal twins is considerably lower, approaching that found between siblings (brothers and sisters born at different times) of .50. The differences between the two sets of correlation coefficients reflect a hereditary difference, although the influence of environment is not completely ruled out. At the same time, the difference in correlation found with ordinary siblings and that shown for fraternal twins suggests the influence of environment. Although fraternal twins may not have identical environments—one may be a girl, the other a boy, with attendant differences in parental actions—they will necessarily have more

TABLE 5.5 RESEMBLANCES BETWEEN TWINS REARED
TOGETHER AND APART

| Measure | *Mean Difference between Twins* | | |
	Fraternal reared together	*Identical reared together*	*Identical reared apart*
Height in cm.	4.4	1.7	1.8
Weight in lbs.	10.0	4.1	9.9
Binet IQ	9.9	5.9	8.2
	Correlation between Twins		
Height	.64	.93	.97
Weight	.63	.92	.89
Binet IQ	.63	.88	.77

similar experiences than two children born at different times. In the latter instance, the age of parents, size and composition of family, economic level of family, and other factors are likely to be different.

In weight and IQ, the identical twins reared apart are more like fraternal twins in the variability shown, again indicating an environmental influence. The differences are more striking if a distinction is made in the extent of difference in the environment of the twins reared apart. When twins are reared in separate homes, the differences in environment may range from small to great. Newman, Holzinger, and Freeman had the environments rated as to the difference in educational and social advantages being provided by the homes. In Table 5.6, the IQ differences are related to educational and social advantage. It can be seen that in nearly every instance in which a large difference existed in the educational advantages offered, the twin with the better environment scored more than five points higher in IQ. In only three instances did the child having the better educational environment score more than five IQ points below his twin, and in each instance these differences were associated with small rather than large environmental differences. When one looks at the effect of differences in social advantages, they appear to have a much less significant effect than differences in educational advantages.

These data indicate that heredity plays a major part in the determination of physical characteristics including intelligence but that sharp differences in environment can produce significant differences in intelligence test score. No one can question the existence of sharp differences in the educational environment of (in rank order) the suburban child, the urban child, the rural child.

Davis' argument that standard intelligence tests underestimate the learning ability of children from lower social classes finds some support in Klineberg's studies of black children migrating from rural to urban areas

TABLE 5.6   EFFECTS ON INTELLIGENCE OF EDUCATIONAL AND SOCIAL ADVANTAGES OF NINETEEN PAIRS OF IDENTICAL TWINS REARED APART*

	5 or more points difference in IQ in favor of lesser environment	*−4 to +4 points difference in IQ*	*5 or more points difference in IQ in favor of better environment*
Large differences in educational advantages		1	8
Small differences in educational advantages	3	6	1
Large differences in social advantages	2	3	5
Small differences in social advantages	2	5	2

*Adapted from Newman, Holzinger, and Freeman as reported by Woodworth, 1940.

and from southern to northern United States. Klineberg (1935) tested black children who had been resident from one to seven years in New York City and found that the longer the city residence, the higher and closer to average the mean intelligence score was. When the argument was advanced that this could be true if migration was selective, i.e., the more capable families moved first, Klineberg showed that the gains occurred when given groups were retested after given intervals of residence. Gains were greater on verbal tests than on non-verbal tests, supporting the hypothesis of environmental influence.

More recent support is found in Lee's (1951) study of the relationship between IQ of black children and length of residence in Philadelphia, shown in Table 5.7.

Three interesting features appear in Table 5.7. The first is the comparative stability of the IQ's of the Philadelphia-born black children; the second, the difference between those children having kindergarten experience and those not having it; and finally, the progressive gains in IQ with length of residence in Philadelphia. The results of this study corroborated earlier studies which showed that gains in mean IQ scores correlated with length of residence in northern cities. Somewhat similar results occurred with black children moving from rural to urban areas in the South. The fact that IQ scores for the same children show gains goes against an explanation based on selective migration, and the fact that more recent studies report higher averages for southern blacks than earlier studies supports an explanation based on variation in environmental and educational opportunity.

Davis' view is that the gains in intelligence test scores in Lee's study support his own hypothesis and that the stable scores of the Philadelphia group are depressed by the general environment associated with a socially disadvantaged group. As Davis puts it: the meaning of social class is that it limits and patterns the learning environment, structuring the social maze in which the child learns his habits and meanings. Lower class people have

TABLE 5.7 MEAN IQ's ON PHILADELPHIA TESTS OF MENTAL AND VERBAL ABILITY*

Group	N	*Test Score in Grade*				
		1	2	4	6	9
Philadelphia-born and attended kindergarten	212	97	96	97	98	97
Philadelphia-born and no kindergarten	424	92	93	95	94	94
Southern-born and entering Philadelphia schools in grades:						
1A	182	86	89	92	93	93
1B-2	109		87	89	91	90
3-4	199			86	87	89
5-6	221				88	90
7-9	219					87

*After Lee, 1951.

a deep anxiety about food, shelter, clothing, heat, and darkness due to their uncertainty about income. When they have money, they eat. But more often they are hungry. They see life as a recurrent series of depressions and peaks with regard to the gratification of their basic needs, quite the opposite of middle class children who learn to accept voluntarily deferred gratification. Aggression is handled differently. In the middle class it is channeled into social and economic skills, into initiative, ambition, even progressiveness. In the lower class, direct expression is encouraged if not required. Thus, expectations, motivations, and behavioral patterns (including problem solving techniques) are shaped by the cultural experiences common to given social strata.

But before an environmental hypothesis can be accepted, one would first have to account for the fact that foster children's intelligence correlates more closely with their natural parents' than with their adopted parents' (Honzik, 1957, 1963), and second for the fact that differences found in IQ's of children when comparison is made on the basis of paternal occupation do not increase with age as would be expected under circumstances of continuing exposure to favorable environment (Bayley, 1954). In other words, differences at age 2 to 3 are practically as great as at age 18. The point that is most significant in consideration of the effect of previous experience on learning is Davis' demonstration of the differential effect of family background and associated experiences upon capacity to answer satisfactorily certain kinds of test items, particularly those having to do with verbal comprehension. Children from middle and upper social classes, whether of superior ability or not, apparently have an advantage in verbal learning (an important asset in school) as a result of previous experience.

The solution is not to be found in changing the content of intelligence tests as much as changing the content of the culture of the socially disadvantaged child, no simple task as the Office of Economic Opportunity has discovered.

Present intelligence tests are extremely useful in various kinds of prediction: performance in school, occupational selection, job performance, military classification, and so on. It has yet to be demonstrated that culturally fair tests provide more accurate predictions, and until they do, they are not as valuable. We should note, as Davis correctly points out, a limitation in present tests. With certain populations, the scores are not highly dependable but are subject to noticeable change in a given period of time. In such instances, long range predictions are not in order. The entire controversy could be avoided if we gave up any notion that our present tests are measuring innate intelligence, innate reasoning ability, capacity to learn from experience, or any other definition of intelligence you may wish to substitute here. Most tests measure rather limited aspects of behavior. The term general intelligence is a misnomer as far as tests are concerned, for in most instances the items being answered are specific rather than general and provide measures of particular abilities or combinations thereof. Granting the charge that currently used intelligence tests are culturally loaded and may contribute to underestimates of the educability of children from lower social strata does not mean that they are useless or that a culturally fair test is more useful. An important measure of the goodness (i.e., the validity) of a test lies in its predictive powers. The culturally fair tests will have to show a higher degree of correlation with various criteria such as academic performance, job performance, and so forth to be preferable. Several considerations militate against such an event—one related to test construction, a second to society, and a third to the effects of social stratification upon individual development. It is difficult to devise new items for tests which surpass carefully selected items in standardized tests. Second, culture exists and societies change slowly. Tests, like people, are immersed in the matrix of culture and must make predictions within the matrix. In many instances, these will be self-fulfilling prophecies. It would be no loss if all group intelligence testing were postponed until fourth grade or later, for learning rates would provide a more immediate index of capacity.

Personality.   Longitudinal studies of changes in intelligence of 140 children at Fels Institute (Kagan et al., 1958; Sontag et al., 1958) were followed from birth to age 10. The group (of superior intelligence with a mean IQ of 120) showed a median change of 18 IQ points, somewhat greater than the median change of 10 IQ points reported in the Honzik, McFarlane, Allan study (1948). The principal purpose of the study was to learn if gains or losses in IQ were associated with personality characteristics. It was reported that children with maximum increases show higher achievement needs, competitive striving, and curiosity than children showing maximum decreases. Emotional dependence in the preschool years proved detrimental to intellectual growth.

It becomes apparent that intelligence is a function of many influences and that it is a misconception to conceive of it as a fixed quantity. Rather, we need some kind of calculus for estimating rates of change under given conditions. At the moment, we must be content with estimates of possible change under divergent conditions. Table 5.8 shows Bloom's (1964) estimate of the potential effects of different environment at given ages of development.

CAPACITY

At any given moment each individual is possessed of certain abilities, that is, available and developed skills for performing acts of varying complexity, and certain capacities or potentials for development of future skills. Abilities are measured by achievement and performance tests; capacities

TABLE 5.8 HYPOTHETICAL EFFECTS OF DIFFERENT ENVIRONMENTS ON
DEVELOPMENT OF INTELLIGENCE IN THREE SELECTED AGE PERIODS.*

| Age Period | Percentage of Mature Intelligence | Variation from normal growth in IQ units under given environmental conditions | | | |
		Deprived	Normal	Abundant	Difference
0-4	50	−5	0	+5	10
4-8	30	−3	0	+3	6
8-17	20	−2	0	+2	4
Total	100	−10	0	+10	20

*B. S. Bloom, *Stability and change in human characteristics* (New York: Wiley, 1964), p. 72.

are measured by intelligence and aptitude tests. Because the tests available
fail to measure all one's abilities and capacities, we are frequently forced
to resort to less reliable guides. With respect to abilities, we can use observation to inform us whether an individual is able to perform given tasks
successfully, and, lacking the opportunity to observe (as is typical in employment interviews), we depend upon questions during interviews or
reports of previous observers. Capacity presents greater difficulty than
ability inasmuch as it involves a guess or prediction as to future level of
performance. The greater the experience of the predictor and the broader
his acquaintance with the individual and skill under consideration, the
better his predictions are likely to be; but they are still fraught with error,
as anyone who has attempted to predict the performance of race horses can
tell, in spite of lengthy geneology and field performance data. Betting odds
represent a ready estimate of the margin of error involved in the prediction.
Another illustration from human performance may be had from spring
training camps of professional baseball teams. Many promising prospects
attend spring training, all estimated by professional observers to possess
considerable capacity and promise; only a minority, however, fulfill the
promise of major league careers. The reasons lie not only in shortcomings in
capacity as such, but also in differences in opportunity, motivation, temperament traits, and so on. The influence of these several variable factors necessitates ascertaining the degree to which capacity controls ultimate performance and its relationship with the other important factors contributing
to successful acquisition of any given skill—in short, the relationship between capacity and learning. We can begin with the concept that a person's
capacity—his potential for learning various skills—is at present only partially measurable. Even so, intelligence tests do provide useful measures of
capacity.

Correlational techniques provide an answer to this question. By correlating intelligence test scores with various external standards of judgment
such as success and failure in different occupations, external validity coefficients provide knowledge regarding the kinds of predictions which
can be made from intelligence test scores. By intercorrelating scores
on different tests and sub-tests, certain common components of tests can

be identified, especially through the use of factorial analysis techniques; with this information, homogeneous tests of single factors can be constructed to serve as measures of single aptitudes. This can be illustrated by comparing aptitude and intelligence tests currently in use.

Since their inception, intelligence tests have been composed of a variety of items: vocabulary, arithmetic computation, identifying missing parts of objects, memory span for numbers, digit-symbol substitution, and the like. They tap a variety of human capacities. Through the use of factor analysis it is possible to group together those segments of tests which have much in common (as shown by high intercorrelation) with each other and little in common with other segments. These constitute aptitude tests, which in general measure a single primary aspect of human behavior. More than a score of such aptitudes have been identified, but the more commonly recognized and used aptitudes are verbal comprehension, abstract reasoning, numerical reasoning, spatial visualization, perceptual speed, rote memory, word fluency, mechanical aptitude, and motor dexterity.

Verbal comprehension and abstract reasoning are two aptitudes which comprise significant portions of most intelligence tests. Verbal comprehension pertains to the understanding and use of words and is tested by such items as vocabulary, synonyms, and definitions of words; abstract reasoning is usually tested by geometrical, pictorial, number series, or verbal items which involve analogies, sequential or logical analysis. The fact that most pencil-and-paper tests are dependent upon reading skill and vocabulary and that even oral or performance tests are dependent upon verbal instructions results in this factor being found in some proportion (however small) in nearly all aptitude tests. This fact plus the further one that aptitude tests show greater than zero correlation with each other supports an argument that there is a general learning ability. Table 5.9 shows the interest correlations of certain of the aptitude tests in the Chicago Primary Mental Abilities battery. It will be noted that the correlation coefficients range from .10 between reasoning and numerical aptitude, to .63 between verbal and reasoning aptitude. Spearman, a noted English psychologist, proposed a two-factor theory of intelligence to account for the correlations, suggesting that a general learning ability exists which underlies all human abilities and that supplementing this general ability are specific aptitudes. Opposed to

TABLE 5.9 INTERCORRELATIONS AMONG CHICAGO PRIMARY MENTAL ABILITIES TESTS (AGE 7-11)

	V	S	R	P	N
Verbal	.....	.24	.63	.33	.25
Spatial		.....	.40	.37	.10
Reasoning			.....	.45	.32
Perceptual				.....	.35
Numerical					.....

this theory is a multi-factor theory proposed by Thurstone, whose primary mental abilities test intercorrelations are shown in Table 5.9. Thurstone's viewpoint is that the aptitudes are discrete, unitary factors and that the intercorrelations occurring are an artifact of test construction in which the pencil-and-paper techniques used depend upon words for communication. Supporting this stand are several studies which show that low intercorrelations between learning tasks are the rule and that gains made in learning tend to be fairly specific to the particular task. Moreover, the intercorrelations between test scores tend to diminish with increasing age, being greater in childhood and smaller in the older groups being tested; the result is that in fairly homogeneous populations such as college students it is possible to construct separate aptitude tests between which the correlations approach zero.

Numerical aptitude involves the ability to work with numbers and to compute elementary quantitative problems such as adding and multiplying rapidly and accurately. Such quantitative reasoning ability is commonly used in test batteries for college admission, particularly in engineering and scientific schools, and in simpler form in elementary school tests predictive of achievement in arithmetic. It is frequently found combined with verbal comprehension and abstract reasoning items in so-called general intelligence tests.

Spatial visualization involves the ability to conceive objects in two or three dimensions, such as one does in looking at a blueprint which presents several two dimensional views of an object, thus requiring the viewer to visualize the appearance of the object in three dimensional form. Perhaps a simpler explanation would be that it is the ability one uses when looking at a parking space to estimate whether or not the automobile will fit in it. Perceptual speed involves the ability to identify similarity and differences in symbols or objects quickly and accurately. Clerical aptitude tests which require the comparison of groups of numbers or letters for likeness or difference utilize this aptitude.

Memory is apparently an ability which may be subdivided into several different components, judging from the research reports produced by the United States Air Force Aviaton Psychology program. Several of the components which have been identified are rote memory, perceptual memory, and memory span. Word fluency is a factor measured by the capacity to recall words quickly and by spelling and grammatical construction items. Games such as Scrabble and Anagrams utilize this aptitude.

Mechanical aptitude appears to be a composite of several aptitudes, rather than a single factor, involving verbal comprehension, abstract reasoning, and acquired mechanical knowledge. Scores on tests of mechanical aptitude also appear to be more susceptible to modification from learning. Motor dexterity, like memory, is a factor which can be subdivided into several aspects involving speed of reaction, fine and gross motor coördination, and other components.

Perhaps the most persistent effort to tie the pieces together is found in the work of J. P. Guilford and his colleagues at the University of Southern California. Figure 5.4 shows Guilford's conception of the structure of intellect based on test factor analysis. In his scheme, 120 different abilities, or combinations of operation, process, and content comprise the intellectual domain. Operations are the kinds of processes performed: discovery or recognition and understanding of information, ability to retain it in memory and reproduce it, ability to reach a known solution on the basis of information available or produce divergent solutions, and the capacity to make judgments about suitability. Products relate to the form that information takes from single units to complex systems and to the transformations and extrapolations made. Content involves the several types of information processed: concrete, symbolic in the form of letters, codes, numbers, semantic in the form of verbal meaning, and non-verbal in the form of manifest actions and feelings.

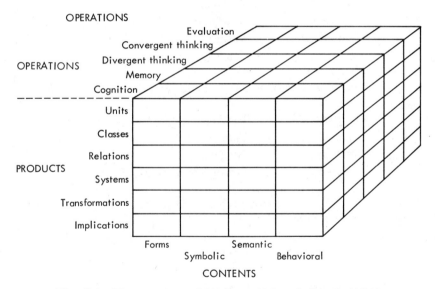

Fig. 5.4 The structure of intellect. (After Guilford, 1956.)

The Relationship Between Intelligence and Motor Learning. As far as younger children are concerned, there appears to be little relationship between intelligence test score and sensori-motor learning. This generalization applies in either direction. Although children differ in the ages in which they pass through the various stages of motor development, their age of walking and attainment of other motor skills of early childhood are not predictive as far as future intelligence is concerned. Nor is the intelligence test score valuable in predicting sensori-motor learning. Mattson's study reported earlier in this chapter showed no relationship between intelligence test score and performance with the rolling ball maze. These findings have been confirmed on other tasks such as throwing quoits, hitting targets, and mirror drawing. Much the same conclusion holds for older children and young adults, due in part to the discrete nature of sensori-motor tasks (Cratty, 1963; Start, 1960; Rhule and Smith, 1959).

The Relationship Between Physical Capacities and Motor Learning. Paralleling the work done with intelligence and aptitude tests, numerous efforts at factor analysis of motor tests and motor skills have been made with the hope of isolating motor aptitudes and a general motor ability which might be comparable to general learning ability and the different mental aptitudes. The results of several studies (McGraw, 1948; Larson, 1941; Seashore, 1942) have classed the fundamental elements underlying the performance of motor skills as:

Strength	Body size
Speed	Reaction time
Accuracy	Steadiness
Endurance	Balance
Agility	Control of voluntary movements

The fundamental skills in physical education were identified as:

Running	Kicking
Jumping	Climbing
Vaulting	Catching
Throwing	Pronograde locomotion

In a comprehensive survey of research in this field, Guilford (1958) reduced the number of factors to six:

Strength	Precision
Speed	Coordination
Impulsion	Flexibility

The first list and Guilford's are quite alike, particularly if body size and endurance are combined under strength. Each of these factors may be considered not only in relation to overall motor performance but also in relation to body parts: trunk, arms, legs, hands, fingers. When consideration is given to the basic skills in physical education listed above, the significance of a difference in leg and arm strength can be seen for climbing versus vaulting. Corroboration of the discreteness of psychomotor abilities comes from Fleishman's (1954) work in which he identifies some twenty-five measures of physical abilities relating the factors to different body parts and performance.

Unlike intellectual abilities, where evidence can be marshaled for the existence of a general intelligence factor, studies indicate that motor learning is dependent upon specific abilities relative to specific motor skills. Seashore (1942) found the correlation between fine motor abilities to average .31, between gross motor abilities .26, and close to zero correlation between the two sets, suggesting that in activities where intellectual ability is not an important factor, learning is a function of the specific musculature involved in the activity (Bachman, 1961).

The more complex the motor skill, the greater the likelihood that it will involve higher mental abilities, i.e., learning will be correlated with intelligence. Some support for this is to be observed in the relationship between intelligence and occupation which shows that higher degrees of intelligence are associated with the more complex trade skills—electrician, tool-and-die maker, pattern maker, and others. However, there are undoubtedly other social factors besides intelligence involved in the selection process, as is indicated by the variability within occupations and the overlap between occupational levels.

In training feeble minded individuals in manual tasks, it has been found necessary to fit the task to the level of intelligence. A boy with a mental age of 7 can sew a broom, but it takes a mental age of 9 or 10 to build up the shoulders of a broom. Girls with a mental age of 6 can learn to crochet, but fancy embroidery calls for a mental age of 9 to 12. An imbecile can tear off the soles from old shoes or pick apples which are to be used for cider, but he cannot operate a burnishing machine nor pick apples for packing without bruising them. The higher grade idiot can be trained to

TABLE 5.10 CORRELATIONS BETWEEN INTELLIGENCE AND ACHIEVEMENT IN DIFFERENT SUBJECTS AT ELEMENTARY SCHOOL LEVEL*

Size of Correlation	Reading	Spelling	Arithmetic	Handwriting
.90 − .99			2	
.80 − .89	6	2	1	
.70 − .79	7	3	6	
.60 − .69	12	7	2	
.50 − .59	5	5	10	
.40 − .49	4	4	6	1
.30 − .39	4	5	6	1
.20 − .29	6	3	1	1
.10 − .19		2		
.0 − .09		1		3
−.10 − −.01	2			1
Median r	.60	.51	.55	.08
Number of r's	46	32	34	7

*J. M. Stephens, *Educational Psychology* (New York: Holt, 1951), p. 228.

TABLE 5.11 CORRELATIONS BETWEEN INTELLIGENCE AND ACHIEVEMENT IN DIFFERENT SUBJECTS AT HIGH SCHOOL LEVEL*

Size of correlation	Average marks	Science	Math.	English	Latin	Commercial subjects
.70 – .79		1		1		
.60 – .69	2		3	2	1	
.50 – .59	13	2	12	2		
.40 – .49	12	1	16	6	1	
.30 – .39	11	4	12	2	3	
.20 – .29	6		4	2	4	
.10 – .19	1				2	2
.00 – .09						2
Median r	.44	.40	.45	.46	.29	.10
Number of r's	45	8	47	15	.11	4

*Ibid., p. 229.

pick up stones and do a few very simple tasks under supervision, but he cannot wash dishes. For dishwashing, the minimum IQ of approximately 26 to 30 is found in the low grade imbeciles. A man with a mental age of 7 can paint a barn under supervision, but he cannot estimate costs or mix paint. An imbecile can learn to milk a cow, but the minimum IQ for general farm work is about 65 or 70. In general, it has been found that the more complex the task, the higher is the minimum mental age needed to master it.

The Relationship Between Mental Capacities and Verbal Learning. Stephens (1951) has compiled and summarized a number of studies reporting the relationship between intelligence test scores and academic achievement. These are shown in the three tables, 5.10, 5.11, and 5.12 which show, respectively, the correlations at elementary, secondary, and college level.

TABLE 5.12 CORRELATIONS BETWEEN INTELLIGENCE AND ACHIEVEMENT IN DIFFERENT SUBJECTS AT COLLEGE LEVEL*

Size of correlation	General college grades	Science	Math.	English	Foreign language	Social studies
.70 – .79	1					
.60 – .69	4		1			
.50 – .59	26	4	2	3	1	1
.40 – .49	44	6	2	3	6	2
.30 – .39	24	5	5	4	10	4
.20 – .29	4	3	2	1	2	2
.10 – .19					3	
.00 – .09						
Median r	.46	.42	.38	.42	.36	.36
Number of r's	103	18	12	11	22	9

*Ibid., p. 230.

The median correlation coefficient is higher for the elementary grades than for either the high school or college level, probably because the range of ability is greater at the elementary level than at the other levels where the less capable tend to be eliminated from school. One of the characteristics of the correlation coefficient is that it is affected by the range of talent in the group. The smaller the range of talent, the smaller the correlation coefficient is likely to be. As would be expected from the content of most intelligence tests, the correlations with verbal and arithmetic phases of the curriculum are somewhat greater than with other aspects such as science and Latin. It is interesting to note that the courses involving the greatest degree of motor skill—handwriting and commercial subjects—produce the lowest correlation coefficients. The size of the coefficients reported has prompted the suggestion that intelligence tests be renamed scholastic aptitude tests because they are most predictive of academic achievement.

Correlation coefficients between aptitude and achievement tests are presented in Table 5.13 showing the relationship between the Thurstone Primary Mental Abilities Test and tested reading and arithmetic achievement.

TABLE 5.13*

| Achievement in | No. in Group | Verbal | Factors | | |
			Spatial	Perceptual	Numerical
Reading	177 age 9 to 9.5	.75	.34	.43	.53
Reading	312 age 10.5 to 11	.85	.40	.40	.48
Arithmetic	463 fourth grade	.50	.30	.37	.44

*Based on Thurstone Primary Mental Abilities Test, 1954, p. 5.

On the whole, the correlations are not greater than those reported for intelligence tests, and particularly interesting is the fact that the numerical aptitude test correlated no more highly with arithmetic than with reading. For purposes of predicting scholastic achievement, specific subject matter achievement tests are more valid. Correlations between achievement tests from one year to the next fall between .85 and .90 and for a span of 4 to 6 years approximate .70. (Bloom, 1964.)

THE EFFECTS OF PHYSICAL HANDICAPS UPON LEARNING

Incidence of Physical Handicaps.   Estimates of the incidence of given handicaps vary with the definition of impairment used. For example, the incidence of blindness varies considerably if a medical definition is used (some degree of loss of vision), a legal definition a(specified degree of loss of vision), or an educational definition (those children who either have no vision or whose visual limitations after correction result in educational handicaps) (Jones, 1963).

Several recent extensive surveys provide a broad picture of illness and impairment among school children. In a national health survey, Schiffer and Hunt (1963) report finding an average of three acute illnesses per child each year, primarily respiratory. Roughly 15 percent of children in the 0 to 4 year age range had a chronic condition—hay fever, asthma, and allergies predominating—which increased to some 30 percent at the 15 to 16 year level. Many of these cause no restriction on function. It is interesting to note that allergies past or present (with hay fever ranking first) were reported by approximately 30 percent of adolescents (Freeman and Johnson, 1964) but these were more frequent among middle and upper socio-economic levels (35 percent) than at the lower socio-economic levels (14 percent). Could it be that allergies are a function of those who can afford them? Jacobziner and others (1963) report an adverse health condition in some 40 percent of children, with a tendency for multiple problems to exist where there is any adverse health condition.

On a more serious level, Mellin (1963) reports congenital malformations occurring in 2.5 to 3.8 percent of children depending upon definition, with more frequent occurrences among infants of older mothers, as has long been known. DeBoer (1962) in a Chicago survey and Corliss, Doster, and Cromwell (1964) in a Denver survey agree on a figure of four per 1000 for organic heart disease.

One of the best objective studies of the relation of physical defects to school achievement was made by Mallory (1922). His findings, based on standard achievement tests and physical examinations, led to the conclusion that physical defects contribute to retardation and that some defects, particularly of hearing and vision, are greater handicaps to progress than others.

Defects of Vision.   The eyes are used so constantly in school learning that any serious impairment of vision is certain to prove a handicap to the pupil. This handicap cannot be adequately measured in terms of actual retardation because many pupils may compensate for it by extra effort, although in so doing they suffer added strain, discomfort, and fatigue. Visual defects appear in many forms and in varying degrees. Less than 20 percent of children *are free* of any visual defect, using an exact medical definition (Dalton, 1943).

Estimates of visual difficulty in the school population vary from around 10 or 12 percent to about 25 percent, no doubt depending upon what degree of deviation from perfect vision the examiner considers a defect and upon the thoroughness of the examining procedures. Jones' (1963) estimate of one educationally handicapped child per 1000 and one blind child per 3000 is conservative.

ERRORS OF REFRACTION.   Among the more common forms of visual defect are the errors of refraction, characterized by faulty focusing of the light upon the retina. In myopia or nearsightedness, the rays of light entering the eye focus before they reach the retina. Vision for near objects is less likely to be impaired than for distant objects by a myopic condition. Thus, the myopic pupil may be able to see fairly well by holding his book or other objects very close to his eyes. He is likely, however, to be unable to see things on the blackboard. Myopia is rarely found in young children, but it appears more frequently in the middle and upper grades. Hypermetropia, or farsightedness, is a condition in which the distance from the lens to the retina is too short for a clear retinal image, or in which the refractive power of the lens is insufficient. This means blurred vision. Hypermetropia is common among young children and appears less frequently in the upper grades and high school.

In astigmatism, the curvature of the lens or cornea of the eye is irregular; this causes uneven focusing of the light on the retina. The child who has astigmatism sees more clearly in one meridian of his visual field than in others. Astigmatism may be either myopic or hypermetropic. The latter is by far the more common among school children.

MUSCULAR DEVIATIONS.   For clear vision, there must be sufficient coördination of the eyes to bring about convergence of the lines of vision on the object to be seen. This convergence is controlled by muscles external to the eyeballs. In a study of 350 poor readers, Eames (1938) found incoördination difficulties at the reading distance in about one half the cases. This defect was marked in more than a fourth of all the cases. For distant vision, deficient coördination was found in about one tenth of the poor readers. Many persons suffer from slight incoördination of the eyes without noticeable effects, though there may be impairment of their binocular vision and strain occasioned by the effort to secure clear vision. In serious cases, there may be inability to fuse the images from the two eyes into single vision. This may lead to the suppression of one and the eventual loss of sight in one of the eyes.

ANISEIKONIA.   The condition known as *aniseikonia* is one in which the ocular images are unequal in shape, in size, or in both shape and size. It is believed by those who have studied this defect extensively that many persons who have such symptoms as headaches, dizziness, or nervousness associated with the use of their eyes and who do not exhibit the ordinary ocular defects may have aniseikonia. It has been found to have a significant relation to reading disability (Dearborn, 1938) and anomalies of visual space perception.

In a typical elementary classroom, one can expect to find three to four children in need of special attention because of visual disabilities— visual acuity between 20/40 and 20/70. An equal number are likely to have minor disabilities which can impair efficiency of learning.

Visual Defects and Learning. Blindness restricts the person's ability to get about in his environment, directly restricting the range and variety of experiences obtained (Harley, 1963) as well as reducing the ability to manipulate and control objects and events in the environment and the self in relation to it (Garry and Ascarelli, 1960; Buell, 1951). The difficulties imposed·are of two kinds: first, limitations in opportunity for normal development, and second, frustration, particularly in social relationships which produce a preference in the blind for retreating from reality. It is a reasonable, though unprovable, assumption that such experiences would have a retarding effect upon intellectual development. It is a fact, as Hayes (1938, 1941) has reported, that when tested on intelligence and achievement tests adapted for use with the blind, a smaller portion of blind children are of average and superior intelligence than the general population and that a greater proportion of intellectually retarded children is found. Young blind children were on a par or superior to sighted children in information on language, literature, and social sciences but inferior in nature study. With advancing years in school, the sighted children surpass the blind, the latter dropping two grades below in general achievement. Undoubtedly, the educational programs for the blind are not as adequate in all instances as for the sighted. Even more difficult is the task of building reading skill in Braille and providing Braille materials for reading. Teaching Braille to children is like teaching shorthand in the elementary school, but it is more difficult than shorthand, for Braille must be written from right to left in the way words would appear if a book were held up to a mirror and the image copied.

Many studies have indicated the relation of defective eyesight to poor reading. In the study of 350 poor readers by Eames, mentioned above, about one third had defective vision when both eyes were used. About two thirds of the right eyes and three fourths of the left eyes exhibited defective vision. Eames states that incoördination of the eyes is the defect most frequently encountered among poor readers and that this factor appears much more frequently among pupils with reading difficulties than among unselected controls. He writes, "It results in the early onset of fatigue, insufficiency of convergence in reading, impaired fusion, irritability, and inattention." Other conditions which Eames finds related to poor reading ability are: farsightedness, anomalies of eyedness, and low fusions of the images from the two eyes. He finds very few astigmatic reading cases, and nearsightedness is reported as an "infrequent offender" with respect to reading. He suggests that a low degree of myopia may even favor reading, as the child will need to exert less than the usual amount of effort to secure adequate accommodation for near vision (1935).

These findings are in substantial agreement with those of Farris (1936) who found that hypermetropia and muscular deviations were associated with poor reading progress but that myopia and myopic astigmatism were associated with better than average progress. Correction lenses aided achievement in the cases of those defects associated with poor reading. Imus (1936) reports from a study of 100 first grade children by the Dartmouth Eye Institute that approximately 25 percent had defective vision to a degree that warranted corrective measures and that some of these cases were probably handicapped in reading by their defects. Schwartz (1940) reports improvement in 71 percent of the cases of poor readers after correction was made for ocular defects. In a study of fifty unselected cases of reading failure, Eames (1943) found that 80 percent had visual trouble of some kind. These were given glasses or treatment. Half of them, those with IQ's below 90, did not gain any more in reading during the year following treatment than they did the year before. But the 40 percent who had eye trouble and whose IQ's were above 90 gained thirteen months in reading age during the ten months following correction or treatment as against a gain of seven months for the year before treatment. Twenty percent of the total group of reading failures had no eye trouble. It is recognized that poor reading may be due to several conditions other than defective vision; but that such defects often are the primary cause of reading disability seems clear (Durrell, 1940; Gray, 1936), and the need for professional examination and ocular therapeutics is definitely indicated.

Teachers should understand that glasses do not always free a child from visual handicaps. Of such cases Eames writes:

> When a child has low vision which is only partially improved by glasses or which cannot be improved at all, the teacher should not expect the pupil to compete with normally seeing children. He should be given a seat in a good light, be given frequent rest periods, be permitted to look out of the window whenever he wants to (because looking out of the window rests the focusing muscles), and be provided with textbooks having large, boldface type. He should be allowed to use a heavy, soft pencil and to write script large enough for him to see clearly. If vision is markedly low, placement in a sight saving class should be considered.

Sato (1937) compared the achievement of 3300 nearsighted, normal, and farsighted children in Tokyo elementary and secondary schools. Markedly nearsighted pupils without glasses showed lower performance on the whole, while few poor students had normal vision. Farsighted students were inadequate in subjects in which use of textbooks was greatest, e.g., language and history. In physics and algebra, where less dependence is placed upon texts, the achievement of the farsighted approximated that of the normals, as it did in such subjects as drawing and gymnastics.

Defects of Hearing and Learning.   Although there is no sharp line of demarcation between the hard-of-hearing and the deaf, the latter are those children who are unable to acquire language because of inability to hear and whose hearing is of no practical value in communicating with others. These individuals may range from the totally deaf to those with considerable sound perception, but in all cases their hearing is of little practical value in the ordinary affairs of life. Those who fall between this range and normal hearing constitute the hard-of-hearing, children whose hearing, though defective, is functional. Deaf children are classified into those who are congenitally deaf and those who are adventitiously deaf as the result of events occurring after birth, such as injury or illness. Deaf children are found at a rate of two to five per 1000 in the general population by McCabe (1963); Powers (1964) found a higher incidence of mild hearing losses, five per 100.

Hearing disability presents an even greater handicap than visual defects, for sound is basic to language and language is basic to learning. A child who cannot hear directions cannot act intelligently. Estimates of the intelligence of deaf children vary according to the type of test used as a measure. In general, the intelligence of deaf children is lower than that of normal children, and there does not appear to be a difference between those congenitally and adventitiously deaf. The deaf appear to be approximately two years retarded intellectually by age 10 to 11. Pintner (1941) reports the IQ of deaf children to be in the mid-80's in a 1928 study of the National Research Council, thus corroborating a more recent survey of English children by Hood (1949) who found one third of the deaf children fell below IQ 85 compared with only one fifth of normal children. This retardation is most noticeable with respect to abstract intelligence and verbal comprehension; for non-verbal performance scales, deaf children apparently perform as well as normal children (Hood, 1949; Springer, 1938; Oleron, 1950).

Similar findings are reported by Pintner and Lev with respect to the hard-of-hearing school child. Comparing verbal intelligence test scores of 1556 normal hearing children with 1404 hard-of-hearing, the mean IQ of the former was 100.6, the latter's 94.7. For marked hearing defects, the mean IQ was 92.4. On a non-language intelligence test, the mean IQ of 372 normally hearing was 102.2 compared to 99.3 for 315 hard-of-hearing children, a difference that was not statistically significant.

The progressive mental retardation noted with respect to intellectual development is paralleled in the academic achievement of the deaf and hard-of-hearing children. Sprunt and Finger (1949) screened 692 pupils in grades three to seven, retested those showing marked hearing loss, and then compared a sample of twenty-eight children with deficient hearing with a matched sample of twenty-eight normally hearing children on a non-verbal intelligence test and on educational achievement. The children with hearing deficiency showed a half-year retardation in academic achievement but no difference in non-verbal test score. In a survey of 1000 children representative of Toronto children in grades five to eight, Conway (1937) found 8 percent hard-of-hearing in one ear, 2.7 percent in both ears. Where the hearing loss was greater than 20 decibels, the retardation in school was between 10 to 15 percent. A survey of the elementary school pupils of New York City indicated that 3.17 percent of all the children had impaired hearing in both ears, and approximately 42 percent of the hard-of-hearing children were retarded one year or more (Caplin, 1937). That poor hearing is a handicap to achievement under ordinary classroom procedures can scarcely be doubted, particularly if the deficiency is severe enough to cause a child to fail to hear much of what is said. Adequate hearing tests should be given to all children in order to discover those whose hearing is deficient. When cases of defective hearing are found, the necessary treatment should be secured not only for the sake of better schoolwork but also to prevent the development of serious deafness. Diseased conditions of the nasal passages and the throat, which tend to block the Eustachian tubes, are credited with being the most prolific sources of impaired hearing. These include diseased and enlarged tonsils and adenoids, and chronic catarrh. Scarlet fever and measles frequently cause inflammations of the middle ear. Aching or discharging ears are indications of trouble and should receive prompt attention. Too frequently, children who have defective hearing are treated as stupid or annoyingly inattentive.

Other Handicaps.   Cerebral palsy, spastic paralysis, cardiac problems, poliomyelitis, osteomyelitis, bone tuberculosis, and epilepsy handicap a much smaller percentage of children than do visual and hearing defects. Zintz (1951) found that approximately one child in 200 had a serious physical handicap in a statewide survey of 11,142 pupils at the sixth to eighth grade levels in Iowa. Not only were the handicapped children retarded four, six, and ten months respectively at the sixth, seventh, and eighth grades, but those having multiple handicaps showed greater retardation. Handicapped children showed a significantly greater degree of withdrawing behavior, lower self-concept and lower self-acceptance (Smits, 1964).

The educational achievement of these pupils was similar to a group of 835 crippled children in a special orthopedic school; these children progressed about .8 of a grade per year. This group (Lee, 1943) included some children with non-orthopedic difficulties (teeth, tonsils, vision, nutrition, speech) as well. Each child averaged two non-orthopedic defects in addition to the orthopedic difficulty. Frequently the assumption is made that a regular academic program can be followed equally well by orthopedically handicapped children, provided that physical and speech therapy are included. When one considers that the mean IQ of crippled children has been placed between 82 and 87 (Lee, 1931; Fouracre, 1950), that the orthopedically handicapped tend to be over-age for grade (Fouracre, 1950) with an average educational retardation in the elementary school of ten months, and that a consistently higher percentage of below average intelligence is found than with normal children, it is questionable if the typical academic curriculum is adequate for these children. The problems become even more acute at high school level when problems of vocational choice and non-dependence must be faced.

MOTIVATION

If capacity is the promise, the potential to be developed, it is motivation which brings it to fulfillment. An engine may be capable of producing a certain amount of horsepower, but fuel is needed to make it do so.

In the beginning, to be alive is to be motivated, to have energy to expend on the environment. Experience soon begins to have its shaping effects, and we find ourselves asking: motivated for what? That is, what is it that we seek or desire? What need gives rise to the goal directed activity we observe? How do we identify the need, account for the particular goal striven for, explain the behavior adopted to achieve the goal? How do we explain the fluctuation in drives, and how do we elicit, provoke, and maintain drives for purposes of learning?

A first question of teachers is: how do I motivate children? The question ignores the fact that children are already motivated. The question should be: how do I identify the child's motives and turn them to educational goals? Equally important: how are my actions affecting the child's motives?

The question: "Motivated for what?" takes cognizance of the fact that motives are internal; they are states or conditions within the organism to be inferred from his behavior. For example, we observe a baby crying:

ACTIVITY	(INFERENCE)	ACTION	EFFECT ON ACTIVITY
Baby cries	(hungry?)	Feed baby	Stops crying (was hungry)
or			
Baby cries	(hungry?)	Feed baby	Cries more (not hungry)
	(wet?)	Change	Stops (was uncomfortable)

When asked to account for the change in behavior, one reasons backward from the observed events, saying that something must have caused the activity—some drive which was satisfied by food—for after feeding, the activity came to an end, and so it must have been a food seeking drive. Or, it didn't come to an end with food, so it wasn't hunger; but it ended with a change in diapers, suggesting an avoidance-of-discomfort drive. The diagram thus appears:

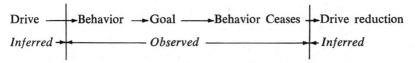

Drive ⟶ Behavior ⟶ Goal ⟶ Behavior Ceases ⟶ Drive reduction
Inferred ⟶ ———————— *Observed* ———————— ⟶ *Inferred*

The inferred drive in the diagram finds verification in the innumerable animal studies in which the subjects are deprived of food or water for periods of time in order to provide them with sufficient drive to perform countless tasks. But the questioning pushes still farther: what produces the drive, what arouses it? Research disclosed that tissue changes produced variations in the sugar content, density, and salinity of the bloodstream, and these in turn triggered glandular responses which produced hunger and thirst drives. Thus was born the homeostatic or equilibrium concept of motivation, that needs basic to survival give rise to drives which produce activity with the purpose of satisfying the drive. Responses could be learned (where to find water) to reduce the variation in activity. When satisfied, the drive ceased, and equilibrium was restored. The concept could as easily, but with much less dignity, be called the hungry dog model. The dog sleeps in the sun until hunger or thirst stirs him; when he is satisfied, he returns to sleep. The model is intriguing in its simplicity, but is too simple for man. He doesn't stop eating when filled or wait until hungry to begin to eat. Some will eat or drink themselves to death, others will refuse to eat during a hunger strike until dead. In other words, certain of man's motives will on occasion outweigh the presumed basic motive of survival. Nevertheless, the concept of equilibrium has pervaded explanations of motivation in many areas. In an article concerning economic psychology by Katona (1954) this point is discussed:

> The notion of "saturation" of the market is based on old-fashioned psychological assumptions which in turn rest on the analogy of biological drives: for example, if an animal is hungry, it is motivated to search for food; after it has eaten, the motive disappears or becomes weak. The saturation concept has resulted in dire predictions about the future of the U. S. economy. Some people point to the large proportion of U. S. families that already possess major goods, such as refrigerators (over 80%) or automobiles (about 70%), and they argue that in the future, sales will be limited largely to replacement needs.
>
> But social motives are different from biological ones. Levels of aspiration—in sports, for school grades, for position, for income, and for goods —mostly rise with achievement. A beginner in golf, for instance, may strive hard to achieve a score of 100; when he has achieved his goal, he invariably raises his sights. We give up aspirations when we have failed, not when we have succeeded. . . .
>
> We translate our needs in demand when we are optimistic, confident, and secure. We are "saturated," on the other hand, when we are pessimistic, insecure, and especially when our past endeavors have been unsuccessful.

The distinction which Katona [2] makes between biological and social motives is a valid one. Man has biological motives which operate similarly to those of animals, but his behavior is more highly variable and the biological needs are so overlaid with acquired response patterns and motives that the equilibrium concept is an incomplete explanation. McClelland (1953) has aptly pointed out that biological drives do not suffice as an explanation of how animal behavior is directed and controlled; much less do they explain the "extraordinary strength characteristic of learned human motives."

This was dramatically demonstrated in a classical study by Roethlisberger and Dickson (1939) in their Hawthorne studies of the relationship between working conditions and productivity. This is one of the few studies in which every effort possible was made to control factors influencing production. A team of girl telephone relay assemblers was put at their work in a room in which different aspects of the physical environment could be controlled—humidity, temperature, light, rest periods, and others. The variables were manipulated with the desire of ascertaining the optimal combination of working conditions as far as maximum output was concerned. With each improvement in light or temperature, production increased. The work week of the girls was reduced first from 48 to 44 hours, then from 44 to 40 hours. With each change, production increased. Rest periods and snack periods were introduced. Production increased. It appeared that improving working conditions improved production. But investigation of production records revealed that when one of the group of five girls was absent for a day, production did not fall off as would be expected if output were near the maximum per person. Puzzled by this, the investigators reversed the experimental conditions, eliminating rest periods, lengthening the work period, and reversing the improvements in illumination and humidity. Production did not fall off as expected; it increased. This began a monumental shift from looking at working conditions and time and motion studies to looking at workers and their attitudes and motivations. The girls on the relay assembly team liked the novelty associated with the experiment; it provided an interest and appeal which their work had lacked; they wished it to continue. As the experimenters made their modifications in working conditions, the girls obligingly improved their work. The direction of the modification made little difference to them. They wanted to continue the project as long as possible. One thing the study did reveal was the intricate nature of motivation and its inevitable relationship to behavior.

[2] Drive and motive are used with different meanings by different authors. One distinction made is between drive as a generalized state of activity and motive as being specifically related to a given goal; a second is between drive used with reference to physiological motivation and motives with reference to personal-social (acquired) motives. In this chapter, the two are used interchangeably. Other terms frequently synonymous are needs, predispositions, and purposes.

As Mowrer points out (1952), it would be convenient if man operated like a temperature thermostat, responding to only two stimuli, hot and cold, with two responses, on and off. However, man not only can make a wide variety of responses to a single stimulus or drive, but he is also capable of separating those acts which work best from those which do not. The basic pattern of motivation is subject to modification by learning in three of its aspects.

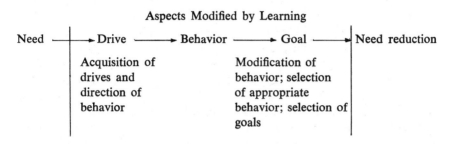

Aspects Modified by Learning

Need	Drive	Behavior	Goal	Need reduction
	Acquisition of drives and direction of behavior	Modification of behavior; selection of appropriate behavior; selection of goals		

Under some circumstances, the basic tissue needs may be modified, as is found to occur with some drug addictions; in general, however, the modification occurs through the acquisition of drives which direct behavior toward given goals, toward the learning of behavior and habit patterns which work successfully to attain goals, and toward the identification and establishment of selected goals.

Most of the work on acquired drives and rewards has been done with animals and is based mainly on experiments involving fear as an acquired drive and fear reduction as a reward, and on studies using hunger as a basis for learned rewards. If the test of a drive or a reward lies in its ability to produce learning or behavioral changes, then fear is a strong, acquired drive. Miller (1948) has demonstrated how rats placed in one compartment of a cage and shocked on repeated trials quickly acquired a conditioned fear of the compartment, so that on subsequent trials they showed immediate agitation and fright on being placed in the compartment, even though not subsequently shocked. They had acquired a fear of what were previously neutral cues. The fear drive was sufficiently strong that they learned to operate a wheel to open a door permitting escape into an adjoining compartment. Their learning curve on manipulating the wheel showed steady improvement. Moreover, when the wheel device was blocked, the rats learned a second response of pressing a bar to escape. Some animals operated the device for several hundred trials without need for further shock, so powerful was their acquired fear. Fears play an important role in human behavior, mainly in safeguarding the individual from real danger but also in protecting him from the discomfort associated with situations perceived as dangerous or threatening. Some persons possess a marked fear of speaking in public. They avoid it if possible but when unable to do so their behavior prior to the event exhibits many symptoms comparable to our friends, the rats. They become extremely tense, nervous, and emotionally upset. One can't hclp but wonder if the frequent errors and embarrassment incurred while reciting before classes during many years of school has any relationship to this fear.

The foregoing studies show acquired drives; experiments using hunger and food show the acquisition of learned rewards or goals. Chimpanzees, for instance, have been trained to work for tokens which they could exchange for food, then to perform a variety of tasks in order to obtain the tokens, thus showing that the tokens had acquired reward value. We are all familiar with the lengthy process of training in which humans learn the value of money. The student will recall from the discussion of Hull's learning theory that he considered reinforcement essential to learning. When behavior results in the attainment of a goal capable of satisfying the drive conditions, drive reduction reinforcing the behavior results. Moreover, Hull and his students believed that secondary reinforcement also occurs and that neutral stimuli associated with the reinforcing state of affairs acquire reinforcement value themselves, as do tokens or money. To illustrate, a child may acquire a drive for affection from being held, fondled, and cuddled as a result of conditions associated with feeding and the resultant primary drive reduction. The explanation is attractive, but it also contains a paradox: how can the same object be simultaneously drive increasing and drive reducing, as money or tokens appear to be, acting as both incentive (spurring drive) and reward (satisfying drive) simultaneously? It is probable that the drive reduction explanation is overly simple. Possibly in younger children drive reduction serves to reinforce responses and terminate behavior, but with increasing age humans develop deferred as well as immcdiatc goals and also aspirations that are relative to the accomplishment of other persons as well.

Our desires may focus on certain objectives, such as college graduation, not only because it is: (1) a way station to a particular vocation or to a higher degree, but also (2) because it may satisfy parental aspirations of importance to us, and (3) it simultaneously satisfies a desire to surpass the achievement of a neighbor, cousin, brother, or sister. The football team, having scored a third touchdown over an opponent, thus providing a comfortable margin (drive reducing) may return to the kickoff line saying, "All right, let's get another one!" (drive stimulating). The problem of developing a theoretical explanation which is consistent and applicable to all situations is difficult.

Mowrer (1952) contends that a distinction must be made between (1) solution learning and (2) sign learning, the former providing the basis by which organisms acquire acts or means which are instrumental in satisfying drives, and the latter being the basis on which they acquire emotions, secondary drives, and meanings. In (1) instrumental learning, an act which contributes to drive redúction becomes attached to the drive through reinforcement. In (2) sign learning, fears and desires depending upon whether the cue signifies an increase in drive (fear) or a decrease in drive (desire) are acquired.

The pattern of motivation so modified appears as follows:

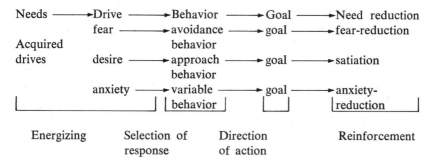

Anxiety has been added as an acquired drive, as distinguished from fear. Although the two are related in that both refer to events which appear dangerous or threaten harm or pain to the individual, fear is commonly considered as being more specific and segmental in nature. We fear dogs, high places, insects, or the like. Anxiety, when allied with fear, is more ambiguous and vague. In more frequent usage, however, particularly in clinical psychology, anxiety refers to a general all-inclusive state of feeling continually apprehensive and threatened.

Earlier it was pointed out that drives are acquired. Responses which are capable of satisfying drives, e.g., reaching rewards or avoiding harm and given goals or rewards are learned. The process of learning can be shown in our eating habits. A balanced diet is attainable in many forms, but different cultures establish preferences for specific foods and aversions for others. Raw meat, rancid fat, squid, snails, rattlesnake meat, sea urchins, to name but a few, are foods which some peoples relish in contradistinction to the preferences of most people in this country. These preferences have been learned as a result of training experiences. The mode of eating is learned as well—the socially approved manner of holding one's fork or one's chopsticks, or using nothing but hands, of belching politely or not, singing during the meal, and so on—all are learned rituals to be performed as necessary or are corollary acts to obtaining and eating food. Our drives, as well, have been modified and added to as a result of learning. Our preferences for given foods and anxieties about tabooed foods, as well as our seeking of money as a means to food, are all acquired drives.

The diagram also points out the three functions of drives: energizing the organism into activity, directing it toward an appropriate goal, and selecting the responses instrumental to reaching the goal. Some learning theorists (Brown, 1953) hold that the concept of motivation should be restricted to the energizing functions and believe that the directing and selecting functions can be adequately explained by habit patterns. This again points up the need for extensive research in the relationship of motivation to human behavior. McClelland and his colleagues (1953) have provided new impetus by suggesting that the distinction that has long been made between primary (biological) and secondary (social) drives or motives be discarded and that all motives be handled as learned. They define a motive as a recall of a change in affect (emotion) by a cue established by association. This view differs from Mowrer's (mentioned above) in placing the emphasis upon the association of a cue to a change in emotional state rather than viewing emotions as acquired drives. According to McClelland, changes in emotional states result from discrepancies between the adaption level and the expectation level of the organism. Small discrepancies produce no emotional reaction, moderate differences produce a positive emotional reaction, and large discrepancies between adaption level and expectation level produce negative affect. Negative affect leads to avoidance behavior; positive affect yields approach behavior. Two quotations from McClelland will illustrate the hypothesis:

> U.S. and Indian populations as groups should show different color preferences according to the principle that moderate discrepancy from different skin color adaptation level bases will yield pleasure in colors of different wave length composition. . . . in India red is the most preferred color and white the color for mourning, whereas in the United States blue-green is the most preferred and black is the color of mourning.

and

> Johnny may develop expectations as to what a model airplane or a solved arithmetic problem looks like, but he may be unable to confirm these expectations at all, or only partially. The result is negative affect, and cues associated with these activities may be expected to evoke avoidance motives. To develop an achievement approach motive, parents or circumstances must contrive to provide opportunities for mastery which, because they are just beyond the child's present knowledge, will provide continuing pleasure. If the opportunities are too limited, boredom should result. . . . if the opportunities are well beyond his capacities, negative affect should result, and he may develop an avoidance motive as far as achievement is concerned.

The proposals are intriguing, promising for research in human motivation, and have many implications for educational practice.

Motivation and Educational Practice.   By the time children reach school, few of their drives are being satisfied on solely an elementary basis. Already a complex hierarchy of goal preferences, response patterns, and approach and avoidance drives, fears, desires, and anxieties will have been established.

The tasks which the child meets in school are usually abstract and intangible, and being plagued by constant evaluation of goodness of performance by teacher, parents, and classmates, he can easily establish neutral or negative emotional reactions. More important still is that many of his acquired motives are social in nature: affection, belonging, acceptance, and the like. To be satisfied, these motives involve interaction with other people, particularly teachers. Children's motives can be satisfied only if the motives of the teacher permit and tolerate the motivational and learned behavior pattern the child has established prior to beginning school. The teacher's own motivations—her fears, anxieties, and desires with respect to discipline and control, authority and school, brightness and stupidity, neatness, and cleanliness—must be such that she is capable of satisfying the social motives of children through herself and her arrangements for the class by guiding them in the acquisition of motives that will contribute to a satisfying life.

As a result, teachers find themselves in an interaction situation in which their motives as a teacher are to: (1) maintain dominance and (2) produce academic achievement in children (her private desires and aversions may be something else again); but her pupils are seeking satisfaction of a set of acquired social motives often only remotely related to the task at hand. Further, what happens during the interaction shapes and develops the future motivational pattern. Given this situation, we will allow this basic discussion of motivation to rest here, turning to it again in Chapter 7, where teacher use of incentives is considered, and more intensively in Chapter 10, where effects of learning on motives and attitudes are discussed.

SUMMARY

Each of the individual variables—maturation, age, sex, previous experience, capacity and motivation—has been considered, and its relationship to the acquisition, retention, and transfer of training of sensori-motor and verbal learning has been reviewed. Most significant are the individual learner's readiness for any learning experience as determined by his maturational level and previous experience, his capacity or potential for development, and the acquired motives which give direction to his energies. All the individual variables must be considered simultaneously by the teacher in planning learning activities for individual children, for the rate of progress is a product of the interaction of the combination of particular capacities and motivation occurring.

When children or adults are instructed in groups, the task is complicated by the wide range of individual differences encountered. It is not uncommon to meet a range of four to six grades in achievement in class groups from intermediate grades up. Numerous factors and conditions contribute, but individual differences in rate of maturation, in experience, and in interest are important. Physical maturation is an important determinant of readiness for learning in young children, but with increasing age, readiness becomes increasingly a matter of having had the appropriate prerequisite experiences. In both motor skill and verbal learning, progressive improvement in learning occurs with increasing age up to adulthood. Beyond age 40 a gradual decline occurs, varying according to the ability under consideration and the activity of the individual concerned.

In general, sex differences are not a vital factor contributing to differences in ability or learning. Although some differences in capacity can be associated with sex, the more important conditions are differences in interest, motivation, and attitudes and the role they play in achievement. These conditions are more closely associated with cultural and experiential, than with genetic, differences.

Tests of intelligence, aptitude, and achievement can be valuable to a degree in estimating possible progress. The value of tests will vary their validity for any single subject; intelligence tests, for instance, are useful predictors of verbal achievement but not of art achievement. Tests must be supplemented by individual observation and judgment in deriving estimates of capacity.

A number of circumstances can contribute to unreliable test scores and consequently, to faulty judgments and predictions. Among these are use of inappropriate tests, inadequate norms, lack of testee motivation, faulty test administration, physical handicaps, practice effects, impoverished environmental backgrounds, and others. Nevertheless in skillful hands, intelligence, achievement, and other tests can be useful aids in planning programs, estimating potential, and analyzing learning difficulties.

Physical handicaps, including visual and auditory disabilities, occur in sufficient frequency in unselected groups of children that special attention is required for their identification and correction in order that learning not be needlessly impaired.

Essential to the learning process is motivation, which energizes the organism, gives direction to activity, and selects the goals deemed valuable. The teacher is concerned not only with utilizing existing motives for educational ends but also with shaping the motives in desirable directions, inasmuch as the results achieved in striving for given goals operate to modify the motives themselves. The end of learning is not only a skill or knowledge but also the acquisition of motives, attitudes, and interests which serve individual, educational, and social needs.

FURTHER READING

Selected Readings

GREEN, D. R. 1964. *Educational Psychology*. Englewood Cliffs, N. J.: Prentice-Hall, pp. 1-31.

MONROE, W. S. 1950. *Encyclopedia of Educational Research.* New York: Macmillan, pp. 137-207.

Selected References

ANASTASIA, ANNE. 1958. *Differential Psychology.* New York: Macmillan.

BLOOM, B. S. 1964. *Stability and Change in Human Characteristics.* New York: Wiley.

DAVIS, A. 1961. *Social Class Influence Upon Learning.* Cambridge, Mass.: Harvard Univ. Press.

FALKNER, E. 1960. *Human Development.* Philadelphia: Saunders.

HUMPHREYS, L. G. and P. L. BOYNTON. 1950. "Intelligence and Intelligence Testing." In W. S. Monroe (ed.), *Encyclopedia of Educational Research.* New York: Macmillan, pp. 600-12.

MUNN, N. L. 1954. "Learning in children." In L. Carmichael (ed.), *Manual of Child Development Psychology.* New York: Wiley, pp. 374-458.

Original Investigations

BAYLEY, NANCY. 1955. On the growth of intelligence. *Amer. Psychol.,* 10: 805-18.

BERLYNE, D. B. 1967. Arousal and Reinforcement. In D. Levine (ed.), *Nebraska Symposium on Motivation.* Univ. of Nebr. Press, pp. 1-110.

BRONFENBRENNER, J. 1961. The changing American child: A speculative analysis. *J. Soc. Issues,* 7: 6-18.

FELDHUSEN, J. F. and H. J. KLAUSMEIER. 1962. Anxiety, intelligence, and achievement in children of low, average, and high intelligence. *Child Developm.,* 33: 403-9.

GUILFORD, J. P. 1959. Three faces of intellect. *Amer. Psychol.,* 14: 469-79.

MATTSON, M. L. 1933. "The relation between the complexity of the habit to be acquired and the form of the learning curve in young children." *Genetic Psychology Monographs,* 13: 299-398.

MEAD, MARGARET. 1935. *Sex and Temperament in Three Primitive Societies.* New York: Morrow.

6

Task Variables

A second important group of variables affecting the course of learning includes those associated with differences in whatever task is to be learned. Tasks vary in length, in difficulty, and in similarity to other tasks. They also differ in their degree of meaningfulness to each individual learner, as well as in their degree of pleasantness or unpleasantness. The major part of the experimental work that has been completed to date on these characteristics of tasks has utilized verbal materials, nonsense syllables, word lists, various kinds of poetry, and prose. A few experiments have been concerned with motor skills.

LENGTH, DIFFICULTY, AND MEANINGFULNESS
OF MATERIAL

Length of Material.   The form of the learning curve is relatively uniform for acquisition of new material of differing lengths. When the total time required to learn verbal tasks of different length is divided into fractions, the percentage learned during given fractions of time is comparable (Robinson and Heron, 1922; Robinson and Darrow, 1924). Some variation occurs in relation to the type of material and the criterion of learning employed, whether memorization of nonsense syllables, verbatim reproduction of word lists or poetry, or learning of the logical meaning of materials.

When the length of the list exceeds the memory span, a noticeable increase in difficulty occurs. Ebbinghaus, for example, was able to recite seven nonsense syllables after one reading, but seventeen readings were required for learning a list of twelve, and thirty readings were necessary to master a sixteen syllable list. As the number of syllables in the list was increased, there was an increase in the number of readings per syllable. Similar results are reported by Lyons (1914). When difficulty is judged in terms of the amount of time required per item, a similar disproportionate increase is usually found. Beyond the region of immediate memory span additional increases in length do not produce disproportionate increases in difficulty. If anything, the longer lists are more readily learned.

The school situation to which the foregoing evidence may be most applicable is learning to spell. The conventions adopted for the spelling of words are in many respects similar to nonsense syllables. The latter make little sense in either form or meaning. Similarly, the spelling of words, though associated with words and meanings comprising part of the child's vocabulary, is inconsistent in many cases with common pronunciation. The rules are of little value because of the numerous exceptions. Consider first the sounds of the following words, then the spelling: "ideeut," "idyut," and "ijut" are common pronunciations of the word spelled *idiot*. "Cooja" and "jeetchet" are spelled *could you* and *did you eat yet*. "Nupshul" and "nup-chooal" present no problem to anyone married, but *nuptial* is strangely spelled and could as easily be "nuptual." Then consider *bleed, mead,* and *Reid,* and *stead* and *bead*. Different spellings are pronounced alike; identical spellings are pronounced differently. Learning the conventional spelling of words is largely rote memory of forms that are frequently as meaningless as nonsense syllables and is better served by short lists within the memory span, with provision for overlearning to increase retention.

This problem is complicated by other factors besides the magnitude of the lists compared. The increase in difficulty with an increase in the amount of material to be learned is apparently influenced by the kind of material and by the distribution of practice. Lyons' study indicated that during continuous learning at one sitting, the time required for memorizing digits and nonsense syllables increased at a proportionately faster rate than the length of the series; but at one reading per day (distributed learning), the increase in time corresponded roughly to the increase in the series. Henmon (1917) reported that in memorizing poetry, the number of repetitions increased proportionately less than the increase in the number of lines or stanzas. Greater economy for the longer passages was also indicated by the greater saving found for them in relearning after twenty-four hours. This difference in retention in favor of the longer selection was relatively greater for poetry than for nonsense syllables. For prose, the number of repetitions remained approximately constant for passages of different lengths. Prose passages of 100, 200, and 300 words required an average of 6.1, 7.3, and 7 repetitions respectively.

Cofer (1941) compared the time and trials required to reach mastery of prose passages of different lengths for both verbatim and logical learning. For logical learning, the learner had only to master the essential ideas of the passage. It was found that verbatim learning not only required more time and repetitions than logical learning but that it was also more affected by increases in the length of the passages. With increases in the amount of material to be learned, difficulty increased at a greater rate for verbatim than for logical learning.

Length of Task and Retention.   Are longer lists or longer lessons remembered better than short lists or short lessons? The answer seems to be "Yes," provided the longer material is learned to the same degree. Ebbinghaus learned lists of nonsense syllables of different lengths and computed the saving when the same lists were relearned after twenty-four hours. The twelve syllable list was relearned with a saving of 35 percent, the twenty-four syllable list with a saving of 49 percent, and the thirty-six syllable list with a saving of 58 percent. The greater savings for the longer lists indicate that a relatively larger amount was retained. This may be owing in part to the fact that the longer lists required more readings. The twelve syllables required seventeen readings, the twenty-four syllables required forty-five readings, and the thirty-six syllable list required fifty-six readings. Thus, each syllable in the longer lists was seen many more times.

These results have been verified in principle by other investigators who have used other materials and other methods. Robinson and Heron (1922) experimented with lists of nonsense syllables, and Robinson and Darrow (1924) with three-place numbers. Their results indicated the tendency toward a greater percentage of retention for the longer lists with both the recall and relearning methods. When controls have been used to prevent overlearning of various units of the longer lists by eliminating them from the series as soon as they are learning, the recall and relearning scores have been found to be approximately the same for lists of differing lengths. This was the finding in an experiment on paired associates learning where each pair was removed as soon as the subject had responded correctly with its second member three times (Sand, 1939).

That the larger number of presentations in the case of the longer lists is not the full explanation of the higher retention rates found for longer materials is indicated by a study made by Woodworth (1938). To a group of twenty-five students he read lists of words arranged in pairs at the rate of one pair every six seconds. The subjects were instructed to learn each pair so that when the first one of the pair was presented, they could recall the second. The lists varied in length, containing five, ten, twenty, and thirty word pairs respectively. The prompting method was used, and each list was read three times. A recall test of retention was given two days later. For immediate recall, the percentages were higher for the shorter lists, but after two days the percentages of the various lists recalled were as follows: five pair list, 4 percent; ten pair list, 16 percent; twenty pair list, 36 percent; thirty pair list, 34 percent. Thus, retention was higher for the longer lists even though they were presented the same number of times as the shorter ones and the same time was allotted to each word pair in all of the lists. The fact, however, that the thirty word list fell short of the twenty word list suggests that there is probably a limit beyond which the returns begin to decrease. Woodworth suggests that in the harder tasks, the subjects were stimulated to a greater degree to find meaningful relations between the paired words.

Position in a Series. It is well known that the first of a series of experiences is likely to have high memory value. As a rule, we easily recall our first day of teaching, our first visit to a particular city, and our first airplane ride after we have forgotten later ones. In memorizing, the beginning and the end of a series are usually learned before the middle part.

In an experiment, three series of fifteen items were presented once to a group of sixty-eight students. The first series consisted of nonsense syllables; the second, of unrelated words; the third, of related words. The number of correct reproductions for each item in the three series is shown in the following table:

Serial position of item:	1	2	3	4	5	6	7	8	9	10	11	12	13	14	15
Nonsense syllables	56	35	24	22	24	8	12	9	6	3	7	3	18	26	51
Unrelated words	65	68	45	37	58	18	44	32	36	15	46	31	49	49	58
Related words	66	68	67	54	67	58	59	58	58	56	52	52	62	52	62

It will be noted that the first and the last nonsense syllables were reproduced with far greater frequency than the others in the series. A similar trend is found in the two meaningful series, although to a lesser degree.

Difficulty of Material and Learning. Krueger's data (1946) reproduced in Figure 6.1 show the learning curves for eight series of nonsense syllables of increasing difficulty, both qualitative and quantitative. The student may question the relevance of experiments dealing with nonsense syllables to human learning, particularly in conjunction with school. Consideration will lead one to the conclusion that many tasks at all grade levels are non sense-making in the respect that the material is novel, abstract, and comparatively foreign to any of the previous experiences the subject has

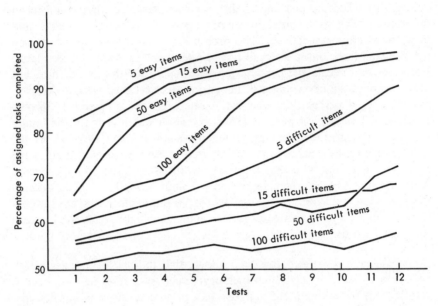

Fig. 6.1 Curves of learning for tasks of increasing difficulty. (After Krueger, 1946.)

had. Figure 6.1 shows a negatively accelerated acquisition curve for easy material (rapid early gains gradually slowing). Rate of learning is linear for intermediate difficulty and positively accelerated for the most difficult material. Few comparable studies have been made of the difficulty of school tasks. One effort is found in a study with Air Force mechanics (Klare, Shuford, and Nichols, 1957) learning technical materials. Two versions were prepared, one difficult, the second easier in that it contained a higher proportion of short, familiar, and frequently used words, shorter sentences, and more concrete than abstract terms. The simpler version produced greater reading efficiency (more words per second and more words per visual fixation as determined by an eye movement camera) and greater retention. The latter result held true when both number of readings and amount of time allowed for reading were controlled.

Gunborg (1939) checked the difficulty of the arithmetic processes of addition, multiplication, subtraction, and division when these processes appeared in combinations of two in a single problem. He attempted to answer the questions of what effect being the first or second step in a problem had upon each process, and what effect being combined with the other three processes had upon difficulty. For instance, in this problem: Alice picked 13 quarts of cherries. Her sister picked six times as many. How many quarts did they both pick together? multiplication is combined with and precedes addition. The problems were graded to a sixth grade level of difficulty and administered to 3831 pupils. Addition and multiplication were easier when the first step in a problem, and division and subtraction when the second step. For all processes in the first position, the order of increasing difficulty was addition, multiplication, subtraction, and division; in the second position, the order was subtraction, addition, division, and multiplication. This held true for all levels of ability. Whether these results are inherent in the processes or are an outgrowth of the method of teaching is not clear, although the number of children involved in the study, taken from six states, would indicate that a wide range of procedure was probably represented in the sample. It has been shown with reading material that the frequency of difficult words is related to progress of reading with primary grade children. When the portion of difficult words exceeds 20 percent, the task of reading becomes too difficult and progress is retarded, probably as a result of reduction in motivation as well as difficulty in comprehension. Between 5 percent and 20 percent of difficult words in the reading material appears to be optimal as far as learning of reading is concerned.

Hildreth (1941) emphasizes that children and adults attempt to simplify a problem which is too difficult for them or beyond their comprehension by reducing it to a level at which it is coherent; in the process, however, they produce errors or distortions which are not chance errors but the product of attempting to give meaning to the problem, and as such are clues to the mental processes of the individual. In reading, a child attempting to make sense out of the visual and auditory symbols may perceive them incorrectly. Observational study of the responses and substitutions provides useful analytic material for evaluating mental development, understanding thought processes, and diagnosing learning problems.

The learning curves for motor skills are similar to that shown in Figure 6.1 for verbal materials, judging from a compilation of studies by Davis (1935). A more rapid initial rise occurs in simple motor tasks than in complex tasks, with fluctuations and plateaus more frequent in the latter. Retention curves for motor skills have typically shown less forgetting than occurs with verbal material, as Figure 6.2 illustrates. Most adults would estimate that their performance in the Sunday picnic baseball game is better after a lapse of several years without practice than their recollection of historical events, although performance at the picnic table probably surpasses both in speed and dexterity. An ingeniously designed study by Van Dusen and Schlosberg (1948) which controlled the differential practice effect, produced the highly similar curves shown in Figure 6.3. Two sets of switches were labeled with nonsense syllables. Subjects were then given paired association learning tasks that involved the simultaneous learning of pairs of switches and pairs of nonsense syllables. Retention was similar for both, suggesting that the usual greater retention of motor skills over a period

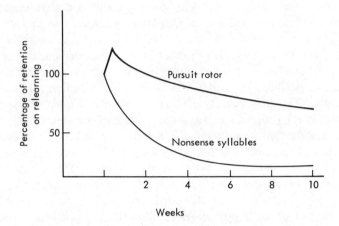

Fig. 6.2 Comparison of retention of motor (pursuit rotor) and verbal learning (nonsense syllables). (After Leavitt-Schlosberg, 1944.)

of time is probably a function of overlearning and degree of organization and integration within the task.

The transfer effects of complex versus simple motor skills were investigated by Jones (1952) in a study involving a complex and simple two-hand coordination tracking task. Four groups of forty-one men learned one of the four possible combinations of the complex and simple tasks (simple-simple, simple-complex, complex-simple, complex-complex). Data showed that the transfer of training from the complex to the simple task was as great as the effect of direct practice on the simple task and was greater than the

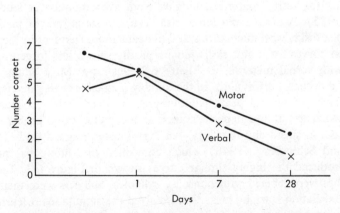

Fig. 6.3 Retention of verbal and motor learning after equal practice. (After Van Dusen and Schlosberg, 1948.)

reverse transfer of simple to complex. Direct practice on the complex task gave greater learning than the transfer from simple to complex, suggesting the possibility that with adults it may be more advantageous to tackle the complex skill directly, e.g., one may learn more golf starting on the golf course than on the driving range. With children, these results would undoubtedly have to be qualified in terms of the restrictions imposed by differences in neuro-muscular development.

Meaningfulness of Material and Learning.   The youngster coming to school for the first time has been hearing and speaking and experiencing his native language for some years. Measures of his spontaneous vocabulary indicate a usage of between 2500 and 3000 words by grade one and possibly a total vocabulary five to ten times as great. These are 2500 sound words, not symbol words. The process of learning to read requires the recognition and association of arbitrarily chosen symbols with sounds and concepts acquired through previous learning. The task seems eminently simple to anyone who can read. Written words are an inescapable and practically constant part of the environment, more numerous in our daily lives than automobiles. For the illiterate, however, these minutely differing symbols are a meaningless hodge-podge. To give you the impression once again of the confusion that goes with learning to read, a series of shorthand symbols has been printed below. Your task is to learn to read them by associating the symbols with the words already known to you, so that you can recognize them when you see them again.

The shorthand sentence reads, "In the primary grades book is the symbol for a word already familiar." Now turn to page 186 and without glancing back at the original, see if you can read the sentence which appears there. (See footnote on page 186 for transcription.) The only change is that which is typical in first grade readers—the same symbols are rearranged in different order.

If you have had the experience of memorizing nonsense syllables, you can appreciate what it means to children to be required to memorize material that has no meaning for them. Experimental evidence clearly indicates the greater ease and facility for memorizing meaningful as compared with meaningless material. Being meaningful means that there has been some previous experience with the material and that some associations have been formed with it. In other words, meaningful material is already learned to some extent. It was for this reason that Ebbinghaus devised and used nonsense syllables in his experiments. He wanted to avoid the uncontrolled variables of previous experience in the interest of more reliable quantitative measures of associative learning.

The importance of meaning for the formation of new associations is revealed by comparing the learning of a list of nonsense syllables and a list of familiar words. In an experiment by the writer, three lists differing in meaning were presented to 348 students. The first series consisted of fifteen nonsense syllables, the second was a list of fifteen three-letter sense words, and the third contained fifteen words meaningfully related to each other. These items were presented one by one on large cards at the rate of one every two seconds. After a single reading, reproductions were made in writing. The mean number of correct reproductions for each of the three series was:

I.	Nonsense syllables	4.47
II.	Unrelated words	9.95
III.	Logically related words	13.55

In the experiments just cited, the series was presented only once; hence, learning was incomplete. The measure of the degree of learning for purposes of comparison was made in terms of the number of members reproduced. Similar differences between meaningful and non-meaningful materials can be demonstrated by the method of complete mastery. Here the subject continues to repeat each series until he can recite it correctly. Learning is measured in terms of the time or the number of repetitions required to reach complete mastery. For the same three lists used in the experiment just described, Guilford (1934) reports the following as the mean number of trials required for complete mastery by 117 subjects:

I.	15 nonsense syllables	20.4 trials
II.	15 unrelated words	8.1 trials
III.	15 related words	3.5 trials

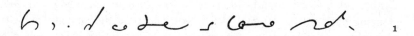

It should be remembered, moreover, that there is a rather wide range of individual differences in the case of all of the measures of learning mentioned here.

Nonsense syllables and the study of human learning are inextricably mixed, for Ebbinghaus invented the one and pioneered the other, and much of the early research reported in this chapter owes its origin to his initial inspiration. Currently, one of the most systematic programs of research on characteristics of materials has been directed by Underwood at Northwestern University. In one of his studies (Underwood and Richard-

[1] Book is a word already familiar in the primary grades.

son, 1956) four serial lists of words were presented to 100 students. Two lists were comprised of nonsense syllables highly meaningful (e.g., nik), two low in association value. In addition, in one of each pair of lists the syllables were high in similarity and low in similarity. The results showed that the higher the meaningfulness, the faster the learning; the lower the meaningfulness, the more similarity within the list retarded learning and increased forgetting. Meaningfulness was important to initial learning more than retention, for its effect here was indirect, offsetting effects of similarity. Further corroboration that meaningfulness is more important to acquisition than retention is provided by Archer (1953) and Dowling and Braun (1957). There is probably very little learning without meaning. Even in learning nonsense syllables, the learner seeks various meaningful associations, telling himself that cows moo for *kuh* and *muh*. With recognizable words the learner builds up meaningful connections between the various words or integrates the members of the series into larger units. One subject, for example, tied together the words *pet, son, cat,* and *box,* by making the sentence, "The *son* put his *pet cat* in the *box.*"

Ausubel has explored the value of such efforts to make material meaningful through the use of what he terms "organizers." For example (Ausubel and Fitzgerald, 1961), 155 college students who were to learn a 2500 word passage on the principles of Buddhism were divided into three groups. Two days before learning the passage, one experimental group studied a 500 word *comparative organizer* which compared the major ideas of Buddhism with Christianity; a second group studied an *expository organizer* which made no reference to Christianity; and the control group studied a historical introduction which did not refer to the ideas of Buddhism. Differences in original knowledge of Christianity were controlled by dividing subjects into those with high and low knowledge. The former group made the greatest retention; the organizers were most effective with the less knowledgeable because they helped relate unfamiliar material to established concepts in the learner's cognitive structure and accomplished this by clarifying the discrimination between the two sets of material.

The practical importance of the influence of meaning is indicated. No pupil should be asked to memorize something he does not understand or in which he is unable to find meaning. All material should be made as meaningful for the child as possible. Number experiences should precede the learning of the combinations in addition and subtraction. A child should know definitely what words mean before attempting to learn their spelling. Poems should be thoroughly comprehended before one undertakes to learn them verbatim. Dates and names of persons and places should not be memorized as isolated bits of information but should be incorporated into larger units of understanding.

In order to meet these requirements for economy in memorizing, the teacher should seek to widen the child's range of associated experiences. Particularly, the material to be learned should be related to his own needs, welfare, and interests. This may be accomplished in various ways: by discussion, by explanations, and by stories of related events. Questions are useful in bringing the child's former experiences into relation with the new material. Meaningful organization may be promoted by a consideration of likenesses and differences, the bearing of one fact upon another, group membership, and the answers to such questions as: Who was involved? When did this incident take place? Where? What were the causes? What were the consequences?

Adults are prone to confuse facts and generalizations. For example, the statements that a plucked violin string vibrates or that the air temperature is 65 degrees are both facts. In contrast, the statements that sound is caused by a vibrating instrument or that condensation results from the cooling of air are more than facts. They are generalizations which can make sense only if one understands the hidden meanings and relationships involved. Memorizing of the generalization makes it possible to reproduce it like a record but does not guarantee any understanding of meaning.

Swenson's (1949) study of the comparative effectiveness of teaching arithmetic to second grade children by the meaning and drill methods substantiates the foregoing views. The experiment involved 332 pupils in fourteen classes, half taught by drill method, half by the meaning method. The one hundred arithmetic facts, $0 + 0$ through $9 + 9$, were divided into three sets. In the groups taught by the generalization methods, the facts which centered around a generalization were presented together and the children were encouraged to discover and formulate their own generalizations, e.g., when you add 0, the other number stays the same; if the numbers are upside down the answer is the same. Practice exercises were given after the generalizations had been achieved to aid understanding. In the drill groups, the addition facts were presented as isolated facts, speed of response was emphasized, using fingers was discouraged, errors were corrected immediately, and drills were varied and made interesting. The total length of the experiment was twenty weeks. The fact that the addition facts were presented in three sets permitted not only measures of initial acquisition, but also of retention, interference and transfer of training between sets. In this study, the advantage went to the group which learned by the generalization method; the initial learning was greater, and there was greater transfer and less interference between sets. Compared with the amount learned, the amount retained was equal for both methods.

INTERFERENCE

The more you learn, the more you forget. True, the more you learn the more you know; but the more you know, the less you will learn. These bald statements dramatize a losing race we all run in our efforts to retain what we know and to learn new materials. What we learn today will interfere with our attempts to retain and recall something learned earlier. This is termed *retroactive inhibition,* backward blocking. What we learn today will interfere with some of tomorrow's attempts at learning. This is *proactive inhibition* or forward blocking.

In the experimental study of the retroactive type of interference, subjects are given certain material to be learned, followed by what is called an interpolated learning task, then asked to recall the original material. In studying the proactive type, the interpolated material is presented first, followed by the original learning. In both cases, the number of trials to master the material after the interpolation is compared without such interpolation as seen in the diagram below.

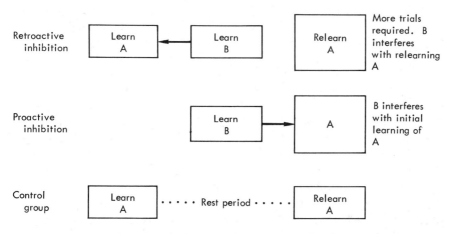

The losing race is not as fruitless as it appears. We know that material which is used is retained, and that forgetting is greater with unused material. And once considered, forgetting is a blessing if not a virtue, for much that is antiquated gets eliminated, as well as much that may be unpleasant. But we find ourselves in a continual struggle between elimination and assimilation, for the useful can be forgotten as well as the non-useful. New material can be related to old, as well as interfere with it, which creates one of teaching's major tasks, that of developing structures, concepts, hierarchies of knowledge and generalizations to which new information can be related and of creating skills in learning how to learn, to look for generalizations, and to relate to existing generalizations. Ever since the first systematic study of retroactive inhibition by Muller and Pilzecker in Germany in 1900, the entire topic of interference in learning has been recognized as vitally important because of its relation to retention and forgetting. In the following paragraphs we shall consider some of the conditions and experimental findings regarding them.

Similarity.   MATERIALS AND OPERATION.   It early became apparent that the amount of retroactive inhibition is related to the degree of similarity between the original learning and the interpolated task. Skaggs (1925) used interpolated activities having different degrees of similarity to the original learning and found that as the similarity increased, the retroactive effect increased. But in some other experiments, he found less retroactive inhibition with a high degree of similarity. From his results, he concluded that retroactive inhibition tends to increase with increases in similarity up to a certain point and that beyond that point further increases in similarity approaching identity bring a reduction in the amount of inhibition.

Robinson (1927) reached a similar conclusion. He believed that if we begin with an interpolated task identical with the original and make it dissimilar by increasing degrees, there will at first be an increase in retroactive inhibition until a maximum is reached, and beyond this point further increases in dissimilarity will result in decreases in retroactive inhibition. He tested this hypothesis by an experiment in which he used lists of eight consonants for learning material. He regarded the learning of the first four consonants of each list as the original task and the learning of the last four as the interpolated task. The degree of similarity of the two tasks was varied by including in the second half of each list zero, one, two, three, or four consonants that were presented in the first half. Thus, the degree of similarity here was a matter of the number of common elements in the learning material of the two tasks. The results showed an increase in retroactive inhibition with the reduction of similarity or number of common elements. Owing probably to the limitations of his learning materials, there was no indication of a reversal of the trend.

Other experimenters with different methods and materials and with other ways of securing different degrees of similarity have tried to test this hypothesis. Results have varied. It appears that the Skaggs-Robinson hypothesis does not hold for all relations of similarity in that under some experimental conditions a decrease in similarity (percentages of identity) produces a corresponding increase in retroactive inhibition, while under other conditions the amount of retroactive inhibition increases with an increase in similarity (Britt, 1935).

Gibson and Gibson (1934) had twenty-six subjects study a list of ten pairs of consonants for two minutes. After a three minute interval spent on an interpolated task, the subjects were tested for recall of the original material. Five groups were employed, and their interpolated tasks differed in materials, in operation, or in both. The five tasks were: first, learning another list of consonants; second, learning ten pairs of digits; third, canceling paired consonants; fourth, canceling paired digits; fifth, looking at pictures. The recall scores for the groups improved in the order in which the tasks were listed. The conclusion was that similarity between the interpolated task and the original learning in either operation or material produces poorer retention than similarity in neither of these aspects of the tasks.

MEANING.   That similarity of meaning as well of operations and materials is a factor conducive to retroactive inhibition has been shown by McGeoch and McDonald (1931). They used a list of adjectives for the original learning and then compared the retroactive effects of learning synonyms and antonyms of these words, unrelated adjectives, nonsense syllables, and three place numbers. The highest retention scores for the original lists were obtained with the numbers, the lowest with the synonyms. The scores with the other materials fell between in the order of their similarity to the original list. When the synonyms were arranged in three groups according to degree of similarity of meaning, it was found that the interpolated list with meanings most similar to the meanings of the words in the original list produced the greatest amount of retroactive inhibition. Similar results were obtained by Johnson (1933), who used lists of nouns for the original learning and synonyms of three different degrees of similarity in meaning for the intervening learning. In a later study, McGeoch and McGeoch (1937) used lists of paired associates and found that there was more loss in retention when the interpolated material was similar to the original list in the first or in both members of the pairs than when it was unrelated or synonymous only in the second members.

METHODS OF LEARNING.   When the materials of the original and interpolated tasks are learned by similar methods, the amount of retroactive inhibition is likely to be greater than when different methods are employed in the two tasks. A demonstration of this fact was made in an experiment by Waters and Peel (1935). Their subjects learned lists serially and by the method of paired associates. The retroactive effect of the interpolated learning was greater when paired associates learning was followed by paired associates learning and when serial learning was followed by serial learning than when one of the forms of learning was followed by the other form.

The pervasive effects of similarity or its reciprocal, dissimilarity, took an unusual turn in an experiment by Bilodeau and Schlosberg (1951). They tested the effects of the interpolated activity on retention when it was learned in two different physical environments, one in a dingy storeroom, the second a bright classroom. Their results suggest that even incidental stimuli associated with learning conditions aid in discrimination, because the interference was reduced by one half as a result of learning the interpolated material in a different environment. This suggests that the optimal location for studying a subject would be the final examination room.

In a variation on the theme, which supported the preceding findings, Greenspoon and Redge (1957) showed that interference was greatest where original and interpolated learning occurred in one environment, and relearning in a different one.

Degree of Learning.   ORIGINAL TASK.   Thorough learning of the original material tends to minimize the adverse effects of the interpolated activity on retention. For example, Pyle (1919) had two groups of subjects, A and B, sort decks of 150 cards into thirty compartments numbered to correspond to the numbers on the cards. The subjects practiced for one hour daily for thirty days. There were two arrangements of the numbering of the compartments. Group A alternated daily from one arrangement to the other. Group B practiced fifteen days on the first scheme and then spent fifteen days on the second. Group B surpassed A both in gains over initial scores and in the final speed attained. Pyle believed that practice on the second scheme inhibited the learning of the first and that the inhibiting effect was less for B because the first arrangement was more thoroughly learned at the time practice on the second was undertaken.

The influence of the degree of learning of the original task on retroactive inhibition was clearly demonstrated by McGeoch (1929). Lists of nine nonsense syllables were presented six, eleven, sixteen, or twenty-six times. For the experimental series, the learning was followed by a rest of thirty seconds, and then another list of nine syllables was presented eleven times. The results indicated a tendency for retroactive inhibition to decrease as the number of repetitions of the original list was increased. The inhibition fell from 108.5 percent at six presentations to 5.3 percent at twenty-six presentations.

INTERPOLATED TASK. Regarding the interpolated activity, it has been found that in the early stages of learning, an increase in the degree to which it is learned increases its retroactive effect but that when the learning is carried to a high degree of mastery, there is sometimes a decrease in the amount of inhibition caused by it (Melton and Irwin, 1940). McGeoch (1932) obtained results indicating that after the interpolated task is completely mastered, additional repetitions do not increase its retroactive effect. In a study in which the interpolated list was presented two, five, ten, or twenty times, retroactive inhibition was found to increase with the increase in the number of repetitions up to the tenth repetition; but for the additional ten repetitions, when the number was stepped up to twenty, there was no further increase in the retroactive effect (Thune and Underwood 1943). The greatest amount of inhibition is believed to occur when the degrees of learning in the two tasks are about equal.

Bunch and McTeer (1932), in a study of human maze learning, used 110 subjects who learned two stylus mazes, one for the original task and the other for the interpolated activity. The experimental condition tested for its effect on retroactive inhibition was the administration of electric shock on the hand for errors. The retroactive effect of learning the second maze on the retention of the first was less than half as great when the original learning took place with punishment for errors as when it was done without shock. Retroactive inhibition was also greatly reduced when the second maze was learned under punishment conditions. Since the administration of shock for errors was conducive to faster learning with fewer errors, it seems likely that these results are related to those considered in the preceding paragraphs. Punishment for errors may reduce retroactive inhibition because it facilitates learning.

Under natural conditions, one may well ask which is the original and which is the interpolated materials, because as we proceed through the school day, each subsequent subject is original for the next and interpolated for the preceding. As a result, one wants to know if any relationship exists between varying degrees of learning of the two. Fortunately, as overlearning on either the original material or on the interpolated material or on both increases, the amount of interference is less (Briggs, 1957; McAllister and Lewis, 1951). Thus, the worst possible study arrangement is to learn two sets of material to a low or intermediate degree, for the retroactive interference increases rapidly with low to moderate amount of learning on the second task. Better to learn either well, best to overlearn on both. Briggs explains these results in terms of Gibson's differentiation theory which states that confusions increase as the strengths of the two response systems (original and interpolated) approach equality because of difficulties in discriminating one from the other. With overlearning, discrimination increases, reducing interference.

Amount of Material Learned. ORIGINAL TASK.   Some of the earlier studies showed a decrease in susceptibility to retroactive inhibition as the amount of material of the original task was increased. This may have been due not simply to the amount of the material itself but to the fact that the longer lists require a higher degree of learning and are retained better. In a more recent experiment, in which lists of six, eight, ten, twelve, and fifteen pairs of nonsense syllables were used, an attempt was made to control the degree of learning by removing each pair as soon as it had been correctly reproduced three times. The groups that learned the four longest lists recalled almost identical percentages of these lists. It appeared, therefore, that increases in length from eight to fifteen pairs of syllables did not produce decreases in retroaction (Sand, 1939).

INTERPOLATED TASK.   In one of McGeoch's studies (1936), it was found that the interpolation of sixteen adjectives after an original list of sixteen had been presented eight times produced more inhibition for relearning after twenty minutes than did the interpolation of lists of eight adjectives. His data indicated that the amount of retroactive inhibition was determined by the relative lengths of the original and interpolated lists.

Another study bearing on the influence of the length of the interpolated task was reported by Twining (1890). He used lists of eight nonsense syllables. After the original list was learned to one perfect trial, he presented, during the thirty minute interval before relearning, one, two, three, four, or five lists ten times each. The recall scores for the original list decreased and the number of relearning trials increased directly as the number of interpolated lists increased. Thus, the length of the interpolated task appears to be one of the factors determining the amount of retroactive inhibition produced by it. By controlling both amount of material and amount of time spent on the interpolated material Slamecka (1962) concluded that it was amount of time rather than material which explained variations in degree of interference.

Temporal Position of the Interpolated Task.   There has been considerable interest in the question of whether the retroactive influence of the interpolated activity varies with its position within the interval between the original learning and the test of retention. Müller and Pilzecker (1900) and Heine (1914) believed that the sooner the interpolated activity was introduced after the original learning, the greater would be its inhibiting effect. Robinson (1920) introduced the interpolated task at four different temporal points of a twenty minute interval and found no relation between the position of this task and its inhibiting influence. Skaggs (1925) concluded that the retroactive effect is greatest when the interpolated activity comes immediately after the original learning. The results of later experiments have not been in agreement on this point. In some experiments, the greatest amount of inhibition has resulted from interpolation immediately after the original learning (Sisson, 1939); in others it has resulted from activity placed just before the recall or relearning of the original material (McGeoch, 1933; Whitely, 1927). The results have sometimes shown no consistent differences in inhibition for different temporal positions of the interpolated task (McGeoch and Nolen, 1933).

In view of the fact that the experimental data suggested two distinct points at which the interpolated learning produced maximum retroactive inhibition—immediately after learning and immediately before recall—Postman and Alper (1946) tested the effect of nine different temporal conditions upon recall. Twenty unrelated word pairs were learned by sixty-three college students, using the anticipation method. They were tested for recall on the list after a sixteen day interval. At nine different points in the interval between learning and recall—immediately after learning, one, two, four, eight, twelve, fourteen, fifteen days, and immediately before recall—an interpolated list of twenty word pairs was learned, in which the first word of each pair was the first word in the original list. A new association was learned for it. The maximum retroactive inhibition occurred when the second list was interpolated one day after original learning, with two other high points at eight days and fifteen days. The authors interpreted their results as showing that the retroactive effects are greatest one day after learning because that is the point by which maximum unlearning had occurred. The interpolation at fifteen days was construed as most disturbing to recall, with the eight day interpolation being a combination of both effects.

Yet the evidence was not all in, and probably still is not, and the results show the slow step-by-step nature of much scientific work, broken occasionally by the brilliance of rare genius. Archer and Underwood (1951) thought the results inconclusive because the degree of learning of the interpolated material had not been controlled, only its temporal location. Arguing that low degrees of learning prior to recall could have effects similar to high degrees occurring a longer time before recall, they varied temporal relations and degree of learning simultaneously and obtained results which attributed the interference to degree of learning alone. Their time span, however, was forty-eight hours, differing considerably from the range that Postman and Alper tested. In a parallel study (Newton and Wickens, 1956), further support is lent this position but not under all conditions of learning.

Organization. Considerable evidence points to the degree of intra-serial integration as a matter of importance in determining the extent to which retention may be impaired by the activity that follows learning. By *intraserial integration* is meant the organization of the unit members of the learning material into a unified whole or pattern by means of the various associations formed between them.

In an attempt to secure gradations in similarity throughout the scale from maximum to minimum similarity, Watson (1938) used ten groups of subjects and ten variations of the interpolated task in an experiment on card sorting. Each group first sorted a deck of eighty cards ten times into sixteen compartments numbered to correspond with the numbers on the cards. Then followed an interpolated sorting with changed arrangement and the final sorting with the original arrrangement. For group I the inter-polated task was exactly the same as the original. This meant that the group simply had additional practice on the same performance. Here was complete similarity, and the effect of the interpolated practice was a slight improve-ment in the performance. For group II four compartment numbers were changed for the interpolated sorting. This meant that the cards bearing these numbers had to be thrown into compartments different from the ones in which they were placed during the original practice. Group III had eight numbers changed; group IV, twelve; and for group V all sixteen numbers were changed. In terms of materials, the first five patterns were completely similar, for numbers were used throughout, but from group I to group V there was increasing change in the organization of movements required. For groups VI to IX letters were substituted for numbers to the extent of four, eight, twelve, and sixteen letters respectively. Here was increasing dissimilarity in terms of materials, while the movement patterns remained the same as in V. The results showed an increase in retroactive inhibition through groups II to V. The change to four letters in group VI did not appreciably diminish the retroactive effect of the interpolated sorting, but from group VI on, there was consistent decrease in retroactive inhibition with the least amount appearing in group IX where all sixteen numbers were changed to letters.

Watson believed that the factor of similarity is insufficient to explain the results and suggested that compatibility also is a factor determining the retroactive effect of the interpolated activity. In his pattern I, there was complete similarity and complete compatibility in the identity of the original and interpolated tasks. In V, where all numbers were changed, there was complete incompatibility and complete similarity. The same numbers were used, but each one was associated with a different response. In IX he found complete dissimilarity and complete compatibility because here the interpolated task was entirely different from the original both in materials and in organization of movements. There was, therefore, no necessity for unlearning the original task in order to learn the interpolated task. He points out that when compatibility and similarity are both high, the retention is high; when compatibility is low, even though similarity is high, retention is low; and that when similarity is low and compatibilty is high, the retention is relatively high.

This investigator found, moreover, that his subjects did not learn the original and interpolated patterns as entirely separate units, but that they tended to organize them into a comprehensive pattern that included the two. In cases where some of the numbers were changed, the subjects apparently reorganized the original pattern to include the needed changes in response. When letters were substituted for the numbers, the original pattern was not repeated (the pattern being the same as for V) and so, with the increase in the number of letters in the interpolated task, the material of the two tasks became less similar. There was then a decrease in the extent to which the interpolated task would disrupt the original organization. These observations led Watson to conclude that "the factor of organization determines the conditions of transfer and inhibition."

Sisson (1938) showed that even the low degree of organization provided by presenting lists of adjectives in the same order on each learning trial produced less interference than when both lists were scrambled after each trial. Such arrangements are tolerable for a few short lists of words, but if the only degree of organization possible was that of a constant order, we should soon sink in the sheer volume. It is here that Ausubel's work, already mentioned, takes on significance. A basic assumption about school curricula is that some form of organization, some rationale for ordering the content, exists. In fact, teachers often blithely assume that requisite prior knowledge and information exist in students who come their ways. Assuming it should lead them to using it, by creating links and contrasts with new material. To illustrate from a study of Ausubel's (1960) on the use of advance organizers: matched groups of experimental and control groups of undergraduate students were set up on the bases of sex, field of specialization, and ability to learn unfamiliar scientific material. The learning task consisted of a 2500 word passage of empirically demonstrated unfamiliarity, dealing with the metallurgical properties of steel. On two separate occasions, forty-eight hours and just before contact with the learning task, the experimental groups studied a 500 word introductory passage containing substantive background material of a conceptual nature presented at a much higher level of generality, abstraction, and inclusiveness than the steel material itself. This passage was empirically shown to contain no information that could be directly helpful in answering the test items on the learning material. The control group studied a traditional type of historical introduction of identical length. Retention of the learning was tested three days later. Learning and retention were greater in the experimental group in support of Ausubel's argument that advance organizers select and mobilize the most relevant existing concepts in the learner's cognitive structure and relate the new material to it.

"Advance organizers" are not to be confused with "study habits." When groups of Air Force trainees were given two passages (2600 and 3800 words) to learn on aerodynamics and communist ideology under different techniques of studying—outlining, summarizing, underscoring main points—these aids did not result in greater comprehension of the materials (Stordahl and Christensen, 1956). The advance organizer functions to relate the concepts in the material to the cognitive structure of the learner through increased discriminability and relevance.

Other Factors. AGE OF THE ASSOCIATIONS. When the degree of retention is about equal for two sets of material and one of them has been retained over a longer period of time, the retention of the older material will be impaired less by an interpolated activity than the retention of the younger. Thus, there appears to be a connection between Jost's law and retroactive inhibition (Britt and Bunch, 1934).

MENTAL SET. An experiment by Lester (1932) showed that instructions given to the subjects tend to reduce the retroactive effects of the interpolated activity when those instructions lead to expectation of recall, to expectation of the interpolated material, and to an understanding of the possible effects of the interpolated material. An even greater reduction of retroactive inhibition resulted from urging the subjects to make an effort to avoid letting the interpolated material interfere with their retention of the original lists.

AFFECTIVE TONING. Memory value has usually been found to be greater for pleasant than for unpleasant materials and also greater for unpleasant than for affectively indifferent materials.

The investigation of this problem has been difficult because of the many complicating factors involved. One of these is the factor of vividness. It is known that the vividness of an impression enhances its retention (Van Buskirk, 1932). Affective experiences are usually more vividly impressed than indifferent ones, and this would tend to increase their frequency of recall. Another fact to be taken into account is the greater frequency for most persons of pleasant experiences than unpleasant ones (Flügel, 1925). The very fact that one has more pleasant experiences would account to some extent for the greater number of pleasant than unpleasant experiences recalled. Then, the degree of affectivity varies for both pleasant and unpleasant experiences, a fact which makes reliable measurement difficult. Also, the affective toning of an experience tends to change with the lapse of time and under repetition.

Because of these features of the problem, the method of free recall of experiences often used in earlier studies is not considered dependable. In this method, individuals were asked to list all the experiences of a given period which they could recall and then rate them as pleasant, unpleasant, or indifferent. In most cases, this method has shown more affective than indifferent memories and more pleasant than unpleasant ones. But the results are obviously affected by factors other than affectivity alone.

A more satisfactory method of dealing with this problem is one in which the subjects learn a list of terms judged to be pleasant, unpleasant, or indifferent; then after an interval they are tested to determine the differences in retention for the three kinds of items. This method, however, is limited by the following facts: words in an experimental list may not have the same affective values as in other situations; a word may have a pleasant or unpleasant meaning without actually arousing the feeling (Young, 1937); and the words in such a list may differ in degree of familiarity or number of associations. In the light of these complicating influences, it is not surprising to find some disagreement among investigators. The gist of the evidence, however, seems to justify the following tentative conclusions: first, pleasant material is usually retained better than unpleasant material; second, the greater retention value of pleasant material tends to increase as time passes, but eventually it decreases as complete forgetting of both kinds of material is approached; third, for children this difference between the retention of pleasant and unpleasant material is much less than for adults; fourth, unpleasant material is usually retained better than indifferent material; fifth, both pleasant and unpleasant experiences tend to lose their affective toning and to approach indifference as time passes, but this tendency is greater in the case of unpleasant experiences; sixth, the factor of vividness plays a part in the recall of affective material, but compared with feeling, its influence is greater for immediate recall than for delayed recall (Beehe-Center, 1932; Cason, 1932; Dudycha, 1941; Gilbert, 1938; Meltzer, 1930).

A study by Bunch and Wientge (1933) of the relative susceptibility of pleasant, unpleasant, and indifferent words to the retroactive effect of interpolated indifferent material showed the least amount of retroactive inhibition for the pleasant words. Frank and Ludvigh (1931) used pairs of nonsense syllables for the original learning and then a series of odors was presented to the subjects. The odors were grouped as "pleasant," "unpleasant," and "indifferent" according to results from previous experiments. Recall was tested after an interval of ten minutes. There was better retention when the learning was followed by pleasant odors than when it was followed by unpleasant ones. It appears that the unpleasant odors had a greater inhibiting effect on the recall of the syllables learned prior to the presentation of the odors.

METHODS OF MEASURING RETENTION.   Several studies have shown that the indicated impairment of retention by interpolated activity is greater when retention is measured by recall than when it is measured by relearning trials (Britt, 1935; Lester, 1932; Dowling and Braun, 1957). The retroactive effects of the interpolated activity on the retention scores tend to diminish as relearning takes place, and after a few trials there may be no difference with respect to retention between the work and rest conditions. How quickly the retroactive effect disappears seems to depend on such conditions as degree of learning and the similarity of the two tasks (McGeoch, 1942; Briggs, 1957). These findings indicate the practical importance of reviews as a means of counteracting the impairment of retention by the activities that follow learning.

When the recognition method has been employed for measuring retention in experiments designed to investigate retroactive inhibition, it has revealed in some cases no difference in retention between the work and rest conditions. When this method has yielded evidence of retroactive inhibition, the amount indicated has usually been small. This is in keeping with the fact, mentioned in an earlier section, that higher percentage scores of retention are usually obtained by the recognition method of testing than by the method of recall. It appears that recognition is affected in essentially the same way as recall, though to a smaller degree, by the activities of the interval (Britt, 1935; McKinney, 1935; Zangwill, 1938).

Forgetting During Sleep.   In one of his studies of retention Ebbinghaus found that the amount forgotten between the twenty-fourth and forty-eighth hours after learning was about three times as great as that lost during a fifteen hour period falling between 8.8 and twenty-four hours after learning. This was not in line with the usual findings that indicated a slower forgetting rate for the intervals further removed from learning. It was observed that the proportion of time spent in sleep was greater for the earlier fifteen hour period than for the later twenty-four hour period, and it was suggested that sleep might favor retention. This explanation was not accepted by Ebbinghaus, who considered forgetting to be a function of time. He attributed these exceptional results to experimental error. But later on, experiments were undertaken by other investigators to discover the relation of sleep to retention.

Jenkins and Dallenbach (1924) made the first real test of the hypothesis, rejected by Ebbinghaus, that forgetting takes place at a slower rate during sleep than during waking periods. Two college seniors served as subjects. They learned lists of ten nonsense syllables to the point of one correct reproduction, some in the morning and some at night just before going to sleep. Tests for recall were given after intervals of from one to eight hours. The results indicated a striking difference between the amount forgotten during periods of sleep and of waking. More than twice as many syllables were correctly recalled after intervals of sleep than after the intervals in which the subjects were awake. Considerably more were reproduced after one and two hours of sleep than for the corresponding intervals of waking. The amount retained continued to drop during the day, but for the periods of sleep there appeared to be no further loss after the second hour. These results led to the conclusion that forgetting is the result of the interfering or obliterating effects of experiences, impressions, and activities which follow learning. This conclusion was in opposition to the view, prevalent at the time, that forgetting is a matter of deterioration of the effects of learning with the passing of time because of disuse.

Later, Van Ormer (1932) investigated retention during sleep and waking by means of the relearning method with the experimental refinement of making corrections for differences in learning efficiency at different periods of the day. It was found that more readings were required to memorize lists of nonsense syllables at night than in the morning. His results were in substantial agreement with the findings of Jenkins and Dallenbach. For the first hour, the rate of forgetting appeared to be about the same, as determined by relearning, for the waking and sleeping intervals; but after that, retention was definitely better during the periods of sleep.

Since the results from nonsense materials do not always apply to meaningful materials, a study by Newman (1939) is particularly significant for educational practices. His subjects were eleven college students, and he used for learning materials three short stories equated for number of points essential and non-essential to the plot. The stories were read at different times of day and reproduced after intervals of approximately eight hours. It was found that the essential points were reproduced much better than the non-essential ones, and that there was practically no difference between the number of essential points reproduced after eight hours of sleep and after an equivalent day interval. But for the non-essential points there was a difference, and the results were in accord with the findings of the previous studies in which nonsense materials had been employed. After the eight hour interval of sleep, the subjects reproduced on the average 47 percent of the non-essential points, while after the two waking periods only 25 percent and 19 percent were recalled. Newman concluded that forgetting is due to interference produced by the events of the interval but that the meaningful organization of the learned material tends to counteract this action.

It can be added parenthetically that if forgetting is reduced during sleep, learning of new material is negligible or nil. As enticing as the idea of learning from records under pillows may be, no substantial evidence exists to show they produce learning, in spite of claims of advertisements. This is consistent with what we know about arousal levels and information processing in the brain. Learning requires alertness. Emmons and Simons (1956) effectively demonstrated this when they played a list of ten one syllable nouns to nine men, ages 18 to 31, while the men were asleep. An electroencephalogram was used continuously to monitor sleep, so that tape recordings which were played regularly during the night could be stopped if there was any doubt. In addition, observations were maintained of wakefulness and comments of subjects during the night. The simplest test of learning was employed, recognition of words heard after awakening. No learning occurred.

Forgetting.   Any efforts to explain retroactive and proactive inhibition are at once explanations of forgetting. The earliest explanation of forgetting was the common-sense one that "things just fade out" as a result of disuse. Unfortunately for common-sense, the law of disuse failed to account for many facts—retention is better after sleeping (non-use) than waking; and further, any individual can recall some information or skill long dormant and under hypnosis or sodium amytal can recall memories apparently completely forgotten. The first effort at theory which took interference into account was Muller and Pilzecker's (1900) *perseveration theory*. In their view, it took a short while after learning for things to jell, and new material introduced immediately following learning interrupted the neural processes required for consolidating and fixating. However, the perseveration theory does not adequately explain the retroactive effect of activities that follow learning by several days, nor for the amount of retroactive inhibition being greater when the materials and methods of the original and interpolated tasks are similar than when they are dissimilar. Further, some forms of activity, even though fairly strenuous, when placed immediately after the learning, do not produce any appreciable amount of retroactive inhibition (McGeoch, 1931).

Two tenable and related theories to explain retroactive and proactive inhibition are McGeoch's *competition of response theory* and Melton and Irwin's *unlearning theory* (1940). In our daily life, we are continually learning new responses to the stimuli previously associated with other responses. McGeoch suggests that the result is a competition between responses to a given stimulus—an interference of new learning with old and vice versa. The fact that less forgetting occurs during sleeping hours than during the intervening activity of waking hours lends support to the hypothesis that forgetting is not the result of disuse but rather of interference between new and old learning. The interference may be viewed as a case of negative transfer of training, with previous learning inhibiting present learning and the latter interfering in the recall of previous learning. The product of the interference is a confusion of the old and the new. The findings on the relation of the degree of similarity between material to the amount of retroactive inhibition and the effect of different temporal relations support an interference theory.

Melton and Irwin extended the interference theory to include what they designate as active unlearning. In a study of the intrusions between lists of nonsense syllables presented as original and interpolated learning, Melton and Irwin came to the conclusion that the competition of responses —the direct interference—was inadequate in accounting for all of the retroactive inhibition. Using lists of eighteen nonsense syllables of low associational value and varying the number of trials on the interpolated list, retroactive inhibition was greater for interpolated lists practiced for five and ten trials than when the amount of practice was greater. The authors concluded that the number of intrusions is insufficient to account for the amount of retroactive inhibition, and suggested that an additional factor which may constitute active unlearning occurs by causing the original learning to become disrupted during the process of learning the interpolated list. This unlearning apparently lessens as the degree of learning of the interpolated and original list increases, suggesting that the higher the degree of organization of material learned, the smaller the degree of interference. Further investigation of the factor of unlearning is needed, but it is not unlikely that retroactive inhibition involves more than the direct knocking out of one response by another and that a more dynamic change may occur. McGeoch and Underwood (1943) have provided some experimental corroboration of Melton and Irwin's hypothesis, but Osgood (1948) contends that even the two factor theory is not adequate to account for all the retroactive inhibition; he suggests that the reciprocal inhibition of antagonistic responses needs investigation.

IMPLICATIONS FOR EDUCATION

The data from the laboratory experiments disclose the following aspects of the task affecting learning, retention, and transfer of training.

1. The perceptual clarity of the task as to relevant cues and appropriate responses.
2. The meaningfulness of the material and understanding obtained.
3. The context in which the skill or knowledge is acquired.
4. The difficulty level and complexity of the task.
5. Conditions contributing to or reducing the interference between tasks, such as similarity of stimuli or responses and degree of overlearning.

In the laboratory we find singular aspects of learning being manipulated under carefully controlled conditions. Ultimately each of the aspects must be seen as part of the total curriculum, not only the formally described set of facts, skills, concepts, and activities which comprise the curriculum but also the provision for individual differences, motivation, interest, and attitudes.

It was a matter of happenstance that the study of the effects of interference concentrated more on retroactive inhibition. One learned A, then B, then looked at the effects of A on recall of B. Schools have a forward thrust rather than a backward, assuming that today's lessons contribute to tomorrow's learning. The more relevant aspect of interference is the proactive inhibition design. Underwood (1957) has argued convincingly, with support from experimental evidence, that proactive inhibition is as significant as retroactive. Only by implication do schools give recognition to its effects by spending September and October in relearning what was supposedly mastered the previous year. Knowing what has been learned about the conditions which produce interference has decided import for the organization of curricula and instructional practices.

Although justice cannot be done in the space possible, a brief glance at organizational patterns of curricula is in order. Curricula can be classified as subject matter centered or experience centered. In effect, a curriculum is an attempt to relate subject matter and individual experience, the logical and psychological, in a way which attains the desired objectives of education. Subject centered curricula have been organized into three types: subject matter, correlated subjects, and broad fields. In the subject matter curriculum, the emphasis is on facts, skill, and knowledge, with the subjects presented as separate tasks during individual periods and at predetermined rates. In the secondary school, time allocation is determined by the number of periods per week assigned a given subject; in the elementary school, though standard periods are lacking, one finds specific amounts of time per day are allocated to a given subject or skill such as reading. The correlated subjects curriculum is an attempt to relate the separate subjects to each other. History and geography, science and health education, or geography and economics, though taught separately, may be presented in a manner that emphasizes the relationships between them. It is a short step to the broad fields curriculum in which the language arts are considered as a whole and the separate phases of communication—listening, speaking, reading, and writing—are treated as parts of the whole. The same approach can be taken with the social sciences, the arts, or other subjects.

The experience curriculum or the developmental activity curriculum places emphasis on the learner, on his interests and abilities, and on his personal, social, and intellectual growth. Its problem is how to use the physical and social environment of the school to provide experiences appropriate to developmental level. In practice, the difference between subject centered and child centered curricula can be difficult to detect, but the difference in emphasis is clear. In the former, knowledge and procedure are preestablished, and the task of the child is to make his responses congruent with the established model. In the latter, the emphasis is on exploring, analyzing, and problem solving. Carried to an extreme, the child would find himself exposed to a range of materials suitable to his interests and developmental level. He could start at any point and proceed at his own pace, assisted and encouraged by the teacher. If this procedure were followed in college, instead of beginning psychology with an introductory course, one could start at any point—social psychology, child psychology, abnormal psychology, and so on—and ultimately because of the basic interrelationship underlying all knowledge, one would move through the entire field of psychological knowledge, as long as interest and ability were equal to the task.

The core curriculum is a type of curriculum which can be applied to any of the preceding curricula, for it identifies central and peripheral learnings. It is more commonly associated with the broad fields and developmental activity curricula, and in this connection puts an emphasis on the study of broad social problems confronting society, the conditions which gave rise to them, and possible solutions.

An analysis of the general types of curricula described in comparison to the conditions producing interference indicates that however well taught the individual subject may be, the total school day or school week combines a complex of tasks in which the probability is:

High	Low
The context is one in which relevant cues and responses are difficult to discriminate.	Structural relationship between parts of curriculum.
Task difficulty is great.	Adaptability to individual differences in ability and interest.
Interference because of similarity of teaching procedures.	Time schedule permitting optimum practice and overlearning.
Rote learning of principles as well as facts.	Opportunity to evolve and apply generalizations.

Most teachers take positive transfer of training for granted, assuming the subjects they teach contribute greatly not only to academic achievement in other areas but also to the student's adaptability to life. Unfortunately, the research provides little comfort, for in the main it shows the degree of positive transfer to be low, forgetting high, and rate of progress slow. In part, the rate of progress is a function of developmental and maturation rates in children, but in greater part the slow rate results from an assumption that the inherent organization in subjects and curricula will be self-revealing to learners. But much of the so-called organization is not inherent in the materials but externally imposed. For example, differences between numbers can be obtained by adding or subtracting, or within these two approaches by resorting to decomposition or equal additions; the perspective one obtains of the Civil War or The War of Secession (depending on one's preference in terminology) is quite different viewed in terms of ultimate victory, military or political. No small difficulty arises from the fact that a sufficiently low degree exists of meaningfulness, of association within and between tasks, and of mastery to create conditions which maximize interference. Yet Ausubel's work (1958) indicates that proactive inhibition in the retention of meaningful school material can be reduced by the use of appropriate organizers introduced at suitable points in time.

SUMMARY

The difficulty of material and the meaningfulness of the task are of significant importance in their influence upon learning. The shape of the learning curve varies with the difficulty of the material to be learned, difficult tasks showing a slow rate of acquisition and verbatim learning requiring more repetitions than the learning of generalizations. The same task varies in difficulty for different children as a result of their capacity and experience differences. Even with this variation, there are tasks more suitable to given age levels than others. Although experimental evidence describing the difficulty level of various school tasks is limited, it is possible for the teacher to empirically arrive at valid judgments by checking the rates of progress of several children within the class, selected at different levels of ability. Tasks which are too simple fail to challenge children, while tasks too difficult discourage them. Learning curves as seen in the middle of Figure 6.1 are desirable. By periodic checks of rate of progress on different material, a teacher can assure herself that it represents an appropriate level of difficulty.

The practical importance of meaningfulness to learning has been pointed out. Rote memorization of meaningless material is a useless waste of the time of teacher and pupil. One of the justifications of a curriculum that is coördinated with the life experiences of children is that it achieves greater meaningfulness by utilizing the daily experiences of children. Words from the child's vocabulary can be read and spelled more readily than words which are strange to his vocabulary, for the latter lack meaning because of inexperience. It is obviously impossible to relate all learning to past experience, but one of the keys to teaching is still available in providing experiences which lend meaning to tasks. This is the function of pictures, exhibits, field trips, and the like—to provide the pegs of meaning upon which abstractions and generalizations may be hung. The teacher of the sixth grade class who lifted a boy out of his seat and turned him upside down in order to teach the class to invert the fraction and multiply when dividing by a fraction had a penchant for vivid illustrations which the class didn't readily forget.

The importance of discovering meaning for oneself cannot be overlooked. As with almost all discovery, it is not the number of errors that counts but the ultimate solution. Errors made in the process of discovery of solutions and generalizations are to be encouraged, for the modification of performance as a result of experience is an essential aspect of learning. One of the main problems with children is to narrow the field of search sufficiently so that a solution is likely. Even in Easter egg hunts, children have to have some idea of where to look. Certainly, in discovering mathematical, scientific, and social generalizations, some clues are necessary as to where to look or what particular aspects of the problem demand attention.

There is no lack of evidence that today's learning interferes with yesterday's and tomorrow's. The smaller the interference the more substantial the learning. Interference between learning tasks is greatest when the meaningfulness of the material is low, when the degree to which the sequential tasks are learned is low, and when tasks have low degrees of organization and near similarity in content, processes involved, and method of presentation. The evidence suggests that a sequence of tasks during the school day should avoid juxtaposition of subjects that are somewhat similar, such as French and Spanish, or Latin and English. Addition and subtraction, and multiplication and division of numbers involve similar processes which may be confused, particularly when aspects of the learning may be incomplete or of insufficient degree. Differences in methods of presentation which contribute to distinction and contrast between present and previous learning serve to reduce interference.

FURTHER READING

Overview

STROUD, J. B. 1940. "Experiments on learning in school situations," *Psychological Bulletin,* 37: 777-807.

Selected References

AUSUBEL, D. P. 1963. *The Psychology of Meaningful Learning.* New York: Grune and Stratton.

HOVLAND, C. I. 1951. "Human learning and retention." In S. S. Stevens (ed.), *Handbook of Experimental Psychology.* New York: Wiley.

KLAUSMEIER, H. J. and C. W. HARRIS. 1960. *Analyses of Concept Learning.* New York: Academic Press.

MC GEOCH, J. A. and A. L. IRION. 1952. *The Psychology of Human Learning,* rev. ed. New York: Longmans, Green.

Original Investigations

AUSUBEL, D. P. and D. FITZGERALD. 1961. "The role of discriminability in meaningful verbal learning and retention," *J. Educ. Psychol.,* 52: 266-74.

KRUEGER, W. C. F. 1946. Rate of progress as related to difficulty of assignment, *J. of Educ. Psychol.,* 37: 24-49.

MELTON, A. W. and JEAN IRWIN. 1940. The influence of degree of interpolated learning on retroactive inhibition and the over transfer of specific responses, *Am. J. of Psychol.,* 53: 173-203.

SWENSON, ESTHER, G. L. ANDERSON, and C. L. STACEY. 1949. Learning Theory in School Situations, *University of Minnesota Studies in Education.* Minneapolis: Univ. of Minnesota Press, pp. 9-39.

UNDERWOOD, B. J. 1957. Interference and forgetting, *Psychol. Rev.,* 64: 49-60.

VAN DUSEN, F. and H. SCHLOSBERG. 1948. Further study of the retention of verbal and motor skills, *J. of Exp. Psychol.,* 38: 526-34.

7

Method Variables

The discussion in the preceding two chapters has centered on the learner and on the nature of the task to be learned. We have ignored the function performed by the teacher: the systematic organization of materials for presentation to individuals. Knowledge of individual differences and of the meaningfulness and difficulty of tasks presented is essential in any attempt to initiate and maintain learning with children; however, the ways in which given tasks may be presented are varied, and the teacher must understand the effects of different presentations or arrangements upon the learning process. Many times, each of us has heard or used the maxim, "Practice makes perfect." It is used to justify continued repetitions of given acts, such as practicing musical scales, rehearsing dramatic plays, drilling in multiplication and addition tables, and practicing football plays, apparently on the assumption that repetition in itself is useful. What purpose does repetition of responses play in learning? How much and how often should practice be given? Does practice function differently in acquiring a skill than in retaining the skill once it is mastered? What factors other than amount of practice should be taken into account in organizing learning tasks? All these questions concern the teacher in her work of facilitating learning.

As a result of his early studies in learning, Thorndike (1916) proposed a law of exercise based on his conclusion that the connection or association between a stimulus and a response is strengthened by mere exercise—the repetition of response in the presence of the stimulus. Thorndike's prolific writing had a profound effect upon educational practice, and his recommendations for organization of learning tasks—arrangement from simple to complex, the use of frequency of occurrence of events as a criterion of importance for learning, and frequent repetition in the process of learning—were widely adopted. Subsequently, after further experimentation, Thorndike changed his opinions on the value of exercise in learning. Unfortunately, many teachers were not aware that Thorndike had shifted his views as a result of his continued studies (1931, 1932), for their chief technique continued to be endless repetition. In *Human Learning,* Thorndike refers to the former acceptance of the view that the mere repetition of a situation in and of itself produces learning and then states that this is not true. In an experiment involving 3000 attempts to draw with eyes closed a line four inches long, the lines drawn in the last two of the twelve sittings were not drawn appreciably better than those in the first and second sittings. The repetition of the situation was not sufficient in itself to cause learning. Here the learner had a task, a goal, but no way of knowing how far he fell short of it each time and no way of knowing in what way to change his performance in order to improve it. The need for some kind of check or appraisal of achievement in terms of the desired outcomes is indicated by the results of this experiment.

The result of such experiments was a shift in emphasis from repetition and drill to such factors as distribution of practice, knowledge of results, overlearning, whole learning versus part learning, incentives, and set, and the relationship of all to learning. Nevertheless, the evidence we have been considering points clearly to a fact every teacher should bear in mind, namely, that the mere repetition of a response is not sufficient, in and of itself, for learning.

DISTRIBUTION OF PRACTICE

Practice, like medicine, may be presented in small or large doses. It may be concentrated into relatively long unbroken periods of work or spread over several short sessions. It is possible, for instance, to organize college curricula so that one studies nothing but psychology one semester, political science the next, and so forth; or it may be arranged so that a student takes a variety of courses in each semester. When practice is concentrated in long unbroken periods, it is referred to as massed practice;

when it is spread out over a period of time, it is referred to as spaced or distributed practice. Almost without exception, the studies concerned with the relative effectiveness of spaced versus massed practice, whether with motor or verbal learning, show that practice should be spaced for best results. A few words in spelling each day for a week will be mastered better than a large number bunched in one lesson.

Three variations may be introduced in distribution of practice. The length of the practice period may be varied, with rest periods constant; the length of the rest period may vary, with amount of work constant; and varying arrangements of work and rest periods may be combined.

Length of the Practice Period.   In general, it appears that the shorter the practice period, the greater the learning that occurs. Typical of the experimental findings is Starch's (1927) study in which two ten minute, one twenty minute, and one forty minute practice periods per day at letter-digit substitution were carried out until a total of 120 minutes had been completed. The shorter work periods were all more effective than a single two hour session, and the two ten minute sessions per day were most productive of all. At the same time, it apppears that there is a limit below which it is not profitable to reduce the length of time spent at one sitting. Pyle (1928), for example, compared the results from practice periods of fifteen, thirty, forty-five, and sixty minutes in a substitution experiment, and found the thirty minute period to be the most effective for gains in speed on the basis of the total time spent in practice. The fifteen minute period was too short for best results in this task, and the forty-five minute and one hour periods were too long. The results for the longer periods indicated very little gain after thirty minutes of practice, presumably because of increased fatigue and work decrement and decreased motivation in the latter part of the hour. The early studies of massed and distributed practice, those done during the 1920s and early 1930s were crudely executed, concentrating on the superficial aspects, the observable phenomena. Nevertheless, the superiority of distributed practice was readily established. It was approximately 1940 when a systematic experimental attack, begun by Hovland at Yale and pursued by Underwood (1961), sought to isolate the specifics involved and relate the results to learning theory, notably Hull's theory of excitatory and inhibitory forces, differential forgetting, and fatigue.

In a comparison of the effectiveness of massed versus spaced practice, one set of findings is the demonstrated superiority of spaced practice where length or amount of material to be learned is the consideration. The greater the amount of material, the greater the advantage of distributed practice, particularly in central portions of the material where acquisition is slowest. The results occur with motor learning as well as with verbal, even where less time is allocated to distributed practice.

Duncan (1951) compared unequal amounts of practice under two conditions. Calling attention to the fact that when the amount of practice is the same for both groups, the distributed practice group requires a greater elapsed time from beginning to end, Duncan held the time for both groups equal to twenty minutes. Each group had two five minute work periods separated by a ten minute rest period. During the five minute work period, one group practiced continually; the other worked ten seconds, then rested twenty, with the result that it had only one third the amount of practice. Nevertheless, the distributed practice groups were superior in both pre-test and post-test sessions. The pre-test massed practice group produced superior performance when switched to distributed practice in the post-rest session.

The evidence supports a conclusion that the shorter the work period, the better, provided it is not too short. Most tasks and activities require an initial period for warm-up. If the work period is too short, the learner probably fails to become oriented to the nature of the task.

But just how long should the periods be, and how long should the intervals between these periods be? The optimal length and spacing of the periods appears to depend upon the nature of the learning task and upon the age of the learner. It is safe to assume that in memorizing large blocks of material the learning should be spread over several periods, that for difficult material the periods should be shorter than for easy material, and that for young children there should be shorter periods than for older learners. In attempting to secure the advantages of distributed effort, we must guard against making the periods either too short or too long.

Hahn and Thorndike (1914) found that for a total of ninety minutes of practice in addition, 22½ minute periods brought greater gains than periods of 11¼ minutes for pupils in the seventh grade. For the sixth grade twenty minute periods were equivalent to periods of ten minutes; in the fifth grade 7½ minute periods were almost as good as periods of fifteen minutes; and for fourth graders ten minute periods were better than five minute periods.

Length of the Rest Period.   How long should the interval between practice periods be? In general, the length of the interval does not appear as important as the fact that rest periods occur, for the variations which occur between rest intervals of different length are smaller than those that occur between having or not having periods of rest. The optimal length of the rest period varies with the type of task or skill being learned. For instance, in an experiment by Dore and Hilgard (1937) utilizing the Koerth pursuit rotor—a target tracking task—three groups practiced for periods of one minute with rest periods of one, three, and eleven minutes respectively. The task was to hold a hinged stylus on a small brass target mounted on the disc of a phonograph turning at the rate of one revolution per second. Within an equal number of trials, the group that rested eleven minutes between trials made the greatest gain. The group resting three minutes was second best, and the group with the one minute intervals was third. A fourth group which had 9 three minute work periods interspaced with one minute rests made the poorest showing of the four groups when comparisons were made for equal trials. Overall efficiency in terms of score attained relative to amount of work done occurred with the group alternating a one minute work period with four minutes of rest. In a further study, Hilgard (1949) had two groups practice on the pursuit rotor, one group receiving decreasing rest intervals, the second, increasing rest intervals. Scores were better under distributed conditions early in practice, but by the end of the experiment differences in performance were negligible, suggesting no particular advantage to a given sequence of rest intervals. The experiments suggest that the extremes of spacing or massing are less advantageous than moderately spaced, even moderately massed, practice.

Denny *et al.* (1955) mixed massed and distributed practice in three sequential practice sessions of six, twelve, and three minutes interspaced with five and three minute rests. The all massed practice worked continuously during the three periods, the all distributed alternating thirty seconds work and thirty seconds rest. In the other six groups various combinations of massed to spaced practice occurred, M-M-D, M-D-D, and so on. Distributed practice was clearly superior during the first period; subsequent shifts to massed practice were accompanied by decrements in performance, possibly from temporary building of inhibition under massed conditions, which dissipated during subsequent rest periods.

Results reported by other experimenters indicate that for a given task there is an upper limit to the advantage of spreading practice out in time. It is possible to have intervals that are too long for best results. In a study of eye-hand coordination with a pursuit oscillator, Travis (1939) compared the results obtained under different interpractice intervals while the practice periods were kept constant at five minutes. Rest intervals of twenty minutes were found to produce better results than rests of five minutes, and intervals of forty-eight hours, seventy-two hours, and 120 hours. Here it appears that for a working period of five minutes on this task, five minute rest periods were too short for maximum gains, while intervals of forty-eight hours and over were too long. It seems that the most effective length of interval varies not only with the nature the learning task but also with the length of the practice period. Within limits, the longer practice period calls for longer rest periods.

Relationship Between Work and Rest Interval. Several studies are available regarding the interaction between work and rest periods of different length. Kimble and Bilodeau (1949) used four combinations of ten second and thirty second work periods with ten second and thirty second rest periods to determine which was the most important variable—work, rest, or interaction between the two. The task used 300 seconds total practice time on the Minnesota Rate of Manipulation Test, which requires the rapid turning and placing of circular blocks. The subjects were forty-eight men and forty-eight women evenly divided between the four groups. The groups with the shorter work period had the higher output, and the shortening of the work period rather than variations in rest period appeared to be the important variable. Interaction between the two was insignificant.

In a more elaborate experiment, Ammons (1947) utilized combinations of one-third, one, five, eight and seventeen minute work periods with one-third, two, five, ten, twenty, sixty, and 310 minute rest periods. All combinations of work and rest periods were followed by a continuous eight minute work period. Thirty-four groups with fourteen subjects in each practiced a rotary-pursuit task in which they were forced to work at a faster than normal rate. Ammons was interested in the rate at which work decrement occurred during the initial work period, was dissipated during the rest interval, and recurred during the post-rest continuous practice. On this task, the work decrement reached a maximum during the eight minute practice group, dissipated rapidly during the first two minutes of rest, reaching a maximum at twenty minutes. Five minute rest intervals appeared optimal for this task. Again the crucial factor was the length of the work period.

Theories Explaining Distributed Practice. Several explanations have been offered to account for the superiority of distributed practice: perseveration, fatigue, motivation, rehearsal, maturation, reactive inhibition, and differential forgetting. The perseveration theory assumes that neural processes continue for a time after the activity ceases, thus assisting in the fixation of responses. Fatigue and motivational explanations are allied in the assumption that continued work increases fatigue and decreases motivation, thus having a negative effect upon learning. In massed practice, both fatigue and decreases in motivation presumably would occur more rapidly. If no activity is introduced during the rest period, it is possible for subjects to rehearse the task implicitly, facilitating improvement of response.

Reactive inhibition is a term used to describe the tendency to avoid repetition of a response once given. The student will recall that Hull developed the concept of excitatory potential and inhibitory potential. Excitatory potential results from drive states and reinforcement. One of the factors in the inhibitory potential is reactive inhibition, a theoretical construct postulated to account for decrement in work resulting from a negative after-effect of responding. Reactive inhibition is believed to dissipate proportionally to the amount of time allowed for rest; this process would account for the improved performance observed in distributed practice when compared to massed practice.

The final theory proposed to account for the advantages of distributed practice is one of differential forgetting (Easley, 1937; McGeoch, 1942). According to this theory, we learn wrong responses as well as right responses during practice, but the wrong ones are not learned as well as the correct ones because the latter are more often reinforced. Since the wrong responses are not learned as well, they are forgotten more rapidly during the intervals of no practice. The rest periods between practice sessions afford an opportunity for the progressive elimination of incorrect responses.

The available evidence supports the reactive inhibition, the differential forgetting, and to some degree, the motivational explanations. Ammons' study, reported earlier, and a study by Kimble support the occurrence of a rapid increase in reactive inhibition early in practice. Kimble (1949) divided 474 subjects into eight groups, six experimental and two control, which were presented with an alphabet printing task in which the letters were printed upside down from right to left, so that when the work sheet was rotated 180 degrees the letters appeared in proper form. All groups had forty trials of twenty-nine seconds. One control had massed trials, the other had thirty second rest intervals between trials. The experimental groups had a single ten minute rest occurring after the fifth trial of the first group, after the tenth trial of the second group, and so forth. Each group showed a marked increase in performance after the rest, which was smaller for the groups in which the rest was longest postponed.

In an experiment similar in design to Kimble's (Wasserman, 1951), high and low motivated groups were added by inducing an ego oriented set in the former by the instructions given them and a task oriented set in the latter. The results which favored the highly motivated group supported the hypothesis that increases in motivation raise the critical level of reactive inhibition.

Hovland (1938, 1939, 1949) and Underwood (1951, 1952) have carried out a series of experiments designed to check the variables influential in the greater effectiveness of distributed practice. Hovland (1938) presented nonsense syllables at different rates, two seconds and four seconds and found distributed practice markedly superior at the faster rate of presentation. In analyzing the results, the advantage of distributed practice was more closely related to the amount of work—that is, the number of trials—than to the degree of learning. Perseveration, rehearsal, and fatigue could not be used to explain the differences. There was no reason to assume that perseveration is greater at a two second rate; color-naming during the rest period was used to prevent rehearsal; nor could fatigue be explained as occurring more rapidly.

The findings, which shed no light on motivational changes, support the reactive inhibition and differential forgetting theories. Hovland (1939, 1949) has shown that distributed practice is more effective in serial learning than in paired associates learning (less interference would be expected on the latter) and is more effective the faster the paired associates are presented. Underwood (1951) and Oseas and Underwood (1952) have tested the effectiveness of distributed practice on learning of concepts where massed practice would be anticipated as better and on learning of partially learned material where the advantage of distributed practice should be less. The experimental results were inconclusive.

From a theoretical viewpoint, motivation, reactive inhibition, and differential forgetting appear to have the greatest support in explaining the effectiveness of distributed practice, although it is more difficult to isolate motivational effects. Increased motivation and decreased reactive inhibition and differential forgetting during the rest periods operate to facilitate performance, if not the learning itself.

Reminiscence.   Retention curves for both verbal and motor learning sometimes show a temporary improvement in performance after practice has stopped. This phenomenon of an initial rise has been labelled *reminiscence,* although technically it is referred to as the *Ward-Hovland Phenomenon* (Ward, 1937; Hovland, 1938). It is usually observed within the first five to ten minutes but may be observed after several days. It is characteristically found with younger rather than older children and adults, and as a result some association with maturation was offered at one time as a possible explanation. Measurement of reminiscence is difficult, for it could be considered a fundamental learning phenomenon; explanation of it in terms of fatigue, motivation, and artifacts of measurement must be eliminated. These problems involve establishing control over:

1. *The effect of immediate recall.* The test of recall constitutes a trial which can produce learning. Hovland established a separate control group to assess the extent of learning at the end of practice.
2. *Rehearsal.* Subjects can voluntarily or involuntarily engage in practice during the rest interval. Again, Hovland controlled rehearsal by introducing an activity such as color naming to occupy the subjects during the rest period.
3. *Interference and positive transfer.* The rest period activity must be sufficiently dissimilar to not interfere with recall of the learned materials; similarly, the materials must be sufficiently novel to avoid transfer from the subject's previous learning.
4. *Motivation.* Subjects should be familiar with the pattern of the experiment in order to make the required shifts from practice to work period, rather than being set to recall after the last trial.

Reminiscence occurs where learning is incomplete. Where a criterion of mastery is used for performance, the ceiling has been reached; where little skill exists, improvement is improbable. Thus, the phenomenon occurs most frequently at intermediate levels of proficiency. Other factors affecting it are:

1. *Materials.* Reminiscence occurs with rote learning rather than with meaningful material and with serial learning rather than with paired associates. The longer the list, the greater the amount of reminiscence.
2. *Method of learning.* More reminiscence occurs with massed practice than with space and faster presentations. Blocks or groups of materials show more reminiscence than single lists.
3. *Individual differences.* Reminiscence is observed with both sexes, varied ages, and varied intelligence levels.

The best supported explanation for the Ward-Hovland Phenomenon is that inhibitory tendencies build up during practice, being higher the greater the amount of material or practice. These inhibitory tendencies dissipate rapidly, faster than forgetting proceeds, immediately following the end of practice, producing the temporary rise before the impact of progressive forgetting is seen. Thus, the change is one of performance, rather than learning. Physical education teachers will not find it difficult to conceive of a number of practical applications of these phenomena in elementary physical education programs and secondary junior varsity sports.

Educational Significance of Distributed Practice Experiments. From the foregoing studies, it appears that when the amount of work involved in a task is great, when the task is complex or not particularly meaningful, when the frequency of error responses is likely to be high, or when motivation is low or amount of effort required high, the practice sessions should be spaced with primary attention devoted to the length of the practice period rather than of the rest period.

In contrast, when the task is highly meaningful (Ash, 1950) or when learning presents the possibility of insight, when the material has been previously learned to a high degree of proficiency but during a prolonged intervening interval the forgetting has been great, when peak performance is required on tasks already well known, or when prolonged warm-up periods are necessary to becoming involved in the task, then massed practice periods are favorable.

New tasks generally should be introduced to school children in small quantities with short initial practice periods and short rest intervals; gradual lengthening of the practice period should follow. The fact that the length of the rest period is less important than the length of the work period permits teachers considerable flexibility in scheduling practice periods. For peak performance, massed practice on well learned material is usually desirable.

DEGREE OF LEARNING

Retention of learned materials is increased if practice continues beyond the point of the first errorless reproduction, for consistently higher degrees of retention have been shown for correspondingly higher degrees of learning. Overlearning works to reduce forgetting and undoubtedly accounts for the retention of skills in some degree after long periods of disuse. Recollection of college songs, game skills, poetry, and various motor skills, even after long periods without use, results from the fact that they were originally oft repeated well beyond the point of initial learning.

That overlearning improves retention for rote learning of meaningful words was demonstrated experimentally by Krueger (1929). The learning material consisted of lists of twelve one syllable nouns. The anticipation method of learning was used. Each list was considered learned to 100 percent when the subject could anticipate correctly all of the words during a single presentation. Two degrees of overlearning were employed. In one (50 percent overlearning), the lists were shown one and one-half times the number of presentations required for 100 percent learning. In the other (100 percent overlearning), the number of presentations was twice that required for 100 percent learning. Tests for retention were given after intervals of one, two, four, seven, fourteen, and twenty-eight days. Both the recall method and the relearning method were used for measuring retention. The scores indicated that the one day interval retention for 50 percent overlearning was about 50 percent better and that the longer the interval, the greater was the superiority of retention from the overlearning. The 100 percent overlearning brought higher test scores after each interval with both recall and relearning than were obtained from 50 percent overlearning, but the superiority of 100 percent overlearning over 50 percent overlearning was less than the superiority of 50 percent overlearning over initial learning. Thus, there appeared to be a diminishing advantage as the degree of overlearning was increased. This study indicates that overlearning, at least to the extent of 50 percent, increases retention, and that the longer the interval, the greater is its value. These findings are significant for memory drills and for all other cases where retention for a long period is desired. It should be noted, however, that to be effective, the repetitions beyond the threshold of recall require the same high degree of attention as those which precede the first perfect recital.

As might be anticipated following the discussion on retroactive effects, less interference or negative transfer accrues from material which is learned to a higher degree. As the amount of training increases, the amount of positive transfer tends to increase; this was revealed in the experiment by Bruce

(1933) involving nine relationships of similarity and identity between the training and test lists of paired nonsense syllable studies. When the training list was presented twice, there was negative transfer in six relationships. With six presentations of the training list, three of these negative cases shifted to positive transfer, and the amount of negative transfer was less for the remaining three. With twelve presentations, only two of the conditions showed negative transfer, and the amount was less in these cases than it was for six presentations. In the case of two conditions which showed positive transfer after two presentations, the amount of positive transfer was increased as the number of presentations was increased to six, and to twelve.

Other studies have shown negative transfer (interference) when the training was meager and positive transfer when it was more extensive. In the submerged target experiment by Hendrickson and Schroeder (1941), the explanations of light refraction differed in completeness for two experimental groups. The group that received the fuller explanation showed greater gains from transfer. These findings led to the definite conclusion that partial or superficial learning is more likely to interfere with other learning than is complete mastery and that for maximum returns in the way of positive transfer effects, thorough training is needed.

The studies on overlearning have one or two practical implications for educational practice. The first is the distinction between practice and drill. In the popular conception of the terms, there is little difference in meaning, except, perhaps, a different occasion for use. One practices the piano and drills in arithmetic, practice perhaps being done singly and drill in groups; but the meaning of both terms incorporates the repetition of given acts. Psychologists give a different meaning to practice which might be described as a condition of learning involving the repetition of an act as a means to a change (presumably improvement) of performance. This is quite different from repeating an act for purposes of fixing or stabilizing the performance. The student will recall that in the original discussion of the process of learning, two aspects were mentioned: the identification of the correct behavior and the subsequent stabilizing of the correct behavior. Practice is the condition under which one learns the correct response, and, as can be seen from the studies on distributed practice, it is desirable to provide situations in which variability of response, continued motivation, and differential forgetting are possible. Once material is correctly learned, drill or overlearning is desirable to stabilize the response. Premature drill produces greater negative transfer as well as stabilization of erroneous responses. The second implication is that drill is desirable, properly located in the learning cycle. In one sense, drill corresponds to massed practice, and consequently is desirable later in practice. It should be apparent also that prolonged drill has diminishing returns, for gains in retention are not proportional to increases in overlearning. In addition, they are likely to suffer from diminished motivation on the part of the learner.

RECITATION DURING LEARNING

It has been reliably demonstrated that reading combined with recitation is superior to reading alone for memorizing both meaningful and non-meaningful material. One of the most widely quoted studies on this subject was made by Gates (1917). He had children and college students memorize nonsense syllables and biographical material. The time devoted to study was divided for different groups so that different amounts were devoted respectively to reading and recitation. The material to be learned was printed on a sheet of paper. Each subject read this until he was given a signal to recite. Then he began reciting to himself and referred to the paper whenever necessary. It was found that for the nonsense material, the amount reproduced was much greater for reading with recitation than for reading alone, that the difference increased as the proportion of time devoted to recitation was increased, and that it was greater for delayed recall than for immediate recall. The difference was not so marked for the meaningful material, although it was sufficient to indicate the value of recitation in memorizing.

Similar results were obtained from a study on this problem by Forlano (1937). His subjects, children in the fifth and sixth grades, learned spelling, arithmetical facts, and vocabulary material under normal school conditions by the recitation method and by reading without recitation. The recitation method was found to be superior to the all-reading method in each of the experiments for both immediate and delayed recall. The superiority of the recitation method was generally greater for delayed recall than for immediate recall. In the case of spelling with one fifth and two fifths of the time devoted to recitation, the results were only slightly better than for reading only. But with three fifths of the time spent in recitation, the superiority over all-reading was significant and only slightly less than for putting in four fifths of the time reciting.

Granting the superiority of the recitation method over the all-reading method, Skaggs (1930) devised an experiment to discover the relative value of grouped and interspersed recitations. After two preliminary readings of a selection of poetry, his subjects—college students—tried four different procedures with regard to reading and recitation. According to the results of this experiment, it is better to have one recitation or attempted recitation after each reading than to have the readings and recitations grouped by twos or threes.

The practice of attempting to recall during the course of learning is conducive to an active attitude, vigorous effort, and concentrated attention; but perhaps the most important reason for its superiority over the all-reading method is that the individual actually practices what he is trying to learn. Just as we learn to write by writing, so to learn to recite, one should practice reciting. It gives the learner an immediate goal, shows him the progress he is making, and reveals the imperfections in his performance that need to be remedied. After a few readings, nearly everyone tries to test himself in some way. This was found to be more or less true in the experiments using the all-reading method.

A practical question arises about when the recitation process should be started. This naturally varies with different types and lengths of material. Except for every short selections, it will first be necessary to read the material through a few times without recitations. Four to eight times has been suggested as optimal for relatively short materials (Skaggs, et al., 1930). Recitation must not be guessing (Forlano and Hoffman, 1937).

It will probably be comforting to many teachers to know that the time-honored classroom procedure of assigning reading and hearing recitations is experimentally justified. Unfortunately, the typical procedure of serial classroom recitation in which students report one by one assumes that *hearing* recitation is as valuable as giving it. In view of conflicting motivations and varying levels of attention, this assumption is hardly tenable. Fortunately, recitation need not be oral to be effective. Spitzer (1939) investigated the effectiveness of the test reviews as a method of recitation. He divided 3600 children drawn from the sixth grade in nine Iowa cities into ten groups of approximately 400 each. Each group was tested at a different interval after initial learning—one, seven, fourteen, twenty-one, twenty-eight, and sixty-three days—on reading material about peanuts and bamboos designed to be relatively new, highly factual, authentic, and of adequate difficulty. Both articles were approximately 600 words in length. Twenty-five item tests having reliability coefficients of above .75 were used as measures. The results showed that review in the form of a test was an effective method of aiding retention and that it can serve as a learning device. It is possible for such a test to fix errors as well, and it was important that corrected tests be returned. The earlier the test was given after initial learning, the greater the review value. These findings were confirmed by Tidemann (1948), who advocated that review tests should be administered immediately after learning and at less frequent intervals as time elapses. He found more forgetting in one day when retention is not aided by review than is forgotten in sixty-three days when two intervening review tests were used as aids to retention.

Jones and Stroud (1940) checked the comparative effectiveness of both test review and reading review at intervals of 1 to 17 days and found that test review is most effective between one to three days but is progressively less effective the longer the interval of time. At intervals of fifteen and seventeen days, reading review was superior to test review. When one considers the form of the forgetting curve—with the initially sharper drop gradually leveling off—it is understandable that early test review permits recall when the amount retained is still comparatively great, but that after the major forgetting has occurred, the residue to be tested for is small. Reading serves to promote relearning, which of course progresses more rapidly than the initial learning. In 1951, the University of Michigan general psychology staff set up an experiment comparing recitation, discussion, and group tutorial teaching procedures (Guetzkov, Kelly, and McKeachie, 1954), in the teaching of general psychology. Two interesting outcomes are reported: higher achievement on the final examinations plus student preference for the recitation group method (weekly and semi-weekly quizzes), but more favorable attitudes and greater interest in majoring in psychology resulting from the other two methods. The higher achievement confirms Hunziker and Douglass' (1937) report two decades earlier, and like Douglass, Guetzkow, Kelly, and McKeachie attribute the results to greater student familiarity and comfort with a recitation procedure. It is also possible that limited teacher skill in other methods and practice effects on test taking have a bearing on the results.

More surprising are the age and the limited number of studies in support of an instructional method so common as to be considered traditional. While no attempt has been made to make an exhaustive survey, one would expect so thoroughly respected a procedure to be firmly based in research. In view of the reading problems, adjustment problems, school drop outs, rates of forgetting, and other educational dilemmas, one would have long since expected penetrating questions about instructional procedure. Fortunately, the winds of change and challenge blow more strongly, as we shall see in considering such developments as teaching machines and television in the next chapter.

Illustrative of the importance of written review is research by Allen (1957, 1960) on the effectiveness of student participation techniques during various forms of audio-visual presentations—films, film strips, film loops —on both verbal and motor learning. He comes to the general conclusions that:

1. Learner participation during a film showing will result in greatly increased learning from the film.
2. The overt verbalization of responses by the learner during the film increases learning.
3. The furnishing of knowledge of results during the film also aids learning.
4. If participation during a film requires the practice of a skill demonstrated, the taking of notes, or the performance of any other activity that may divide the attention between the observation of the film and the performance of the activity, the film must be paced slowly enough to eliminate the distraction caused by such a diversion of attention.
5. Mental practice of skills demonstrated, information communicated, or questions asked during or after a film showing will increase the learning under certain conditions.

The important consideration for educational practice is that written review can be effective and has the advantage of providing a group procedure which permits everybody in the class to review the material. The review need not be as formalized as a test, with possible negative affect on the part of the students, but may be incorporated into small group procedures in which pupils check one another, one pupil having the answers. Review may be in the form of simple recognition or recall, or it may involve higher levels of organization, depending upon the ingenuity of the teacher in developing her questions for review. This procedure can be especially valuable with pupils of below average ability, with whom Spitzer found the most rapid forgetting.

KNOWLEDGE OF RESULTS

At the heart of the traditional method of teaching insofar as its effectiveness is concerned is the provision of knowledge of results. At a minimum, the student gets a confirmation or not in the teacher's "correct" or "no, try again," and often some information in the form of cues regarding the nature of the error or the correct response. Unfortunately, the procedure is a ghastly waste of time, for the knowledge of results is beneficial only to the student reciting and to those of his classmates who are "with it," formulating answers on their part rather than waiting to respond and wondering what their question will be. For the same reason, most homework assignments are usually ineffective for want of knowledge of results at the time the work (the responses) is performed.

Studies of knowledge of results, or feedback as it is often called, show it to be *the most important variable* at the teacher's command for controlling performance and learning, certainly with perceptual motor and verbal learning, and probably conceptual learning. An experiment by Bilodeaus and Schumsky (1959) confirms in one study what has been demonstrated many times, *that there is no improvement without knowledge of results, there is progressive improvement with it, and deterioration after its withdrawal,* in this instance in reference to a lever positioning response. With certain behaviors, such as speech and tracking, performance is seriously disrupted by delays in feedback as short as one second.

Earlier in the chapter mention was made of an experiment, reported by Thorndike, in which the subject attempted 3000 times to draw a four inch line with his eyes closed. No improvement was made as a result of all these trials. But suppose the subject were informed after each trial about the magnitude of his error. This was demonstrated in an experiment carried out in the writer's laboratory with results shown in the table below. Group A_1 attempted to draw four inch lines (in blocks of 20 tries) with eyes closed, thus eliminating visual feedback and receiving no knowledge of the results from the experimenter. Their error was as great on the twentieth trial as on the first and remained at the same magnitude for the entire series. After each trial in the second series (A_2), the same students measured their line with a four inch rule, and the immediate improvement as a function of knowledge of results is shown in the table (figures represent errors expressed in one sixteenth of an inch; thus sixteen equals an error of one inch. Group B had only twenty trials (eyes closed), with the same visual feedback provided by a measure, and their performance parallels A_2. Group C made twenty attempts with eyes closed but were informed by the experimenter regarding the extent of their error. The auditory approaches but does not reach the same degree of improvement as visual feedback.

The mean error scores for the first, fifth, tenth, fifteenth, and twentieth trials in the four series were as follows:

| Group | A_1 | A_2 | B | C |
Feedback	None	Visual	Visual	Auditory
Number of subjects	7	7	14	15
Mean scores:				
1st trial	16	21	22	22
5th trial	16	3	6	7
10th trial	11	3	4	4
15th trial	13	5	3	5
20th trial	17	2	2	4

The results of this experiment were confirmed by Trowbridge and Cason (1932) with the additional observation that the degree of improvement was directly related to amount of information provided. The more specific the knowledge regarding the nature of the error, the greater the improvement (Bartlett, 1950).

The amount of information provided by knowledge of results can vary from low to high and vary in the combination of sensory modalities involved. The greater the amount of information received that is *specifically relevant to the performance desired,* the greater the improvement. A distinct shortcoming of most college courses is that the final examinations are seldom returned to students to provide them with essential knowledge of results regarding their performance. Gilbert (1956) carried out an experiment at the University of Nebraska in which the amount of information from examinations was varied. Four groups used a self-scoring device which informed them whether or not their examination response was correct, permitting them to vary their responses until obtaining a correct response. In effect, these groups received a right-wrong feedback with no further information. The time requirement of the device was such that in the same amount of time, the four comparison groups could complete the examination on standard answer sheets and have time available for discussion of the answers, hence receiving greater information. With gain as a criterion, these discussion groups received significantly higher scores. In a somewhat more systematic approach, Irion and Briggs (1957) used three procedures: a one-try with right-wrong feedback, a one-try followed by immediate identification of the correct answer, and the try-until-right method. Complete knowledge of results was superior, with the immediate identification of results slightly but not significantly superior than try-until-right in which full information is delayed by trial and error. Immediate information prevents practice on multiple errors and permits immediate implicit practice of the correct response. Such results may vary by age level and learning task, but evidence is needed. There is no question that feedback is crucial to communication between individuals; Leavitt and Mueller (1951) show its importance as an element in the learning situation between teachers and students, and Smith and Knight (1959) show it applies in behavior as complex as group problem solving and self-insight.

In many learning situations, particularly perceptual motor learning, knowledge of results is intrinsically linked to the responses. Tracking, handwriting, vehicle operation, speech, and other responses provide visual, auditory, or proprioceptive stimuli which provide immediate information regarding the appropriateness and accuracy of the responses. Often a combination exists, as we well realize on arising in the dark to journey to the bathroom. In many learning situations, progress is dependent upon some external display regulated by an instructor. The novice diver trying his first back dive, the young violin player struggling for tone control, the graduate student's research design, possibly even the solution to the married couple's quarrels, involve faults which are not easily apprehended. The error may involve failure to identify and respond to the correct signals, utilizing inappropriate responses, or generalizing incorrectly. An interesting illustration of such a complex situation is the use of films by professional football teams for knowledge of results and analysis of error. The information provides tangible evidence for analysis by the coach and greater refinement in judgment. An illustration of the opposite, which a government could ill afford, was the first Battle of Bull Run, in which both sides were temporarily defeated and accurate knowledge of results could have turned the outcome either way, before the arrival of southern reinforcements.

WHOLE AND PART LEARNING

When the vogue was rote learning the memorizing of facts whether of literature or life, a natural question was whether one should memorize by *parts* or by the *whole* method. By the whole method, one reads and re-reads the entire block of material to be learned, be it a list of terms in physiology or French, a selection of prose from Machiavelli or *Mad Magazine,* or a poem of Cummings or Chaucer. By the part method, one goes at it a section at a time, mastering that section before proceeding. As a natural consequence, the early studies use verbal and particularly memorizing tasks; more recently a noticeable shift to motor tasks has occurred from problems of attempting to train airmen in complex motor skills.

The early studies were equivocal; differences were observed, now in favor of the part method, now in favor of the whole method. For example, Jensen and Lemaire (1937), reporting on ten experiments, give the nod to the whole method in six instances. A closer look at the results shows that the superiority of one method or the other depended on less than half the students. Only 34 percent did better by one method or the other. To confuse methods, these children did not always do better by their habitual method. A child, left to his own choices, often fails to choose the more effective method. In view of the fact that effectiveness of method is affected by the complexity of the task, the previous experiences of the learner and his attitudes, such findings are not surprising.

Children are not alone in having difficulty making a choice of the preferable procedure. Knapp and Dixon (1952), expecting a combined method of part and whole to prove superior in learning to juggle three ping-pong balls, compared matched groups on whole, part, combined, and free choice method. Daily five minute practice sessions were given and time required to master the skill was the measure of performance used. For the part method, a rigid procedure involving practice on a progressive number of balls was used, while the whole method used all three from the beginning. In the other two groups, these methods were combined, as required and by choice. Contrary to expectations, the combined method proved second best to the whole method and free choice was worst of all, suggesting that instructors have something to contribute to learning.

The basic and essential advantage of the whole method is that it provides an overview of the total task or skill to be mastered. From the start, the items can be associated in proper relation to the total. It utilizes the consolidating values of meaning and this favors good retention.

First, the *character of the material* itself has much to do with the relative advantages of the part and whole methods. The superiority of the whole method depends largely upon how compact and meaningful a unit the entire selection is. If it is not too long and the material is closely knit together on one theme, the whole method will probably bring better results. Studies by Northway with school children, for example, indicated that for memorizing poems, the whole method is advantageous for poems understood as a whole (1937). When the parts themselves are more closely integrated than is the whole selection, we may expect the part method to be superior (Seagoe, 1936). Many skills combine a series of sub-component parts into a complex whole. Operation of an airplane combines both lateral and vertical dimensions of control; driving an automobile combines lateral control and velocity; a bicycle, lateral control, velocity, and balance.

The evidence suggests that with complex motor tasks, practice on the whole is preferable, providing greater transfer to the parts than the reverse, and that pure part approaches are less efficient (Briggs and Waters, 1958; Briggs and Brogden, 1954). Even simplified wholes facilitate learning more than a pure part approach.

The preferred organization of practice on parts and wholes will depend in large part on previous experience of the individual learner. Gross evidence can be found in cultural differences, e.g., foreign pilot trainees coming from non-mechanized cultural backgrounds score at levels of mechanical aptitude equivalent to American girls. Closer to home, age and skill differences will affect learning rates and integration of parts and wholes because of positive and negative transfer from prior learning (Welford, 1951).

There is no doubt that the *attitude* of the learner toward the whole method is an important factor in determining how well it works. Children often prefer the part method, and unpracticed adults are often skeptical of the advantages of the whole method. With the whole method, much more time and work are required before any results of learning are manifest. One may read a long poem through a dozen times without being able to recite a single line, while with the same amount of work by the part method the learner would probably be able to recite several stanzas. For this reason, a learner gets the feeling of success sooner with the part method. The recitations of parts become sub-goals, which provide a series of steps toward the main goal, the ability to recite the whole. These intermediate goals and the satisfactions derived from reaching them no doubt favor the part method, particularly with children and with adults unaccustomed to rote memory work. The whole method is likely to be discouraging because the learner has to work so long before he can see any returns for his effort.

SENSORY MODALITY

In his review of research on variables affecting the visual and auditory modalities, Lumsdaine (1963) summarized the situation by describing the problem as a complex one involving a number of variables, not the least of which is the interaction between the individual learner, his capacities and skills, and the task to be learned. Gollin and Baron (1954), searching for possible consistency in learning of perceptual and verbal tasks, found wide individual differences in response to differing perceptual situations. In teaching abstract science concepts to first graders, Wittrock (1963) showed that conditioning verbalization to the audio-visual stimuli used helped average children master the concepts but that it was not needed by superior children. At present, a definitive statement cannot be made in favor of any modality—although the immense sale of audio-visual equipment under the federal Elementary and Secondary School Education Act presumes an answer. The practical course for the best interests of all when dealing with a number of children is to use different modes of impression and procedures to bring different senses and various combinations of senses into play—a multi-modal approach. Adams and Chambers (1962) demonstrated visual and auditory stimuli are more effective than either alone in a tracking test. Yet such a generalization is too facile; aren't the various senses already operative in any learning situation? The task for research, and one which is being pursued, is to identify combinations or systems of presentation relative to given stimulus conditions.

The use of audio-visual materials in the classroom is justified on the basis of a multi-sensory approach, but the mere use of a multi-modal stimulus does not insure greater learning. An enthusiastic but naïve use of recordings and films, silent or sound, can produce as much confusion as learning. Extensive research completed during the past decade has demonstrated that audio-visual devices, television, and sound films can provide as much learning as a teacher using a variety of teaching techniques—e.g., lecture, discussion, and others—and further that an effective teaching film can surpass a poor teacher. A number of limitations to the use of films have been observed and bear repeating. The influence is greatest when the film content reinforces and extends previous knowledge and attitudes. It has the least influence, particularly upon attitudes, when previous knowledge is inadequate or when content is antagonistic to prevailing attitudes. Films are most effective where the skill or knowledge concerned is specific rather than general. Variations in audience reactions which are functions of age, intelligence, education, sex, and attitude influence the nature of the learning that occurs, particularly if the film content is general. For audio-visual aids to be most effective, they should be supplemented by desirable conditions of learning: appropriate set, opportunity for recitation and review, examination, knowledge of results, and so on. More detailed consideration of these media is presented in the following chapter.

SET

The intent to learn is an important factor for successful learning. While it is true that associations are formed in many cases without intent to learn, little progress in the school situation may be expected from mere exposure to material. A teacher may read a poem to children several times for the purpose of having them learn it verbatim and find that he cannot recite it himself after the children are able to do so.

The influence of the learner's goal set on his learning has been demonstrated in an experiment previously referred to. A series of ten cards, each bearing a word and a number, was presented eight times to a group of ten students. Below the number on each card was a strip of colored paper, the color being different for each card. As the cards were presented, the students were instructed to observe carefully the word on each card and the number appearing with it, so that they would be able to reproduce the words together with the correct number for each. Nothing was said about the colors. Following each presentation of all ten cards, the students were asked to write down as many of the word-number pairs as they could recall. After the series had been presented eight times, they were asked to name the color which was presented with each word. The means of the reproductions for the eight trials were as follows:

Trials:	1	2	3	4	5	6	7	8
Word-number pairs	3.7	5.6	7.0	7.2	8.3	8.7	8.8	9.7
Word-color pairs	—	—	—	—	—	—	—	2.9

It will be seen that more word-number pairs were recalled after a single presentation than word-color pairs after eight presentations. After the eighth presentation, all but one of the group gave correctly all ten word-number pairs. The one who had not reached complete learning reproduced seven correctly. Yet the mean number of word-color pairs reproduced was only 2.9. When allowance for successful guessing is made, it is evident that there was very little learning of the word-color combinations.

The set illustrated in the word-color task is a *perceptual set,* a specific predisposition to respond in a given way, in this instance because of the instruction provided. In a more general form, attitudes are predispositions to respond on a more general scale to a class of objects—we may be prejudiced, dislike school, be eager for sports, set to respond in more general fashion. In manuals describing appropriate use of films, a common recommendation is to provide the audience with a film guide, or at a minimum, to identify key items to be seen. Such instructions create a perceptual set found valuable, particularly with younger children, in increasing the effectiveness of film presentations. Prestidigitators and magicians use perceptual sets efficiently to distract the audience from their crucial maneuvers. A second kind of set is an *operational set,* a predisposition to perform certain operations under given conditions. For example, insert the next number in the following sequence:

$$1 \quad 2 \quad 3 \quad 4 \quad 5 \quad 6 \quad 7 \quad 8$$

In all probability you inserted a 9 because of the well established habit associated with the sequence of numbers. The correct response is 100.[1] In an early experiment on problem solving, Maier (1931) presented his subjects

---

[1] 22 has been added to the original number (12) and successively added to each result.

(college students) with the task of tying together two strings which were suspended from the ceiling at such a distance that it was impossible to reach the two simultaneously. The only available tool was a pair of pliers. The solution was simple (once known): tie the pliers to one of the strings, start it swinging like a pendulum, and catch it while holding onto the second string. Yet the typical uses of pliers created an operational set which blocked solution for a number of the students.

Earlier, in Chapter 6, Ausubel's work on the use of advance organizers was discussed in facilitating learning. In a follow-up study, Wittrock (1963), believing that more was involved than selecting and mobilizing the most relevant concepts of the learner, gave his subjects the same passage on Buddhism to study but without the advance organizer comparing Buddhism and Christianity. Instead, three of his four groups were given instructions (1) to note similarities between the two religions, (2) to note differences, and group (3) to note both. The fourth group had straightforward instructions to remember the content. Two of the groups (2, 3) proved superior both on immediate learning and retention after three weeks, supporting Wittrock's contention that advance organizers create sets as well as help organize.

Operational sets may relate to the functional use perceived for given tools, objects, or equipment; they may consist of certain modes of attack on problem situations (there are the jig-saw puzzle fans who start with the edge pieces, those who first assemble colors, those who begin randomly to fit pieces together on the basis of form, and those who don't even bother to look at the picture); or they may be sets to attend to certain stimuli and ignore others. Irion (1948, 1949) contends that the forgetting which occurs in retroactive inhibition experiments with the control group which has the rest period is illusory, and that what occurs rather, is a dissipation in set which is not restored until the retention trial is underway. By providing a warm-up experience on a related activity, he showed that retention was greater than anticipated.

Sets are established in several ways. Familiarity and accustomed usage, as with the pliers in Maier's experiment, is one means. Yet, to watch a young child or a rhesus monkey explore and manipulate a tool or gadget leads one to realize that some unconventional uses exist. Another source of set is partial success in some operation. A not uncommon set is whether or not one pumps the gas throttle in starting the automobile on a cold morning. If a few pumps seem to be working, pumping will continue, often to the point of flooding the motor. In an anagrams puzzle situation, Adamson (1959) was more systematic in manipulating the zero, partial, and complete success frequency and observed that partial success created a set which was more resistant to extinction than complete success. Most significant is the fact that instruction can create and maintain sets. At a minimum, *attention* is needed, and this is not always easily obtained. Vivid and novel impressions have strong memory value, probably because of heightened attention. More than attention or a set to work is needed, as Ausubel and Wittrock show. There must be attention to the relevant stimuli and the significant aspects of the responses. In complex learning situations, this is a vital instructional function, for appropriate sets are significant in the acquisition phase more than in the retention. Admonishments to "be sure to remember" seem to have little effectiveness (Ausubel, *et al.,* 1957).

GUIDANCE AND CUES IN LEARNING

There is a real art in knowing when to step in and give instruction and guidance and when to let the learner practice on his own. Errors are unavoidable in the course of learning and they are helpful as long as they contribute to a knowledge of the appropriate actions. In fact, an unfortunate effect of instructional practice is the feeling on the part of the children that errors per se are bad, with the consequent reluctance to try for fear of making errors. Sufficient evidence is available to provide definite guidelines regarding when and how much to prompt the learner. Carr (1930) and his students investigated the question of guidance with respect to motor learning, using both animal and human subjects. Carr's results showed that guidance given in small amounts early in practice was beneficial but that if it was deferred, its effectiveness decreased the farther it occurred from initial practice. Two to four guided trials in maze learning were sufficient. More guidance impeded learning. The evidence suggests that if a learner is to acquire a skill, he must perform the required tasks with limited amounts of outside help. The findings undoubtedly apply as much to parents and assistance with homework as they do to teachers.

The available evidence suggests that the same generalizations apply to learning which involves higher mental processes (Swenson, 1949; Stacey, 1949). Stacey distributed 100 sixth grade pupils into five equated groups and presented them with learning material consisting of fifty items in which one of the five words composing each item did not belong with the other four. The five groups were given different amounts of information regarding the task ranging from the brief instruction that one of the words did not belong with the others up to being told what the word was and the basis or principle as to why it did not belong with the other four. The latter group, the most informed, had the greatest opportunity to practice without error, the opposite being true of the group given the least information. Stacey concluded from his results that the process of active participation involved in self-discovery made for more effective learning than a process which involves mere identification of information previously given. Although the least informed group made a greater number of errors in the process of discovery, their errors were eliminated more quickly and with less detrimental effect than those of the highly informed group, which tended to perseverate in their errors once made.

Such findings suggest that guidance plays a less important role in learning than does knowledge of results and that too much and too late guidance can have a detrimental effect. It should be pointed out, however, that the subjects in these experiments had knowledge of what the task or goal was which served to direct their behavior. It is very likely that guidance is effective in the degree to which it helps establish the appropriate sets.

A possible qualification to the preceding generalizations regarding guidance is suggested in a study of Maier and Klee (1945). In studies concerned with the effectiveness of trial-and-error and guidance in changing fixated behavior which the animal was unable to modify even though aware of the correct response to be made, Maier and Klee came to the conclusion that trial-and-error procedures are more effective in learning new responses and that guidance was effective in breaking old, fixated responses but ineffective in the learning of new responses. Guidance should be discontinued as soon as the old response is broken, i.e., when the new adjustment has been successfully made. Undoubtedly, the limited effectiveness of guidance is related to the problems in complex learning of discriminating between relevant and irrelevant cues and external and internal stimuli—external physical environment, posture, self-instruction, and the like—all of which are part of the stimulating conditions during learning.

Three studies which provide information regarding effective guidance of learning are Arrow's (1958), Kimble and Wulff's (1961), and Maccoby and Sheffield's (1958). Arrow was interested in what he termed "consistent" and "inconsistent" guidance. The task for eighty-eight college students was to guide a stylus through a maze without error. The control group was self-instructed in that they received no information from the experimenter. One of the two experimental groups received a confirming signal (green light) for every correct turn, the second group were given incorrect information at 30 percent of the choice points. The results in terms of time, number of trials, and number of errors are shown for the original learning and for transfer to a second maze.

		Learning Maze Mean Scores			Transfer Maze Mean Scores	
	Time	Trials	Errors	Time	Errors
Group 1	7+ min.	16	52	6	48
Group 2	11 min.	33	86	11	109
Control	9 min.	19	56	7	57

Performance of the guided and self-instructed groups are similar, with a small advantage to the former. Group 2, misled by inconsistent information, produced the worst performance, showing in addition signs of confusion and frustration. A few in the group ignored the faulty confirmations they were receiving and performed as well as control subjects. The inference of the research is that guidance or prompting has to be accurate and consistent to be effective.

Kimble and Wulff used a combination of film strips and work books to teach the use of the slide rule. Short visual presentations were alternated with short work segments. Various kinds of cues were provided in the practice segments to narrow the range of response possible on the problems. The control group worked the problems without cues. Not only was learning superior with the experimental subjects, they showed greater facility on more difficult items and greater transfer of training to similar tasks. Thus, another function of guidance is to reduce the probability of frequency and kind of error. In the Maccoby–Sheffield experiment, they demonstrated that when a complex task (assembly of an ignition distributor) was subdivided into suitable steps (difficulty was such that 75 percent could not perform it following demonstration), the best results occurred when practice followed immediately after a segment, rather than after demonstration of the total operation (combined segments) or after a progressive sequence of shifting to larger segments. In other circumstances, the latter procedure has proved effective. The results indicate the importance of proper timing of guidance. Like knowledge of results, delays in time make guidance less effective.

The entire issue of the value of error in learning, its appropriate proportion and place, is very much a live issue in instruction, particularly in programmed instruction. No simple solution is likely to ensue, one principle which relates both to the kind of learning and the criterion of learning adopted, e.g., efficiency of acquisition, retention, transfer, and so forth. A suggestion is found in an experiment by Wittrock (1963) on an abstract task of deciphering codes. Greatest prompting was provided by giving both rules and solutions, least by giving neither. Intermediate guidance, which consisted of giving one or the other to the 292 college students participating, produced the greatest retention and transfer, but maximum guidance yielded greatest initial learning.

PROVIDING GUIDANCE DURING INSTRUCTION

Careful analysis of any given skill is needed in order to contrive learning exercises which yield the development of the desired skill with minimal efforts. Several steps should be followed in guiding learning activities:

1. Analyze the skill. What are the desired terminal behaviors? What are the sub-components?
2. Demonstrate the skill by part or whole.

3. Guide initial responses.
4. Provide appropriate exercises.
5. Provide knowledge of results, preferably intrinsically.
6. Help the learner evaluate performance.

Analyze the Skill.   It is essential that the instructor clarify his understanding of the task so that he can teach the component parts in the simplest fashion possible. Confusion is the result when an amateur dance instructor begins with, "You start off with your weight on your right foot; step forward with your right foot; no, that is wrong, your weight is on both feet." The results of such analysis can be conveyed to the learner in the form of exercises and demonstrations. Several years back, it was common practice in skiing to instruct the learner on the various weight and balance shifts occurring in a given turn: "As you are traversing the slope, your skis are parallel, slightly more weight on the downhill ski. As you approach the turn, put your weight on your downhill ski; counter-rotate your shoulders and hips; stem one ski; release the edges of your skis by leaning down the fall-line. As your skis come into the fall-line, rotate hips and shoulders and shift weight to the downhill ski as you complete the turn." A novice has difficulty merely recalling the sequence of events, much less executing them, and his perception of movements is sufficiently delayed that the action gets away from him.

Today the same instruction would begin by dividing the sequence into a series of component parts, each of which is an integrated unit, not a meaningless fraction, and devising an exercise which demonstrates the movement. For instance, the first step would be to have the student traverse a gentle slope, skis together, repeatedly lifting his uphill ski slightly and replacing. One cannot lift the uphill ski until weight is on the downhill. The next step in the sequence is to instruct the student to raise the uphill ski as he has been doing, then step out on it, and lean down as if to pick up a bucket. This maneuver provides the stemmed ski and the shift in weight needed to produce a turn.

Demonstrate the Skill.   Although little attention is paid to imitation in formal discussion of learning, it serves many purposes which go unrecognized, particularly in motor learning. The skill has to be demonstrated in the way it will be perceived by the student. An instructor who has his students facing him is providing them with a reversed demonstration. For instance, training in the assembly of a piece of equipment or the operation of a machine is more effective if the learners are behind the instructor rather than surrounding him in a circle. The mere presence of the model isn't sufficient: it must be a model who demonstrates clearly what to do. The effectiveness of filmed demonstrations and closed-circuit television in medical schools is ample testimony to the value of demonstration. Ample research evidence exists to support the empirical demonstrations of such techniques as surgical operations to demonstrate the value of the enlarged visual image provided by film, not only for demonstrations of technique but also of general principles.

Imitation provides a major avenue through which children learn motor skills, acquire language patterns, gestures, attitudes, and a wide variety of social behaviors. There is no question regarding the role that imitation and, reciprocally, demonstration plays in learning. In fact, the educational value of the so-called educational toys which are replicas of household equipment find their educational value in the presence of a model who provides repeated demonstrations. Nash (1958) has reported how the complex skill of operating a cotton textile machine is taught the young Cantelense in Guatemala entirely by demonstration. The apprentice stands by the machine and observes the operator perform the series of responses required to operate the machine. The training proceeds entirely by demonstration and observation, without any instructions, questions, or opportunities to practice. When the apprentice thinks she has mastered the procedure, the machine is turned over to her, usually with successful results.

Guide Initial Responses.   Many skills have two component parts, a motor part and a perceptual part. Dancing, skiing, running have high motor components but low perceptual components. The cues to performance are kinesthetic and have to be sensed internally. Learning follows a course of gradual approximation and refinement of the correct response. Verbal instruction is easily overdone and confusing because of its failure to call attention to the correct cues for judging and correcting performance. The child learning to row a boat for the first time and keep it going in a straight line will become quickly confused and discouraged by a series of verbal commands attempting to correct the veering: "You're going in a curve!, pull harder on the right oar!, you pulled too hard, now pull on the left oar; don't put your left oar so deep into the water," and so forth. A much more meaningful instruction would be: "You turn by pulling on one oar alone. To go straight, sit in the middle of the seat and pull with both arms. Try to keep your hands together when you pull and the oarblades against the water." Manual guidance can be of assistance where the pattern of movement is not clear, but the fact that learning a motor skill requires voluntary control of movements regulated by the central nervous system places definite limits on its value. Reading, speaking, and map reading are skills with high perceptual and low motor components. Verbal guidance can be valuable, but it should be positive and focus on the appropriate cues. The learner should be told what *to* do rather than what *not* to do, by concentrating on the goal to be achieved.

Provide Appropriate Exercises.   The analysis made by the teacher should lead to the development of exercises which foster the sub-skills needed. A vivid memory of superb teaching is that of a French phonetician instructing a group of men for an hour at a driving pace on the distinction in the pronunciation of two sounds, the vowel sounds in *je* and *j'ai*. The task is seemingly such a simple discrimination that it would seem impossible and unnecessary to hold a group of adults, even though novices, at the task for that length of time. Making the demonstration more intriguing was the fact that the group of fifteen men were from a dozen different countries in Asia, Africa, and the Americas. The exercises proceeded through a series of simple repetitions of single sounds which the teacher corrected man by man, then of combinations of the two vowel sounds with the same consonant, then through a series of progressively longer and more intricate combinations of consonant and vowel sounds requiring finer discriminations, both in listening and speaking, in order to accurately distinguish the intended meaning. With an ear as acute as a symphony conductor's for a false note, she would detect faults in pronunciation, locate the erring member, and then work with him quickly on a particular combination. Her talent was such that she was able to provide special drills for particular errors according to one's country. For example, the North American, the South American, and the Japanese have different difficulties in learning to pronounce the French "r," because in each of their native languages the closest native sound is created differently.

Provide Knowledge of Results.   An effective guide to improved performance is to have knowledge of the results of any response. In perceptual motor learning, the outcome is an inherent part of most situations and automatically yields feedback on results. The pilot landing a plane is aware of an angle of approach that is too steep, even before the jar of the wheels on the ground. The overstroked tennis drive on its way out-of-bounds is sensed immediately. In other forms of learning, performance is not as readily judged. The pronunciation of sounds in a foreign language depends not only upon vocal mechanisms but upon auditory discrimination. A faultily produced sound or word may sound correct because of the lack of fine auditory discrimination. In cognitive learning, errors are still more difficult to perceive. Nevertheless, improvement requires knowledge of results.

INCENTIVES

Games of chance and gambling are among the oldest of human diversions and not the least popular, judging by the stack of games on Christmas store counters, the college bridge players, and the ticket sales of the Irish Sweepstakes. Some $15 billion changes hands legally in the United States each year, and estimates indicate another $60 billion illegally, as much as one dollar of every ten in the national income. To be sure, the same dollar may change hands more than once, so that all of the good citizens may not be participants, yet all of the good citizens have been participants, having participated in some game of chance, with or without a wager. And probably nearly all have stated at some time or another: I'll bet you. And at some time, most have backed some bet with a nickel or better.

Now a wager is an event with a definite pay-off—one loses, one wins; one is punished or rewarded. Thus, the consequences are definite. On turning to the behavior of adults—some gamble, some do not; the question of the functional relationship between punishments and rewards, between present behavior and historical antecedents naturally arises. Some of the aversion to gambling may stem from external as well as natural consequences of wagering—parents and preachers make punishment the wages of sin, but as much may arise from the frequency and magnitude of the rewards and punishment experienced.

A slot machine parlor (?—one searches for an appropriate term) is an interesting location for observing human behavior, probably the nearest equivalent to a human Skinner box (with the exception that entrance and exit are voluntary). Unlike many of the more lavish arrangements for gambling provided by Reno and Las Vegas, the SMP is devoid of embellishments. Rows of slot machines, graduated by degrees of punishment (dime, quarter, dollar) stand back to back with barely enough space for the human operators to pull the levers without bumping. The doors, if they exist, are open to the street, the climate itself providing natural optimal working conditions. The initial behavior of those entering will vary considerably, an obvious result of their previous experience—familiarity with the environment, experience at wagering, and motivation. But look only at the naïve subjects: some will enter, stand, look about, and leave without risking a coin; another will enter, look about, saying: "I'll try it once and see what happens." A less cautious person but one with good impulse control will say: "I'll play five dollars and win or lose, I'll leave." Then, there is the plunger who walks up to the one-armed bandit saying: "Let's see what happens," or, "I'll bet I'll be lucky."

Casino operators learned long ago what Humphreys demonstrated experimentally in 1939, that partial reinforcement is more powerful than total reinforcement, i.e., we persist longer at behavior rewarded occasionally than behavior rewarded every time. As a result the behavior of the participants will change as a result of what occurs while they engage in their pastime. Even the person who only entered and looked may find his resolve or his fear weakened by what he observes: many do it, they seem to win (the seem-to-win observation is biased because his attention is attracted to the clatter of coins being received by the winners while he overlooks the moment of silence following three lemons). Among the participants, the changes will be observable. Rare is the man who stays with his initial intention of five dollars only, unless he is unfortunate enough (casino operators set the reward level to discourage such discouragement) to lose it without return or with returns which are negligible. Particularly those who enter with an open mind (and leave with an open wallet) tend to show noticeable shifts in behavior—in terms of effort (money used), rate of responding (frequency and speed of pulling levers), and emotional responses (of pleasure or disappointment, often largely suppressed because of the protocol of the poker-face).

If the digression seems lengthy, it is short in comparison to the years spent in that "parlor of learning," the classroom. And in this Skinner box, because of compulsory school laws which even the Amish find implacable, the only escape comes with age, fantasy, or passive avoidance.[2] Like all analogies, this one has its limits, because schools offer a great variety of rewards from learning, mastery, friendships, whereas slot machines are a solitary and disappointing pursuit. Nevertheless, in the matter of incentives, the analogy has merit, for the teacher like the casino operator wants to keep the players working. She is the regulator of rewards, at least some of them, for peer groups and parents enter the equation. Her management of incentives will shape the *behavior* and in turn, the *motives* of the students. Some will become addicted to learning, discovering Dionysian delights in the activity, others will want out, acquiring strong aversion to intellectuals and their activities. These effects are important to the teacher because her professional motivation, unlike that of the casino operator, is to develop talents, not exhaust resources.

Before discussing the effects of incentives, a distinction between incentives and motives is needed. In Chapter 5, the development of motivation and the acquisition of social motives were described briefly. Motives are those *internal states* or conditions which cause an individual to seek particular goals. Motives and goals, as well as the appropriate behavior for reaching the goals, are established and modified as a result of learning.

Incentives are those objects, situations, or events, external to the individual, capable of satisfying a motive. In many instances, goals and incentive are identical; in some they are not. The differences in the two situations are of especial interest. An incentive may be objectively described; a goal can be defined only in terms of the motive conditions and as such is more speculative. More important, the incentive which an individual seeks may not be the goal. We commonly strive for money—a few persons for the sake of the money itself, but most for different reasons—to provide economic security, to satisfy various appetites for a new automobile or boat, or to achieve the prestige of being wealthy. Money may be an incentive sought by many, but their motives for seeking it, the why of seeking it, and thus their goals may be quite different. A pupil in a class may strive for a perfect mark in an arithmetic or spelling lesson not because that is his goal, but because it may symbolize teacher approval, which is what he

[2] Graduation is considered success behavior rather than escape behavior.

basically desires; or, he may wish to avoid parental criticism for less than perfect work. The incentive of the perfect paper is not his goal.

It is also possible for the incentive to be synonymous with the goal. A youngster may work hard sanding, glueing, and painting a model airplane for the sole satisfaction he derives from the completed model. The distinction that has been made between incentives and goals is an important one for the teacher because she manipulates incentives—praise and blame, reward and punishment, sarcasm and ridicule, gold stars and grades, competition and cooperation. Not infrequently, these incentives are manipulated in ways which *satisfy the teacher's motivation* by the results which are produced. A junior high school teacher who sarcastically ridiculed individual pupils in her English class was thought to be very humorous by her students—until one by one nearly all of them became the butt of her ridicule. The few who escaped still thought her humorous, but most of the others developed a strong dislike for the teacher because her approach conflicted with their personal motivation.

We are so habituated to marking and grading, rewarding and punishing, testing and measuring that we think the entire learning enterprise would end abruptly were we to dispense with them. Not to use them would be to fail as educators. The entrenchment of this concept in educational thinking was observed recently in conjunction with a project of the Massachusetts Council for Public Schools for providing foreign language instruction via television—*Parlons Français*—to the 150 school systems participating in The 21″ Classrooms' in-school television broadcasts. Two fifteen minute programs per week are provided children in the intermediate grades to which are added two fifteen minute practice sessions by the classroom teacher. Where administrative support and teacher enthusiasm are high, the children show considerable progress in learning to speak French. The learning that occurs is self-evident and is further corroborated by end-of-year tests (Garry, 1964). In instituting the program of instruction, the teachers were encouraged not to concern themselves with grading or evaluation, in the knowledge that the direct satisfaction of learning to speak a foreign language would be satisfying and motivating to the children.

One need not administer tests to determine if an instructional program in foreign language is going well. If the only time the children engage in a second language is during the practice sessions, if they make no spontaneous use of it and cannot respond to simple questions or directions, they are not learning a language. If during practice sessions the teacher does most of the talking, the children speak haltingly or not at all, the practice consists mainly of games, songs, and mimicking, then the instructional program is inadequate. Yet such observational evidence did not satisfy many administrators and teachers. They believed that if they didn't test and didn't grade, the instructional program was not educationally respectable. They gauged their effectiveness by the procedures being used rather than by the performance of the children and the satisfactions found in learning and mastering a second language.

Incentive conditions are only one of many factors affecting the motivational climate of a classroom. When young children enter school, their needs for approval of adults and for maintaining and developing their self-esteem are quite strong. Their approach to school is a mixture of obedience, curiosity, fear, anticipation, and uncertainty. Gradually, if conditions are favorable, they develop desires to master the tasks which confront them and the confidence that they can do it. They also develop an awareness of the emerging peer group and a desire for a place in it and approval from it. Research increasingly supports the principle that the learning that occurs in any classroom is functionally related to the kind of personal relationships existing between teacher and pupils and between pupils themselves. One's basic needs for self-esteem, recognition, and acceptance find their satisfaction in this matrix of interpersonal relationships, and in comparison to self-acceptance, teacher acceptance, and group acceptance, the specific incentive conditions used are of secondary importance. Part of their importance hinges on what they signify about the teacher-pupil relationship. If they are low pressure, work-centered, and related to information about progress, they are useful; but if they are high pressure, personal, and competitive, they are partially self-defeating for they prove effective only with those children who can and will respond to such conditions.

Incentives may be classified into two kinds: *intrinsic* and *extrinsic*. Intrinsic incentives are those which operate to functionally relate the task and the goal. Extrinsic incentives are those which have no functional relationship to the task. Taking again the arithmetic or spelling lesson, successfully spelling words which had been previously missed, indicating improvement, or correctly answering all the arithmetic examples are satisfying ends in themselves and are functionally related to the task being performed. Having a teacher put a gold star on the paper or receiving a grade of A at report time has only an arbitrarily established artificial relationship and as such is an extrinsic incentive.

Calling grades artificially related to learning tasks may be a surprise. Ask yourself for a moment what C means. Your answer is probably that it is average. Investigate the meaning of the letter "C" in a dictionary; no connotation of average is given. At best, the dictionary will say that it may be used as a symbol to arbitrarily designate a class or group, usually third in order. For the moment, let us accept the meaning of average and ask, "Average in what? In relation to a particular group of students? But are they capable students?" If so, the average is different than if they are retarded. The symbol as used is not only artificial, but relatively meaningless. A teacher might as well give a ten-penny nail for average work and a 20-penny nail for superior work. In either situation, it is by the authority of the teacher that a given symbol is chosen; some prefer cowboy stickers or flowers to gold stars. To know the meaning of the symbol requires knowl-edge of the teachers' standards, which vary considerably. The author has met three teachers who would not give any A's, the first because she couldn't stand to give F's and wanted to be "fair," the second because she thought only God was perfection, and the third because he didn't want any pupil to think he was really that good.

In considering the effect of various incentives, it is well to keep in mind that many at the disposal of the teacher are extrinsic—rewards, punishment, praise, and so on. We use them because many of the learning tasks we present to children provide no intrinsic satisfaction, at least in initial stages. We use these incentives because they work; but invariably we use them badly.

Rewards and Punishment.   Reinforcement is one of the cornerstones of learning. Hedonistic explanations of learning have a long history cul-minating in Thorndike's law of effect and Hull's theory of primary and sec-ondary reinforcement. In effect, satisfying outcomes reinforce the behavior which leads to the reward because of the reduction in drive which the re-ward provides. Whether the explanation lies in the reduction of drive, or in a change in the stimulus conditions associated with the termination of behavior, or in an increment to the probability of a repetition of the be-havior, as the more sophisticated applications of modern statistical learning theory suggests (Estes, 1959), reward and reinforcement have both a theo-retical and practical role in learning. Regardless of theoretical explanation, it is essential that reward be linked with the kind of behavior desired. If quality of work is important, then this is what has to be rewarded, not punctuality, attitude, or some other characteristic. The specificity indicated lends added support to the earlier discussion of the general motivational conditions. This can be illustrated by the manner in which students vary their preparation for an examination, depending upon the type of examina-tion being given. The student adopts the study technique most likely to yield the favorable mark contingent upon high examination score. The variety of ways in which satisfaction of the interpersonal[3] motives of desire for recognition, approval, and acceptance can be provided in the elementary and secondary schools offers the teacher a range of procedures varying from smiles to grades.

Three aspects of reinforcement are important: speed, magnitude, and frequency. A firmly established fact with mice and men is that rewards and punishments, to be effective in shaping behavior, should follow quickly on the heels of the behavior (Estes, 1956). This is especially true with children, who have yet to develop mediating behaviors which in a sense are self-informative and support continued effort to achieve deferred goals.

[3] Interpersonal in the sense that their satisfaction is contingent upon favorable response by another person.

Sheer quantity of reward is less significant as long as it is sufficient to be accepted as existing. Established expectancies affect thresholds, i.e., a child accustomed to candy bars will sniff at M & M's. Given the discrete nature of most classes and classrooms, one teacher's molehill can be another teacher's mountain, i.e., students will work as hard for a grudging "Well done" from one teacher as for a second's effusive "How marvelous!" But within a given situation, variations in magnitude of rewards will count (Spence, 1956). Students can discriminate those behaviors which are more highly rewarded and take their cues accordingly. Hence, if enthusiasm for impressionistic paintings is what sends the art teacher, the students won't talk up Jackson Pollack. Finally, the frequency of reinforcement is probably the most significant of the three. Skinner (1938, 1953, 1968) and his students have studied the effects of different ratios of reinforcement upon behavior with pigeons and rats, more recently extending the research to human subjects. The results of his research are dramatic and relevant to human behavior, as is testified by the current enthusiasm for the application of operant conditioning to modifying human behavior.

Skinner's work could readily have been considered with other learning theorists, however he considers himself an empiricist rather than a theorist; and because his research has such relevance to teaching practices, it is better considered here.

The distinction between classical conditioning and operant conditioning was described in Chapter 2. Skinner has pursued the study of operant behavior, the effects of different reinforcement schedules, and the implication of his discoveries for the shaping and modification of human behavior. Reinforcement schedules fall into two main types: (1) non-intermittent and (2) intermittent. Skinner has extensively studied various arrangements of intermittent reinforcement.

   I. Non-intermittent schedules
      a. Continuous—Every response is reinforced
      b. Extinction—No response is reinforced

  II. Intermittent schedules
      a. Fixed interval—The first response after a specified time interval is rewarded. If one minute intervals are established, the first response following each elapsed minute will receive a reward.
      b. Fixed ratio—Reinforcement occurs after a specified number of responses, e.g., every tenth or every one hundredth.
      c. Variable interval—A response will be rewarded on the average of every five minutes or other arbitrarily determined mean, but the actual interval between reinforcements may vary between a few seconds and many minutes.

    d. Variable ratio—On the average, every tenth, twentieth, or other frequence of response will be rewarded, but the actual reinforcement will fluctuate within predetermined limits.

The basic schedules have also been combined in varying patterns with the interesting result that the organism learns to recognize and respond to the differences in patterns. For example, under a mixed schedule, a pigeon will run off a large number of responses, running past the point where reinforcement would have occurred on a fixed interval schedule. Failing to receive reinforcement in ratio to the number of responses given, the organism stops responding, then gradually picks up as the interval end approaches. Secondly, organisms will shift patterns of responses in association with the discrimination of specified stimuli. Thus, they will respond one way to a black disc, another to a white disc, and still another to a red disc.

When reinforcements are given at regular intervals (fixed interval reinforcement), a fixed rate of responding develops which is low just after reinforcement, gradually increasing as the interval passes, reaching a peak rate just prior to the end of the interval and reinforcement—not unlike the behavior of children just prior to report cards. When fixed ratio schedules are in force, output is high though not uniform, with the curious occurrence that the less frequent the reinforcement, the higher the rates of responding. However, this state of affairs is a result of training schedules, starting with reinforcement of each act and gradually reducing the frequency. Something of this nature happens naturally in the training of infants and young children, e.g., in toilet training, with a progressive decrease of reward as the habit becomes entrenched. Thus, the first evidence of bowel or bladder control is effusively rewarded; then as mastery is evidenced, the control is taken for granted and no longer rewarded. But it will take only a few consecutive lapses (perhaps occasioned by the birth of a sibling) to get the parent going again on another reinforcement schedule, although this time the parent is more likely to resort to punishment than praise. However, there is a significant principle involved here. The reinforcement schedules of the parent or teacher are as much controlled by the responses of the learner as the latter are controlled by rewards. In other words, reinforcement has to be meticulously applied if it is to shape behavior, which means one has to be ready and willing to reward whenever the learner produces the desired behavior. Herein lies one of the basic weaknesses in parent and teacher management of behavior. They reward as the spirit moves them rather than as the response occurs!

Variable interval reinforcement produces a high and uniform rate of responses, which is preferable to mixed schedules, for the latter produces variable response patterns. Yet it is the latter type of rewarding which is more often characteristic of teachers with their report cards and rewards variably applied from child to child in an almost random arrangement.

Secondary reinforcement assumes an important role in operant conditioning, in the form of *generalized reinforcers* (Skinner, 1953). These once neutral stimuli, which acquire their reinforcing power by virtue of having been repeatedly paired with primary reinforcement, become significant because of their very ubiquitousness. Money is a means to the satisfaction of many needs and desires, primitive or sophisticated. Thus, it can be used to reinforce a great variety of responses. So also attention, which provides a sense of recognition, of approval, of self-esteem; in short, it is capable of satisfying many motives.

The perverse nature of reinforcement is seen in the development of "superstitious" behavior. If by chance a response is accidentally rewarded, the probability of the response recurring is increased. If the response is emitted more frequently, the chances of its receiving further reinforcement increase; hence, it becomes established as a habitual response. An interesting illustration of this is reported in many divergent forms by professional baseball players, particularly pitchers. For example, a pitcher may wear a particular hat or pair of shoes or follow a different sequence in dressing for the game (attention to the behavior being heightened because it is an important game). Victory in the game (reinforcement) strengthens the pattern of behavior leading up to the game. Obviously, such behavior will be further strengthened by a winning season or extinguished by repeated failure.

Skinner recognizes both positive and negative reinforcers, distinguishing the latter from punishment, whereby an *undesired* response results in punishment. Both positive and negative reinforcers serve to strengthen desired responses. In many instances, negative reinforcement takes the form of withdrawal of affection, i.e., denial of the availability of positive reinforcers. In other instances, it may be defined by the implied consequences of undesired behavior. For example, in a situation in which a teacher is using positive reinforcement to get a child to remain seated and pay attention and negative reinforcement to prevent his walking out of the classroom without permission, the negative reinforcement may be the threat that either he remains in the classroom or else goes home. If home means facing various tribulations with parents, then this alternative serves to strengthen school behavior.

The significance of positive and negative reinforcers for teaching is easily overlooked. Determine the *specific* behavior desired from a child. Begin with responses of which the child is capable, i.e., simple and readily available rather than complex and difficult. Behavior has to occur before it can be rewarded, so it is better to begin with responses that are likely to occur! Systematically, we repeat, systematically (for the strength of any response is correlated with the number of rewards—Strassburger, 1950) reward every occurrence of the desired behavior until it becomes habitual, then reward less frequently. At this point, rewards can shift to the next level of behavior desired. Note that rewards are to be determined by what the child will work for, not by what the teacher thinks nice. Thus, the teacher has to ask: what can I give or do that the child will find rewarding?

The importance of specifying the behavior to be rewarded and tying reinforcement to it is shown when reinforcement is linked to irrelevant responses, not unlike what occurs in "superstitious" behavior, as noted above. Experiments with animals have shown that if a response made because of one motive is followed by an effect that satisfies some other motive, the effect, though irrelevant to the first motive, serves to reinforce the response. Thus, the scratching by a rat is relevant to irritation but not to escape or eating. Yet, when rats were released from a problem box and rewarded by food following the activity of scratching, the tendency to scratch was reinforced by the reward. The rats thus rewarded learned to scratch as a means of escape (Lorge, 1936). The strengthening effect of irrelevant satisfying aftereffects has also been experimentally demonstrated with human subjects (Thorndike, 1933). A considerable amount of learning appears to result from outcomes which are irrelevant to the motive prompting the activity. When a child completes his arithmetic assignment and then is rewarded for accuracy and neatness by a special privilege or honor, the satisfying effects of the reward will tend to reinforce his efforts to secure neatness and accuracy in his work.

With children who are obtaining general satisfaction in school, the matter is less important than with children unable to function at the rudimentary levels of organization and attention necessary for learning. Specificity and frequency of reinforcement are crucial with the latter; but it is important with the former if learning outcomes are to be relevant to educational goals.

The early significance of intermittent or partial reinforcement is shown in two studies with preschool children. In the first (Brackbill, 1958), eight infants between the age of 3 and 5 months were initially observed to establish their existing rate of smiling. Then all the infants were picked up each time they smiled and were held and talked to until they were responding at a regular rate. Then, half the infants were shifted to intermittent fixed ratio reinforcement. Effects were measured by rate of smiling during an unreinforced extinction period. The intermittent reinforcement group was highest. The second study (Fattu, Mech, and Auble, 1955) involved preschool children operating a Skinner box arrangement which gave candy pellets instead of the customary animal food. The children (ages 3 to 5) were invited to play a game which consisted of operating the rod which caused the candy to drop into a tray. Three schedules of ratio reinforcement were used: 25 percent, 50 percent and 100 percent for a dozen trials, following which responding rates were observed for an eight minute period. Highest extinction rate occurred with the partial reinforcement and with the 25 percent rate in particular. These two studies have been cited because of their simplicity; most situations are more complex, with reinforcements coming from multiple sources (classmates as well as teachers) and in relation to multiple motives. As a result, differential effects occur. For example, Stevenson (1961) shows that effects vary with age; older children use verbal hypotheses to guide their behavior. In another example, Rosenblum (1956) used three reinforcement schedules (100 percent, 50 percent and 0 percent) on ten trials on copying designs, then asked his fourth and fifth grade subjects how confident they would be of success during a subsequent series of ten trials, gauged by the number of poker chips they would risk. The 100 percent group indicated significantly higher levels of confidence than either of the partial reinforcement groups. The rate of responding is possibly not the sole result of variations in reinforcement schedules. Subjective estimates of success and failure may be affected as well, and self-confidence may be a term applied to risk taking behavior derived from success-failure ratios. One hundred percent success ratios may be as disastrous for self-confidence as total failure rates because of the trauma of unexpected failure. Yet research indicates that probabilities of response are affected by stimulus frequencies and reinforcement ratios, often unconsciously (Grant, Hake, Hornseth, 1951).

Experiments using punishment have produced paradoxical results. In some instances, punishment will function similar to rewards (Tolman, Hall, Bretnall, 1932), in another it will suppress responses temporarily (Estes, 1944), and in others suppress them to the extent that forgetting is apparently complete (Freudian repression). Two recent summaries (Church, 1963; Solomon, 1964) bring some order to the diverse results. The effects of punishment will vary with rapidity and intensity, with the strength of the habit being punished, with the degree of adaptation of the subject to the punishment, and with the nature of the habit and how it was acquired, i.e., through previous reward or punishment. A number of inferences from empirical and experimental data can be made with respect to the usefulness of punishment as an incentive in changing behavior.

The greater the habit strength (the longer its duration and the more it has been reinforced in previous history), the more resistant it is to extinction; further, the more familiar the subject with the kinds of punishment utilized, the less effective it is likely to be. Thus, gradual buildups in punishment are likely to be ineffective in eliminating entrenched habits. Yet such is precisely the procedure commonly used by parents and principals— criticisms, mild threats, strong threats, mild punishments, strong punishments, permitting a gradual adaptation to the sequence of punishment. It was a wise man who observed that force is more effective in potential than in action, for once applied it is much less frightening.

Two practical reasons rendering punishment ineffective is that like rewards, swiftness of administration is important, but to be effective, it has to be isolated from any rewards present, else it may serve to strengthen rather than reduce responses. In the average classroom, such an arrangement is difficult to achieve, both because of the multiple demands which the teacher must simultaneously handle and the uncertainty with respect to the potential rewards present (Sechrest, 1963).

In mild amounts (the teacher would scarcely consider them punishments), punishment can produce greater arousal, call attention to cues, and reinforce desired behavior. The daily run of instruction contains its full share of warnings (mild punishments): careful now, on your toes, you're guessing, now I'm sure you know the answer, stop guessing and think, pay attention, etc., etc. These function primarily as cues and intensifiers. Stronger degrees of punishment can temporarily suppress behavior only to have it show itself another day; or partially suppress it, i.e., it won't appear in the classroom but will on the playground or out of school. In either case, success is only partial, for suppression is but one step toward the training goal; the other is substitution of an alternate form of desirable behavior. Finally, complete suppression can conceivably be attained by traumatic degrees of punishment.

The experimental and empirical results indicate that punishment does affect behavior and learning, but primarily to suppress, secondarily to modify. Humanitarian convictions oppose punishment, but equally important, it is impractical because it is unlikely to be effective within the range of options available to the teacher. Its usefulness will occur where it can be used temporarily to regulate or control one kind of behavior, while it is being replaced by alternate forms of responses which are being rewarded.

The discussion to this point has concerned itself with the effects of punishment on instrumental acts acquired as means of fulfilling certain motives. Certain other aspects of punishment need consideration. Rarely is the teacher familiar with the kinds of incentives utilized by parents, with the adaptations and expectations which a given child brings to school with him. Habits which have been acquired through punishment are highly resistant to change by further punishment, especially in the degree available to school personnel; emotionally based habits such as thumbsucking, masturbating, nail biting, and others are more likely to be fixated by punishment than changed. Finally, emotional arousal and upset are the companions of punishment. Emotional arousal often disrupts learning by reducing attention to relevant cues; further, more negative and hostile feelings will often be directed to the punisher, lessening the likelihood of subsequent responsive learning. A ready example is seen in the comment of a junior high school teacher: "I made a serious mistake with that boy. I saw him copying on a quiz, took his paper and tore it up in front of the class. From that day on, he'd have nothing to do with me. Whatever the effect on his cheating, I destroyed my effectiveness as his teacher."

In looking at the effects of incentive conditions in shaping behavior, consideration must be given to not only the immediate outcomes but also to long term effects on developing motives of children. In laboratory experiments, it is possible to arrange incentive conditions so that physiological drives are being manipulated, but rarely are these primary drives operant in classrooms. Instead, a complex system of acquired social motives is being met. Incentive conditions within the classroom should be such that not only are the motives harnessed to the task of learning, but also that the way in which they are used shapes them to individually and socially desirable ends. Two unfortunate effects of mismanagement are seen in drop-outs and cheating. When reward conditions are such that only a few can attain them, as is the case with A's and Honor Rolls, a major fraction of the students are denied the sense of accomplishment signified by "good grades." These students develop a progressive sense of failure and see little purpose in striving for an unattainable goal. The result is lower motivation, a contributing condition to a major portion of the drop-outs. It would surprise no teacher to know that in a group of adults asked to run three blocks for a prize of $10, a few wouldn't start and most wouldn't finish. Those finishing would be the ones who thought themselves close and those who completed as a matter of personal pride. Yet we somehow expect children to persist in the fact of continued failure made even more painful by being public.

A second disadvantage to such incentive conditions is that grades and honor rolls and similar symbolic rewards become ends in themselves, often to be gained at any price, including cheating. When 20 to 80 percent of pupils in twenty second to sixth grade classes (median of 40 percent parallels college data) change answers during self-correction of quizzes (Thurlow, 1959), the effects of the desires for "good grades" can be seen. Such a large portion of our lives is spent in study and work that the most desirable condition would be to enjoy these activities for their own sake. Hopefully, the student's main satisfaction in preparation for the science fair should be the enjoyment derived from a successful project rather than the award or prize to be won. Studying, working, learning, producing should be satisfying in and of themselves. There should be no need for artificial incentives such as prizes, rewards, winning a competition, honor rolls, and magna cum laude degrees. Often these have the unfortunate effect of developing a "what's it worth" or "what's in it for me" attitude. Individual motivation being what it is, the world of work and the inept matching of men and jobs being what they are, non-functional incentives will exist for some time, at least until technology and the economy of abundance provide leisure for all. Yet our use of incentives can be subordinated to the intrinsic satisfactions to be found in achievement, so well characterized in Mallory's comment on why he tried to climb Mt. Everest, "Because it's there." This is much the same motivation that prompts the exploration of space.

The distinction to be made is not whether to use incentives or not, but rather how to use them, when to use them, and to what educational purpose. Incentives have their value and their place. They encourage effort, particularly in early stages of learning when intrinsic satisfactions are low; they provide knowledge of results, but they have an unhappy capacity for becoming ends in themselves as a result of overdependence on them. We overlook more basic motivational conditions in any learning situation and we neglect the effects of our incentive conditions on the developing motives of children, in our desires to spur short term pupil effort for immediate learning.

Praise and Reproof.   Illustrative of several early experiments on motivation concerning the influence of incentives such as praise and blame, reward and punishment, and success and failure upon school work was Hurlock's (1925) study of praise and reproof. One hundred and six fourth and sixth grade children of both sexes were divided into four matched groups on the basis of intelligence tests and arithmetic skill. A fifteen minute daily practice period in addition was given to the groups for five consecutive days and progress recorded. One of the four groups served as the control group and received its tests separately without comment as to performance. The remaining three had their tests together but under different incentive conditions. Irrespective of score obtained, each of the three remaining groups received consistent praise or reproof or was ignored. The children in the praised group were called by name and told of their excellent results and encouraged to improve. The reproved group was called out and criticized for poor work, careless mistakes, and lack of improvement. The ignored group received no recognition, merely heard what occurred to the other two groups. Figure 7.1 provides a diagram of the results. The praised group showed the greatest gain, with the reproved group second. The ignored group improved only slightly more than the control group. The praised group was the only one to make consistent gains. When the results were compared for other individual differences, it was observed that girls in the praised group showed greater gains than boys, but the reverse was true in the reproof group. The less capable pupils made the greater gains. Superior pupils were more affected by reproof. These latter results were confirmed by later studies by Forlano (1936). He showed that the effects of given incentives were related to personality differences as well; shy and inadequate pupils, for instance, respond more favorably to praise than criticism.

Knowledge of Results as an Incentive.   There is a considerable amount of experimental evidence that indicates the stimulating value of the learner's knowledge of his score, his successes and errors, and the progress he is making (Fay, 1937). There is satisfaction in bettering one's previous score, in seeing the errors disappear, and in watching one's curve of accomplishment

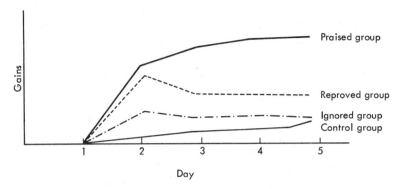

Fig. 7.1   Schematic diagram of gains made in addition by fourth and sixth grade pupils under different incentive conditions. (After Hurlock, 1925.)

rise to new heights; that is, of course, if one is trying to improve. Pointing out to a child his errors or other deficiencies in his work is the classroom analogue of the laboratory announcement of "Wrong" for incorrect responses or electric shock at the end of a blind alley. Through their informative value, they both accelerate learning. Likewise, informing the child of the good points in his work and the gains he has made is equivalent to mild shock or "Right" for correct responses in the laboratory. The critical evaluation of a pupil's work will be more effective as an incentive to improvement when it is specific with respect to particular defects, errors, and good points than when it is general and indefinite, as in such comments as "Your work is poor," or "That is very good." Forlano (1936) compared the effectiveness with fifth grade pupils of immediate and delayed knowledge of results as an incentive when it was combined with a monetary reward. The gains in achievement with knowledge of results alone were as great as those obtained with a supplementary reward. Annett (1963) makes a vital distinction in stating that the informational content of knowledge of results is important for learning whereas the motivational aspect is important for performance.

Competition and Cooperation.   Many a teacher has been able to secure enthusiastic effort by means of a competitive enterprise when other methods of motivation have failed. For such motivation to be effective, a child must have a fair chance of winning. If a child knows from repeated experiences that he does not have a chance, he not only will not be stimulated to exert himself, but he may develop an attitude of hopelessness and a sense of inferiority or a resentment against the whole classroom situation. While generally considered more desirable from the standpoint of wholesome social attitudes, group competition appears to be less effective as an incentive than individual competition (Maller, 1929; Sims, 1928).

In one experimental study on rivalry 155 fourth and sixth grade pupils were divided into two approximately equivalent groups for each grade on the basis of initial ability, sex, and age. The experimental group then was divided into two sub-groups who were told that they were to try to surpass each other. The work consisted of addition exercises in arithmetic. Rivalry was further stimulated between the two subdivisions of the experimental group by putting the scores of each on the board and calling out the names of the members of the winning group. This procedure was continued over a period of one week. The results indicated clearly that the rivalry had been a strong incentive, for the experimental group made considerably higher scores than the controls. Here the effect of rivalry was greater for the younger children and for those less gifted intellectually (Hurlock, 1927).

The use of organized competition and rivalry in the classroom, while it no doubt does provide a strong incentive, is not generally regarded as a first-rate teaching procedure. It may work when other and better means fail. But it has numerous disadvantages. Aside from the fact that it is conducive to antagonisms and other undesirable social attitudes, it is probably the most artificial of artificial incentives. The interest is in beating the other fellow or the other group, not in the studies or in improvement. When the competitive conditions are removed, there is little likelihood of any transfer of interest or continuance of effect thus artificially aroused. A case in point is that of a teacher whose pupils had been coming to school without being properly washed. Urging and coaxing had failed to secure the desired handwashing. So she arranged for competition between boys and girls. Boys were lined up in one row, girls in another. Hands were held out as the teacher walked down the rows to see whether boys or girls had the cleaner hands. After a time the practice was discontinued. Then one morning one of these boys started off to school without his usual washing of hands and face. His mother caught him just in time and said, "Here, you haven't washed up yet." "Oh, we don't have to wash any more," was the youngster's reply.

In interpreting the value of competition, one must bear in mind its acceptance in our society. In other groups which do not sanction competition, such as the Arapesh in New Guinea or the Zuñi in the United States, experimentally induced competitive situations would very likely produce different results. Competition, like soup-spooning, is learned. It can be of value in providing considerable zest to classroom activities on a number of occasions, provided the individuals on competing teams are evenly matched. As a long term procedure, however, it can have disastrous results, unless one is concerned only with the winners. Those who constantly lose (and some are almost certain to be constant losers in academic competition) ultimately, in self-defense, reject the competition and, in rejecting it, they cease trying.

Success and Failure.   If A's, honor rolls, and victory in competition are attainable by only a a few, success is available to all, provided that success is defined as achieving one's goal. Success has the advantage of coming in degrees, in contrast to rewards, which are more likely to be an all-or-none affair. One at least derives satisfaction from progress toward a goal and this is having success in degree. The mere setting of a goal is satisfying, as any college student who has spent two to three years at college without a definite objective can aver. Progress toward a goal and attaining proximity to the goal region are still more satisfying. The Sears have carried out several studies of the effects of success and failure upon motivation. In one study (1937) Sears demonstrated that in an experiment in which half the group received consistent failure in attaining the goals which had been set in a speed of card sorting task, they showed progressively slower progress than the success group which made consistent gains. In another study of the level of aspiration of academically unsuccessful students, Sears (1940) found that their failure resulted in unrealistic goal setting. They either set goals so low that no hazard was involved (note that a too-easy success is not satisfying) or so high that success was impossible. Academically successful students were realistic in estimating their improvement. Other related studies have shown that successful attainment of goals contributes to realistic levels of aspiration.

Levels of aspiration are modified not only by the attained results, success or not, but also by certain group influences. Few college students will acknowledge before an examination that they are well prepared even though they may believe they are, because to do so would be to invite the disfavor of the group. Neither will they acknowledge that an excellent score was the result of preparation; rather, they will dissemble, attributing the result to "luck."

The effect of a steady diet of failure is easily seen in pupils held in school against their wishes because of minimum age laws for leaving school or in non-promoted students whose goals shift from learning to getting out of school. Few teachers will say that such pupils are incapable of learning more than they know; rather, they complain about the lack of interest or motivation which prevents their learning and makes the teacher's life difficult. One solution offered is to change the law; another that should be considered is changing school practices—to encourage pupils to progress to the limits of their own abilities by aiding them to set attainable goals, which would have to be short range goals in the elementary school for the period, the day, or the week. This would require teachers to see value in progress itself, not solely in excellent scholarship. It would necessitate a realistic estimate of what progress she can expect a pupil to make, not what she would like to see made by all. It would mean seeing that school children are not too often discouraged nor too easily satisfied.

Placing the emphasis upon success and failure to reach goals realistically set would tend to overcome other disadvantages of incentives. The first is the limitation found in the arbitrarily established standards of adults. Maturation requires the attainment of independence from parents and teachers—the adult authority figures in children's lives. With the coming of adolescence, the struggle for independence is usually intensified, and in the struggle it is inevitable that symbols the adults hold dear—such as grades and similar incentives—should become subject to some degree of rejection. It is usually junior high school teachers who first complain of the indifference of pupils to grades. Second, incentives tend to lose their appeal in the absence of satisfaction of motivation. Secondary rewards need periodic strengthening unless they become goals in themselves. The operation of this in practice is easily seen in the giving of monetary rewards for good report cards, which in a sense constitutes bait or a bribe for learning. Interestingly enough, in a study conducted by the author among 700 students in a junior high school, it was the students having poorer academic records whose parents used the giving and taking away of monetary rewards and allowances to a significantly greater extent. Third, unattainable incentives lose their appeal except under unusual drive conditions. When incentives such as grades and honor rolls and teacher praise are so rigged as to be accessible to only a few—the students having the advantage of greater ability, superior academic achievement from grade to grade, and so on—it is these few who alone will continue to strive for them, while the remainder gradually lose interest in attaining the impossible.

SUMMARY

The methods of the teacher can make a considerable difference in the learning that occurs. The tasks she presents, the amount of practice given, the distribution of practice, provision for drill and recitation, furnishing knowledge of results, and adopting effective incentive conditions fall within the available methods by which the teacher can influence the course of learning.

A number of general principles result from the experimental literature on teacher procedures and the preceding discussion.

Establish a set to learn.   If the learner sees purpose in what he is learning and has some knowledge of the value of the task, he will learn more than when he pays incidental attention. Attitude is a generalized set. Lack of confidence, dislike of school or teacher, inability to see value in assignments unfavorably affect children's efforts to learn.

Clarify the task; define the problem.   The learning situation should be such that unnecessary errors are avoided. Errors which contribute knowledge or results and hence lead to improvement are useful, but those which result from confusion only produce more confusion.

Provide a model, a demonstration, verbal guidance, and cues.   A demonstration of the skill provides a model to be simulated; verbal guidance and cues help the learner direct his efforts by informing him of what to do and how to do it.

Provide adequate amounts of time and distribute practice.   Spaced practice with rest periods facilitates learning. Initial short periods which are gradually lengthened as skill develops are desirable. The early phases of practice periods are more effective inasmuch as efficiency decreases as fatigue and boredom increase.

It is advisable to space practice when: the amount of work involved or the length of the task is great, the task is not meaningful, the task is complex, the frequency of error response is likely to be high (especially during initial stages), or motivation is low or amount of effort required high.

Massed practice is preferable when: the task is highly meaningful, insightful learning is possible, a high degree of transfer from previous learning is likely, skill has been previously learned to a high level of proficiency (even though considerable forgetting has occurred), peak performance on well known knowledge or skills is required, or a prolonged warm-up period is necessary for productivity.

Practice the task as a whole if it is simple or short. Break more complex tasks into natural components.   Children tend to learn better by the part method, adults by the whole method if they have had some experience with it. In the whole method, progress is not readily apparent, a factor which can be discouraging to young children. Complete mastery of each part is not needed before introducing the sequential part.

Insure accurate or correct initial responses.   Avoid errors as far as possible and check them on their first appearance, unless to do so inhibits the motivation or effort of the learner.

Encourage meaningful associations.   Associations within the material encourage the development of an internal organization. Learning is facilitated by a contextual organization. Transfer of training from previous experience is desirable.

Provide for recall and recitation.   Meaningful recall in any degree is conducive to favorable attitudes, contributes to meaningful learning, and allows for more effective distribution of practice. Too early recall, however, leads to guessing and retards learning.

Provide immediate knowledge of results.   Accurate information as to progress is as valuable as reward in promoting learning. Delayed knowledge of results, e.g., returning examinations a week later, is not as helpful.

Overlearn once mastery is attained.   Retention is increased, positive transfer of training promoted, and interference with other learning reduced by any degree of overlearning. Drill should be meaningful, similar to the situation in which the skill is to be used, and command the attention of the student.

Reward liberally and early.   Rewards reinforce behavior. They are best when they are an intrinsic part of the activity. Artificial incentives are useful in maintaining effort until some sense of achievement and mastery evolves.

Apply the skill or learning.   Have children make use of what they learn in order to foster retention and produce transfer of training.

Help the learner to analyze his performance.   Realistic appraisal and critical analysis are importantly related outcomes of learning.

The incentive conditions used in the classroom are of considerable significance not only because they determine the direction of immediate effort, but more because they determine in degree the future motivation of the learning. Because drives and motives are to a large degree learned—at least the major portion of personal-social motivation—the effect of differing incentive conditions upon the kind of motives acquired should be carefully considered. The typically used incentives of grades and similar devices, which permit only a few to experience success, create artificial goals in those who can attain them and a rejection of such incentives by those who cannot. Repeated failure to obtain the incentive produces increasing feelings of inadequacy accompanied by negative motivation and hostility and aggression toward others. The creation of sound personal and group mental health in the classroom is closely allied with the incentives employed by the teacher. Realistic goals—those which are attainable—toward which one can progress and ultimately achieve with the related sense of success are preferable to the run of praise, punishment, competition, reward, cooperation, ridicule, and the like. However, it cannot be denied that the latter incentives can be effective in producing and prompting learning.

FURTHER READING

Overview

MELTON, A. W. 1950. Learning. In W. S. Monroe (ed.) *Encyclopedia of Educational Research*. New York: Macmillan, 668-90.

Selected References

GAGE, N. L. 1963. *Handbook of Research on Teaching*. Chicago: Rand-Mc-Nally.

GAGNE, R. M. 1964. *The Conditions of Learning.* New York: Holt, Rinehart, & Winston.

MC GEOCH, J. A. and A. L. IRION. 1952. *The Psychology of Human Learning (rev.).* New York: Longmans, Green.

MASSERMAN, J. M. 1943. *Behavior and Neurosis.* Chicago: Univ. of Chicago Press.

SKINNER, B. F. 1968. *The Technology of Teaching.* New York: Appleton-Century-Crofts.

SPENCE, K. W. 1960. *Behavior Theory and Learning: Selected Papers.* Englewood Cliffs, N. J.: Prentice-Hall.

Original Investigations

BRUNER, J. S. 1961. The act of discovery. *Harvard Educ. Rev.,* 31: 21-32.

CHURCH, R. M. 1963. The varied effects of punishment on behavior. *Psychol. Rev.,* 70: 369-402.

SEARS, PAULINE. 1940. Levels of aspiration in academically successful and unsuccessful school children. *J. Abn. Soc. Psychol.,* 35: 498-536.

SKINNER, B. F. 1954. The science of learning and the art of teaching. *Harvard Educ. Rev.,* 24: 86-97.

TABA, HILDA and DEBORAH ELKINS. 1966. *Teaching Strategies for the Culturally Disadvantaged.* Chicago: Rand-McNally.

8

Individual Differences
and
Educational Practices

The focus in the preceding chapters has been on the variables which affect learning. They have been treated singly, often without reference to a particular learner, task, or teacher, and as subjects of inquiry for which certain experimental and empirical data existed from which a set of generalizations could be drawn. The psychology of learning is concerned with the "how" of teaching and learning. It is intermediate between the social value system, which establishes the educational objectives of the community, and the teacher in the classroom, concerned with a specific group of children. (See Figure 8.1.) As useful as the generalizations are, they have limitations that are immediately apparent when one begins to work with an individual child or a class, for here decisions have to be made as to what to do when. The art of teaching lies in the ability to translate generalizations into action, and especially in recognizing where they do not apply.

In the school and classroom a number of sociological and psychological factors are operating to create special conditions which influence the course of events:

1. Each child presents a unique combination of abilities, traits, attitudes, experiences, and interests. Ideally, learning tasks and teaching procedures should be varied to suit each child. This is possible in a tutorial situation, much less so in the group situation. However, considerable accommodation is necessary and possible.

2. Each child is a member of a series of social groups which direct and control his actions. His primary group is his family which creates his basic character. The family participates in a given social class, ethnic, and religious milieux which set values, norms of behavior, social and personal attitudes on a variety of subjects: attitudes towards school, expression of aggression, level of aspiration, sexual behavior, work, time, nature of man, and others. Most children participate in neighborhood play groups and friendship groups which develop their own goals, value systems, and interests, and which influence children's behavior as long as they desire to maintain membership in the group.

3. The school is a social unit with a given mission and a prescribed field of action. The hierarchy of community values and the control of the school board establish permissible areas of action and prohibit others. For example, the freedom to discuss religion, sex, community politics, family budgets, and the like is usually quite restricted. It is much safer to discuss the segregation in South Africa than that in the United States; and if discussing the latter, it is better to discuss some other region of the country in preference to one's own community. In addition, expectations are established for the teachers, in part by the community and to a considerable degree by the school administration. A school acquires its own "personality," which is related to the principal's attitudes and expectations. There are quiet schools, active schools, confused schools, rigid schools. The teachers themselves constitute an in-group that demands conformity and support in conflict.

4. Within this framework, each class exists as a separate unit with its own operating procedure, its own social climate, its own interplay between students and teacher.

Children are reared in a man-made environment, consisting not only of the physical objects and tools which man has created and invented but also the language, customs, skills, attitudes, and beliefs which he has devised and transmitted from generation to generation. Large scale differences can be distinguished between recognizable cultural groups in different regions of the world. Although such differences are of no immediate concern to the teacher, their existence is mute testimony to the importance of cultural and social factors in shaping the behavior of members of a given society, and of the need for awareness of the patterns adopted by a particular group. Many so-called sub-cultures exist within this country—some identified with minority groups, some with urban-rural differences, some with socio-economic differences. The differences associated with these sub-groups have important implications for the classroom teacher. Prolonged isolation and economic and social deprivation have been shown to have negative effects upon intelligence test performance (Anastasi, 1958). The quality and amount of formal schooling show considerable variation by such sub-groups; the differences have been particularly conspicuous in connection with social class and ethnic minority groups and, to a lesser extent, urban-rural differences. The quality of educational service available and economic factors undoubtedly contribute, but attitudinal differences and motivational factors associated with these varying sub-groups play an important role (Hollingshead, 1949).

Group differences associated with cultural variation have limited significance for the teacher working with a particular child inasmuch as the differences within any such group are larger than the differences between sub-groups within a culture. The teacher must meet the particular combination of aptitudes, personality, attitudes, and behaviors present in a given child. The fact that a particular child is from a lower class family does not establish that his attitudes toward school will be negative. However, the tasks faced by a teacher extend beyond working with individual children, for most of her work with them is in groups. Yet the common attitudes brought by the children from the out-of-school environment establish in part the environment within the classroom; they prevail unless they are modified by in-school experiences. A number of studies substantiate the importance of such influences. Milner (1951), analyzing data from parent-child interviews, suggests that the relationship she observed among social status index, reading readiness, and linguistic development of first grade children may be explained by the more positive family atmosphere enjoyed by middle class children. Not only did these children have more opportunities for verbal interaction with adults, they also developed the motivation essential to success in adult directed learning. Several studies have shown the significance of socializing techniques on achievement oriented behavior. The interaction of parent approval-disapproval and success-failure in studies by Child (1946), Keister (1937), and Wolf (1938) affects the achievement and persistence of children. In these studies, high levels of persistence were associated with demand levels properly adjusted to the level of children's ability, low persistence with insufficient or unreasonable demands, and also with social approval of persistent striving for achievement and disapproval of its absence.

Although the home is the primary socializing agency defining the child's status in society and interpreting his experiences for him, the teacher is the formal agent of society. Her task goes beyond the transmission of knowledge and skill and includes developing and shaping attitudes, motives, and values. Her effectiveness in this role is dependent upon her ability to function as a group leader. Each child enters school with a unique biological, psychological, and social heritage evidenced in his aptitudes, personality, and behavior patterns. His entrance into school marks a psychological and social separation from the home. Prior to his entrance to school, his group membership has been limited to the home; now he is on the verge of friendships which will expand to membership in a group of peers. The developments that occur in his attitudes, motives, and values will be determined to a large extent by his membership and roles in the groups in which he comes to participate. The extent to which the school is a major factor in shaping his attitudes, motives, and values will depend on the ability of teachers to shape and influence groups of children and their attitudes. A study by McCandless (1942) illustrates the difference that the kind of direction provided can have on acceptability and status within a group. McCandless predicted and observed that, under autocratic adult leadership, adolescent boys in a training school would admire the openly dominant boy "because he dares to react in the fashion which all boys would . . . were it not for the fear of punishment or failure involved." When the leadership in an experimental cottage was changed from adult dominated to a form of greater self-government, the correlation between dominance (determined by ratings by adult supervisors) and socio-metric popularity dropped; indeed, the popularity of the six boys originally rated least dominant increased. In contrast, the correlation between dominance and popularity increased in the control group during the eight months of the study, reflecting not only the stability of group structure once established but also the influence of the adult directors on its nature.

Eight dimensions of the instructional group require consideration. Three are relatively inflexible, the remaining five flexible, in point of teacher's power to modify:

Inflexible	*Flexible*
Major goals	Climate–atmosphere
Leadership–authority	Interaction
Group membership	Communication
	Structure
	Norms

The major goals of the instructional group are determined by school board policy, curriculum, and the teaching materials available. Within this framework, subordinate goals such as projects or activities may be determined by the group, but the range of freedom is relatively narrow. The teacher is established as leader, and the amount of authority she can share with or delegate to members of the class is not great. Students are required by law to be in attendance; rarely do they have any choice of school, teacher, or fellow classmates.

The remaining elements are susceptible to teacher influence and the more so, the younger the pupils. Whenever individuals—children or adults —form a group, consensus rises quickly as to who is and who is not accepted, who is perceived as expert, who is not, who has power to get his way, who does not, and the status of each individual. These rapidly formed positions remain stable over time in spite of an individual's efforts to improve or modify his acceptability, power, or status. The teacher is in a key position to influence the development and functioning of groups. She has the power to determine the patterns of interaction. These may be restricted to teacher-pupil interaction which denies students access to each other, at least in the classroom; or they may range to spontaneous, student-determined interaction. In most classrooms, interaction is regulated by the teacher, both as to frequency and type, e.g., whether or not it shall be competitive or cooperative. The teacher is determiner of the rate of student output and the direction, pattern, and spread of the communication network. She plays a central role in establishing the norm system, the set of shared expectations regarding appropriate behavior, and the extent to which the students will share in determining it (Davidson and Girard, 1960).

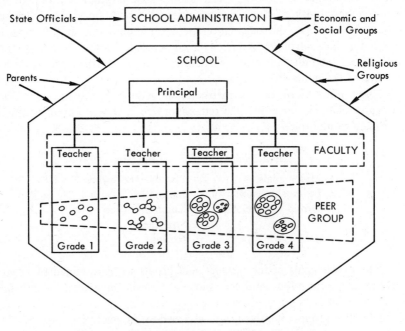

Fig. 8.1 Social pressures affecting the teacher.

The particular group structure that emerges in any class results from the interplay of many forces—the differences in ability and motivation of the members of the group and the individual needs of the teacher set in a matrix of social forces (Moos and Speisman, 1962). Figure 8.1 diagrams the professional and community forces bearing on the school, the formal administrative responsibility, the expectations established and shared by the faculty, the individual students, and the emerging and progressively more important peer group, which establishes its own social structure and norm system. In the diagram, an attempt has been made to indicate variations in the teacher's role—the teacher functioning now as a group member, now aloof from the group, now detached and dominant—suggesting differences in the group climate being created. The climate created by the teacher determines common modes of response which the students will adopt toward each other, toward authority, and toward learning. She determines whether it is supportive (encouraging mutual listening, harmonizing, and problem solving) or defensive (characterized by advice giving, blaming, controlling, persuading, and punishing). She encourages or inhibits the initiation and testing of ideas, the regulation and control of actions, the acquisition and evaluation of information, and courses of action. Every teacher creates a unique climate in her classroom, the result of her own personality as it is affected by the matrix of forces in which she finds herself. A number of brief descriptions illustrate some of these differences:

1. A teacher so lacking in emotional spontaneity and expression that the children never laughed or smiled in class.
2. A teacher whose skill in group work results in a continuous workshop atmosphere with groups of students working independently on projects using her as consultant and arbiter of conflict.
3. A teacher whose bent for sarcasm seems quite humorous until every student becomes the target. The outcome: a group which claws each other with fault finding.
4. A teacher who relates herself to the students individually rather than as a group, and who uses the interplay between her encouragement and individual relationship to create high rivalry between pupils and generally high achievement in the competition for her favor, but with several students each year developing severe situational adjustment problems in their inability to keep pace.

There are probably as many variations as there are teachers, but withal, the climate which a teacher creates and the roles she plays are essential determinants of class behavior, development, and achievement. She is an emotional thermostat playing a dominant emotional role in the class; she is organizer and director of activities; she is sanctioner and approver of behavior. The emotional climate she creates is determined by her personality and by her motives in teaching, for the latter determine the points at which her frustrations will occur. Her motives for becoming a teacher are numerous and varied: family pressures, interest in a particular field of knowledge, desire for status, love of children, identification with a former teacher, desire for security, desire to contribute to improvement of society, inadequacy in working with adults, satisfaction of needs for dominance, or some combination of these. The degree to which her needs are satisfied or thwarted and events in her life situation (financial problems, illness, family conflict, failure to marry) will determine the stresses and satisfactions she experiences and will contribute to her emotional capacities relative to children.

Figure 8.2 indicates three aspects of the classroom situation affecting climate and morale. Within any group situation there are kinds of behavior that are prohibited or forbidden; there are kinds of behavior which are subject to rules and regulations; there are kinds of behavior which are open to choice. In our society, aggression, treason, and certain kinds of sexual behavior are forbidden; taxes, automobiles, and burials are regulated; food and clothing preferences and child rearing practices are subject to individual volition. The classroom is similar in its operations. A suitable atmosphere exists when a balance of the three modes of behavior and avenues for the satisfaction of human motives, rather than their denial, is achieved. A classroom in which there is no room for choice may be efficient and achievement high, but it is not healthy. Instead, it is like a prison, for

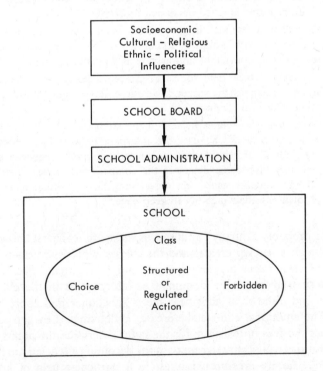

Fig. 8.2   Diagram of socio-psychological factors influencing class.

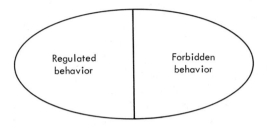

Fig. 8.2a   Diagram of prison environment and some classroom conditions, i.e. no choice permitted.

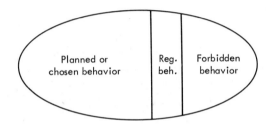

Fig. 8.2b   Diagram of "open-structure" plan reducing regulations to a minimum and substituting planned or choice of behavior.

all behavior is regulated—what you do, when you do it, who you do it with, when you eat, when you can talk, what you can talk about, when you come and go, and so on. This is scarcely preparation for living in today's world with its interminable choices.

A teacher can very easily check her performance by asking herself, at the end of the day or a week, "At what points and on what subjects did the students have any freedom of choice?" That freedom will have been rare, perhaps nonexistent. Usually a teacher continually imposes her purposes on her class, instead of relating her purposes to student needs, motives, and interests.

The area of regulated behavior may be established by teacher dictum or it may be achieved through shared authority. The process of creating rules and regulations is a valuable learning experience in itself, for through it children develop standards of their own creation for evaluating their performance. Hopefully, it would not be done as an abstract exercise in the promulgation of rules but done piecemeal, as need arises. One of the purposes of regulations is to provide a system for getting necessary work done in complex social situations; another is to prevent difficulties by setting bounds to behavior. Greater flexibility should exist in the classroom. It is possible to prevent difficulties by preestablished rules and regulations, but such an arrangement can work to deny children important learning experiences (Minuchin, 1965).

Perhaps an illustration can be taken from administration. Many times an administrator bemoans the problems he is faced with and wishes there would come an end to them. Regardless of how we might sympathize with his plight, we should recognize that finding solutions to problems is the *raison d'être* of an administrator. A teacher in her classroom is in an analogous situation. Her goal should not be an environment in which no problems occur, but rather one in which their occurrence provides an experience resulting in learning—of moral standards, ways of treating one another, concerted action to achieve common goals, and so on. Rules are better if they evolve as expressions of developing concepts rather than as preordained determiners of behavior.

The kinds of action and behavior which are prohibited should be those which not only are socially taboo but also those which foster destructive or harmful behavior. Too often the prohibitions do the opposite— deny the expression of healthy, constructive motives. For instance, a cafeteria in which talk is forbidden denies children healthy, natural intercourse. If conversation interferes with the cafeteria regimen, there are alternate or compromise solutions. A junior high school with a regulation that students must walk single file when passing from class to class is absurd. It merely indicates that the administration is unwilling or incompetent to meet whatever problems exist educationally.

Within the given context, the teacher has many roles to play. The ones she selects will depend on her concept of herself, her motives, the student's conception of a teacher, and administrative and community expectations of her. The teacher can serve as:

1. Representative of society imposing social demands
2. Source of knowledge and information
3. Guide or helper in learning
4. Referee or arbiter of disagreements
5. Evaluator and judge of performance
6. Detective of forbidden behavior
7. Object of identification
8. Reducer of anxiety
9. Ego supporter
10. Group leader
11. Parent substitute
12. Individual friend and confidante
13. Object of affection
14. Target of hostility

15. Tyrannical overseer
16. Administrative agent or clerk
17. Protector and defender

Some of the roles are forced upon unwilling teachers, but within the range of choice open, the roles which stimulate children toward more appropriate kinds of behavior are: (1) the source of knowledge, the experienced person who guides, helps, and assists with explanations and suggestions; (2) the standard setter who evaluates performance and establishes limits and bounds; (3) the referee who mediates conflicts and reconciles differences; (4) the ego supporter whose encouragement and support can be depended on; (5) guide, helper, and counselor who encourages the development of self-understanding; and (6) the friend, confidante, and member of the group who shares feelings and experiences (Symonds, 1955).

Equally significant in the modification of behavior is the influence of one's classmates, exercised informally but influentially to the degree to which group structure and group membership exists. As individuals establish interpersonal relationships, a group structure emerges in which different roles and status are assigned to various members and a set of group norms is established. The group norms are shared because of the potential gratifications deriving from doing so and fear of the penalties for not. It is difficult to determine the degree of sharing or the result of conflicts in norms resulting from membership in different groups. The group is a vehicle through which change in individual attitudes can be achieved and is, to some degree, susceptible to teacher direction (Mann and Mann, 1959). Comparing the individual and group motives in play in a classroom situation shows a number of significant motives which are group oriented:

Group	*Individual*
Group loyalty	Supporting or resisting authority
Gaining status or attention from group	Gaining status or attention from teacher
Competition	Achieving standards of performance
Power	Work for rewards
Gaining acceptance	Work to avoid anxiety
Friendly interplay	Intrinsic interest in work
Affiliation with group	Self-esteem

Within this milieu of motivation, a teacher can bring about behavioral change if she can structure a situation so that a higher order of satisfaction will be derived from a change of behavior than from maintenance of the current behavior. The increment in degree of satisfaction has to be sufficient to overcome established habit patterns. Involved here is a creation or selection of reinforcement conditions to bring about change. This includes the agent of reinforcement (teacher, class, work); the object of reinforcement (individual or group behavior); the nature of the reinforcements (rewards, punishment, whatever); the appropriateness of the reinforcements (as it is task or person oriented and as it is a natural stimulus or consequence); and the schedule of reinforcement (the frequency and conditions under which it occurs). Although this may sound unnecessarily complicated, an illustration will be of value:

> When a sociogram was made in an eighth grade class, it revealed that Jean was an isolate. This didn't surprise the teacher because whenever she would divide the class into groups for work, Jean inevitably started an argument about how to divide the work and ended by stalking away to sulk. The teacher was conscious of two other difficulties: one a reticence in reciting, the second, a difficulty in accepting an appropriate feminine role.
>
> Jean was an attractive girl by adolescent standards, healthy and energetic. She came from a middle class family in which both parents worked. She had two older brothers, one in the Army, the other in high school. They played various sports together and Jean had become quite skilled. During recess period, she was much sought after because she could hit and field a baseball as well as any of the boys. She scorned the idea of playing baseball with any of the girls, "because every run they made was on errors." The same boys who wanted her on their team ignored her on other occasions, however.
>
> She had high average intelligence and her achievement was at grade level. When called upon to recite in class, she'd straddle her desk, give a brief answer, and thump down into her seat. Asked to elaborate, she would respond, "I just told you." She usually dressed in stiffly starched boy's shirts, skirts, and saddle-type oxfords, using a boy's mackinaw or wool shirt for a jacket.
>
> In regrouping her class following the sociogram, the teacher grouped her with a highly feminine but very capable girl and a boy who was not only capable in both studies and sports but also very sociable. Both were highly chosen individuals on the sociogram.

The teacher was purposefully attempting to create a group in which Jean would find acceptance. Recognizing that the girl presented a group with difficulties, she selected two students capable of meeting the problem and who could serve too as models of femininity and masculinity.

> At first the conversations flowed around Jean, but gradually she became involved in them. As she was good at drawing, she was given the job of drawing a map of Grant's Mississippi Campaign, part of the social studies work. When the group came to report, they delegated Jean the job of giving a "chalk-talk" on the campaign, and when the class chose to use her map as a bulletin board display, she really beamed. Though she was becoming more expansive verbally and socially, she still scorned girls' activities. When the time came for the Christmas program and dance,

Jean would have no part of it. When the girls came to the teacher saying that Jean wouldn't help with the decorations, the teacher utilized group pressure by suggesting they ask Jean to help make a fireplace out of orange crates (a masculine activity). When the girls asked Jean to do this, she told them to get the boys to do it, but decided to do it after the girls complained that the boys weren't responsible. Before she was finished, Jean took a group of the girls home to cover the crates with crepe paper she had at home, and they ended making fudge and watching television.

On the day of the party, Jean said she wasn't coming, but that night she brought in a cake her mother had made (the teacher had earlier discussed her plans with the mother). After bringing the cake, she started to leave, but the girls asked her to help with a decoration that had fallen (Jean was the steadiest person on a ladder). She started to leave again, but the teacher asked her to help serve. Ultimately she stayed, enjoyed playing charades, even though she didn't dance. That winter, the teacher got Jean to play on the girls' basketball team "to help the girls learn to shoot baskets like the boys."

Interplay of individual and group reinforcement is seen in the gradual modification of Jean's behavior, both personal and academic, almost in spite of herself. The overall education activity has to function in an analogous manner. The efforts of a second grade teacher to apply the principles of learning to a developmental-activity unit in science is described here. These are the principles and objectives she took into account:

1. Allow for individual difference in ability, need, interest.
2. Provide for physical, emotional, and social growth as well as mental growth. Such growth requires more than subject matter mastery and requires an expansion of subject matter rather than minimizing it.
3. Basic considerations: readiness, preparation, motivation, appropriate practice, drill, reinforcement through reward, and success.
4. Conditions needed for learning: security (a sense of belonging in the class); confidence (the child feels equal to the task); effort (the child learns what he does); meaningful experience (encourage the child to question, observe, engage in activity); success.
5. Emphasize interest, meaningfulness, variety in presentation, knowledge of progress; minimize contests and competition, rewards, punishments, and restrictions.

This particular unit got its impetus from a child who was reading Dr. Seuss's book *Horton Hears a Who*. She was enjoying the book so much that the teacher read it to the class during their story period. Taking advantage of the children's interest in the story about the elephant, the teacher asked the class if they would like to see an animal show. Getting an affirmative answer, she asked each to tell about some animal he had seen, an activity that carried over to the next day.

The teacher obtained from the school librarian all the available animal books on the first to third grade levels and arranged them according to the reading ability of the pupils. She scheduled a film on zoo animals and also placed some colored animal photographs at the front of the room. This stimulated further discussion, and during the art period that day the children drew various animal pictures which the teacher placed with the colored photographs. When the children explained their drawings, they began to ask questions about the various animals and turned to the teacher for information. She suggested books in the special section of the library appropriate to the children's reading level. Where available reading material was too difficult, the teacher suggested other animals, knowing what was available.

On the following day the film was available for story time. After the film, the children wanted to tell what they had learned, but the teacher suggested they take their books home and see how many interesting things they could discover. Asked if they would like to study animals, the class responded enthusiastically but developed too long a list of animals, considering the long list of questions they had generated. They cut down the list, and the teacher divided the class into groups, based on animals the children were interested in, and picked a leader for each group. Each group decided which of the questions they wished to answer (each group having two animals) and the form in which they would report their information. Thereafter, the unit took up all class periods except the basal reading and arithmetic drill period. Exhibits were put on display, and the endeavor ended with the presentation of a play to the school.

The objectives were achieved to a fairly high degree, and the pupils learned to work quietly together and to cooperate in locating information. They learned something about many animals, notably their values and their methods of protecting themselves and obtaining food. Most difficult to evaluate was the extent to which attitudes and appreciation of animals changed.

OBJECTIVES

Teacher	*Pupil*
Gather and organize material	Learn about different kinds of wild animals
Develop leadership and initiative	
Develop responsibility in carrying out tasks, in caring for materials.	Learn about animal homes
	Learn about how animals get their food and protect themselves

DEVELOPMENT OF UNIT

Selection of animals, committee assignments, and reporting:

1. Bear, elephant   Scrapbook
2. Hippopotamus, monkey   Mural   } plus
3. Whale, tiger   Clay models   individual
4. Lion, giraffe   Booklets   reports
5. Kangaroo, rhinoceros   Animal charades

Committee functions:

Divide up and assign questions to be answered.
Decide how and where to obtain information.
Select procedure for reporting.

Questions developed by pupils:

How much does animal weigh?
How tall is he?
Are their teeth sharp?
Do they have fur or skin?
Do they make good pets?
Can they run fast?
Can they carry heavy loads?
Can they be trained?
What kind of feet do they have?
Do they have claws?
Do they keep their claws sharp?
Do they drink differently?
Do they run or jump?
Can they swim, climb trees?
Do sea animals sleep?
Can they see well?
Can they hear well?
Does he drink much water?

Do they lay eggs?
How do they find their babies?
Do they carry their babies?
How many babies do they have?
Where do they hide?
How do they protect themselves?
Where do they live?
How do they protect their babies?
Do they have winter homes?
Do you find them in a zoo?
Do you find them in a circus?
Are they friendly?
Are they dangerous?
How do they fight?
How long do they live?
Do they kill for food, or just because they like to?

CORRELATION WITH OTHER SUBJECTS

Language arts:
Reading widely used in gathering information.
Writing used when children wrote short animal stories and letters of invitation to other classes.
Oral language used by all pupils in reports, in discussion of zoos, circuses, experiences with animals.
Children selected and learned to spell names of twenty animals.

Social studies and science (direct study more than correlation):
Pupils learned the kinds of food used, how obtained, how animals protect themselves and the provision nature makes for protection. They learned about the size and appearance of the animals and about their homes.
Pupils learned what different countries the animals lived in.

Arithmetic:
Comparison of height, weight, size.
Problems involving size of animal families computed.
Ages of animals compared.
Some learning of four digit numbers required for weights of elephant, hippopotamus, rhinoceros, whale.
Some learning of terms such as pound, tons, miles, yards, feet, inches, bushels.

Music:
A variety of songs were learned: "Monkey Song," "See That Elephant," "Big Brown Bear," "Have You Seen the Zoo?" "Animal Talk," and others.

Health and safety:
How animals are cared for in the zoo and circus.
How the public is protected from dangerous animals at zoo and circus.
What animals eat.

Art:
Animals modeled from clay.
Jungle of cardboard, construction paper, and clay animals.
Freehand drawing and coloring of animals.
Stencils and freehand drawing used in making mural.
Spatter work used in making animal booklets.

Although only the barest outline of the unit has been presented and illustrated, the applications in an operational setting of the generalizations regarding learning are:

1. Begin where the learner is. This requires knowledge about the child's physical characteristics and health, capacities, personality, previous experiences, and level of achievement.
2. Adjust the pace of presentation to the learner. Flexible sub-groupings are necessary in order to work with groups of children at common levels of achievement.
3. Select and introduce activities consistent with educational objectives in points of content, pupil activities, resources, and evaluation procedures. Execution requires alertness and flexibility rather than rigid schedules, appropriate feedback on progress, and periodic summary and evaluation. The activities selected and procedures followed should be linked to specific behavioral changes in doing, knowing, feeling.
4. Motivate by providing for learner satisfactions—directly from the intrinsic satisfaction of learning, indirectly through incentives, or concomitantly through satisfaction of security, status, friendship, and self-esteem needs.
5. Create a physical and emotional environment that contributes to healthy personal and social development as well as to intellectual development. The interpersonal relationships of teacher and class, group processes, and disciplinary procedures used establish the social climate.
6. Evaluate and redirect, using tests and observation to determine degree to which objectives are being achieved and the kinds of modifications of plan which appear needed.

GROUPING

It would be convenient if each pupil were uniform in degree of aptitude and ability in all areas. Under such circumstances it would be possible to establish fairly stable and homogeneous groups for purposes of instruction and to standardize teaching practices for the different groups. When intelligence tests were first developed, a certain naïve faith ensued that at last we had a magic mirror in which we could see all. By obtaining intelligence test scores, it would be possible to group children with others of like ability, all of whom could be taught by standardized procedures utilizing standardized materials; educated persons could be mass produced in the same manner as automobiles. The rude awakening came all too abruptly. Intelligence tests provided no magic key to analyzing human capacity; instead, they proved to be crude measuring devices of a restricted aspect of human capacity. When children of the same mathematical aptitude are grouped together, they are heterogeneous (highly varied) for any other aspect of aptitude such as language, art, music, etc. They are not even homogeneous (similar) as far as achievement in mathematics is concerned. To test this statement, compare the range of *achievement* in mathematics or reading ability of any group of youngsters having average mathematical or verbal aptitude; the range of their achievement will be found to be nearly as great as for the entire unsorted group. (See Figure 5.1.) Unfortunate as this outcome may be for educational practice—for it makes the task of teaching by groups more difficult—it redounds to the benefit of society. Man's evolution has become dependent upon establishing new ways of behaving, individually and socially, rather than upon the selection of organically better adapted species. To this end, a homogeneous populace of uniformly trained people is ill suited.

In spite of the non-homogeneity of so-called homogeneous groups based upon any single criterion such as intelligence tests, the practice of homogeneous grouping has persisted in education, particularly at the junior high school level. While it is true that it is a convenience to be able to teach a group of children who approximate each other in aptitude and achievement, mainly because the instruction can be carried on with less diversified materials, it should be apparent that the frequently observed junior high school practice of subdividing children into groups on the basis of intelligence, achievement, or any other criterion, and leaving them in these fixed groups for all subjects, fails in its purpose. What often occurs is that the groups become more homogeneous in attitude and motivation, negative or positive; the inferior groups become less motivated, and the superior groups become anxious about maintaining their status.

The elementary school organization in which the classes are heterogeneous provides the teacher with the necessary flexibility in arranging her sub-groups so that she can have comparatively homogeneous sub-groups for a particular subject or activity, whether it be reading, singing, spelling, auditory discrimination, or other tasks. This permits her to adapt methods and materials to a particular task for particular groups of children. The student who investigates the question of the relative superiority of homogeneous versus heterogeneous groupings will find the results of the many research studies favoring one as much as the other. The question is not which method is superior but, rather, which method should be used with what group of children under what circumstances. In the question of grouping, the extent to which the teacher can adapt her materials and procedures to the particular grouping arrangement appears to be the important consideration.

Another problem of educational practice associated with the variability in learners is that of making adequate provision for exceptional children—those who deviate markedly from the average of the group in intelligence, physical development, and other characteristics. It is apparent that individuals learn at different rates and that it is desirable to have all individuals learning at an optimum rate. Gifted children learn more rapidly, while intellectually retarded children learn more slowly; both differ in qualitative aspects as well as quantitative aspects of learning. Physically handicapped children have special problems to be faced in overcoming the degree of isolation that handicaps impose, just as children with personality disturbances encounter an isolation resulting from their difficulty. The customary procedure in educational practice for meeting the problems presented by individual differences is not to tamper with the organization of the curriculum and the courses of study (i.e., the sixth grade teacher would teach "sixth grade work"; High School English was High School English!) and to vary the volume of work or the placement of the student within the program. Three general modifications were used: *adaptation, segregation,* or *acceleration*. Adaptation is merely the provision of specially suited tasks within the regular program, usually under the euphemism of "enriching" the program. The precise nature of what was enriching about the assigned tasks, or why all could not benefit from such privilege often goes unanswered. In theory, adaptation for the gifted child consists of enriching the program by providing special opportunity for investigating and learning at a more intensive level or in more extensive areas than for the average child. Adaptation for the less intelligent consists of simplifying and reducing the degree of abstraction.

Segregation (in educational rather than sociological terms) is a procedure for setting up special classes or special schools. Some school systems have established schools or special curricula within schools for either the gifted or retarded. These children are separated from the average children and are provided with special programs. Such a solution is more difficult for a small school system than for a large one, for if the intellectual deviates constitute between 2 and 5 percent at either end of the distribution curve, a school system would need a minimum of 200 pupils entering school each year to fill special classes and a larger number for special classes for other handicaps. Sorting on the basis of intelligence or achievement test scores frequently has the corollary effect of dividing groups along social class or ethnic lines.

Acceleration consists of advancing or retarding children to the grade level at which they are capable of performing. The gifted children would be advanced and the intellectually retarded children would be held at grade level and advanced more slowly through the educational program. Advanced placement programs provide a current illustration of an accelerated program. In practice, they are often sweatshops for the swift rather than providers for individual differences. It's quite true that they get able students "through" more rapidly, but through what? Kendall (1966) crystallizes the problem somewhat humorously by describing the plight of the avid, able reader. Given a boy at 15 able to read 500 words per minute who, because of his passion for reading spends a generous six hours per day at it, how much could he read in a lifetime? He would cover some four billion words in 44,000 books, barely enough to complete the books and government pamphlets published last year in the United States. (The average college graduate manages to read at a rate of 325 words per minute and spends twelve hours a *month* on "culture," of which only five hours are devoted to reading.) The question is basically not how much, but what, which brings it to whether teacher interests or pupil differences are to be served.

A variety of arguments favoring and opposing all three procedures can be advanced. To mention a few: special classes can be adapted to individual needs providing a special program impossible in the regular classes; enrichment provides a wider and deeper range of experiences and at the same time permits a youngster to participate with other children who are at his same level of development both socially and emotionally; and acceleration challenges a youngster to work up to capacity, avoids his wasting time, permits him to complete lengthy academic training sooner and become a contributing member of the community at an earlier date. In the opposite vein: special classes create artificial cleavages between children—the gifted become vain and the dullards discouraged—thus defeating basic democratic principles of mutual respect; enrichment is so difficult to attain in the regular classroom that it can be had only at the expense of the majority of the children; and acceleration and retardation place individual children in groups in which they are unable to participate because of differences in maturation. The fundamental criticism is that all three attempt to marry the child to a rigid curriculum, rather than seeking a harmonious union of culture and child.

MEETING INDIVIDUAL DIFFERENCES

Two developments during the past decade hold considerable promise for more effective provision for individual differences, both of teachers and learners. For generations the school systems and the universities have functioned with an egg crate organization. Each class was a spatially isolated unit presided over by an individual teacher. She was lord of all she surveyed, all 125 square feet. The more advanced school systems supplemented her efforts (at elementary level) with supervisors, specialists, consultants, as the term may be, in art, music, physical education—the "soft" subjects, basically those in which classroom teachers felt most inadequate. At the secondary level, the cubicle arrangement was maintained but with a subject matter specialist (hopefully) in each room, supplemented by a counseling staff to help the students adjust to the world in the form of the school. But teachers vary in interests, in abilities, in knowledge. A program which can capitalize on these differences for the benefit of the educational program promises greater yield. Critics of the administrative organization of schools, arguing from the analogy that events which have increased industrial efficiency will also increase educational efficiency, point out that the manufacturing process has become more productive as a result of subdividing the process into single skills in which one person could be highly proficient (as well as rapidly trained from unskilled to semi-skilled status). If you accept the premise that a child is like a vacuum tube, then the course of action is clear.

If you accept the criticism, without the premise, to the effect that present organizational arrangements fail to make most effective utilization of teacher talents, then a somewhat different course of action follows: one called *team teaching*. This is an attempt to utilize the abilities of teachers more effectively. In its simplest form one finds several teachers, e.g., three sixth grade teachers, deciding among themselves who will teach the reading, the science, the social studies or what have you, on the basis of their known interests and perceived competencies, then shifting the pupils to permit this. In a slightly more advanced form, one finds the ungraded school—more often the primary grades—in which a number of teachers are responsible for a number of pupils, and they sort them from time to time during the school day for the purposes of instruction in reading, numbers, and the like. Here, obviously, is a more efficient homogeneous grouping. Both types fall far short of the industrial model of both horizontal and vertical hierarchies and subdivision of ability and operation. In more developed models, usually seen in the secondary school and often in conjunction with televised or automated instruction, a given department or combination of departments— English-social studies, mathematics-science, languages, and so on—will organize itself to utilize different techniques of instruction—lecture, demonstration, discussion, television, tutoring, independent study, and so forth— provided by different members of the staff in accordance with their individual competencies.

The educational literature is full of studies comparing different instructional techniques—lecture versus demonstration, teacher-centered versus student-centered, lecture-demonstration versus problem solving, informational TV versus problem solving-TV, individualized reading versus traditional reading, decomposition subtraction versus equal additions subtraction, autocratic versus democratic, etc., etc., ad infinitum (see for example, Barnard, 1942; Koontz, 1961; Walker, 1961; Bernard, 1958; Hart, 1959; Edmiston and Benter, 1949). For every significant difference on the side of the devil, a matching one can be found on the side of the angels (which may be the nature of the universe). The fallibility of such studies stems from three sources: (1) too often there is inadequate control, (2) the independent variables are too broad, masking the effects of several more specific variables, and (3) a theoretical or logical link is basically lacking between independent and dependent variables.

The research evidence available on the effectiveness of team teaching is largely descriptive, rather than experimental, hence difficult to evaluate. Yet logically, the argument is sound, provided the energy demanded in coördinating teaching enhances rather than detracts from the input into teaching. An underlying assumption in more developed forms of team teaching is that class size is not an important variable in determining learning outcomes; team teaching advocates would argue that they are in a better position to utilize class size as a variable for purposes of instruction. Given the research data available (e.g., Goodlad, 1955; Otto, 1953; Siegel, Adams, and Macomber, 1960), there is little to suggest that class size affects achievement, attitudes, work habits, or discipline. There is no reason to suggest that a lecture to thirty should produce results different from a lecture to 300, if all 300 can hear it. This will disappoint teacher associations that have long struggled for smaller classes. Their efforts rest upon conviction rather than evidence. They can argue that the measures used to this point tap only a limited number of educational outcomes. True. They can argue that conservation of teacher energy is a function of small classes. True. They can argue that the potential of small classes has yet to be tapped. True. But these are arguments, not facts. Enough is known from research about size of group to show that small and large groups function differently as a result of resources available within the group, leadership potentials, individual demands for satisfaction, etc. This is a matrix yet to be explored if schools are to be more than transmitters of traditional culture.

A second procedure directed at providing for individual differences among pupils rather than among teachers is the type of team teaching called "mutual aid instruction" developed by Durrell and his students at Boston University. The basic procedure lies in combining small groups of two to five pupils who are at a common point in achievement on a given subject. Inasmuch as the pupils will be working independently (the teacher's function is as periodic supervisor, consultant, and evaluator), a series of "job sheets" is needed. These sheets constitute in effect assignments of given amounts of work to be executed in class by each group. The members of the group work to solve the task, compare results, argue the differences, call for the teacher where agreement is impossible. By introducing concepts, clarifying confusions, and testing to determine achievement, the teacher assists and checks on progress. Analysis of error permits appropriate review. Rate of progress is determined by the pupils themselves rather than the teacher or the progress of the entire class. Such team learning has the advantage of permitting reshuffling of groups by subject and over time as needed, organizing combinations of children for personal-social development as well as academic and varying group size from two up, according to the instructional task (Batty, 1949; Bixby, 1958). In short, it provides an organization procedure for sorting students which fits the rationale of a multiplex system incorporating the mass instruction seen in educational television and the tutorial procedures found with teaching machines. Moreover, the success of team learning depends on the job sheets, that is on having ready and available a wide range of prepared materials divided into functional sub-units.

INSTRUCTIONAL TELEVISION

Whatever the medium or technique that instructors have devised, be they books or films, lectures or seminars, laboratories or field trips, poorly designed or well designed, man and child have learned from it. Research of the past decade reveals that they also learn from television. Educational television is almost unique among educational innovations for the degree of research it has generated at applied, developmental, and field testing levels. Although information, communication, and learning theories have served as orienting factors in this research, practical problems have dominated it. The results of research on these problems show that television can be an effective instructional device. Schramm (1962), Kumata (1956), Holmes (1959), and Stickell (1963), have systematically reviewed and critically analyzed much of the research comparing the effectiveness of instructional television with other methods of classroom teaching. Generally, the findings show that the potential of television for accepting, distributing, and presenting formal instruction to a variety of students, using diverse content or subject matter diversely presented, compares favorably with direct personal teacher-to-student instruction. Though used in its primitive stages of development, television has at least not adversely affected the quality of instruction.

Experiments with instructional television have used the content of mathematics, physics, chemistry, biology, psychology, sociology, political science, literature, English, foreign languages, and many other subjects. Research shows that when lessons are prepared for specified content, then presented via television to appropriate students, learning occurs. This generalization holds over a variety of instructional situations. The credit for success must go first to the creativity of the devised program, second, to the medium (television) which carries it.

The results of recent research suggest that television for teaching should be greatly broadened. Limitations may be imposed when superior picture, sound or color definitions are required. Television can probably be used to teach complex as well as simple material. Television can function to develop concepts, increase problem solving ability, and teach creative thinking no less than direct conventional methods of instruction. The crucial task is to acquire the same confidence with which we now produce materials yielding these outcomes with conventional methods.

Televised instruction need not be passive instruction. Recent research proves that programs that demand constant learning responses and practice to provide needed reinforcement can be televised. Television can be effectively coordinated with other instructional procedures. In most of the research, teachers have presented the instructional material by television, thereby limiting the kinds of stimulus materials and conditions. Only limited exploration has been made of providing *direct interaction or transaction between students and stimulus materials* without the intervention of the teacher. The research indicates that television is not the principal or overriding influence on learning; the quality of the stimulus materials and the interaction of students with them are primary. Conventional techniques apparently yield equivalent results whether administered face-to-face or by television. One of the interesting results of the comparison research is the number of "no significant differences" reports which occur.

Stickell reports that the more rigorous the experimental design and controls, the fewer the statistically significant differences. Carpenter concludes that when significant difference occurs in a relatively exact comparison between televised and direct teacher-to-student instruction, something was wrong with the experiment. Such equivalence of effect offers school administrators procedural options. Since quality may be obtained by alternate methods, the decision to televise or not can be based on other considerations such as:

1. *The kinds of content required* and its preparation and organization into effective patterns of instruction.
2. *The available staff* and relevant competencies with respect to the options available.
3. *Availability of funds* to cover capital investment and operating costs.
4. *The student population* to be served including grade levels, numbers, distribution in space, mobility, and conditions of instruction.
5. *Appropriateness and acceptability* of the selected option relative to instructional objectives and people affected by the selected option.

Television as Part of an Instructional System.   Television has mainly been used to distribute conventional instructional materials over wide geographic areas. It has supplemented or temporarily replaced the regular teacher. But television is only one medium of communication. Books, films, teaching machines, and teachers are others. One of the problems in the improvement of education is how to incorporate the various media and materials into integrated systems which are more efficient in producing specified learning outcomes. A number of decisions are required to accomplish this:

1. *Determining the information to be transmitted to the learners:* the facts, rules, and concepts relating to the psychomotor, cognitive, and affective behaviors desired. These are decisions pertaining to curriculum, course, and lesson content and require the selection, assembling, organizing, and storing of relevant information.

2. *Determining the specific learning outcomes for given learners:* the operationally-defined pupil behavior to be acquired, selecting the appropriate information for transmission, evaluating the potential of the various media available—books, teachers, films, teaching machines, television, and others.

3. *Determining the media to be used:* the particular content and the form of its presentation, i.e., direct versus indirect approach, inductive versus deductive, and the like.

4. *Programming the material for presentation.*

Critical decisions must be made in each phase. If television is selected, consideration of its special potentials and limitations is necessary. Some of the most important of these are: (1) its capacity to transmit a wide range of both video and audio materials, (2) its ability to function in concert with or to incorporate many other carriers of stimulus materials such as recordings, projectives, graphics, printed materials, and so forth, (3) its capacity to span space and reach large numbers of students with low unit cost, (4) its recording capacity which permits pretesting, revision, and repetition of materials, (5) its potential for magnification and amplification insuring clear perception of specific instructional materials. Also to be considered are television's limitations on learning, e.g., the interests, previous learning, or individual differences in ability of the students to be addressed.

In programmed instruction where one student interacts with a machine or with a textbook, individual differences among students are adjusted for by the level at which the lesson materials are prepared, by pretesting the materials with the students at that level, and by allowing each student to select his learning pace. When programmed instruction is presented by means of such media as films or television, the interaction occurs between the device and many students. During such a fixed learning period, the pace is determined not by the individual student but by the schedule of the presentation which itself obtains for all students.

All media possess assets for some purposes and liabilities for others. An ideal education system, employing a variety of media, depends upon the optimum matching of capabilities and objectives, and on the maximum potential for offsetting the limitations. A typical educational system will fall short of the ideal and will derive from the trade-offs between assets and

POSITIVE	NEGATIVE

Individual

Programs suitable to all ages, IQ's, and aptitudes can be developed.	Not suited for certain subjects such as literature, critical analysis, and the like.
Branching programs are much better for brighter students.	Bright children will get bored by repetitive nature of program.
Allow for individual differences in pacing and rate of progress.	No opportunity is provided for discovery, intuitive perception, or the use of tacit promises in a logical sequence.
The machine records student performance permitting continuous evaluation and a cumulative record for research.	Stifle curiosity.
Differences in level of readiness are provided for by small step structure.	

Task

Material is covered more rapidly at all levels.	The learning is empty verbalism detached from real experience.
Difficulty level is controlled; private tutoring provided.	Insufficient evidence is available on retention and transfer of programmed material compared to non-programmed instruction.
Teachers can devote more time to enrichment and creativity.	
Specialists can program materials giving students access to the best.	High density of materials in small-step procedure lowers motivation.
There is continuous, non-threatening testing while learning.	Learning involves emotions as well as verbal symbols.
Obsolete materials can be readily replaced.	
Quality of instruction is predetermined.	
Student is encouraged to think through material step-by-step.	

Method

There are immediate confirmation, reward, and reinforcement without dependence upon teacher provided incentives, and avoidance use of negative incentives.	The learning process is dehumanized.
Competition is against self — not group.	Teaching machines will render the modern school building obsolete.
There is continuous participation while learning.	No time is provided for reflection or for consideration of the implications of materials.
Overlearning is provided for.	
Cheating is prevented. A correct response is required to advance. Responses are monitored, guided, and corrected at each step.	Provide only for individualization through pacing, but not through variations in program content. All students learn the same material the same way.
There are no problems of attention, arousal, or maintenance.	Learning is organized on a part-to-whole basis which has disadvantages.
Corrections are work-centered, impersonal, unemotional.	Program has no control over learner set.
There is better opportunity for systematic study at home by sick or invalid children.	
The machine is "unhumanly kind and unhumanly knowledgeable."	
Machine relieves teacher of responsibility for drill; increases efficiency of process.	

liabilities. Cost is one basis for assessing the outcome of such trade-offs, student achievement another. In the case of television, it would appear undesirable to use it for subject matter which can be taught as well or better by other less costly media. The more complicated and costly television or film media are better reserved for subject matters containing dynamic or transient stimuli. Science demonstrations of principles of physics or chemistry or laboratory procedures involving non-verbal, visual stimuli are excellent examples. Similar aspects can be found in art appreciation, social studies, and foreign languages.

The capability of a medium to present the relevant subject matter *content* is a first criterion in its selection. A second involves the capability of the medium to provide *control over the presentation process*. The medium should have the capability of exercising control over the amount of stimulus material presented at a given time and over the duration of its presentation, over the opportunity for student response, and over the opportunity to provide confirmation. Television does possess most of these control features.

Factors or conditions affecting the learning process and hence to be brought under control are: (1) the *source and resources* of the stimulus materials, their characteristics, sign-symbol modes, authenticity, structure, significance, and scope; (2) the *stimulus materials* which are selected, ordered or organized, transformed and adapted for presentation to learners; (3) the immediate surroundings or *environment* in which the stimulus materials are presented to students; (4) the *learning responses,* reactions and transactions of students with stimulus materials; (5) *the amounts and appriateness of the kinds of reactions,* which are performed, whether overt or covert, the schedule of these reactions and their effects on the learning tasks; (6) the *evaluations and comparisons* (especially by students themselves), or achievement rates and terminal performance levels with the purposes, objectives, and standards set for the learning tasks. Implicit in this set of conditions are the several facets of teacher behavior: motivating, presenting, organizing, evaluating, and counseling, however managed, by teacher, television, book, film, teaching machine, demonstration, model, field trip, or any combination thereof.

Currently, few instructional television programs exist which qualified experts agree are well prepared and approach their potential. Neither the science nor the art of preparing such materials has progressed to the point where adequate presentations can be produced and distributed with assurance that the instruction goals are being met. A part of the difficulty is that adequate testing criteria are yet to be developed. Currently, instructional television suffers the technological void that test construction experienced during its early phases. The first objective tests were largely "off the top of the head," but later the criteria for evaluating tests and the knowledge for preparing them went far beyond the rote learning and recognition of concept conditions characteristic of tests a generation ago.

Recent research on instructional films, teaching machines and education shows certain relating conceptual trends. It suggests guidelines to the planning and preparation of program materials.

1. *The content of a televised lesson must be adapted to the particular purpose* of instruction intended at a given time. It seems unlikely that many ETV programs can be made which are applicable in a wide variety of instructional situations.

2. *The content of a televised lesson must be adapted to the experience, aptitude, and readiness of the learner.* It may be that for particular subjects it will be necessary to have several lessons, each adapted to the capabilities of a particular set of learners.

3. *The lesson content should aim to motivate the learner,* particularly because acquiring the appropriate knowledge or skills is likely to be dependent on subsequent activities.

4. *The television lesson must be directed at clearly defined* behavioral goals. The key word is behavior. The desired performance is described in terms of the specific, measurable behaviors involved. Avoid general statements such as, "Understand the meaning of Boyle's Law." Preferable is, "Compute the volume of gas, given information about pressure and temperature." Such explicit statements about end behavior provide not only a clear-cut determination of the goal but a non-ambiguous criterion for judging success in reaching it. Such statements can readily include not only acts of recognition or recall but also performance of simple or complex tasks.

5. *The content of a televised lesson must be presented in appropriately sized content steps and goal steps* if it is to be effectively communicated and mastered by the learner. If the steps are too small, boredom may ensue; if too great, acquiring the behavior may be impaired; if not related to prior skill and knowledge of the learner, interference may result.

6. The content of the televised lesson must be *optimally sequenced and organized.*

7. The content must be planned and arranged to provide for the *active participation* of the learner and the *practice* of the desired behavior.

8. *Provision is necessary for reinforcement and feedback of information* to the learner regarding the appropriateness of his responses.

Immediately apparent in the foregoing set of statements is a relationship between principles of learning and organization of filmed or televised instructional materials—concerning motivation, defining behavioral goals, appropriately sizing and sequencing steps of instruction, active participation by the learner, and provision for knowledge of results and reinforcement. Yet curiously, there was a long delay in applying these principles of learning to audio-visual instruction. It is only within the last decade (due to federally supported research) that audio-visual instruction has utilized these principles and this is as much a result of cross-fertilization from programmed learning as from a direct application of learning theory. The change is evidenced by the newly-named Learning Media Centers, which were once termed A–V Centers. Originally, the motion picture projector and subsequently, the television set made their way into the classroom as auxiliary devices, presumably enriching the learning experience of the child by bringing to him experiences which he could not obtain for himself. What happened to the school is similarly happening to the home as a result of developments and economies in the use of film. With satellites available for broadcasting purposes, plus developments in laser holography, the technical capacity to bring experience to the individual is becoming so extended (in contrast to taking the individual to the experience by means of travel) that one can literally have "instant experience." But if learning is to prove effective, more than experience is necessary; rather, some ordering and organizing of it are required, which introduces a second aspect of educational technology.

The first aspect of educational technology is the technical means, the equipment or hardware needed to perform a given task. The second aspect is the nature of the experience to be provided. Television sets or computers provide little gain in the instructional process if the programs presented fail to provide effective learning experiences. Not infrequently, our technical capacities get ahead of our emotional and intellectual capacities for proper use of them. Given our penchant for believing that the purchase of a piece of equipment automatically insures its proper use in solving problems, it is not surprising to observe a large scale use of film and television without an adequate base in program development.

Lumsdaine provides us with two figures which illustrate first (Figure 8.3), the interplay between the two technologies, i.e., equipment and instructional practice, and second (Figure 8.4), that between behavioral science and current concepts of programmed instruction.

It is not by accident that Skinner's name falls in a central position in Figure 8.4, for it was he who gave the impetus for the shift (1954, 1958) from merely observing learning, as one does in the laboratory, to managing it, as one hopes to do in the classroom. Skinner sees any educational subject as consisting of a cumulative set of behaviors which can be analyzed into component parts and segmented into a series of steps in learning which provide for gradual approximation of the skill and its ultimate mastery. The student will see here a direct application of S-R theory, the concept that mastery of skill or knowledge is achieved by the assembly of the requisite pieces, rather than by its acquisition through insight of a global Gestalt. Actually, two theories come to bear, Guthrie's as well as Skinner's. Guthrie's views were that the simple contiguity in time of stimulus and response sufficed for learning, whereas Skinner underscores the importance of rein-

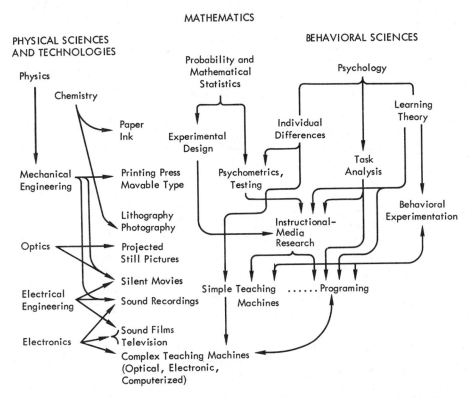

Fig. 8.3 Some of the interrelationships among developments in physical and behavioral sciences related to educational technology. (From Lumsdaine, 1964.)

forcement in learning. The actual pattern of many instructional programs simply provides the stimulus situation designed to elicit a given response, then provides confirmation of the appropriateness or the error of the response. Unless this knowledge of results is interpreted to constitute a reinforcement, the design follows Guthrie's concepts more than Skinner's. Nevertheless it was Skinner, with his strong empirical bent, who produced the marriage of psychological principle and educational practice.

Central to Skinner's work in programming, is his view that it is the response (the operant) which is crucial. Thus he would and does criticize audio-visual techniques for the assumption that all that is needed is to provide the stimuli, i.e., the film or picture.

Skinner would very likely deny the aphorism that "one picture is as good as a thousand words," arguing that a picture is only as good as the number of desired responses which it produces. Thus, Skinner makes the programmer responsible for the learning; faulty learning indicates the need

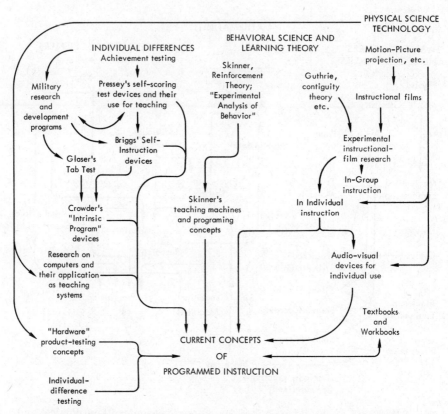

Fig. 8.4 Converging streams of influence affecting present concepts and practices in programmed instruction. (From Lumsdaine, 1964.)

for revising the program, not chastising the learner. Consequently, a program may be defined as a sequenced combination of instructional events designed to produce predictable and specifiable changes in learner behavior. (Note that the definition is independent of the form the program takes! It applies equally well to a teacher's unit of instruction, a television program, or a teaching machine.)

MACHINE TEACHING

The latest report from the Dean
In praise of the teaching machine
Is that Oedipus Rex
Could have learned about sex
By himself, and not bothered the Queen

Whether such a happy or unhappy millennium, depending on one's views on incest and sex, will be achieved by automated instruction is highly doubtful. Yet the classrooms and school systems are in the initial stages of a technological revolution. The quiet marriages of electronic firms and publishing houses, the appointment of a former United States Commissioner of Education to head such a firm symbolizes the times. Indeed, many schools thought the revolution could be achieved by the purchase of teaching machines, only to discover that it was programs that counted, not levers and gears.

Actually, Sidney Pressey developed teaching machines forty years ago but the *Zeitgeist* was not propitious for their acceptance. In another form, instructional machines have been in use for some years to improve reading instruction but without significant effect (Thompson, 1956; Bottomley, 1961; McDowell, 1964). Reading can be improved by using machines; it can be improved equally well with other forms of instruction not using machines. The typical reading machine is a very modest device compared to the more sophisticated types of teaching machines now available. More sophisticated approaches include:

1. Individual viewing and listening equipment for slides, film strips, motion pictures and recordings, including language laboratories of all types.
2. Printed programmed materials, such as scrambled textbooks.
3. Teaching machines of the Skinner or Crowder type containing carefully developed verbal or pictorial programs, with various ingenious mechanical or electrical arrangements to test a student's reaction and to inform him of errors and progress. In their ultimate form, the programs are linked with a computer to provide flexible and responsive environments.
4. The use of computers, linked to typewriters, visual displays and other response devices to provide a responsive environment, i.e., the pupil interacts with the computer program. The use of computers makes it possible to vary the items presented the learner according to the trend of his responses, and a continuous analysis of his errors.

It is readily seen that any teaching that the machines do comes in the form of a carefully developed set of instructional material sequentially presented by a mechanical device. All teaching machines represent some form of the Socratic method of teaching in that they present the student with a series of questions and answers organized along Cartesian lines of analysis into the smallest parts and ordered from simple to complex. In general, the apparatus presents a verbal, symbolic, or pictorial bit of information or a problem, usually in question form. The student is provided with some means of responding (he may press a key, write an answer, type a response, move an indicator, and the like); and then the machine provides him with knowledge of results regarding the correctness of his response. Basic features of the program consist of a pretested sequence of small steps, cueing, active responding, immediate confirmation, and self-pacing. Much in the same manner that tests are pretested to insure reliability and item validity, so too are programs pretested by trying them out on designated groups of learners and revising them on the basis of their errors, so that the progression of questions minimizes errors. The advantages of active responding and the provision of immediate knowledge of results need no explanation. Machines have the advantage of allowing the learner to move through the program at his own rate, be he slow or swift in a subject, for they are, as it were, his private tutor.

Two main approaches to programming currently exist—a linear program developed by Skinner at Harvard (representing an application of his basic research in learning) and branching or scrambled programs which originated with Norman Crowder. The former requires the learner to supply an answer by writing a missing word or phrase, much in the form of the short answer or completion type test item, except that in this situation the learner has little or no prior knowledge. Therefore, the items are carefully constructed to minimize error in response through the use of contextual or semantic cues within the framework of each item. In this linear program, each step is taken in sequence; there is no opportunity to attempt larger units or bypass known information. It depends on an elicited response at each step. One can see the relationship between operant conditioning and linear programs. In both instances, the learner's behavior is being shaped and brought under control of external stimuli.

The branching technique usually presents the learner with a longer unit of materials followed by a multiple choice type of item. His response to the item determines which of several units he will be directed to work on next. Crowder tries to anticipate mistakes and use them as an integral part of his program instruction. He believes the student must be given a chance to be wrong, for his error will provide clues as to what he does not know, what he needs to review, and so on. Furthermore, it provides the option of skipping that which is sufficiently known. Thus in branching programs, the program sequence is indirectly under student control because it is his response which determines the next move.

The question of the appropriate level of error and the functional role of error in learning is a crucial difference between the two concepts of programming. In either case, blind errors and cul-de-sacs represent time and effort wasted. Beyond that, the question hinges on the extent to which errors facilitate or impede mastery of knowledge and skill and more important, how they relate to transfer of training. At the moment, the answers to these questions are matters of conjecture. The relative merit of each concept of programming is likely to depend on the type of learning involved.

Simple discrimination, perceptual learning, and serial learning tasks of both verbal and motor types are probably better suited to a linear type program, whereas problem solving and various analytical tasks are better served by branching programs.

The positive and negative features claimed for teaching machines follow. Some are definite, others speculative, as they relate to individual, task, and method variables.

Anyone evaluating the application of teaching machines to specific, present day educational situations can safely discount current predictions regarding the upper limits of machine development, not because the automated classroom will not happen, but merely because the achievement of such a level is bound to come slowly due to financial ramifications and human inertia. The crucial question is not the technological and engineering aspects but the implication (Galanter, 1959) that in developing teaching machines, learning theory is being developed which will eventually regulate a mass standardized educational program. Such educational theory should be the result of conscious philosophical thought more than technical possibilities. When Skinner counters the cries about mechanization with, "There is no reason why the schoolroom should be any less mechanized than, for example, the kitchen," one can't avoid the thought that there is more than cakes to be cooked in the classroom. More fundamentally, the question comes down to the concept of "the educated man." Whose concept shall it be, the technicians? Unfortunately, philosophy has a way of following on the heels of fashion, as much as shaping it. Given the present system of control of education, many of the objections to teaching machines can be discounted, for control is distributed over many groups varying from publisher to purchaser and user, providing a system of checks if only by the number of individuals involved. Objections that focus on the limitations of teaching machines should also be discounted because of the probability that future technological developments will overcome most current operational limitations. Already this can be seen in the Edison Responsive Environment Machine, which uses a computer's capacity to provide flexible responses to children's learning attempts.

Already the research on films, television, and teaching machines indicates that they are as effective in informational and skill learning as conventional teaching methods. Films and TV can induce changes both in attitude and in motivation, although they play a secondary role to other social agencies. The concern and subsequent reassurance about new teaching aids not replacing the teacher (which is usually offered as an afterthought to reassure teachers that they are irreplaceable) fail to view the change that these aids are imposing on teachers and curricula. For example, large numbers of elementary school classrooms are attempting to learn to speak French or Spanish by means of televised instruction.

There is no question but that schools, like industry, will adapt to automation, with a resulting reallocation of manpower and skills. The nature of children and learning being as they are, the probability is that few teachers will be displaced; rather, in any situation where the device can instruct as effectively as a teacher but at a lower unit of cost, it will be used. If the result is to provide greater learning with the same resources, a replacement of less competent teachers by those with a higher order skill, or a better provision for individual differences, we should utilize such equipment. Certainly our provision for individual differences has been most inadequate to date; our annual convoy type of education and our ability to manage attitudinal, social, and conceptual learning are most uncertain and haphazard. The major task ahead is to learn how instructional devices can be most effectively incorporated into the educational process; to learn how to integrate the teachers, materials, programs, and learners; and most important, to extend our knowledge in areas of learning other than information acquisition and motor-skill development.

SYSTEMS ANALYSIS PROCEDURES

Many of the objections to programmed learning stem from hasty or naïve conceptions. If, for the sake of argument, the educational process can be oversimplified and considered a two-step process consisting of the acquisition of knowledge and the development of skills for the attainment of cultural, social and personal goals, then the situation can be imagined in which the machines will handle most of the first step, and teachers the second. Films may be used in teaching motor skills to demonstrate skills, provide analysis of techniques, illustrate strategies and tactics, but teams require players, and crafts require mechanics, and both require coaching. Perceptions can be sharpened and information and concepts transmitted, but the application to the field, be it geology, anthropology, or deer hunting requires more than audio-visual techniques. Skimming of material, organizing meaningful relationships, creating metaphors, inventing, chairing a meeting, leading a group, living compatibly, even catching a fish, are but a few aspects of various kinds of learning where live teaching is needed.

The facts are that we have bumbled along with our educational programs, doing a surprisingly good job considering our goal of universal education compared with the limited resources we have been willing to allocate. However, the spoilage rate—25 to 30 percent judging by the drop-outs—is excessive. We are approaching the point where we possess the technological, scientific, and social skill to remedy the matter. The implications of team teaching, team learning, television, and teaching machines are clear. They provide the possibility for organizing a system which, linked with teachers, can produce a learning environment which will not only accomplish the traditional task of information and skill learning but go beyond it to develop the personal and social competencies needed. This will necessitate an analysis of the kinds of outcomes and competencies desired and a subdivision of tasks among the component parts of the system (anyone of the above four T's plus the teaching staff), guided by operational research to evaluate and increase the effectiveness of the program. In all probability, more teachers will be needed, for schools have operated at minimal staffing; the kinds of specialization will go well beyond today's subject matter specialist, who is competent mainly to organize materials for presentation to learners. This function will be replaced by competency in diagnosis and analysis of learning difficulties, selection of appropriate training activities, skill in organization and leadership of groups, and a coterie of such skills. Teaching will finally become a profession, rather than a stopover on the way to marriage. The teacher will be a pivotal person in the interaction of a set of contingencies: (1) the application of acquired knowledge about learning from experimental psychology; (2) the inter-action between individual children and teachers in group situations; (3) the community, its size, number of children and available resources; and (4) the community's social objectives and value systems.

GRADING AND PROMOTION

Grading and promotion are two aspects of educational practice of much concern to the teacher because of their relation to motivation. Three or four times during a school year, teachers go through the ritual of grading. Few derive any satisfaction from the practice and many have their misgivings. Concurrently, the children work harder, pretend to be better than they are, apple polish, and resort to other devious tactics to insure favorable grades. Few will be satisfied, many disappointed, and all can well question the procedure. For all practical purposes, grades and report cards could be dispensed with today without serious loss. College admission programs would not suffer, parents would not know less, and teachers could devote their time to educational activity. But like many rituals, grades and report cards will persist.

Grades and report cards have three main features: (1) they are measures; (2) they constitute a communication system; and (3) they serve as incentives affecting motivation. As measures, they provide information on individual and group progress and knowledge of results to children and parents. As measuring systems, they suffer the usual problems of validity and reliability: what do they measure and how consistently do they measure it? In the total sense, the composite average of teacher grades is as good a predictor of scholastic achievement as is available—as good as tests. The sum total of all the grades a child receives constitutes a composite measure of aptitude, achievement, motivation, deportment, study habits, initiative, *et al.* But taken individually, it is difficult to determine what a grade represents. Each teacher establishes her own basis for grading. Seldom do two teachers have the same basis. Some base their grades on achievement, some on achievement relative to ability, others on effort, others on gain, others on attitude, and so on. Worse, only a few teachers tell children the bases upon which they are grading, with the result that the learner doesn't know the direction his efforts should take, much less what the grade means when he receives it.

The first step in grading is to make clear what it is that is being judged or measured—quality of work, quantity of work, effort, or whatever—and to recognize that, for each aspect to be measured, a separate grade is needed (if it is to be meaningful without further explanation, inasmuch as a grade is no more than a symbolic representation of standing in some characteristic). The teacher and the pupil should both be clear on the meaning of the grade. Second, once the attribute being judged has been selected, the basis of comparison should be established. Three such bases are possible: (1) comparison with the performance of others; (2) comparison with the potential performance of the individual, e.g., degree of improvement; (3) comparison with some absolute external standard. Adopting the foregoing steps in establishing criteria for grades will increase both validity and reliability.

Grades are part of a communication system informing the pupil and his parents on his progress. As a communication system, it is only as good as the amount of information conveyed in relation to the amount of energy expended. Previous comment has been made on the relative meaninglessness of letter grades. In spite of this, the conventional A-F grading system has two advantages in conserving energy: the first is that parents think they know what the grade means and ask for no further information; the second is that if grading is unavoidable, this method is as convenient as any. As for the pupil, his information is more accurate in spite of the grades, for he knows from daily performance how he is progressing in his various subjects. To improve grades and report cards as communication systems requires providing more explicit information, possibly in the form of check lists, letters, parent-teacher conferences, and the like—no small task.

It would be helpful if pupils and parents could divorce the informational aspects of grades from their motivational aspects, utilizing grades purely for knowledge of performance. But grades are incentives and operate with the effects described in this chapter. From the viewpoint of educational practice, it is important that the grades do not become a deterrent to motivation. Considering the central position of motivation in learning, any losses in motivation are mutually defeating to the purposes of both pupil and teacher.

Promotional policy similarly influences learning by virtue of its effect upon motivation. In general, two choices are available: holding the pupil at the grade level of the tasks he is capable of performing, which necessitates retaining the pupil at a given grade until he succeeds in the tasks; or keeping him with the pupils of his same physical-social-emotional development, irrespective of his performance on tasks. The former is called non-promotion or retention, the latter social promotion. Research shows that a policy of non-promotion does not assure any more mastery of subject matter or any faster progress than social promotion (Collinson, 1940; Cook, 1941), but that it does have a negative effect upon motivation (Sandin, 1942; Trainor and Rogers, 1955) in that non-promoted pupils, when compared with socially promoted pupils, show more symptoms of maladjustment, are more hostile toward schools, are more often socially rejected by their new classmates, and are more often viewed unfavorably by their teachers. While this evidence strongly favors a policy of social promotion, it does not justify a conclusion that social promotion can be depended upon for learning. In either case, learning proceeds only if capacity, task, and method have been adequately considered. A child can remain illiterate under either procedure if suitable provision for learning is not made.

SUMMARY

The classroom is a multi-variate situation in which innumerable influential factors are in simultaneous operation—individual abilities, attitudes, interests, experiences, instructional programs, and the like. The teacher plays a key role in orchestrating these variables. Among the major dimensions of the instructional group three (goals, authority, and group membership) are prescribed by the curriculum and administrative policy. The remaining five (climate, groupings, communication, group structure, and norms) are subject to teacher control. Key dimensions of the teacher role are: (1) source of knowledge; (2) nurturing adult; (3) organizer; and (4) authority figure.

Flexibility in grouping is essential in providing for individual differences. Support can be found for nearly all administrative arrangements: homogeneous and heterogeneous grouping; adaptation, segregation, and acceleration; team teaching and team learning. Equally, failure of such administrative arrangements is easily documented. No single procedure is best. Most comparisons of various arrangements fail from an oversimplified conceptual plan. What is required is consideration for total instructional systems which are coherent wholes. These will incorporate composite arrangements, including varied organization of instructional staff, multi-media modes of presentation, and a closer relationship between learning theory, experimental research, and educational practice.

FURTHER READING

Overview

HARRIS, C. W. 1960. *Encyclopedia of Educational Research.* New York: Macmillan. Selected topics: school progress; marks and marking system; curriculum development; social climate of classrooms; teaching machines; television.

Selected References

GAGE, N. L. 1963. *Readings in Social Psychology Applied to the Classroom.* Boston: Allyn, Bacon.

HILGARD, E. R. 1964. *Theories of Learning and Instruction, 63rd Yearbook,* NSSE.

PRESCOTT, D. A. 1957. *The Child in the Educative Process.* New York: McGraw-Hill.

SEIDMAN, J. M. 1955. *Readings in Educational Psychology.* Boston: Houghton-Mifflin.

LUMSDAINE, A. A. 1960. Instruments and media of instruction. In N. L. Gage (ed.) *Handbook of Research on Teaching.* Chicago: Rand-McNally, p. 609-54.

LUMSDAINE, A. A. and R. GLASER (eds.). 1960. *Teaching Machines and Programmed Learning: A Source Book.* Washington, D. C.: NEA, Dept. AV Instr.

Original Investigations

FINN, J. D. 1960. Automation and education. In Technology and the instructional process. *A.V. Communic. Rev.* Winter: 5-26.

GLANSER, M. and R. GLASER. 1961. Techniques for the study of group structure and behavior: II. Empirical studies of the effects of structure in small groups. *Psychol. Bul.,* 58:27.

SKINNER, B. F. 1958. Teaching machines, *Science,* 128: 969-77.

three

LEARNING
IN
BEHAVIORAL
AREAS

9

The Objectives
of Education

Education is fraught with much conflict. There is first the question of
who should be educated and at whose expense. There are some who
would educate only the gifted, although considering man's relations to his
fellow man, "gifted" may be misconstrued to mean those from a given
social class rather than those of a given capacity. There are those who
would educate all, on the premise that the successful development of
democratic society depends upon an educated citizenry. Whatever the
preference of people, there is no unanimity of opinion, and even those
who espouse the cause of universal education are not enthusiastic about its
cost. It is reasonably safe to say that the general philosophy within North
America is that all children shall at least have equal opportunity for
education; and if at times the boundary lines of what constitutes "equal"
are stretched, the acceptance of the philosophy justifies efforts to make
"equal" mean the same. This leaves the questions of what the education
shall be, of what studies shall be incorporated, of whether or not personal

or social development of children shall have equal place with academic and scholastic development, of what values shall be stressed, and of whether or not religion shall be incorporated in the curriculum, and, if so, whose religion. In general, these are philosophical questions which in modern societies are decided by some agency of government to which the general public has varying degrees of access. In the United States, the authority as to what shall be taught rests with locally constituted school committees, usually elected by the constituency served. That conflict can exist in this area of decision can be seen in the controversies that have arisen in recent years regarding world government, the United Nations, and the United Nations Educational and Social Organization, and their appropriate place or lack of place in a course of study.

If groups of adults are asked to identify the skills, achievements, and competencies which they would like to have their children attain by the end of twelve grades of school, the list they prepare will usually include:

1. Able to read, write, speak effectively
2. Able to think and reason
3. Able to get along with others
4. Able to appreciate art and music
5. Able to select a suitable vocation
6. Have some knowledge of history, government, and science
7. Have a hobby, and leisure or sport skills
8. Have a working philosophy of life
9. Have the ability to lead a happy, well adjusted life

The lists vary from group to group, being sometimes longer or shorter, and sometimes phrased in different terms, just as lists of educational objectives prepared by various committees over the past fifty years have varied in the number of items in their lists; but in essence, they say much the same thing. The foregoing list of items may be grouped under three headings:

1. Cultural
2. Social
3. Personal

Cultural items are those which involve learning to live in the man-made part of the environment, that is, using the language and the customs, the tools and utensils, and the machinery and equipment that a particular group of men have adopted for their use. The so-called fundamental skills are fundamental only to a particular society; they are far from being universal.

The items grouped under the second heading—social—are those related to living successfully with other human beings in a given society. This involves certain formal knowledge about the customs and institutionalized procedures—how the government operates, when to pay taxes, what accepted religious procedures are, and the informal procedures involved in maintaining satisfactory relationships with those persons met on a face-to-face basis—one's family, friends, and fellow-workers. Again, these vary from social group to social group even within a country; witness the variations in prejudice in different sections of the United States. The third group of items includes those concerned with personal adjustment—having a philosophy, a way of working, knowing one's assets and liabilities and accepting them for what they are, and knowing how to satisfy one's motives without infringing on the rights and privileges of others: in all, being personally well adjusted.

The order in which these objectives have been listed and described is the order in which they have been taught, an order of priority. We begin with the transmission of culture: the basic skills and the basic information—reading, arithmetic, social studies, and science. The informal social skills are left to chance, and the personal goals of self-knowledge, motivation, philosophy, and decision making may receive the attention of a thoughtful counselor at the secondary level. Knowledge and skills are the goals of education, judging from what occurs in schools; process and motives or values are other matters.

As long as cultural change was a sedimentary process, each generation depositing its thin layer on that of its predecessors, the transmission of knowledge and skill could be justified. They represented a finite, stable, and enduring body of information and behavior that would stand the test of a lifetime. That epoch has reached its end. The liberal education no longer lasts a lifetime.

In establishing priorities among educational goals, we should pause to consider the nature of *our* reservation. A review of the Statistical Abstracts of the United States will reveal that since 1900 any city (25,000 people) has increased fivefold if it has grown slowly, and up to a hundredfold if it's Los Angeles, for example. If population predictions hold, each urban area will have twice as many people by the end of the century as it does now. A glimpse of the future is at hand in the ten story row-houses in Holland. The New York Port Authority plan to build a twin skyscraper complex, five times as large as the Pan-Am building and containing 150,000 people, is a city within a city. These few data only point up probabilities in a situation wherein we have yet to find the solutions, namely how to live in a huge city. This is but one set of problems associated with the quantity of people. More critical for educational objectives is the present state of knowledge. Information in printed form dates back to Gutenberg's print shop of 1446. More books have been published in the last sixty years than in the previous five centuries, and three out of four of these books are new titles, not a new edition of an old classic.

Consider mathematics. Geometry got its start with Thales before the age of Pericles; Diophantus invented algebra two centuries after Christ; the seventeenth century saw analytic geometry, the calculus, and probability theory born, with non-Euclidean geometry coming along in the nineteenth century. A secondary school graduate was doing well if he got through the first three, and more recently we take pride in having added the calculus to the advanced secondary school programs. Where, then, put probability theory or non-Euclidean geometry, not to mention games theory, topology, group theory, symbolic logic, and the new algebras all invented in this century. Several of these, such as probability, game theory, and symbolic logic, are more relevant than geometry to our life. As much new mathematics has been developed in this century as in all previous centuries. For example, the number of mathematical papers published doubled between 1940 and 1950, again between 1950 and 1960, and have more than doubled again in this decade. Goethe is reputedly the last man who had a working mastery of the sum of man's knowledge, and Gauss (1776-1855) is supposed to have been the last man to know the all of the existing mathematics. If population is expanding, knowledge is mushrooming even faster.

Given the complexity of social organization on one side and a body of knowledge expanding at a logarithmic rate on the other, an inversion in the priorities of education may be in order, with the traditional culture in last rather than first place. This will be heresy to anyone convinced that a classical education is the prerequisite for teaching. However, if one accepts the information explosion, the population explosion, and the philosophical explosion as realities, then we face changes of the magnitude of the Renaissance or more. It was at that point that Copernicus started the earth travelling around the sun, ending its stay, as man viewed it, at the center of the universe. Feudalism fell and with it the divine right of kings. Man replaced kings as God's chosen, for wasn't man the acme of creation?

An equally dramatic change has occurred; in a short span of time our world has accepted the idea of possible life at other points in the universe, not in human form necessarily, but possibly possessed of the ability to communicate. This acceptance portends a shift in man's concept of where the pinnacle of creation is, which, viewed alongside the rise of existentialist philosophy, is indicative of certain doubts regarding the traditional concept of man as God's chosen. We may be searching for a new set of anchoring points, new identity in a changing intellectual environment. But numbers of people, amounts of information, and shifting philosophical concepts are the smallest part of impending change, if one takes seriously the technological revolution and the biological revolution, and we dare not do otherwise. Originally, when man lived by hunting, nearly all of his energies went into survival. With the invention of agriculture, some human energy was freed from toil, and the astronomer, mathematician, and priest emerged. With the invention of the machine, still more energy was freed for a variety of "non-productive" tasks. In fact, the United States is the first to have a majority of its work force engaged in service, rather than in manufacturing, production and allied work. These services range from menial work to medicine; nevertheless, fewer than half the work force produces enough food, goods, and so on, for the entire population. Now, with the development of automation, cybernetics, and computers, a vastly greater portion of human energy and time will be freed—for what?

Before writing was invented, the extent of a man's influence was limited by the range of his lifetime contacts—friends, fellows, and family. The possible exception was the epic tale passed along through the oral tradition. Writing made communication over generations possible; and print over time and space. Film and television, linked to satellites, make possible immediate access to any point on earth, and laser holography can make it possible to bring a three dimensional image of any person to any location. Technically, if we choose to put the resources into the development, man could sit in a cell and have his experience brought to him by means of TV and other technical processes. But what experiences? And this question holds, whether we bring the experience to man the learner, or take man to the experience: how shall one spend, fill, occupy leisure? And how shall we determine human worth when rewards are no longer based on the production of goods, capital, or services?

Then, there is the biological revolution. Consider this statement made by a biologist (from Fabun, 1968, VI-22):

> Only ten or fifteen years hence, it could be possible for a housewife to walk into a new kind of commissary, look down a row of packets not unlike flower-seed packages, and pick her baby by label. Each packet would contain a frozen one-day old embryo, and the label would tell the shopper what color of hair and eyes to expect as well as the probable size and IQ of the child. It would also offer assurance of freedom from genetic defects. After making her selection, the lady would take the packet to her doctor and have the embryo implanted in herself, where it would grow for nine months, like any baby of her own.

When one considers that human eggs have been fertilized and maintained in test tubes until cell division has commenced, and that implanting embryos is now done with certain domesticated animals, the above prediction is not implausible. Even more crucial is the slowly developing power to synthesize and manipulate the basic building blocks of life, the nucleonic acids. Given these Promethean powers, how shall man use them? By what set of values shall we decide the future?

If these considerations have merit, then our educational objectives need reordering, giving priority to values, social symbiosis, and information processing. The first is the most difficult, yet the most critical, for it first requires establishing a set of anchoring points for a new frame of reference, then making them explicit educational goals. We have been struggling to adapt to urban life a set of values which emerged from small town, agricultural, frontier democracy. The struggles going on in the cities over community control of schools is but one manifestation of this. Now we face the task of deciding which of our traditional values are valid for the life and times ahead, and the form in which they will manifest themselves.

Next comes the problem of the relationship between men (and women, and children). Various forms of symbiosis are observable and available, exploitative, reciprocal, dominant-submissive, and so forth. Again, the rate of social change makes consideration of the question imperative.

A century and a half ago most men in this country were self-sufficient. Most were self-employed farmers, living with their families, raising their food, making their clothes. Social interactions were intermittent—barn raisings, harvesting, occasional trips to town. Today, it takes only a strike of any of a dozen different labor unions to make only too clear how intricately interdependent we have become. Social symbiosis being unavoidable, man will have to be able to live, work, and play with others in high density social situations. Such accommodations are not easily achieved, yet they become as basic a learning task as arithmetic fundamentals.

Finally, there is the matter of knowledge. No man will be able or need to carry with him all the information he needs to deal with the contingencies of a lifetime, if for no other reason than the obsolescence rates in information. He will need skills in information processing which will include wanting information, knowing where to get it, and how to use it, that is, how to transform it in order to make it applicable to diverse problems. Learning how to learn will be a basic work skill. The implication for education is a shift from product to process. Already this change is occurring in mathematics. The beauty of the new math is not that children are doing algebra. There is no more virtue in doing algebra at six than at sixty. It is that they understand the thinking processes they are using which have a base in algebra. They are learning why and when as much as what and how. The memorized 100 basic arithmetic facts no longer suffice. Many of today's children may never encounter the calculus or topology or the laws of probability in a formal manner. Yet they will use, with comprehension, processes involved in all three. They will thus comprehend the difference between a Mercator projection and a polar projection.

Similarly, motivation is taking on an all-important look. The events of schooling have an impact on motivation as important as their impact on information. The management of groups and experiences in such a way as to maximize their positive potential for motivation and group processes is an essential precursor to the solution of the complex social problems existing and foreseeable. An inherent part of this management is the development of value systems that will serve as dependable fixed points. Thus the *kind* of information is subordinate to the *process,* and the process subordinate to the individual, rather than the present inverted order where the objectives specify a given body of knowledge to be mastered. Instead, knowledge becomes a means to an end, rather than an end in itself. If man is to continue to survive on the basis of his capacity to invent new ways of behaving, rather than new species, then an open-ended system which permits novel acts is prerequisite. With it, an educational system is needed which at a minimum does not deter inventiveness and flexibility, and at a maximum facilitates them.

Given a revised organization of methods and materials based on systems analysis and a revised focus on objectives, the task for the teacher is staggering, even more so for the schools of education. Changes are occurring at varying rates in different aspects of the curricula. Human habit lending the inertia it does, evolution may be slow, but the pressures are there in novel plant designs, in new curricula in science, mathematics, and foreign language, and now in the recently established regional educational research centers.

In relating the psychological variables to education, the distinction between content and process is utilized. Instead of the traditional educational organization of knowledge, skill, attitude, and behavior, i.e., the products, the focus is on the processes involved. This makes a certain psychological sense, because many learning tasks (e.g., reading, science laboratory, art, physical education) have affective motor, perceptual, symbolic, and cognitive aspects. Hence, each of these psychological aspects is considered in a separate chapter. The categories established are not mutually discrete, for it is virtually impossible to avoid some overlapping of functions, no matter what scheme is used. The purpose is to provide a framework within which the individual task and method variables reviewed in Part Two can be related to the work of the teacher. The chapters are ordered from what can be viewed as simple to complex learning, beginning with respondent behavior associated with the autonomic nervous system involving feelings and attitudes; then operant behavior involving the peripheral nervous system and simple trial and error problem solving, habits, and skills, with reinforcement playing its part; and finally complex problem solving utilizing the central nervous system and so-called higher mental processes. The prospects are that the compromise embodied in this scheme of categories will soon prove artificial as research gradually erodes the boundaries and identifies the processes common to all learning (motor, affective, cognitive).

An unfortunate outgrowth of concern with methods of teaching is an impression that a specific, approved technique exists for meeting any problem which arises and for providing immediate and easy solutions. It can be said only that there are better and worse techniques but that for any immediate educational problem there are probably several avenues to a successful solution, just as there are several procedures by which one may add a column of numbers and obtain a correct answer. The skill in teaching lies in being able to select the knowledge pertaining to a given situation and to adapt and apply it. Just as frequently, the skill lies in knowing that a procedure doesn't apply and feeling free to depart from convention.

Children are individuals, like others in the main but unique in part. Psychological experimentation, at best, provides guidelines for action, not specific answers for given individual children. The results of experiments depend upon averages. One can almost make the generalization that there are no average children, no children who are exactly average in all characteristics. The experimental result provides a useful point upon which to base decisions, but variations must be allowed for. It is in this ability that the art of teaching is distinguished from the sciences of education and psychology. In approaching the following chapters, the student may well consider the following questions:

How are *motives* shaped by the events of learning? Do understanding and insight play significant parts in emotional development, or do conditioning and reinforcement predominate? How do children acquire fears? How can their fears be met and controlled? How are attitudes learned? How changed? Can ideals and values be taught directly, or are they acquired indirectly? How does group behavior affect attitudes? How does appreciation for art, music, literature develop? To what extent should the teacher regulate her own attitudes and values in the classroom? To what extent is the teacher justified in attempting to develop ideals?

Can *motor skills* be learned blindly, automatically? What part do perception and thinking play in motor learning? Can motor skill be increased without direct practice? Are the usual practice periods for piano, football, or other motor skills too long? Would as much be learned in less time?

How do *perceptions* develop? How are they modified? How does motivation affect perception? Does learning proceed slowly in initial phases because it is more often organized on a logical basis rather than on a psychological basis? How can tasks be presented so that the learner perceives clearly what is to be done and what to be learned? How can the teacher sharpen the differences and the similarities and make clear the discriminations that have to be made?

Can *rote learning* really be considered learning by the teacher? In a classroom where rote learning is the vogue, could we not eliminate the teacher and do a more effective job with television teaching and self-checking devices? Where memorizing proceeds without comprehension, is anything ever retained for more than a short time?

Does correct usage of words indicate *comprehension?* Can abstract ideas and concepts be developed in the absence of actual experience? How can audio-visual aids be used as a substitute for direct experience? Can the teacher teach children how to learn?

What are the essential characteristics of problems? Do pupils react to problems as problems with a need to solve them or to problems as tasks to be performed? To what extent can *problem solving* ability be developed? To what extent do teaching methods defeat the development of problem solving ability? Can one think without using words or symbols? Are children capable of thinking and solving problems?

To what extent does schooling make a difference in the lives of children? Are the skills learned in school carried over into the out-of-school life? How much *transfer of training* occurs and how can it be increased? Do some subjects have greater transfer value than others? How do memory and reasoning ability develop? Do certain subjects develop such abilities?

FURTHER READING

Overview

BRUNER, J. (ed.) 1966. *Learning About Learning: A Conference Report.* Washington, D. C.: U. S. Dept. of Health, Education, Welfare.

Selected References

A.S.C.D. 1957. *Research for Curriculum Improvement.* Washington, D. C.: NEA, The Association.

BLOOM, B. (ed.). 1956. *Taxonomy of Educational Objectives.* New York: Longmans.

ERIKSON, E. 1950. *Childhood and Society.* New York: Norton.

FABUN, D. 1968. *The Dynamics of Change.* Englewood Cliffs, N. J.: Prentice-Hall.

MELTON, A. 1964. *Categories of Human Learning.* New York: Academic Press.

NASH, P. 1965. *The Educated Man.* New York: Wiley.

Original Investigations

AIKEN, W. M. 1942. *The Story of the Eight-Year Study.* New York: Harper.

BRISTOW, W. H. and D. A. ABRAMSON. 1966. Curriculum planning and development. *Rev. of Educ. Res.,* 36: 339-98.

NASH, P. 1965. Two Cheers for Equality. *Teachers College Record,* 67: 217-23.

SCHOELER, H. and G. S. LESSER. 1967. *Teacher Education and the New Media.* Washington, D. C.: AACTE.

TORKELSON, G. M. (ed.). 1968. Instructional Materials: Educational Media and Technology. *Rev. of Educ. Res.,* 38: 1-195.

10

Affective Learning:
Motives
and Emotions

Teachers as a group, when asked to designate topics connected with learning that they wish to study, invariably rank motivation and discipline high in importance. Motivation is recognized as important because without it, learning progresses slowly; discipline is important to teachers because it involves behavior motivated toward goals other than those which the teacher has selected or designated or deemed proper. A common fallacy that teachers express is their desire "to motivate" students to learn, thus confessing failure to recognize that children *are* motivated. They are exceedingly active, curious, and enthusiastic, all of which indicate motives in operation, but the motives may have no affinity for the arithmetic lesson or the chemistry experiment or whatever the item on the daily schedule of the teacher. Furthermore, the desire "to motivate" implies as often a desire to regulate behavior, to be able to turn it on or off as the teacher desires. Each person's and each child's motives are intrinsically his own, useful if they can be tapped, malleable if guided, but resistant if thwarted.

One of the problems, then, is to harness motives to educational goals; a second is to manage learning situations so that their effect is to foster motives which are personally and socially beneficial to the student.

In the initial discussion of motivation in the chapter on individual differences (Chapter 5), the following diagram for physiological drives such as hunger and thirst was introduced along with the acquisition of motives through the medium of reinforcement and drive reduction.

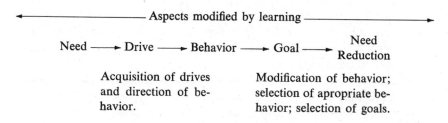

Classes of Motives.   On the basis of such a formulation, one can argue the development of a hierarchy of motives, beginning with the rudimentary physiological drives and culminating in the self-directing adult. The sequence of development as Maslow views it is:

Need	*Defined as*
Physical	Having the basic physiological needs provided for.
Safety	Assurance of being cared for and protected by dependable adults.
Affiliation	Need for love and affection; existence of person on whom one can depend.
Approval	Recognition of approval–disapproval and desire to obtain the approval of the person in power who establishes the reward.
Esteem	The standards by which one has been judged are internalized as standards for judging oneself; desire for those things which provide self-approval, status, recognition.
Mastery	Need to achieve, to accomplish, to master skills, surpass others.
Independence	Desire to be autonomous, self-maintaining person.

In reviewing the list, one sees the gradual acquisition and development of these classes of motives over time. The physical needs exist at birth and satisfaction must be immediately provided. Closely allied are safety or security needs, the basic assurance of being cared for and protected, psychologically as well as physically. Maslow believes these are fundamental, and that until they are reasonably well satisfied, the adequate development of the higher motives is impaired. The affiliative needs include love and affection, both of which find their basis in the early patterns of child care. The needs for approval and self-esteem are seen to emerge during the preschool years, mastery and independence during school years. This is not to suggest that achievement and autonomy do not have roots in early experience, rather that they emerge more gradually. Anyone who has watched a three-year old evade its mother in a supermarket or exclaim: "I did it!" on buttoning a button realizes that the roots of independence and mastery sprout early in childhood.

Where Maslow has provided a hierarchical ordering of general classes of motives as they develop, Henry Murray (1938) proposed a list of social motives based on intensive case studies with normal subjects. His purpose was to identify the psychological needs manifest in the behavior of his subjects. He was less concerned with the evolution of the needs than with their nature. Murray made particular use of projective tests in identifying the "psychogenic needs," to use his words. His approach is a dynamic one in which behavior is viewed as the result of the interplay of the needs and the environmental "presses," as Murray termed them.

The following list provides descriptions of the needs that Murray identified and relates them somewhat roughly to Maslow's hierarchy. The match is inexact in a few instances like Sex, Exhibition, and Order, which fall between categories. A careful consideration of the list will show that most of our actions and inferentially our needs (other than the basic physiological ones which are not included) can be fitted to one or another of the listed needs.

Describing motives and developing a classification scheme is an important first step in understanding motivation, but naming is not explaining. Calling a seagull a seagull doesn't mean we know anything about him. The designation of motives is helpful to the degree to which it corresponds with, describes, and helps explain behavior. On the human level, most of our knowledge of motivation is descriptive. Most of the experimental work has been carried out with sub-human species because of the possibility of controlling the propagation, feeding schedules, handling, and other experience. Even here, the problems are complex. On the human level, it is still more difficult to isolate a single motive. One man's desire for dominance may be satisfied by being a professor, another's by operating a bulldozer, a third's by simulating a heart attack when threatened. The very pervasiveness of motives makes it difficult to delimit them in ways which satisfy rigorous experimental design. The same behavior in different persons may derive from entirely different motives. Caring and fondness for animals may be a substitution for childlessness in one, an escape from inadequacy in social

Maslow's hierarchy of needs	Murray's psychogenic needs*	Defined as the need to
Physical	Sex	establish and maintain an erotic relationship.
	Sentience	seek and enjoy sensuous impressions.
	Acquisition	gain possession of objects and property.
Safety	Succorance	seek help, aid, love, support, or protection.
	Harm avoidance	avoid pain, injury, illness, danger, death.
Affiliation	Nurturance	give help, love, protection, care, support.
	Rejection	ignore, snub, discriminate, exclude another.
	Dominance	control one's human environment by seduction, suggestion, persuasion, or command.
	Aggression	attack, harm, punish, or kill another by word or deed.
Approval	Deference	yield to another's influence; admire, follow, and support a superior; conform to custom.
	Infavoidance	avoid failure, shame, ridicule, derision.
	Exhibition	impress others, attract attention, excite.
Esteem	Recognition	obtain praise and commendation; want respect.
	Defendance	defend self against attack, criticism, blame; conceal failure or fault; justify self.
	Abasement	comply, accept or seek blame and punishment, belittle self, confess and atone.
	Counteraction	overcome failure by restriving; overcome weakness or fear; maintain respect and pride.
Mastery	Achievement	accomplish the difficult rapidly and independently; master, organize, and manage people, objects, or ideas; excel.
	Understanding	know for the sake of knowing; speculate, analyze, formulate, generalize.
	Order	achieve organization, order, balance, precision, neatness, or cleanliness.
Independence	Autonomy	be independent and free, unconfined and uncoerced; be unattached or unconventional.
	Play	be relaxed, amused, diverted, entertained.

*Murray's original list contained 28 psychogenic needs, but seven have been omitted here because they appear to overlap one or more of the needs listed. These are: conservation, retention, construction, superiority, inviolacy, blamavoidance, and similance.

relationships for a second, a directly satisfying vocational interest for a third, or a combination of all in yet another.

The most intensive effort to provide an experimental account of motivation originated with Clark Hull and his students and their studies of instrumental conditioning. In explaining learning and habit formation, Hull made reinforcement and drive reduction central to his theory. Responses are learned because they occur in association with reinforcement. Simultaneously, neutral stimuli, occurring in association with drive reduction, acquire a capacity to reinforce. Behaviorists extend this concept to explain the learning of social motives.

PRIMARY AND SECONDARY DRIVES

In both classical and operant conditioning, a response or sequence of responses is brought under the control of new stimuli through the manipulation of reward and reinforcement schedules. The new stimuli, once neutral, acquire a capacity to elicit behavior which was earlier dependent on primary reinforcement such as food or water. Applied to the learning of human motives, the explanation would be: when an infant is fed, primary drives—hunger and thirst—are reduced. Neutral stimuli, associated with the drive reduction, acquire a reinforcing capacity of their own. Being held, caressed, talked to by the mother become what are known as secondary reinforcers, secondary because they do not reduce a primary drive. Just as food is something to obtain, so the repeated contact, holding, cuddling by mother—or as we might call it, affection—is something to be obtained also. According to this theory, our personal social motives are derived by conditioning through association with primary drive reduction.

No one will contend that neutral stimuli associated with primary drive reduction do not acquire reinforcing power, but to use this fact as an explanation of all human motives is cumbersome, if not impossible. Consider a few examples of man's unique, sometimes bizarre, behavior. The college student attends a college to further his education but as often as not cannot decide about education on or for what. He avoids eight o'clock classes like a plague, in fact he avoids as many classes as possible, preferring contract bridge, coffee, and chit-chat in the commons to study. He will join a fraternity not because the accommodations are any more comfortable or less expensive but for status, subjecting himself voluntarily to a variety of indignities during "hell week." Just prior to examinations, he will voluntarily work day and night long after all other higher and lower forms of life have retired to rest (with the exception of rats, bats, and burglars), smoking and drinking coffee endlessly to stay awake in order to cram sufficient information into his memory to pass an examination, information which will be forgotten within a fortnight. Or take man *en masse*. He lives in cities and commutes to factories in the suburbs. He lives in the suburbs and commutes to offices in the city. He spends half or more of his wealth building armaments to destroy other men's wealth, fearful all the time that they will destroy his own. He reduces the death rate and increases the birth rate and ignores over-population. He writes symphonic and folk music for his pleasure. He invents tools and machines to make work easier, then fears being made idle by his inventions. He dies from heart attacks from overwork and by dysentery from under-sanitation, yet permits both to continue. He employs psychologists and psychiatrists to study himself but is unimpressed by their findings. He could control his numbers but won't, satisfied to overpopulate and pollute his environment. Indeed, man is a complex, oftentimes strange creature.

Limitations of Reinforcement Theory. Perhaps the major weakness of the theory deriving social motives from the reinforcement of the survival needs of hunger and thirst is the fact that secondary reinforcers require repeated exposure in conjunction with primary reduction if they are to retain their reinforcing capacity. Without it, they are rapidly extinguished. Second, the theory assumes that activity is dependent on deprivation. The conditioning patterns explain instrumental learning—how we acquire the behavior which makes goal attainment possible—better than they do the acquisition of personal–social motives.

Several lines of experimentation offer clues which promise to reconcile the limitations of the secondary reinforcement theory. The first suggests that affectional needs may be primary rather than secondary drive states. Harlow and his associates at the University of Wisconsin have carried out a series of interesting studies with monkeys in which they provide infant monkeys with artificial mothers, then study various aspects of subsequent development. Their first study compared the relative strengths of contact comfort with nursing comfort. Two artificial mothers were constructed. The first was made of wood, covered with rubber, and enclosed in terry cloth; the second was made of wire mesh in the same shape. Both radiated heat (from a light bulb) and both gave milk in the conventional location by means of a mechanical feeding device. In Harlow's words:

> It is our opinion that we engineered a very superior monkey mother . . . soft, warm, and tender, a mother with infinite patience, a mother available 24 hours a day, a mother that never scolded her infant, and never struck or bit her baby in anger . . . although this position is not held universally by the monkey fathers.

To carry out the first study, four newborn monkeys received all their milk from the cloth mother, four more from the wire mother. The time each infant spent with the surrogate mothers was automatically recorded. Figure 10.1 shows the time spent each day with each mother from the first day to approximately six months of age.

It can be readily seen that both groups spent a predominant amount of time with the cloth mother. As Harlow points out, a drive reduction theory would expect the greatest strength of response to the source of feeding, but these results give priority to contact comfort. Exposed to various fear-producing stimuli, the monkeys sought the comfort of the terry cloth mother rather than the wire mother. Harlow's conjecture from this continuing series of studies is that contact comfort is a primary drive basic to the developing of

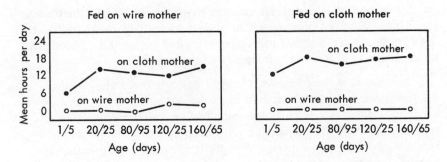

Fig. 10.1 Hours of contact spent on wire and cloth mothers for monkeys fed on wire and cloth mothers. (From Harlow, 1958.)

affectional bonds between mothers and children, or more abstractly, between the "objects" which provide comfort and the child. This conclusion will give comfort to mothers who enjoy holding their infants. In further experiments at the Wisconsin laboratory, Harlow has shown that monkeys will manipulate mechanical devices and puzzles for the direct satisfaction involved, without any involvement of reward in the usual sense.

Some thirty years ago, Dennis (1935) started a line of experiments which adds an important dimension to curiosity and exploratory behavior as motives. He was studying habit formation beginning with the customary assumption that the initial behavior of the rats was helter-skelter. Many adults make similar assumptions about children's behavior, that it is random unless regulated by adults. The assumption is erroneous in both instances.

Dennis observed that the rats' early behavior was not random but systematically variable. For example, if the rat turned one way on his first trial in a maze, on the next he would turn the opposite. Dennis was curious about the possible causes. Two or three explanations suggest themselves. The first derives from Hull's concept of reactive inhibition to the effect that following the performance of an act, there is a temporary resistance to repeating the act immediately, and the greater the effort, the greater the resistance. The second possibility is that the animal is "curious," i.e., he wants to seek out novel stimuli, and that reinforcement comes from drive increase rather than drive reduction. A third and related explanation was suggested by Glanzer (1953) and tested in a series of experiments (Glanzer, 1958).

Inhibition or Boredom?   Glanzer argues that it is not responses which become inhibited but stimuli which become satiated, or crudely put, we become "fed up" with seeing the same old things. The distinguishing characteristic between "curiosity" and stimulus satiation is that the former works through increased responsiveness to new stimuli, the latter by decreased responsiveness to old. In effect, one is turning toward the novel, the second, turning away from the familiar. These last two have obvious overlap; testing either against the reactive inhibition explanation is simpler. The initial experiment was to give an animal a choice of turning in a new direction into familiar territory, or turning in the old direction into new territory. If he chooses the latter, he is preferring new stimuli in spite of the reactive inhibition to be overcome in repeating the same turn. The animal is first rewarded for making a right turn in a maze shaped like a plus sign.

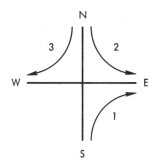

On the first run the animal starts at S, turns right, and is fed at E. On the second run he starts at N. A right turn will take him to W. If he is resistant to making the right turn because it is a repetition of the previous response, he will turn left. If curious, he will turn into the new alley to W. When tested, the animals preferred the new territory. Thus started a line of experimental studies of conditions affecting choices, leading up to what Dember (1965) calls a Theory of Choice.

The Theory of Choice starts with the premise that an organism is an information processing system in much the same way that it can be considered a food processing system. Just as it has certain food requirements, it also has certain information requirements which it will attempt to satisfy. These requirements are set by past experience. At the same time, all objects, events, and situations in the environment convey information, not in the notion of so many facts but in the technical sense of so much "news." The familiar is redundant; it says the "same old thing." The novel, unfamiliar conveys more information, more "news," hence possesses the capacity to arouse interest. According to Dember, all objects or events have their information value, or "complexity" value as he termed it, and this complexity is the crucial property with respect to motivation.

If the assumption holds that human beings are information processing systems with requirements set by past experience, this suggests they will seek objects or events which are (a) interesting and attention-getting and (b) "compatible" with past experience. One feature of compatibility is an appropriate level of complexity. The theory suggests that the appropriate level is an experience which provides some new information, but not 100 percent novelty. The old familiar lacks complexity or mystery and is boring.

(A parallel between this theory and that of McClelland's discussed in the final pages of Chapter 5 occurs, but we will return to this later.)

A study which illustrates the theory is found in an intriguing experiment with nursery school children. They were first allowed to familiarize themselves with a small group of toys, then given the opportunity to choose another table at which they wanted to play. One of the tables contained all new toys, another all the familiar toys. The remaining three tables contained mixtures of the familiar and novel, varying 2:6, 4:4, and 6:2. The children chose those three tables, containing a mixture of novel and familiar, in preference to the totally novel or the totally familiar. One is tempted to ask: I wonder if there were any personality differences between the children choosing 6:2 versus 2:6? Quite possibly such "personality" differences are merely differences in previous levels of information flow. Theoretically, one would expect children living in stimulus rich environments to develop different expectations and capacities from children of impoverished or disadvantaged environments.

Dember's theory not only builds on the research mentioned, but has had some preliminary tests with rats and college students—those perennial subjects—which suggest the validity of the desire to move from the less complex to the more complex, and to prefer levels of complexity correlated with levels of preference, i.e. past experience.

INTRINSIC MOTIVATION

Again, Dember's theory corresponds with arguments advanced by Hunt that suggest that labelling certain behavior as curiosity, manipulation, and play is an unfortunate result of labelling a *need* in accord with the *activity*. Hunt suggests that the explanation of the fact that animals seek stimulation, once primary needs such as hunger and thirst are satisfied, lies in the fact that such stimulation is intrinsically motivating, that there is satisfaction to be derived from the processing of information, i.e., making use of the distance receptors, the eyes and ears. In the primitive state, survival has depended as much on efficient use of eyes and ears, as it has on physiological drives. Both senses are rich sources of information, and the surviving man is he who efficiently uses them. In effect, Hunt argues that an eyeful is as appealing as a gutful. The main stumbling block in such a cognitive theory of motivation, as opposed to the drive reduction theory, is answering the instigating question: under what conditions will one seek or avoid stimulation?

The answer is expressed in differing ways by Glanzer, Dember, and McClelland: (1) increasing information and decreasing avoidance, (2) increasing stimulus complexity, and (3) increasing pleasurable or decreasing unpleasant affect. Similarly, Hunt thinks the answer to the instigating question lies in incongruities at the physiological level between physical demands and food and water supply which activate organisms to seek them, and at the psychological level between standards or expectations and events which lead to action. A novel situation is incongruous in the fact that it differs from expectations. Some novel situations attract, as in the studies of curiosity; others frighten or repel, as with children or chimpanzees who are frightened by strangers (and adults frightened by riots). Hunt accounts for such events by pointing to research evidence which suggests that small incongruencies or discrepancies between adaptation levels and the stimulus input are attractive and pleasurable, while large discrepancies are unpleasant and unattractive. Thus, children preferred the mixture of toys which contained both familiar and novel to the all familiar or all novel. The latter presented too great a discrepancy from what they were accustomed to; the former were boring because the children were completely accustomed to them. This level is technically referred to as the adaptation level, the term stemming from studies in perception showing that organisms adapt to the intensity level of stimulus input being encountered; e.g., one "forgets" (gets accustomed to) how fast a speed of seventy miles per hour is until one has to stop suddenly. Thus, organisms seek change about given adaptation levels, given expectations, given standards. These may be physiological (dietary), perceptual, conceptual, attitudinal. They derive from past experience. The positive and negative affect in relation to variations, great and small, from adaptation level is shown diagrammatically in Figure 10.2.

The diagram provides an explanation of arousal or attention or interest as a function of incongruities in stimulation. Humans avoid both a continuously homogeneous stimulus field and one in which incongruities are too great, seeking in preference moderate degrees of discrepancies. This is an explanation of temporary activity; but a successful explanation of human

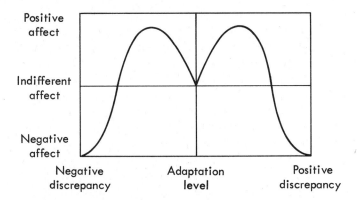

Fig. 10.2 Affective value as a theoretical function of discrepancy level of stimulation from adaption level. (From Hunt, 1965, p. 217.)

motivation must account for the enduring efforts that characterize so much significant human behavior. Hunt suggests that such efforts arise from persistent attempts to reduce the discrepancies or differences between present status and learned expectations or as it has been expressed, between the self-concept and the self-ideal.

During the past fifteen years, research has begun to yield more detailed information on the functioning of the nervous system and its manner of handling incoming stimuli. The stimulus world of the newborn infant has been described as an inchoate buzzing confusion of sounds, sights, smells, and feels in which he will in time find some order and organization. The fact of the matter is that the world is almost always a buzzing confusion of stimuli. Simultanously stacked up like layers in a French pastry are sounds from outside traffic, the radiator crackling, the footsteps upstairs, the wind, the children, the radio, the plane overhead, the typewriter, and more. Visual stimuli from the desk, papers, floor, hand movements, and so forth are received. The feel of the chair, hands, and elbows on the desk, the tight collar, and the pull of clothes across the back are experienced as well as internal sensations. All of these sensations are relayed to the brain, which somehow is not swamped, as telephone switchboards often are, by the flood of signals. The traffic flow is not only handled but monitored for variations. Consider the mother who without paying special attention detects a quieting in her youngster's play noises to indicate that he may have gotten into something possibly undesirable. This variation is detected, often in the middle of a conversation or a television program or cooking—in short, while she is engaged in a concurrent activity requiring her attention. Two studies which have a bearing on such abilities indicate the interaction between central processes and receptors. Hernandez-Péon (1956) exposed cats to loud tones and recorded the neural activity in their ears by means of implanted electrodes. When the cats were simultaneously given sight of mice in a jar and the smell of fish, the neural activity in the ears dropped markedly even though intensity of tone remained at the same level. Apparently, the inputs from eyes and nose produced an inhibition of the auditory input through some means of central cortical control. Berlyne (1960) reports a Russian study in which a vascular response (change in blood pressure) was evoked by pairing a tone with an electric shock in close sequence. With repeated presentation, the vascular response gradually disappeared. At this point, presenting the tone alone without the electric shock evoked the previously extinguished vascular response. In the course of conditioning, the human subjects gradually adapted to the expectation of the shock, in the same manner that we adapt to, i.e., gradually come to ignore, noise in the environment. But a change in stimulus pattern evoked an arousal. Such capacity for adaptation is essential to adjustment, for lacking it we would be slaves to the sheer physical properties of stimuli and subject to excessive demand.

The discovery that the brain had a rhythmic electrical beat (Berger, 1929) which could be recorded on an electroencephalogram (EEG) and that these oscillations were independent of the sensory influx just described (Adrian, 1931) opened an important avenue to understanding the functioning of the central nervous system. Records of these minute electrical waves show a pattern during relaxation of large, slow-frequency waves, called *alpha waves,* which occur ten times per second. During sleep, the number per second drops still lower. The graph of these waves may be compared to the continuous sequence of ocean waves at a distance from the shore. In fact, the major difference on a graph between ocean waves and the EEG of a man lying relaxed in a steamer deck chair is their frequency. But let the ship's horn sound or a commotion at the rail indicate an approaching ship and the man's EEG changes abruptly. The regular alpha rhythm is reduced and gives way to short, quick *beta waves* occurring at two to three times the alpha rate. If the ship's horn indicates a sudden emergency, the beta waves predominate and shift to a pattern which is rapid, irregular and desynchronized.

At this point several sets of events are underway: specific sensory areas of the brain are involved; at the same time a state of general arousal occurs, mediated by a general barrage of the cortex from the ascending reticular activating system or ARAS. The ARAS plays the monitoring role with the flood of stimuli and the activating role with respect to behavior. In particular, the ARAS is responsive to suddenness of stimulation, set, anticipation, and attention rather than to sheer volume of stimulation. Table 10.1 shows conditions along the continuum from sleep to excitement and the correlated behavioral states.

The ARAS is not a single part of the brain like the medulla or the hypothalamus. It is an intricate network of nerves originating in the lower brain stem and extending upward into the cortex. Several levels of functioning have been identified, as seen in Table 10.1, but primarily these represent a shift from sleep to wakefulness when the alpha rhythms predominate, from wakefulness to general arousal when beta rhythms appear, and finally from a state of general to specific arousal when beta rhythms predominate. At this last stage, the ARAS appears to enter into the specific focusing of or attending to particular stimulus conditions. In much the same way in which the hypothalamus was shown to play a role in smoothing the severity of muscular response in maintaining posture, the ARAS appears to integrate and smooth complex responses to a complex of stimuli, for it responds not only to external stimuli but also to stimuli received from the cortex. The interchange between the ARAS and the cortex is two-way. Presumably, then, memory, perceptual, and conceptual functions of the cortex can serve either as stimuli to the ARAS or enter into the equations determining response patterns of the organism. How the process of differentiation between sensory signals and integration of stimuli occurs

TABLE 10.1   PSYCHOLOGICAL STATES AND THEIR EEG, CONSCIOUS AND BEHAVIORAL CORRELATES

Behavioral Continuum	Electro-encephalogram	State of Awareness	Behavioral Efficiency
Strong, excited emotion: fear, rage anxiety	Desynchronized, low to moderate amplitude; fast, mixed frequencies.	Restricted awareness; divided attention; diffuse, hazy; "confusion."	Poor: lack of control, freezing up, disorganized.
Alert attentiveness	Partially synchronized; mainly fast, low amplitude waves.	Selective attention, but may vary or shift. Concentration, anticipation, Set.	Good: efficient, selective, quick, reactions. Organized for serial responses.
Relaxed wakefulness	Synchronized, optimal alpha rhythm.	Attention wanders, not forced. Favors free association.	Good: routine reactions and creative thought
Drowsiness	Reduced alpha and occasional low-amplitude slow wave.	Borderline, partial awareness. Imagery and reverie. Dream-like states.	Poor: uncoordinated, sporadic, lacking sequential timing.
Light Sleep	Spindle bursts and slow waves (larger). Loss of alphas.	Markedly reduced consciousness (loss of consciousness). Dream states.	Absent
Deep Sleep	Large and very slow waves (synchrony but on slow time base). Random irregular pattern.	Complete loss of awareness (no memory for stimulation or dreams).	Absent
Coma	Isoelectric to irregular slow waves.	Complete loss of consciousness (little or no response to stimulation): amnesia.	Absent
Death	Isoelectric: gradual and permanent disappearance of all electrical activity.	Complete loss of awareness as death ensues.	Absent

*From Lindsley, 1964.

is not known, but the sensitivity of the ARAS to changes in stimuli and to attention very likely enters into the results obtained by Campbell and Sheffield showing that hungry rats are no more active than satiated rats as long as they are kept under restricted stimulus conditions but that changes in external stimuli result in greater activity.

The primary function of the ARAS appears to be that of arousing the organism to activity. In doing so, it provides a capacity for adapting to and taking care of constancies in stimuli and for responding to changes. Conceivably, it could lead to a seeking of change in stimuli for the sake of activation.

AROUSAL AND AFFECT

Now, information does not convey much warmth, and even when we speak of preference for novelty and complexity, it conveys a rather neutral impression. In fact, we speak of emotional arousal as disrupting information processing, implying some conflict between the two. So, explanatory provision for feelings is necessary.

As we have seen, physical needs are one source of stimuli which activate the organism, external stimuli are a second. Looking at Table 10.1 reveals that the organism is always active, not only in the functioning of life processes such as metabolism but also in the processing of information from internal and external sources. Certain drives such as hunger and thirst may produce physical activity directed toward certain goals, but even in their absence, the organism is energy producing and interacting with the energies impinging on his senses.

Stimulus Preferences.   Over the past two decades, Young (1967) has reported a series of studies concerning the intrinsic pleasure-displeasure associated with certain rudimentary stimuli such as tastes, smells, and the like. That these exist, independent of experience, is suggested by Figure 10.3 which shows preferences of three age groups for a range of odors. (It is interesting to note that the least experienced responded more positively to the contrast provided by the absence of odor and that the adults placed no odor accurately in a scale of pleasant to unpleasant.)

Although the exact structure of the neural mechanisms involved in affective arousal is not known, the evidence indicates the existence of a regulatory mechanism within the ARAS which produces general excitation or inhibition associated with subjective feelings of pleasantness or unpleasantness. This suggests that stimuli impinging on receptors possess intrinsic capacity for eliciting affective responses as well as cognitive responses. Young points out, however, that whereas need-free rats will normally choose sucrose to casein, protein-starved rats do the opposite, unless a prior sugar preference habit has been established, in which case

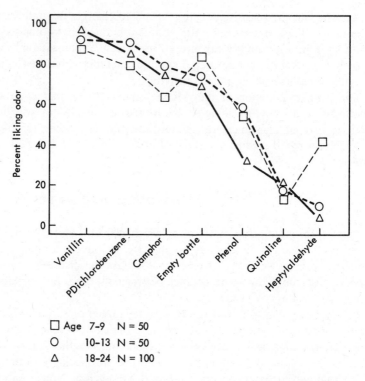

Fig. 10.3 Affective reactions to odors of three age groups. (After Young, 1967.)

the sweet is preferred in spite of metabolic needs. This suggests that learning plays a role not only in the acquisition of adaptation levels with respect to informational needs, but also with respect to affective arousal. As noted earlier, McClelland makes a shift of affect central to his definition of motive. Such a shift may be either pleasurable or painful, leading to approach or avoidance behavior. As a result, affective arousals are directive, regulative, and evaluative, paralleling shifts in stimulus complexity which have been shown to result in selection, seeking, and learning. The picture of motivation, then, is that of an energetic organism responding simultaneously along both cognitive and affective continua. Emotions thus make their contribution to response patterns, and the role of learning and habit has to be considered in this aspect of motivation as well.

EMOTIONS

Being emotional carries negative connotations, of being irrational, out of control, unstable, and so on. Much of this can be traced to historical prejudices which man has developed about himself as homo sapiens, the rational creature, the talking, thinking, tool and symbol manipulating animal, the best that evolution has produced. Rational thinking being man's noblest and distinguishing characteristic, sensuality and emotion seemed his most ignominious. A multitude of events contributing to this notion can and have been traced, but these are more properly the province of history and philosophy. Nevertheless, whatever the reasons, we have been reluctant to look at man as a sentient creature until recently. Systematic research on emotional activity has been limited. Our knowledge is derived in large part from clinical psychology. This partially accounts for the fact that more information is available on fear, anxiety, and aggression than on pleasurable states. Second, the feelings associated with emotional response are primarily internal and as a result dependent upon oral report. Behaviorist psychology, with its emphasis on objectivity and measurement, has been traditionally suspicious of introspection and verbal report. Efforts to identify physiological states which correspond with each emotion have not proved successful. To complicate the situation still more, emotions have their origins in infancy; many are well established before any reasonable kind of verbal report is possible. Finally, the interlock with motivation is such that emotions have been sidetracked in the course of research on motivation until Hull's students, notably Miller, began to look at fear and aggression.

Motives have been defined as internal states stimulating the organism toward specific goals. They are essentially internally oriented to physiological and psychological needs of the organism, although they can be evoked by external stimuli and lead to stimulus seeking. Counterbalanced against these internal needs is the necessity of responding to unsolicited external stimuli. Survival requires an ability to evaluate events and a capacity for rapid mobilization of physical resources. The former requires learned, cognitive ability to recognize danger signals, the latter preparation for defense, flight, or other appropriate reaction. Anticipation and readiness for rapid response are crucial to survival.

Emotions are patterned bodily reactions involving both a response and a preparation to respond to external stimulation. In more primitive days, when man or his immediate ancestors lived a life requiring more direct coping with the physical environment, his scales of judgment possibly had fewer degrees of variation: hungry-fed, sheltered-exposed, safe-endangered, fear-fight, and so on. Even such rudimentary scales involved not only the arousal dimension from passive to active but also dimensions of pleasant-unpleasant and approach-avoid. Increasing intellectual capacity amplified the more rudimentary emotional responses associated with the limbic system of the cerebrum and brought with it more highly differentiated responses ranging from a diffuse sense of well being to ecstasy on the pleasure side and mild aversion to overpowering fear on the negative side.

One of the functions of emotions which has been noted is the rapid preparation for responding to emergencies, an alarm response. A number of physiological responses occur during a state of alarm:

Adrenal gland secretes adrenalin.

Liver increases supply of blood sugar.

Heart beat rapidly increases.

Blood supply to heart and skeletal muscles increases.

Blood supply to skin and abdominal viscera decreases.

Stomach, intestines, rectum and bladder inhibited.

Eyes dilate.

Sweat glands secrete.

Skin hair erects (goose flesh).

Salivary glands increase secretion.

The effect of such responses is to increase the immediately available fuel supply, to stoke up the furnace as it were, to increase the blood pressure and fuel consumption rate, to shut off non-essential gastro-intestinal activity, to increase alertness, and to increase the all important supply of blood for sensory, cerebral, and motor activity. These changes are produced by the activity of the sympathetic section of the autonomic nervous system, the regulator of smooth muscles and glands. When we exercise, become cold, are threatened with asphyxiation, experience pain, or are frightened or made angry, the sympathetic section institutes the actions listed. Counterbalancing the action of the sympathetic section is what is known as the parasympathetic section which serves to counteract the alarm state when the need is over. However, the actions of the parasympathetic section are not as extensive, and it operates in a piecemeal more than an all-or-none manner.

Three Aspects of Emotion. If we consider the total emotional event, at least three major aspects are to be taken into account. These are skeletal or overt behavior, visceral behavior, and the emotional experience.

1. The skeletal behavior consists of the kind of activity we observe in another when he is angered, frightened, jeaolus, surprised, joyful, bitterly disappointed, disgusted, or grieved. We note the shrieks of fear, the threatening fist, scowls, smiles, laughter, sobs, and the like. Such behavior provides the clues which often, though not always, reveal to others the character of the emotion. The effectors for this behavior are the striated or skeletal muscles.

2. The visceral behavior, being internal, is not readily observed in another. Some of the observable effects of visceral components are the reddened or paled face, changes in breathing, dryness of the mouth, loss of appetite, urination, or defecation, all of which may occur in times of

strong emotional excitement. In addition, there are the internal changes reflecting emotion such as increased pulse and breathing rates, increased blood pressure and blood sugar, and so forth. These changes are produced involuntarily through the agency of the sympathetic section of the autonomic nervous system and the smooth muscles. While this widespread visceral activity is a characteristic part of general emotional disturbance, many of these reactions occur in other circumstances, such as violent exercise, exposure to cold, painful experiences, and loss of blood.

3. The third aspect of emotion is the experiential accompaniment of these visceral changes and the overt behavior. This is not open to direct observation by anyone except the one who is experiencing it, but for him it is the most significant thing about emotion. It consists chiefly of a complex of organic and kinesthetic sensations toned by a high degree of unpleasantness or pleasantness together with awareness of the emotional situation.

How Different Emotions Are Distinguished.   The fact that we detect and respond to different kinds of emotion in children and adults leads us to the question of how we distinguish one emotion from another or tell what sort of emotion we have before us. In the first place, we find few differentiae in the visceral reactions. These reactions have been found to be similar in fear and anger, the emotions in which they have been most thoroughly studied. Some recent research indicates that instead of the single adrenal hormone, adrenalin, which was credited with controlling bodily reactions, there are two or more, with adrenalin linked to fear and noradrenalin to anger.

The overt behavior of another person furnishes us with clues regarding the nature of his emotion. The rising voice, violent words, and threatening gestures commonly indicate anger; sobs and weeping, grief. Laughter and smiles are associated with joy, the pale face, trembling, and fleeing are common signs of fear. Studies of the ability of persons to judge emotions from facial expressions as shown in photographs have generally revealed better than a chance percentage of successful responses. Yet the overt behavior does not always reveal the true emotion. The various emotions often contain similar kinds of behavior. For example, crying appears in anger, grief, joy, and fear. As the individual grows up, he finds it socially expedient or even necessary to conceal and disguise his emotions. A person may smile to conceal his anger or laugh to disguise his sorrow or fear. He may manifest a serious demeanor when courtesy demands it even though actually he is amused, or he may appear to be delighted when unwelcome guests arrive.

Facial expression provides a second set of cues. Schlosberg (1954) reports three dimensions of expression which provide good agreement for ratings of different expression: (1) pleasant-unpleasant, (2) attraction-aversion, and (3) aroused-passive. Finally, the nature of the stimulus conditions provides a third means for classifying emotional responses. In a study by Sherman (1927), infants were subjected to various forms of stimulation to arouse emotional reactions, and observers were asked to name the resulting emotions displayed by the infants. Stimulation consisted of dropping a short distance, hunger, needle prick, and restraint of movement. Some observers were shown motion pictures of both the stimulating situation and the ensuing behavior. Other observers saw the behavior without knowing the antecedent stimulating conditions.

The results indicated that the judgments of the observers were dependent in large measure on seeing the conditions which aroused the reactions. When the observers did not see the stimulation, they were unable to agree on the nature of the emotion. When they saw the true stimulating conditions, they agreed in naming the emotion and did so in accordance with what one would expect.

DEVELOPMENTAL CHANGES IN EMOTIONS

Widely spread differences exist in the concepts of the development of the emotions in children. Watson (1930) believed that a trained observer could detect neonatal differences in the reaction patterns of infants for the three emotions of fear, love, and rage. According to the psychoanalytic school of thought, the child comes into the world lonely, helpless and afraid, stunned by the event of birth, and made anxious by the change from a placid to an unstable environment. Though incomplete in all other respects, the child was thought capable of adult emotional experiences. The evidence suggests that the initial state of emotion is one of general excitability from which results a gradual differentiation of emotional reactions influenced by maturation and learning. Bridges (1932) describes the emotional development as a process of differentiation, the first stages being distress and delight states. These occur in the first three months, the distress state being differentiated into fear, aversion, and anger by the middle of the first year, while affection is distinguished from elation by the end of the first year. Following this, still greater refinements occur until the adult emotional response patterns are established.

As development goes forward, many varieties of fear, love, and anger appear. Probably there are as many variations in emotions as there are different ways of perceiving emotional situations and different impulses to react to them. Yet, the familiar terms *fear, anger,* and *love* represent fundamental types and provide a convenient form of grouping for purposes of discussion. We may, therefore, consider the developmental changes in these as fairly typical of what takes place in the development of the emotional life.

FEAR

Careful observations and experiments with infants indicate that fear is naturally aroused by very few forms of stimulation. It has been quite definitely established that without conditioning an infant does not fear the dark, fire, furry animals, or snakes, although fear of these things is commonly acquired rather early. The stimuli which elicit fear without previous experience are those which come suddenly. Quite generally, sudden, intense, and strange stimuli evoke fear reactions in infants, and these are presumed to do so apart from previous experience. In experimental studies by Watson and others, the fear reactions were aroused by a sudden loud noise, by jerking the sheet on which the infant was lying, and by dropping the infant a short distance. It is noteworthy that this element of *insecurity* is the critical feature of all fear situations throughout life.

Changes in the Sources of Fear.   During the preschool period, the number of fear stimuli is rapidly increased. At about the age of five or six months, a child sometimes shows signs of fear at the approach of strangers. This manifestation presumably is directly related to his growth in ability to perceive. A careful investigation of children's fears by Jersild and Holmes (1933, 1935) revealed that the most common fear objects of children under seven years of age were animals, noises and events previously associated with noises, falling or danger of falling, pain or persons and things which have been connected with painful experiences, strange persons, strange objects, and strange situations. During these first six years, there is a decline in some fears and an increase in others. The percentage of children five and six years of age showing fear of noises, pain, falling, and strange persons and things was smaller than for the younger children. But the older children exhibited more fears of bodily injury, darkness, being left alone, and imaginary creatures such as ghosts.

Whether or not a given object will elicit fear depends greatly upon the general surroundings and the condition of the child. For example, a child does not fear a dog if his mother is present but is terrified if the dog comes upon him suddenly when he is alone. A loud noise does not frighten a child who is making it for fun. A child who enjoys being tossed up and caught again by his father may show fear if this is done to him by someone else.

In later childhood, a new kind of fear situation appears, one that is most troublesome. It is the imagined situation which is not limited by the boundaries of space, time, or objective reality. Jersild, Markey, and Jersild (1933) compared children's fears and children's description of the "worst happenings" that they could remember and discovered that children's fears center on different aspects of life than the day-to-day vicissitudes. The main fears of children aged 5 to 12 were (1) supernatural and mysterious events, (2) attack by animals, (3) being alone, lost, in a dark or strange place, and (4) being injured by accident. Almost exclusively, the worst event in children's lives was described as an accident, injury, or other physical hurt. It is, of course, possible to place several different interpretations on such data. They may be taken literally. They can be interpreted as a product of increasing conceptual development and consequent awareness of the environment. They can be interpreted as symbolic evidence suggesting greater insecurity, anxiety, and the like.

Although studies of children's fears made in the school setting probably produce an exaggerated number of concerns regarding school work, it is safe to conclude that fear and anxiety about school work is important from the intermediate grades on. One third of a large group of high school students report fears and worries regarding school tests and grades, one quarter about class recitation and teachers (Noble, 1951).

During the adolescent years, physical violence and suffering continue to be important sources of fear but to a lesser extent than in the preadolescent period. Teenage boys and girls are extremeley sensitive about what others think of them, especially members of their own "crowd." Their fears center largely around social situations and relationships. Clothes, appearance, lack of poise, money enough to do as other young folks do, invitations to the right parties, the family's social standing, hurting other people's feelings, and the impression they make on others are some of the more common causes of anxiety and worry for them. They appear also to be the greatest sufferers from discrimination due to racial prejudices.

Fears Acquired by Conditioning.   The fear reactions, like other forms of response, are subject to modification by conditioning. Many objects become provokers of fear by being associated or identified with something which causes fear. A high school teacher became frightened whenever a door or drawer stuck when she was trying to open it. Her trouble originated with a fright she had when a child. She was playing with her younger sister in the attic of their home. The younger child climbed into an old trunk, the lid of which fell down and became fastened. The older sister was terrified when she could not open the trunk, for she thought the child in it would smother to death before help could be summoned.

A little boy was brought to the school psychologist for a mental test. The child seemed afraid of her and all her efforts to secure his coöperation were futile. The examiner, realizing that there was no use in insisting, arranged for the boy to be brought back again in the afternoon. When he came in the afternoon, he behaved like a different child. He was most cheerful and coöperative. The examiner asked him why he would not do the things she asked of him in the morning. The child replied that he was afraid of her. When asked why he was afraid of her in the morning and not now, he pointed out that she had worn a white dress in the morning. He was not afraid during the second visit because the examiner had changed her dress during the lunch hour. A painful hospital experience had conditioned in him a fear of women dressed in white.

Fears Acquired by Threats, Suggestion, and Imitation. It is likely that before the child learns to understand spoken language, most of his specific fears are acquired by conditioning. But when language is acquired, a new source of fear is opened. Suggestions of danger and dire consequences carried by casual remarks which a child may only partially understand, threats implied or directly made to the child, and stories of disaster and tragedy often serve to implant fear of a situation which had previously been faced with calm or even feelings of pleasure. An electric storm, for example, may become a frightful thing to a child as a result of hearing his elders tell of some person being killed by lightning. One child developed a great fear of death because an older boy had said as they gazed upon the worm-eaten carcass of a cat, "We'll be like that some day."

The negative form of reassurance found in saying, "Now don't be afraid. Mother is right here with you. She won't let anything hurt you," can hardly be expected to develop courage in any child. It is significant in this connection that children in countries subjected to bombing by air raids have shown much greater fear in anticipating the raids than when subjected to the real thing. The source of their anticipatory fear is probably the talk of the dangers and hazards by their elders.

A child is, moreover, sensitive to the fears of others and tends to adopt them. If the first time he sees a snake, his companions show fright, their fear may cause him to perceive the wriggling reptile as a frightful thing, and he will probably react to it as they do. Children tend to imitate the fears of their parents. Hagman (1932) found a correlation of .66 between the number of fears of children and those of their mothers as reported by the mothers. Mothers tend to pass their own fears along to their children. Reports on the conduct of children during air raids indicate that the youngsters tend to reflect the emotional reactions of the older folks around them. If the adults remain calm and quiet, the children are less likely to become terrified than if their elders become panicky. As a result of suggestions, chance remarks, threats, and observing anxiety or panic in others the child learns to perceive situations as harmful or injurious, and the list of his fears grows longer. Research on imitation demonstrates that, unlike the relatively slow process of instrumental training, when a model is provided, patterns of behavior are rapidly acquired in large segments or in their entirety (Bandura, 1962). The pervasiveness of this form of learning is also clearly evident in naturalistic observations of children's play in which they frequently reproduce the entire parental role behavior including appropriate mannerisms, voice inflections and attitudes, much to the parents' surprise and embarrassment (Bandura, 1963).

Unfortunately, there are numerous exceptions to the normal course of development described above. Some fears, especially those conditioned by a severe shock or painful experience, are very persistent. They carry over from childhood into adult life and constitute the unreasonable and childlike fears which we frequently see in adults. The unfortunate individuals who are afflicted by such fears do not discriminate between the insecurity element and what constituted its harmless concomitants in the situation at the time of conditioning, and they continue to be frightened by perfectly harmless situations in which these concomitants occur. So, we have adults who are afraid of the dark, open bodies of water, open places, closed places, cats, fire, knives, and all sorts of objects because these things were connected with some terrifying experience of childhood. To be afraid of poor health, inflation, financial problems, and unemployment would be more realistic.

The School and Loss of Self-Esteem as Sources of Fear.   That the conduct of some teachers contributes to the increase of children's fears cannot be denied. In a study of the worries of school children, Pintner and Lev (1940) found that most of the worries of children in grades 5 and 6 were about matters connected with the family and the school. These writers characterized the school worries as "excessive" and stated that their results indicated that there was too much emphasis in school on failing a test, not passing, tardiness, and poor report cards.

Fears may be engendered by harsh criticism, ridicule, sarcasm, blustering, and displays of temper on the part of the teacher; also by unwise punishments or threats of punishment, by threats of failure, and by humiliating experiences in the presence of other children.

The school is a major influence in the self-esteem and the social acceptance held by a child. Children in the classroom reflect the values and attitudes of teachers in judging the worthiness of other children and in deriving a concept of their own worth. That teachers value excellent scholastic performance and submissive behavior can scarcely be questioned. Few children can be excellent scholars when they are judged competitively, for we must accept the fact that half of the population is below average in intelligence (by definition) and this obviously precludes the winning of competitive honors. Yet, persistently falling short in attaining the teacher's warmest approval promotes a lowered degree of self-esteem and an increase in susceptibility to anxiety and fear. Lazurus and Erickson (1952) demonstrated the deleterious effects of ego threatening stress based on failure upon college students. When two matched groups repeated a sub-test of the Wechsler-Bellevue, the group placed in the stress situation showed a greater spread of scores than the control group which decreased in variability. The greater spread resulted from the improved performance of students having the higher scholastic standing and from the worst performance of those having lower scholastic standing. Keep in mind that both groups, by virtue of being in college, have probably experienced more success than failure during grade school.

Overcoming Fears.   The method most frequently used by parents in attempting to relieve their children of fears is that of verbal assurance, which is not very effective if used alone. Its use in connection with other procedures is recommended. A recognition of the unreasonableness of a fear, while a help in many cases, does not always enable one to overcome it. Also of little value are the practcies of ridiculing or shaming the child, ignoring his fears, or forcing him to face or participate in the feared situation.

More effective than trying to talk a child out of his fear is an example of fearlessness. If the child sees that his parents, his teacher, or other children are not afraid, he will usually be able to face the situation more courageously. Basically, the intent is to provide a model, which if imitated, may thereby provide an adequate method of reacting to the situation.

A method which has been rather successful in overcoming fears in children is to present the feared object as a secondary part of a total situation that is pleasant. The procedure is to present the feared object first at a safe distance while the child is enjoying himself himself in some activity such as eating, and to bring it gradually nearer and nearer as the child becomes accustomed to facing it without emotional upset. Jones (1924) found that in this way children's fear reactions to rabbits or other small animals could be eliminated.

A study by Jersild and Holmes (1935) of methods used by parents in attempting to help their children eliminate fears indicated that the most successful procedures are: first, those which provide for the child opportunities for becoming acquainted with the fear situation by coming in contact with it frequently in his own normal activity; second, those which provide for contact with the fear stimulus first in a slight degree and then with gradually increasing intensity until it is encountered in its entirety; and third, those which help the child to develop skills which will enable him to cope successfully with the situation. A situation ceases to agitate and overwhelm an individual when he is able to make an adequate response to it.

George, a boy of nine years, was afflicted with an acute fear of the water. He was an only child; his father was a physician, his mother a college graduate. His parents wanted to send him to a boys' camp but believed he should learn to swim before going. The instructor of swimming to whom he was sent understood his fear problem and inquired into its origin. She learned that while at the beach, when he was three years old, two aunts of the boy took him into the water, where he was knocked down by a large wave and severely choked by the water. The unhappy incident had conditioned his fear.

The swimming lessons were given in a pool. The instructor spent the first half hour coaxing the boy to walk across the shallow end with repeated assurances that nothing could harm him. As George timorously ventured to do it, he constantly clutched the edge of the pool. The boy did not want his instructor to go into the water with him. She surmised that he was afraid she would push or duck him, and was later convinced of this when the mother and one of the aunts came to watch the boy during one of his lessons. Impatient with the boy's hesitation, they both shouted, "Push him in!"

Becoming accustomed to the shallow water, George learned to swim a few strokes. But after he learned to swim, he avoided the deeper water. The instructor then placed numbers at the side of the pool and urged him to work out to a farther number. This the boy tried, but all the time he clutched the gutter. He would not swim the length of the pool even with the aid of water wings or pole. He was afraid to jump into the water, but the instructor overcame that by having him work up from the lowest rung of the ladder, until finally he had the courage to jump from the edge of the pool into the shallow water. But he still avoided the deep water.

Finally on the day of the last lesson George did try jumping into the deeper water and enjoyed it. He kept on doing it past the hour for the lesson and asked the instructor if he couldn't do it some more. She told him he could if he would swim the length of the pool with the water wings. He did that and then kept on jumping for a long time. The following summer he became a good swimmer and learned to do several kinds of diving.

In this case, we have a combined use of the various methods mentioned above. The instructor used verbal explanation and assurance, she set an example of fearlessness, she provided contact with the fear stimulus by gradually increasing degrees, she did not try to force him into the water, and she taught him a skill (swimming) for adequately coping with the deep water situation. As for the value of this treatment to the boy, if George had gone to camp with this fear, he probably would have been mercilessly teased and humiliated. What might have happened if he had fallen into the hands of a less sympathetic instructor who lacked the insight and skill of this teacher in dealing with his emotional difficulty?

ANXIETY AND STRESS

Anxiety is commonly viewed as a generalized state of apprehension where the danger stimulus is non-specific and subjective in nature (although it may become attached to specific objects or situations). As such, it represents a chronic response to an environment perceived as being ever threatening. It is distinguished from fear which is considered a response to an external, realistic danger with fairly clear differentiation and perception of the dangerous situation. In other words, anxiety is a vague foreboding of danger; fear is specific in that the source can be identified. We are afraid of *something*. Both fear and anxiety function as drive states, the former producing responses to avoid the fear provoking stimuli, the latter producing responses to reduce the cues and feelings associated with anxiety, to escape stress. Anxiety can have both physiological and psychological accompaniments. It may be associated with hypertension, gastro-intestinal disturbance, fatigue, insomnia, worry, depression, or other symptoms seen with faulty adaptions to life stress and strain. We know that drive states can become associated with a variety of cues and responses, with the result that the symptoms manifested by any individual are likely to be idiosyncratic. Fundamental to them will be a pervasive insecurity, frequently laid down by threatened loss of parental love or repeated failure to find need satisfaction and cope with environmental demands.

All individuals are subject to stress. All individuals experience events which elicit alarm reactions—startle, fright, freezing-up, and the physiological reactions described earlier in the chapter. The general purpose of the responses is to protect the individual and mobilize his energies. As a result of experience, some individuals develop a chronic susceptibility to being threatened and alarmed. In a world in which the dangers become more global, more overpowering, more unpredictable, and the individual becomes more isolated, detached, and infinitesimal in his capacity to come to grips with them, susceptibility to anxiety cannot be escaped.

Another look at Table 10.1 will suggest that stress reactions can have differential effects, depending upon the level of activation of the individuals. For individuals low on the scale, stress and anxiety provoking situations can increase arousal and raise efficiency of performance. Actors, musicians, public speakers, and test takers experience such feelings. For individuals already highly aroused (anxious), exposure to stress or threat can increase the level of arousal to the point where performance disintegrates. Such results have been amply demonstrated in experimental studies. Sarason (1960) reports that the majority of studies of the relationships between anxiety and intelligence indicate that anxiety interferes with test performance (which is after all one measure of capacity to produce maximum performance on general learnings). Taylor (1955, 1958) initiated a series of studies, corroborated by other researchers, which show improved performance by anxious subjects on simple learning tasks but impeded performance on complex tasks.

Stress has been induced in the laboratory by varied means—electric shock, fear of test failure, frustration, threat, time pressure, derogatory comments reflecting on performance or personality, and others. Aside from elevation or depression in efficiency of performance, anxious subjects reveal themselves as being more susceptible to stress, prone to become more rigid in approaching problems, less discriminating in responses, and more variable in performance.

The specificity of fears makes them more susceptible to attack, at least those fears of children as they develop in the normal course of events. Persistent, exaggerated fears and phobias are more complicated. Nevertheless, fears possess a "tangible" quality, something one can get a hold of. Anxiety, more pervasive, vaguer, provoked by uncertain stimuli derived from unknown events, is more difficult. Nevertheless, it is not immutable. Having opportunity to verbalize one's feelings helps bring them into perspective. Making allowance for individual differences in work rates, motivation, and personality reduces stress. One of the disadvantages of homogeneous grouping is that it ignores such factors by placing the emphasis exclusively on performance and on expected equivalence. It also helps to create conditions which cast the teacher or instructor in a threatening, power exercising, status maintaining, arbitrary role rather than a supportive one. Merely feeling able to communicate with the teacher helps. Young children find security in consistency in routines, which lends stability to their world and their expectations. In short, actions which recognize the anxious student, minimize stress, increase security, and build confidence in a capacity to cope with events contribute to a reduction in anxiety and a capacity to manage it when it inevitably occurs.

ANGER

In the case of anger, as in fear, changes both in the source and in the behavior occur through experience. Most children engage in displays of anger more often than they manifest fear. This may be due to the fact that outbursts of anger are found useful for attracting attention and getting what the children want, while fears are more often concealed. Boys usually display anger more often than girls, perhaps because boys are more successful in using it to gain their ends.

Changes in the Causes of Anger.   Manifestations of anger in young children are associated with bodily restraint, interference with activities in progress, and frustration of desires. Throughout life, the essential source of anger is some form of interference which retards the individual's advance toward his goal or frustration which blocks the way to successful achievement of his purposes. In the young child, the most frequent forms of interference are those which impede or prevent free bodily movement. Frustration appears in not being able to get some object of desire or in being prevented from continuing with some activity that has been started.

As the child begins to walk and becomes more active in manipulating things in his environment, the range of possible sources of interference and frustration rapidly increases. The mastery of language also opens new sources of irritation. At the age of six months, he will not be angered by taunting remarks or by having someone call him "names." At a later age, however, he will be quick to resent such insults. They interfere with his good thoughts of himself and conflict with his desire to command respect from others. In his play with other children, conflicts arise over playthings, and over the part to be taken in games. These developmental changes result from both maturation and learning.

As the child grows to maturity, the fundamental causes of anger are the same, though the situations differ. In general, the outbursts due to interference with physical activities decrease. During the period of adolescence, the sources of resentment and retaliation are most often encountered in social situations. For the adult, the causes of anger are often the same as those for children and adolescents; but if he is emotionally mature, he does not so often become angry at inanimate objects that impede his progress, and the social situations that arouse his resentment and indignation are less often personal, i.e., social injustice, brutal or criminal conduct toward defenseless persons, exploitation of the weak, and ruthless acts of aggression by nations.

In anger, as in fear, the provoking situations normally change as understanding develops. It is the meaning which the situation has for the individual that determines its effect on him, and meanings change with intellectual growth.

Changes in the Overt Behavior of Anger.   The infant's reactions to restraint are explosive and diffuse in character, poorly suited to eliminate the cause of his annoyance. Through early childhood his behavior becomes less random and more and more directed toward the thing which arouses his anger. He is likely to resort to various forms of attack, such as biting, slapping, striking, or scratching other children who interfere with his activity. If these forms of behavior are unsuccessful or are promptly squelched by elders or other children, they will soon be abandoned. If the child triumphs in his purposes to get what he wants when he wants it, such forms of behavior may become his habitual method of dealing with interference. If they do not work, he may shift to other less aggressive forms such as sulking to force others to yield to his demands.

Olson (1949), in reporting his observations, reveals the wide range of vocal and motor behavior utilized by nursery school children in temper outbursts. The main vocal symptoms were crying, refusing, and screaming; but threatening, whimpering, and whining plus several other kinds of vocalizing were reported. Motor behavior was primarily pushing or struggling, tensing the body, striking, refusing to move, kicking, stamping, and flight, which were only half the repertoire of responses. Whereas infant outbursts of anger are explosive reactions, by age 4 the anger is directed toward a frustrating object in half the instances.

Anger is displayed by children more often than fear because situations which are psychologically or physically restraining or frustrating increase tensions contributing to aggressive behavior. It should not be construed that all aggressive behavior is undesirable in either children or adults. The direct aggressive actions of young children which ensue from exploratory and energetic behavior are a source of popularity among their classmates, and it is in their direct expression that aggressive behavior becomes channeled into socially constructive activities. The distinction between aggressive and hostile feelings which are an unavoidable result of social living on one hand and aggressive behavior directed to destructive or injurious ends on the other is an important step in child development. Failure to accept anger and hostile feelings in children by shaming or censuring the feelings creates guilt feelings which find displacement in self-disparagement or in more aggressive acts. With young children, acceptance of feelings followed by redirecting or diversion of behavior produces greater success in developing positive controls of behavior than direct challenging of the aggressive behavior.

The adult usually finds it expedient to restrain gross angry behavior. Resort to fist fighting between individuals is not considered respectable in most circles. Social custom dictates the legitimate manner in which insults and other annoying conduct may be redressed. The fighting of a duel was once the socially approved method of redeeming one's honor. Today, the approved methods of attack are ridicule, verbal criticism, blame, speech making, lawsuit, and warfare.

Aggressive feelings may be released in several ways: verbally through joking, teasing, swearing, and criticizing; in fantasy by dreaming or imagining varied misfortunes happening to the thwarting person or object; through displacement by cruelty to a weaker person such as a younger brother or sister or animal, which act may attain quite cruel and destructive proportions; in projection such as prejudice, which rids oneself of hostile feelings by attributing them to others; in delinquency and other anti-social acts; and in self-punishment. Some of the releases are more socially acceptable than others, and some are healthier than others. For example, individuals, particularly males who can express anger verbally without guilt rather than deny it, have shown better achievement in two studies (Weiner and Ader, 1965; Wyer *et al.*, 1965).

OTHER EMOTIONS

There is a temptation to dwell on the negative aspects of children's behavior, particularly aggressive behavior, because it interferes with classroom programs and disturbs other individuals. While an understanding of fear, anger, frustration, aggression, and conflict is essential, it is also important for the teacher to adopt a positive approach to children's emotions in order to foster healthy development. The satisfactory social climate of the classroom depends upon the teacher's ability to foster affectionate and pleasant interpersonal relationships. Fortunately, the positive affect of most children's groups and children far outstrips the negative. Sociometric studies reveal that choices between children usually exceed rejections by a 3 to 1 or 4 to 1 ratio, thus suggesting that teachers may be unduly concerned about "control" of children in assuming that children are innately uncontrolled, destructive, and aggressive. Fortunately, many teachers have discarded the notion that gloom and goodness go arm in arm or that a serious countenance is an essential condition of learning. Just as personality is modified through the control and channeling of negative responses to emotion, so does it develop through the nurturing of positive emotions such as happiness, love, affection, and sympathy.

The many other forms of emotional activity such as joy, love, surprise, mirth, and grief also go through developmental changes under the combined operation of maturation and learning. Joy usually comes from some signal success or the sudden fulfillment of a great desire. But with development from childhood to adulthood, the desires change and so does the character of the situations of success. The child is delighted with a new toy, the adult with a profitable business transaction or the securing of a professional honor.

The emotion designated "love" by Watson was aroused in the infant in his experiments by stimulating erogenous zones of the body. It appears that in the infant, at least, pleasure and happy states are the result of bodily stimulation. The young child's interests are primarily egocentric. His emotional attachment to his parents is probably conditioned by their association with the satisfactions of his physical wants. The gang stage just prior to adolescence shows the appearance of attachments to other persons outside the family circle. Such attachments are as a rule with members of the same sex. At this time, boys like and associate with other boys but shun girls. In adolescence comes the turning to the opposite sex and the emergence of heterosexual interests and attachments. That biological factors of physiological growth, inwardly determined but stimulated from without, play a major role in this development is not to be doubted. Yet the conduct at these various stages is largely dependent upon learning in the form of becoming acquainted with the social norms and conventions and with the importance of conformity to them. In some parts of the world, the approved and generally practiced forms of courtship and love making are quite different from those which are customary among American youth. Whatever form it takes, contact comfort may be as important to man's psychological comfort as it was to Harlow's monkeys.

EMOTIONS AND MOTIVATION

The discussion of emotions reveals several perspectives on them. The first is that emotions function as drive states, equivalent to motives. This is most clearly seen in connection with fear and anxiety, and possibly with anger, with their characteristic physiological reactions plus flight or fight patterns of behavior. A second view puts emotions in the role of feeling states accompanying motivated behavior. In this view, motives are the internal states associated with arousal and direction of behavior, emotions are the accompanying feeling states. An inherent problem in such an interpretation is the assumption of emotional states corollary with given adaptive behavior. In any given behavioral sequence intended to fulfill a given motive, varied and transient emotional states can and do occur. We may eagerly anticipate a project, respond with enthusiasm in getting started, subsequently get disgusted with progress and dolefully reflect on whatever stupidity prompted such an undertaking, only to end exhilarated by a successful achievement or depressed by a failure. Thus, a given motive finds not one but a sequence of possible accompanying emotional responses.

The third view of emotions is that they function as ends in themselves. The phrases, "I did it just for kicks," or, "We were just stirring up a little excitement," suggest that emotional arousal—the excitement, thrill, or pleasure—serves as an end in itself, independent of the specific activity. Principles of primary and secondary reinforcement could be applied to explain how emotional responses, occurring in conjunction with reduction of primary drives, would acquire incentive value of their own. Recall McClelland's making a change in emotional affect central to his theory of motivation (1953). Small increases or decreases in emotional arousal thus strengthen, and large changes have aversive consequence. Such a view closely parallels Hunt's incongruency-congruency theory of motivation, except that Hunt refers to changes occurring in the cognitive, rather than the emotional realm. Finally, the concept of stimulus saturation and Dember's Theory of Choice can be aligned with this last view of emotions. We seem to have arrived at a point of asking when is a motive a motive and not an emotion, or not a cognition.

If we return for the moment to our definition of a motive as an internal state giving rise to activity directed toward a goal, emotions are not excluded. Fear and anxiety, at least, clearly satisfy the definition. They vary in degree of arousal and they produce approach-avoidance behavior with respect to given objects or events. Part of our problem stems from labeling motives in terms of the behavior manifested and the goals sought; part of it stems from early research which began with survival needs and the homeostatic mechanism. Motives are indiscriminate in the particular habits they arouse and incentives they cause to be sought. Second, the concept of homeostasis need not be taken literally, in the physiological sense, in discussing all aspects of motivation. While it functions to maintain the organism at an optimal level physiologically, it may serve a different function psychologically and take a different form in the psychological realm. If in the latter case it is inappropriate to use the term for reasons of technical communication (thus one finds the terms congruency-incongruency in vogue), it is equally inappropriate to transfer the meaning literally.

If we avoid the *cul-de-sac* that arousal is dependent upon a physiological deficit or tension which produces activity to relieve the deficit or tension, and instead begin with an energy producing and consuming organism in a more or less constant state of arousal, our inquiry into motivation takes a different bent. We then can ask: what are the conditions which direct (motivate) the organism toward one goal or another? And we have to ask further: how does the organism keep from getting swamped by stimuli? We can answer both questions if we assume a series of homeostats which (consistent with the views of W. B. Cannon, the physiologist who proposed the concept) free the organism from constant attention to everything. Otherwise, like the rat killing terriers introduced into Wake Island, which went berserk at the numbers of rats, we would soon be exhausted attending to all the information put into our sensory system.

A concept of *discrepancies* linked to a series of homeostats offers an explanation of emotions and motives. Certain of the homeostats are innate, certain acquired, none are absolutely fixed, although they may become progressively so as a function of age.

The first and best known are the physiological needs stemming from lacks and distentions—hunger, thirst, sex and excretory functions. Activity and pain avoidance may be added on the primitive response level. Hunger, thirst, and pressure constitute built-in standards which motivate satisfaction seeking activity, namely, that which reduces the discrepancy by satisfying tissue needs.

Next, as a result of maturation and experience, we acquire three other kinds of standards: emotional, perceptual, and cognitive. Stimuli possess intrinsic yet varying capacity to satisfy, but these are soon affected by learning through association by contiguity and reinforcement, conditioning classical and instrumental. We develop sets of expectations regarding the environment against which we compare the influx of information. That which is consistent with the expectations or adaptation levels can be ignored; that which deviates requires attention. Conversely, by virtue of being active, stimulation is sought. Much as the blind child will rock endlessly, creating stimulus input, we expend energy seeking events which vary from but do not contradict, which are not too radical with regard to established expectations. As language and cognitive development proceed, expectations add an abstract and symbolic dimension. Attitudes represent sets to respond along a positive-negative, approach-avoidance continuum to specified aspects or objects in the environment. Ideals and values add a cognitive dimension. Given these different sets of expectations and more or less permanent or stable adaptation levels, both responses to and seeking of stimuli can be evaluated relative to the degree of discrepancy or incongruity—moderate deviations attracting, drastic ones repelling in accordance with Figure 10.2.

This discrepancy hypothesis fits short run variations in goal seeking behavior, possibly better than long term. It suggests that man's lot contains no permanent satisfaction, no Nirvana. If one considers fashions, automobiles, television programs, and other contemporary aspects of our society, nothing appears permanent other than slight change. It is more difficult to judge its applicability to long term motives, but interaction between the physiological, perceptual, emotional and cognitive components of motivation at both literal and symbolic levels provides enough permutations and development over time to account for persistent motivation.

IMPLICATIONS FOR EDUCATION

If we pause to consider a description of the characteristics of the mature person, we find them falling into three categories: relationships with self, with others, and with the world.

Essential in our feelings about ourself is a sense of being worthy and thinking ourselves good. We accept ourselves and our bodies and can gratify our physical needs adequately. We are consistent within ourselves and realistic in self-evaluation: we know our assets and liabilities and our strengths and weaknesses, and have knowledge of what motivates us and what mechanisms we resort to to maintain psychological comfort. In short, we are internally consistent, neither torn by conflict nor duped by self-deception. In our relationships with others, we are able to give and receive affection, to share others' emotions, to express our own feelings with vigor and spontaneity, to be loyal to friends and tolerant of people without sacrificing integrity, to accept and understand social customs and restrain our behavior accordingly, to be responsible to ourself and others, remaining at the same time sufficiently independent of group opinion and judgment to have some degree of originality and uniqueness.

In our view of the world and our place in it, we have to establish goals which are attainable, seen as socially acceptable, and toward which we can strive with some persistence. We must be able to learn from experience and to design and adapt our plans and procedures to the realities which surround us.

Running through these characteristics are a series of standards and accommodations to them: feeling worthy, accepting our physical needs, consistent within ourselves, knowing assets and weaknesses, loyal and tolerant, having attainable goals, adapting plans to realities. These standards contain elements which are physical, perceptual, emotional, and cognitive.

By the time the child begins school, the basic patterns of motivation and emotional response have been laid down at the physical and emotional, and to some degree, at the perceptual and cognitive levels, but much is yet to come. The role of the teacher is to build, develop, and modify these standards and expectations for selecting, evaluating, and responding to the environment. First is the task of creating expectations. Basically, arousal and interest are sought, a willingness to try the activities proffered by the school. If an aversive set has not been previously established by hearsay, the average child begins with a state of tentative willingness to try the school, accompanied by some degree of anxiety stemming from entering a strange environment. The teacher's task is to allay the anxiety and provoke interest, first by providing comfort by saying such things as: it isn't so different, you know some of the children, you've seen some of the stories, you've played some of the games, and then here are things to try. Like any beginning swimmer, the child has to try the water on his own terms, test his expectations and his capacities. This suggests that fixed standards for all comers are futile, for they are self-defeating; the job is at once to establish goals and standards of performance the child can meet, and at the same time provide less than 100 percent assurance to the child. This last is not to be construed as meaning that the teacher should never be completely satisfied, but that she should be completely satisfied only sometimes. Festinger (1960) has pointed out that one of the effects on individuals of partial rewards is increased performance and motivation.

Unfortunately, one of the effects of pre-established teacher standards is that many pupils receive limited rewards and develop an expectation for repeated failure in school learning situations. The effects are debilitating. If one deliberately attempted to foster hatred for school, i.e., negative motivation or avoidance behavior, one would adopt many practices currently used by teachers: competitive situations, uncertainty of success, arbitrary standards, frequent criticism, repeated public announcement of faults, arbitrary shifts from one activity to another without regard to task completion or level of motivation, repetitious stress situations utilizing time pressure, fault finding, and ego deflating experiences. *Obviously, the opposite is indicated.*

Finally, variation in activity is indicated in order to capitalize on the intrinsic incentives obtained from novel materials and different ways of presenting tasks. It has not been too many years since teachers felt betrayed by television, feeling that children were being taught to expect standards of performance and amusement with which teachers could never hope to compete. Today, the situation is reversed. Any teacher, with a little imagination, can attract children from the ennui of television with its endless repetitions and in the doing, help children develop standards for directing their behavior.

SUMMARY

Drives and motives are internal states giving rise to activity directed toward the attainment of particular goals. Motives are inferred from observed behavior, hence are psychological constructs utilized to account for behavior.

Physiological drives, referred to as primary drives because they are innate, are produced by changes in the internal environment resulting from deprivation, pain, and pressures which instigate chemical and nervous system activities leading to hunger, thirst, pain avoidance, sexual activities, and other survival drives. Primary drives are characterized by cycles of deprivation and replenishment or tensions for release. The process by which a balance is maintained is known as homeostasis.

Activity levels range from quiescence to overexcitement. Activity is instigated by the ascending reticulary activity system (ARAS) which functions as an unspecific sensory system, alerting the organism to changes in stimulus conditions. Interaction between ARAS and cortical and other areas of the brain permit monitoring and selective attention to particular aspects of stimulus input. Changes in activation level are accompanied by changes in EEG patterns of brain wave activity.

Research indicates that once primary needs are satisfied, animals and humans seek stimulation for its intrinsically motivating value, and that the stimulus of increased complexity and increased pleasure will be sought. Levels of expectation derived from experience provide the adaptation levels determining stimulus selection, with small discrepancies being appealing and large ones being avoided.

Emotions are patterned bodily reactions involving both a response and a preparation to respond to external stimulation. Emotions involve skeletal and visceral responses and changes in feeling tone. The repertoire of emotional behavior develops through a process of differentiation resulting from the interaction of maturation and learning. Fear, anxiety, and aggression are prominent emotions which function similar to drives.

In addition to the innate standards for evaluating need provided by homeostasis, learning provides additional sets of expectation in the perceptual, emotional, and cognitive areas which mediate in determining the conditions for arousal. The school has an important role in determining the expectations and shaping the social motives of children.

FURTHER READING

Overview

MARX, M. H. 1960. Motivation. In C. W. Harris (ed.) *Encyclopedia of Educational Research*. New York: Macmillan, pp. 888-901.

Selected References

BANDURA, A. 1966. Social learning theory of identificatory processes. In D. A. Goslin and D. C. Glass (eds.) *Handbook of Socialization Theory and Research*. Chicago: Rand-McNally.

BERLYNE, D. E. 1960. *Conflict, Arousal, and Curiosity*. New York: McGraw-Hill.

JERSILD, A. R. 1954. Emotional development. In L. Carmichael (ed.) *Manual of Child Psychology*. New York: Wiley, pp. 833-901.

LEVINE, D. (ed.). 1965. *Nebraska Symposium on Motivation*. Lincoln, Neb.: Univ. of Nebraska Press.

MC CLELLAND, D., *et al.* 1953. *The Achievement Motive*. New York: Appleton-Century-Crofts.

MURRAY, E. J. 1964. *Motivation and Emotion*. Englewood Cliffs, N. J.: Prentice-Hall.

Original Investigations

GLANZER, M. 1958. Curiosity, exploratory drive, and stimulus satiation. *Psychol. Bul.,* 55: 302-15.

HARLOW, H. F. 1958. The nature of love. *Amer. Psychol.,* 13: 673-85.

JERSILD, A. R. and F. B. HOLMES. 1935. Children's fears. *Child Developm. Monogr.* #20.

OLDS, J. 1969. The central nervous system and the reinforcement of behavior. *Amer. Psychol.,* 24: 114-32.

11

The Development
of Motor Skills

From birth to death, proficient if not skilled performance of many motor skills is essential to meet the demands posed by the environment—skills involving bodily movements however gross or fine, simple or complex. The supposedly helpless infant has a surprising repertoire of available actions— kicking, flailing, crying, sucking, head turning and so on, which steadily expand in scope and increase in refinement. Simple crawling and walking are quickly augmented by climbing, jumping, running, kicking. By kindergarten, motor activities include marching, buttoning, cutting, coloring, drawing, singing. The school child undertakes instruction in reading and writing skills which he will utilize as long as he lives. Many aspects of the upper school curriculum are predominantly skill learning—physical education, typing, arts and crafts. Earning a living, from unskilled work to professional, involves a variety of motor skills—shovelling, machine operation, construction, hair setting, accounting, advertising, surgery, engineering, to name a few. If for want of competence we cannot acquire needed skills, or by virtue of senescence we cannot maintain our skills, we are unable to function independently.

Every normal individual acquires many skills, some for their functional, others for their monetary or social value. Possessing them is an asset in many ways; they make for efficiency in work, enhancement of self-esteem, social recognition, or intrinsic pleasure. We enjoy performing skill feats; we enjoy watching skilled performance. The clever handling of a crane soon draws a crowd of interested spectators. The juggler and acrobat have a secure place in the entertainment world. A cleverly executed football play is admired, even by the opposing team.

Occasionally, one can acquire skill without a conscious plan of what he is about. Most infants learn to suck almost blindly; there is the occasional swimmer who got his start from being thrown into the water; and if one survives his first toboggan or bob-sled run, he undoubtedly learns something about the sport. Such events are more often the stuff of motion picture comedy than serious skill learning. The usual approach to learning a motor skill, self-taught or otherwise, involves having some idea, some plan of what is required. Occasionally, the plan is self-conceived as with the diver, figure-skater, or aerial performer attempting to develop an original show stopping act. Commonly, the plan is provided by a "teacher." The plan may be in the form of verbal instructions provided by book or teacher; it may be a demonstration, live or filmed; it may be an arrangement in the form of a musical score or choreograph. Whatever the source of the plan, the learner's task is to convert it into a sea of actions which represent a reasonable facsimile of the original.

PROGRESSIVE CHANGES IN ACTION
UNDER REPETITION

In the teaching act, the instructor possesses the total plan; he knows the whole of the skill, the various parts, and how they fit into the whole. He has a strategy, a program for teaching the skill. Basically, his goal is to transfer the program to the learner. The latter begins a process of building a detailed concept from vague beginnings and a total performance from piecemeal attempts. His ultimate goal is to blend these discrete pieces into the continuous sequence of movements which characterize skilled performance. And he hopes for a degree of skill which is sufficiently stable so that it can run off automatically with minimum need for voluntary control—in short, a habit pattern.

By definition, a habit is a highly predictable, learned response to a particular stimulus. It is the human equivalent of instinctive behavior in lower species. Beginning with a capacity for highly variable response patterns, man acquires a number of habits. Some are standard routines pertaining to commonly experienced events such as eating, drinking, introducing, venerating, etc. Certain ones are peculiar to specific situations and occupations such as operating, tackling, netting, stitching, and so forth. Whether standard routines or extraordinary, habits, like instincts, are prompted by certain provoking or releasing stimuli. Again, habits are like instinctual responses in being automatic. But they differ in that they are under greater voluntary control, are more variable, and are typically interlocked with a complex stimulus situation. For example, the football tackle or guard has a number of moves (habitual defensive or offensive tactics) available to him. His particular response on a given play will vary according to the immediate offensive or defensive formation and with his interpretation of the play as it develops. Nevertheless, his reaction will be instigated by the signals called by the quarterbacks. Its automatism in response to given stimuli is seen when the quarterback unexpectedly shifts his signals for putting the ball in play in order to trick the defensive lineman into an offside. Between this slightly variable, highly skilled, automatic, habitual response of the college or professional player and the haphazard actions of the sandlot footballer lies a sequence of development common to motor skill learning.

We can begin by asking, Does a unit plan exist for motor skills? In an interesting book, *Plans and the Structure of Behavior,* resulting from their year together at the Center for the Study of Behavior at Stanford, Miller, Galanter, and Pribram (1960) propose a unit which they label the TOTE unit. The term is an acronym for the sequence, *Test–Operate–Test–Exit,* which they judge to be the basic unit of behavior. Diagrammatically, the sequence is seen in Figure 11.1A. Using Miller, Galanter, and Pribram's illustration of hammering a nail, one checks (Test$_1$) to see if the nail is flush with the board. If not, one hits it with the hammer (Operate$_1$), then checks again to see if the nail is flush (Test$_2$). If it is, one stops

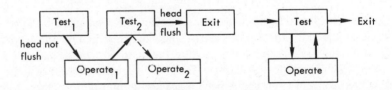

(Exit); if not, one strikes again (Operate$_2$). Inasmuch as the same test is applied after each stroke, the unit takes the form shown in Figure 11.1B. After each operation, a test is made. If the test is satisfied, action stops; if not, action continues until the test is satisfied (dotted arrow in Figure 11.1A). In actuality, the TOTE units incorporate two sub-phases which Woodworth (1958) refers to as the preparatory and consummatory phases of motor units. Before striking with a hammer, the hammer has to be lifted and aimed; after this preparatory action, the consummatory phase of striking can be carried out. Hitting a ball requires drawing the bat or racket back preparatory to swinging, i.e., preparation and consummation. Skilled behavior consists of what Woodworth terms *"polyphase motor units,"* or chains of TOTE units combined into sequences and sets.

The single TOTE unit described for hammering can be observed in children trying to hammer a nail for the first time. After each hit, they will look to see if they have successfully driven the nail. In skilled performance, the test is held in suspension until the discrepancy (distance between head of nail and board) is eliminated by a series of blows. In semi-skilled performance, a series of prior or parallel tests occur. For example: Is the nail going straight? Is the nail bent? Is the wood splitting? Developing skilled performance necessitates building the basic units into a hierarchy of sub-routines which ultimately become integrated into a smoothly flowing performance. Skiing provides a ready illustration, one which we shall return to at various points in discussing motor skill. To the person seeing Olympic competitions on television or to the person in the ski lodge watching instructors taking their preschool morning run, skiing appears to be a smooth, flowing, simple, effortless rhythm. To the novice, it is an awkward, disconnected, complex, near impossibility. Between the two lies a series of developmental phases which occur in learning many different motor skills.

The Snow-Bunny Phase. Skiing, like swimming, represents a novel form of locomotion when it is first tried. In walking or running, we hold ourselves in an erect, balanced position by continuous muscular effort; in swimming, balance and buoyancy are provided by the water. Again, in walking and running, we literally alternate falling and not falling by thrusting our body forward with one leg and checking it with the forward motion of the other leg. Change of direction is obtained by thrusting or falling toward the direction we wish to move. In skiing, a different set of actions is required. Walking on level ground is similar in both instances, but in sliding down a slope the task is no longer an alternation of fall-check. Instead, the task is nearly opposite—to prevent the body getting ahead of or behind the feet. And changing direction in skiing, as in swimming, requires a weight shift or thrust in the opposite direction to that desired. The very first efforts may go well because of the similarity of kicking in swimming and walking in skiing to motions already available in the learner's repertoire. Very few learners, once infancy is past, have no motor skills to bring to bear on a new task, unless it be weightless movements in space travel. But as soon as the skill requires new actions, the learning problems of the Snow-Bunny become apparent.

In this early phase, whether self-taught or taught by a friend or instructor, a first task is to *comprehend the instructions,* and execute a series of preliminary trials involving one or more sub-routines. The advantage of competent instruction lies in the ability to *identify the basic sub-routines,* provide an uncomplicated exposition of what each requires, and *feedback knowledge of results in a manner useful* to the novice. This last service is particularly essential where feedback comes in unfamiliar channels. For example, we are more conscious of information in visual and auditory channels than kinesthetic. At least we are not alert to how our weight is distributed, so that if an instruction calls for weight on right foot in dancing, or on down hill foot in skiing, few know whether their weight is there or not. This sequence can be illustrated from two early instructional segments in skiing. One of the first steps, once the rudimentary act of walking has been accomplished, is to teach the Snow-Bunny to traverse. Starting at the top of a gradual slope, he is shown how to position his body over his skis so that he faces down the mountain regardless of the direction of his skis. As he starts sliding slowly across the slope, he attempts to execute an instruction to lift his uphill ski. This simple act necessitates carrying the weight on the down-hill ski. The first turn in motion introduced in standardized ski instruction programs is the snow-plow, so-called because of the V position in which the skis are held. The novice stands in a fixed position over his skis, ski tips together and tails spread, knees bent, moving forward down the slope. Turning is achieved by simple weight shifts to one ski or the other, producing a turn in the direction opposite to the weight shift.

The plan for the motor sequence is provided by the instructor. During this stage the general sequence of operations performed by the learner involves *make-ready—recall—act—evaluate*. The first is the reception phase of alertness to stimulus conditions and preparedness to respond. The second calls for the recollection of the TOTE units to be performed, the third their execution, and the final phase the checking on performance based on knowledge of results. In skiing, one is immediately aware of a failure in execution. Falls or near falls are frequent, but evaluation is difficult because of the crude perception of the actions leading to the fall. Here instruction is valuable in providing feedback, as it is originally in providing a plan of action.

Repetition of an act normally brings about habituation. It does so by producing progressive change in various aspects of the total operation. At various stages of learning and with various amounts of repetition, we find different degrees of habituation. In considering the modifications which result from repetition, we shall be concerned with changes in the following features: (1) the task, (2) perception, (3) accessory responses, (4) feeling tone, (5) integration, (6) speed and accuracy, and (7) fatigue effects.

CHANGES IN THE TASK. The novice begins a sequence of actions with a given plan of action. The plan is ordinarily derived from some external source such as a book or instructor and is modified and reinterpreted by the learner in the process of attempting to comprehend it. He selects some portion of the plan, a sub-routine to be held in immediate memory, and proceeds to execute the short sequence, sampling the feedback from his own responses plus that provided by any instructor available.

Adding this information to that already in memory, he repeats or proceeds to the next sequence of movements. As he learns, the sequences become longer, the executive plan more effective, the dependence on feedback reduced. As proficiency increases, the sequence of make-ready, recall, act, evaluate is modified. The need for conscious recollection of the task drops out, and the need to evaluate minimized.

The dropping out of the task means that the subject does not have to formulate the act in his mind. He does not, as he confronts the situation, have to think, "Now I'll do this particular thing." The perception of the situation touches off without conscious intent or purpose the sequence of movements previously made. This permits an enormous economy for the individual in getting things done, because his attention may be given to other matters while the habituated performance goes forward. In the case of writing a letter, the movements of the fingers and hand do the writing quite automatically while the writer's attention is free for the non-habituated activity of thinking what to write.

CHANGES IN PERCEPTION.   In non-habituated activity, perception plays an important role. As indicated above, it leads to the formulation of the task, and through it the learner is made aware of various objects involved in the course of action, of the various movements made, and of the changes in the situation effected by the movements. In the course of habituation, however, perception diminishes. First, it narrows to those aspects of the situation most vital to the action. The perception of irrelevant factors tends to drop out fairly early. Then it is reduced with respect to those features of the situation of vital concern to the performance. In learning to play the piano, the novice sees each individual note. But with practice comes a reduction of perception.

In many skills where one's sequence of movements must be suited to changing aspects of the situation, as in automobile driving, a residuum of attention is indispensable. One must watch the traffic and curves in the road. But the extent to which perception changes in this activity can be seen by the fact that one may drive under familiar conditions with his mind absorbed in conversation or the topics of the day. The vaguest kind of perception, with reduced cues and obscure reference to the sides of the road or the traffic lines, enables the driver to keep his car on the road and in the right lane. Without conscious intent he turns the steering wheel upon approaching slight curves and depresses the accelerator as he comes to an upgrade. These movements, originally deliberate sub-routines demanding clear perception of curves and hills when learning to drive, now follow the barest flash of perceptual meaning. Such perceptions may emerge again as active parts in the performance when the driver encounters a traffic snarl or unusual road conditions, for here he is thrown back to a less practiced level of activity.

Because of the great amount of repetition of the acts involved in driving a car, the whole process tends to become automatized, and yet one cannot drive safely without being attentively alert. Lapses of attention, the normal result of automatization, constitute a threat to safe driving. They are responsible for many accidents.

CHANGES IN ACCESSORY RESPONSES. The novice usually displays a number of responses which are more or less accessory to the action. Superficially, these appear to be irrelevant and to mark the behavior of an inexperienced performer. Yet they are integral features of the course of resolution. They reflect the status of the performance at the moment and sometimes appear to effect changes in the procedure. The accessory factors include various comments, facetious remarks, giggling, squirming, sighs, exclamations, emotional reactions, self-instructions in the way of admonitions to be more careful or to try for speed and let the errors take care of themselves, and flashes of reference to self indicated by such questions as "How am I doing?" To illustrate these features of untrained action we quote from the record of the first trial by a subject in the mirror-drawing experiment. The drawing made by this subject in this trial is shown in the first star of Figure 11.2.

> Trial No. 1. At the beginning S smiled, then laughed in embarrassment. "It's awful! I can't start to go in the right direction. Now, if I push it that way. . . . Oh, I'm only going back and forth. How do I ever go forward?" The hand of S, grasping the pencil tightly, shook as it bore heavily on the paper. Leaning over in a hunched, cramped position, S exhibited marked attention. Exclamations of disgust were frequent. Having gone around the first point, she remarked, "A little better!" There were sighs as she went along the side of the second point, making many errors. After tracing around the third point, she said complainingly, "Oh-oh, stuck again!" Her mouth was closed tightly. Just before the fifth point she crossed the line several times, exclaiming, "Oh, dear! I'm slipping out again!" According to her own introspective report, she felt "awfully hot!" Her attention, she said, was not steady because part of the time she was trying to think out the process; then, she decided to pay attention. Her thoughts also dwelt on the instruction to keep between the lines. She was conscious of the fact that she was making many mistakes.

Under repetition, these accessory responses tend to drop out. As this experiment went forward, fewer comments were made by the subject. In trial fourteen, the drawing of which appears in Figure 11.2, there were no comments at all. There was a calm, businesslike demeanor, with uniform attention on the image of the star in the mirror. The subject reported that her hand was just "going of its own accord," and that she was "not being of much help to it." Accessory factors sometimes persist. In the thirteenth trial of this experiment, for example, the subject decided to take more time and try to make the tracing as perfect as she could (self-instruction);

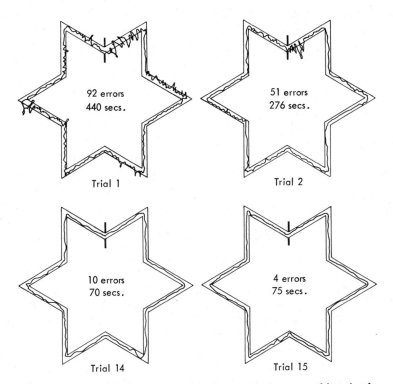

Fig. 11.2 Tracings of the star outline made by one subject in the mirror drawing experiment. *The drawings for the first two and the last two of the fifteen trials are shown. The stars were 5 inches from tip to opposite tip, and the distance between the lines was one eighth of an inch.*

a contortion of the face occurred during the tracing. Longwell (1938) reports that accessory factors do not drop out altogether but that they tend to disappear or to become stabilized as a result of repetition.

CHANGES IN FEELING TONE.   Actions are frequently toned by feelings of pleasantness or unpleasantness, by satisfaction and annoyance. These feeling tones, like other features of action, tend to change under repetition. In general, the feeling which accompanies an action shifts from the unpleasant and disagreeable to the pleasant and agreeable. The tensions, uncertainties, misgivings, awkwardness, and mistakes of the earlier tries are annoying, as are the distressing frustrations due to faulty performance, miscalculations, getting off on a wrong course, running into blind alleys, or the chagrin occasioned by one's ineptitude and the fear of being compared unfavorably with others. To be sure, a new action is not always unpleasant. Its novelty may provide the exhilaration of a new adventure, or the delight in being able to take the initial step toward a new skill.

The changes identified this far are found most frequently in the early phase of learning. With the increasing skill resulting from continued practice come confidence, self-assurance, pride in ability, sometimes even a sense of superiority.

The Intermediate or Hook-Up Phase. In the middle phase of skill learning, the several polyphasic sequences or routines become integrated and changes in speed and accuracy occur. The discrete units merge into a continuous process producing shifts in the factor structure involved in the processes being employed. Fleishman (1957) gave 200 trainee airmen extended practice on several different psychomotor tasks in which some eight factors were involved: speed of arm movement, visualization, perceptual speed, mechanical experience, spatial orientation, response orientation, fine control, and a within-task factor. Proficiency of performance was found to depend on different factors at different stages in learning, and as proficiency increased, the number of significant factors involved were reduced. Reynolds' (1951) study of the predictability of motor performance adds an additional perspective which supports these conclusions. Reynolds correlated scores on successive trials on a complex coordination test administered repeatedly during a series of training trials. The correlation between any two sets of scores decreased as a function of the amount of practice separating them. Correlations between successive sets of scores increased with the amount of practice. Thus, early and late scores showed lower correlation than intermediate scores with either; and late sets correlated more highly than early sets, indicating increasing stability of performance with greater amounts of practice.

INTEGRATION OF MOVEMENTS. Under the influence of repetition, movements undergo considerable transformation. In the beginning, as one undertakes to develop a motor skill, his movements are likely to be jerky, hesitant, clumsy, and awkward. The movements vary from trial to trial. As practice proceeds, the useless movements drop out and digressions are eliminated. Those movements that prove useful in bringing the person to his goal are made with greater promptness and precision and become coordinated into a smoothly flowing sequence. The performance becomes unified, stable, and highly integrated.

In learning to send messages by telegraphy, improvement depends largely upon developing *higher units* of action. The dots and dashes which stand for each letter are first produced as discrete movements, but the constant repetition of the series for each letter soon enables the sender to tap out each letter as a unit. He does not have to think of each movement but only of the letter. Here the letter unit is a higher unit when compared to the separate movements involved in tapping out the letter. The learner may continue for some time on the letter sending level, spelling the words and tapping out each letter as a separate act. As the letter units become familiar and more automatized through practice, they are made with greater ease and while the movements for one letter are still in progress, the sender's attention reaches ahead to the next letter. The second letter-unit of action then is actually begun before the first is completed. We then have overlapping. Soon the letter habits are tied together into action units incorporating all the movements for whole words. Then the sender does not have to think of each letter as he taps out his message. He has passed from letter habits to word habits. Thinking the word "arrived" sets off the rhythmical unified pattern of finger movements for the whole word.

In considering this matter of the integration of the discrete units of a total action function, it should not be assumed that there is no framework to hold these units together at the beginning of practice. Building a skill is not merely the adding of one movement to another. From the beginning, some cognitive set exists by which is envisaged the goal of the total performance. The various units of action are steps taken to reach this goal. The selection and integration of certain movements and the elimination of others is a matter of their congruity or incongruity with the individual's aims. Repetition affords the opportunity for developing better methods of accomplishing that which is to be done.

SPEED AND ACCURACY. As a consequence of the changes we have been considering, there is usually an increase in the speed and accuracy of performance. The typist writes faster and with fewer mistakes. The mail dispatcher does not require so long to sort his letters and throw them into the right sacks. The skater glides smoothly and swiftly without losing his balance. The trained worker gets more done with less effort and does it better.

An example of reduction of errors in motor learning is presented in the reproductions of the tracings of star outlines by a subject in the mirror drawing experiment. Mirror drawing provides a good example of sensorimotor learning, and it is well suited to experimental study. It presents a novel task, and, in a conveniently short period of time, one can observe the stages and changes characteristic of this form of learning.

In the experiment from which these drawings were selected, the star forms were placed on the baseboard of the apparatus and a shield was adjusted so that the subject was able to see the star only by looking into the mirror. He was instructed to trace the star outline by drawing a line along the path between the lines of the star. An error was defined as touching or crossing the line on either side of the path. Fifteen stars were traced. The first two and the last two are shown in Figure 11.2. A comparison will show the extent of improvement in the subject's ability to keep within the lines.

The reduction of time and errors with practice is shown graphically in Figure 11.3. The curves are based on the average scores for each trial made by fifty students. The dotted line is the curve for errors; the solid line

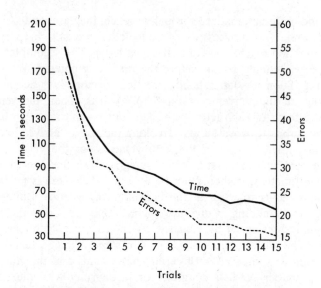

Fig. 11.3 Learning curves for time and errors, based on the mean scores of fifty subjects in the mirror drawing experiment.

is the curve for time scores. Improvement in both speed and accuracy is indicated by the steady decline of the curves throughout the fifteen trials.

CHANGES IN FATIGUE EFFECTS. As a rule, practice reduces the amount of fatigue resulting from performing a given task. We refer here, of course, to the fatigue produced by a single performance, not the cumulative effects of a long series of trials. Early trials are sometimes very exhausting. One is likely to begin with a great deal of muscular tension; nervous energy is dissipated and effort is wastefully expended in surplus motion. Energy is consumed by anxiety and fear. In the practiced performance, energy is expended more economically. The skilled performer takes his work more calmly and performs it with greater ease. A person's first day's work on a new job is likely to leave him pretty well worn out. It is difficult for a teacher to realize how fatiguing are the child's first exercises in penmanship. The experienced teacher will appreciate this point if he will recall how tired he became on the first day he taught in school. The effect of such fatigue is a drop in proficiency of performance rather than an impairment of learning (Alderman, 1965). A circular relationship exists between skill and fatigue—the less proficient the performance, the greater the fatigue effects leading to reduced performance. The greater the proficiency, the less fatigue, with the result that performance continues at a more efficient level over longer periods of time.

The Late Phase of Skill Learning.   Most individuals are content with modest degrees of skill—typing at 40 words or taking shorthand at 80 words per minute, "getting by" in a foreign language, playing a "fair" game of tennis, and the like. Such contentment is understood when one considers the sheer volume of practice required to attain high levels of skill. Improvement follows a logarithmic relationship to the amount of practice. The greatest gains occur early in practice. To attain an increment approximate to that attained in the first 100 trials, an additional 900 are required. To push the skill an equivalent notch, another 9,000 trials are needed. Thus, it is not surprising that few are willing to invest the time and energy required to attain professional performance. Corroboration of the demands in effort and energy are found in any sports page describing the training routine of athletes of championship caliber. Assuming for the moment constancy in motivation and other important conditions, the upper limits of performance are a function of the amount of practice possible before physical deterioration commences.

GUIDANCE OF SKILL LEARNING

The preceding identification of phases of skill learning is necessarily artificial and arbitrary, adopted primarily for descriptive purposes. Skill learning is a continuous process of attempting to master a given space-time sequence of actions. Changes occur progressively, rather than segmentally. The plateaus seen in learning when apparently no improvement in performance is occurring are assumed to reflect deficiencies in the measures or observations being taken, a decline in motivation, or some allied factors, rather than a true stage in the learning process.

Rarely does any learner undertake the acquisition of a new skill without possessing a number of developed abilities which are applicable. Some are general, such as the ability to understand instructions; others are specific, such as the basic motor skills identified in Chapter 5. Thus the learner begins with an organized system of skills and concepts. *The instructor's tasks are to assist the learner to develop a concept of the skill to be performed, to establish an appropriate cognitive set for discriminating the significant stimuli, to differentiate between appropriate and inappropriate available responses, and to organize these into appropriate sub-routines and hierarchies until an adequate level of skill is achieved.* Skills vary in a number of characteristics which affect learning programs and learning rates. Many of our inefficiencies in learning and teaching skills stem from limitations in the analyses of the skills in terms of these characteristics. Skills vary in their continuity, redundancy, and complexity. They vary in the pattern of space-time actions and in the stimulus-response-feedback conditions. Finally they vary in the coördination, timing, anticipation, and gradation of response involved. Several examples can be offered to illustrate these differences. Automobile driving is a continuous task in which a steady flow of information must be processed and responded to. It is highly redundant in that the same or similar sequence of operations repeatedly occurs. Yet it is a comparatively simple skill as judged by the number and kinds of stimuli to be attended to and the responses required. Compare operating an airplane with its complex instrument panel and the eye-hand-foot coördination required. It is probably a safe assumption that accident rates with airplanes would be higher than with automobiles if the same number of both were being operated—an index of difference in level of skill required.

Judging from observed performance on the highways, modest degrees of coördination are needed to operate an automobile; a crude gradation in response suffices. The skill level difference between ordinary motor vehicle operation and racing is great. Redundancy is greater in racing, e.g., the same turns are repeatedly taken in the same direction, whereas complexity is similar. The great differences occur in the coördination, timing, and anticipation required because of the speeds involved, and the gradation of responses needed because of the narrow tolerances involved. Essential differences between skills become apparent when viewed in terms of these characteristics. Deer hunting and the amusement park shooting gallery both call for a similar sequence of actions in firing the gun, but the differences in redundancy, complexity, timing, anticipation, and gradation of response are great. Viewing skills in such a fashion permits identification of critical differences affecting instructional programming.

Initial Steps. Adequate instruction for a good beginning involves more than placing before a child a perfect model or completed sample of a product of the skill he is to acquire. A child may have as his goal acquiring the ability to write. But when he begins, he must start by making particular letters, the letter *a,* and *h,* and all the rest. Now suppose we hand him a well written copy of the letter *a* and merely tell him to reproduce it. With a specimen of writing before him and with no direction except to copy it, there is no particular reason why the child should not begin to write at the right hand side of the page and work backward. He might build up his reproduction in sections, making the letter *R* by drawing a circle and putting two legs on it. These only suggest the many faulty habits a small child might form if left to learn to write without instructions. For a good start, he must be taught what movements are necessary and the sequence in which they should be made. This calls for directions with explanations and demonstrations.

In some cases of motor learning, a clear verbal explanation, simply telling the learner what to do and how to do it, may be sufficient. This will depend on having a background of experience or knowledge sufficient for comprehension of what he is told, adequate attention to the explanation, and a memory for the essential details of the instructions. Thus, an 18-year-old who has ridden in a car might be able to fix in his mind the necessary procedure for starting a car from verbal directions. But an adult who has had no acquaintance whatsoever with the language of golf would probably be baffled if his instructor in his first lesson in golf tells him he must play his iron shots off the center of the body.

The instructor's first responsibility is to have a clearly thought out program. It is often said that the surest way to learn something is to attempt to teach it. In effect, this is to say that the attempt to teach forces one to organize his understanding of the skill involved. Hopefully, instruction begins after this point rather than before with an analysis of the activity in terms of the several characteristics noted above. The advantage of such analyses is shown by Scott (1954) in a program designed to overcome the discouragingly slow progress common to beginning adult swimmers. Recognizing that a complex set of factors involving motor abilities, attitude, water temperature, and instructional sequence affected progress, Scott's program sequenced breathing, floating, backstroke, vertical float, treading, and side-stroke; but emphasis was given to an accelerated rate of the presentation of skills, early introduction of vertical float, treading, and entry into deep water, plus continuous relaxed swimming to develop endurance. Rate of progress was greater than in conventional programs.

Given such analysis, the instructor's task is to transmit his program to his student. Invariably, two decisions occur, whether to proceed by a whole or a part method and to decide the size and sequence of instructional units. There is no intrinsic advantage to either the part or whole method. Both can be used effectively. As one illustration, Wickstom (1958) taught two groups of male, college level novices, equated for physical ability, a set of seventeen tumbling and bar stunts. After a description and demonstration, one group proceeded to practice each stunt as a unit; the other practiced the stunts by steps, finally combining the steps into a total unit. The stunts varied from elementary to advanced. Equal amounts of practice were given. Although a tendency in favor of the whole method occurred, as it often does with adults, only one stunt of the seventeen showed a statistically significant difference.

Research evidence suggests that children may prefer the part method, largely because of a sense of progress derived from small successes; adults with their greater time perspective have more tolerance for the greater time required to master a total task. Furthermore, individuals tend to be more proficient with whichever approach is the more familiar. In general, some combination of the two is likely to be more productive, but the basic choices are determined more by the nature of the material than by the method. For example, skiing is a skill which progresses more effectively by starting with sub-routines which can be combined as mastery of each occurs, whereas piloting a plane is less readily subdivided into pieces because of the dynamic interplay of velocity, gravity, and control surfaces on the plane. Even here, take-offs and landings represent discrete sub-routines which can be delayed until sufficient skill in control of the plane has been achieved. With complex skills involving the interplay of a dynamic set of conditions, such as piloting an airplane, simplified wholes tend to be more instructive than subdivision into simple elements.

A study by Battig and others (1957) indicates that preliminary verbal instructions are most useful with simple tasks, but that as the complexity of the task increases, the efficacy of verbal instruction disappears. The instructions are most helpful in developing the appropriate cognitive set but cannot compensate for the practice needed to execute more difficult tasks. The importance of the effect of the cognitive set induced by instructions is seen in its effect upon speed and accuracy of performance.

Speed and Accuracy. The nature of proficient final performance determines whether emphasis should begin on speed, accuracy, or both. A commonly accepted viewpoint is that accuracy should be emphasized during early phases of learning, then speed should be developed. Research indicates otherwise. Where speed is important in the ultimate performance, practice should be at as rapid a pace as possible. Where quality of performance is important, as it might be in dress-making, cooking, portrait-painting, or cabinet-making, efforts in practice should be directed to doing the task as well as possible.

Where both speed and accuracy are important, as in typewriting or handwriting, to meet the requirements of expert performance, effort must be directed in such a way as to secure advancement in both. In the mirror drawing experiment, in which subjects are instructed to work as rapidly and at the same time as accurately as possible, it has been found that some students improve more in speed while others improve more in accuracy. A comparison of the gain in speed and in accuracy for a group of fifty subjects reveals that twenty-seven gained more in accuracy, whereas twenty-three made greater gains in speed. Reports of the subjects indicate that self-instruction frequently operates to shift effort from speed to accuracy or the reverse.

In an experiment bearing on the topic, Solley (1952) gave three groups of forty randomly selected subjects different instructions during an initial training period and studied the effects on subsequent performance. The experimental equipment involved a twelve-ring target, a striking instrument, a 1/100 second clock, a photo-electric system, and a scoreboard for timing and scoring thrusts at the target. Each group had ninety training trials distributed on six days over a three-week period, one stressing speed in striking the target, one stressing accuracy, and the third placing equal emphasis on both. Subjects' scores were computed and they were informed of performance after each day. At the end of the initial training period, statistically significant differences in speed and accuracy demonstrating the effectiveness of the sets obtained from verbal instruction were obtained between the three groups. During a second three-week period, all groups were instructed to place equal emphasis on both speed and accuracy. The results showed that the initial training period had a pronounced effect upon subsequent performance. Speed developed under initial emphasis of speed readily transferred into performance during the equal emphasis period, whereas accuracy gained at low rates of speed was lost almost immediately when the rate of performance was increased. The result indicates that in motor skills where speed is to be a significant factor in ultimate performance, the emphasis should start on speed, with accuracy secondary; but, where both speed and accuracy are to be combined in performance, the initial training should incorporate both.

Form of Instruction. Experimental evidence and teaching experience indicate that when a child is being directed concerning the form his activity is to take, he should be told what *to* do rather than what *not* to do. From the instructions arises the task which determines the course of action. The instructions, therefore, should be aimed at the results desired. Negative instructions may serve to inhibit undesirable responses, but when imposed upon the child as he is about to enter upon a new kind of motor performance, they may serve to distract and divide his attention and lessen his chances of success. Direct measures must sometimes be taken to block error and break up faulty methods, as we shall consider later; but in the beginning when we are trying to help the child to a good start, his attention should be directed to his goal and the movements to be made in order to reach it rather than toward the undesirable or forbidden modes of response. The best way to prevent the formation of faulty habits is to have a strong set and undivided attention directed toward the correct means of gaining one's end.

With this general guideline, a variety of procedures can be used to facilitate learning. For example, Howell (1956) demonstrated that a graphic analysis of the response pattern of a complex, rapid motor act presented to learners after each performance helped them to understand the physical principles involved, visualize their errors, and correct them. The motor skill was sprinting, the subjects were beginners, the graphic record was obtained from a device which recorded a clear, continuous graph of the force exerted by each foot, the manner in which the force was exerted, and the time taken to complete each movement. These patterns could be compared with the characteristic pattern recorded by good sprinters. The experimental group improved rapidly; after the third day (eight trials per day), they surpassed the control group and maintained their superiority thereafter. Further, they were less variable in performance than the control group.

As technological skill increases, it is natural that it should produce modifications in instructional procedures. One finds an increasing use, for example, of films, film strips, and film loops in various aspects of instruction. A number of studies (Bream and Messersmith, 1948; Damron, 1955; Nelson, 1958) describe the use of such techniques in teaching such varied skills as tumbling, golf swing, and defensive football formations. In all instances, they proved effective, but no more so than conventional procedures. Such results recall the findings with television instruction, that equivalent outcomes can be obtained, and that the more rigorous the experimental controls, the fewer the number of significant differences obtained when instructional procedures are compared. The limitations of such procedures is that they are parallel, rather than composite. Increases in instructional efficiency are likely to come from analysis of skill requirement and adaptation and utilization of instructional techniques peculiarly applicable to given aspects of the skill, rather than from comparisons of alternate, overall procedures.

Egstrom (1964) has demonstrated that time spent in conceptualizing the skill to be performed can contribute to skill acquisition; and Smith and Harrison (1962) show similar results with varied forms of practice—visual, motor, mental, and guided practice. Of interest is the fact that certain forms of practice can be more effective in improvement of speed, others in reduction of errors. The interaction between form of instruction and locus of skill is clearly seen in Wilden's comparison of authoritarian and pupil dominated methods of teaching basketball to junior high school girls. Two groups of girls were matched for age, motor ability, basketball knowledge, and socio-metric status. Both groups were given similar instruction in rules, fundamental skills, and basic tactics, following which team play was controlled by the coach for one group, with the second group being self-directing. Independent observers ignorant of the experiment rated performance of both groups, crediting the coached group with better skills, the pupil-dominated group with greater knowledge of rules and better team performance. In retrospect, these results appear as an intrinsic part of the instructional format.

Demonstration. The essential purpose of the initial instruction is to give the learner a clear idea of what he must try to do. If verbal explanation and directions are not sufficient to accomplish this, the instructor must show the learner. Because a young child is less capable of strict attention than a mature person and since his ability to comprehend and remember what he is told is more restricted, he, more often than an adult, will need to be taught by means of demonstration. Lack of attention can be as much a result of incomplete understanding as a cause of it.

In giving a demonstration of the performance to be learned, the instructor must take care that his pupil is in a position to observe the essential details of the demonstration and that his attention is being given to it. It must not be hurried but should be given slowly enough for each step to be witnessed and understood. In the case of a demonstration involving several steps, it may be necessary to repeat it several times. In most cases, explanation should accompany the demonstration.

Common mistakes of an inexperienced teacher are to cover too many details in a single explanation, to give too many directions all at once, or to demonstrate more than a beginner can possibly assimilate at one time. The instructor should remember that the role of his instruction is to establish a set in the mind of the learner—a task—and that the capacity of any person is limited with respect to the number of steps that can be incorporated into a single task. It is poor teaching, for example, to take a young person out for his first lesson in driving a car, and proceed to tell him all you know about handling a car. He will not be able to remember more than four or five items of instruction at a time. The complex processes must be taken up a few steps at a time. As these are practiced and mastered, new steps can be added and the whole process integrated by practicing all the steps together.

Reversed View of the Demonstration.   A demonstration of a motor performance may be very confusing if the instructor and learner face each other. The reason for this is that the learner, in such a position, sees the movements in a right-left reversal of the way he must make them himself. The reader may observe this difficulty if he faces someone who is trying to show him how to tie a new kind of knot. It will be much easier to see how the knot is tied if he stands beside the demonstrator; he can thus see the movements from the direction from which he will see his own movements when he attempts to tie the knot himself. An instructor of surveying reports that his students learn to use the surveying instruments more readily if he has them stand behind him and look over his shoulder as he gives his demonstrations.

Manual Direction.   Sometimes in teaching a motor skill, manual guidance of the learner's movements is employed by the instructor. This procedure involves taking hold of the learner's hands, feet, or whatever part of the body he is to use in the skill to be acquired and pushing them through the desired movements in the proper sequence. Piano teachers sometimes place a child's hand in position and push his fingers down to strike the keys. For beginners in manuscript writing, the letter forms cut from emery paper are sometimes used. The child traces these forms with his fingers. In the first trials, his hand may be guided manually by the teacher.

What we have here is a form of demonstration. It is a way of showing the learner what to do and how to do it. As a form of demonstration, it has certain advantages over merely observing the teacher's performance. It avoids the difficulties of a reversed demonstration described in the preceding section. The learner sees his own members moving in the manner in which he must make them go himself. This should be helpful in selecting and identifying the proper movements.

There is another possible advantage of this kind of demonstration: the kinesthetic element involved. The child not only sees his hands or other members in the various positions but also feels them there and feels the movement from one position to another. The value of this is somewhat uncertain since the kinesthesis involved in having someone else move your arm about cannot be identical with that which comes from your own execution of the movement. Some individuals seem to depend on kinesthesis more than others in learning movements. A student in the writer's laboratory was found to be entirely lacking in visual imagery according to all our tests. She was given a learning problem that consisted of reproducing a nonsense design after a five-second exposure. Most students have been found to make a reasonably good reproduction after four or five trials. This student was unable after many trials to make any headway in learning the design well enough to reproduce it. Finally, she adopted the scheme of tracing the design in the air with her finger during the exposure period. By doing this, she was able after three trials to make a very good reproduction of the figure.

Although manual guidance may be, in some cases, a good way of showing the learner how to carry out the performance, it does not take the place of the individual's own efforts and practice. To learn a skill is to modify the controls or determination of movements involved in the action. The center for these controls is in the central nervous system, and the modification of them is brought about by the learner's activity, not by the activity of the teacher.

Self-Instruction and Motor Learning. In the absence of knowledge of how to proceed to develop a new type of skill, and with no one to give the learner directions, it would seem that an individual might in some cases be able to think out the proper procedure. Perhaps this is sometimes done, though it is probably safe to say that it is rarely done. To think out the best method of performing a task requires a certain amount of knowledge or experience relevant to the task, an acquaintance with principles involved, and the ability to restrain the impulse to experiment blindly. It is probably more often the expert or a person who has already acquired more proficiency than the novice who actually thinks out a better way of doing a thing. Repeatedly, students have reported that prior to their start on the mirror drawing experiment, they thought that they could manage the tracings easily by simply going in the opposite way from that which was normal because they were aware of the fact that the mirror reverses the image of the star outline. Here is an example of trying to solve the problem of procedure by thinking. But the actual benefit of such reflections is invariably slight. Usually the subject soon becomes baffled and finds that his deductions lead only to confusion. He then casts aside his logic and plunges into a try-this-and-try-that method. Efforts at verbal solution to problems involving perceptual motor skills have the advantage of being more systematic, though not necessarily more successful, than manipulative approaches (Ray, 1957).

When reflective thinking is helpful, its contribution is of the same sort as that made by the instruction of a teacher or of a book. It provides suggestions of how to proceed. Of itself it can never yield a motor skill. It may, if good, foreshorten trial and error and thereby contribute to the efficiency of learning.

The development of skill requires practice on the part of the learner; however, mental practice can assist the process. Vandell, Davis, and Clergston (1943) divided twelve males from each of three school levels, college, senior and junior high school, into matched experimental and control groups. The groups having actual practice or mental practice showed improvement in basketball shooting, with the groups having actual practice making the greater gain. Control groups showed no improvement.

These early findings regarding the usefulness of mental practice have been subsequently confirmed (Twining, 1949; Clark, 1960; Jones, 1965), although all studies have involved comparatively simple skills.

Having demonstrated the usefulness of mental practice in skill learning, the researchers are prone to give it equal status with direct practice, overlooking the fact that the skills with which this effectiveness has been demonstrated are comparatively simple ones for which transfer potentials are considerable, e.g., ring toss, basketball shot, badminton. Mental practice is not likely to prove as effective with novel and complex skills.

EFFECTIVE PRACTICE CONDITIONS

We can now consider some of the factors which make for economy and efficiency in acquiring motor skills. From the great amount of work done on this subject, it is possible to state several generalizations that should be helpful to one desiring to secure the maximum return for the time and effort expended. The factors to be considered are motives, working conditions, essentials of effective practice, and correction of faulty performance.

Motivation.   Adequate motivation is always an essential for effective learning activity. When it is a motor skill that is to be acquired, probably the best motive is the desire to possess the skill. When there is no such desire, the teacher's first concern is to create it if possible. In many cases, it will be sufficient to point out the benefits to be derived from the skill. If the learner is a younger child and the advantages offered by the skill are so remote that they do not appeal to him, then other motives must be enlisted. Among these are the desires for social approval, prestige, and play. Athletic skills offer intrinsic satisfaction because of the potential fun involved and the status to be derived from possessing the skill, even in the elementary grades. Boys in particular need such skill to gain the respect of their peers, which explains in part why we observe boys seeking such experience and showing superior proficiency with increasing age in spite of the relatively equal physical capacities of boys and girls up to early adolescence. Unfortunately, the school curricula too often center on competitive athletics and high organization team sports. Under such a system, most individuals become watchers of games, not players.

Once the novelty wears off, early phases of learning involve considerable frustration. Each practice trial produces some resistance to repeating the act (reactive inhibition). Some of the resistance is physiological and dissipates rapidly, some is psychological. The advange of high levels of motivation is that it works to postpone the build-up of resistance to the repetition needed to gain proficiency (Wasserman, 1951). Finally, frequent and consistent use of reinforcement is important, particularly in the early stages of learning. Given the overt nature of responses in motor learning, reinforcement should be specific rather than general, linked to and calling attention to appropriate responses which approximate the desired behavior.

Working Conditions and Instruments.   Favorable working conditions and good tools or instruments have much to do with efficiency and economy of motor learning. Room temperature and humidity should be conducive to bodily comfort. Lighting should be adequate for clear vision without strain. The height of chair, desk, or table used should be adjusted to avoid fatiguing positions. Instruments should be placed within natural reaching distances and, where several are used, arranged so that a minimum of effort is expended in shifting from one to another.

Poor working tools may retard learning or, because of necessary adjustment required to offset their defects, they may even be the source of habits that may later have to be overcome. The beginner in typewriting should have a machine that responds normally when the keys are struck, and the child learning to play the piano should have an instrument that is well tuned.

Goals and Sub-Routines.   For instruction to be effective, the learner needs a clear idea of the goal of instruction and the ways and means for reaching the goal. Awareness of a goal without knowledge of the sub-routines involved in achieving it leads to trial and error efforts to discover how to accomplish it. Similarly, emphasis on the steps to the exclusion of the goal is ineffective.

After a proper start has been made, practice should be aimed at the end to be achieved. Practice on difficult parts may require definite attention to the steps, but the steps should be regarded as the means for achieving the final goal. The goal gives meaning to the steps.

As an example of emphasis on steps without due regard for the final goal, we cite the case of a friend who is now past 70 years of age. When she was about 10 years old, the aunt with whom she lived wanted her to learn to make a quilt. Her task, set by her aunt, was to sew together small pieces of calico cloth to make one "square" every Saturday morning. The child's goal, therefore, was not to make a quilt, but to piece a square every Saturday morning. After she had completed a square, the task for that day was done. Now, at 70 years of age, she still has the collection of completed squares but she has never put them together to make a quilt. Here was emphasis on steps to the neglect of the real and ultimate goal. The goal is needed to secure the integration of the steps into the total performance.

Conditions Under Which Practice Should Be Conducted. *Practice should be conducted under conditions similar to those which will attend the use of the skill, and the procedures practiced should be those in which skill is desired.* One learns what one practices. After the steps necessary for a good beginning have been taken, attention during practice should be directed toward the desired results. If it is skill in throwing a ball that is sought, the eyes should be fixed on the target when throwing. Although some useful bits of information regarding what to do in the water may be acquired on land, one must, to become a skillful swimmer, practice in the water. To be able to tackle well, the football player requires practice in real game situations. In the shop, the student should have real machines and make real things.

Older methods of drill for students of typewriting called for a great amount of drill on nonsense syllables, assuming that the finger movements acquired would transfer directly to typing words in sentences. No doubt some transfer occurred, but the same dexterity can be obtained by use of meaningful letter combinations. Modern methods call for the student to start practicing on sentences just as soon as the keyboard is learned, providing him practice in accordance with his goal, which is to be able to type sentences skillfully. Similar changes have occurred in foreign language instruction. Instead of the vocabulary lists to be memorized, but not recalled when needed in a sentence, the present emphasis is on first obtaining mastery of basic linguistic forms, e.g., declarations, questions, and the like, within which various vocabulary items can be interchanged. During this early phase, vocabulary is deliberately held down until fluency in the basic structures is achieved.

Warm-Up. From the time children reach school age, they bring to any new motor skill a number of motor abilities. With increasing age, the variety increases. Speed of learning a new skill is a function of the transfer of these skills to the new task. Where the variety of skills possessed is great, as it is with adults, opportunities exist for negative as well as positive transfer. The provision of short warm-up periods helps to dissipate negative transfer effects, as well as create appropriate sets for performance of the task. In an experiment involving twenty-four groups of twenty college students (Silver, 1952), the task was to print the alphabet upside down and right to left. Both negative and positive transfer occurs with such a task. The experimenter systematically varied the amounts of warm-up under both spaced and massed practice conditions. The performance of the warm-up groups was significantly superior to those having no warm-up, and spaced practice was superior to massed. Learning to write in shorthand is somewhat similar. Adults are familiar with all the motions needed to form the symbols but use them in differing combinations and rhythms. Furthermore, they use them intermittently, so that one alternates learning shorthand with normal writing. Simple warm-up drills—forming right and left ovals, chaining dashes in rhythmic sequence—create a cognitive and motor set which counteracts negative transfer potential.

Distribution of Practice. As shown by Silver's experiment described above, spaced practice is more effective than massed. For the more difficult and complex skills, practice should be liberally distributed. The length of the practice period should be short when new motor tasks are being introduced for the first time. This is especially true with elementary school children whose differences in maturation, attention span, and interest span are noticeable. Many motor skills not only involve complexity in the physical movements involved but also depend upon complex mental or social processes which increase the learning difficulty, thus augmenting the need for spaced practice. For example, handwriting involves intricate thought and grammatical processes, as well as minute finger movement; team games such as volleyball, baseball, and basketball embrace complex group actions and detailed rules of action, as well as highly coordinated motor movements. Great individual differences occur in the amount of practice needed to learn a specific skill due to differences in capacity as well as in motivation. As practice continues, efficiency decreases due to fatigue and boredom. Individuals vary in degree of persistence, which is another factor influencing performance. Although a massive body of evidence has developed supporting the advantages of distributed practice and continues to find additional supporting experimental evidence (Duncan, 1951; Ammons and Willig,

1956; Oxendine, 1965), conditions exist under which massed practice may be desirable in learning motor skills. A wide range of individual differences in motor ability exists within any group. For those with greater ability, massed practice may be preferable because of the potential positive transfer effects. In many instances, massed practice will produce equivalent or greater learning. A distinction is needed between performance and learning. Performance may appear lower under massed conditions because of either a work decrement or self-pacing (Reynolds and Bilodeau, 1952; Bilodeau, 1954). Second, the choice of methods will vary with the task. For example, massed practice proved more effective with adults for archery than badminton (Young, 1954) and less effective in learning a new basketball skill. A choice will be based on potential facilitating or interfering effects from other motor abilities.

Rhythm.   The development of motor skills involves both spatial and temporal coördination of movements. Rhythm is an aid in establishing temporal coördination. The playing of music with lively rhythm will help to speed up the slow worker. Since it operates to reduce tensions in muscles not directly used in the task being practiced, rhythm tends to lessen the fatigue effects of practice. It is desirable to have children practice their writing exercises in rhythm. Music may be used to set the pattern of rhythm. The rhythm of music, counting, or tapping is used to advantage in pacing the strokes for typewriting drills, in directing calisthenics, in establishing the proper timing of movements needed for giving artificial respiration, and in promoting graceful dancing.

But to secure the advantages of rhythm, one must know at what stages to use it. A reasonable familiarity with the task, ability to make the various movements, and proper form are essential prerequisites to the use of rhythm drills. A young teacher who had been working in her first position only a few weeks complained that she could not keep her pupils together in group drills in typewriting because they had to stop and look for the keys. Students will not be able to type rhythmically until they have learned the position of the keys. Children will be able to write rhythmically only when it is no longer necessary for them to stop to think of the various movements required to form the letters or of the correct position of their fingers and hands. According to Freeman (1914), writing becomes rhythmical for most children at the age of 9 or 10. He suggests that this is the age when writing drills requiring rhythm may be suitably given.

Moreover, group drills in which rhythm is used will not in the later stages of practice be suitable for developing maximum speed. There will be individual differences in capacity for speed which will render any pace unsuitable for all members of the group. If the tempo is suited to the average, those who could go faster will be held back, while certain slow ones will not be able to keep up or will work under too great a strain in doing so. In order to attain the greatest possible speed, the individual must practice at his own best speed.

The advantages of a diagnostic approach are revealed in a study by Rowley (1938). She wanted to know if slow writers in grades four, five, and six were inferior in motor coördination to the fast writers. On the basis of suitable speed tests of handwriting, two groups of children were selected, one made up of the slowest and the other of the fastest writers. Each group included twenty-five children. The members of the two groups were paired for sex, C.A., M.A., and I.Q. These children then were given the tapping test for the right and left hands. By means of special apparatus, a test was made to determine the speed for making short vertical finger movements similar to those used in writing. Tests were also made for speed in making similar movements with the arm. The scores of the slow writers on these tests were compared with the scores made by the fast writers. There was no significant difference between the scores of these two groups on any of the tests. It was concluded that the difference between these slow writers and these fast writers was due mainly to training factors, not to a difference in native endowment with respect to capacity for speed or motor coördination. The findings indicated the possibility of successful remedial instruction for improving the speed of slow writers.

Knowledge of Results. One of the most effective guides to improvement of performance is having knowledge of results. This has been discussed in greater detail in a preceding chapter, but an additional study will re-emphasize its value. Helmstadter (1952) divided 100 college undergraduates into four groups and compared their performance curves on the Minnesota Rate of Manipulation Test (a block turning test) under four different conditions. One group received immediate knowledge of its performance; each of the other three groups had performance goals set by one of three different procedures: a self-set goal, an externally established goal, and a goal of improvement. All groups showed similar performance curves, in contradiction to the hypothesis that goal setting procedures would provide stronger motivation. Knowledge of results provided as great an incentive as the varied goal setting procedures. It would be more accurate to say that knowledge of results alone was as effective as knowledge of results plus an established goal. The simplicity of the task may have induced only limited amounts of ego involvement restricting the effectiveness of goal setting procedures, yet, if true, the situation is not unlike many learning situations in which the participant's interest is comparatively slight.

One advantage which many motor skill learning situations provide is immediate knowledge of results. The baseball is hit or missed, the golf ball lands on the fairway or in the rough, the paint brush spreads paint smoothly or splatters paint. Knowledge of results is immediately apparent, and self-instruction directed at correcting and improving performance follows. It is essential that the self-instruction be accurate and that the analysis of behavior lead to improvement, not to further distortion in performance. This is precisely one of the main functions of a teacher.

Punishment, Emphasis, and Extraneous Cues.   It is a common practice in training animals and children to punish undesirable forms of behavior. The belief behind this practice is that the unpleasant aftereffects of an act tend to prevent its recurrence. As noted in Chapter 7, many experiments have been performed with animals to determine the effect of punishment for "errors." It has been found that an electric shock accompanying wrong responses generally serves to hasten the elimination of errors. The explanation in terms of the law of effect was that the tendency to make the wrong responses was weakened by the annoying result. This explanation has been proven inadequate by recent studies, which have shown that shock on right responses or in an alley between turns also tends to facilitate learning. These findings have led some writers to believe that the effect of the shock is not to inhibit the wrong responses but rather to make the learner more alert to the significant cues and to emphasize the fact that the response is either right or wrong (Reed, 1935). Muenzinger concluded that the effect of the shock was general rather than specific (1934).

Bernard and Gilbert (1941) report an experiment on maze learning with fifty-two college students as subjects; it was designed to determine whether the effect of shock on entering blind alleys was general or specific. They found that the alleys in which shock was received were eliminated more readily than those in which no shock was received. From this they concluded that the shock did have a specific effect in modifying the reactions it accompanied as well as the general effect on the learner's alertness demonstrated by other studies.

These writers also point out that the use of the words *reward* and *punishment* may be misleading in considering the effect of extraneous stimuli on learning. For a stimulus which may be annoying as a signal that an error has been made may be satisfying when it means that a right choice has been made. Shock, when used to announce errors, usually has punishment value, but it has been found to have about the same effect as a reward when used on right responses. Bernard and Gilbert (1941) make the following significant comments on this point:

> From the evidence available it seems reasonable to postulate that any well-defined stimulus introduced consistently in connection with either right or wrong responses will tend to favor their repetition if they are right or their elimination if they are wrong, provided that the stimulus is not of such a type or strength as to introduce a distracting effect. In other words, any stimulus which is not highly distracting may act either as a "punishment" or a "reward," depending upon whether it accompanies responses which are arbitrarily designated as right or wrong. . . .

In human subjects, knowledge of a "punishment" stimulus appears to mean much more than direct affective reactions to the stimulus. In the present investigation most of the subjects reported that they tried to avoid shock mainly because it signified error rather than because it was disagreeable, in spite of the fact that they all reported the shock to be decidedly uncomfortable. Their reports also indicated that they tried to avoid un-shocked blind alleys as instructed, but that they tended to forget where these alleys were in the maze and that they often failed completely to perceive that they had entered a blind alley. On the other hand, the shock which was given in the "shock" alleys announced the errors in a definite and clean-cut manner and enabled the subjects to mark the location more accurately.

If an extraneous stimulus serves to facilitate learning by way of emphasizing right or wrong responses, is it better to emphasize the right responses or the wrong responses? An answer to this question is provided by an experiment reported by Silleck and Lapha (1937). A punchboard maze, containing thirty pairs of holes, was used. One hole of each pair had an electric connection with a bell which rang when the stylus was inserted. One group of subjects was instructed to place the stylus only in holes which rang the bell, while another group was instructed to place the stylus only in the holes which did not sound the bell. For one group, the bell meant an error, for the other group it signaled success. The mean number of trials required for an errorless performance was 11.7 for the Bell-Right response, and 15.7 for the Bell-Wrong response group. The findings are in accord with other experimental data in indicating that emphasis on right responses is more favorable for learning than emphasis on wrong responses.

Criticism. Evaluation of a student's performance is an essential part of any teacher's work. This includes the pointing out of errors and faults. Its purpose is to promote improvement. To accomplish its purpose criticism should be specific, constructive, and encouraging. For example, it will not help the child very much to tell him merely that his writing is poor and that he should do better. To be effective, it must point the way to better performance. Emphasis should be on what is being done correctly, rather than on errors.

In offering criticism, the teacher should seek to avoid discouraging or antagonizing the learner. Some sensitive persons cannot take graciously even the kindest and most constructive kind of criticism. In dealing with little children, we should be careful when criticizing their work that we do not discourage them or make them feel that they are incapable or less capable than other children. Some children who are not doing well simply need to be told that they can do better. The teacher should show appreciation of good work, should commend the child for advances he is making. If adverse criticism is preceded by a recognition of merit, it will be easier to take, and it will be more likely to stimulate effort to improve. The effort of criticism will depend largely upon the spirit and manner in which it is given.

One possible way to avoid the negative effects of criticism is to encourage the learner to criticize his own work, to find the errors he has made, and to locate for himself, where possible, the strong and weak points in his performance. The practice of autocriticism should make for self-reliance and initiative in promoting one's own progress.

Amount of Guidance.   While the services of a teacher in directing learning may serve to hasten it and prevent much waste effort on the part of the learners, it sometimes happens that guidance is overdone. This may occur when the teacher, in her zeal to prevent all errors, dictates precisely just what is to be done step-by-step. Too much guidance may destroy the initiative of the pupil and thus deprive him of the opportunity to learn. When each step is dictated, the child may learn to perform the steps, under dictation, but fail to develop the ability to perform the whole task without aid. The end sought should be the child's ability to carry out skillfully the whole performance by himself, not the ability to follow step-by-step the teacher's directions. Verbal guidance plays an important part in transfer and retention of a skill.

OTHER FACTORS

Maturation.   A number of generalizations can be made with regard to the influence of such different factors as maturation and capacity, on motor learning. Studies of the motor achievement of individuals in different stages of growth have indicated the important relationship between motor development and maturation. In the studies considered, the term maturation refers not only to chronological age, but embraces also skeletal and physiological advancement.

1. It is possible to predict the stage of growth at which an individual can acquire certain motor skills. This is particularly true in infants and young children.
2. There is noted wide variation in the motor achievement of individuals within any age range. This is most apparent in adolescence.
3. Strength, rather than chronological age, intelligence, or school grade, is a primary determinant of the degree of motor ability.
4. Motor skill development tends to coincide with the growth curve. Early or late physiological maturation affects motor performance.
5. Although gross motor skills are better performed at adolescence due to the strength increment during puberty, those motor skills which are dependent on flexibility, coördination and control appear to be less ably performed during the period of rapid growth.

6. Until puberty, boys and girls compare favorably with one another in many motor skills; after puberty, however, boys tend to excel, especially in the gross motor skills.

Capacity.   The capacity of an individual for the learning of motor skills may be divided into physical and mental capacities, which have been analyzed through factor analysis techniques. The result has been the identification of a large number of separate factors which may be classified into three general categories: fundamental elements underlying the performance of a skill such as strength, speed, and accuracy; fundamental skills in physical education such as running, jumping, and throwing; and complex skills such as basketball or football.

1. The efficiency of physical factors increases with age up to maturity; age influences are equivalent to maturational influences. In general, this means that a child will learn a given motor skill with greater efficiency and with less practice as he approaches maturity.
2. The requirements for intelligence are dependent upon the complexity of the skill to be learned and the instructions to be understood.
3. Individuals with higher intelligence generally learn new motor skills with greater ease and speed than individuals with lower intelligence.
4. It is doubtful whether there are any motor skills which do not require some intelligence, although some studies seem to suggest that there are some "pure" motor activities, independent of intelligence.

SUMMARY

Three phases are apparent in motor skill learning. First there is the beginning phase in which comprehending instructions and identifying basic sub-routines are of primary importance. In this stage, preparation, recall, action, and evaluation are accompanied by changes in perception of the task, the procedures, and in feeling tone.

In the middle phase, the discrete units begin to merge into a continuous process. For example, the child who knows all the sounds associated with the letters of the alphabet begins to sequence the sounds (on viewing a word) in order to produce the sound of a word.

In the final phase, various accessory responses disappear; conscious control of responses is no longer needed as they become automatic.

The instructor's task is assisting the learner to develop a concept of the skill to be performed, establishing an appropriate cognitive set for discriminating the significant stimuli, differentiating between appropriate and inappropriate available responses, and organizing these in appropriate sub-routines and hierarchies until an adequate level of skill is achieved.

In any instruction, but especially in motor skill learning, emphasis should be on the *correct* response, rather than on what *not* to do. This applies both to development of perception of the act, with accompanying mental practice, as well as to commending the correct response. Assuming readiness of the learner, effective conditions of practice call for: (1) a motivated learner, (2) analysis of the skill into identifiable sub-routines, (3) distribution of practice under realistic or simulated conditions, (4) appropriate amounts of guidance, (5) immediate knowledge of results, and (6) systematic reinforcement.

FURTHER READING

Overview

AMMONS, R. B. *Skills.* 1960. In Harris, C. (ed.) *Encyclopedia of Educational Research.* New York: Macmillan, pp. 1281-87.

Selected References

AMMONS, R. B. 1947. Acquisition of motor skill: quantitative analysis and theoretical formulation. *Psychol. Rev.,* 54: 263-81.

BARKER, R. G., BEATRICE WRIGHT, and MOLLIE GONICK. 1946. *Adjustment to Physical Handicap and Illness: A Survey of the Social Psychology of Physique and Disability.* New York: Social Science Research Council. Bull. No. 55.

FITTS, P. M. 1964. Skill learning. In A. W. Melton (ed.) 1964. *Categories of Human Learning.* New York: Academic Press, pp. 243-85.

FITTS, P. M., H. P. BAHRICK, M. E. NOBLE, and G. E. BRIGGS. 1966. *Skilled Performance.* New York: Wiley.

MILLER, G. A., E. GALANTER, and K. H. PRIBRAM. 1960. *Plans and The Structure of Behavior.* New York: Holt.

WATSON, E. H. and G. H. LOWREY. 1951. *Growth and Development of Children.* Chicago: Yearbook.

Original Investigations

BILODEAU, E. 1954. Rate recovery in a repetitive motor task as a function of successive rest periods. *J. Exper. Psychol.,* 48: 197-203.

LEAVITT, H. J. and H. SCHLOSBERG. 1944. The retention of verbal and motor skills. *J. of Exp. Psycho.,* 34: 404-17.

OXENDINE, R. J. 1965. Effects of progressively changing practice schedules on the learning of a motor skill. *Res. Quart.,* 36: 307-15.

SOLLEY, W. H. 1952. The effects of verbal instruction upon the learning of a motor skill. *Res. Quart.,* 23: 231-40.

12

The Development
of Perception

We live under a continuous barrage of light and sound and touch and smell from without, mood and movement, posture and position from within. If we are to direct our energies effectively, we need to be able to respond to the significant and salient features of this barrage arising from an ever changing flow of situations. Otherwise, we should soon be exhausted. We also need to be able to respond in a relevant manner to any given situation.

Although we may begin our day in routine fashion, as we move on into it new and different events occur demanding variations in behavior. It is impossible to have a habitual response to every event. There are simply too many variations to be met. Simpler organisms living in more restricted environments can depend on built-in response systems (instincts) that are linked to specific stimulus situations. Man cannot. Variability of response is essential to survival. Yet variability poses a different problem, that of establishing the appropriateness of response when many responses are available. Economy of effort demands some means of recognizing significant features of stimulus situations and ordering and selecting appropriate courses of action. Perception provides the means.

The perceptual skill that is involved in daily performance is easily overlooked. Not until someone challenges us with the need for a perception which we are unable to make do we become aware of the discrimination which occurs in perception. The city-bred person has difficulty making the fine discrimination needed to see a deer, hidden among the brush on a hillside when his woodsman companion points at the animal. The difference is not one of visual acuity but of perceptual training. Driving an automobile in traffic involves a gamut of perceptions impinging in a steady stream upon different sensory organs and involving perception ranging from literal to highly enriched interpretations. The judgments of speed, direction, and angles of movement of other automobiles on the highway involve the literal perception of objects in space. In some instances, the perception may be impoverished by limitations of stimulation, for example, driving in fog or snow. Or in contrast, many of the perceptions may be highly enriched by previous experience. The green and red signal lights have meaning because we have learned green means "Go" and red means "Stop." The westerner arriving in New England for the first time doesn't know how to respond when he observes both red and yellow showing simultaneously, a signal meaning "Pedestrians move, automobiles stationary." More skillful discriminations are involved in anticipating the movements of the car ahead from slight changes in speed, shifts in position in the traffic lane, or other variations foretelling a left or right turn or the intention to pass or stop. Errors in interpreting cues occur. A common misinterpretation of stimuli is imagining that one sees water lying in a dip in the road when the reflected light is right. Lapses in attention or concentration on matters irrelevant to driving frequently produce failures to observe stop signs or the entry of other vehicles, occasionally with fatal results.

Perception plays an important role in our social behavior. Living effectively with other people requires recognition of their intentions and their reactions toward us and understanding them. Often quite subtle cues must be recognized and correctly interpreted in making these judgments. When we meet strangers, we look for clues in facial expression, dress, speech, and gesture which will allow identification as to how compatible or not he may be with respect to our own views and attitudes. We would make many more faux pas if everybody dressed and talked alike. Clothes differences not only enhance personal appearance; they provide information.

Perception ranges from a minimal level of barely sensing stimuli through the literal interpretation of cues as to size, shape, motion, texture, distance, and the like, to those which involve a wealth of past experience and training in order to provide the appropriate interpretation of a stimulus. The tobacco buyer who can identify by its texture, color, and shape the particular area from which a batch of leaf tobacco came or the wine taster who can identify the vineyard and year of production of wines from their body and flavor have learned to respond to and interpret stimuli which others do not perceive. The conditions affecting detection, discrimination, recognition, identification, and judgment, the processes by which perception develops, and the influence of attitudes, sets, motives, and group norms upon perception are of prime importance.

THE GENERAL NATURE OF PERCEPTION

Perception is a fundamental psychological activity. It is something the individual does. It is not, as we consider it, a faculty of the mind, nor merely a cluster of sensations. When we perceive, we translate impressions made upon our senses by the stimuli from our environment into awareness of objects or events. Moreover, the temporal reference is to the present, for the objects and events of which we become aware are regarded in perception as present and as going on. This activity of perceiving is such a universal and intimate feature of our mental life that it is often difficult to realize that objects of the physical world do not merely present themselves and that we do anything more than open our minds to receive them as they really are. It is easy to overlook the fact that we construct our world of things and events out of our sensory processes and that physical objects as we know them through sight, sound, taste, smell, and touch are the products of our own perceptions.

Essential Features of Perception. Perceptions depend on sensory experience. This includes the various qualities of experience derived from the stimulation of the sense receptors by the appropriate physical stimuli. Visual sensory experience consists of many thousands of different visual qualities. These include all shades of grays and the colors—reds, yellows, greens, blues, and their intermediates in all degrees of saturation from the richest colors to grays and in all tints and shades from lightest to darkest. In hearing, we have tones and the various kinds of noises. The tones vary in pitch, and a good ear can distinguish approximately 11,000 differences in the range from the lowest to highest. Sweet, salty, sour, and bitter are the primary taste qualities. In the olfactory group are a great variety of odors. From the receptors in the skin and in the internal organs we get such qualities of experience as sensory pressure, pain, warmth, and cold; and from the proprioceptors in the muscles we get the strains and pressures of kinesthetic experience. These widely differing qualities of sensory experience depend on the organs of sense and on the nervous system. They are the basis of our knowledge of the world about us. Without them there would be no awareness of anything.

Considerable interest has been shown in recent years about the effect of sensory deprivation on perception. When adults are subjected to several days of continuous isolation during which any kind of sensation is at a minimum, they exhibit gross perceptual disturbances. Objects appear displaced in the visual field; shapes of objects, planes and lines show continuous change; and the color characteristics of objects are altered (Heron, 1961). These distortions are short-lived (Doane *et al.,* 1959). The temporary effects of isolation on values and attitudes in prisoner-of-war camps in China after the Korean War have been widely reported.

Some of our perceptions are bound to stimuli, others are affected by learning. The sensory field in perception is organized first with respect to *figure and ground.* The thing perceived stands out against a background, as when a ship at sea is seen against a background in an indefinite expanse of water and sky, when a farmhouse stands out against the fields and hills of the landscape, or when a star shines against the darkened dome of the heavens.

In Figure 12.1, the black area is figure, and the white area is ground when one sees a black face looking toward the right. When it is reversed, the white area is figure and the black portion is ground. It is to be noted that the change in figure-ground relations appears without a change in the designs themselves, but with this change comes a different meaning. Something different is seen. Thus, the figure-ground aspect of perception is an arrangement of the sensory field. It is a fundamental determiner of what one sees and of what one learns by way of observation.

Fig. 12.1   Reversible figure-ground relations. *Either of the two faces may be perceived, according to which area, the black or the white, becomes the figure.*

Certain characteristic differences between the figure and ground are to be noted. In the first place, the figure has more or less definite form. It is marked off by fairly distinct boundary lines. The figure may be complex, but its parts in clear perception are always closely patterned to form a unified whole. The ground, on the other hand, is formless and indefinite. The figure seems to stand forth, usually in front of the ground or surrounded by it. Elements of the sensory field not incorporated into the figure lack significance and seem not to belong to anything in particular. Notice that when the black portion of Figure 12.1 is perceived as the face looking to the right, the black dot in the white area is not related to the other parts at all, and it has no particular meaning. But when the white part is figure and a white profile is seen, the black dot occupies an essential position in the figure and definitely is an eye. The part is what it is by virtue of its relation to and membership in the whole figure. The common experience of failing to see some object before one's eyes, even when attending to it, is probably often due to failure to incorporate it into a definite figure pattern.

Figure-ground relations, moreover, are not restricted to visual perception. They appear in perceptions of sound, taste, smell, and touch, though in these the boundaries may be less sharply defined. The grouping of the sound elements into tonal patterns in music is controlled largely by the stimulus pattern set forth by the instruments. Rhythmical units may be established by regular variations of intensity, pitch, or length of interval.

The Stimulus Pattern and Perceptual Organization.   Several features of the stimulus pattern act to determine how it will be perceived.

PROXIMITY.   The parts of the stimulus pattern which are close together tend to be perceived in groups. Their proximity in time or space affects the organization of the field in perception. To one walking in the wood, trees or bushes will appear in clusters and groups according to their proximity, whereas in a nursery field, in which the plants are uniformly distant from each other, the very uniformity makes it difficult to view it other than as a whole. The way the dots are printed in Figure 12.2 produces a perception of the two sets as a cluster of four and a cluster of eight.

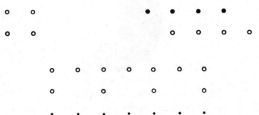

Fig. 12.2   The influence of the stimulus pattern on the organization of the perceptual field.

SIMILARITY.   The more similar objects are, the more likely that they will be perceived together. Even while seeing the whole of the nursery field just mentioned, one is aware of variations between groups of plants differing in size, color, or type. One sees a section of evergreen trees, some flowering plants, and so on. Look again at the top right set of dots in Figure 12.2; if you did not see it as a cluster of eight, you saw it as two sets, one black and the other white, grouping those which were similar.

CONTINUITY.   The lower dots in Figure 12.2 are seen in rows, and the top and bottom row are more readily perceived because of the continuity of the line. It is not merely the nearness of the dots, but also the regular, continuous sequence, which enables one to see them as rows.

CLOSURE.   Individuals strive to reach a satisfactory end-state of equilibrium. Incomplete forms, missing parts, gaps in information, and the like are completed or filled in by the perceiver. Most readers will read the symbols in Figure 12.3 as "Tom," by adding the missing parts in order to complete the stimulus, yet it can as readily be read as "Pam." Perhaps more forcefully, the principle of closure is illustrated in rumor spreading. The situation is usually one in which some degree of tension and ambiguity exists. The tension is eased and the ambiguity eliminated by the creation of rumor (supposition) amplified by details which will change as the story moves from one person to the next, as each one attempts to achieve and maintain a perception which provides a satisfying end-state.

As far as perception is concerned, closure is to Gestalt psychology what reward is to association theory. It produces the satisfying, tension relieving end-state which terminates activity.

Fig. 12.3   Incomplete figure.

Anticipatory set, expectation, and motivation can all play a significant role in the closure that results in a given situation. Mark Twain provides a ready illustration of this in Tom Sawyer, whose Aunt Polly was ever ready to attribute to Tom any mischief that occurred, even though his cousin Sydney was frequently the perpetrator.

Perceptual Constancies.   Our perception of various characteristics of objects does not correspond to the actual stimuli they provide us. The way in which we see brightness, size, color, and shape is closer to our knowledge of their appearance than to their actual appearance. This phenomenon occurs where discrepancies exist. For example, if a picture of a blue woman's coat is projected onto a yellow screen we see it as blue; yet if a blue square of the same color is projected, it appears neutral gray, as it should from what we know of color mixture. Yet in the former instance, we saw the coat as bluer because of our object reference. A more systematic illustration of the color constancy effect is seen in the experiment by Bruner, Postman, and Rodrigues (1951) in which subjects were asked to view a series of food objects which had been cut out of the same piece of orange paper. Each subject looked at the orange colored banana, lemon, carrot, tomato, and so forth, one at a time, then turned away to a color wheel and selected the color to match what he had just seen. The subjects consistently chose matching colors which were distorted in the direction of the natural color of the object.

If you look at the coffee cup on the table in front of you, it will appear to have a round top. Yet if you hold your thumbs and forefingers in front of your eyes in such a way that one hand appears to be touching top and bottom of the cup's top, and the other hand the two sides of the top, you will notice that the distances between your thumb and forefinger are unequal, indicating an elliptical shape, not round. If, now, you glance at another cup across the table or on another table, the two cups will look to be the same size or close to it. Again, if you hold your fingers so as to compare the relative sizes of the two images, they will be much different, providing you crude illustrations of shape and size constancy effects.

The degree of constancy effect which occurs is relative to the amount of discrepancy between the visual stimuli and the object being considered. It represents a compromise between the two, whether it is size, brightness, shape or color that is being considered. The greater the difference in the stimulus conditions, the greater the degree of distortion that occurs in making the compromise. Such constancy effects serve a useful purpose, for they facilitate discrimination. We see, not the temporary pattern of stimulus that a specific object offers but a compromise in which essential features are exaggerated, those features which from prior experience provide the sharpest discrimination. Our environment would be considerably more hazardous if all objects appeared in their true size against their backgrounds.

ATTENTION AND PERCEPTION

Attention as a Selective Process. The activity of perceiving starts with the excitation of the sense receptors by physical stimuli and runs its course with the transmission of neural impulses to the cortex and the organization of the resulting sensory qualities into meaningful patterns. At any moment, however, the organism is assailed by a multiplicity of stimuli too great to be utilized. Hence, a selection must be made. This process of selection is attention.

Attention is not a mental power but a device whereby the organism favors certain stimuli and disregards others according to its own needs, inclinations, and momentary activity. Some of these conditions which determine the selection are transient, as for example, the sets induced by a command from the teacher or the increase in volume which accompanies radio or TV commercials. Others, which have their sources in the history of the organism and its development, are more constant factors. These sets, biases, and habits give orderliness to the apprehending of our surroundings by providing a right-of-way for clarity of perception in one area of stimulation while other areas are disregarded or are made to wait their turn.

Studies of the attention aspect of perception have been largely concerned with three problems: first, the relation of attention to clearness of the experiential pattern; second, the number of things that can be attended to at one time; and third, the factors which determine attention.

Fluidity in Perception. Through introspection, one may observe the effects of attentive selection on conscious experience. If the reader will for a moment observe his patterns of experience, he will note that they are constantly shifting and that at any given moment, some parts of the conscious field stand out clearly while other parts are obscure. As you look at the clock on the mantel, the visual pattern is dominant. You are only vaguely aware of other objects in the room. The radio sounds are unclear and you fail to hear what the announcer says. If your attention shifts to the speaker's voice, the vocal sounds become focal and clear, while the visual qualities become obscure. Perceptual experience is organized with respect to different degrees of clearness into a foreground-background pattern. The constant shifting of the foreground gives emphasis now to one, then to another part of the general scene.

One of the practical problems of a teacher is that of sustaining the attention of a class. Children are sometimes said to be incapable of sustained attention, but this is hardly accurate. The attention of a little child is more completely governed by the characteristics of the things that appeal to his receptors than is the adult's. His attention is likely to shift rapidly from one thing to another in his environment. He is readily distracted by noises, bright colors, moving things, and bodily discomfort—more so than the older child or adult. This is as we should expect in view of the fact that he has not had time to acquire the strong social motives and the controlling interests that play so important a part in the determination of attention in the adult. Solley and Murphy (1960) point out that a simple pleasure-pain principle operates in predicting what will be organized as figure in a figure-ground learning experiment with young children. Under the right conditions a child can give attention over a considerable period of time. It is largely a matter of motivation. At the movie, at the circus, or in hearing an interesting story the child will have little trouble in keeping his attention from wandering. Attention is so important a matter for learning that it must be aroused, directed, and sustained by the teacher if he is to meet with any degree of success in his work. It is futile merely to demand attention and then proceed with a dull, monotonous, and meaningless presentation of facts. The secrets of securing and maintaining attention are change, novelty, interest, and meeting a need.

The Span of Attention. One really attends to one thing at a time. Quick shifts of attention may enable a person to observe several things in a few seconds or to carry on two operations that require attention. When several things occupy attention at the same moment, they are taken as a unit. One may apprehend clearly a group of five dots, a flock of chickens, or a forest. In such cases, one does not attend to the individual dots, chickens, or trees any more than one watches all the ballplayers on a team simultaneously.

The primary determiners of attention are certain characteristics of objects or stimuli that usually are potent for securing attention. Large, moving, novel, unusual, or isolated objects in contrast with their surroundings are usually favored items of attention. Intense, continuous, repeated, or changing stimuli make a strong bid for attention. These factors appear to dominate the attention of animals and play a relatively larger part in controlling the attention of children than of adults. Finally, there are certain regularities of stimulus conditions and certain salient features which gradually become predominant. Most parents have had a child anticipate them with a statement such as: "I know what you're going to say: GO TO BED."

BEHAVIORAL DETERMINANTS OF ATTENTION AND PERCEPTION

Early research on perception was concentrated on the psycho-physical aspects—the level of stimulation needed to be perceptible, the degree of change in stimulus conditions which was perceptible, the constancy and autokinetic effects, and so on. Research has been and still is vigorous. During the last ten to fifteen years research has flourished on how individual differences in the observer affect perception. For example, the traits associated with women's faces (in photographs) varied with the age of the judges whether college age or older males (Secord and Mulhard, 1955); personality characteristics such as extrovert-introvert (Taft and Coventry, 1958) or authoritarian-liberal (Scodel and Massen, 1953) were associated with perception of body position and self-other perception.

Typically such studies rely on either the differences in speed with which pictures or words can be recognized in a tachistoscope or the distortions introduced when subjects view pictures or compare objects. Both types of studies have been used to indicate the existence of differential effects as a result of cultural or sociological events. For example, Bruner and Postman (1947), McGinnies (1949) and Weiner (1955) show that socially tabooed words such as raped, whore, bitch require longer exposure times for recognition than neutral words. As an example of the second technique two groups (Solby and Sommer, 1957), one Mexican, one American, ages 16-42, were matched for age, sex, occupation, and socio-economic status. All had 20/20 vision, and none had first-hand information of the other culture. Each subject viewed ten pairs of photo slides through a prism lens stereoscope. Each pair of photo slides was composed of a typical American scene and a typical Mexican scene which were similar to each other in form, control of mass, texture, light and shadow. The left-right position of the pictures was randomized to correct for eye dominance in individual subjects. Exposure was standardized. Each subject was asked to report what he saw. The experimenters found that the scenes from a subject's own culture were perceptually dominant suggesting a differential perception associated with events of personal significance. In similar fashion, perception to politically neutral (50/50) material will be biased according to the political affiliations of the reader.

Set is a condition resulting from instruction which yields variations in perceptions. It was interesting to see that the delayed recognition times to tabooed words disappeared when subjects were instructed to expect to see such words (Aronfreed *et al.,* 1953; Freeman, 1954). Often our attention is channeled by sets which become established as a result of familiarity. When a group of twenty-eight college students were shown playing cards for a fraction of a second in a tachistoscope, their recognition of the cards was immediate. Certain cards, however, had color and suit reversed; e.g., there was a black three of diamonds. Each card was presented until correct recognition occurred three times. The time required for recognition of the trick cards was significantly greater because of dominance or disruption in response. A majority showed preferences for either form or color in responding, ignored contradictory features, and were disrupted when the incongruities became apparent, all of which resulted in longer response times. As multiplicity in set is increased, length of time for correct perception increases (Postman and Bruner, 1949).

Motivation, Reward and Punishment.   Early studies of the effect of motivation on perception utilized hunger as the motive, different lengths of time without food as an index of degree of hunger, and sensitivity to food stimuli as a measure of the effect upon perception (Levine, Chein, and Murphy, 1942). The increase in the number of food associations showed the influence of need on perception, yet a simple need-fulfillment or wish-fulfillment explanation was inadequate. As hunger increased, the number of food associations reached a peak, and then instead of slow steady increase relative to hunger, decreased; and it became evident that not only strength of motivation had to be considered but also the means by which a person dealt with his motivation and strove to satisfy it. A not unusual response is to temporarily suppress it.

Schafer and Murphy (1943) capitalized on figure-ground phenomena to test the differential effect of reward and punishment. Subjects were shown the four faces seen in Figure 12.4 twenty-five times each in mixed order in a tachistoscope. They were required to learn the names which went with each picture. Subjects were rewarded with a small amount of money when either of two of the faces appeared and punished by a loss of an equal amount when the other two appeared. In the test situation,

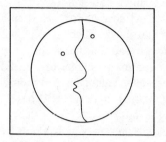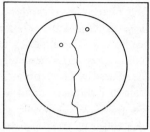

Fig. 12.4 Test figures for differential effects of reward and punishment in perception. (From Schafer and Murphy, 1943.)

the faces were combined as shown and the comparative effect of reward and punishment measured by the name given to the combined figure. The responses given by a 4/1 ratio were the names of the pictures which had been rewarded. Comparable results were obtained by Solby and Sommer (1957) with 5 to 7 year old children.

Values and Attitudes. Bruner and Goodman (1947) stimulated a number of studies of the effect of values and attitudes on perception by taking three groups of boys of 10 to 11 years in age, 10 rich, 10 poor, and 10 unspecified as a control group. The boys were asked to adjust the size of a circular spot of light until it matched their impression of coins ranging from a penny to a half-dollar. The boys were asked to make their estimates from memory, and then again with the coin present. Bruner and Goodman's assumptions were that differences in social class attitudes toward money existed and that these would be reflected in the subjects' perception of the size or magnitude of money. Their assumptions were borne out. All the children overestimated the size of the coins (except half-dollars); the degree of overestimation varied with the value, not the size of the coin, and was greater for poor boys than rich. In a subsequent variation, Lambert, Solomon and Watson (1952) had an experimental group of children turn a crank to receive a white poker chip which could be put into a vending machine for candy. Control children did the same but got the candy directly without the use of the poker chip. Comparisons were made between the size adjustment of a spot of light prior to the experiment, after ten days of positive reinforcement, and after a single day without reward followed by a single day's resumption of reward. The experimental group showed a significant increase in their estimate of the size of the poker chip from the first to the tenth day. This increased estimate disappeared and then reappeared with the one day without reward followed by the one day resumption of reward.

Wittreich and Radcliffe (1954, 1956) have shown heightened perceptual sensitivity to authority figures (petty officers) by navy recruits after seven weeks of training, and to simulated mutilated figures by navy medical corpsmen.

Expectancies and Meaning.   The effects of attitudes, interests, needs, prejudices, and training experiences of various kinds is to restrict the number and kind of cues to which we respond and to increase our sensitivity to certain cues, either positively or negatively. Instead of regarding all aspects of a person, we look to selected features of face, speech, dress, or skin. In each situation, we identify, classify and categorize; in effect, we both recognize salient features of the stimulus field and arrange the field in accord with the expectancies we bring from past experience. Perception is not a passive recording of events but an active attending and interpreting in order to make sense of the world. Such expectancies permit efficient functioning with only a minimum of effort. But they can cause misperceptions as well. As an illustration of this, Zillig (1928) trained one group of five popular girls to deliberately make mistakes in the performance of certain calisthenics and a second group of five disliked girls to perform the calisthenics perfectly. When their classmates were asked to observe their performance and then list the names of those who performed correctly and those who did not, a higher proportion of correct responses were attributed to the popular girls, none of whom had performed correctly.

In the detection of spelling and arithmetic errors, teachers have been shown to be biased in favor of the abler students. Thus, one advantage of an expectancy is speed and efficiency in performance; a disadvantage is failure to recognize contradictory information.

Finally, there is the interpretation of meaning associated with the stimuli we perceive. The quiet swish of an infant emptying the tissue box holds special meaning for the mother, just as an explosive pop near a pond would mean beaver to a woodsman. From our experience, we build up a comprehension of the meaning of sight, sound, and other stimuli which is partially unique to our particular experience and partially common to all people.

The mere experience of a particular color, sound, taste, smell, or touch appears without learning. We do not have to learn in order to sense the color blue, the rumbling sound of thunder, the odor of violets, a salty taste, or a pain. But we do have to learn what the color is a color of. We have to learn to identify one noise as that of thunder, another as the roar of an airplane, and another as the report of a pistol. We learn to perceive objects, but we have sensory experience directly as the result of the impact of environmental forces upon the sense organs.

When the qualities of conscious experience refer to an object or event in the physical world, they are said to have *meaning*. All perceiving involves the factor of meaning. When we see a chair, a tree, or a house, we perceive the objective fact. The thing-out-there is the meaning that the pattern of colors and lights has for us. The relation between sensory experience and meaning is mainly the product of learning.

DEVELOPMENT OF PERCEPTION

Despite its importance to our functioning, we know comparatively little about the development of perception in the child. Fantz (1961) demonstrated the existence of pattern preferences as early as the first week of infant life. Operating on the knowledge that infants look longer at a patterned object than a plain one, he presented infants pairs of cards—one with black stripes of varying widths, the other gray—and closely observed their eye movements in response. Second, he presented different patterns in pairs— bull's-eye and stripes, checkerboard and square, circle and cross. A month-old baby could discriminate 1/8 inch stripes and with increasing age showed finer and finer discrimination, reaching 1/64 inch at 6 months. Distinct preferences were shown for particular patterns, bull's-eye and checkerboard, with a change in preferences occurring over time. In spite of the incomplete development of visual areas of the brain at birth, infants at birth or very soon thereafter show crude visual acuity and ability to discriminate pattern differences.

Maturation, functional use, and learning all enter into the development of the perceptual skills of the child and adult. A variety of species have been reared in the dark—chicks, rats, kittens, monkeys, chimpanzees, and humans (the congenitally blind)—and the effects of lack of visual experience observed. Rats and chicks showed no effects, kittens showed some delay in visual discriminations but once in the light recovered quickly without special training. Monkeys, chimpanzees, and humans show more significant effects. Riesen (1947) raised two chimpanzees in the dark to the age of 16 months. Brought into light conditions, the eyes functioned adequately and visual tracking movements were present, but object recognition, form perception, and spatial orientation were lacking. They bumped into objects, could not locate objects in space, were unable to recognize the food bottle by sight (although immediately by touch). Some fifty hours of training were required to bring them to normal functioning. Comparable retardation in the use of the sense of touch has been observed in chimps having restricted motor experience during their first two years. Senden (1960) reports the experience of human subjects for whom sight had been restored by surgical removal of cataracts of the eyes. Object recognition and form perception were poor. Color responses were initially dominant. In attempting to discriminate a square from a triangle, resort to counting corners occurred; and even after discrimination was established, the changing of the color of the patterns disrupted accurate perception. A minimum of a month was required to initiate rudimentary perceptions. Senden's material was largely taken from case histories from the last century and as a result, is incomplete in many respects.

Campbell (1941) describes the experience of a person (97 percent blind) recovering sight at 18 years of age. He reported that when the light first flooded his eyes, everything seemed hazy, with no definite forms or arrangement and with no perspective. The room seemed full of new and strange objects. He did not recognize anything about him at first. The doctor took him to the window and asked him if he saw the hedge across the street. He replied, "No, Sir," for, as he said, he had no idea which among the many strange forms was the hedge. He had to learn what a hedge looks like. Then he asked the doctor where the curb of the street was. The doctor explained which form was the curb. He could see it then. Later, he went to a motion picture theater. He found it very confusing because so many things were portrayed that he did not recognize. When he came from the theater, he saw the stars for the first time. He was so amazed and delighted that he thought it strange that other people were not looking at them too. When he returned to school and old friends came up to congratulate him, he could not tell who they were until he heard them speak. He misjudged distances at first. He had experiences such as reaching for an object and having his hand go beyond it. There was much trial and error in his learning to judge distances from shapes, shadows, and angles.

None of these results can be explained by innate capacity, maturation, or learning alone. Capacity is needed and maturation affects its rate of development, but in higher organisms, functional use and learning enter into a complex interplay. Denied experience at appropriate levels of maturation, blind persons require extensive training to acquire the visual-perceptual skills which develop so casually in the sighted.

Children's Perceptions. Although the broad outlines of the development of children's perception is known, much less information is available about their specific perceptions. In a period in which organized visual activity, i.e., television, dominates the leisure hour of the child (purportedly with disastrous effects), we know very little of what the child actually sees when he views the television screen and what meaning he associates with it. At a time when televised instruction is becoming widespread, our research evidence on how to manipulate visual images is limited (Gropper, 1962).

In general, the child's perceptions are meager, vague, indefinite, and lacking in detail. They involve, for the most part, reactions to gross and unanalyzed wholes. The infant first becomes aware of certain elements of his environment that stand out as strikingly different from the rest of the surroundings. A loud noise against the otherwise comparative quiet of the room, an abrupt tug on the blanket that covers him, a face that comes into view, or the contact of his lips with the nipple set off certain reactions. At first, these things are fused with the general situation. As he reacts to these in different settings, they gradually become disentangled from the mass situation, take on the quality of individuality, and become more or less distinct items of the objective world. The sequence of development, like that of motor activity, is from mass to specific. Upon looking at the books in the psychology section of a library, for example, an infant probably would experience only a broad, loosely patterned, variegated expanse; the 5-year-old would see a lot of books; the high school student would see many books on psychology; and the college student of psychology would see the particular works of several well known psychologists.

In the first weeks of life, the sense organs appear to be capable of effective functioning, but the experiences arising from them are indistinct and poorly organized. The perceptual ability of the infant develops rapidly during the first year. His behavior reveals his growing awareness of objects. In the first few months, he acquires the ability to distinguish persons from inanimate objects. His eyes follow an object moved in front of his face. He reaches for and grasps small objects, inspects and manipulates them, and turns his head toward the source of sound. The ability to recognize his mother is manifest about the third month. When first her face is singled out as an object of perception, it appears that he sees it as a whole. Later the eyes, nose, and mouth are distinguished as discrete parts. By the fifth or sixth month, he discriminates between strangers and familiar persons and begins to show fear of strangers. About this time, he first distinguishes between a friendly voice and an angry or threatening voice. The ability to learn to distinguish between simple geometric forms such as circles, squares, and triangles has been found in children as young as 6 months (Ling, 1941). By the end of the first year, the child's world contains many objects known and recognized by him through perception, including recognition of himself (Dixon, 1957). His needs and the outcomes of his reactions are important factors in determining what perceptions develop during this period.

During the preschool period, the perception of objects continues to develop in the direction of distinctness and precision. Spatial and temporal relations are, however, discerned very imperfectly. Three-year-old children have very imperfect notions of the meaning of "near" and "far." Even 4-year-olds have not completely learned to use the spatial cues of relative size, shadows, and converging lines. Children's perception of size is frequently faulty because they have not learned to allow for the factor of distance. Curti (1938) reports the case of a little boy of 3 who thought horses seen at a distance were tiny horses, and of a little girl 4 years old who thought her father was getting smaller as he walked away from her. In effect, the child's perceptions are truer to reality, i.e., the size of the field occupied by the image. Size constancies have yet to develop. Early space perceptions in children appear to depend mainly on touch and exploratory movements. These are gradually transferred to vision. The ability to localize points touched on the skin is well developed before the age of 3, and school children are as adept as adults in two-point tactual discrimination.

A number of studies have revealed that young children are woefully ignorant of the most commonplace things. It appears that much that passes before their eyes is never seen. They usually know best the things they handle and the things they encounter in their home life. Their knowledge of things encountered in their walks and travels is less exact. New experiences are interpreted in terms of former experiences; hence, observations for which there is inadequate preparation or background are likely to be unreliable sources of knowledge. After about the third year, children's imagination becomes very active. This often colors and distorts their perceptions, sometimes making them fantastic. Individual differences restrict the value of generalizations here as in all matters of human development. Yet, certain general trends of perceptual growth may be observed. By the end of the second year, the perception of objects is fairly well established, but throughout early childhood, objects and persons are likely to be apprehended as more or less isolated or disconnected items. A child of 3 years can enumerate objects seen in a picture, but description and interpretation require a higher degree of mental development. Perceptions of size, distance, and form are relatively crude in the preschool child, and spatial and temporal relations are imperfectly grasped at this age. The ability to apprehend relations improves as the child grows older and learns to interpret the various cues commonly employed.

As the child grows to maturity, his perceptions become richer and more definite in detail, his past experience playing an ever increasing part in his observations. This gives stability to the perceptive functions. The small child's perceptions are much influenced by his present mental set, his emotions, and suggestion. This is true of an older person's perceptions also but to a lesser extent because of the greater weight of past experience. If, for example, you were walking along a dark street with a small child and pointed out the dark form of a bush and said, "See that bear over there," he would probably see a bear. But this would not occur with an adolescent unless he was in an unfamiliar forest.

As adolescence is approached, the qualitative analysis of objects appears and perceptions become more abstractive in character. A further development, which comes as the child moves toward maturity, is the acquiring of symbolic perceptions in which the object is perceived, not for itself, but for what it represents. Examples are found in the meanings of words acquired as language is learned and in the meanings of various signs.

Sensory Discrimination. The efficacy of perception depends upon the range of distinguishable sensory elements. Certain color-blind persons, for example, are not capable of sensing the difference between stimuli that yield the colors red and green for normal vision, and they find it impossible to distinguish between red and green objects that are alike except for the color. Things that look exactly alike cannot be distinguished in visual perception. If a distinction is made, other senses or other cues are used. If a person's hearing was so dull that he could not distinguish more than ten tonal pitch differences, his perception of music would lack most of the fine variations and harmonies we normally know as music. If one could hear only one tone, he could distinguish differences in sounds only on the basis of variations in intensity and duration. Thus, the greater the range of noticeable differences in the qualities of sensory experiences, the greater will be the possibilities of making fine distinctions in perception.

Maturation plays an important role in the development of the capacity for sensory discrimination, and judging from studies with primates (rigorously controlled experimental conditions would not be possible with human infants), once the capacity for object discrimination is present, learning of such discriminations proceeds rapidly (Zimmerman, 1960; Harlow, 1960).

Can sensory discrimination be improved? If this question is interpreted as referring to perception, the answer is "Yes." If we interpret it to mean the improvement of the capacity for sensing, or sensory acuity, the answer is "No." If a person is dull in hearing, training will not improve that hearing capacity. Color blindness cannot be cured by practice in looking at colors. Perhaps, in some instances, certain exercises may help to minimize certain sensory defects, but the experimental evidence does not support such claims (Gibson, 1953). The sensory mechanisms are limited regarding the variety of experimental qualities they can provide. Training does not change this capacity, but it may greatly improve the use of one's sensory capacity in distinguishing small differences. For example, children improve in their ability to distinguish between letter patterns in learning to read.

The Various Objects of Perception.   Not all the objects of perception are concrete, particular, space-filling material objects. We perceive melody, rhythm, and patterns of sound in music. We note the passing of time and realize that some events transpire quickly, while others run on and on. We observe that the table is made of walnut, the apples are ripe, the coffee needs sugar, the potatoes are cooked, the man is old—a variety of attributes. Moreover, we perceive objects not for what they are but for what they represent, their symbolic meanings. The flashing yellow lights on the highway are not there for illumination but to indicate a need for caution. Printed and spoken words, numbers, and codes are symbols which initiate a higher order of meaning.

Then there are perceptions through which we realize the moods, emotions, and motives of other persons and of ourselves as well, important perceptions in living. We perceive complacency, indifference, happiness, and sorrow. There are also esthetic perceptions affording the realization of beauty and the enjoyment of humor. Finally, there is the perception of relationships, in the concrete dimensions of height, weight, size, and so on, and in the abstract dimensions of power, affection, dependency, authority, need, and the like.

Changes in Sensory Patterns.   There is no doubt that the way older individuals organize their sensory field is influenced by tendencies and predispositions resulting from their earlier activities. The establishment of a particular pattern inclines the observer toward such an organization of his perceptual field on subsequent occasions. Once we have discovered the hidden figures of a puzzle picture, these figures are usually very persistent and compelling in later perceptions of the picture.

In an experiment by Siao-Sung (1937), a series of twelve simple, irregular figures formed by dotted lines were first shown to a group of subjects. Later, these figures were presented again but as parts of larger and more complex figures, the larger figures thus masking those of the original series. To a control group, the larger figures were presented without the previous showing of the simple figures. It was found that the experimental group tended to see readily the masked figures as units in their respective complexes because they had previously observed these figures in isolation. The control group saw the masked figures much less frequently because no predisposition had been established for them in previous experience as in the case of the experimental group. The latter saw the masked figures as units in the larger figures twenty times more often than did the control subjects. It is evident that what we see depends upon the organization of our visual field and that this organization is greatly influenced by previous experiences. Perhaps the most widespread example available is the difference in our perception of letters and words, once we have begun to read.

Changes in Meaning.   As experiences increase, perceptual meanings change, tending as a rule to become more definite and more effective as a means of adjustment. An acquaintance walking along a dimly lighted street on a rainy night came to a crossing where the pavement was broken. He saw a dull, irregular patch of gray which he took to be a piece of the broken cement pavement. It appeared high and dry, so he proceeded to step on it. To his consternation, his foot splashed into a puddle of muddy water. Hearing the splash and feeling his foot slipping into the mud quickly changed the meaning of his visual pattern from *cement* to *mud puddle*. In both instances, the interpretation resulted from past events.

In other cases, the pattern of learning involved in the development of perceptual meaning is dependent on association. A child who is learning to read is shown the word *house*. He does not know what it means, but the teacher says, "House." He knows the meaning of the spoken word. By the association of the spoken word with the printed symbol, the latter takes on the meaning of the former. Needless to say, the associations can become highly abstract, as for instance in the study of European history, when our concepts of royalty and revolution are determined more by imagination and stereotype than reality.

Cue Reduction. A special case of the change of meaning in perception is cue reduction. From the name, it might seem to be more appropriate to describe this as a change in the perceptual pattern without change in the meaning. There is a change in pattern because certain parts of it are dropped out and the meaning carried by the original pattern is now attached to the remaining portion. On the other hand, we have a change of the meaning borne by the part which remains. You hear a voice over the telephone and do not recognize the person speaking. He must tell you his name. Later you get well acquainted with this person. He calls you on the telephone, and you recognize him by his voice at once. The quality of this particular voice is now sufficient for the apprehension of the person calling. It has taken on a meaning which at first it did not have.

In cue reduction, a part stands for the whole, or at least renders the same service for perception as it rendered earlier only in conjunction with other stimuli. Thus, the sight of a human foot means that a whole person is present; a particular noise indicates an airplane overhead; and a scorchy odor reveals that the potatoes have boiled dry.

Cue reduction serves a useful purpose, for it permits us to speed our responses by acting on minimal information. You experience something similar when you dial a wrong number for a non-existent telephone. Before you complete dialing, a special tone interrupts, preventing you from tying up switchboard space. In many situations, the number of alternate responses available to us is considerable. If we waited until we had complete information, then paused to select among the various responses available, we would never get our food purchased and cooked, much less eaten. Imagine going to the store, viewing the display, returning to review recipes and menus, and going back to purchase.

Cue reduction permits an anticipation of the event and a readying to meet it. In short, we ready ourselves to respond based on a matching of perceptions with probable sequences in the environment. Where probabilities are high, we are able to short-circuit the comparatively lengthy process of discrimination and judgment required in situations where alternatives are numerous or conditions ambiguous. It is unfortunately the case that in many circumstances which social conditions present, we *act* as if probabilities were high and alternatives few (do you recall coming to like someone whom you initially rejected?). We ignore contradictory information and force the situation to fit our anticipations. Many a child with a reputation of being a troublemaker has been accused of perpetrating a misdeed because such judgment fitted the teacher's anticipation, not because he did it.

THE IMPROVEMENT OF PERCEPTION

At first reading, the term perceptual learning seems synonymous with audio-visual education, emphasizing the vital role that perception plays in learning. There is a second aspect of perceptual learning to consider, namely, the extent to which we learn to perceive. Both are important to the practical problems of education and training. Our concern here is with the extent to which perception can be improved, for even the most casual observer will grant perception an important role in learning. A review of the various theories of how perception and learning are related all have in common the assumption that we receive more information through our senses than our nervous system can transmit. Early theorists, Helmholtz and Tichenor, assumed past experience accumulated and was expressed in subconscious inferences which imposed limitations on the information being considered. Brunswik's (1955) probabilistic functionalism is a derivative theory. The Gestalt psychologists thought the sensory field was self-organizing and that it imposed certain configurations on the perceiver. Stimulus conditions can be found which support this view. More recently, J. J. Gibson (1959) has argued for the primacy of stimulus arrays in perception. In recent years, a synthesis has been emerging which includes the view that perception is learned.

Perception is of such basic importance to the individual and his educational progress that its improvement becomes a part of the task of every teacher. Because it does attain a considerable degree of respectability before the child comes to school and because it develops to such a large degree through incidental learning, it is too often accepted as a ready-made vehicle for stocking the child with information. However, the facts revealed by the study of perception make clear the need for serious attention to the deliberate cultivation and training of this ability. Probably the best work in this type of training has been done in the kindergarten and in our schools for the feeble-minded. (See the Montessori and the Fernald methods.) Here, the need for such work is more easily appreciated because the lack of perceptual development is more apparent in the very young and in the mentally deficient. But much can and should be done at all levels of the educational program. To illustrate the need, two groups of rural southern and urban northern high school students heard a tape recording of twenty non-verbal sounds, then wrote brief descriptions identifying the source of the sound (Frymier, 1958). In both quantitative and qualitative analysis, the northern pupils made more correct identifications. The southern rural pupils had more correct identifications related to farms and machinery. If one could count on lifelong residence in a given environment, such differences would be of less concern; but in a mobile and changing society, perceptual skills need appropriate development.

The results of perceptual training may be seen in the alertness of the proofreader, in detecting mistakes in printing. The trained professional buyer for a clothing store is especially adept at distinguishing the various qualities of cloth. Expert tea tasters are noted for their acute perceptions of minute differences in the quality of the brew. The experienced hunter knows by the tracks in the snow what game has passed. The musician detects in tones the slight defect which passes unnoticed by the untrained listener. In every field of human art and endeavor, the perception of the expert—the well trained and the fully experienced—is keener, more critical, and more analytical than is that of the novice or the uninitiated.

Gibson (1953), after making an extensive summary of the experimental studies pertaining to the effect of training upon perceptual judgment, concludes that the studies confirm the influence of practice upon improvement of judgment over a wide range of relative and absolute discriminations of visual and auditory stimuli. The improvement of perception requires consideration of five different aspects: detection, discrimination, recognition, identification, and judgment.

Detection. Exploration consumes a major portion of the time of the preschool child. He comes to know his immediate world by first-hand sensori-motor experience—by touching, tasting, feeling, smelling, regarding, and hitting various objects to learn their sound. In the process, he develops various motor skills, some knowledge of function and some rudimentary concepts, but he is also learning essential characteristics of objects. Reactions to objects are essential for the growth of ability to perceive adequately. Both empirical and experimental evidence (Gibson, 1953; Newton, 1956; Bevan and Zener, 1952) indicate that thresholds of sensitivity can be changed by training. Herein lies the value of permitting children the freedom to run about, to explore their environments, to handle, taste and smell the things they encounter, to dig in the dirt, splash in the water, tear paper, stroke kittens, handle ice, smell flowers, and play with other children. As convenient as the play-pen is, it is a cage designed to constrain and ultimately, like the zoo, produce passive behavior. Nor are the toys which can be added a satisfactory substitute for extended experience. The extreme illustration of this was the 3½-year-old congenitally blind girl seen by the writer who had spent her life in a crib, parents' arms, and stroller and who could not walk, crawl or talk; she could only express irritation at being separated from others.

The kindergarten is well adapted to contributing experiences that have excellent developmental value. Here, the child's perceptual possibilities are drawn out by his play with other children, by making forms in sand or clay, by weaving which calls for the discrimination of colors, by singing, by finger painting, and by the many other interesting activities that afford direct sensory stimulation and the opportunity to respond, explore, and manipulate. But such experience should not begin and end in kinder-garten, else the upper schools provide little more than second-hand experi-ence detached from reality.

To develop perceptual skills, the first step is to obtain awareness. The objects and materials to be observed are important. Natural objects, models, charts, and other concrete materials are useful. The child can describe what he sees, draw pictures of it, or write a composition on it. Questions give direction to perception. A child may be led to see many details which otherwise might entirely escape his attention. Another means is to show a group of objects or a picture for a few seconds and have the children later tell how many things they can remember. This may be made into a sort of game. Group discussion of a picture or of what is seen on a field trip may be made stimulating. In all these procedures, the teacher has the opportunity for correcting faulty observations and for helping the child to become more accurate.

Children naturally seek adventure and new experiences. They like to explore. One teacher succeeded in arousing the interest of a boy who was indifferent to his school work by telling him he was to describe to her every morning one interesting thing he had seen on the way to school. This assignment included the subtle suggestion that if he noticed things around him, he would find interesting things. This boy was soon reporting to his teacher not one but several interesting things he had seen, and his attitude toward his work quickly improved. By instructing the child to watch for certain things, by directing his observations, and by seeing to it that the experience brings satisfaction, teachers create awareness, inter-est, and attention and in the doing fulfill an essential function of the teach-ing role.

Discrimination. In her summary on perceptual learning, Gibson (1953) points out that improved skill in discrimination plays an important role in such learning. The earlier discussion on attention is pertinent, for part of the task is identifying the relevant stimulus dimensions and cues to which to respond in making a discrimination. As the number of alterna-tives increase within a dimension (Krulee, Podell, and Ronco, 1954) or the number of stimulus dimensions increase, discrimination becomes pro-gressively more difficult. Nearly all learning experiences except specially designed laboratory experiences present a complex of stimuli. For example, a judgment of depth involves consideration of shading, size, distance, tex-ture, and perspective. The task in instruction is to make the essential dimen-sions recognizable and more easily discriminated, at least initially. Consider the task of locating a word in the dictionary. Assuming the word to be spelled correctly, the task is essentially a matching task requiring knowledge of the alphabet. Yet most middle-grade children have difficulty with this task long after they have memorized the alphabet because their rote repetition beginning at A creates a barrier. The essential discrimination is that of knowing the location of the first (and subsequent) letter of the word in relation to all the other letters in the alphabet—in short, to know the alphabet forward and backward from any point in it. Specifically, if you open the dictionary at M and are looking for *jewel,* you need to know that J precedes M. Knowing this, the secondary cues of the order of letters within the word and the page headings are useful. Until then they are confusing.

The use of contrast is important in speeding discrimination, but it should be along the relevant dimension. For example. discriminating the sounds "f" and "v," "p" and "b," and other similar pairs is difficult. Greater contrast makes the discrimination initially easier, with progression in difficulty occurring subsequently.

The child's auditory perception at the age when he is learning to talk is very imperfect. He may have normal hearing and the pronunciation he hears may be faultless, yet his own pronunciation may be faulty because he fails to hear the fine variations and delicate shadings of sounds characteristic of good speech. Children often need special training to improve their ability to hear various word sounds accurately. This imperfect auditory perception of word sounds may affect not only the child's pronunciation unfavorably, but may be responsible for confusion in the next language steps and his learning to read and spell. For example, in a composition by a seventh grade girl appeared the following errors in spelling: *hunerds,* for hundreds, *Washinton,* for Washington, and *witch* for which. The relation of these errors to faulty pronunciation is obvious. This child wrote these words as they sounded to her and as she herself pronounced them. Her difficulty was not due to home influence nor to bad pronunciation by the teacher. Her parents were well educated and spoke plainly. Failure to hear properly was a basic cause here of bad spelling. This child needed "eartraining" to help her hear the word sounds correctly.

In order to learn to read successfully, a child must be capable of good auditory and visual discrimination. Reading begins with the child's oral vocabulary. He knows the spoken word first. This is associated with the printed word. Then, after the pattern of learning by conditioning, the visual form takes on the meaning carried by the speech sound. If the learner does not hear the essential and distinguishing elements of the spoken word, he may have trouble in making this shift to the printed form. A large proportion of the children referred to the Boston University Educational Clinic as reading difficulty cases have shown lack of ability to notice similarities and differences in the sounds of spoken words (Murphy, 1943).

Visual discrimination is essential for reading, for if the learner does not distinguish relatively small differences in word forms, he will confuse such similar letter patterns as *house, louse,* and *horse.* To distinguish between *new* and *mew,* for instance, requires rather keen perceptual discrimination, and it is not surprising, in view of the fact that perceptions are so imperfectly developed at the first- and second-grade levels, to find that these words look alike to some children.

Contrast has to occur along the *relevant stimulus dimension*. One occasionally sees color and size differences in the print in beginning readers. Generally such variations do little to facilitate learning to read, for the new words have to be distinguished from old, e.g., *dig* from *dog,* on the basis of difference in form, not size or color. In complex skills, levels of discrimination occur. Fleishman and Fruchter (1960) showed by factor analysis that in the early stages of learning Morse code, auditory rhythm discrimination and auditory perceptual speed were important, but that at later stages speed of closure was significant. It is likely that such stages occur in learning oral and written language, e.g., discrimination between verb endings in French or noun endings in German prior to comprehension of sentence meaning.

Recognition and Identification.   If perception is the process mediating between sensation and interpretation, i.e., between stimulation and meaning, the dividing line falls indistinctly between recognition and identification. We often recognize a stimulus pattern without being able to identify it, e.g., recognizing someone without remembering who he is or when and where we knew him. Identification calls for greater supply from memory. Recognition occurs because we know the salient features in a stimulus pattern— the singular voice qualities, stride, gesture, or outline that characterize a friend or relative. Identification is influenced by set—calling to someone we thought we recognized. A simple illustration of the effect of set upon identification is seen in a study by Bruner and Minturn (1955) who presented a group of college students a broken B under rapid and slow exposure conditions. When the broken letter was contained in a group of capital letters, it was seen as B; but when it was contained in a group of two-digit numbers, it was seen as 13. Under slow exposure, identification was accurate in spite of set.

Recognition can occur along many dimensions. In a carefully controlled study, Eames (1947) compared the speed of object recognition and word recognition of 329 children between the ages of 6 and 13. Seventy-five children were passing in all school subjects, 254 were failing. The speed of object and word recognition was the same for succeeding students, but markedly disparate for failing students, with speed of word recognition falling behind object recognition between ages 6 and 12. Eames explains these results in terms of an artifact of the educational program which places emphasis upon sight vocabulary and oral reading during the elementary grades, thus permitting the lack of speed of recognition of words to go unnoticed.

Such perceptual skills appear to be quite specific. Several studies have shown a correlation between perceptual span, perceptual speed, and speed of reading, but they have failed to show that improving perceptual span or perceptual speed produces a concomitant improvement in reading (Sutherland, 1946; Smith and Tate, 1953; Freeburne, 1949). The three studies mentioned have utilized such devices as flashmeters, ophthalmographs, tachistoscopes, and reading rate controllers with which the reader could progressively advance his reading rate. Marked increases in perceptual speed of recognition have been shown in all instances (using college students as subjects), and also (where the reading rate controller was used) in reading speed as a result of training. Unfortunately, the increases transferred in such small amounts to normal reading situations that direct work at increasing reading speed appears equally if not more beneficial. Such results point up the importance of diversified perceptual training as well as relating such skills to higher order skills and concepts.

One of the tasks of the initial stages in language learning consists of learning labels such as *Daddy, Mommy,* and the like. Subsequently, in learning to read, we learn visual labels corresponding to the oral ones. The learning of labels goes faster if we have had firsthand experience on which it can be based. This is one of the arguments supporting the use of audio-visual methods in education. They approach firsthand experience. The last decade has seen a tremendous increase in the use of audio-visual methods as a result of the development of educational television and because of the impact of the National Defense Education Act of 1958 which provided funds for equipment and research in the "new educational media." An estimated million children receive some instruction by means of television. The rapid development has contributed to the unquestioned transfer of classical instructional procedures to the screen with the result that students are shown teachers talking from a screen rather than from the front of a classroom. On the average, only some 20 percent of present programs make use of the screen for *visual* presentation of the subjects. The rest is talk. Even with this fraction, there is an implicit assumption that visual presentation will succeed where teachers have often failed. Much the same assumption is made for field trips. There is no question that it is possible, but it is not automatic. Without prior preparation in how to look, i.e., perceptual training, films and field trips often fall short of expectations.

The relationship between perception and labeling appears to be reciprocal, i.e., having labels ready facilitates perception. In a series of studies, Spiker (1956a, 1956b) has shown among other results that having labels available facilitates discrimination and retention. Spiker's work has been with younger children and with particular tasks, but if the results can be generalized, as learning theory would indicate, the so-called experience centered curriculum is not a complete answer. For example, some knowledge of the existence of Neo-classical, Romantic, and Realist schools of art and their essential differences would be as valuable to a museum trip, as the museum trip would be to an introduction to nineteenth century painting. Without the labels of the various schools, the trip would emerge as a blur of paintings. With labels available, some recognition and identification are likely.

Interest probably functions in a manner similar to sets and labels in focusing attention and in speeding the recognition of selected aspects of the stimulus field.

Judgment.   Various illusions are often used to impress us with the susceptibility of our perception to false impressions, pointing up the fact that ultimately we are faced with the task of relating our perception to external reality (viridical standards) to some degree. This involves eliminating what psychologists call constant errors, as opposed to variable errors. When you type, you make occasional errors which vary; however, if you shift your hands one row of keys to the right or left, all words will be misspelled (for touch-typists) as a result of a constant error. It could be argued that some forms of functional insanity manifest themselves in an inability to bring perceptions into congruence with external realities, as defined by some set of measurements or observations.

On the basis of our experience, we build a set of meanings or concepts—of the essential and distinguishing characteristics of given classes of objects or events and of the relationships between them. On the basis of these, we develop certain expectancies or hypotheses with which we approach different situations—the shriek of brakes implies danger, to ourselves in traffic, to others if we're in the house. The same sound would be meaningless in the woods. These expectancies apply to people as well as objects. We may learn to anticipate fathers as understanding and sympathetic or arbitrary and indifferent and perhaps extend this to men in general. As we view the range of personalities and competencies which survive, we understand that a range of tolerance exists. To stay within this range requires continuous judgment of what is occurring, what response is needed, and a verification of its appropriateness.

We use various means to check or test our perceptions and our actions. We use the perception of the other sensory modalities to verify one against the other. We can tell if the car is turning or the chair is tipping by the kinesthetic [1] cues provided. We use the difference in sounds produced by the tires on ice to check the visual perception of a slick surface. We use knowledge of results and feedback of information as other means of testing our judgments. It is interesting to note the number of games which allow multiple serves or tries. The degree of failure of the first try leads to an adjustment on the rest of the series as one tries to improve the results. Feedback often comes from two sources: internal and external. In learning the

---

[1] Kinesthesis: the feeling of movement within the muscles, joints and tendons, as distinct from the sense of touch.

forearm stroke in tennis, we get information from the feel of the movements made, the sound of the impact of racket on ball, and the direction the ball takes. Simultaneously, the coach may be saying, "You dropped the head of your racket." Laboratory studies suggest that intrinsic feedback is more valuable than extrinsic (Annett, 1959; Pearson and Hauty, 1960). This would indicate that the baseball pitcher's feelings for what went wrong with a pitch are more useful to him than the umpire's calling it a "ball."

External information of another sort is often available for checking the simultaneous judgment made by another. Consider how frequently you check your neighbor's lecture notes to determine if you both heard something the same way. A fairly extensive literature has evolved regarding the effects of group norms on perception. Illustrative of this is an experiment by Bovard (1951). Two sets of experimental groups existed, the first organized on a leader centered basis for the semester, the second, group centered. At semester end, the groups were asked to judge the length of a green paper rectangle before and after the announcement of the mean judgments made by the group. All groups shifted toward the group norm, with the group centered group making a greater shift, indicating not only the use of the group norm to verify perceptions, but a difference in willingness to accommodate it. Judging from the greater shift in group centered groups, a motivational aspect as well as the information offered apparently influenced the outcome. This would not be inconsistent with the earlier discussion of the effects of motivation on perception. The Schafer and Murphy experiment (Figure 12.4) indicates that reinforcement can be influential in the determination of perceptual judgments.

WHAT PERCEPTIONS SHALL WE TRAIN?

No attempt will be made here to list all of the perceptions which the school can develop. The needs of various individuals are so diverse and the demands of different vocations so varied with respect to effective perception that only general objectives can be listed. Perceptual skills essential to survival have been needed since the days of the cave. Today's dangers lie with the automobile and the autocrat instead of the mammoth and the sabre-toothed tiger. If the ends of life be primitive self-perpetuation, then such perceptions as protect that goal should suffice; beyond this, perceptions that enhance the development of the person and his mutual existence with his fellow are necessary.

Perception of Physical Objects. Every individual must get on in a world of natural and man-made objects. A good start has been made on the perception of objects, their nature, qualities, and form by the time the child enters school. However, imperfections and limitations are still so great that the school has both opportunity and duty for enrichment, extension, and refinement. Nature study and science classes, the field trip and the laboratory provide opportunities whereby the pupils' observational skills can be quickened to see more penetratingly into the marvels and miseries of man and nature, whether they be hoar frost or forest fire, monumental river dams or factory slag heaps and city streets.

Space Perception and Orientation.   Because adjustments of various kinds must be made to the spatial aspects of the contents of one's environment, the individual needs a well developed ability to apprehend spatial relationships. The time is not too far past when a man could learn his geography first-hand, on foot or horseback; but these no longer dictate the bounds of his world. With the geographic limits extended by jet plane and camera and with the senses extended by television, microscope, radio, oscillograph, radar, laser, and other inventions into space and into structure, we need training in reading and understanding the information provided by press, picture, equipment, and experience.

At a mundane level, we need effective procedures for teaching the ability to make quick estimates of distance and speed if the automobile is to become less lethal; at an abstract level we need to understand man's relationship to his physical and ecological environment and the effects of his actions on them.

Social Perceptions.   If the population increase is going to leave standing room only, we should consider whether we prefer a world which seems like a subway car at peak hours, with each man elbowing his anonymous neighbor, or one offering more accommodation between world residents. The social disorganization and personal breakdown which exist indicate a certain need for improved ability to perceive others and ourselves in relation to them, to recognize the meaning of behavior in relation to the intentions of others as well as of ourselves. More than superficial etiquette is needed for social relationships to become graceful; living requires the perceptual skills prerequisite to knowing others at some depth.

Esthetic Perception.   Every child should learn to see the beauty in his surroundings. The enjoyment of a beautiful sunset, landscape, picture, or music depends upon the degree to which perception has been established. To appreciate good music, one must be sensitive to the figures and patterns of tones that make it good. To appreciate art, the pupil must be able to see the shadings, rhythm, and balance by which the artist has expressed his purpose. The domestic science class should be taught to see the pleasing details of an artistically arranged dinner table and the fine points of good taste and design in clothing. The botany class should learn to see the beauty of the color patterns of flowers, not merely stamens, pistils, and petals. The literature class should be taught to see the beauty of the total pattern of the poem, not merely to tear good literature to pieces in a search for similes and metaphors. Scarcely any better starting place could be found than the program seen on the ubiquitous television set, largely ignored by teachers, for one might say that taste, like charity, begins at home.

SUMMARY

Perception mediates between the continuous stream of stimulus arrays impinging on our senses and the variety of emotional, cognitive, and motor responses available. Living between two stimulus worlds, one internal, the other external, we need a procedure for selecting, ordering, and responding that is efficient in terms of the appropriateness of response and the energy exchange involved. The perceptual processes make this possible. We approach the environment with certain expectancies born of past experience, present interest, attitudes, and set that influence the particular aspect of the stimulus field to which we attend. We seek stimulus cues that confirm or refute and in the process discriminate, recognize, and identify essential features. Sensory thresholds, figure-ground relationships, and constancy effects impose limitations, configurations and priorities. Ambiguity, motivation, set, and group pressures affect the kinds and amount of information needed to confirm our expectations.

Perception is an activity upon which much of our learning depends. At the same time, it is modified and developed through learning. Sensory thresholds, discrimination skills, and meaning and interpretations can be improved through training. The perceptions of young children are meager, crude, indefinite, and lacking in detail. They improve gradually over time, partially as a function of maturation and progressively as a function of experience. For the school to ignore perceptual training is to minimize its potential impact on child and society.

FURTHER READING

Overview

HILGARD, E. R. 1957. Perception. *Introduction to Psychology, 2nd ed.* New York: Harcourt, Brace, pp. 331-89.

Selected References

BLAKE, R. R. and G. V. RAMSEY (eds.) 1951. *Perception: An Approach to Personality.* New York: Ronald.

KOCH, S. (ed.) 1959. *Psychology: A Study of a Science.* Vol. I. New York: McGraw-Hill.

WOHLWILL, J. F. 1960. Developmental studies of perception. *Psychol. Bull.,* 57: 249-88.

Original Investigations

BOVARD, E. W., JR. 1951. Group structure and perception. *J. Abn. and Soc. Psychol.,* 46: 398-405.

GAGE, N. L. and G. SOUCI. 1951. Social perception and teacher-pupil relationships. *J. of Educ. Psychol.,* 427: 145-52.

GIBSON, ELEANOR. 1953. Improvement in perceptual judgments as a function of controlled practice or training. *Psychol. Bull.,* 50: 401-31.

GYR, J. W. *et al.* 1966. Computer simulation and psychological theories of perception. *Psychol. Bull.,* 65: 174-92.

POSTMAN, L. and R. CRUTCHFIELD. 1952. The interaction of need, set and stimulus in a cognitive task. *Amer. J. of Psychol.,* 65: 196-218.

SOLBY, C. M. and SOMMER, R. 1957. Perceptual autism in children. *J. Gen. Psychol.,* 56: 3-11.

13

Rote Learning
and Retention

Try not remembering or not thinking. One can accomplish this for several seconds by concentrated attention on looking or listening. But not to remember or not to think is almost like not breathing. Like thinking, breathing can be stopped momentarily, but both, like feeling, are inherent in being alive.

The intricacies of the brain delay understanding of how it functions in learning and in recalling. Gradually, as refined techniques for studying brain function develop, our knowledge expands, and with it our concepts of what occurs when we learn, think, or remember. A century ago, when mapping of the brain became more definitive and localized areas relating to speech, vision, and motor actions were identified, the assumption was made that a memory area and a thinking area existed. In fact, the faculty psychology in vogue at the time assumed a range of human faculties such as memory, reason, will, perseverance, and the like, each with its specific area in the brain. It was known that damage to specific areas of the brain impaired speech and vision, but the same could not be demonstrated for memory.

When the electrical potentials associated with nerve and brain function were discovered, these were naturally incorporated into attempted explanations. It is not surprising that the telephone switchboard was used as a model of central nervous system operations, or that today the computer provides a newer model. One had only to plug into the correct circuit to get the correct number, i.e., recall the needed information. In fact, the analogy has been made that a ten story telephone switchboard building would be required to provide as many circuits as the brain possesses.

One of the difficulties with analogies as explanations is the temptation to take them literally. It is true that the discharge of electrical energy in the brain is a continuous process and that its flow in circuits can be demonstrated, not unlike that in the wires of a house, ready to produce a response if the proper button is pushed. But recordable electrical activity in the brains of animals and humans can be abolished by cooling them markedly for short periods of time, without significant effects upon memory. A similar analogy is that of storage, taken from computer technology. Because certain information is stored on tapes or discs for use in a given computer program, we extend the analogy that information is stored in the brain. We conjure up visions of file cabinets in cerebral attics, holding all of life's information, i.e., all we have experienced. The fact of the matter is that six months after completing a college course, we cannot call up half of what once we knew. Possibly it is lost, i.e., one doesn't know where to look, but equally possible, the information may no longer exist because there never was a file cabinet, or rather, the brain doesn't function like a computer. We do know that the brain functions much slower than computers, as far as speed of transmission of impulse, yet the brain can often operate more rapidly than a computer as far as recall of information is concerned. Thus the analogy, though helpful, has its limits.

As biochemists discovered the part played by certain chemicals in transmission of nerve impulses at synapses, conjectures were offered assigning them a central role in memory and thought. More recently as scientists have shown how genetic information can be reproduced and communicated through chemical codes carried by ribonucleic acid (RNA) and desoxyribonucleic acid (DNA) molecules, the idea of an equivalent process in the brain has been suggested. Wechsler (1962) argues that memories do not exist before being recalled, any more than melodies are stored in pianos. Recall is thus a form of response, made possible by some modifications in the organism's capacities as a function of experience, much as a guitar would respond differently if the tension on the strings were changed. By this thesis, to account for memory requires explaining the nature of the changes in the organism's capacities. Nor is any inference to be made that the changes are permanent, any more than our reaction time or visual acuity is unchanging. Fatigue, drugs, age, and experience affect these capacities, just as they affect memory. What is indicated is a plasticity, a changing over time by virtue of the events of life, suggesting that very little is permanently retained in memory. One's immediate counter is to ask: Why then do I retain that inconsequential, earliest childhood memory? Most likely because it has been often recited, hence repeatedly recalled. To some extent, memory may function like a tape which has been repeatedly used for recording. To begin with, it yields no sound when put on Play. Once recorded on, it plays back, yet each play loses a little in fidelity. It becomes less and less identical with the original sound. One can record over the first recording; however, occasional sounds from the first recording can, like early memories, still be heard.

PHYSIOLOGY AND MEMORY

In spite of the limitations regarding detailed functioning of the brain, some reasonable conjectures can be made regarding memory. From birth to death, the brain is continuously active. Variations in electrical activity in different areas of the brain associated with variations in degree of arousal and stimulation of the organism can be shown by means of electroencephalographic recordings. The brain is subject to a continuous stream of stimulation, even during sleep, from within and without the body. By means of afferent neurons, eyes, ears, nose, and other senses, the organs transmit a continuous series of signals, some of which receive attention, others being ignored. Driving an automobile at a constant speed on the highway provides an illustration. We are seeing, hearing, smelling, feeling continuously, with attention directed to looking. But let a slight knock in the motor begin, or a wobble in the wheel, or a smell of burnt rubber occur, and our attention shifts immediately. Yet the flow of stimulation from all sources continues without interruption, without regard to our shift in attention.

The afferent neurons bringing impulses to the central nervous system, including the brain, are like an interstate highway system on which traffic flows in one direction only, with occasional intersections or exits to other one-way highways. The brain itself consists of a mass of associative neurons, more like a city consisting entirely of one-way streets. Estimates have been made that the brain contains some nine to ten billion nerve cells, intricately interlocked like city streets. The electrical impulses being transmitted along and between neurons can be likened to automobiles in a downtown section, some moving along the streets, intersecting with other lines of traffic, others circling the block, the entire section active. Traffic is heavy at certain periods of the day, light at others, varying from one section to another, but always with some traffic somewhere. The difference is that the traffic in the brain consists of electro-chemical impulses being routed through clusters of neurons. And one of these neurons may have some fifty branches and be able to influence four thousand other neurons, constituting a more intricate network than any web of city streets. The stimuli from the afferent neurons sets these clusters, which have been termed reverberating circuits, into operation. One supposition is that these reverberating circuits constitute immediate memory, the short-term awareness of information and events.

If permanent memory were automatic, that is, every stimulus experienced were permanently retained, even ten billion brain cells would not suffice. Fortunately, the reverberating circuits of immediate memory are like merry-go-round rides at an amusement park, short-lived and quickly forgotten. As a result, most of the stimulation being received is ignored, certain selected for attention. Some of that selected for attention will be retained in long-term memory. The process is fortunate, for it means that most of the irrelevant can be ignored, that which is no longer useful forgotten, and that which was shameful or painful escaped.

We know from experimental studies with animals and clinical studies with human subjects that electrical shock disrupts memory for events immediately preceding the shock but not long-term memory. The inference is that the shock disrupts the impulses occurring in the reverberating circuits. Normally, our experience is less cataclysmic. We must look to less dramatic causes of disruption. We shift attention, for instance. The shift may occur as a result of a change in the pattern of stimulation. Music on the radio catches our attention and distracts us from what we were reading; the telephone rings; someone rises from the row ahead to leave the theatre, and so on. Or our motives shift; we think of lunch and wish the lecture would end. Possibly a new set is created; the instructor announces a surprise quiz to end the period. Events such as these suffice to disrupt immediate memory enough to erase it, as easily as the second introduction at a party erases memory of the first-named.

Long-term memory appears to be dependent upon chemical changes in brain cells, rather than electrical changes. Although evidence is circumstantial, it is plausible if not convincing. The best understood mechanism for the storage and transmission of information is that involved in heredity and the transmission of genetic information. Information is conveyed from cells of the parent to the child through the medium of the nucleic acids (DNA and RNA) which are essential building-blocks of the chromosomes of plants and animals.

We also know from research on immunity to disease, that the body possesses the capacity to produce antibodies capable of identifying and defending the body against specific disease producing agents. This capacity may result from natural causes such as a prior occurrence of the disease, or artificially by vaccination and other forms of immunization. Nevertheless, to perform this function, the antibodies have to "store" the information which makes recognition of the disease producing agent possible. And such information is specific, not general, just as the ability to distinguish a Ferrari or an Austin-Healy is specific. Furthermore, this chemical memory varies in length for different diseases. For some, like measles, immunity is apparently life-long, at least in most individuals. For others, repeated vaccinations are needed. It may be that such "permanent" memory is kept refreshed by repeated exposure and that with rarer diseases, the immunity response needs artificial reinforcement; but this is speculation.

More direct evidence of the significance of chemistry for memory is found in studies which show that direct injection of RNA has a beneficial effect upon memory and that chemicals which inhibit RNA operation, such as puromycin, an antibiotic which blocks protein synthesis, prevent the establishment of permanent memory. Such evidence lends credence to the argument that permanent memory is achieved by chemical changes which occur in the molecules of brain cells or combinations of brain cells, under given conditions of stimulation. Lacking detailed knowledge, any generalizations that can be made about the functioning of memory are based on global, and hence cruder, evidence. Nevertheless, in very simple terms, it is possible to see how the development of perceptual constancies which stabilize perceptual responses to the environment, conditioning experiences which link new sets of stimuli and responses, and the development of concepts which permit generalized responses constitute modifications of the organism's capacity to respond.

ROTE MEMORIZING

A first inclination, when thinking of memorizing, is to consider deliberate efforts to memorize a poem, lecture notes, multiplication tables, or some other form of verbal material. Somehow the equivalent effort to distinguish a Doric from an Ionic column, a red from a white blood corpuscle, or to lift a dry fly out of the lake and flip it back without thinking of the sequence of movements escapes us when discussing memorizing. Yet each of these is a form of memorizing: establishing an available capacity to provide the appropriate response on future occasion. Small wonder, then, that much of our knowledge of conditions affecting memory stem from studies on rote verbal learning. Nevertheless, rote learning is not restricted to verbal materials. It is probably more accurate to say that most of our knowledge, verbal or motor, is acquired by a sequence of gradual approximations of the ideal or perfect performance, at least during the initial stages of learning, and that much of our interest in concept learning and learning by discovery stems from a desire to speed the process and increase the efficiency of learning. But learning by discovery is not yet the prototype of learning. Whether by accident, ignorance, design, or necessity, much of school learning is rote learning, the commitment to memory of predetermined responses, with the hope that in the process of commitment to memory, understanding will also occur.

Most of us have formed a great many associations with the things which we meet frequently in the course of our daily living. Thus, *church* may suggest: worship, preacher, building, bell, sermon, hymns, usher, pew, aisle, wedding, music, congregation, deacon, contributions, or Sunday school. Now, the chances are that on different occasions with different attitudes and sets, the mention of *church* will bring to mind different ones of these associated experiences. If you are hungry, you may think of the church supper. At Christmas time, you may think of the music of your church. In other words, the total situation governs associative recall, and the response to a stimulus made in one situation may be altogether different from that made to the same word in another situation. What appears depends on purpose, problem, attitude, mood, and other sets.

In such cases as we have just mentioned, most of our associations are formed incidentally. In rote memorizing, however, there is normally a definite purpose to acquire the ability to recite or reproduce in a fixed manner. An attempt is made to form a particular associative train and to strengthen it by repetition, so that the recurrence of a particular item of experience or verbal reaction will invariably be succeeded by the one that followed it in the learning situation. So, the poem is read and reread until every word in every line can be recited in the precise order in which it is read. Spelling must be learned so that for each word the exact sequence of letters can be reproduced. A deviation from the serial order experienced in learning is considered an error, and the learning in that case would be regarded as imperfect or incomplete.

In paired associates learning, where two items are learned together, the pair is repeated until the learner, upon experiencing the first member, will be able to recall the second, for example, learning the dates of historical events or the capitals of states. Memorizing is, then, the process of developing associations strong enough to make it probable that specific responses will be prompted in the presence of specific stimuli.

The two procedures just described, serial order learning and paired associates learning, are the most frequently utilized in studies of rote learning in the laboratory, with nonsense syllables playing a prominent part as material to be learned. The virtue of the nonsense syllable is that it permits some control over the influence of the prior experience of the learner. Even so-called nonsense syllables vary in meaning, as one can readily see in comparing MEX, KUJ, and LVK. In serial order learning, a list of syllables or words, such as that shown below, are presented one at a time, with two seconds exposure being typical. Each word serves as the prompt for the next. The words may be unrelated, as in the second column, or conceptual or syntactical cues may be provided. The importance of such cues should not be underestimated, for by kindergarten, children possess sufficient control over the grammar system to use syntactic cues to deduce the meaning of unfamiliar words, and with increasing age and education make progressively greater use of such knowledge (Kean and Yamamoto, 1965). Such procedures permit study of the effect of variations in meaning, distribution of practice, associative frequency of letters and syllables, and other variables on rate of acquisition and retention. In paired associates learning, a pair of syllables or words is used. For example, the syllables in the first column may be linked with the words in the second, e.g., TAJ with HAND, and so forth.

TAJ	HAND
YIC	CARD
HUZ	DOCK
CEX	PACK
YAD	MILE
MEP	COAT

Verbal discrimination learning is a variation on paired associates learning which calls for recognition rather than recall. Here the learner has to identify which of a series of pairs being presented is correct. A simple illustration is seen in a 3-year-old asking her mother: Is this hug? and, Is this kiss? as she carried out what she hoped was the appropriate action. Her confusion about the discrimination was readily understandable. Both words had been used unsystematically in the same situation. Sometimes the child was hugged, sometimes kissed, sometimes both, the action carried out with and without verbal accompaniment. Finally, by testing her understanding, the child learned to verbally discriminate the two.

One finds less use of verbal discrimination tasks in the laboratory and less use of what is known as free learning tasks. In the latter procedure, order of presentation and order of recall may vary. Such a procedure poses obvious difficulties for control in laboratory settings, but one need only consider the order in which questions in a final examination may be arranged to recognize that the order in which we are likely to be expected to reproduce our learning in school or life settings can be highly variable.

It should not be surprising to learn that most of the studies of rote verbal learning and retention, using the experimental procedures described, have been conducted with adult subjects, college students especially. One of the prime complications in using adults stems from the variations in associations which they bring to the experiment as a result of prior experience, the transfer of training which ensues, and particularly their applying their learning habits and skills to the tasks presented them. Children offer some advantages as experimental subjects in this respect by virtue of their greater naïveté. However, from a review of the results of verbal learning studies with children, Keppel (1964) has concluded that there is a reasonable correspondence in the effective variables reported and in the relationships which have been identified with adult subjects. This is particularly true for associative values for experimental verbal material (Gaeth and Allen, 1965).

QUANTITATIVE CHANGES IN TIME

Detailed consideration was given in earlier chapters to the variables influencing the form of the curve of retention, so that a brief review and some elaboration will serve to point out their importance with regard to remembering and forgetting.

Modes of Impression.   Several different modes of impression are available for rote learning—visual, auditory, kinesthetic, vocomotor. Material may be memorized silently or aloud from listening or reading. Material may be written as an aid to learning, and several combinations of the modalities may be combined.

It is quite probable that individuals differ in the modality through which they perceive best. Whether or not such differences are innate or learned is unknown. The author recalls a boy in the first grade who could repeat the words in a vocabulary drill perfectly when the entire list was written in several widely spaced columns on the blackboard but could not recognize the same words presented on flashcards. The repetition of the words on the blackboard was not dependent upon the serial order of the list because the boy could name the words in mixed order. The discrepancy in performance prompted the author to ask the boy if he could recall the words on the blackboard if blindfolded. The boy tried and succeeded, because he had associated the sound of the word and the position of the word on the blackboard. Such individual differences in modes of learning exist even though there is limited experimental confirmation.

Attempts to obtain definitive evidence on modality of presentation encounter several formidable problems concerning subjects, tasks, and measures which require solution before differences can be attributed to modality. To begin with, individuals are likely to be randomly assigned to experimental groups with the result that studies concerning modality of presentation usually involve composite groups. The results of such studies have been equivocal. They offer little assistance to the teacher who asks if certain modes of presentation will be more effective with certain children. Compounding the problem even more is the fact that individuals are not likely to respond in a unitary fashion to given modes of presentation, but an interrelationship with modality and material is likely. In an early study, Brener (1940) demonstrated that the memory span of college subjects varied with material. He used both visual and auditory methods of presentation to test memory span for a variety of materials—digits, consonants and colors, concrete words, geometrical designs, and abstract words, nonsense syllables, and sentences. About the same time, van Tilborg (1936) showed that verbal and non-verbal learning (paired nonsense syllables versus a finger maze) was retained equally well where the tasks were equated, in the face of the supposition that non-verbal habits are better retained. More recently, Runquist and Hutt (1961) attempted to study the acquisition of verbal concepts by high school students with two forms of stimuli presentation, verbal and pictorial. The results, which favored verbal presentation, were confounded by two conditions of the experiment: first, responses were verbal, permitting the intrusion of association between modes of presentation and response; and second, certain of the concepts involved, such as soft, sharp, and shiny, were primarily tactual rather than visual. Finally, Stroud and Schier (1959) obtained only moderate correlations between differing measures of retention, with verbal and pictorial materials learned to the same level of performance.

None of the studies allowed for individual differences in the preferences of the students learning the materials. In a study of paired associates learning, Postman and Riley (1957) paired numbers and nonsense syllables. These were designated as *unlike* pairs. Where S and R were both numbers or both nonsense syllables, they were termed *like* pairs. When each list which was presented consisted of all *like* pairs or all *unlike* pairs, they were learned with equal rapidity. However, when the lists were mixed, *like* pairs were learned more rapidly than *unlike* pairs, indicating that the subjects selected first those items which they preferred to learn.

Unequivocal answers regarding mode or presentation are not easily obtained. In general, it may be said that as far as groups of children are concerned, no single modality is superior to others but that a multi-modal approach combining auditory, visual, and kinesthetic stimuli is likely to surpass a unimodal presentation. The application of a systems approach to instruction, with testing of variations in the form of the components, promises better answers to the problem.

Meaning.   Meaningfulness of the material learned and the degree to which it is related to earlier learning are important factors in retention. In one study, the retention curve for nonsense syllables fell considerably below the curve for poems and appeared to drop faster between the second and tenth month (Woodworth, 1938). Experiments on the retention of words, poetry, and factual prose in which the recall method was used have not shown as large a percentage of loss during the first few hours after learning as was found by Ebbinghaus for nonsense syllables by the relearning method. There is little question that we remember better what we understand than what we do not understand. English and Edwards (1939) showed that retention tested immediately, thirty, and ninety days after hearing and reading an unfamiliar passage was greater for substance learning than for rote learning. Significantly greater amounts of material learned by rote were forgotten than with sense or substance learning, even when the items were equated for differences in difficulty. The argument for the use of concrete rather than abstract materials, and direct experience rather than second- or third-hand experience, particularly with young children, rests upon such studies showing the greater learning and retention of meaningful materials.

Underwood has been responsible for an intensive series of studies at Northwestern University on the relationship of meaningfulness to verbal learning and retention. Early association theory credited contiguity of stimulus and response and frequency of repetition with considerable importance in learning. Since Thorndike's revision of his theory in 1930, practice alone in the absence of reinforcement has been minimized and frequency of reinforcement and drive reduction given center stage. Underwood does not ignore the importance of reinforcement, but he believes that meaningfulness can be explained by the differential frequency with which the units of language have been encountered. He began by correlating the meaningfulness of nonsense syllables as listed in the Glaze (1928) and Noble (1952) lists with the frequency with which letters, syllables, and words occurred in the English language and found that the correlation between meaningfulness and frequency was high. Having established the fact that the more frequently a verbal unit is experienced, the greater is its meaningfulness, he next attempted to identify the role that frequency plays in verbal learning. Underwood began by formulating the "spew hypothesis" which states that the frequency with which verbal units have been experienced directly determines their availability as responses in new associative connections; i.e., if a subject is presented with a stimulus, his most likely response will be that which has been experienced most frequently. Free association studies show that the responses most frequently given to stimuli are words which have high frequency in everyday usage. What followed were a series of laboratory experiments designed to test the theory that frequency was the fundamental variable underlying meaningfulness. For example, in one study four groups were given different amounts of familiarization (one, ten, twenty, and forty presentations) with forty nonsense syllables of low association value. Both amount learned and percentage recalled varied with degree of familiarity. Underwood extended his experiments to include letter frequency and syllable frequency with positive results. On syllable integration, results were mixed. The theory held for both high and low integrated trigrams—those made up of letters occurring in high or low frequency—but not for intermediate degrees. Underwood operated on the assumption that the meaningfulness of the trigram was determined by the combined frequencies of the individual letters. Conceivably, the subjects invest more variability to responses at intermediate levels than at either extreme.

Sufficient recent evidence exists supporting Underwood's thesis (Hall,

1954) but also identifying other variables which influence meaningfulness. For example, the method of learning—logical versus verbatim (King and Russell, 1966), the presence of contextual clues (Peterson and Peterson, 1957), the amount of material and the possibility of intra-list associations (Deese, 1960), the associate clustering and grouping with the material to be learned (Bousfield, *et al.,* 1958; Justesen and Bourne, 1963)—is a variable affecting the meaningfulness of the material to be learned. All of these variables, including frequency of occurrence, can assist the learner in identifying the appropriate response and connecting it with the appropriate stimulus, the two stages which Underwood sees as significant aspects of verbal response learning, a view positing a parallel between verbal and motor learning.

Overlearning. Associations once learned are stabilized and habituated by memory drills. Reviews preferably should be frequent at first because forgetting is greater in the initial stages, but they may be scheduled at progressively greater intervals. Several studies have shown that verbal material will be retained as well as motor skills if initially learned to the same degree.

Drill is purposeless prior to the mastery of a skill or the acquisition of knowledge, for it fixates error responses or produces negative transfer. An appropriate illustration is the commonly used practice in spelling of instructing children to write each word five times. In copying words from the blackboard, a child is likely to copy the word on the board, then copy the word he has written. An intelligent fourth grade boy carrying out this assignment produced the following:

> November
> Noveber
> Novebr
> Nvebr

His final spelling resulted in part from his difficulty in reading his own handwriting, which, producing a confused stimulus, resulted in such perceptual phenomena as the sharpening of certain salient stimulus features and the leveling of others. But it also occurred from the drill of error responses. Instead of looking back to the board each time for the correct stimulus, he looked back to his reproductions and whatever errors they included. It is thus essential that mastery precede drill or overlearning.

Drills should be staged at times when the pupils are actually overlearning in order that they serve to consolidate and fix performance changes which are permanently desirable. Brownell and Chazal (1935) inquired into the effects of premature drill on the learning of third grade arithmetic. When they analyzed the procedures used by a group of sixty-three third graders who had been taught addition and subtraction by the drill method in grades one and two, they found that only 49 percent based their answers to addition combinations on immediate recall; nearly half used counting or guessing to obtain answers, while the remainder obtained a solution by indirect methods. After a month of daily drill in the third grade, the proportion using immediate recall and indirect solutions had increased to 64 percent at the expense of counting and guessing. Following another month in which no special drills were provided, the recall and indirect solution group had reached 71 percent. The study illustrates the limitation of drill as a teaching method and especially as a procedure for developing the higher mental processes involved in quantitative thinking.

Distribution of Practice.   From the evidence available on practice, the repetitions in memorizing should be distributed rather than massed. Short rest intervals appear to be as effective as longer ones. The length of the work period will vary with the task to be learned, but in general the less meaningful the task, the shorter the desirable work period. In instances where distributed practice is not possible, the evidence suggests that the part-method of learning may be preferable to the whole. Stroud and Ridgeway (1933) compared the number of trials needed to learn three poems (meaningful material) in massed practice by three different procedures: part, progressive-part, and whole. The whole method was inferior to the other two.

Review and Retention.   For some time it has been advocated, in view of the negative acceleration of forgetting, that to secure the best results in retention one should review frequently at short intervals soon after learning and then after longer and longer intervals as the temporal distance from the original learning increases. This appears to be a sound principle in general, particularly for rote learning. But if a child has just read and clearly understood a story or a lesson in history, an immediate rereading may be rather dull and less stimulating than a multiple choice test over the materials read. A review may be made by recalls as well as by rereading. Tests provide review by recall.

It has been found that the most advantageous temporal position differs for these two forms of review. Jones and Stroud (1940) made a comparison of the effectiveness of review by multiple choice testing and by rereading for three different temporal positions within an interval of forty-two days following learning. About 1300 seventh-grade pupils spent twenty minutes studying an article on the history and methods of making paper. Ten minute reviews were given by testing or by rereading for different groups on the first and third, on the eighth and fifteenth, or on the fifteenth and seventeenth days after the original learning. When the reviews occurred on the first and third days, the review by testing was significantly more effective than the review by rereading; but for the reviews placed later in the interval, the advantage was in favor of the rereading. The farther the review is removed from the original learning the more, of course, will forgetting have taken place; therefore, less and less of the content will be available for review by testing as the elapsed time increases. Tests and examinations have a salutary effect on retention, both as a means of stimulating reviews in preparing for them and for securing recall while taking them.

A study of retention under various testing procedures was made by Spitzer (1939) with 3605 sixth-grade pupils as subjects. The learning material consisted of a printed article, which was studied for eight minutes. Some groups were tested immediately after learning and retested later. Others were tested at intervals varying from one to sixty-three days. The groups tested immediately made definitely higher scores on the later tests. Without recall, forgetting was rapid during the first day. Pupils of superior ability did not forget as rapidly as those of lesser ability. The data clearly indicated that the recall in tests given immediately after learning was a distinct aid to retention.

The advantages of recitation go beyond memorizing. Verbalization during learning can be a facilitating factor with both children and adults. Applying relevant labels assisted young children in learning reversal shifts, i.e., to attend to size rather than color as the significant stimulus (Kendler and Kendler, 1961), and verbalizing during the course of a demonstration aided children in repeating the demonstration (Seidman, 1955). It is worth noting the importance in both studies of relevant verbalization.

Set. One often has many possible responses for a given stimulus. In such cases, the individual's set and other subjective conditions may affect the course taken in recall. Hunger is likely to steer recall toward food. Thirst makes one think of water or places where it may be obtained.

Sets are more often psychological than physiological, being established by prior experiences, by attitudes, by instructions, and even by the task itself. An investigation by Levine and Murphy (1943), even though it suffers from the small number of subjects involved, clearly illustrates the effect of a set in the perception of controversial material and its subsequent effect upon recall and forgetting. Two small homogeneous groups of students of college age, one pro-Communist, the other anti-Communist, were selected. Each subject was presented with two prose passages, one anti-Communist, the other pro-Communist and instructed to read each twice. After fifteen minutes, subjects were instructed to reproduce the passages as accurately as possible. Again, at weekly intervals, the subjects were asked to reproduce both paragraphs. Sharp differences in both learning (first reproduction) and memory (subsequent reproduction) were shown. The differences in learning approached the .01 level of statistical significance and the differences in retention reached the .01 level, with the anti-Communist group showing marked superiority on anti-Soviet material and vice versa.

Abom (1953) showed that material acquired with a set to learn was more resistant to forgetting under an ego threatening condition than was the same information acquired incidentally. The materials used were color plates, from standard color vision tests, which one group learned with a set to learn, the second incidentally. Under the circumstances of experimentally induced failure, which was presumed to be ego threatening, the incidental learning group showed significantly lower memory scores than its counterpart group. Abom concluded that the lack of set resulted in less effort to counteract the effects of threat by rehearsal, overlearning, or increased motivation. Thus, motives, attitudes, and level of aspiration constitute built-in sets to be taken into account in instruction.

Varied tactics have been used to induce sets or what may be roughly grouped under the rubric of set. As illustrated, one approach is to mobilize or induce existing motives or to tap given attitudes. In the discussion of Underwood's studies in meaningfulness, familiarization with desired responses proved helpful. Calling attention to the relevant stimuli is another approach. The verbalization used in the Kendler study of reversal learning maintains attention to the shift in stimulus conditions associated with correct response. Levin, Watson, and Feldman (1964) show that pretraining of first grade children on initial and terminal letters to be encountered in selected words provided them with cues which assisted subsequent learning of word recognition. Providing rules and examples of their application prior to introduction of new material is beneficial (Wittrock, 1963b). In certain situations, the procedures used in establishing given sets are tantamount to introducing a concept about which information can subsequently be organized. Ausubel and Fitzgerald (1961, 1962) have used what they term "advance organizers" to create a set for approaching new materials. The organizer is a short overview providing an ideational framework, for example, a short passage on the similarities and differences between Christianity and Buddhism, prior to the introduction of material to be learned about Buddhism. Such sets have proved particularly useful with college students of lower verbal ability or where inadequate prior knowledge of the material existed. Reynolds (1966) has shown that establishing a set to link new materials to a previously meaningful structure produces positive results. A variety of possibilities are thus available to create meaningful relationships among learning tasks by the use of appropriate sets. This approach is quite in contrast with the approach often seen at secondary and college levels where an assignment or homework is given with little direction. The able students manage, but the less competent stumble through with less success than they could achieve, given better direction.

Meaningfulness of material, frequency of presentation, degree of learning, and other features of the material are not the only factors affecting retention. The arousal level of the learner, his motives and attitudes, the affective toning of the material, the success or failure experienced in learning and the amount of associated stress are conditions to be considered.

Affective Toning. Among the experiences most easily recalled are those emotionally toned, or markedly pleasant or unpleasant (Dudycha, 1933). The question arises regarding what influence the affective qualities may have upon learning. Experimentation on this problem is difficult, for one can never be sure what feeling tone may be aroused by a particular situation, nor can one assume that material, pleasant for one subject, may not be indifferent or unpleasant for another. There is always need for report on this feature of the experience by the subject himself (Rett, 1965). Regarding the material itself, it appears that affectively toned materials tend to make a more lasting impression than indifferent material. In an experiment by White and Ratliff (1934), college students learned a list of pleasantly toned words, such as *flower, smile,* and *home,* and a list of unpleasantly toned words, such as *vomit, disgrace,* and *insult.* After complete learning, the two kinds of words were recalled about equally well in a test given shortly after learning and then one week later.

If one pauses to recall outstanding memories from earlier schooling, invariably the situations that are spontaneously recalled are those which in the main were markedly pleasant or unpleasant. Favorite subjects are as frequently associated with favorable relationships with a given teacher as with the pleasure derived from the subject itself. Perhaps more significant as far as retention of learning is concerned is the comparative indifference of many students toward their studies. At best, their motivation is mild and the affective toning of the material being learned is neutral, neither factor constituting the most desirable circumstances. Apparently, it is the intensity of feeling tone rather than the quailty that affects the extent of recall (Postman and Murphy, 1943; Weiner, 1966).

Motivation. The hint that the effects of motivation would be complex was found in the first studies on memory for completed and incompleted tasks. Zeigarnik (1927) tested the effect of interrupting a person during the performance of an engrossing task on his memory for the task. Students of different ages were given a variety of tasks to perform, such as solving puzzles and matching blocks to given designs. On half of the tasks the subject was interrupted. After the series of tasks was completed and put away, the subject was asked to recall the tasks upon which he had worked. A higher percentage of the interrupted tasks was recalled than of the completed tasks. But it was not quite this simple. Certain conditions prevent the occurrence of what has come to be known as the Zeigarnik effect. As might be expected, fatigue prevents it, time dissipates it, and emotional disturbance disrupts it. Interrupted tasks which are too difficult tend to be forgotten, giving confirmation to the level of aspiration studies which show that a task has to be seen as offering some likelihood for success if subjects are to become involved with it. The satisfaction or dissatisfaction of the subject with the solution, irrespective of what the experimenter thought, influenced its retention in memory. And if a single task were seen as endless, or if all the tasks were seen as part of a whole rather than as separate tasks, the effects of interruption were lost.

Various explanations have been offered to reconcile the contradictory results appearing here and in subsequent experiments (Rozenzweig, 1943; Glixman, 1949; Boguslavsky and Guthrie, 1941). Atkinson (1953) argues that subjects high in need achievement will recall more incomplete tasks if they are motivated in the experimental situation. Alper (1957) and Rozenzweig believe that the effects are explained according to the ego strength of the individual and whether or not he is task oriented or ego oriented. The extent to which subjects interpret their performance as being successful or failing affects their speed of learning and subsequent level of performance (Weiner, 1965, 1966), offering a possible explanation. Frequent methodological shortcomings in the experiments in failing to provide independent measures of task orientation, ego defensiveness, and ego enhancement leave the explanation of the effects ambiguous. Suffice it to say that motivational dispositions, response to threat, and perceptions of success or failure affect speed of learning, selectivity of learning, and subsequent recall. The significant fact is that subjects tend to remember what appeared to them to be their failures or their not attaining a successful completion. In view of the reluctance of children generally to persist with eagerness in a task at which they appear to be failing, and in view of the high frequency with which attention is called to errors during the course of the school day, it would appear wise to minimize this effect by making sub-tasks the parts of a whole having a definite terminal point at which success can be experienced.

Arousal, Anxiety, and Stress.   Clear-cut distinctions between arousal, anxiety, and stress are difficult to establish in experimental terms. Arousal has been measured in terms of muscular tension and skin resistance, the most frequent measure of anxiety is scored on the Taylor Manifest Anxiety Scale, a questionnaire requiring reports by the subject of behavior characterized as anxious. Stress has usually been defined in terms of a set established by the experimenter, indicating to the subject that poor performance on the forthcoming task will be indicative of low ability or low intelligence. Stress becomes an induced threatening situation, and anxiety by definition is a built-in hypersensitivity to being threatened; either can provoke higher degrees of arousal with little qualitative distinction.

Studies of motivation indicate that there are optimal degrees of motivation as well as excessive degrees. One of the effects of anxiety is heightened drive state. Associated with the heightened drive are physiological and psychological responses associated with apprehension and fear reactions. Whether anxiety is an effect as well as a cause is not clear, but its presence is associated with poorer performance on intelligence and achievement tests. In learning situations, anxiety appears to facilitate simple learning where responses are clearly identifiable, but it impedes learning on complex tasks.

A number of studies have shown that stress can function positively in low anxiety subjects but that it is disorganizing for those in whom reported anxiety is high. The general effect of both arousal and stress appears to apply to recall and retention more than to learning, with a positive relationship evidenced (Kleinsmith, Kaplan and Tarte, 1963; Weiner, 1966).

QUALITATIVE CHANGES IN TIME

A number of qualitative changes in retained material take place during the interval prior to recall. In recitations and examinations, children show not only a loss of much that they have learned but also various deviations from the original material. From the standpoint of school learning, it is obvious that this feature of retention is quite as important as the quantitative loss. The facts of quantitative decline are significant for all cases of rote learning, such as the memorizing of arithmetic combinations, spelling, and verbatim learning of poems and rules. But the qualitative changes which include insertions of new elements—transpositions, distortions, substitutions, omissions of particular details, and the like—are common, and for the teacher who is trying to build up topical understanding they are of vital concern.

Interference and Intrusions. The studies on retroactive inhibition have shown that the insertion of a second learning activity between the original learning and recall results in interference, which impairs retention. But beside this it is found that sometimes items from the interpolated lists of learning materials appear as erroneous responses during the recall of the original material (Melton and Irwin, 1940). Thus, we find that from experiences occurring during the interval, various elements may be blended with what has been learned so as to cause errors in reproduction. A classroom illustration would be the case of a child who reads two stories in succession and then into his reproduction of the first inserts characters or events from the second. An example from everyday life would be the case of a person who sees an automobile accident and afterward hears another witness tell something about it which he himself did not observe, and who later in court testifies to having seen what he only heard from the other witness after the accident.

One of the factors influencing intrusions is the similarity of the inter-polated and original material. Early research treated the similarity factor alone, but a study by the Gibsons (1934) systematically modifies both method and material. Five matched groups of twenty-six college students learned lists of ten pairs of consonants for two minute periods. After a three minute interval spent on an interpolated task which was alike or different in method of operation and material, the subjects were tested for recall of the original material. The control group which spent the intervening interval looking at pictures had the highest percentage of recall. In the other four groups, the interpolated task was alike in both method of operation and material, dissimilar in one but alike in the other, or unlike in both. The interference resulting from the interpolated task was at a minimum when both operation and material were dissimilar but was greater when either operation or material was similar.

The interference caused by similarity is pronounced during the early phases of learning but not so pronounced in recalling verbal material once it is learned (Beecroft, 1956). It is greatest when similarity exists between both stimulus and response words, thus maximizing the number of com-peting associations. With material of low meaningfulness, the interference can be produced by literal similarity in the form of the material to be learned; but with more meaningful materials, the similarity of the material may be associative, e.g., *bread* and *loaf* are more similar than *bread* and *bead* (unless you were unfamiliar with English, in which case the latter are similar in form only, having low meaningfulness). Finally, similarity can be conceptual in that one item is a member of the class represented by the sec-ond, e.g., boat and ship (Schoer, 1963; Lovell, 1963). In all instances, in-terference is greater for low ability students than high, and this appears to hold for children as well as adults (Gaeth and Allen, 1966). In the face of such competing associations, prior familiarization with responses and dis-tribution of practice work reduce interference (Underwood and Schulz, 1959; Underwood, Runquist, and Schulz, 1959).

Stories and Other Comprehended Materials.   When children or older subjects are asked to reproduce stories or other topical material, a number of discrepancies are usually found when their reproductions are compared with the original. Omissions, alterations, and additions are frequent. Points not essential to the plot as understood drop out. Uncomprehended elements are omitted. The general meaning of the story or topic dominates the reproduction, and elements that were not incorporated into the general meaning structure are not recalled. Where gaps occur in recall, the subject fills in from his own general fund of experience. His account is thus, more than reproduction; it is in part a creation (Bartlett, 1932). When a story is passed along from person to person, the accumulation of alterations sometimes produces a remarkable transformation that bears little resemblance to the original. Titles and names of persons and places are the most unstable elements of the story. The story shortens as it is passed along. Minor details drop out first, incidents and events are transposed, and the language is changed to patterns more familiar to the members of the group (Morris, 1939).

Memory changes for objects tend to follow a course similar to that found for stories. Minor details tend to drop out rather early. The recalled object tends to become less distinctive and to approach a type according to the individual's general experience with many objects of the class to which the particular one belongs. Certain essential features become stereotyped. For example, one sees an elephant at a circus; as time passes, the particular characteristics of this elephant disappear from memory and the features common to all the elephants one has seen remain. If, however, the object possesses some unusual feature that receives special attention and arouses interest, this feature may not only persist in memory but it may dominate the recalled structure.

Pictures and Nonsense Figures.   In a number of studies on this problem, pictures and nonsense figures have been used as learning materials, and retention has been tested after an interval by means of drawings. As in the case of retelling stories, this test is not a measure of retention alone. In addition to what is actually recalled, such drawings represent the creative activity by means of which the subject fills in the gaps in his recall in order to complete the picture. The results of such studies indicate that the details tend to drop out sooner than the main outlines of the picture or figure and that with the lapse of time, there is a drift toward a schematized type. Sometimes the figure changes so that it comes to resemble something else. This appears in some cases to be due to verbal labeling or to an associated idea. For example, if the subject sees a nonsense design and thinks, "It looks like a cat," his reproductions are likely to look more and more like a cat as time passes (Crosland, 1921). Under repeated reproductions, an irregular or unsymmetrical figure tends to become more regular or to shift toward symmetry (Perkins, 1932). Figures resembling to some degree a more familiar form tend to be drawn more like the familiar form. Lines that in the presented figure are fairly close to parallel, vertical, or horizontal tend to be drawn as parallel, vertical, or horizontal. A peculiar feature of the picture may be exaggerated, and certain writers partial to the Gestalt point of view hold that under repeated reproductions figures tend to improve through structural change (Wulf, 1922).

It is clear, therefore, that qualitative changes in the material learned, as well as changes in the amount retained, take place during the interval following learning. These changes are due to previously acquired knowledge, to experiences which precede learning, to verbal description and analysis, and to various events or experiences of the interval.

The Range and Accuracy of Report.   The range and accuracy of the report are influenced by several factors. In the first place, in order to get a full and reliable report, the individual's observation must be thorough and accurate. His perception of the scene or incident may be defective because of failure to attend adequately or because of emotional excitement or an indifferent attitude. His report may be erroneous because of his poor judgments with respect to spatial and temporal relations; it may be incomplete because of forgetting; and it may be distorted by what the individual hears or sees between the incident and his report. Its accuracy and completeness are, moreover, influenced by the form of the report, by the character of the questions the individual is called upon to answer, and also by the factors of age and training.

The report may be made in *narrative* form, in which the individual lists all the objects he can remember, or recounts, without prompting and in as full detail as possible, the story of what he saw. A second form of report is the *interrogatory* type. Here the individual is asked a series of questions or is presented with a list of questions about the scene or incident. The narrative form is usually more reliable than reports given by answering questions. On the other hand, the interrogatory form is suited to bring out more details. The range is usually greater for the interrogatory report because of the prompting value of the questions, but this form of report is less reliable than the narrative because of the misleading suggestions often contained in the questions (Cady, 1924). With the lapse of time, there is a decrease in both the reliability of the report and in the amount reported; but for both the narrative and the interrogatory reports, the decrease is more rapid for accuracy than for amount (Dallenbach, 1913).

The manner in which the question is phrased may greatly influence the subject's response. Some years ago Muscio (1916) made a systematic study of the relation of various types of questions to caution or uncertainty, suggestiveness, and reliability of the answer. Among other things, he found that the use of the definite article *the* in place of the indefinite *a* tends to make the individual less cautious, and the answer less reliable. The use of the negative *not* gives a question greater suggestiveness and decreases caution and reliability. Example: "Didn't you see a dog?" A question that simply asks whether certain things happened or were present is conducive to less caution in answering and to less reliability of the answer than one that asks the individual whether he saw or heard them. Of all the forms of questions studied, the implicative type, such as "Was the dog black?" which implies that there was a dog, was found to be least conducive to caution and reliability. This investigator concluded that for the most reliable answer, the question should not contain the definite article or the negative, and that it should be specifically directed toward what the individual actually observed.

Children are inferior to adults in both range and reliability of reports on what they have seen and heard. This is due to the child's more limited experience, immature judgment, imperfect understanding, and greater suggestibility. As he grows older, the range of his report increases faster than its accuracy. The reports of very young children in picture tests are usually mere enumerations of objects. Later the ability to describe in terms of relationships develops and at the age of 10 or 12, children are usually able to evaluate and interpret.

RETENTION OF SCHOOL LEARNING

It is sometimes felt that the use of nonsense materials in the laboratory precludes application of the findings to school learning. However, a comparison of the results of school learning with those obtained from laboratory experiments shows that the same fundamental principles apply in both situations. After all, the materials presented for learning in school are nonsense materials until some learning of them has been done. The fact that they are meaningful simply means that they have already been learned to some degree and the study of them means additional learning. The use of nonsense materials enables us to start nearer the zero point and makes possible a more exact accounting of the many factors that contribute to learning and retention. The writer agrees with the suggestion made by Stroud (1940) "that differences in the materials employed in the two fields of research (the laboratory and the classroom) are not so serious as those involving the use that is made of them. The fact that lists learned in the laboratory are usually made up of nonsense syllables does not present so great an obstacle to applicability in school as does the fact that the learning activity is memorization."

Studies on the rate of forgetting of school subjects usually show a negatively accelerated rate of forgetting of the same general form as the typical Ebbinghaus curve. This has been found in studies on the retention of history, physics, chemistry, botany, and zoölogy. Of course, as we have already noted, one usually retains a greater percentage of meaningful material than of nonsense material; the curve of retention does not drop so swiftly for meaningful material.

When children or students are tested after a considerable period with no formal instruction in a subject, a big loss is indicated for factual content. In a study by Greene (1931) 1064 university students were given in October the same examinations they had taken at the end of three courses the previous June. The repeated examinations showed a loss for the four months of about half of the information that had been reported correctly in the June examinations. Similar results have been reported by other investigators (Smeltz, 1956).

Retention During the Summer Vacation.   Children have been tested in various subjects in a number of studies at the end of the school year and again after the summer vacation. The results sometimes show losses, sometimes no change, and sometimes they actually show a gain. Reports on reading for the first three grades vary from slight losses to slight gains, and for the intermediate grades, the trend toward gains appears to be stronger than toward losses. Gains have been reported for history and literature. A study of the retention of American history by junior high school pupils indicated a loss of about 13 percent after four months, approximately 19 percent after eight months, and about 23 percent after one year (Brown, 1928). Losses are found for spelling and arithmetic, particularly for the computational skills. Bright pupils have been found to gain more or lose less than their less intelligent classmates (Schrepel and Laslett, 1936; Swenson, 1941). The gains reported probably may be attributed to practice or additional information picked up during the summer, since they are found most often in the subjects which may most easily be reviewed, practiced, or supplemented by incidental learning. Where actual losses occur, it sometimes requires several weeks after school reopens to recover from the setback caused by forgetting.

Factual Information Compared with Other Learning Outcomes.   There is a considerable amount of evidence which indicates that factual information is forgotten faster than the ability to explain, interpret, and apply general principles. Computational skills in arithmetic have been found to deteriorate more over the summer vacation than the ability to solve problems in arithmetical reasoning. College seniors who had not studied geometry since high school did better on a geometry test that was in part a test of ability to reason than they did on tests in chemistry and physics (Eikenberry, 1923). Results of a test in zoölogy, given to eighty-two students at Ohio State University fifteen months after the completion of the course, showed the greatest loss in technical material or information and no apparent loss in ability to apply to new situations principles that had been learned (Tyler, 1933). In terms of percentages of the gains made by boys and girls during a course in high school chemistry, retention after one year for five selected objectives of the course was found by retest to be as follows: application of principles, 92 percent; selection of facts, 84 percent; balancing equations, 72 percent; symbols, formulas, and valence, 70 percent; and terminology, 66 percent (Frutchey, 1937). Other studies have shown that retention of the substance of paragraphs, as measured by recognition of sentences that

summarized the meaning of the paragraphs, is superior to verbatim retention as measured by the recognition of sentences drawn verbatim from the
text (Edwards and English, 1939).

Attitudes, also, are apparently more permanent acquisitions than
factual material. The evidence that a number of important learning outcomes are more stable and lasting than factual information and verbatim
learning is encouraging to the educator. It should not, however, be construed to mean that factual teaching is altogether unnecessary, for such
teaching has its place in fostering the development of concepts and the
comprehension of principles. These findings bring to our attention again
the need for clearly defined teaching objectives and suggest that our tests,
as well as our teaching, should be suited to these objectives.

Rote and Nonrote Responding.   Foreign language learning probably
corresponds more closely to rote verbal learning than any of the school
subjects. For years, the traditional method of instruction consisted of paired
associate learning of vocabulary, i.e., foreign words paired with native,
and serial rote translation of sentences, forward and backward. Meaningfulness of material was low, so too was motivation. The results can be
summed up in the following dialogue:

A. Did you study a foreign language in school?
B. Of course.
A. What?
B. French.
A. Really? How long?
B. Four years.
A. Wonderful! Do you speak French?
B. No.
A. But you can read French?
B. I used to but I've forgotten most of it.

Since Sputnik underscored our need to be compatible with the rest of the
world, we have experienced a great push on foreign language instruction.
Recognizing the inadequacies of the traditional form of instruction by
reading and translation, the audio-lingual method has been substituted.
The rationale is: learn the language the way the natives do, by learning to
speak it from hearing it. The method works for them, even their morons,
why not for you? As a result, the audio-perceptual and -lingual aspects
are stressed; the visual-motor aspects, as exemplified by textbooks and
writing, are postponed.

The result is that one form of rote learning has been substituted for
another. Learning of grammar, vocabulary, and pronunciation is accomplished through the pattern drill, in order to avoid speech habits acquired
in learning to speak one's native language. A leading advocate, Brooks

(1961), states that the single paramount fact about language learning is that it concerns not problem solving but the formation and performance of habits and further (1961), that the pattern drill is exercise in structural dexterity undertaken solely for the sake of practice in order that performance may become habitual and automatic. The effect is that imitation, practice, intensive drill, and avoidance of the mother tongue are obtained at the price of motivation and meaningfulness.

Either procedure overlooks the learner and his motives. And these prove to be confounding effects with second languages as much as with laboratory experiments involving nonsense syllables. By the time the child reaches the point in school where he encounters a foreign language, usually age 9 or more, he has achieved a fair mastery of his native tongue—the greater part of the grammatical structure, an extensive vocabulary, and more significant, a varying grasp of the concepts represented by language. As an infant, he may have stretched his powers to recognize and pronounce the sounds and understand the meaning of a word or phrase. But as a child, even though he may need massed drill to correctly make the Spanish or French "r" sound, it doesn't take him long to figure out and get bored with repeating: *Buenos días, como esta usted?* or, *Bon jour, Madame, comment allez vous?* And he has no real reason to ask where the railroad station is.

There is probably no question that intensive practice is required to obtain correct speech sounds and intonational patterns because of competing vocal responses derived from long established habits in speaking one's native language. Nevertheless, any procedure involving rote learning has to confront the known facts which have been identified earlier in this chapter: competing associations between stimuli and responses related to similarity, meaningfulness versus meaninglessness of materials, learner motivation, effects of perceived success or failure, and other variables. Further, the learner is not a passive recipient, as is occasionally inferred in laboratory experiments. Given a task of learning nonsense syllables, he will devise some plan for going about the job other than mere repetition. Given the syllables MEX, KUJ, LVK to memorize, a learner is certainly likely to think of Mexican or mix to help with the first syllable, and even to attempt to link them together (e.g., "Mexican, couldja leave, kid?") with a mental note to omit the suffixes. The shift to audio-lingual approaches in foreign languages thus may facilitate learning *to speak* a language rather than read it, but it has not come to grips with the problem of rote learning and conversely, how to capitalize on the existing conceptual development of the learners.

Another aspect of the social arena dominated by rote learning is manners and etiquette, standardized ways of responding appropriately in given situations. The behavior may be meaningless; apparently a bow, curtsy, handshake, kissed cheeks, clasped fingers touched to lips, or other gestures all serve equally well as gestures of greeting. The banalities of parting can be equally meaningless, even fraudulent: Had a delightful time; We must do it again, sometime; So enjoyed meeting you, etc., etc. Again, rote learning, but useful because it provides everyone sharing a common culture with a standardized form for meeting given situations and hence, serves to minimize tension and anxiety arising from ignorance about the appropriate actions. Anyone who has visited a foreign land and been concerned about avoiding faux pas can testify to the fatigue engendered by the lack of rote responses. The result of such rote social learning is to provide persons with sets of expectations and modes of response which are mutually satisfying. As such, they are socially facilitating. To suggest this model as the ideal for all social situations is to propose rote learning as the paradigm.

In many social relationships, expectations get established which tend to impose rote behavior. For example, professors are supposed to lecture and stop at the appropriate time. If not, there is a subtle flurry of putting away pencils and closing books. Presidents are supposed to reassure, appear in command of events; athletes are supposed to say sporting things exemplifying fair play; and Beatles are supposed to beat and be asinine or absurd when interviewed, but with *their* penchant for subtle exaggeration, they went too far recently, failing to fulfill the expectations of the press, for all they said to all questions was: "Woof, Woof." Hopefully not apocryphal, the anecdote reports an unwillingness to fulfill the rote expectations of the press interview with rote responses. If this twist on expectations represents an ironical fulfillment of a ritual (or rotual!) established by social expectations, an interview with another popular contemporary singer exemplifies the refusal to fulfill such expectations, i.e., a "put-on":

> Q: What made you decide to go the rock-n'-roll route?
> A: Carelessness. I lost my one true love. I started drinking. The first thing I know, I'm in a card game. Then I'm in a crap game. I wake up in a pool hall. Then this big Mexican lady drags me off the table, takes me to Philadelphia. She leaves me alone in her house and it burns down. I wind up in Phoenix. I get a job as a Chinaman. . . .
> Q: And that's how you became a rock-n'-roll singer?
> A: No, that's how I got tuberculosis.

If rote learning in principle represents the submission of the learner to stimulus control (the automization of response), the foregoing interchange represents its abreaction, rejection of the relevance of the stimulus. In both situations, the situation hinges on motivation via either frustration or values. However pertinent rote responding is to both, the learner enters into account in each.

SUMMARY

To this point in time, verbal learning has been the foundation of our educational program. Perhaps television may visualize the procedure, but until that time verbal learning, with some of it by rote, will continue. It should be evident that no one procedure of instruction is best for all conditions. Nevertheless, a number of suggestions based on the experimental evidence can serve as guides in formulating suitable procedures.

Associate new material with meaningful concepts to facilitate learning.

Provide familiarization in advance with the material to be learned, or with the kinds of responses required, or provide an overview in the form of advanced organizers, relating past to coming instruction.

Establish appropriate learning sets through clear and explicit instructions.

The best procedures for directing memorizing vary with the age and intelligence of the learner, his former experience, and the nature of the material to be learned.

Things to be recalled together should be presented together and in the order in which they are to be recalled.

Use the whole method for short and easy passages and a combination of the whole and part methods for long and difficult passages. Give special attention to the more difficult parts.

Use precaution to insure accurate first impressions. Avoid errors so far as possible, and check them on their first appearance.

Let the pupils practice some form of recall during memorizing, for this is conducive to a favorable attitude and provides practice on the functions which the learning is supposed to develop. Such recital, however, should not come so early as to encourage guessing. Errors made by guessing may seriously interfere with correct learning.

Secure the advantage of using rhythm when possible. For very young children, this may be accomplished by the method of reading or reciting aloud in concert.

Make use of artificial memory aids or mnemonic devices sparingly and only in the case of very difficult associations.

Provide for a sufficient number of repetitions or rehearsals to insure an adequate amount of overlearning. Learning to the point of immediate recall only is not sufficient for schoolwork. For permanent retention, review often at first. The length of the interval between reviews may be increased as time passes.

Distribute the repetitions liberally. Make memory drills short and stop at the first signs of fatigue. In selecting the most apropriate length of learning periods and intervals, consider the age and ability of the child, the difficulty of the task, and the stage of learning.

Secure and maintain a desire to learn. Help the child to appreciate the value for him of mastering the material.

Commend earnest effort and inform the learner of his progress.

Secure and maintain full attention by starting promptly, by varying methods, and by using novel devices to make the work pleasant and interesting.

See that the child understands what he is to learn before he starts. The learning of meaningless material is sheer drudgery and an absolute waste of time for the school child.

Do not require children to memorize anything that will not serve some useful purpose or provide some pleasure or satisfaction for them. We cannot justify rote memorizing on the grounds that it improves the "faculty of memory."

Have the children make use of what they learn. Words from spelling lessons should be used in sentences and compositions and arithmetic facts in problems; gems of poetry may be recited on programs or quoted by the pupils in their own writings.

Avoid sequential presentation of materials of high similarity.

FURTHER READING

Overview

HOVLAND, C. I. 1951. Human learning and retention. In S. S. Stevens (ed.) *Handbook of Experimental Psychology*. New York: Wiley, pp. 613-89.

Selected References

BILODEAU, E. A. 1966. *Acquisitions of Skills*. New York: Academic Press.

HUMPHREY, G. and R. V. COXON. 1963. *The Chemistry of Thinking*. Springfield, Ill.: Charles C Thomas.

MC GEOCH, J. A. and A. L. IRION. 1952. *The Psychology of Human Learning*. New York: Longmans, Green.

UNDERWOOD, B. J. and R. W. SCHULZ. 1960. *Meaningfulness and Verbal Learning*. New York: Lippincott.

Original Investigations

AUSUBEL, D. P. 1960. The use of advance organizers in the learning and retention of meaningful verbal material. *J. Educ. Psychol.*, 51: 267-72.

KREUGER, W. C. 1929. The effect of overlearning on retention. *J. Exper. Psychol.,* 12: 71-78.

WEINER, B. 1966. Effects of motivation on the availability and retrieval of memory traces. *Psychol. Bull.,* 65: 24-37.

WITTROCK, M. C. 1963. Effect of certain sets upon complex verbal learning. *J. Educ. Psychol.,* 54: 85-88.

14

Comprehension:
The Development
of Understanding

Interrelated with the perceptual processes discussed previously is the development of understanding and comprehension. Both depend upon complex, highly developed responses, but comprehension goes beyond perception in being an organizing, synthesizing process in which experiences are integrated into compact, meaningful units which can be utilized symbol-concepts which in themselves represent abstractions from perceptions. Perically. Comprehension is a cognitive activity involving the attainment of ception is tied to the objective world of stimuli; comprehension is tied to cognitive processes in which concepts are abstracted from their various contexts and organized into unitary constructs.

THE DEVELOPMENT OF UNDERSTANDING

Our concepts are the understanding we have of certain generalized and abstracted aspects of many experiences. Our understanding of what we hear others say or what we read involves more than the meanings of the various words as perceived. These various meanings are important to understanding, but in the process of comprehending they fuse; the fusion yields a larger total meaning for the sentence, paragraph, or lecture as a whole. Comprehension is an organizing synthesizing process that integrates experiences into larger meaningful units.

Comprehension in the Classroom.   No other psychological function is used more in the classroom for purposes of learning than is the one we are now considering. Without it, no reading could be worth anything, no study could be successful, no explanation or demonstration by the teacher could accomplish its purpose, and every lecture would be a waste of time. Without comprehension, no assignment would set the pupil for the performance of the learning exercise planned by the teacher. Whether we teach in the lower grades, in the high school, or in the university, we spend a large part of our time explaining, lecturing, and prescribing reading with the expectation that through comprehension, our pupils will become better informed and acquire an understanding of the subject we teach. The discovery method of teaching rests on the assumption that discovery produces greater comprehension.

CONCEPT FORMATION

When we use a term such as *banana, apple,* or *pineapple* we are employing a label, a word, or name to refer to a specific kind of object or event. But when we use a term such as *fruit* or *food* we are employing a concept, a common response to dissimilar stimuli. Apples and bananas are dissimilar in appearance, but in spite of the dissimilarity, we recognize them as alike not only by our verbal response but also by our behavior, e.g., eating them, separating them from vegetables in stores and storage. As a result of learning, we have come to perceive them as alike. Further, we group fruit under the more generic term of food in spite of the differences between meats, leaf vegetables, corn flakes, fruit, frozen vegetables, and so on. In effect, we have learned to act under certain circumstances as if all were alike.

Both discrimination and generalization are implicit in such behavior. Discrimination (or abstracting, as it may be termed) is suggested because certain common features of the various objects have been identified and we have also discriminated between those occasions which call for the common response and those which do not. Discrimination of both stimuli and response has occurred. Generalization is implied whenever this common response is extended to any object possessing similar stimuli.

The procedure by which we develop concepts is informal yet systematic—informal in that it derives primarily from the events of personal experience, systematic in that the events encountered in our environments, including the behavior of parents and others, occur and recur with a certain regularity. Although parents tend to be less consistent than the school, the efforts of both parents and school in child rearing show a regularity associated with social and cultural objectives. The 18-months-old child who calls "Mummy" when she wants out of her crib, or says "Mummy" to mother, father, or maid, or takes a cup from a cupboard and returning to mother says "Mummy" as she extends it obviously has her labelling wrong, but she also has a rudimentary concept of the functional equivalence of certain adults in caring for her needs. Although this illustration runs counter to the proposition that children's conceptual development proceeds from the concrete to the abstract, it is consistent with Brown's (1958) argument that children's vocabulary does not invariably build from the concrete to the abstract. He contends that adults determine which name to give a thing on the basis of functional utility; the specific names of individuals are thus likely to be learned before class terms such as men, women, or people. Conversely, generic terms such as fish are understood and learned before such specifics as perch or trout or an abstract term such as vertebrate. The sequence in which words are acquired is determined by adults and may be specific or general as utility dictates. Thus the labelling process, at least in early stages of development, is largely determined by adult language usage, but conceptual development is determined by the child's perceptions and the confirmation, correction, and reinforcement which he experiences. For example, the 4-year-old who asked one mid-morning, "Mommy, is hungry when I eat something and thirsty when I drink?" was busy identifying certain distinguishing features of designated physical conditions. The same child had been using the two words appropriately yet indiscriminately for over a year, at or near mealtime. Undoubtedly, she had been asked at mealtime, "Are you hungry?" or heard other members of the family exclaim, "I'm hungry," or, "I'm thirsty." Her use of the words prompted such adult responses as an offer of milk in response to "I'm thirsty," which she would accept or reject depending on whether she really wanted fluid or food. Finally, she was clarifying the concept. At the same point in time, she was struggling on a more rudimentary level with a more difficult concept: anger. She would repeatedly ask her parents, "Are you mad?" The more frequent reply would be "No," or, "No, I'm thinking," or, "No, I'm tired," or, "No, the sun hurts my eyes." There would be the occasional confirmation, "Yes, I am." When the child was asked, "What makes you think I'm mad?" her response was to frown, imitating parental facial expression. Here the child was searching for the correct cues and applying the correct label to what might be considered a happy–not happy level of categorization.

Kinds, Characteristics, and Functions of Concepts. Research on concept development has progressed slowly with the result that our knowledge is much fuzzier than with motor or verbal learning, or for that matter, problem solving, which has been a more popular topic for inquiry. The last two decades have seen a marked increase in effort to apply experimental methods to concept formation and problem solving. By way of evidence, research on these two topics was summarized for the first time in the 1957 and 1961 issues of the *Annual Review of Psychology*. Our concept of concepts is being gradually delineated.

Berlyne (1965) identifies two kinds of concepts which he terms "situational" and "transformational." The first is illustrated by the behavior describing the child struggling with the concepts of hunger or anger. In effect, she was attempting to distinguish the positive and negative attributes of each concept. Transformational concepts involve an operation. For example, given the IQ of a school child, what inference could be made about his academic achievement or about the size of his shoe? In each instance, the concept of intelligence is linked with a second concept, each of which must be understood. Finally, the concept of correlation and its use to inference is required. Gagné (1966) argues that the distinguishing feature between the two is how they are achieved—the former through observation of contrasting positive and negative instances, the latter by definition. For example, to square a number is to multiply it by itself. Rules and principles thus represent a higher order of concepts because they involve relationships between concepts. In an experimental study of concepts, Bruner, Goodnow, and Austin (1956) classified them as conjunctive, disjunctive, and relational. These overlap the Berlyne-Gagné categories.

The following examples labelled A, B, C, D on page 461 illustrate the various types.

	ASPECTS		OPERATIONS
Berlyne	Situational		Transformational
Gagné	Observation		Definition
Bruner	Conjunctive	Dysjunctive	Relational
Example	A	B C	D

PROBLEM: Can animals other than those classified as birds, fly?
FACTS: A. All birds have feathers.
          B. Bats bear their young alive.
          C. Bats are night animals.
          D. Bats do not have feathers.
          E. Bats can fly.

In A the distinguishing attributes of birds are identified along with certain characteristics of bats. Flying is a positive attribute but bearing young alive is negative; hence, the observation indicates that bats are not birds.

B like A is taken from a test in problem solving developed for fifth grade pupils, both B and A containing items which were not dependent on prior information for solution. In the case of A, the essential information is provided; and given these observations (dependent in this case on sufficient skill in reading), the question is whether or not the child can formulate the appropriate concept. In the following example, the items were pretested in order to establish that fifth graders knew the animals. The solution requires a search for some attribute of the animals listed which is functionally equivalent, although differing in outward appearance (see Figure 14.1).

Science Reasoning Test—Verbal Classification

Four of the five are alike in some way. One of them does not belong in the group. Which one of the five does not have something that the other four have? Mark on the answer sheet the one that does not belong in the group.

25. (a) Apricot (b) Peach (c) Banana (d) Plum (e) Pear
26. (a) Oyster (b) Lobster (c) Clam (d) Scallop (e) Mussel
27. (a) Cow (b) Goat (c) Horse (d) Sheep (e) Pig
28. (a) Dog (b) Cat (c) Wolf (d) Hamster (e) Rabbit
29. (a) Boston terrier (b) Boxer (c) Beagle (d) Dachshund
    (e) Collie
30. (a) Pear (b) Radish (c) Tomato (d) Beet (e) Cherry

Similarly, C is disjunctive. In spite of the fact that all can be committed to an institution, and the psychotic may commit acts identical with any of the others, by definition only four of the cases presented are criminal.

Which is not a criminal?
  Burglar   Forger
  Felon   Psychotic
        Robber

Finally, the figure used in conjunction with a test of stimulus satiation versus response inhibition in Chapter 10, page 311 not only involves these two concepts but more, a conceptualization of an operation which tests the contradiction between the two.

One of the dimensions underlying these different types of concepts is complexity, which of itself may be defined in several ways. One aspect of complexity which appears in the ordering of concepts is a crude hierarchy ranging from those which have observable attributes to those involving relationships. Observable attributes may range from concrete to abstract, as in toys to tolerance. Relationships may begin with the observable (e.g., between wind direction and weather) and end with concepts involving relationships between concepts (e.g., the general theory of relativity). The order in which we acquire our concepts is affected but not determined by this dimension of complexity. More important are the developing capacities of the child and the demands and experiences he encounters. The same child can be trying to clarify the concepts of hunger and kinship at one time. For instance, the concept of mother is abstract and definitional. Consider the youngster attempting to understand this concept: My mother is the mother of others, and she is not the mother of my father because she is his wife, but she too is the daughter of her mother as I am the daughter of my mother, but why is she only the stepmother of Billy? It is not simple; and yet we want children from an early age at least to have their kinship labels straight. Hence, we give them continuous experience.

Complexity varies along another dimension, that of the relevance–irrelevance of the available information to the concept to be identified. A number of studies in which Archer (1962) and Bourne (1965) have been principals indicate that the amount, and probably the discriminability, of relevant and irrelevant information available is an important determinant of the speed with which a concept will be identified. Difficulty increases with too much of either. The concept of *bird* is likely to come easier than that of *dog,* largely because the amount of irrelevant information is low and the essential discriminating feature, flying, is immediately apparent. Other relevant stimuli such as feathers, eggs, accessibility (of wild birds), and sound are secondary. In contrast, the irrelevant stimuli associated with *dog* are many: size, shape, color, sound, docility, and the like. Yet the relevant stimuli, while few in number when compared with the more complex concept of tolerance, are not readily discriminated. Although it is difficult to envisage any learning situation in which discrimination is not called for, it is at the heart of concept learning, hence the effects of relevance of available information. Teaching for concepts necessitates determining the relevant information from among all which is available.

Another important characteristic of concepts is their potential for transfer, for sorting out information, for dealing with new situations. Perhaps no better illustration can be offered than the game of "Twenty Questions." Essentially an isolated and/or known bit of information can be identified by sequential application of concepts—human or not, dead or alive, American or European, and so on. Without concepts, the game would become guesswork, more like a dog sniffing along a sidewalk (which, of course, is a human's concept of what a dog can tell from sniffing).

This power of concepts exemplifies its most important function, that of reducing the complexity of the environment through identification of commonalities, which reciprocally makes rapid identification of unique features possible. We have seen, with respect to both motivation and perception, how we develop sets and standards for selecting and evaluating environmental events. Concepts serve an equivalent function in cognitive behavior. They permit a ready interpretation of environmental events and a rapid mobilization of the responses appropriate to the occasion. Concepts reduce the complexity of the environment. Lacking them, we should be faced with the energy draining task of constantly paying close attention to all events and constantly being engaged in learning, adjusting our actions in response to discrete, apparently unrelated events. Moreover, it is the stability which concepts provide that allows us the freedom to seek or respond to events in terms of motivational needs, rather than being totally absorbed in meeting environmental demands.

This discussion of the functional characteristics of concepts has ignored the substantive dimension, the particular attributes of people and places to be learned. Any curriculum constitutes a given concept of the organization of knowledge for purposes of learning. The kinds of subdivisions which fall within such broad conceptions encompass some ordering and arranging of given concepts. Whatever the order, we find concepts of number, of time and space, of self and society, and of esthetics and philosophy. However labelled—mathematics, history, geography, social studies, science, or whatever—each subdivision will incorporate certain kinds of concepts to be mastered. There will be concepts of attributes and qualities, of form and structure, and of process and relationship to be mastered. Each kind will involve its own hierarchy from simple to complex.

Concept Development in Children.   Early research on concepts centers on naturalistic and structured observation of children. From the works of Curti (1950) and Buhler (1930) one learns that conceptual development follows a general sequence of: (1) identifying, (2) grouping, (3) explaining, (4) defining, and (5) generalizing. The first step is the identification of particular persons or objects, first evident in pleasure or avoidance reactions, and subsequently evident in the ability to name the person or object. At first, the object must be present, but later the behavior of the infant will indicate memory for and reaction toward absent persons or objects. Concept development begins when the child can separate a variety of similar objects into different categories—cups, dishes, glasses, and so on. Glasses vary in appearance, dishes also, and the child's ability to name them or to pick them correctly on command indicates that he has discriminated certain uniformities of appearance or usage in spite of their variations. His attempts to apply these new concepts often prove wrong, as when he points to a cat and says "doggie," but out of this testing process emerges a more accurate definition of the essential attributes of a given class of objects or events, and with it a hierarchy of classes: apples, pineapples, prunes; fresh fruit, canned fruits, dried fruits; fruits in general; and food. These developments are not restricted to physical objects but include qualities, conditions, and actions such as quarreling, making, being good, and the like. Paralleling these events is a gradual awareness and increasing understanding of causality. No better illustration can be found than the barrage of why, where, and when questions of the preschool child. Finally, the child begins to generalize from his concepts: Do birds have beds? Is my blood carried in pipes like the water? Although errors may be frequent, his concepts provide a basis for managing the myriad conditions to be faced in a multi-faceted world.

This sequence should not be thought of as a series of stages, through which all children proceed at set rates, but rather as overlapping aspects in the process of concept formation. Welch and Long (1940, 1942, 1943) carried out a number of studies with children concerning the development of hierarchies of concepts in children. They concluded from their work that infants discriminate and generalize in the preverbal stage and apply language to such discriminations when they can, sometimes as early as 18 months. About the age of 2, the child has grasped his first genus–species relationship such as food–fruit. His categorizations continue at the one- and two-level stage until his fifth year when both vertical and horizontal expansion occur: e.g., food–fruit–banana, and fruit–fresh fruit–canned fruit. Subsequently, one finds a gradual increase in the number of categories and the levels in the hierarchy of categories that the child can manage. Generally, children find concrete concepts easier to acquire than abstract ones, such as form and number. Color concepts are intermediate when the task involves the use of color in discriminating the relevant attribute but more difficult when the task involves generalization (Heidbreder, 1948; Wohlwill, 1957).

One could easily form the impression from the work of Welch, Long, and others that children's conceptual ability has been underestimated. In one sense, this impression is true and is reflected in the reorganization of the elementary school curriculum in mathematics and science. If the material being presented is made meaningful (presented at a conceptual level that children can grasp), children can understand basic algebraic concepts and scientific concepts such as the principles of sound and light (Nelson, 1957). When the learning situations are primarily verbal and abstract rather than concrete and perceptual, conceptual development proceeds slowly. Nevertheless, higher order concepts are inherently more abstract and therefore less easily attained. For example, in mathematics the first concept to emerge is that of one versus many. The child may consequently count readily by rote but is in his fifth year before he understands the meaning of 2, 3, both, most, and biggest. At about age 6, he can handle simple addition and simple fractions, but his ability to apply statements of quantity and measures is limited. Similarly with spatial concepts: he is able to look at and point out objects from an early age but is 4 to 5 years old before words such as up, down, on, here, and gone hold much meaning. And many adults have never mastered either compass orientation or the abstract spatial concepts expressed in maps, particularly the various projections which depict geographic relationships on the earth's surface. The importance of relevant perceptual experience to the development of spatial concepts in children is seen in the difficulty and delay that blind children experience in establishing spatial and topographical orientation (Garry and Ascarelli, 1960). Many such children have difficulty developing any objectivity in their concept of space. Their view remains essentially egotistic, for instead of conceiving of established order in space (i.e., walls and doors remain in the same position regardless of one's personal position), the world appears to shift and turn in relation to their own movement.

Time presents some of the most difficult of the common concepts. Kindergarten children understand the meaning of daytime, nighttime, morning, and afternoon but not "a long time ago" (a common introduction in children's stories) or "a short time ago." In fact, a sense of historical time is not well established until adolescence, when the ability to conceive of such abstract ideas as future and past take on some time perspective.

Piaget's Work. One of the major contributors over the past thirty years to the understanding of thought, reasoning, and conceptual development in children has been Jean Piaget at L'Institut des Petits in Geneva. Using procedures which combine observation and interview of children in semistructured situations, he has produced a detailed and extensive body of knowledge on the development of intelligence, reasoning ability, language, moral judgments, and social behavior. Many American psychologists, trained in the experimental tradition, take exception to the validity of some of Piaget's findings because of his less rigorous methods. But the sheer volume of his work, coupled with his concepts of child development, make him a man to be reckoned with for some time to come. Piaget conceives of development as proceeding in a sequence of definite stages, with the age of seven years being a major turning point in the child's conceptual ability and 11 to 12 years as a secondary one.

According to Piaget, conceptual development occurs in the following stages:

1. *Sensori-motor (age 0 to 2) stage.* Lacking language and symbolic ability, the infant is unable to form concepts. His view of the world is dominated by his perceptions. During this period, his perceptions and reality are identical. Gradually he develops an awareness that the world contains objects which are permanent in shape and appearance as well as in being, and of himself as one among them. He comes to realize that some objects are capable of voluntary movement, as well as appearing to move as a result of his own movements.

2. *Preconceptual period (2 to 4 years).* The ability of the child to imitate permits him to use actions and images as representative of objects and events, and his capacity to use words signals an identification of

objects. Nevertheless, he is unable to make, as adults do, the distinction between internal and external events, between word and object, between thought and the thing thought about.

3. *Intuitive thought (4 to 7 years).* Although the child is able to differentiate between himself and other objects, his explanation of events is a projection of his own experience. Thus, sun and moon move because they want to. If a scratch hurts him, it must hurt the table. Perceptions still dominate; thus, the fact that in perceiving one focuses on a selected aspect of the event to the exclusion of others leads the child to concentrate on one feature in making judgments. In watching a full cup of beads being poured into a bowl, the child will conclude there are fewer beads because the bowl isn't as full as the cup (inability to conceive of conservation of mass). If ten buttons are placed in a line three feet long, he will conclude there are more buttons than when they are side by side in line.

4. *Concrete operations (7 to 11 years).* For the first time the child is able to free himself from his perceptions and deal with events on a conceptual basis involving classes and relationships between classes. Piaget believes this is possible because thought processes can proceed independently of perceptions. Various possibilities can be entertained, symbolically manipulated through the medium of language, and accepted or rejected.

5. *Formal operations (11 to 15 years).* The development of socialized speech during the preceding period contributes to an ability to reason about the beliefs of others and to solve problems on an abstract basis. Formal manipulations at the symbolic level using propositions, models, and simultaneous consideration of combinations of events is possible.

Piaget attributes the dramatic shift at age 7 to the child's mastery of language. Until this time, he sees the child as egocentric, tied to his perceptions and the immediacy of events. The child's use of language during the preschool years is personal, but as his language ability proceeds, it exposes him to social influence concerning the perceptions of others, their evaluations, and their experiences. This interpersonal aspect of language usage makes it possible for the child to detach himself from the world and himself from himself, thus permitting an objective view of the world about him. It is at this point that the child becomes logical.

Piaget's work has stimulated consideration of the appropriateness of curriculum and instructional procedures, especially in mathematics and science. In part, this is due to the fact that the changes being advocated need theoretical support and find it in Piaget's work. His work has also provoked experiments intended to verify his conclusions. The results of such research indicate that Piaget's conclusions about the sequence of development are more valid than his conclusions pointing to definite stages of development, especially his conclusion that the age of 7 marks a definite turning point in the development of the child's conceptualization. When larger and less selected samples of children are used and more rigorous experimental conditions established, variation in age occurs associated with both the kind of task and the experiential levels of the children.

Bruner (1964) has outlined a sequence of cognitive growth which may prove fruitful in relating divergent viewpoints. He begins with the fact that man has survived as a species and extended his domain by modifying his behavior rather than by evolutionary changes in physical structure. This has occurred, according to Bruner, because man has linked himself to three general kinds of implement systems: those which extend his motor capacities such as various tools; those which extend his sensory capacities such as radar, sonar, television; and those which extend his rational capacities such as language and logic. Cognitive growth consists in part of the development of systems of representation for the information associated with each of these implement systems and for developing integrated plans of behavior for mastering the patterned nature of the social and cultural environment.

To function in the environment, we need to be able to remember the environment, its regularities and their relationships. This requires modes of representing the environment in memory, which permit ready and functionally useful retrieval of information when needed. Bruner suggests we have such representational systems at three levels: motor, perceptual, and symbolic (his terms are "enactive," "iconic," and "symbolic"). For an example of environmental representation at the motor level, we are able to move about our rooms or homes in the dark without bumping into walls or objects. So, too, are we able to execute complex motor sequences without apparent thought—knitting, skiing, and the like. The limitation of representation at this level is that it offers no means of recapturing the action once performed or of holding action present. For this reason, professional football teams make extensive use of motion pictures of previous games in order to be able to represent specifically the success or failure of performance on certain plays.

Percepts and images are the representational modes at the iconic level. The advantage, and at once the disadvantage, of representation at this level is, to use Piaget's terms, its "centeredness" and "non-reversibility." Perception focuses on selected aspects and ignores others thereby misrepresenting or distorting the environment. Being non-reversible, percepts limit the freedom and flexibility of manipulation. Bruner reports an interesting illustration of this in a modification of a Piaget and Inhelder experiment involving the conservation of liquid volume across transformation in appearance. In the original experiment, children between the ages of 4 and 7 were presented two identical bottles containing the same amount of water. One of the bottles was poured into a second container. If the water level after pouring, now stood higher than in the remaining bottle, the children claimed there was more water. If the water level was lower because the new bottle was wider, the children claimed there was less water. Piaget and Inhelder state that children at this age are not able to grasp the idea that the volume of water remains the same despite its apparent difference, or as Piaget puts it, children at this age are not able to conserve the concept of liquid volume across transformation in appearance. In the variation reported by Bruner, the original Piaget procedure was followed to establish a baseline. None of the 4 year olds tested, 20 percent of the 5 year olds, and 50 percent of the 6 year olds responded correctly that the volume of the water was the same after being poured. Subsequently, the experiment was repeated. The jars were exposed, then the water was poured from the original to the second jar. But the pouring occurred behind a screen, making it impossible to see the new water level. Asked to guess the water level, the proportion of correct answers jumped to 50 percent, 90 percent, and 100 percent respectively for the three age levels. The climax occurred when the screen was removed. At this point, as Bruner puts it, the 4 year olds who guessed correctly were overwhelmed by the visual display and they reversed themselves, concluding that the larger, second jar had less water. Most of the 5 year olds and all of the 6 and 7 year olds stuck to their judgment. Bruner attributes these results to the dominance of the perceptual mode of representation and proceeds to describe the gradual emergence of concepts which depend less on perceptual configuration than on functional and symbolic attributes, and the critical role which language plays in this development. As Piaget suggests, language permits the transformation, the combination and recombination of experience independent of time, place, and event.

If cognitive growth proceeds as Bruner believes, each phase builds on the preceding level with no sharp division between the stages. The fact that the child devotes most of his attention and energy to motor activity during his first two years and that his language growth does not show marked acceleration until his fourth year does not preclude perceptual and cognitive growth during the preschool years. In fact, the three are to some degree interdependent. Nor do the ages of 7, 11, 15, or 50 guarantee an end to egocentricity or the exclusive utilization of symbolic representation.

LANGUAGE AND COMPREHENSION

It is a truism that language plays a key role in cognitive processes, but it is a truism not easily explained. Although many of our concepts derive from immediate experience, others such as spatial relations, number, and in fact most of the higher order concepts depend on language. One has only to consider the extent to which college studies are based on verbal manipulations rather than direct experience to realize the role of language and symbols. Even in a visual medium such as instructional television, several surveys found less than a quarter of the program content to be visual, the balance verbal. Even though the statistic indicates failure to capitalize on the strengths of television, language plays a prominent role. Earlier in the chapter, reference was made to the distinction between labels and concepts. The acquisition of labels and the development of concepts proceed apace and the two are inextricably mixed. However, the presence and correct use of a label does not necessarily imply the existence of a concept. For example, an American studying French could readily learn to label a woman's right hand as *la baisse-main* (literally: the kiss hand) but if he had never observed (live or filmed) the greeting in which a man kisses a woman's hand, the term, though correctly applied, would be relatively meaningless. The same person, observing variations in etiquette (handshaking by all on meeting and parting, cheek-kissing by some on meeting, women entering restaurants first but mounting stairs last when accompanied by a man) would acquire a concept of appropriate social behavior even though ignorant of any of the labels commonly employed: *la politesse, la courtoisie, la galanterie,* and so on. Similar events occur with children. The child who recognizes a difference between family and strangers and between family and acquaintances has a rudimentary concept. And the concept can be demonstrated by differences in his responses even though no labels may as yet exist. For example children feel freer to act aggressively with peers than with adults, even though unable to express it. Yet without labels and language, concept development would be highly restricted.

Beside its declarative and manipulative effects, language serves a number of important functions in comprehension.

1. Language helps intensify the child's awareness of particular features of the environment, and through repeated attention calling, fosters retention.
2. Naming facilitates learning. Even nonsense names aid preschool children in locating hidden toys more rapidly than no names.
3. Verbalizing during play and exploration aids perception, recall, imagination, and prediction. To deal with new situations, remembering and imagination are needed to bring the past forward and to anticipate the consequences of actions.
4. As situations become increasingly complex, verbal and numerical symbols are essential. Language makes it possible to go beyond first-hand experience.
5. Language plays a vital role in concept development: in single classification, in multiple classification involving two or more attributes, in serial ordering, and in the formulating of principles.

Language is not always a help, for it can underscore past experience and create perceptual sets which actually block the learning of new concepts or meeting novel situations. Even worse, by virtue of the verbal nature of education, words become ends in themselves instead of handmaidens to the concepts they symbolize. The result is empty verbalism. It occurs too frequently; for example, the bright fifth-grader who could parrot a definition of peninsula but couldn't apply it to Boston, even when looking at a map.

The acquisition of labels can be explained in terms of conditioning. Figure 14.2 illustrates the association of the label *apple* with the object. The fruit itself is capable of eliciting a complex set of sensory–motor–attitudinal responses which may include among others recognition from sight, shape, odor, wanting it or not, reaching, feeling, holding, and so forth. By means of conditioning, the word *apple* becomes capable of eliciting fractional parts of this complex of responses. This does not imply that on hearing the word *apple* a person automatically reaches. However the question, Would you like an apple? elicits a response $\longrightarrow$ $\boxed{r_a - - - - - s_a}$ $\longrightarrow$ which may include such motor responses as looking to judge the apple's attractiveness, salivating, and sniffing; attitudinal responses involving a degree of liking–disliking; judgment of state of hunger and possibilities of getting a more preferred fruit, and the like. These fractional responses associated with the apple per se need not be overt. They do serve, as indicated in the diagram, to mediate the next steps (R) in the ensuing sequence of responses, both covert and overt. By conditioning, such mediating responses associated with labels may be acquired for other fruits and other objects and come to represent the "meanings" of the labels.

Figure 14.1 illustrates the development of a concept such as fruit or vegetables based on the meanings associated with the labels. The dashed lines running from the separate fruits to fruit represent the process of abstraction by which fractional but salient features are combined into a higher order concept such as FRUIT. Certain features such as color, shape, size, and so on have to be ignored (discriminated as negative stimuli) and others such as seed, flesh, growing above ground must be identified (discriminated as positive stimuli). By a similar process, a hierarchy of concepts can be built up, e.g., food, nutrition, and so forth. At this point, the diagram has been simplified, for the concept of FOOD would derive from the individual objects as well as from the broader concepts of FRUIT and VEGETABLE. Concepts can emerge as a result of trial and error learning, from systematic instructions, from problem solving situations, and even incidental to some other activity.

Sources of Misunderstanding.   Spoken language is a vehicle of communication, but each person builds his own understanding of what he hears in terms of his own previous experience and conditioning. His construc-

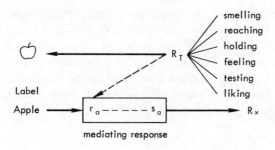

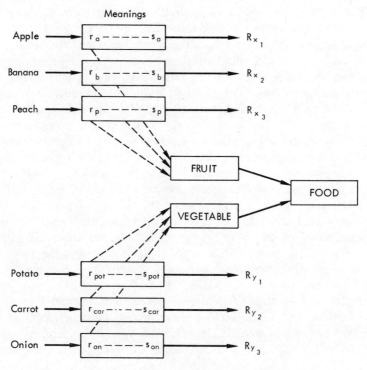

Fig. 14.1 A = Acquisition of labels
B = Acquisition of concepts

tions are, moreover, subject to his own mental set, interests, biases, and moods of the moment. Mutual understanding requires a common background of experiences. When the hearer's *experience background* differs from that of the speaker, the former may put an entirely different construction upon the words of the speaker than that which was intended. A newspaper report told of two bandits who entered the office of a firm in New York, covered the employees with pistols, and demanded the payroll. "Let 'em have it," said the proprietor to his employees, meaning that they should hand over to the holdup men the $5500 payroll. But these words carried a different meaning for the bandits. They thought the proprietor was telling someone to shoot them, so they opened fire. Two bullets struck and killed the man. The bandits fled without the payroll.

A statement may be misunderstood because of an inappropriate meaning conveyed by some key word. This misunderstanding may be traceable to differences with respect to the *word meaning*. A man who was seeking employment was told that a job was open at the Eagle Laundry, but he did not think he could qualify because he had never washed an eagle.

Words that sound alike but that have various meanings are frequently sources of faulty comprehension, particularly when a child is more familiar with an inappropriate meaning than with the one needed. This type of confusion is shown by the student who wrote on his geometry paper, "A hole is equal to some of its parts." Children often reveal their misconceptions in drawings made to illustrate the poems or other matter read to them. After reading the poem "Barbara Fritchie" to a group of young children, a teacher asked her class to draw some pictures to illustrate it. One little girl produced the sketch shown in Figure 14.2, and explained that it was a picture of "Stonewall Jackson riding a head."

Children acquire word meanings according to the usage in the community where they live. When they move to another locality where usages

Fig. 14.2 A child's conception of "Stonewall Jackson riding ahead."

are different, they frequently encounter difficulties in comprehending what they hear. This was a major difficulty for children evacuees from England during World War II. Catherine Coyne (1941) tells of a little girl who wrote to her mother that in this country a *jumper* is called a "sweater," a *lorry* is a "truck," a *tram* is a "streetcar," and a *lift* is an "elevator." The following account of a conversation between a boy from England and an American boy outside a suburban garage is quoted from Miss Coyne's article.

. . . . The Briton had been startled by a placard reading, "Flats fixed here."

"That's a strange thing," he remarked to his friend. "Why should a garage be interested in flats?"

"That's their business," the American explained patiently.

"How can a garage be interested in flats?"

"Because an automobile can't run if the tire is flat, so the garage fixes it."

"Oh, I thought—Oh, I'm sorry, I thought it meant a real flat, you know, what you call an apartment."

The two boys continued to inspect the sign, and the Briton volunteered that in England a flat tire was called a puncture. Then he said, "But why should they fix it?"

The American, exasperated by the cross-purposes of their conversation, asked tartly, "Well, what would you do with it?"

"I'd repair it," the Briton said calmly.

"Well, what does the sign say?" the American asked warily.

"It says they would fix it, and that means they'd stick it, or keep it the way it is."

Another source of error in comprehension is *inadequate perception* of certain key words. This may result from inadequate sensory perception or misinterpretation of data. A friend was standing by the elevator shaft waiting to go down. As the elevator came down from the floor above, the operator called out, "Going down?" The young man sprightly replied, "Yup." As the elevator passed by him he shouted "Down!" The operator stopped the car, brought it back to the floor where the fellow was standing, remarking apologetically, "I thought you said, 'Up'."

Written Language. The signs we comprehend may be graphic or pictorial. Cartoons deliver many timely messages in concise form, and television provides a new visual dimension to living. Yet most of our communication (despite McLuhan) is dependent on language, much of it in written form. The first requirement in reading is *perception* of the word or printed symbol. Comprehension may be blocked at this point by defective eyesight, inadequate illumination, or distraction. Next there must be *word recognition.* One may be able to perceive a word as a word but not be able to recognize it, just as one may realize the passage written in Russian constitutes a sequence of words involving a similar alphabet but be unable to recognize a single word. Beyond *recognition* there must be *word meaning.* Beginning students of foreign language are soon able to recognize and pronounce words, yet have no conception of their significance.

In learning to read, the child usually acquires word meanings by associating an object or its oral symbol, the spoken word, with the printed symbol. When the association or conditioning is complete, the printed word carries for him the same meaning as does the spoken word. Later he may be able to derive the word meanings from printed definitions, explanation, or context.

Finally, the reading process involves *sentence and paragraph comprehension.* Without this there is no true reading. The process of comprehending the meaning of a sentence or paragraph in reading is essentially the same as for comprehending speech. From the word meanings, the reader formulates the topical meaning of the whole. Correct word meanings are essential for adequate comprehension in reading. We understand what we read in terms of our previous experience and according to our present attitudes. To be understood, the reading matter assigned to children must deal with things within the range of their experience. If it does not, the teacher must provide the experiences necessary for comprehension. Explanations of new terms, allusions, figures of speech, principles involved, or the use of pictures, diagrams, specimens, and the like may serve to give the child the necessary background for comprehending a passage that transcends his past experiences.

Vocabulary.   In any field of study, the lack of a sufficient knowledge of the special vocabulary of that field impedes progress. Until we know the meanings of the special terms of a science, a business, or an art, we cannot read the literature in that field with adequate comprehension. Experimental studies have shown the value of systematic vocabulary training as an aid to the comprehension of subject matter. Ninth grade algebra students, for example, who were given special instruction designed to help them understand the mathematical terms and expressions with which they were unfamiliar, made better records on achievement tests than did pupils of a control group who were not given such instruction (Drake, 1940). Likewise, special training on the meaning of certain geographical terms encountered in historical matter served to improve the comprehension of this material (Tormey, 1934).

Various attempts have been made to secure better comprehension of the meaning of content by simplification of the vocabulary. In the case of some literary selections, this has been successful. It should be remembered, however, that simplification of vocabulary will not be helpful unless it involves the substitution of words known to the reader for those that are not familiar. The mere substitution of shorter words or of words selected from a list derived from counting those occurring most frequently in printed matter will not necessarily make the material easier to grasp. In an attempt to discover the merits of simplifying vocabulary as an aid to comprehension, Nolte (1937) revised selections of reading matter by substituting words taken from the Thorndike Word List and also by translating them into basic English. Care was taken to preserve the original meanings. This investigator concluded that such simplification did not make the passages significantly easier to understand.

While a knowledge of the meaning of the words is a primary essential for reading comprehension, there are other factors involved. One might know the meaning of every single word in a sentence and still not be able to grasp correctly the meaning of the sentence as a whole. Beside the subjective factors of set, there are the arrangement and complexity of sentence structure and the relation of the idea expressed to the experience of the reader. A sentence made up of easy words may express an idea which cannot be grasped by the reader because of its remoteness from his experience, or the sequence of phrases and a multiplicity of clauses may cause confusion. For example, the line, "Grant that love needs pity's fury," is not simply or easily comprehended even when put in context.

Verbalism.   The term *verbalism* connotes the use of words without a knowledge of their meaning. All too frequently, the student, unable to understand what he reads and faced with a test of recitation, proceeds to memorize statements from the textbook in order to have something to present to the teacher. He then reproduces words or passages he does not comprehend. This educational evil is fostered by bookish teaching, by asking questions framed in the language of the textbook, by accepting as answers words lifted from the book, by assigning material to be memorized without first seeing that the pupil understands it, and by failure to relate the material to the child's own experience.

A child of twelve in the eighth grade of a junior high school of good repute was doing her homework in arithmetic. It was memory work, and after she had studied for a long time, she asked her father to take her book to see whether she could recite her assignment. The father was surprised to see that the asssignment was the flat memorizing of six tables of weights and measures. They were in the back of the book under the heading, "For Reference." They included measures never heard of by most adults, much less used by them. But aside from the utter waste of time and energy involved in memorizing them, they were absolutely foreign to the child's understanding. After passing grams, grains, gills, the number of square yards in a square rod, and the number of square rods in an acre, the child came to the table of cubic measure. She recited "1728 cubic inches equals one cubic foot, 27 cubic feet equals one cubic yard." Then her father interrupted and asked what that meant. She said she did not know. The father then explained the meaning of a *cubic inch, cubic foot,* and *cubic yard.* The child understood that readily. Then he asked her if she knew how to figure out how many cubic inches there are in a cubic foot in case she should not remember the number. She did not, and so was shown how to compute the cube of a number. When shown that all she needed to remember was to multiply $12 \times 12 \times 12$ to get the number of cubic inches in a cubic foot, or to find the number of cubic feet in a cubic yard all she needed to do was to take $3 \times 3 \times 3$, she grasped the principle at once. But it was a new idea to her. The teacher had said nothing of the meaning of the word *cubic,* nor had she mentioned the procedure for finding the cube of a number. Two things were wrong with the teacher's assignment. In the first place, there was no sense in having the child memorize meaningless material. In the second place, even if meaningful it was relatively useless.

That the salute to the flag and the routine concert recital of the pledge of allegiance is but an empty sham and devoid of meaning to a large portion of the children of whom it is required is indicated by what children write when they are asked to write out the pledge. A revealing study was made of such written pledges collected from children in grades five to eight. In a group of thirty fifth graders who recited the pledge twice a week, sixteen wrote, "I pledge a (or the) legion." The word *indivisible,* in "one nation indivisible," was written in twenty-five different ways, but not once was it written correctly. The following are some of the ways it was written:

"in the verble," "in diblise," "into besinble," "in vissilta," "into viszable," "intervisbul," "inda vevsable," "in vestable," "invisible," "in the visble," "and davisable," "in the Vizbee," "into visable," "inves abull."

The phrase "for which it stands" was frequently distorted, and "justice for all" was quoted as "just for all," "just as for all," "just is for all," and "busted for all." The following are exact reproductions of the whole pledge as written by three of these fifth graders.

"I brith the flage of the United States of dismed and to the spries and it stands one monton in the besble with hevties and gustees and all."

"I pledge the legion to our flag of the United States of America, and to the republican for which we stand one nation and davisable with liberty of and justice for all."

"I blidge a legion to my Amiacan flag and which it stand one nacion in the vizble and libdy of busted for all."

FOSTERING COMPREHENSION AND
CONCEPT DEVELOPMENT

Perceptual Aids to Comprehension.   For centuries, education in our schools has been predominantly verbal and bookish. The revival of interest in early Greek and Latin classical writings in the fifteenth century and the invention of printing established the educational tradition that to be educated was to be well read, and this conception of education has prevailed in spite of the protests of educational realists who have repeatedly pointed out the need for learning about things from first-hand experience with them. With the invention and use of such modern devices as the motion picture, film strips, radio, and television, a new insistence on the use of concrete materials has developed.

We have seen that comprehension rests on experiences which the individual has already had, that concepts grow from concrete experiences, and that the meaning of a word is clear only when one knows the thing it signifies. Perception of concrete things is basic to all understanding; yet, ignoring this or remaining in ignorance of it, we have too often taught words without the experiential background necessary to give them real meaning. Next to the object itself in point of directness of experience are pictures of the objects. Besides giving a more accurate impression of the thing being studied, pictures and real objects have greater interest and attention value for children than their verbal representatives. This makes for more vivid impressions and better retention than can be secured from verbal discussions. Perceptual aids which may be employed in certain cases with profit to the pupil are blackboard drawings, graphs, and diagrams; charts, maps, and globes; slides, films and film strips; models, demonstrations, and dramatizations. The proper role of such materials of instruction is to supply experiences needed for comprehension. Such perceptual experiences as they provide must be directed toward the formation of concepts and generalizations in verbal terms. Meaningful experience naturally begins with the perception of the real object, but learning should move toward the level of comprehension where more varied and richer meanings can be assimilated from books and oral discussions.

Numerous experimental studies have shown the values for classroom instruction of motion pictures and other perceptual aids. They have also shown the futility of indiscriminate use of them. In general, their use has been found helpful in those cases where the experiential background of the pupils is insufficient to enable them to comprehend verbal discourse. By means of pictures, children can get a better idea than from words alone of the appearance of people and of scenes in foreign countries or of ancient times even though these may differ considerably from the peoples and scenes familiar to them.

The effective use of classroom films or of the field trip calls for careful preparation of the pupils in what they are to notice and for the direction of their observations. Without such direction, attention may be focused on some interesting detail which has no significant connection with the topic to the exclusion of more important matters. Also, some kind of follow-up work or discussion is usually needed in order to emphasize important points, to correct erroneous conceptions, and to place the observations in their proper relations to the subject being studied.

The presence of a television set in practically all homes in the urban areas and in nearly all rural areas presents a window to the world for children in developing understanding and comprehension of a variety of topics. The television experiences of children have scarcely been tapped by the teacher as adjuncts to the classroom in concept development, with the result that children undoubtedly possess many semi-organized concepts which are in need of clarification. Concept development needs not only assistance from the teacher but also the critical evaluation of the observed programs.

Laboratory Experience.   The laboratory method of instruction is another means of providing first-hand experience. It has proven its value as an aid to the comprehension of principles of science. Under the microscope, the student sees what his textbook tells about. In the laboratory he witnesses the chemical change taking place in the test tube, measures electrical current, obtains water by the explosion of hydrogen, and sees the effect of air pressure on the tin can from which air has been expelled. His observations provide the basis for understanding scientific generalizations and the procedures that have developed our scientific knowledge. What he learns by his own experiments, he is not likely to forget, provided he is not merely going through the motions of an experiment and blindly following the directions of the manual, with no real appreciation of the problem and without discovering the significance of the results.

Simulation and Group Activities.   In recognition of the necessity for actual concrete experiences as a basis for learning, many modern schools have adopted a plan of instruction known as an activity program. This plan conforms to the view that through engaging in various forms of activity, physical, mental, and emotional, the child develops an understanding and an appreciation of his environment and a knowledge of the society in which he lives. In the early grades, the activities usually pertain to the child's immediate social environment, such as the means of obtaining food, clothing, and shelter for the family. Later they may deal with the lives of people more remote from their immediate environment, extending to the peoples of other lands and other times. Indians, Vikings, Pilgrims, and other historical groups thus become the object of study and reliving through projects and dramatizations. Such vivid experiences offer children a much fuller understanding and appreciation of historical life than could possibly be obtained from reading only.

Developing Concepts. While the meaning of a sentence is ordinarily comprehended in a few seconds, the development of a concept may extend over a period of months or years. However, the process is similar, for in both cases a topical meaning emerges from a series of related experiences. The meaningful reference of the concept is not to a particular object but to a class of objects or to some common feature of many different experiences. Our concept of *rain,* for example, carries a broader meaning than that derived from perceiving a particular rainfall. It is what we know about rain in general. It is derived from seeing rain, from having it wet our clothing, from feeling it on our faces, from hearing its patter on the roof, and from observing its connection with dark clouds, flooded streets, dripping eaves, and the growth of plants. From these varied experiences with rain, that which is common to them all—water falling from the sky in a vast multitude of drops—emerges as the universal property of rain. So, in the development of any concept, the qualities or properties common to a variety of experiences are detached or isolated from those other features which vary from one of the experiences to another, and these common qualities or universal features are organized into a new unit of understanding.

Many concepts develop slowly simply because the experiences from which they are to be derived occur infrequently. Even where experiences occur daily, they come in a sequential arrangement. Concept development hangs on memory and the accident of occurrence. The great advantage of instruction is the possibility of contiguous presentation of relevant stimuli and the focusing of attention on them. Dominowski (1965), in reviewing the role of memory in concept development, concluded that the acquisition of a concept was directly affected by the degree to which contiguous instances of the concept occurred. By means of simultaneous presentation of multiple instances involving a given concept and pointing out the salient features through instruction, the multiple discriminations necessary for abstracting the concept are more readily achieved. A further advantage is the opportunity which instruction provides for confirmation of responses and for facilitating generalizations which are freed from the literal aspects of the stimuli.

For promoting the development of abstract concepts in children, two steps are indicated: first, the *location* and identification of the property to be abstracted by an examination of concrete objects or situations possessing it; and second, the *isolation* or discrimination of that property by varying its concomitants and by contrast. Suppose, for example, we wish to build up the concept of *river*. The child must first observe the essential features of a river. This calls for a detailed examination of some typical rivers. The child should note that each one examined is a natural stream of water, that it has a source, that it runs its course between banks toward some larger body of water situated at a lower level, and that it is part of a great drainage system. These features common to all rivers must then be dissociated from those characteristics of particular rivers that are not found in all rivers. We vary these irrelevant concomitants by the study of many different rivers. It will soon be discovered that some rivers flow north, some south, some east, some west, and many meander in various directions. Particular direction is then eliminated in favor of *any* direction. In like manner, the essential features are to be divorced from particulars of location, sources, depth, length, width, and outlet. Isolation by contrast calls for a comparison with brooks, lakes, bays, and oceans, with a recognition of differences between these and rivers.

For the development of general ideas and an understanding of principles, rules, and laws, the use of a number of illustrations or examples is usually necessary. To serve their designed purpose, these illustrations themselves must be readily understood. The use of a single illustration is frequently insufficient to secure the isolation of the essential features common to all cases covered by the rule, definition, or law. Such a failure to generalize from a single example is seen in the following case. A lecturer had described a form board test as an example of performance tests of intelligence. When asked later to explain performance tests, a student wrote, "A performance test is a test given with little blocks." Apparently other types of performance tests had not been incorporated into his concept.

In developing generalizations, it will not be necessary to start at the primitive level of concrete experience in every case. Explanations framed in general terms already familiar to the student may be effective. It may be expected also that children of relatively high intelligence will require fewer concrete examples to reach a generalization than less gifted children (Ray, 1936).

Harding and Bryant (1943) illustrate how simple personal experience projects, which incorporate concrete number experiences and assistance in abstracting and generalizing, promote number concepts. Using equated control and experimental groups of fourth grade pupils, who at the beginning of training were five months below grade level in achievement, Harding and Bryant found that providing the experimental group with functional activities produced a significantly greater gain in arithmetic reasoning and a gain in computation equal to that of the control group which had a textbook-drill procedure. These results occurred in spite of the fact that the experimental group had little or no drill. It is also interesting to observe that the range of individual differences in skill in the experimental group was greater than in the control group at the end of the study.

The development of time concepts is an understanding that comes slowly. Friedman (1944) showed that children do not obtain a full understanding of our conventional time system until they are about 11 years old. Concepts of the immediate past and subsequently the more distant past appear to develop before concepts of future time. Marked gains are seen at the fifth and sixth grade level, but many inadequacies in time concept exist through high school, particularly in translating pre-Christian dates. Pistor's (1940) study has shown little improvement in time concepts resulting from history instruction in the sixth grade, but Friedman and Marti (1946) have shown that history instruction of itself is of little value in developing comprehension of time concepts unless it incorporates specific instruction regarding time lines, historical sequences, time concepts, and the like. The latter study was completed with twelfth grade students. Whether or not the same result will occur at a sixth grade level is not known. But the foregoing studies confirm Katona's report (1939) that students who learn by understanding develop greater ability to transfer their skills to the solution of new problems than those students who acquire knowledge by mechanical memorizing.

STUDY FOR COMPREHENSION OF CONTENT

The term *study* is used to cover a wide variety of learning activities and various forms of learning. In this section, we shall consider those forms of study which are aimed at comprehension of the larger units of subject matter. Such study involves the organization into topics of meanings obtained from reading matter. In reading for comprehension of content, we seek to clarify our understanding and to extend our knowledge; in rote memorizing, the aim is to be able to recite words in a fixed order. The reading assignments in such subjects as history, geography, social studies, and psychology should be comprehended, not memorized.

Study Habits. A number of investigations have shown that the study practices of students in high schools and in colleges differ widely (Dynes, 1932; Parr, 1930). It appears that many do not know how to study efficiently and that a great amount of time and effort is wasted through ineffectual procedures and poor study habits. The methods used by a large proportion of students have resulted from a trial and error process of striving to meet the demands made upon them. Instruction in study procedures has for the most part been sporadic or incidental.

Experiments on Training for Effective Study. The results of a number of studies indicate the value of special training in methods of study. Some of these studies have dealt with particular procedures in connection with a particular subject. For example, Newlun (1930) found that training in the summarization of historical material in the fifth grade improved the learning of history. Barton (1930) found that training in outlining and selecting the important points of content was an effective aid to comprehension.

An experiment is reported by Wagner and Strabel (1935) in which groups composed mainly of high school juniors were given extensive training in how to study. During the junior year, the work of the trained pupils was significantly superior to that of the untrained control pupils with whom they were matched for intelligence, age, grade, sex, curriculum, and previous school record. Although the trained groups lost some of their advantage after the training period, they continued to make higher marks than the controls. They also carried more work and failed fewer subjects than did the members of the groups that were not trained in study methods.

Suggestions for Effective Study.   It is possible to state, in a general way, certain principles of effective study in the light of the results of many different investigations made on this subject. The teacher will realize in the light of the foregoing discussion that these are not absolute rules, that they will not guarantee excellence under all conditions, and that it will be necessary to make adaptations to the requirements of particular cases and special circumstances.

1. *Time.* An adequate amount of time must be provided for the study of each lesson if satisfactory progress is to be made. The planning and budgeting of one's time with a suitable apportionment for each essential task will help one to meet this primary requirement and will promote the efficient use of available time.

2. *Place.* Efficiency is promoted by regular work habits. For best results from study, one should have a regular place for study, free from all unnecessary distractions. The desk or table should be clear of things that tend to divert attention from the work to be done.

3. *Set.* The time required for settling down to work is reduced and concentration is encouraged by the following practices: a prompt and determined start with the purpose of the assignment clearly in mind, a quick preliminary survey of the chapter by skimming or by glancing over the division headings, and reading the summary at the end of the chapter before undertaking intensive reading. Having in mind at the start what the chapter is about in a general way helps the reader to select the most essential points and makes it easier to organize them into topics.

4. *Practicing recall.* The practice of attempting at the end of paragraphs or sections the recall of the main points presented in them is an aid to the mastery of content. It is a good practice also to summarize in one's own words at the end of the chapter the main points of the whole chapter.

5. *Organization.* The ideas obtained from reading should be related and organized. In longer and more difficult material, this may be promoted by outlining. A good outline will make the principal ideas stand out and show the relation of secondary or minor points to the major ones. Meaningful associations with previous experiences are helpful both to comprehension and to retention. Their number may be increased by thinking of

original illustrations, by relating the new material to previous study, by using what has been learned in other courses to verify or evaluate the statements of the author, by making comparisons, and by thinking of possible practical applications of the principles presented in the text.

6. *Dictionary*. The dictionary should be used when new words are encountered if their meaning is not clear from the context.

7. *Application of effort*. Best results call for the application of wholehearted effort to the task at hand. Intensive work, however, requires an occasional pause for relaxation. The length of the period during which full effort may be sustained will vary with the nature of the subject matter. In fairly heavy reading, one hour is probably as long as most high school or college students can apply themselves efficiently without a change. The value for efficiency of interspersed rest periods has been amply demonstrated, and this holds true for study as well as for other work. There are emergencies in life where a person must drive himself beyond the fatigue point, but this is unwise and seldom necessary in the sphere of study.

8. *Cramming*. One cannot accomplish in a few hours of intense and continuous effort what should have been spread over several weeks. Cramming is not an efficient method of study. Good students, more than poor ones, keep their work up by daily study. When this is done, there is no need for cramming. The habit of letting work pile up through neglect is found more often among poor students. They, more often than high ranking students, sit up late and study long hours before examinations. This practice leads to confusion and fatigue, both of which are unfavorable to a good performance in examinations.

9. *Review*. For retention, reviews are usually necessary. But reviews also have value for comprehension. Frequently, a second reading brings to light points missed in the first. In the light of the thought of the whole chapter as grasped in the first reading, new meanings may be found or more accurate interpretations may be given to various paragraphs.

10. *Notes*. The taking of notes is a good practice when it serves as a stimulus to the selection of the most important points, and when the notes are used for making a quick review of these points. If notes do not serve in either of these two ways, their value is questionable. Note taking on a lecture or on reading should be selective. It has been found that poor students more often than superior students take notes on lectures as fast as they can write (Pressey, 1927).

11. *Study questions*. Study is more effective when the student has a definite objective. For the less mature learner, this advantage may be secured if the teacher will supply questions to be answered from the material to be studied. Such questions will serve to guide the pupil's efforts toward the discovery of the points which the teacher wishes to stress.

12. *Written exercises*. The writing of a theme, term paper, or thesis on a topic is a good exercise for the promotion of comprehension of that

topic. This is true for the following reasons: it calls for the gathering of information; it requires the systematic organization of one's ideas; and it brings to light hazy conceptions and stimulates the writer to clarify his own thought. This applies also to writing reports on field trips, laboratory experiments, collateral reading, or topics discussed in class.

SUMMARY

Comprehension is the process through which we acquire an understanding of concepts. A large part of school learning takes place through comprehension. Concepts are developed through the enrichment of experience, the differentiation of details, and the organization of these details into new structural units.

Concepts represent a common response to a class of objects or events, regardless of dissimilarity. Discrimination and generalization are essential aspects of concept formation. Concepts may be acquired through observations of varied instances or by definition; they vary in being situational or transformational.

Concept development follows a general sequence of identifying, grouping, explaining, defining, and generalizing. Concepts develop gradually in children and are relevant to their age and experience. They depend on representational systems at three levels—motor, perceptual, and symbolic.

Language serves a number of important functions in concept development and comprehension—focusing attention, naming attributes, recalling past experience, formulating generalizations and principles. We comprehend both oral and written language in terms of our own previous experience and training and according to our attitude or set. Lack of appropriate experiential background interferes with comprehension; so, too, does faulty perception of words.

The development of concepts is important to comprehension. Our concept of an object includes all that we have learned from many different experiences with it.

Abstractions emerge from particular experiences through location of the common quality or characteristic in the midst of its concomitants, and by the isolation of this feature through variation of concomitants and by contrast. Generalizations are developed in much the same way. A general idea refers to the characteristics common to a group or class of objects. Rules, laws, definitions, and principles are generalizations which apply to many different particular situations. The teaching of abstractions and generalizations usually calls for the use of several illustrations. A single illustration often results in incomplete isolation of the essential features of the concept from irrelevant features of particular cases.

Some classroom practices which facilitate or improve comprehension are: the employment of such perceptual aids as field trips, real objects, and pictures; laboratory exercises; and the participation in group activities centered around a topic of study.

Investigations have shown that students differ widely in their study practices, and a number of experiments have indicated the value of special training in effective study procedures. Studies of the differences between good and poor students indicate that academic achievement is influenced by a large number of factors. Important among these are intelligence, time spent on study, study habits, and emotional disturbances. Recommendations for efficient study for comprehension of content include: provision for sufficient time, a regular place for study, preliminary skimming or reading of summaries, practicing recall, organization of as many meaningful relations as possible, looking up new words, working intensively but not too long at a time, day-by-day study as opposed to last minute cramming, reviews, taking notes on long and difficult material, and using study guides.

FURTHER READING

Overview

RUSSELL, D. H. 1960. *Concepts.* In C. W. Harris (ed.) *Encyclopedia of Educational Research.* New York: Macmillan, pp. 323-29.

Selected References

BERLYNE, D. E. 1956. *Structure and Direction in Thinking.* New York: Wiley.

BROWN, R. W. 1958. *Words and Things.* Glencoe, Ill.: Free Press.

BROWNELL, W. A. and G. HENDRICKSON. 1950. How children learn information, concepts, and generalizations. *Natl. Soc. Study of Educ., 49th Yrbk.* Chicago: Univ. of Chicago Press, Part I: 92-128.

KLAUSMEIER, H. J. and C. W. HARRIS. 1966. *Analyses of Concept Learning.* New York: Academic Press.

Original Investigations

DOMINOWSKI, R. L. 1965. Role of memory in concept learning. *Psychol. Bull.,* 63: 271-80.

KATES, S. L. and L. YUDIN. 1962. Concept attainment and memory. *J. Educ. Psychol.,* 55: 103-9.

SAFIER, G. 1964. A study in relationships between the life and earth concepts in children. *J. Genet. Psychol.,* 105: 283-94.

SUPPES, P. 1966. Mathematical concept formation in children. *Amer. Psychol.,* 21: 139-50.

15

Solving Problems
by Thinking

We consider thinking the most exalted of psychological processes possibly because we believe man alone capable of it. Why else coin the term "higher mental processes?" Yet thinking, like most other aspects of behavior is composite rather than unitary, diversified rather than singular. To provide you with an illustration of this, read to the end of this paragraph and when you reach it stop. Read no further until you THINK. Ready? Now THINK.

What did you do in the blank page provided for you to think? If curiosity did not lead you to jump to the next printed line, like the person who reads the end of the mystery story first, you probably drew a blank, as the expression goes. Why? Because you had nothing to think about, suggesting that thinking is not substantive, as are looking, perceiving, walking, and eating but, rather, a process to be applied. Then THINK about something; THINK about an apple.

TYPES OF THINKING

This time several things could happen depending on the sequence of thoughts conjured up by the idea of an apple: the images of apples, apple pie, apple tree, worms in apples, apples' fragrance, color, shape, or other features, wherever the stream of consciousness took you in the process of *associative thinking*. Now think about the motion picture, television program, or theatre play which you most recently saw. What did you think about it?

Your initial reactions are to recall what you saw last, then recollect the plot or players, ending probably with some judgment as to whether you liked it or not. The process here was different from that of associative thinking, for it involved a memory search directed at the identification of the appropriate event and the recollection of its content followed by a judgment which involved both the application of some standards of critical evaluation and a degree of affective response involving like and dislike. This is a very simple illustration of *critical thinking,* which can encompass varied actions —self-analysis, propaganda analysis, and the like.

Another variety of thinking is *problem solving,* which begins with a stimulus situation and instructions which establish the thinker's set and define the goal. The instructions may be implicit in the situation, provided by oneself or by someone else such as an instructor.

The second phase of problem solving typically involves a search for relevant knowledge, information, or concepts which are applicable to the problem situation, and sometimes involves the invention of a solution or possible solutions including their respective courses of action. This leads to the third phase, that of determining which course to follow.

In the problem presented on page 432, all the necessary information was given; thus, the search phase could be skipped, a choice made between alternate possibilities, and finally, the decision verified to see if the facts chosen supported the decision. The illustration given is characteristic of much of so-called "problems" to be solved in school. The goal is established by the instructor, and much or all of the information is provided, so that the demands are for direct recall without invention. At the same time, the goal of the student is to get the work done in the shortest time in order to satisfy the instructor, *rather than understand the process for solving the problem.*

Quite a different situation arises when, during the course of a 500-mile, three-day trip, the automobile motor begins to buck slightly when accelerated, starts readily when the motor is cold but not without pushing when warm, finally begins to falter and backfire regularly regardless of speed, ultimately quits abruptly in open country forty miles from home. The problem here is a real one, for getting home is dependent upon getting the automobile started or finding an alternate means of transportation. If the driver has no relevant information or concepts, i.e., knows nothing about automobiles except where and when to add gasoline, his probable course of action would be either to send for help or find an alternate way home. If his family is present, additional contingencies must be considered. In contrast, if the driver is a mechanic, the problem becomes one of trouble-shooting, requiring little in the way of concept formation or invention (search phase), only the adoption of a strategy which pinpoints the trouble.

In contrast, the person who knows a little about motors must invent a solution. While driving, he was probably conjecturing about possibilities: seems like it isn't getting the gasoline when I accelerate—could it be dirt, poor gasoline, fuel pump breakdown, carburetor malfunction? But the rapid deterioration and abrupt quitting seem to exclude the likelihood of the difficulty being connected with fuel and points instead to ignition, because

SCIENCE CONCEPT TEST

Which of the following imaginary animals would you call a mammal?

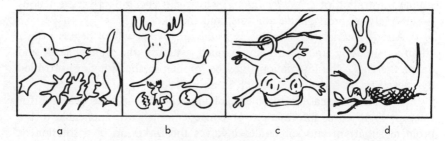

a   b   c   d

Which of the following birds would be the most apt to eat mice?

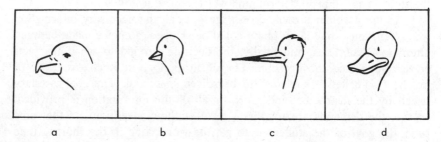

a   b   c   d

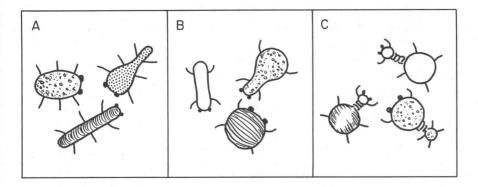

Study the above groups of figures. Determine how the figures in each group are alike. Then study the shapes drawn below and decide in which of the above groups each figure belongs. Mark your choice in the "B" or "C" column on the answer sheet. If you feel that the figure does not belong in any of the three groups mark the "D" column.

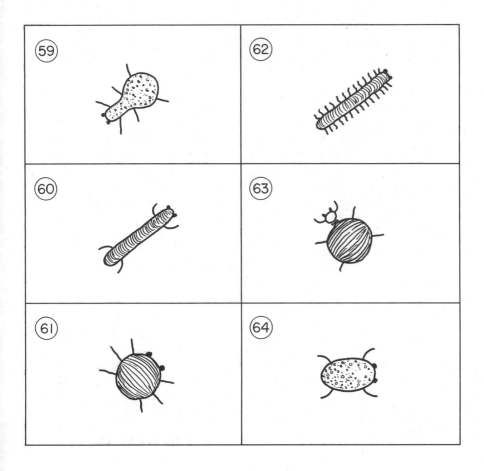

of the backfiring and abrupt end. Could the coil have failed; could a wire be disconnected? What else could be happening? These steps illustrate the efforts to formulate a concept of a possible solution based on both present information and past experience, leading to obvious efforts to test the solutions and locate the difficulty.

A fourth type of thinking is often referred to as *creative thinking*. The distinction from problem solving is not always clear, for finding a solution often involves creative activity as far as the individual is concerned, even though it may in no way be novel to other people. However, a distinction exists between the discovery of knowledge which already exists and the creation of new knowledge, whether scientific, philosophical, or artistic. Yet painting, often thought of as being highly creative, illustrates fully the difficulty of defining creativity. Fra Angelica, Memling, Tintoretto, Rubens, Rembrandt, Van Gogh, Picasso, all paint in their unique style. Yet the origins of their styles can be found in their predecessors and teachers. It is occasionally said that Giotto and Cézanne were *the* two inventors in painting since the Middle Ages, the first turning to nature rather than religion, the second to structure rather than substance. To give a brief illustration, however, of creative thinking, identify the changes you would have to order if you were the protocol officer for the United Nations and responsible for arranging the reception (and making a favorable impression) on the first Ambassador from Mars. Our space explorers report that Martians have no thumbs, only four fingers. Consider the effects. What changes would you order in silverware, cups, buttonholes, razors, etc., etc., to make life comfortable. From the various illustrations provided, one readily sees that thinking is a composite process involving many abilities such as memory, perception, imagination, and so on, and that it takes a number of forms: associative, problem solving, critical, and creative—to adopt Russell's (1960) classification scheme. Implicit in all forms of thinking (with the possible exception of associative thinking) are cognitive or discovery factors, production of convergent or divergent thinking, and evaluation and decision making (Guilford, 1956).

Learning and thinking are inextricably related, not only because we learn to think, but because it is not too great an exaggeration to consider thinking as self-instructed learning. When learning was defined as the changing of behavior by means of practice or training, it implied motivation on the part of the instructor. The use of instruction as a means for learning suggests its greater efficiency in modifying behavior, both as to goal attainment for the learner and for achievement of the ends of instruction. If the environment were non-changing and behavior perfectly adaptive and completely satisfying, then efficiency in learning could be defined solely in terms of the acquisition and retention of established knowledge and behavior patterns.

In a variable and changing environment, as ours is, efficiency cannot be equated with mastery of established knowledge. It requires a capacity for subsequent modification of behavior: (a) to vary responses in new or different situations, (b) to transfer relevant training from former to novel situations, and (c) to acquire a systematic method of modifying behavior, or learning how to learn. The various forms that learning takes—conditioning, trial and error, rote learning, acquiring insight—can be ranked for efficiency in these terms, and it becomes readily apparent that some combination of trial and error learning and acquiring insight is essential to effective environmental adaptation and that such a procedure should be able to function on an anticipatory basis, i.e., the overt act should not have to be taken to discover the consequences. This is essentially what thinking involves, be it problem solving, critical, or creative. The available alternates —blind trial and error, following tradition, avoiding new situations, jumping to conclusions, unquestioned acceptance of decisions of others—do not sound promising.

PROBLEM SOLVING

We encounter a problem when, for any reason, we are deterred in our efforts to reach some goal. Any problem situation implies the existence of constraints, which often may be irremediable, as when a parent refuses permission to engage in some activity or a teacher detains a pupil, or even stronger, as when there is a commitment to prison. Even this last is rarely unsolvable. One has only to think of appeals, escapes, pardons, and paroles to realize that possible solutions exist. The characteristic situation is that of an organism directly seeking to attain some goal, encountering a barrier, and being faced with the problem of how to circumvent it, how to find a solution in the face of the imposed constraints. Thinking is one type of activity which follows as an organism, human or animal, meets, recognizes, and attempts to solve a problem.

Most students are familiar, in one form or another, with Dewey's (1910) so-called five steps in problem solving: (1) experiencing the felt difficulty, (2) defining the problem, (3) suggesting possible solutions, (4) using reason to deduce the implications of possible solutions, and (5) testing the solution. These steps suggest that problem solving is a rational, systematic procedure. Possibly such was the case for as able a scholar as Dewey, but at the more ordinary level of human affairs, problem solving is much less systematic and much more involved. It is true that one must be aware of the existence of a problem before any effort at solution can be attempted, but beyond that point procedures for obtaining a solution can range from haphazard to orderly, relying on trial and error as much as reason, memory as much as imagination. At one end of the scale of difficulty of problems are the problems in Asia, Africa, and Latin America being faced by the "big power" governments, not to mention their own domestic social problems. The complex of political, social, and economic morasses existing on those continents are the product of centuries and scarcely solvable within any presidential career. Yet actions taken, attempted solutions, carry high risk of life and limb, as much as of wealth and power. Perhaps on the same level of difficulty in terms of hidden information and of the permutations possible may be a defensive lead against a slam bid in contract bridge. At the opposite end of the scale of difficulties of problems is a last-minute run in a stocking. Under such a range of circumstances, no ready-made pattern for problem solving is conceivable. However, we can examine the steps in the process and the factors which seem to affect the efficiency with which solutions are attained.

   Steps in Problem Solving.   Given the problem situation in whatever form it occurs—expenses exceed income, the car won't start, a child is ill, a skunk is digging holes in the lawn, water appears on the ceiling from an undisclosed leak in the plumbing, the opposing army initiates the use of a new and deadlier weapon—obtaining a solution involves three main phases: (1) the search phase, (2) the functional solution phase, and (3) verification of the final solution.

   The search phase yields a narrowing of the range within which a solution is to be found, the crucial area or point in the situation where the difficulty lies. At first the nature of the difficulty may not be clearly grasped. Before being able to attempt a solution, unless approaching it randomly, one must clarify the problem. This is in some respects the most critical step. The most difficult aspect of scientific research is formulating the answerable question, in short, defining the problem. The physician has to diagnose the illness before considering the type of treatment. The expert auto mechanic locates the reason for the car's not starting before attempting repairs. The attack during this phase is primarily analytic, a seeking of relevant information in the situation and from past experience. The analysis typically proceeds on a piecemeal basis rather than comprehensively. Hildreth (1941) reports that when the original form of a problem proves too difficult, both adults and children attempt to reduce it to simpler terms in an effort to make it meaningful and also to ease tension. Errors occur frequently in the effort to make the problem congruent with prior concepts or experience.

   We often speak of putting our finger on the problem, implying that after analysis of the problem in relation to the desired goal, the point of difficulty has been identified. Each unsuccessful attempt to clarify the problem leads to a reformulation of the problem—a could-it-be? no-it-isn't, then-perhaps-it-may-be series. Efficient problem solvers were shown to spend a higher proportion of time in the analysis of the problem, ask a greater proportion of their questions during this period, ask more unique and less redundant questions, and ask them at a slower rate (Blatt and Stein, 1959). In short, careful analysis characterized efficient problem solving. Less efficient individuals moved into the intermediate phase too soon, attempting to synthesize a solution before having sufficient information.

Once clarified, the process moves into the functional solution phase, an attempt to combine the elements into proposed solutions. The dividing line between the two phases is not as clear as the change in attack. From the data assembled through observation, recall, or imagination, inferences are made as to possible solutions. Whatever the procedure adopted in this phase, the attempts are not blind. For example, returning to the stalled car situation, if the problem has been narrowed to being an electrical one and the key to the ignition is on and there is gas in the tank, one doesn't move around the automobile opening and shutting windows, doors, or trunk. One checks to see if the spark plugs are firing, or if a loose connection exists, and the like.

In this second phase of problem solving, search continues but of a different nature. One attempts to recall from past experience any information which would prove useful in developing a solution. If one has seen a mechanic use a screwdriver to short-circuit the spark to the block, he may use it to see if electrical current is getting to the spark plugs. An experiment of Weaver and Madden (1949) repeating an original study of Maier (1930) with similar results shows the relevance of past experience to problem solving. The problem was to make a pendulum which would swing and make chalk marks at two spots on the floor (see Figure 15.2). Fifty-two college students were divided into four groups and given adjustable poles, heavy string, a heavy clamp which could hold the chalk and provide enough weight for the pendulum, and chalk. The groups varied in the amount of "experience" and "directions" given. One group was given only the problem. A second was given the problem plus a demonstration of the parts. The third was given a hint (direction) as to the solution. And the last group was given both a demonstration (relevant experience with the parts) plus directions. Solutions were highest in the second and fourth groups. Only one student in the directions-only group and none in the problem-only group solved the problem.

Any solution depends on its functional effectiveness. Considering the automobile problem again, one may accidentally locate a loose wire, but unless the procedure is functionally related to the analysis—i.e., a systematic check of wires, distributor, and so on—solution is improbable. During this phase, each tentative solution, even if unsuccessful, restructures the problem (Morgan, 1945). For example, if a check of the ignition system

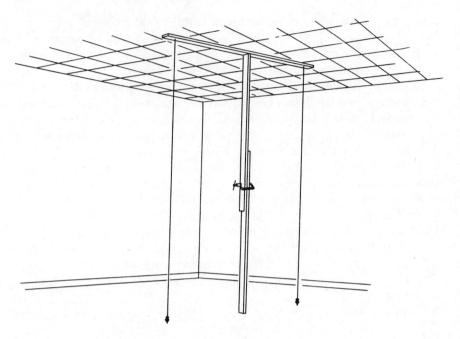

Fig. 15.2 Swing pendulum problem designed by Maier (1930) for the study of reasoning.

fails to solve the problem, one will turn to check gasoline delivery as a possibility.

The third phase is the development of the actual solution. The first phase delineated the problem; the second phase involved the development of a mode of attack; in the third phase the mode of attack is applied until the solution is obtained. One may discover that the automobile stalled because the cable connecting the foot throttle to the carburetor had come apart. The separated pieces may be difficult to reach for want of an appropriate tool or because of the danger of being burned by the hot motor. At this point in the process, efforts are sharply directed toward reaching the conclusion of the task. Validation of the solution to most problems comes quickly, although not always. The validation of Einstein's theory of relativity waited upon the occurrence of particular astronomical events. A number of solutions to problems of delinquency have been proposed and tested with dubious results and thus have not been validated.

Problem Solving by Children.   The young child's behavior in experimental problematic situations indicates that he learns by his own exploration and manipulation the possibilities of using various instruments or objects in such a way as to secure desired results (Richardson, 1932). When children 2 or 3 years old attack new problems, such as those involving the stacking of two boxes or the joining of two sticks, the method employed is usually of the trial and error type. If, then, another problem is encountered similar to one already mastered, there may be some transfer of experience bringing an immediate solution (Alpert, 1928). Older children, having a greater fund of experience, solve more difficult problems and, in solving them, manifest more insight. Their behavior in problematic situations indicates a greater ability to formulate and maintain an assault on a problem. Their attacks are more deliberate and systematic.

Oakes (1947), utilizing an interview procedure with groups of children between kindergarten and sixth grade, inquired into their explanations of natural phenomena and observed a steady increase in physical explanations grade by grade. Cause and effect explanations were characteristic of the brighter children. The steady growth of conceptual developmental and logical reasoning was demonstrated in a field study by Strauss and Schuessler (1951), who followed an interview technique with a group of children between the ages of 4½ and 11. The questions pertained to money and its use and were asked during a sequence of interviews of fifteen to thirty minutes. Children's concepts were seen to develop by stages. The typical 5-year-old, for instance, could distinguish one or two small coins but was unable to identify the remaining coins, whereas with increasing age children understood the function of a storekeeper.

The ability to think out the solutions of problems develops gradually and increases with age (Heidbreder, 1928). There is no specific point in the child's development where trial and error ceases to be the method for discovering solutions and where thinking takes over. Some degree of insight appears in young children when they see a significant relation between some object in the situation and their goal, as in the case where a stick is apprehended not merely as a stick but as a means for drawing a toy within reach. This has been observed in the behavior of apes and in children about 2 years old. A little later memory and imagination may be brought to play upon the problem. First it may be an object not present in the perceptual field that is thought of as a means for reaching the goal. As understanding develops, concepts are used to advantage and we see the gradual emergence of more abstract forms of reasoning. Symbolic materials become available through the functions of memory, imagination, and comprehension. Suggestions for solutions may be derived more and more from past experiences and the need for the exploratory manipulation of objects grows less. The appropriateness of the suggestions, also, is weighed and estimated more by thinking of their implications rather than being discovered through precipitous attempts to act upon them.

Sporadic bits of associative thinking are sometimes observed in young children. They are limited in each case to the child's range of experience and interests. A child four years old, while watching the water run off from the kitchen sink, asked, "Is it like a little hill?" Though we cannot be sure just what the remark indicates, it appears that this child was bringing his knowledge to bear on the question of why the water was disappearing. A boy of six years asked his grandmother what *double* means. She replied that it means *two*. The boy came back with the remark, "Then Grace is double because she is two." Grace was his 2-year-old sister. The outcome was faulty, but it was a clear case of inference, and the error was due to inadequate concepts rather than to the process itself. The effective use of general principles demands a clear understanding of the principles. An adult, when trying to reason with insufficient knowledge, makes errors similar to those found in the thinking of children. In novel situations, when the adult is unable to find in what he has learned anything to help him out, he frequently reverts to trial and error in attempting to solve his problem.

Piaget (1950) describes the intellectual function of a young child as being primarily at a sensori-motor level. However, preschool children vary markedly in their ability to deal with problem solving situations, and their abilities in this direction are related more closely with experience than mental age. The observed correlation between socio-economic status and problem solving ability is probably an outgrowth of differences in both amount and kind of such experiences. Children are more successful in attaining solutions to problems in the presence of objects than in working with problems which have been presented entirely verbally. Yet both the previous experiences with an object and the presence of the object have negative aspects as well, for they tend to limit perception of object properties. For example, a hammer will be perceived as something to hit with rather than a possible weight. In fact, casual observations of young children indicate that on first encounter they respond to the primary functional purposes of tools—they will dig with a spoon and stick with a fork. Attempts to explore various other uses, such as using a spoon as a hammer, as a drumstick, or to ping glasses, are stopped by adults, indirectly inhibiting an important feature of problem solving ability, the capacity to vary response.

Children of school age use verbal hypotheses to guide their behavior. They can induce generalizations from repeated observation of phenomena and utilize these generalizations to explain events and to suggest solutions. The ability to verbalize freely and to understand concepts are closely related. Where younger children perceive words as concrete ideas and emphasize isolated or particular aspects, older children stress the abstract, class, or conceptual features of word meaning. As they grow older they utilize synonyms and explanational types of definition more frequently.

Adults, in general, can do better at thinking out the solution of problems than children. They are able to take a more objective attitude toward problems. Having greater emotional stability and control, they are likely to have less interference from emotional reactions. They can usually keep their attention on the problem over a longer period of time and hence are less likely to be thrown off course by the intrusion of a new interest. The most important reasons for the greater thinking ability of adults, however, are their greater range of experience, better understanding, larger fund of well developed concepts, and the fact that they have acquired certain general procedures for meeting and working out their difficulties.

A young child's needs are comparatively simple and, for the most part, are satisfied by other persons. The responsibilities of adults are often sources of problems. Lacking these, the child does not encounter problems as often. Not only is the child often blind to difficulties which present problems to more mature persons, but his limited knowledge makes him less able to comprehend the nature of the difficulties he does realize.

In the next stage of the thinking out process, the child's comparatively limited range of experience and his meager fund of generalizations place restrictions on his ability to arrive at a successful solution. Excellence in thinking of this kind requires a fertility of suggestions for solution, and this depends upon the thinker's associative resources. The child is usually not able to bring to mind as many possibilities for solution as one with greater understanding and more extensive experience in the field of the problem.

Finally, the child generally lacks critical judgment. He is less capable of developing the implications of a suggestion and of determining its propriety by reasoning. This, too, is due to his limited range of information and understanding. It requires knowledge to be able to evaluate and judge correctly.

Conditions Affecting Problem Solving.   Problem solving is not a unitary ability but a complex of a number of abilities. Research involving factor analysis indicates the importance of inductive and deductive reasoning abilities independent of intelligence. Problem solving incorporates a variety of related thinking processes involving relationships, the synthesis of isolated experiences, and the reorganization and recentering of materials. Four factors which affect problem solving processes are indicated; these concern the type of problem, the characteristics of the problem solver, the method of attack, and the social and group factors in the situation.

It is not surprising that prior experience with a pattern of events, whether they evolve from the experimental situation or previous experience, should affect choices in a problem situation. It is of interest to note that a close relationship emerges between the choice distributions and the event probabilities (Goodnow and Postman, 1955). Even when individuals are searching for a lawful solution to a problem, they learn to discriminate between probabilities of events, even though the latter are not explicit.

The risks involved or the potential rewards influence behavior. The effect of probabilities shift when the less frequent events are linked to larger rewards (Edwards, 1956).

Problems can vary in complexity and hence in the probability of solution, from simple recognition tasks such as locating a piece in a jig-saw puzzle to as complex a problem as the invasion of Europe in 1944. Not only do problems vary as to type, difficulty, and complexity, but they frequently vary in the risk involved. There is little risk involved in haphazardly trying piece after possible piece in a jig-saw puzzle, but a great risk in haphazardly throwing military units onto the Normandy coast. In fact, the increase in risk posed by a threatened change in the weather almost resulted in a delay in the invasion. Another feature in which problems vary is in the degree of personal involvement. A considerable difference exists between the care taken in reaching the solution of a bridge problem in the newspaper and one at the card table, especially if the latter involves some kind of competition. Differences in tension associated with the two situations affect performance; so too does the ego involvement of the participant. Combs and Taylor (1952) demonstrated this in an experiment in which men and women undergraduates learned a code to a satisfactory level of performance, then were given coded sentences of equal difficulty to translate. One series of sentences was neutral, the second threatening in that it contained embarrassing or repugnant ideas. In addition, external threats were applied in the form of time pressure and questions about individual capability. Translation time and number of errors increased under threatening conditions.

In addition to the variation introduced in problem solving by the nature of the problem, individual characteristics of the problem solver affect his method of attack. Klausmeier and Loughlin (1961) studied the characteristics of children of different levels of intelligence in solving problems graded according to their level of ability. Three groups of fifth grade children of different levels of intelligence were used: 55-80 IQ, 90-110 IQ, 120-146 IQ. Problems of equal difficulty, determined by an equal length of time necessary to reach a solution, were presented to each group. Differences in problem solving were noted, in spite of the gradation of problems. Low ability groups showed less persistence, greater acceptance of incorrect solutions, and greater use of random attack than the other two groups. Conversely, high ability groups took greater note of mistakes and their correction, verifications of solutions, and logical sequence in problem solving.

Variations in performance at problem solving occur with respect to sex, motivation, expectancy for success, and training. These variables interact with the nature of the task, so that simple generalizations cannot be offered. In a study in which memory for isolated items interfered with solution to new and difficult problems, Saugstand (1952) found girls solving fewer problems than boys but being less deterred by incidental memory. The problems presented, however, involved spatial aptitude on which sex differences occur. Problem solving was affected by prior training in mathematics and physics. This last effect may result from experience in the use of principles in solving problems (Cross and Gaier, 1955). More recently, Klausmeier and Wiersma (1964) found that the sex differences were related to the task, boys being superior at tasks involving convergent thinking, girls at those involving divergent thinking. Some part of the differences in performance relates to differences in attitudes between boys and girls toward problem solving (Carey, 1958).

It would be expected that individuals high in achievement motivation will persist longer at attempts to solve problems, obtain a greater number of solutions, and solve problems more rapidly (French, 1958; French and Thomas, 1958). Performance is affected by the expectations for success, and this in turn depends not only on individual motivation but on the degree of success or failure experienced. Expectations of success increase with actual proportions of success (Tyler, 1958). In predicting success or failure, adults tend to overpredict the proportion of success, and this overprediction increases as the number of failures increases (De Soto *et al.,* 1960; Feather, 1963). Furthermore, as expected from studies on anxiety, these experiences interlock with other personality components to affect variability in the performance (Mandler and Sarason, 1953) e.g., individuals who have had a history of low success are more subject to the stress effects of failing under experimental conditions. A number of studies indicate that success in problem solving can be improved through a variety of training procedures. The nature of the set with which individuals approach problems affects their success. Encouragement to expect success (Tyler, 1958) improves performance, as does a set to view situations as problems and look for alternative solutions rather than adopt the obvious solution. The result is an increase in the quality and number of solutions, both with children and adult groups (Maier and Solem, 1962; Ackerman and Levin, 1958).

If willingness and ability to shift set and seek alternatives (McNemar, 1955) leads to greater success, the antithesis, rigidity, limits effectiveness. Rigidity occurs when one persists in responding to a limited number of cues of an object or in a situation or is fixated in mode of attack. For example, for years the writer has given puppies a rag tied up in knots to keep them from chewing on shoes. Most books on training puppies make reference to such a gadget. Today in pet stores, one can find hard deerskin shaped like a bone with a knot at each end. Someone was ingenious enough and sufficiently flexible in his thinking to consider making the gadget of leather at a handsome profit. Our tendency to see objects in terms of customary usage—rulers as rulers, coathangers as coathangers—limits our flexibility in conjuring up other uses for them in finding solutions to problems. Such learned sets impair problem solving effectiveness (Schroder and Rotter, 1953). Everyone has engaged in inflexible modes of attack. The most common experience involves searching for a misplaced object. One will persist in circling the room or house or going through the same file repeatedly, refusing to accept the fact that the misplaced item could be elsewhere, or to consider alternate solutions.

Rigidity cannot be conceived of as a separate isolated factor. It can be the product of past experience and familiarity with the stimuli. In effect, instruction is a form of induced rigidity, for the learner is encouraged to attend to selected aspects of the materials at hand and to procedures for dealing with them. Such action is a necessary and desirable aspect of instructional strategy, so long as it is not overcontrolling. Obviously, training in flexibility and adaptability of approach can shift such tendencies, and this in effect is what the technique of "brainstorming" encourages. (Knight (1963) has shown that the greater the amount of effort expended in obtaining solutions, the greater the persistence in the use of the solution procedure with subsequent problems. In addition to situational influences, personality characteristics contribute to rigidity of attack. Nonconformity, flexibility, and positive adjustment are associated with ability to overcome set in solving problems (Cowen and Thompson, 1951; Nakamura, 1958).

Considerable research has been completed with subjects ranging from school age to adults on group problem solving, with the general finding that the average group is superior to the average individual. This holds for spatial as well as verbal problems and for human relations and social problems but less so for mathematical problems. The superiority of the group does not derive from any inherent greater effectiveness of groups as such, but rather from the probability of getting a good solution from some member of the group (Tuckman and Lorge, 1962). The effectiveness of the group depends on the efforts and ability of the most able member to communicate his knowledge and gain its acceptance by other members of the group. Centralized groups and highly cohesive groups emerge as less efficient than less cohesive groups (Phillips, 1956) apparently because of restrictions on interaction. Even though students working cooperatively in a group produce better solutions, the problem solving ability of any one individual does not improve (Hudgins, 1960). If time consumed rather than quality of solution is taken as the criterion of effectiveness, group problem solving is less effective for it is more time consuming.

In reviewing the conditions which affect problem solving both positively and negatively, the value of a group situation becomes apparent. Having a number of individuals is tantamount to having a range of solutions proposed, overcoming set and rigidity. Low cohesive groups in particular provide greater flexibility. Further, the climate of a group can reduce the inhibiting effects of stress and fear of failure, for responsibility is spread. Finally, interaction can contribute to greater persistence in problem solving efforts, as well as greater acceptance of solutions achieved (Hoffman and Maier, 1961).

CONVERGENT AND DIVERGENT THINKING

In the process of problem solving, thinking plays a vital part. Once the difficulty which we identify as a problem has been experienced, thinking enters the process at several stages—in attempts to clarify and define the problem, in ordering and arranging the facts, observations or evidence in order to formulate a tentative hypothesis, and finally, in the application of reasoning to test a hypothesis. Essentially, thinking consists of arranging past and present experience into patterns. Various attempts have been made to classify steps in thinking. One distinction that has been made is that between inductive and deductive thinking: moving from specific cases to a principle in contrast to the opposite, making conclusions about specifics on the basis of a general truth or principle. For example, given a basket of green apples, one could pick an apple at random and taste it to find that it was hard and sour. After two or three repetitions, one may be ready to make a generalization that hard, green apples are sour (inductive reasoning) and then on the basis of the generalization, to conclude that this holds true for the remainder of the basket (deduction). Another classification scheme looks at thinking in terms of its products—associate, convergent, and divergent thinking.

It would be convenient if we could nimbly explain thinking as the conscious, symbolic manipulation of concepts. But all thinking is not conscious. Let your chain of thoughts run beginning with *lover*. In a few seconds, you will produce a series of complex associated thoughts which seemingly leap to mind from nowhere. If you reject such automatic associations as a form of thinking, consider the number of times you have put aside a problem because of being unable to find a solution, only to have the solution occur in the middle of some other activity. Apparently, you continued to think about the problem on an unconscious level. This intuitive solution, occurring after a period of incubation, is reported often enough to be more than a chance phenomenon. Furthermore, thinking is not exclusively a mental process. When individuals are instructed to think about lifting an arm, a measurable difference in the electrical potentials of the nerves associated with the muscles and minute muscular movements can be detected. Moreover, mental practice has demonstrable effects on skill improvement. Thus, thinking is a process which not only involves sensations, perceptions, and associations but goes beyond them. Symbols and concepts make this possible. In convergent thinking, we essentially attempt to close a gap between a starting and ending position. Bartlett (1900) refers to this as thinking in closed systems. In the series below

$$1 \quad 3 \quad 2 \quad 5 \quad 3 \quad 7 \quad \text{————}$$

A By ———— ———— ———— ———— ———— *Homework*

the task is to find a unifying concept which will account for or provide a pattern which explains the group of divergent ideas. In the first, the task is to identify the number progression sequence which produces 4 as a solution. In the second, both partial and totally correct solutions are possible. One can begin the third word with C, the fourth with D, and so on; or one can insert a three letter word, then a four letter word, and on to the eight letter word, *homework*. Both partially correct solutions provide a sequence which either ends with the initial H of *homework* or the eight letter word which *homework* is. The fully correct solution is the progress which shifts the initial letter—C, D, E, F, G—and also increases the length of each successive word by one letter.

Another form of thinking occurs in what Bartlett has termed open systems, where one must move from the known to the unknown in seeking a solution. Guilford identifies this as divergent thinking. Other authors apply the term creative thinking. Finally, we often make reference to critical thinking, referring to the application of standards of judgment to ideas, plans, products, and the like. This may occur in propaganda analysis, in weighing evidence, in selecting between alternative proposals, and in other forms of judgment.

It is clear that we use the term, thinking, in a variety of ways: If I had only thought of that (divergent production) . . . What do you think of (critical thinking) . . . Do you think that (convergent thinking) . . . I couldn't think of (associative thinking). Thinking becomes a general term covering a variety of behaviors ranging from straightforward association to complex problem solving. At one point, we use thinking to refer to concept formation, in the next to refer to divergent production. Used so broadly, thinking is not particularly useful as a descriptive term.

Gagné has suggested a hierarchy which provides a more helpful ordering of types of human learning.

CREATIVE THINKING

Studies of creativity include biographical data concerning creative people, introspective statements by creative thinkers, tests of individual

Response learning	S-R	Establishment of a response connection to a stimulus specified along physical dimensions
Chaining	S-R→S-R	Establishment of chains of S-R connections.
Verbal learning	S-r→(s-R)	Establishment of labeling responses to stimuli varying physically within limits of primary stimulus generalization. Previous response learning assumed (as indicated by brackets).
Concept learning	$S_1 - r_1 - s$ $S_2 - r_2 - s$ → Concept $S_3 - r_3 - s$	Establishment of mediating response to stimuli which differ from each other physically.
Principle learning	Concept → Rule Concept	Establishment of a process which functions like a rule "if A, then B" where A and B are concepts.
Problem solving	Rule → Higher Order Rule → Rule	Establishment of a process which combines two or more previously learned rules in a "higher-order rule."

differences of various creative individuals such as artists, scientists, poets, and the like, experimental studies of creativity, and efforts at teaching creativity. We also have descriptions of inventions and reflections by men and women best in a position to observe and understand, the thinkers and artists themselves. These observations show that the process differs tremendously from person to person and from problem to problem. Our present knowledge is characterized more by confusion than clarity.

Wallas (1926) provided an early description of four main steps in the creative process: preparation, incubation, illumination, and verification. More recently, Osborn (1957) expanded these to seven steps: orientation or pointing up a problem, preparation and gathering of data, analysis, ideation or identifying alternatives, incubation and illumination, synthesis or putting the pieces together, and evaluation. From this series of steps, it is difficult to distinguish creativity from problem solving. Just as the distinction between inductive and deductive reasoning breaks down in actual practice, so too does an attempt to distinguish creativity as an independent process. Experimental evidence shows no sharp definition between the so-called steps, nor does research indicate any common procedure characterizing creative individuals.

Creativity is currently an important area of interest in education. *Psychological Abstracts* reports over 120 abstracts for a four year period. Yet a review of the research reveals little agreement on what is meant by creativity. To some, the word is synonymous with intelligent behavior, although the work of Getzels and Jackson (1962) and Torrance (1960) indicate that creativity and intelligence are relatively independent of each other, at least in groups of superior ability. For some researchers, *creative* is a glamorous way of saying *gifted;* for others, it is synonymous with imagination. Perhaps the connotation implied by the majority is the potential to produce unexpected responses. From data regarding writing, drama, music, symbolic thinking, and fluency of thought processes (Miller, 1962), at least a moderate correlation between creativity and intelligence appears (MacKinnon, 1962) but not to the extent that would indicate that all gifted children are creative. Consistent with his structure of intellect, Guilford (1956) contends that independent factors can be identified which characterize creativity, but the tests he has devised have demonstrated inconsistent results as measures of creativity.

Another dimension of creativity is that of personality. Rogers (1959) suggests three aspects closely associated with creative acts: (1) an "openness to experience" meaning lack of rigidity, a tolerance for ambiguity, and the ability to accept conflicting information without premature closure, (2) an "internal locus of evaluation" by means of which an individual makes his own judgments of worth independent of external pressures, and (3) "the ability to toy with elements and concepts." Such abilities are based in ego strength, self-worth, and psychological freedom. Such a conception makes creativity an outgrowth of cognitive, life-style, or motivational interaction with the environment.

In short, it appears that at the present writing, problems of establishing criteria for measurement of a complex set of behaviors preclude definitive statements regarding the nature of creativity; yet the fact, however ambiguous, that it can be nurtured seems clear (Ray, 1966; Golann, 1963; Drevdahl, 1961; Maltzman, 1960). Although feelings of security and self-worth may be the product of early development, the ability to ask questions, to propose alternative solutions, to tolerate ambiguity, and to defer judgment appear as outgrowths of the educational process. Highly structured, authoritarian, uniform method instructional procedures tend to inhibit the thought processes essential to the ability to order old and new experience in different patterns.

DIRECTING AND TRAINING PUPILS IN PROBLEM SOLVING

The Problem Method of Teaching. The good teacher will provide opportunity for children to learn by thinking out problems. There are certain definite advantages in this method of teaching. First, it is conducive to an alert attitude favorable to learning. A good problem is a good motive for learning. Second, it is conducive to the building up of confidence in one's ability to work things out for himself. This has definite value for the individual's mental health, for one of the first principles of mental hygiene is that difficulties should be regarded as problems to be solved rather than as emergencies to be evaded. Third, the memory value is exceptionally good for results obtained by solving a problem, and, if these results are forgotten, they may be thought out again in most cases more easily than the first time. Finally, this method of learning provides valuable training in facing and working out solutions of problems. Through it, with wise direction by the teacher, the pupil may learn the art of sound thinking. To secure a transfer from a particular field of instruction to problems in other fields, however, it is essential that the student be made aware of the general aspects of the methods and procedures which bring good results (Ulmer, 1939).

A number of experiments have been done on different teaching techniques—lecture versus discussion, teacher centered versus student centered and the like, usually with equivocal results. Several comparisons of the lecture-demonstration method with the problem solving method were made utilizing college students as experimental and control groups. Although the differences obtained usually were not statistically significant as far as determining which is the preferable method, qualitative differences occurred. For instance, on specific information learned, the lecture-demonstration group surpassed the problem solving group; the latter, however, had greater understanding of generalizations. While the lecture method tends to be superior for informational gains, the utilization of problem solving techniques in teaching is necessary if the teacher is to develop problem solving skills.

Reviewing educational research on problem solving approaches used in conjunction with the teaching of social studies, Broadhead and Dimond (1950) reported that high school students using a problem solving approach showed greater development in critical thinking as well as in subsidiary research and study skills.

CREATING THE PROBLEM.   First of all, in securing and directing problem solving activity, the teacher must set the stage for the problem. One of the simplest ways in which this may be done is to ask a thought question. Such a question is not one that can be answered directly by repeating something that has been read, heard, or otherwise learned but one that calls for the production by real thinking of a new bit of knowledge, a new opinion, or a new belief. Problems also may be aroused by the assignment of exercises or tasks that bring the child into new situations for which his established modes of response are inadequate. It could be the problem of finding an effective means for raising funds to buy a new flag for the schoolroom, how to secure suitable costumes for the class play, or the need for making the school paper more appealing to the pupils.

Whatever its source, the problem must be adapted to the pupil's level of experience and understanding. For young children, it should be comparatively simple and related to a concrete situation and familiar materials. More difficult problems may be introduced to older children. For them imaginary situations and more abstract propositions may be employed.

Although the teacher may suggest a problem, it must become the child's own problem if it is to motivate thinking on his part. The teacher's assignment or question has aroused a real problem only when the child or student himself feels a need or desire to find the answer or solution. It is for this reason that the most effective thought questions are those that appeal to the learner's curiosity or are related to his own interests and welfare. A thought provoking question is one that delivers a challenge, not one that strikes down a child and leaves him with a sense of failure or incapacity.

It takes more skill and originality on the part of the teacher to ask good thought questions, to arrange thought provoking projects and activities, and, on the higher levels, to direct research, than merely to ask questions of fact based on a textbook or pass out information by way of telling or lecturing. An investigation, in which the number and kinds of questions asked by fifty-six sixth grade teachers of history were compared with the scores these teachers made on intelligence tests while in college, revealed that the teachers with higher intelligence asked a smaller total number of questions but more thought questions than did the teachers who rated lower in intelligence (Haynes, 1936). When the teachers were divided into four groups from lowest to highest according to their intelligence scores, it was found that the percentage of thought questions asked varied directly with the intelligence of the teachers. Assuming that thought questions stimulate thinking, we see that these results indicate that the more intelligent teachers secure a greater amount of thinking than the less intelligent ones.

COMPREHENDING THE PROBLEM.   When the problem is established and the difficulty felt, the pupil is ready for the next step which involves the clarification of the problem, its definition, and precise location. The significance of the question may be but vaguely grasped or the nature of the difficulty may be incompletely comprehended. A vaguely defined problem leads to mental fumbling and floundering. If a pupil is to learn how to think, he must be made to realize the need for determining, at the start, the nature of his problem. He should be warned of the danger of making false assumptions. He may need to be told to reread the statement of the problem and to examine its conditions more carefully. His attention may need to be called to some condition that he has overlooked. Sometimes a well-put question may help him to see more clearly the essential features of the problem. In some cases, as in a proposed research undertaking, it will be helpful to have the student write out a precise statement of the problem which he intends to explore.

Hildreth (1942) demonstrated the importance of having some understanding of the nature of a problem by dividing 100 boys and girls between the ages of 7 and 10 years into two groups, one of which had the opportunity to see the jig-saw puzzle whole before working on it, the other having no idea of the puzzle solution. Time scores and number of moves made were recorded. The uninstructed group was significantly slower than the instructed group and engaged in more trial and error behavior. Interestingly enough, the children tended to be in action all the time they were working, very few stopping to *think* without making moves. Although it may be argued that jig-saw puzzles are not problems in the usual adult understanding of the word, they are appropriate as tasks for children, who function more effectively on a concrete than on an abstract level.

SEARCHING FOR CLUES.   Superficial thinking and erroneous conclusions are the penalty for trying to solve problems with insufficient information. The discovery of relevant data frequently demands exploration and search. If the problem falls within a field in which the person has an abundance of experience or concerning which he is well informed, he may call upon his associative resources to great advantage. He may be able to solve the problem at once by recalling relevant facts and by reorganizing them in such a manner as to meet the requirements of the situation. In many cases, it is necessary for one to collect and organize new material bearing on the problem. Here, the teacher may render valuable assistance without depriving the pupil of the opportunity to work out his own solution and may provide training that will extend beyond the particular exercise at hand.

In the first place, the teacher can acquaint the pupil with the various sources of information and the proper way to consult them for securing needed material. She may suggest procedures for reaching and consulting the most suitable and reliable sources of information.

Besides knowing where and how to find material pertinent to his problem, the pupil should be taught to evaluate the sources. He should be able to distinguish between original and secondary sources and between statements of established fact and interpretations or opinions. He should be sensitive to the particular biases or viewpoints of the author consulted.

Finally, in order that the collected material may be most provocative of suggestions for solving the problem, the material must be organized or arranged according to a meaningful pattern.

Problem solving apparently necessitates not only the bringing of salient information to bear on the problem but also flexibility in not being bound by previous experience and solutions.

SECURING SUGGESTIONS FOR SOLUTION, AND THEIR EVALUATION.   The good teacher will avoid both the giving of too much help and the mere exhortation to think. The pupil should be allowed to do his own thinking, but the teacher can be of service by directing his attention to significant elements in the situation which he has failed to notice or by asking an appropriate question to stimulate the recall of some principle or fact which has an important bearing on the problem.

If inferences do not appear readily, the pupil should be encouraged to search diligently for the right clue. His suggestions for solution or his hypotheses depend upon the relations he discovers among the facts and principles organized around the problem.

If the pupil seems blocked by a false assumption regarding the requirements of the problem, he should be asked to re-examine the problem.

If he persists in repeating a fruitless attack, he should be encouraged to vary his procedure and try out new leads. A good thinker is one who can readily change his approach.

If he is inclined to give up too easily, the teacher should urge him on and point out some of the possibilities which he has not explored. To become a good thinker, the pupil must learn to be persistent.

If he appears tired, confused, or emotionally disturbed, he should be allowed to drop the matter for a while and return to it later. After a period of rest, one is often able to pick up a new lead or see a clue which before had escaped his attention.

The teacher should point out to the pupil the need for an openminded attitude and freedom from prejudice, for biases and preconceived notions are often fatal to sound thinking.

A willingness to venture a guess should be encouraged, not a random guess but an assumption made deliberately with all the available facts in mind. Such an assumption is a hypothesis. Its merits will be determined by studying its implications to see whether it meets the requirements of the situation. No harm is done if it proves to be a false lead. It can be abandoned if it proves to be inadequate, but it might turn out to be a satisfactory solution. Great thinkers sometimes try out hundreds of leads before they find the right one.

The effective direction and training of pupils in problem solving activity will foster a critical attitude toward the suggestions for the solution of a problem. To become a good thinker, the child must learn that when an idea for a solution comes to his mind, it should be regarded as a possibility to be tested before it is accepted as final. He should be taught the importance of suspending judgment until all the available data on the subject are examined for evidence and of seeing the merits and disadvantages of the proposed solution in the light of all the information at hand.

There are a number of things to consider in dealing with faulty proposals for a solution or an erroneous answer to a thought question. If a sensitive child happens to give a ridiculous answer and is laughed at or is made to feel ashamed because of it, he is likely to "close up" and refuse to attempt any further suggestions. Repeated authoritative rebuttals or denunciations by the teacher are likely to produce the same results. When a pupil suggests an absurd answer in good faith, his efforts should be met with a respectful request to tell why he thinks it is a good answer or by questioning that will lead him to discover its defects. If he appears to be merely guessing at random, he should be reminded that he is supposed to find the answer by thinking over what he knows about the subject. In some cases when the child lacks sufficient information to see why his answer or proposal is inadequate, it may be necessary for the teacher to explain why his offering is not correct or sound.

Failure to detect the shortcomings of a proposal for solution may be due to faulty conception of the problem, lack of sufficient information, misinformation, biases and prejudices, unwillingness or lack of desire to exert further effort, or a false assumption of relationship. In helping the pupil to detect the weakness of his hypothesis or the error of his answer, the teacher should take notice of its source and make the attack from that point.

SUMMARY

Thinking is an activity through which an individual arrives at the solution of a problem. The problem is a felt difficulty, and the solution is a new bit of knowledge or a new belief. An important feature of this form of thinking is its employment of symbolic materials. Symbolic meanings provide clues, evidence, and flashes of insight. Just as all thinking is not problem solving, so all problems are not solved by thinking. We often avoid thinking by accepting solutions provided by imagination or memory. When experience or knowledge is lacking, we are prone to resort to overt trial and error.

The characteristic phases in the process of thinking out the solution of a problem are: (1) a difficulty is felt, (2) the problem is clarified and defined, (3) a search for clues is made, (4) various suggestions for solution appear and are evaluated or tested, (5) a solution is accepted or the thinker gives up in defeat, and (6) the solution is tested.

The ability to solve problems by thinking can be improved by training. This improvement results from acquiring the means (knowledge and symbols) to think with and also from learning the best procedures for using these materials effectively. Learning and thinking are linked in two ways: first, we learn by thinking, and second, we improve our ability to think by learning.

Young children solve problematic situations mainly by overt trial and error exploration and manipulation. The ability to solve problems by thinking develops gradually with growth in experience and understanding. Children are inferior to adults in problem thinking principally because of their smaller range of experience. They are less sensitive to problems, have fewer concepts to work with, lack critical judgment, are less capable of sustained attention, and are less able to take an objective attitude toward their problems.

The problem method of teaching secures learning through the solving of problems. Its advantages are: (1) it promotes an active attitude, (2) it fosters confidence in ability to work things out for one's self, (3) the memory value is especially good for things learned in this way, and (4) it provides training in the procedures for thinking out solutions to problems.

In directing and training pupils in problem solving, the teacher's task is: (1) to set the stage for the problem by asking thought questions and by devising and assigning problem exercises, (2) to assist the pupils in clarifying and defining their problem, (3) to stimulate fertility of suggestions for solution and direct the pupil to sources of data bearing on the problem, and (4) to foster a critical attitude toward the suggestions so that they will be properly evaluated and tested before being finally accepted as solutions.

FURTHER READING

Overview

GETZELS, J. W. 1965. Creative thinking, problem-solving, and instruction. In E. R. Hilgard (ed.) *Theories of learning and instruction.* 63rd Yearbook. Chicago: National Soc. for Study of Educ., pp. 240-67.

Selected References

ASCHNER, MARY JANE and C. E. BISH (eds.) 1965. *Productive Thinking in Education.* New York: Nat'l. Educ. Assn. and the Carnegie Corporation.

RUSSELL, D. H. 1956. *Children's Thinking.* Boston: Ginn.

SHULMAN, L. S. and E. R. KEISLAR. 1966. *Learning by Discovery: A Critical Appraisal.* Chicago: Rand-McNally.

VINACKE, W. E. 1952. *The Psychology of Thinking.* New York: McGraw-Hill.

Original Investigations

ANDERSON, H. C. 1965. Can first graders learn an advanced problem solving skill? *J. Educ. Psychol.*, 56: 283-94.

BIRCH, H. C. and H. S. RABINOWITZ. 1951. The negative effect of previous experience on productive thinking. *J. Exper. Psychol.*, 41: 121-25.

DUNCAN, C. P. 1959. Recent research on human problem solving. *Psychol. Bull.*, 56: 397-429.

GOLANN, S. E. 1963. Psychological study of creativity. *Psychol. Bull.,* 60: 548-65.

KERSH, B. 1962. The motivating effect of learning by directed discovery. *J. Educ. Psychol.,* 53: 65-71.

MARQUART, DOROTHY. 1965. Group problem solving. *J. Abn. Soc. Psychol.,* 41: 103-13.

NEWELL, A. and H. SIMON. 1961. Computer simulation of human thinking. *Science,* 134: 2011-16.

SCHRODER, H. M. and J. B. ROTTER. 1953. Rigidity as learned behavior. *J. Exper. Psychol.,* 44: 141-50.

16

The Development of
Attitudes and Ideals

Significant social attitudes are learned in early childhood under parental influence and with strong emotional reinforcement. They include basic values, ideals, and conscious attitudes, which often change very little throughout life. A review of the literature of psychology reveals many different connotations of the term *attitude*. It is used to mean almost any form of set from organic urge, bodily posture, or habit to purposes and ideals. This loose and varied use of the term simply means that a common definition or conception has not been universally adopted. G. W. Allport (1935) provides the following definition after sifting many definitions for their commonalities: "An attitude is a mental and neural state of readiness, organized through experience, exerting a directive or dynamic influence upon the individual's response to all objects and situations to which it is related." More briefly, an attitude is an acquired readiness directing responses to classes of objects. As such it is *inferred* from certain consistencies in behavior patterns.

A similarity between attitudes and motives and concepts is immediately discernible, for we have defined motives as internal states stimulating the organism toward specific goals; and concepts were identified as common responses to dissimilar stimuli. Both are similar to attitudes in being mental and neural states of readiness organized through experience. The differences hinge on activity-passivity and on affective content. Motives are goal oriented and need satisfying, demanding activity by the organism for their satisfaction. Attitudes are latent sets to respond to instigations arising in the environment. Thus, one may be prejudiced against Negroes, although never having encountered one and thus never having had the occasion to respond directly in terms of this attitude. In contrast to concepts, attitudes have an affective dimension, an approach-avoidance direction of feeling and an intensity that is lacking with concepts. All three are acquired forms of behavior, but attitudes are distinguished by the approach-avoidance dimension, the affective content and the intensity of response, and the dependence on the environment for elicitation. Attitudes, then, are acquired and enduring states of readiness to respond in a consistent fashion to a set of social objects—persons, events, or things. Attitudes differ from interests. Interest refers to positive actions directed toward specific objects or events. Attitudes may be either positive or negative and encompass a class or group of social objects; thus they are more general. Attitudes are similar to habits in being consistent response sets, but again they are less specific than habits and involve an emotional content that many habits lack.

Rosenberg and Hovland (1960) diagram the bridge that attitudes provide between environmental events and behavior as follows.

Schematic Conception of Attitudes

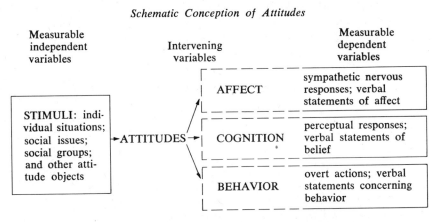

The diagram suggests that attitudes incorporate both feelings and beliefs and evaluation of objects and events on both an emotional and cognitive level. In the latter domain, attitudes overlap beliefs, values, and ideals and rationalized convictions of right and wrong, of the good and the ideal. Attitudes serve both personal and social functions. Like concepts, they provide ready-made bases for evaluating and responding to environmental events. They serve a protective function and an energy conservation function. Socially, they insure a sufficient uniformity of group response necessary to a stable social order. Each group, each society sets standards for its members to follow. Each teaches what to value, whom to admire and emulate, and whom to dislike and avoid. These established prejudgments serve as a basis for collective response. For example, the value we attach to law and order and the subordinate attitude toward criminals provide for an immediate mobilization of social reaction to a riot: it violates an important value, the behavior is criminal, therefore the perpetrators or participants are to be so treated. No need to inquire further; our predispositions provide the basis for forming a judgment and acting. So the prevailing attitude two generations ago about "foreigners," "immigrants," and "socialists" permitted a social acceptance of the Sacco-Vanzetti conviction which is now in question in retrospect. And the historical view of the peasants' revolt and the Thirty Years' War following the Protestant Reformation differs from that of the German landowners and Luther himself. In a like manner, history will render a different perspective of race relations in this country during the last half of this century.

We are all conscious of the fact that our attitudes change, although we are not sure how much or why. We do not know whether it is because of aging, reading, watching television, listening to influential friends, or other conditions which produce the change. An important demonstration of change in attitude among a fairly homogeneous group of women graduates of Vassar College is provided by Freedman (1966). The data are responses to questions in the California Public Opinion Survey (Adorno et al., 1950) taken between 1956 and 1961 of women who graduated during the years indicated in Table 16.1.

ATTITUDE MEASUREMENT

If, as pointed out, attitudes are predispositions to respond in given ways derived from earlier experience, then a description of an attitude, qualitative or quantitative, has to be inferred from certain aspects and certain consistencies of behavior. Statements such as: She has a positive attitude toward life, or, He's certainly rabid about communists, or, Don't get her started talking about pewter, contain inferences about attitudes based on observed regularities in behavior. The Rosenberg-Hovland diagram suggests two sets of variables; those found in the situation, those in the individual. Primary in the latter are the affective and cognitive dimensions, but other characteristics such as motives, interests, perceptions, and so on, influence behavior. Verbal responses are distinguished from overt behavior; not because the verbal responses are not overt, but to allow for

TABLE 16.1   ITEM FROM CALIFORNIA PUBLIC OPINION SURVEY*

| | Percentage of favorable responses given by women graduates of classes of | | | |
| | *1904* | *1921-1924* | *1940-1943* | *1956* |
N =	85	73	77	200
What this country needs most, more than laws and political programs, is a few courageous, tireless, devoted leaders in whom people can put their faith.	83	68	43	56
Obedience and respect for authority are the most important virtues that children should learn.	65	48	23	49
Human nature being what it is, there will always be war and conflict.	56	79	63	70
Science has its place but there are many important things that can never possibly be understood by the human mind.	71	63	58	61

*From Freedman, 1966.

the fact that words and actions can differ—we often do not practice what we preach.

Measures of attitudes rely heavily on verbal responses, which we know will differ from behavior. Reconciliation of the discrepancy lies less in discounting verbal statements than in recognizing that different sets of variables are operable. Verbal statements are likely to give greater credence to ideals or to isolated factors where actions are governed by the specifics of given situations, often involving multiple cross-currents. Thus, two college graduates may profess democratic sentiments, but only the one threatened with loss of education for his children may act to desegregate schools rather than close them. This event involves a conflict in attitudes felt by one but not the other. A quite different discrepancy is seen when voters state they are undecided about whom to vote for. Some will be truly uncertain, others will not want to tell the interviewer who their choice is.

Cook and Sellitz (1964) list five major kinds of attitude measures:

1. Those depending on self-report of beliefs, feelings, behavior, and so on, about a class of objects.
   Example: Questionnaires of interviews in which respondents agree or disagree with statements, e.g., Table 16.1.
2. Measures based on inferences from observed behavior.
   Examples: Inferences made from role playing in specified situations; program selections of television viewers.
3. Measures permitting inferences from reactions to partially structured material pertaining to an object.

Examples: Projective tests involving selected objects; drawings of children about "my family."

4. Inferences made from task performance which is subject to influence from disposition toward the object.

Examples: Differences in retention of memorized materials which are favorable and unfavorable toward the objects; assigning statements along a favorable–unfavorable continuum as with a Thurstone type scale, or designating attributes on a Semantic Differential scale.

5. Measures involving physiological reactions.

Examples: Recording of eye blinking, palm sweating, or pulse in connection with exposure to given objects.

Each technique assumes a high correlation between the overt response and the private attitude and assumes also that it successfully excludes the intrusion of non-attitudinal determinants of response. Success in the first instance is determined by the extent to which the purpose of the task— whether it is an interview, a questionnaire, or some other task—is apparent to the person being tested, whether or not the implications of responses to specific items are clear and subject to conscious control. Each technique has its advantages and disadvantages. The intent of questions is discernible. Blind questions can be included to mislead the respondent; role playing requires a speed of response in a semi-fluid situation which makes conscious control difficult; projective techniques gain in ambiguity but lose in the extent to which they exclude extraneous influences. In all situations, pressure to agree with perceived norms exists—social norms which are both general and implicit in the situation and personal norms implicit in the self-image one desires to maintain. For example, a young man on a commercial vehicle in the South may avoid sitting with Negroes; his counterpart in the North may not hesitate to do so; both may be equally prejudiced but are governed by social norms. Both may act alike in riding in an Army truck, though their attitudes may remain the same. Finally, both may change their attitudes and behavior as a result of service under combat conditions. The correspondence of stated and actual behavior, of behavior under different social conditions, and behavior under different conditions of personal involvement, all operate to produce inconsistency in the different measures of attitude. These will continue in spite of increased sophistication of the respondents (they are less easily misled) and in spite of the increased sophistication of attitude measures (they are more indirect in their tactics).

STUDIES OF ATTITUDES OF CHILDREN AND STUDENTS

We are living in a world of rapidly changing social conditions. Old procedures and old solutions are inadequate to cope with the new problems which the changing order presents. Given the accelerating rate of change, the demands to be faced by future generations will be such that fixed patterns of response based on past or present conditions will be inadequate. The problems challenge their versatility and resourcefulness. Changes will inevitably come, and there must be a readiness to adjust to them. If social change is not to outrun our democratic processes, the school must instill in the young certain democratic attitudes and ideals. These, if developed, may be expected to direct creative effort along the lines of a democratic order.

Reports of studies made of the attitudes of school pupils indicate that our schools have not been particularly successful in instilling democratic attitudes. The findings indicate that a large proportion of the young people are possessed of prejudices and views which are not in keeping with democratic principles. For example, H. E. Jones (1938) found that 62 percent of the first year pupils of a favorably situated high school expressed a dislike for all radicals, 65 percent agreed that foreign radicals should not be allowed to visit the United States, 71 percent would not allow radical agitators to speak publicly in parks and streets, and 24 percent supported the statement that armies are necessary in dealing with backward peoples. Recent studies by Remmers at Purdue a decade ago show that a generation has made small change. A majority of adolescents can be found in possession of attitudes which run counter to constitutional rights. The fact is less a failure by the school than a default, even recognizing that attitudes stem from many sources besides school. The schools have assumed that reference to and discussion of values and ideals will suffice, ignoring the affective and behavioral dimensions. As a result, students know about values, but do not necessarily believe in them.

Democracy cannot prosper in a nation whose people are heavily loaded with religious and racial prejudices and class hatreds and antagonisms. Education for democratic citizenship calls for the prevention and removal of such inimical attitudes and the establishment of such favorable ones as:

1. Belief in the "inalienable rights" of the individual.
2. Acceptance of the principle of equality of privilege.
3. Tolerance of the views of others and a willingness to allow these views to be expressed.
4. Respect for the individuality of other persons.
5. A willingness to accept social responsibilities.
6. A willingness to abide by the decisions of the majority.
7. A willingness to protect minority rights.
8. A willingness to arbitrate conflicts of interests.

Many studies have been made to determine the nature of the attitudes of children and students. These studies have dealt with a large variety of subjects, such as racial preferences, views on various social issues, preferences for school subjects, and attitudes toward God and the church. No attempt is made here to summarize all this literature. A few studies are mentioned briefly for the purpose of illustrating the character of the work done in this field.

Racial Preferences and Prejudices. Zeligs (1950, 1951, 1954) has completed several investigations of intergroup attitudes among elementary school children; these provide information regarding the prejudices and attitudes of children, and have the advantage of being comparisons of similar groups of children at a thirteen year interval. In comparing the attitudes of sixth grade children in the same school in a midwestern community toward Irish, Finnish, several middle-European, Hindu, and Filipino groups, Zeligs found a negligible change in thirteen years in the proportions of favorable and unfavorable attitudes but a slight increase in neutral attitudes, possibly because of lack of familiarity with some of the groups mentioned. Granting the limitations inherent in attitude measurement, which aside from the technical problems assumes a close relationship between verbal response and actual behavior, the author concluded that education aimed at creating favorable intercultural attitudes left much to be desired. When asked reasons for preferences and rejections of various nationality groups listed, a series of characteristics stressing cultural similarities and differences, stereotypes with respect to intelligence, honesty, fairplay, and the like were given. In the thirteen year period, the reasons reported reflected a shift from racial and physical characteristics to form of government and kind of leader as a basis for preference. The fact that the follow-up study occurred during the war years leads one to believe that the shift reflects wartime allegiances and attitudes. But attitudes and prejudices are in part built upon group-held norms and are not dependent upon actual experience with the discriminated group.

In her most recent study, Zeligs points out the persistence of attitudes and prejudices ingrained in early childhood. However, she notes some lessening of anti-Negro prejudice, some increase in expressed sympathy, and some increase in feelings of guilt and social responsibility. Stevenson and Stewart (1958) and Frenkel-Brunswik and Havel (1953) corroborate these conclusions. The former, studying Negro and white children between the ages of 3 and 7 conclude that white children distinguish and discriminate between races at a younger age and show a greater preference for their own race. By the age of school, Negro children show less preference for their own race than white children and assign more negative roles to Negroes. The Frenkel-Brunswik and Havel population was older—1500 children of ages 14-17—from which highly prejudiced, moderate, and tolerant samples were studied. Frenkel-Brunswik and Havel concluded that the children as a group were prejudiced and the feelings were deep-seated. Again, Bevan, Katz and Secerd (1956) find white students exaggerating the stereotypical responses to the Negro as superstitious, lazy, emotional, and immoral in contrast to assigning more favorable attributes to whites. Of interest was the heightened perception of Negroes in a mixed group of photographs by both anti-Negro and pro-Negro adolescents in contrast with impartial judges.

Two early studies of attitudes (Bogardus, 1927; Katz and Brady, 1933) repeated after approximately a twenty year interval (Bogardus, 1947; Gilbert, 1951) show the persistence of cultural norms. Bogardus developed a Social Distance Scale in which subjects were asked if they would be willing to admit members of various national groups to close kinships by marriage, to a club as a personal friend, to the same street, to the same employment, or to United States citizenship. In both the original survey and the follow-up, the sample exceeded 1500 native-born Americans having high school education or better. Results are seen in Table 16.2.

TABLE 16.2   SOCIAL DISTANCE EXPRESSED TOWARDS SPECIFIC
GROUPS.

Social distance: Willing to accept in	English	German	German Jew	Negro
marriage	94%	54%	8%	1%
friendship	97	67	22	9
neighborhood	97	79	26	12
employment	95	83	40	39
citizenship	96	87	54	57

*After Bogardus, 1927.

Results of the follow-up study showed a modest shift towards more favorable attitudes but essentially the same ranking. Recounting the existence of prejudice confirms what we know. Its continuity over time testifies to its resistance to change in the face of intellectual and social efforts to the contrary. The pervasiveness of prejudice is seen not only in the preschool Negro children who exhibit the formation of unfavorable self-images but in the fact that Negro college students parallel the Katz and Brady Princeton men in typing the Negro as a group with the same stereotype even though perceiving themselves individually in a more favorable light (Bayton, 1941; Gray and Thompson, 1953).

In a study of a large number of Negro adolescents, Beckham (1934) found that by the age of twelve most of them had experienced some form of unfavorable discrimination or humiliation because of their race. The effects most often produced were resentment, aloofness, antagonism, and in some cases, a strong desire for personal achievement. A majority thought white teachers were usually fair, but a number complained that teachers showed discrimination in favor of white children in grades, positions of leadership, seating, sympathy, derogatory remarks about Negroes, and in discouraging the Negro pupils from taking part in extracurricular activities. In exploring the experiences of Negro youth in Miami, Florida, Hindman

(1953) found that contact between Negro and white students was limited, occurring mainly in stores, on public transportation, and on jobs. Prejudicial attitudes were supported by maintaining social distance, and verbal antagonism was listed as a frequent unpleasant experience. Negroes are not alone in this experience. Minority groups commonly encounter social rejection, although the Negro is more easily singled out.

Winnowing out the impact of prejudice on attitude is a complex task, because it becomes involved with a variety of other variables such as parental attitudes, educational and economic opportunities, availability of economic and social resources, personality factors, and the like. Three studies in differing disciplines indicate a generally negative effect. Hammer (1953) had the drawings of Negro and white children from segregated schools in a border state evaluated anonymously by clinicians for aggression and found a higher incidence of frustration and aggression in both white and Negro children, giving support to the theories of Symonds and Maslow that social discrimination is perceived as rejection with consequent aggressive responses. Roens (1960) predicted a general denigrating effect expressed in an observed greater correlation between lower intelligence test scores, lack of self-confidence, anxiety, and adjustment, than occurred in a group of white, comparable group of soldiers matched for age, education, parental occupation, geographic origin, and length of military service. These findings agree with those of Clark (1962) showing more hostility, withdrawal, and defeatest attitudes among Negro children in New York. Underscoring these negative effects, McQueen and Churn (1960) found that Negro and white children, matched for age, sex, grade, years in elementary school, father's occupation, and proximity of dwelling in an integrated community with stable Negro and white population, showed non-significant differences in intelligence test scores, achievement, and attitude toward school. The validity of racial comparisons hinges on the adequacy of sampling and the representativeness of the groups tested, and many interpretations can be ventured. However, the bias introduced by deficiencies in sampling are probably not as serious as the biases introduced by differences in the attitudes of the observers.

Academic Preferences.   In any ordering of preference for school subjects, the rankings will be bound by the experience and exposure of the students. The result is that we find the conventional subjects ordered. The same holds true in the ranking of preferences for television programs. One can only rank what he has been presented; little opportunity occurs to express opinions about programs which might be offered. Given curricular limitations, subjects such as spelling and arithmetic receive higher rankings than social studies or history (S. Josephina, 1959; Mosher, 1952). A more general finding at both high school (Brodie, 1964) and college levels (Brown, 1954) is the link between an attitude of expressed satisfaction with school, both academically and in social acceptance, and scholastic success in school.

However, satisfaction with school is also linked with socio-economic status (Coster, 1958; Montague, 1962) with the result that cause and effect are confused. Children from middle class levels approach school with more positive attitudes, which when reinforced by success, auger for satisfaction. Success, however, is not restricted to such children.

Various studies have shown that the reading interests of boys and girls differ somewhat both in childhood and in the adolescent period. Boys in the elementary school years are likely to be most interested in reading about war, athletics, and adventure whereas girls like fairy tales and stories dealing with home or school life. Girls become interested in romantic novels earlier than boys. In adolescence, girls favor love stories and reading that deals with travel and home life. Boys of the adolescent age generally prefer such subjects as sports, outdoor life, adventure, inventions, and machinery. Annual studies by Witty at Northwestern University of TV program preferences of children show comparable developments in choice.

So far as attitude toward school is concerned, Tenenbaum (1944) reports that 20 percent of 639 sixth and seventh grade New York City school pupils were dissatisfied with school and 40 percent were critical of many phases. Girls reflected more favorable attitudes than boys. Fortunately for teachers, the negative feelings were directed against the school as an institution rather than against the teacher as a person, which confirms findings of the author. Perhaps it is premature to say, "fortunately for teachers," for the possibility is real that children are reluctant and fearful of directing their criticism against an authority figure and substitute the school as a safer target. In general, however, the concept of going to school is the one that is established rather than going to a teacher, so that the attitude is more likely to be generalized.

Religious Attitudes.   The results of an investigation of students' attitudes toward God and church at three large universities and three denominational colleges indicated that few students were inclined to be atheistic. There appeared to be no important differences between the attitudes of the two sexes and little change in religious attitudes during the four years in college. The attitudes of the students in the denominational colleges were somewhat more favorable than those of university students.

A study by Spoerl (1951) suggests possible differential effects of religion on attitudes. Using a group of 926 college students, drawn one-third from a single public school system and Jewish, Protestant, and Catholic in a ratio of 1:2:3, Spoerl gave each student a Bogardus Social Distance Scale on which they indicated preference for various national and racial groups, ranging from a high of "willing to marry" to a low of "exclude from this country." Although no significant differences in the average prejudice occurred between the three religious groups, differences in the pattern of prejudice appeared. The Protestant and Catholic students emerged from the given school system more tolerant, the Jewish students less tolerant than those from outside the system. Protestant prejudice was directed toward "minority" groups, Jewish toward "majority" groups, and the Catholic against what was termed "heathen." Differential effects of religion on attitudes have been reported by Remmers in his surveys of adolescent interests. However, the limited number of studies involving religious biases precludes definitive statements. Seemingly, sex behavior is less private than religious beliefs.

Young adolescents are generally rather conservative with respect to sociological matters, and the tendency is for them to become more liberal with increase in knowledge and personal experience with the issues. A number of studies have thrown light on the attitudes of youths relative to social and economic problems. In regard to such issues as prohibition and communism, adolescent attitudes differ to about the same extent as those of adults and probably reflect the opinions and feelings of the older persons with whom these young people are associated. More detail will be presented in the section on attitude change.

War.   During the years before World War II, a large number of studies were made of the attitudes of high school and college students toward war. In practically all of these where definite scores were obtained by means of attitude scales, the mean scores for both men and women fill in the divisions labeled "mildly pacifistic," "strongly pacifistic," or "moderately opposed to war." The women usually were found to be slightly more pacifistic than the men. In a number of cases, the same students were retested later in their course to discover whether there were shifts in their attitudes. There were shifts in some cases by some individuals toward greater pacifism; these were offset by shifts of others in the opposite direction, leaving the mean score of the group about the same (Dudycha, 1942). But several retest studies indicated a small but definite shift toward greater pacifism (Corey, 1940; Farnsworth, 1937; Jones, 1938, 1942).

With the outbreak of war in Europe, there was some indication of a shift away from the pacifist attitude. Then came the Pearl Harbor attack and our entry into the war in full force. Students who had been taught by the school, the church, the radio, the movies, and the press to regard war as a horrible thing and futile as a means of settling disputes between nations— students who had acquired from their teachers, parents, and pastors attitudes which set them against war—were suddenly told that they must become soldiers, fighters, and killers because arbitration and conciliation had failed. The result was confusion, doubt, and disillusionment. The emotional shock to many was great.

It was not easy to embark on a course absolutely opposed to one's deep-seated feelings and convictions. But social pressure and law made it practically impossible to do otherwise. High-pressure propaganda, fear of consequences if the war were not won, and war hysteria did much to make over the feelings and opinions of many. Others, not being able to escape from years of training, entered upon their duties with resentment against war but sustained by an urgent desire to get the "dirty mess" over as soon as possible, a faith in the possibility of an enduring peace, and confidence in their ability to manage in the future the affairs of the nation more successfully than their elders had done it.

No one who has had contact with young adults in recent history can escape seeing the lack of enthusiasm and the conflict in feelings engendered by both the Korean and Vietnam conflicts. Overt opposition has been freely expressed by a minority; as for the majority, their attitudes express a sense of unavoidable social responsibility in conflict with opposing personal desires, not unlike their parents at the time of World War II.

ACQUISITION OF ATTITUDES

Attempting to isolate the sources of attitude is impossible, for they are so intricately imbedded in the matrix of social experience; identifying the processes by which attitudes develop is possible because they are fewer. However well we can describe the process, weighing their relative contribution is beyond our present state of knowledge. Where the objects which frighten us or provoke our anxieties are idiosyncratic, our attitudes are social—predispositions held in common by members of a group. Understanding them requires understanding culture and society and their functioning.

Each culture, however unique, is a functional solution to the problems of living in a given environment. Its continuity requires its being transmitted from generation to generation; the process we call socialization is essentially the transformation of a child into an adult, the person who behaves, more or less, as prescribed by the society. This means respecting the values, possessing the attitudes, and behaving appropriately. One aspect of being socialized is acquiring the prevailing attitudes existing within a society. Primitive societies, by virtue of smaller numbers and greater stability over time, possessed greater uniformity; a pluralistic society, by definition, suggests a diversity of values and attitudes, but even these fall within certain bounds. A certain range of economic, religious, political, and social views is tolerated, others are oppressed. The Amish, Jehovah's Witnesses, Communists, pacifists experience pressures to conform to various prescribed standards. Certainly, primary social attitudes can scarcely be viewed apart from the society as a whole. Heer (1959) points out the ecological factors in a study which supported the premises that the variation in percentages of the segregationist vote in southern counties would be correlated with the social and economic gains resulting therefrom, using density of Negro population and percentage of white farm population as indicators. Social class status is another of the sociological factors associated with attitudes, in addition to the economic, political and demographic. Middle and lower class families differ, for example, in their attitudes toward education. Such differences communicated to children affect their motivation toward school.

An interesting illustration of the generality of the process of socialization within a culture is seen in two studies of attitudes, the first conducted at three Ivy League colleges by Allport and Kramer (1946), the second an exact replication in nine South Dakota colleges, both public and denominational, by Rosenblith (1949). The findings, which will only be touched on here, were quite similar, despite the geographic and economic differences in the groups:

1. Similar anti-Negro–anti-Semitic prejudices.
2. The more equal status contacts, the less prejudice.
3. A positive correlation between religious training and prejudice.
4. College trained parents have less prejudiced children.
5. Association between prejudice and clinging to parental patterns.
6. Disapproval of civil rights legislation linked with prejudice.
7. Acquisition of prejudice against minorities without having direct experience with them.
8. Prejudices take root where people view the world as threatening and hostile.

Imitation and Role Playing. Although imitation was early identified by sociologists as a process by which social behavior was acquired, the dominance of S-R psychology and reinforcement in experimental psychology and psychoanalytic concepts in clinical psychology resulted in its being given little attention as a factor in learning until recently. One way in which children acquire behavior patterns, including related emotional and attitudinal features, is through imitating their parents and other models —in short, learning by observation and replication. Such efforts at imitation do not go unrewarded, if by no more than an indulgent smile of amusement or prohibition when the child imitates paternal profanity with proper emphasis. But much imitation goes on privately and persistently as young children create play situations, minor duplications of daily life dramas. If each parent, sibling, or other model engaged in unique behavior patterns, imitation would serve personal development more than socialization. But the adults we encounter are engaged in carrying out certain roles in the social order, each with their particular patterns of behavior. By definition, roles are consistent patterns of behavior associated with specified positions in a social structure and possessed of certain obligations and rewards. Thus, most fathers, most policemen, most doctors, most teachers act more or less alike. They fulfill the behavior expected of one holding their position. Teachers expect children to obey, defer, change activity on direction, ask permission, and so on. Teachers are expected to organize, to follow the curriculum, to avoid controversial issues, to not be ostentatious, and the like. For teachers, it is cloth coats and print dresses, not minks and miniskirts. Bandura and several associates at Stanford University (Ross, Walters and McDonald) have carried out a series of studies demonstrating the im-

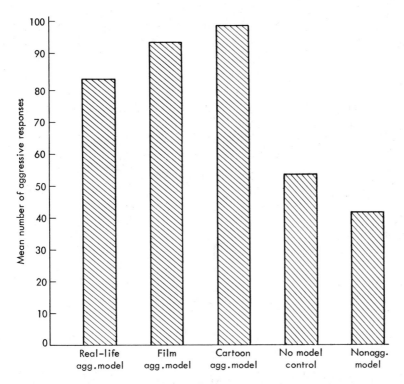

Fig. 16.1 Mean frequency of aggressive responses performed by control children and by those who had been exposed to aggressive and inhibited models. (From Bandura: NIH Grant, M5162, 1964.)

portance of imitation of models in the developing behavioral and attitudinal patterns of young children. In one study (Bandura, Ross and Ross, 1961), four groups of nursery school children observed adult models engaging in aggressive behavior of different degrees of relatively unique forms of physical and verbal aggression toward a large, inflated Bobo-doll. A fifth group served as a control group. One group saw a highly aggressive human model; the second saw a film of the same behavior; a third group saw a milder model; the fourth saw a cartoon version. During the acquisition period, the children simply watched the model's behavior. Subsequently, they were mildly frustrated then tested for the amount of imitative and non-matching aggressive behavior. As Figure 16.1 shows, imitation of the precise aggressive behavior occurred in higher frequency with aggressive models.

As Bandura points out (1964), exposure to models has several effects: (1) opportunity to learn new response patterns, (2) strengthening or weakening of inhibitions about engaging in the observed behavior, (3) eliciting previously acquired but dormant responses.

Imitation does not occur in a vacuum, not so long as adults are present. It was pointed out earlier how some imitative response will be rewarded, others discouraged. Bandura pursued the interaction of reinforcement and modeling behavior. Figure 16.2 shows certain results of the interaction of sex differences, social approval of the models' behavior, and rewarded child behavior. To explain: under one condition, the child not only observed the behavior of the model but saw it generously rewarded; in the second, the model was punished; and consequences occurred to the third. Subsequently, the children were provided opportunity to engage in similar behavior. First noted was the greater inclination of the boys to engage in the observed behavior regardless of whether the model had been rewarded or not. Both boys and girls were less likely to engage in behavior which they had seen punished, i.e., which received social disapproval. However, these differences in willingness to perform the observed behavior were no indication of their having learned what they observed, for when incentives were offered the children, all groups showed equivalent learning.

Thus, the interplay of modeled behavior, consequences to the model, incentive and motivational conditions provide a complex set of determinants

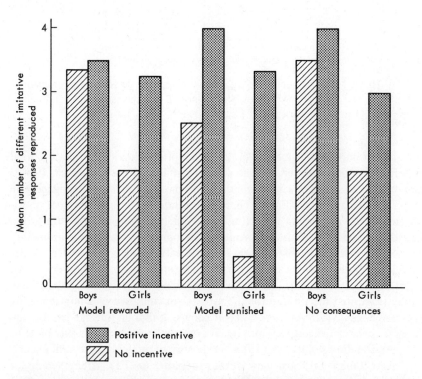

Fig. 16.2 Mean number of matching different responses reproduced by children as a function of response consequences to the model and positive incentives. (From Bandura: NIH Grant, M5162, 1964.)

of both acquisition of responses and their performance. Motivational dispositions focus attention on selected aspects of the complex patterns of behavior to which a child is exposed. Obviously, conceptual development will limit what the child can comprehend, but within this range one may find a young boy imitating his father's gestures, while a girl may imitate a tone of voice taken from the same set of circumstances. Contiguity in time of response and stimulus conditions appear to suffice for learning to occur. Reinforcement appears as a determinant of whether or not and under what circumstances the acquired behavior will be performed. When the consequences to the model are unfavorable, the response may be inhibited. (Such is our social theory justifying execution for murder. Make an example of murderers in order to deter imitative social behavior. Here, however, the factors producing homicide differ from those producing acquisition of responses by imitation. Most murderers know their victims and highly involved motivational conditions exist.) Finally, where incentives exist, the observed behavior may be produced regardless of the consequences to the model. Pop singers and the fads they induce may receive the general disapproval of parents, but their behavior is adopted by teenagers.

Imitation does not imply an exact replication of the observed behavior. For one thing, the significant individuals in our lives, those who serve as our models, exhibit variations in their behavior in response to similar situations, permitting some choice to the observer. The way in which each of us resolves these discrepancies in behavior is affected by our own needs and personality. In fact, we acquire a concept of ourselves based on reactions of others to us, demands imposed, and a growing self-awareness. This self-concept adds a personal dimension to the kinds of choices we make of whom we will imitate and how. Finally, we do not have direct personal experience with all referent individuals. Cultures have their heroes, presented in story and film, replete with the full panoply of legend, providing each person the opportunity to select his ideal and conjure his own vision of how he acted.

Group Pressures.   Parents, older siblings, and friends not only provide models but possess the added power of authority. Where the television performer may appeal to us because of his prestige, the groups to which we belong can impose direct sanctions to govern our behavior. Behavior in early childhood and the acquisition of attitudes is dominated by parental action. In a survey of 3000 children in New York, Martin (1952) found that favorable attitudes in children are associated with parents who accept children, help them, participate with them in some activities, and exhibit coöperative attitudes with each other. Rejection, deprivation, overprotection, and exploitation contribute to negative attitudes. These broad generalizations that attitudes of children are formed in the context of parental opinion, belief, and prejudice find support in more limited but better controlled studies linking parent action to child attitude and behavior. Two important variables are the degree of dominance or authority exerted and the degree of acceptance–rejection. Dependent, submissive, or highly punished children develop greater deference to authority, more rigidity and orderliness, and higher degrees of prejudice. The Adorno, *et al.* (1950) study was an extensive investigation into the roots of ethnocentrism and prejudice. Much simpler in scale is the more recent study of Weatherly (1963) linking anti-Semitism in daughters to the severity of punishment by their mothers. Severity of punishment in conjunction with sex of parent has been shown to be an important determinant in aggressive feelings and its mode of expression. Paralleling this generalization is that of Kounin and Gump (1961) showing that school children (urban, lower and middle class first graders) having punitive teachers manifest more aggression in misconduct, more conflict about it, and more negative attitudes toward school.

In the American culture, the impact of the nuclear family on developing attitudes is heightened by the intensity of the emotional relationships existing within the small family group. Notwithstanding, groups play a key role in mediating the reciprocal needs of society and individuals. Social institutions would overpower individuals were it not for small groups. The stereotype of the Marine leatherneck suggests the subordination of the individual to the institution; that of the hippie the rejection of social institutions. Small groups serve as the intermediary, protecting the individual and allowing him latitude, at the same time requiring conformance with group standards for continued acceptance within the group. Figure 16.3, taken from Marple's study of comparative susceptibility to influence, indicates the importance of a group judgment in shaping opinion. Studies by Sherif and by Asch during the last two decades amply demonstrate the susceptibility of individual to group judgments. The more ambiguous the situation, the younger the subject, the less crucial the issue, and the greater the consensus of opinion, the greater the willingness of individuals to ignore their own perceptions and conform to the group judgment. The closer the issue to deep-seated beliefs or the presence of some support, the more individuals will stand by their judgment.

Groups serve two further functions beside that of persuasion. They provide standards for comparison, and they establish norms for behavior. Groups vary along a continuum from those in which we interact with only nominal degrees of affiliation such as work groups, to those with high degrees of identity such as family and friendship. Somewhere between are groups which can be designated as valuation groups because of the points of reference they provide—professional organizations, labor groups, political groups, church groups, and the like.

Attempts to identify the influence of schools on attitudes have failed to show significant effects. In the next section on attitude change, the role of the school will be discussed further, but certain observations are relevant at this point. One of the difficulties in tracing their influence is the assumption that the attitudes and values supported by the school differ from those of the families. To the extent that family and school are congruent, the in-

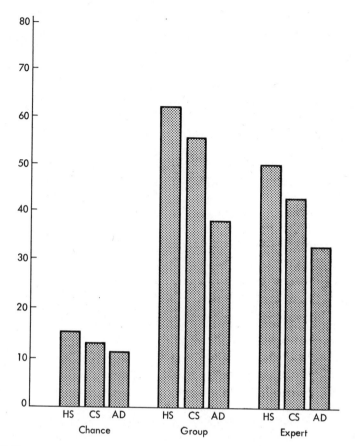

Fig. 16.3
Changes in opinion due to "chance," to "group," and to "expert" opinion, for a high school group, a college group, and an adult group. In all three instances, influences decreased with age. (From Clare H. Marple. 1933. The Comparative Susceptibility of Three Age Levels to the Suggestion of Group Versus Expert Opinion. *J. of Social Psychol.*, 4:176-86.)

fluence of the family will appear predominant. Further, although teachers often serve in a model role, providing observations of appropriate behavior and also offering cognitive information about values, they generally ignore the natural children's groups which exist, the norms they hold, and the attitude-shaping role they play. Teacher influence is greater with younger children but with adolescents, the influence of adults, including that of teachers, wanes relative to the power of the peer group in shaping values. To the extent that differing values or differing interpretations need to evolve in the face of social changes, this independence provides such opportunity. To the extent that some attitudes such as prejudice are socially destructive, this failure to exert an influence is socially damaging. Nevertheless, if schools wish to become a systematic influence on attitudes, greater cognizance of group processes will be required.

Personal Development and Experience.   In addition to the social influences in the formation of attitudes, a variety of kinds of individual experience and personal events serve as predisposing or formative conditions in the development or changing of attitudes. We engage in a continuous stream of experiences, some of which have the potential for initiating or changing attitudes. Wrightman and Noble (1965) showed that one effect of the assassination of President Kennedy on college students who identified with him was a disillusionment with human nature, which proved on retest to be temporary. This effect was not observed on those with neutral or negative feeling about Kennedy. Here was a single, traumatic event, which momentarily at least, produced a shift in attitudes. In a similar but less traumatic vein, Maccoby and Wilson (1957) showed seventh grade pupils identified with certain film characters—in relation to their own aspirations, sex, and motives—and recalled those characters' words and actions better than those of other characters.

Sex, ordinal position in the family, and personality characteristics relate to certain attitudes. Both first-born children and women tend to conform more to group opinion or be more persuasible than their opposites (Scheidel, 1963; Arrowood and Amoroso, 1965). In a small sample of college students, Stock (1949) found those holding negative feelings toward themselves inclined to hold negative feelings toward others, and the feelings toward others grew positive as the student's self-concept improved. Thus, attitude formation is not entirely the absorption of social prescription but the interaction of personality with environmental events.

Finally, instruction can have both direct and indirect effects upon attitude formation. In an ingenious demonstration of conditioning, Staats and Staats (1958) systematically paired positive or negative evaluative words spoken aloud with national names such as Swedish or Dutch as the latter were flashed on a screen for five seconds. Control was provided by allowing other national names such as Greek or German to remain neutral. A similar procedure was followed with selected masculine names such as Tom or Bill. Testing subsequent reactions with a semantic differential scale, the experimenters found their group of ninety-three college students subsequently responded to the selected names with a negative or positive reaction related to the test pairing to a significant degree. An indirect effect with elementary school children resulted from foreign language training (Riestra and Johnson, 1964). One by-product of the language instruction was more favorable attitudes toward Spanish-speaking people.

The permanence of the effects on attitudes of personal experiences of the kind just described is not known. Some are undoubtedly transitory, but others become one in a sequence of events which shape attitudes.

Emotional Experiences.   Attitudes—particularly likes and dislikes, attractions and aversions, interests and antagonisms—are often traceable to some strong emotional experience or to incidents or associations of a definitely pleasant or unpleasant nature. So strong is the tendency for one to assume a favorable or unfavorable attitude toward persons or things associated with a pleasant or unpleasant experience that the process through which such attitudes are established appears to be a form of conditioning.

A teacher writes:

> As a child, I spent a summer vacation with an aunt who had no children and, I suppose, didn't know what to expect of a child of my age. She believed that every girl must be a good seamstress. I had done very simple sewing before, more in the way of play than anything else, but she gave me things to do that really were too difficult for any child of my age. Naturally, I had a very hard time trying to do what she told me to do, to say nothing about sticking the needle into myself often. Invariably, what I did turned out badly and I was reprimanded severely for it each time. The effect of that has always stayed with me. Even to this day, I hate sewing and never do any unless it is absolutely necessary. That one summer's experience destroyed any desire on my part to sew, although I had previously enjoyed making dolls' clothes, even though they were not great successes. Another and far more serious effect was that I took a dislike to that aunt and never wanted to visit there again.

THE MODIFICATION OF ATTITUDES

Given all the conditions which affect the acquisition of attitudes, one may end with the impression that attitudes are in a constant state of change, depending upon momentary influences. While it is true that attitudes are constantly changing, the rate of change may be like that of the earth's crust. The external appearance of the surface of the earth is slowly changing through natural and artificial events. Accumulating geological data suggest a slow change in the movement of the continents and in the surfaces beneath the ocean. On the time scale of a lifetime, attitudes undergo an analogous change, in the way they manifest themselves externally and in their internal structure. A dramatic example of change in recent years is the present willingness to accept the possibility of living beings at other points in the universe. Within a generation, the belief that earthman was an exclusive creation has given way to a tentative acceptance of the probability of life in some form, and possibly in complex organic form, elsewhere in the universe, if not in our galaxy.

Once attitudes are acquired, the question arises as to the conditions which cause them to change. In general, the influences operating are those identified above—social, group, and personality factors. More narrowly, the question concerns the susceptibility to persuasion, and the many variables operating can be viewed with regard to the extent that they induce change from an existing position. A wide gamut of studies which bear on the question is available in the fields of social psychology, communication and mass media, and experimental psychology. Hovland (1959) provides a helpful starting point in summarizing a number of conditions which affect the degree of attitude change occurring as a result of exposure to communication.

Field studies and laboratory studies of the impact of communications upon an audience show considerable discrepancy, field studies showing small changes at best whereas laboratory studies indicate that large shifts in attitude are possible. Some of the differences are inherent in the methodology of the studies (survey versus controlled experiment), more of the differences are associated with the differential affects of the same variables as they interact with one another. The influential variables and the manner in which they differ in field and laboratory are listed and discussed below.

The most frequent subjects of laboratory studies of persuasion are students, usually college students. They are more homogeneous with regard to intelligence, education, and socio-economic background than is a random sample of the general population. Whatever the effects of the message in producing a shift in attitude, it is likely to be more similar for such a group than with a heterogeneous sample, where differing effects can cancel out. Another factor accounting for greater change with college students is that attitude change is more likely to occur in cognitively complex individuals (Lundy and Berkowitz, 1957).

Under laboratory conditions, various kinds of sets are deliberately created and tested, often with selected material which is not familiar. Lana (1964) shows that it is difficult to change opinion through the use of persuasive communication when the person is familiar with the topic and possessed of strong conviction, a fact well known in political circles. When the topic is unfamiliar, thus creating an expectancy, a set, or a conclusion, this

	Variable	Field	Laboratory
1.	Population sampled	heterogeneous	homogeneous
2.	Set	existing	created
3.	Ego involvement	average to high	variable
4.	Exposure	selective	forced
5.	Unit measure	large	small
6.	Time period	extended	limited
7.	Communicator credibility	variable	high
8.	Degree of discrepancy between message and audience	low to average	low to high
9.	Post-communication interaction with others	high	low
10.	Reinforcement	consistent	negligible

establishes greater acceptance of pro and resistance to contrary argument. Sets can be created by using labels, by presenting a conclusion (e.g., a newspaper headline), by suggesting subsequent events (e.g., trial balloons about pending tax increases or cuts) by the big lie, by emotional appeal, and other tactics. Under ordinary circumstances, the audience brings its sets, as determined by attitudes and motives, with it.

Personality variables are too complex to be adequately considered here. High and low ego-defensive women are more resistant to change involving prejudice than moderately defensive women (Katz, McClintock, and Sarnoff, 1956). Other factors than defensiveness may take primacy with the low group. Greater reality orientation and other characteristics influence results (McClintock, 1958). However, when ego involvement and commitment of an individual to a position are high, as is more likely in the public issues sampled in surveys (e.g., war, race relations, election candidates), susceptibility to change is less than in the laboratory where more neutral topics such as health or science are typically presented.

Another factor contributing to smaller changes in field studies is what Klapper (1960) terms selective exposure. Simply put, Republicans listen to their candidates as Democrats listen to theirs; the result is that each receives a confirmation of his already existing position. In the laboratory, the subjects cannot escape the full range of exposure, whatever it may be. Hence, the possibility of a greater degree of change exists because of a clear difference between message and belief. In the same context, surveys sample global issues over extended time periods. As a result, change is harder to produce than on a miniscule issue and is more likely to dissipate itself over days, weeks, and months, as did the effects of Kennedy's assassination mentioned above.

The credibility of the communicator interacts with other conditions to produce differential effects. Credibility has several aspects—the prestige of the communicator, his acknowledged expertise, the sincerity with which he presents his case. Communicators also vary in their degree of familiarity and acceptance. Thus, close friends can be more persuasive than strangers, however expert, particularly where ego involvement is high (Zimbardo, 1958). Such conditions help explain the successful pressure groups in producing conformity. When exposure to highly credible but unfamiliar communicators occurs, change is more likely when the position advocated is not too disparate from the attitude of the listener. Discrepancies which are too great produce a boomerang effect. The audience protects its position by discrediting the communicator, permitting a rejection of the message or distorting it to fit existing views, a form of selective perception. Propaganda consistently has this effect. In discrediting it, the intended recipient gets his existing views reinforced. Children who have experienced marked rejection are suspicious of adults who offer them affection and acceptance and attempt to provoke disapproval in order to remain convinced in their distrust. In either field or laboratory, communicator credibility and degree of discrepancy of message can vary, but in life situations we tend to seek those which are relatively congruent (consistent with the discrepancy theory of motivation) with our views. In the laboratory, the degree of variation is likely to be greater (Hovland, Harvey and Sherif, 1957).

In certain respects, the school is similar to the laboratory in that the students are required to be present and they experience forced exposure to the communicator (the teacher) and to the attitudes espoused. Attention is repeatedly directed to the difference in attitudes between school personnel and children from lower socio-economic levels, with the parallel problem of school drop-outs—the rejection of the promise of the school. The entire problem of drop-outs cannot be explained by attitude discrepancy alone, but it undoubtedly is a factor to be considered in attempts to develop school environments with greater holding power.

Finally, given the opportunity to measure the impact of communications on attitude immediately following exposure, the laboratory has the advantage of testing results without the countereffect of post-exposure interaction with others. A quite different situation exists with regard to the average televised message. Even if we view it alone, we subsequently interact with family or friends, with opportunity to discuss. Even without such, an environment perpetuates its own values. Closely interlocked is the presence or absence of reinforcement. Television advertisement achieves reinforcement by repeated bombardment; political campaigners attempt the same strategy. Most messages suffer for want of repetition or reinforcement. Again, reinforcement is high in groups, which helps to explain their persuasiveness. Several studies (Bostrom, Vlandes, and Rosenbaum, 1961; Scott, 1957; Lublin, 1965; Insko, 1965) attest to the effectiveness of reinforcement, in school and out, attainable by grades, success, and verbal reinforcement. In contrast, threat tends to have little or no effect on attitude change.

VALUES AND IDEALS

The distinction between attitudes and values is not sharply drawn, but two differences can be identified. The first is that attitudes are response oriented; that is, they are affective sets to respond positively or negatively to certain kinds of experience. Values and ideals are goal oriented, hence action oriented. They represent something an individual seeks or will strive for. A second difference is that values have a cognitive dimension. They represent certain convictions, a basis for making decisions about actions.

Each society determines for itself the good, the right, and the ideal, both as to the goals for which men should strive and the behavior they should adopt in achieving their goals. If the story content presented by the mass media reflects the values of our culture, we prize power, wealth, success, and aggressive behavior. But such a conclusion is too simple, for in a society with as many diverse cultural antecedents as ours, there is no simple set of moral rules such as the Ten Commandments to which all uniformly adhere. Instead, almost a cultivated conflict in values is maintained—between conformity and individuality, looking out for self and looking after others, giving and taking, independence and dependence, aggression and gentleness, etc., etc. In such circumstances, each individual has to strike a balance between the external pressures to conform to one set of values or another and his own individuality.

Children primarily acquire their values from their parents and peers, with schools, church, and media playing secondary roles. The actual extent of the influence of school, church, or media is not clear because of limited research and the difficulties of separating parental from school and church influence because of the likely congruence between the three.

The development of character has been long ignored, by both school and psychologist. Schools oprate on the assumption that a combination of well meaning teachers and verbally espoused "boy scout" codes suffice; psychologists have been more concerned with structure and other aspects of personality. Piaget was an exception with his 1932 description of moral judgment in children. More recently, Peck and Havighurst (1960) and Kohlberg (1964) have taken the initiative in this field of study. The general trend of development is a progression from the infant modifying his behavior as a result of the natural consequences of events, through stages of conformity to adults and peers (where the former administer rewards and punishments and the latter group, approval or disapproval), to the final stage where behavior is regulated by personal convictions.

Peck and Havighurst identify five types of character:

1. *Amoral*—concerned with impulse gratification only, without regard for welfare of others. Children who experience few gratifications from parents, high rejection and/or disapproval; lacking in trust.

2. *Expedient*—seeks maximum gratification with regard for others only as a means to an end. Will behave conventionally out of self interest. Need for approval is developed; they seek admiration and applause, but not to the extent of reciprocal gratification.

3. *Conforming*—conforms to group patterns because of valuing conformity for its own sake. Parents of these children tend to be consistent, autocratic, moderate to severe disciplinarians.

4. *Irrational-conscientious*—blind obedience to super-ego without rational criticism of self or situation.

5. *Rational-altruistic*—rational philosophy subject to critical examination guides behavior directed to greatest good. Derived from common participation, shared confidence, trust, leniency, approval.

Peck and Havighurst found a sizable minority in the first two groups and over 50 percent in the two types of conformity (numbers 3 and 4)—the good citizens, the martyrs, the "men-of-principle"—and approximately 25 percent in the rational-altruistic class.

Kohlberg's three levels are similar if somewhat broader:

1. Pre-moral—behavior regulated by fear of punishment (obedience) and hedonism (impulse gratification).
2. Morality of conventional role conformity—in which behavior results from obedience to authority or desire to maintain good relations and have the approval of others.
3. Morality of self-accepted moral principles—in which the morality of contract, of individual rights, of democratically accepted law, or the morality of individual principles of conscience direct behavior.

More significantly, Kohlberg identifies a series of changes in moral development which he contends are independent of culture, social class, or religion —in short, universal. According to him, these changes are

1. A shift from judging acts by their physical consequences to judging them on the basis of their intentions.
2. An increased relativism of judgment, i.e., events are not black and white, good or bad, but vary in terms of the standards which apply.
3. Recognition of the independence of sanctions.
4. Recognition of reciprocity, the adult interpretation of the Golden Rule.
5. Rehabilitation and restitution as objectives of punishment rather than punishment for its own sake.
6. Not viewing natural misfortunes or accidents as punishments for misdeeds, as "immanent justice".

According to Kohlberg, these six are basic aspects of developments in moral judgment during the grammer school years. In particular, the first four of these six are linked to cognitive development. This is the first essential feature, that of conceptual development; a second and third are capacity and consent. The first is knowing what to do or what should be done. This problem is subject to direct teaching on the verbal-conceptual level. The second is linked to experience rather than IQ. It suggests the need for having relevant social experience appropriate to age and developmental levels. It suggests that a "curriculum" for moral development is as necessary as for reading. The third aspect, consent, implies obtaining the willingness, the motivation of the child to abide by, to adopt for his own, the particular values or ideals which we espouse—in essence, obtaining a commitment to certain values.

In describing steps in attitude change, Kelman (1958) distinguished three different processes—compliance, identification, and internalization.

Krathwohl, Bloom, and Masia (1964), speaking of the development of values, specify the steps in this process of internalization as follows. In hierarchical order, from lowest to highest:

1. Receiving (attending)—being aware what one is expected to learn
     Awareness
     Willingness to receive
     Controlled or selected attention
2. Responding—learning to give the desired responses
     Acquiescence in responding
     Willingness to respond
     Satisfaction in response
3. Valuing—believing the behavior to be of worth
     Acceptance of a value
     Preference for a value
     Commitment (conviction)
4. Organization—of an internally consistent system
     Conceptualization of a value
     Organization of a value system
5. Characterization by a value or value system—living by the values as a philosophical set
     Generalized set
     Characterization

The significance of the hierarchy for the teaching of values or ideals can be seen. For example, if a teacher were to desire to promote autonomy, self-direction, and responsibility as one constellation of valued behavior, the first step would be to describe the desired behavior, such as an increased ability to plan and execute a plan, a decrease in instances of seeking direction from the teacher, initiative in extending knowledge (voluntary actions to do more and learn more), and a decrease in obedience simply to obtain rewards, favors, or to avoid punishment are illustrations of behaviors which would fall within this rubric. Social experiences could be designed to produce awareness and valuing; classroom organization could be arranged to provide opportunities for responding. The ultimate organization of an internally consistent system of values would be a long-term if not lifetime goal, but short of that, commitment to specified values and ideals could be fostered. Raths (1966) identifies a variety of teaching procedures specifically designed for such purposes.

SUMMARY

Significant social attitudes are learned in early childhood, under parental influence and with strong emotional reinforcement. They include basic values, ideals, and conscious attitudes which often change very little throughout life. Attitudes are sets to respond positively or negatively to given objects, persons, or events, when values and ideals are learned goals to which the individual is emotionally committed. All possess cognitive as well as affective features.

Family and friends play a primary role in the development of attitudes and ideals, with schools, church, media, and other sources of influence playing a secondary role, although not always restricted to the lesser role. The lack of longitudinal studies of the development of attitudes and ideals circumscribes our knowledge in this area. Laboratory studies show that large shifts in an attitude can be produced under controlled conditions in contrast to field studies where shifts are generally smaller in degree due in part to the interplay of a greater number of influences and possibly to inadequacies of the controls and measures utilized.

Attitudes are acquired by imitation and role playing, from emotional experiences and conditioning, from various kinds of informative experiences, and by deliberate cultivation. Schools have been haphazard in efforts to foster socially desirable attitudes, in spite of evidence which shows schools can be influential. In addition to the emotional commitment involved in ideals, relevant social and intellectual experiences are needed to produce awareness, response sets, and conceptual development. Such activities fall within the domain and the responsibility of schools.

A number of attitude tests have been devised, usually arranged so that variation in degree of favorableness or unfavorableness to a given topic can be indicated by score. In general, the attitudes scales assume a high correspondence between verbal report and actual behavior.

FURTHER READING

Overview

HARRIS, D. B. 1950. How children learn interest, motives, attitudes. *49th Yearbook of the National Society for the Study of Education.* Chicago: Univ. of Chicago Press. Part 1, pp. 129-82.

Selected References

HALLORAN, J. D. 1967. *Attitude Formation and Change.* Leicester, England: Leicester Univ. Press.

HOFFMAN, M. L. and LOIS HOFFMAN. 1966. *Child Development Research.* New York: Russell Sage Foundation.

KRASNER, L. and P. ULLMANN. 1965. *Research in Behavior Modification.* New York: Rinehart-Winston.

LEWIN, G. 1948. *Resolving Social Conflict.* New York: Harper.

LINDZEY, G. 1953. *Handbook of Social Psychology*. Boston: Addison.

MOWRER, O. H. 1950. *Learning Theory and Personality Dynamics*. New York: Ronald.

Original Investigations

ADORNO, T. W., E. FRENKEL-BRUNSWIK, D. J. LEVINSON, and R. N. SANFORD. 1950. *The Authoritarian Personality*. New York: Harper.

BANDURA, A., DOROTHEA ROSS, and SHEILA ROSS. 1963. Imitation of film-mediated aggressive models. *J. Abn. Soc. Psychol.,* 66: 3-11.

HOVLAND, C. I., O. J. HARVEY, and M. SHERIF. 1957. Assimilation and content effects in reaction to communication and attitude change. *J. Abn. Soc. Psychol.,* 55: 244-52.

LEWIN, K., R. LIPPITT, and R. WHITE. 1939. Patterns of aggressive behavior in experimentally created "social climates." *J. of Soc. Psychol.,* 10: 271-99.

MEAD, A. R. 1951. What schools can do to improve social attitudes. *Educ. Leaders,* 9: 183-87.

17

Transfer of Training

When training in one situation or one form of activity affects one's ability in other types of activity or one's performance in different situations we have what is commonly understood as transfer of training. An attempt to operate a tractor or a truck based upon one's knowledge of operating an automobile requires transfer of training in order to succeed in the task. In countless ways we use the results of past learning to meet the demands of new situations. In many ways the results of past learning interfere with new learning, for instance, the difficulty we experience in correctly pronouncing a foreign language because of our habitual manner of pronouncing sounds. From a social viewpoint, the real measure of the effectiveness of education is the degree to which it is transferred into daily life. A fundamental premise on which the school is based is that the training obtained in school will be useful outside of school—in short, that it is transferable.

There is probably no question concerning learning which has occupied the thoughts of educational philosophers and in turn affected the actual course of educational history more than that of its transfer or applicability to lines of endeavor beyond the limits of the sphere of actual training. Such momentous issues as what subjects shall make up the content of the curriculum and the aims and methods of instruction are inevitably decided according to the views, convictions, and prejudices held by the leaders of educational thought in regard to this problem.

Formal Discipline.   The modern scientific investigations of the problem of transfer of training are set against a background of several centuries of rationalistic inquiry concerning the mind and its training. Conspicuous in this background is the doctrine of formal discipline. Based upon a psychology known as *faculty psychology,* it held that the mind is composed of a set of faculties or mental powers such as the will, memory, attention, judgment, observation, reason, and the like.

It was believed by educational theorists that the chief concern of education was to develop and strengthen these faculties. They reasoned, furthermore, that it was the process of learning that mattered most, not what was acquired in the way of information or skills to be used. The mental faculties were believed subject to improvement, strengthening, or enlargement by exercise, much as a muscle is strengthened by use. For this reason, subjects were included or retained in the curriculum, not because they contributed usable information but because of their supposed value as instruments for sharpening the intellect and toughening the fibers of the mind.

The outstanding example of the consequences of this doctrine is seen in the dominant place held by the ancient languages in education. Latin, which had dominated the schools of the Middle Ages and of the Renaissance, had by the end of the seventeenth century lost its exalted position as the language of the clergy, diplomacy, the universities, and writers because of the emergence and adoption of the vernacular languages. Having ceased to be the exclusive language of culture and the humanities, its place in the curriculum was made secure by the argument that no other subject, except possibly formal mathematics, could equal it as an instrument of mental discipline. This view was supported by educational tradition and conservatism.

Now, according to this conception of mental training, it was supposed that the intellect or the faculties of the mind were strengthened by appropriate discipline and in that way the individual was best prepared for all of the demands of life. We have here the notion of a sort of blanket transfer of training from one kind of learning to any situation or activity no matter how different and remote.

In the elementary school, arithmetic was full of useless material selected for its supposed value in training the mind. The process of weeding this out has been occupying the attention of educators only in very recent years. Spelling included the memorizing of thousands of words the child would never use in his own writing. Much attention was given to formal grammar, not to promote good English usage, but to discipline the mind. Methods of teaching were strict and in conformity with the view that, not what the child learned, but the discipline he received in the process was the important consideration.

Although the doctrine of formal discipline has been discredited by modern research, it is still reflected in the practices of some teachers.

Unfortunately, there are still some teachers who require their pupils to memorize lists and tables of factual items which have no immediate or future value for the pupils, with a vague notion that somehow the arduous labor of memorizing will itself improve in some way the mental caliber of the victims of such practices.

During the time when knowledge accumulated slowly, and technology remained fairly stable, the information, knowledge, facts, and skills one learned, in school or on the job, stood one in good stead for a lifetime, regardless of the educational philosophy used to support instruction. Even though the concept of faculty psychology was basically invalid, the learning acquired proved useful. In a society in a rapid state of technological change and a high rate of obsolescence of information because of new knowledge being generated, the knowledge and skills acquired in school are not likely to suffice a lifetime. Hence transfer of training and learning how to learn become critically important to maintaining a livelihood. This reality is producing a de-emphasis on a storing up of facts in school and increasing emphasis on concept development, learning of principles, and development of skills in learning. In this change, we find a germ of an idea proposed under the doctrine of formal discipline recast in modern form, that it is the process of learning which matters most.

PROCEDURES AND PROBLEMS
IN STUDYING TRANSFER

In the early studies on transfer effects, the usual procedure was first to test a group to determine their ability in some one type of performance, provide them training in a different activity, then retest them again on the first task. If performance improved, the transfer from the intervening activity was assumed to be responsible. It was equivalent to asserting that if students progressed better in English after studying Latin, the transfer effect of Latin was demonstrated. Two weaknesses in the experimental paradigm occur: no allowance is made for practice effects, nor is any comparison provided. Individuals generally do better on a second test of any activity because of the practice provided on the first. Thus, scores on intelligence tests are generally higher on a repeat of the same test. In fact, the second trial in ordinary learning starts with the gains and forgetting which occurred on the first. Further, the comparison is something versus nothing, or more accurately of something specified versus something unknown, for one cannot assume that the learners would be doing nothing under other circumstances.

Providing preliminary practice served to meet the objection regarding practice effects stemming from familiarization and providing control groups permitted comparison of transfer from different activities. The general experimental design for study of transfer of training is:

Experimental group	Pre-test Activity A	Training Activity B	Post-test Activity A
Control group	Pre-test Activity A	No training	Post-test Activity A

Gains: post-test scores minus pretest scores
Transfer of training: difference in gains between experimental and control group

The fact that no training is provided the control group infers no activity on their part during the intervening period, an assumption which is hardly defensible. As a result, the experimental pattern usually includes more than one experimental group as well as a control group.

Woodrow's experiment (1927) on memorizing provides an excellent illustration of the experimental method. Woodrow used two experimental groups, one receiving seventy-two hours training in memorizing nonsense syllables and poetry and the second devoting thirty-six hours to the same activity but spending the other thirty-six hours in learning how to memorize, e.g., looking for meaningful associations, using rhythmical grouping, and so on. Both groups were compared with a control group on the gains made between a pre-test and a post-test measuring their memorizing ability for poetry, prose, Turkish–English vocabulary, factual items, and historical dates. The test used was a broad measure of memorizing ability. The group which spent all their time memorizing made only slightly greater gains than the control group in direct contradiction of the claims of faculty psychology, while the second experimental group made the significant gain.

The student will perceive the similarity between the experimental paradigm for studying transfer effects and that for studying interference effects—retroactive and proactive inhibition. One of the difficulties is to sort out the conditions under which positive or negative transfer—interference—will occur. That this is not a simple task is evident by the fact that rarely if ever are experimental subjects totally naïve. This is especially true with school children who are always in between what they have been learning and what they are expected to learn. The rate of improvement for a given amount of practice varies at different stages of mastery, with the result that transfer effects may well vary, if not vanish, depending on the sophistication of the experimental subjects. When individuals are given a series of similar tasks, such as lists of nonsense syllables (Ward, 1937) of equal difficulty, they require fewer trials to learn each successive list. But the improvement is greatest on early trials and gradually levels out, indicating a cumulative positive transfer gradually diminishing. At the same time, the greater the number of lists learned the progressively worse the recall of the initial learning (Twining, 1940). Simultaneously, we observe a combination of proactive facilitation and retroactive interference. Under other conditions, the proactive effect, instead of facilitating learning, impedes it producing negative transfer.

The task of sorting out the effects requires consideration of similarity of method and materials, of the degree of learning, and of temporal relationships between the sets of materials. Further, it requires isolating the effects of similarity with respect to stimuli and responses. It was noted early, in studies of response generalization, that the same response could be generalized more readily to similar stimuli than could varied responses. Following a review of the literature, Osgood concluded that (1) where the same response occurred in relation to varying stimuli, positive transfer was facilitated by increasing similarity of stimuli, but (2) varied responses occurring in relation to the same stimulus produced negative transfer which decreased as the responses became more similar, and (3) where both stimuli and responses varied, negative transfer occurred and was greater the more similar the stimuli. Entwisle and Huggins (1964) demonstrated the last generalization in a study which involved instruction on theory of electrical circuits to college sophomores. Negative transfer was thought likely because circuit theory involves many dual sets of closely related principles. For example, the experimenters taught the principles of voltages and currents in sequence to one group, but taught only one of these principles to a control group, presenting non-relevant material (computer programming) in the empty period. Negative transfer, both proactive and retroactive, was significantly higher in the experimental group.

Negative Transfer. When the interference is greater than the positive carryover, the result is called negative transfer. This has been demonstrated, for example, in card sorting experiments in which the subject practices the sorting of cards into compartments numbered to correspond to the cards. After considerable facility has been acquired, the order of the compartments is changed and the subject is asked to place the cards according to the new arrangement. In performing the second task, the previously formed habits tend to carry the hand in the direction of the former positions of the compartments. This interferes with the making of the proper movements and retards the second learning

If one is to master two such interfering sets of habits as those mentioned above, it has been shown experimentally that the most economical procedure is to master one thoroughly before starting practice on the second.

Pyle (1928) describes an experiment in which a group of subjects sorted cards with one arrangement of boxes an hour a day for fifteen days, and then switched to practice with a different arrangement of boxes for an additional fifteen days. Another group practiced the two arrangements for thirty days but practiced each arrangement on alternate days throughout the whole period. Better results were obtained from the first procedure. Pyle points out by way of application of this principle that it is not advisable to attempt to learn two different systems of writing or two foreign languages at the same time.

Transfer in Motor Skills.   In sensori-motor and perceptual learning, training in one sensory modality can increase speed of learning using another modality (Sinha and Sinha, 1960) and practice with one part of the body or set of muscles can transfer to other muscular mechanisms involving the same or different movement.

Training that transfers to corresponding members of the opposite side of the body is called bilateral transfer. An experiment by Munn (1932) will illustrate the character of this work and the usual findings. The activity in this experiment called for eye-hand coördination. The apparatus used consisted of a wooden cup attached to a long handle from the bottom of which was suspended, by means of a string, a wooden ball. The task was to grasp the handle and flip the ball into the cup. The subjects were 100 college students, fifty men and fifty women. There were two training groups of twenty-five students each, and two control groups of the same number. The training groups were given fifty trials with the left hand, then 500 practice trials with the right hand, and finally fifty additional trials with the left hand. The controls received no practice with the right hand. They were given fifty trials with the left hand, rested for forty-five to sixty minutes, and then practiced for fifty more trials with the left hand. The average increase in facility with the left hand from the first fifty trials to the second fifty trials was 61.14 percent for the experimental groups and 28.5 percent for the controls. Thus, a difference of 32.6 percent was found in favor of the groups that practiced with the right hand, due, apparently, to the transfer effects of that practice to the use of the left hand.

A number of experiments have shown transfer from the right to the left hand in mirror tracing and in other forms of sensori-motor learning. Positive transfer has also been found from the left hand to the right, from hands to feet, and from each foot to the other in the learning of an irregular maze pattern. In some experiments, the advantage of previous practice with a different member appeared mostly in the early trials and diminished as practice was continued. This advantage appears to be due to an acquaintance with the problem, familiarity with the experimental situation, greater ease and confidence, and a knowledge of procedures or movements best suited to accomplish the desired results. Having discovered during the previous practice ways and means of dealing with the situation and applying equally well to the performance with another member, the second task is partially learned when practice on it is begun.

Another experimenter studied transfer in motor learning by measuring the effect of learning one maze upon the learning of several others. He found in each case definite evidence of positive transfer effects. However, the amount of transfer varied widely, from 20 to 77 percent, as measured by trials for the different mazes. One of the mazes used in the transfer series was similar to the maze previously learned except for a section of it which was made a blind alley. To master this maze, the subjects had to break the previously acquired habit of turning into this section. There was considerable interference from the previous practice in the mastery of this part, for the subjects who had learned the otherwise similar maze had greater difficulty in eliminating this section than did controls who had not learned that maze. For this maze as a whole, however, there was positive transfer. It appeared that the transfer effect was the net result of both facilitation and interference. Moreover, as was pointed out in the report, the wide variation in the amount of transfer for the different mazes strongly indicates that the amount of transfer from any learning depends upon the nature of the task to which the shift is made.

A series of studies has been carried out by Gagné and his colleagues (Baker, Foster, and Wylie, 1949-1950). One finding which was confirmed by Duncan (1958) is that practice on a variety of tasks contributes to greater positive transfer, with the amount decreasing as similarity in responses decreases and as differences in difficulty of the tasks occurs. Both pictorial presentations and verbal training facilitate subsequent learning of a motor skill. The amount of positive transfer increases with more trials on a paper-and-pencil pictorial presentation. Where groups received differing numbers of trials ranging from eight to forty-eight (Gagné and Foster, 1949), facilitating effects were greatest at sixteen trials, greater at higher numbers of trials than at eight. An interesting counterpoint is seen in a study of Duncan and Underwood (1953) indicating that interference effects follow a similar pattern reaching a maximum, then declining. At optimum, organization of instruction would attempt to foster positive transfer and minimize interference, for both are likely to be occurring in any learning situation. In actual practice, little account is taken of either. The general assumption is to count on positive transfer from similar activities, and ignore possible competing skills. A ready example is seen in learning to play either squash or badminton after tennis. The objective is the same in all three, to hit a moving object beyond reach of an opponent. Attempts to use a tennis stroke are ineffective, because of the demands for wrist action rather than arm strength. Yet without instruction, the tyro in squash or badminton will attempt to bludgeon along with his tennis stroke, reaping the undesirable effects of negative transfer. The interference and facilitating effects are influenced by the degree of similarity and the amount of practice. Varying responses to similar stimuli produces interference. Practice on the component part can be facilitating, provided enough practice is had. Otherwise, small amounts of practice are more likely to interfere.

Transfer in Verbal Learning. The generalization identified in the preceding section and in the introductory discussion of transfer relate to verbal learning as well (Mandler and Heineman, 1956), particularly that involving nonsense syllables. Verbal learning has an added dimension which complicates efforts to specify transfer effects—namely, the semantic or meaning dimension. In the discussion of concepts, the acquisition of labels was described. Generalization between such responses on the basis of meaning has been demonstrated in experiments on what is known as semantic conditioning. For example, a conditioned response to *bread* will generalize to *loaf* (similar semantically) but not to *bead* (similar form). The variation in amount and kind of transfer is readily seen in Table 17.1. In some cases transfer is positive, in others negative or near zero. No particular kind of material is uniformly superior. In general, the experimental literature shows that transfer occurs where the trained and tested activities are highly similar. For example, practice in memorizing nonsense syllables increased ability to memorize other lists of such syllables, but resulted in no significant improvement with prose selections or other dissimilar materials. The amount of transfer varies with different conditions, and the aim of many of the recent studies has been to discover more specifically the conditions favorable to the maximum amount of transfer. It has been noted that transfer frequently appeared as the result of acquiring better procedures. During the practice series, the subjects learned how to learn. This was illustrated in the previously cited Woodrow experiment on memorizing.

Language plays a ubiquitous role in transfer, for not only are there direct effects possible but also functional effects. For example, words can provide cues which facilitate transfer. Wittrock and Keislar (1965) report a study with second and third grade children which shows that the specific naming of response or having a word denoting a correct concept such as color facilitated solutions to matching tasks on subsequent series where cues were omitted.

Transfer in Problem Solving. A significant series of studies conducted by Harlow (1949) and his students at the University of Wisconsin concerns the formation of learning sets by both children and monkeys. Instead of the ordinary experimental design in which the same task is presented over a series of trials and the amount of learning measured in terms of number of trials needed to reach a given level of proficiency, Harlow presented his subjects with a series of problems and plotted the improvement in performance over the series. A tray containing food wells was presented to a monkey. Covering the wells were two objects which differed from each other in several characteristics such as color, shape, size. The monkey's task was to choose the rewarded one of the two objects by correctly discriminating the particular difference in characteristics of the objects. With children, beads and toys were substituted for the food reward.

A series of 344 problems was presented using 344 different pairs of stimuli. The first thirty-two problems were run for fifty trials each. The second 200 problems were run for six trials each. The last 112 problems were run for an average of nine trials. The question was whether or not the subjects could *learn how to learn,* that is to improve in their ability to learn object-quality discrimination problems. Figure 17.1, adapted from Harlow's data, shows the percent of correct responses obtained during trials on early, middle, and late sets of problems.

The correct responses on the first trial of each series are at the chance level. In the first series of trials, improvement comes slowly, in contrast to the last series of problems in which the subject's responses indicate insight following a single trial as indicated by near perfect responses on the next attempt. The experience obtained on previous trials shows increasingly greater transfer the later the series. The animals and children *learned how to learn* on the discrimination problems, just as Woodrow's subjects had learned how to memorize in his experiment on memory. Before the formation of learning sets, improvement from trial to trial was slight, but after their formation the sudden and sharp improvement shown suggests the gradual development of insight into how to go about obtaining correct solutions. The subjects were also able to utilize the learning sets when the problems were reversed and when the task was shifted from a quality discrimination to a position discrimination. The significance of Harlow's studies lies in providing some understanding of how human and infrahuman organisms may acquire problem solving approaches rather than trial and error approaches to the range of demands to be faced in any environment. Learning how to learn efficiently in a new situation, how to approach problem situations, and how to utilize previous experience to

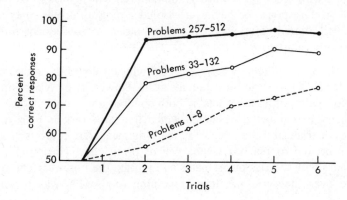

Fig. 17.1

permit insight into newly encountered events permit a transformation from creatures who blindly respond either by fixed habit or by chance to creatures who can adapt "intelligently." In addition, these studies offer a possible explanation of the varying degrees of transfer which have been reported in the different studies on transfer of training.

Other studies show how experience in problem solving may transfer positively or negatively to subsequent problems. Ruger (1926), in an experiment with mechanical puzzles, found definite transfer from practice in taking a puzzle apart to putting it together. In one case, a subject took a puzzle apart 400 times without putting it together or seeing it put together. He then put it together five times. His average time for putting the puzzle together was just one tenth the average time for the first five trials in taking it apart. Since the movements involved were reversed, Ruger believed that the transfer was not due to the carryover of motor habits but to an understanding of the construction of the puzzle acquired during practice in taking it apart.

Different positions of the puzzles required different initial manipulation. Positive transfer from one position to another was found when the subject clearly saw by analysis what adjustments were needed to use the practiced habits in the new position. But when such insight into the process required for solution was lacking, the old habits produced interference when the puzzle was changed to a new position. Practice with one puzzle transferred positively to the solution of another puzzle involving similar procedure when the subject discovered by analysis during practice the underlying principle and devised a formula for solution that was appropriate for the new puzzle. Motor habits, carried over without the benefit of analysis and generalization of procedure, led to error and negative transfer effects when they were inappropriate and to positive effects when they happened to be appropriate. Among the factors promoting transfer in puzzle solving listed by Ruger are: heightened attention to the task, shift from self-consciousness to a problem attitude, improved methods of attack, analysis and generalization of procedure, and an awareness of the similarity of the new case to the old.

Barlow (1937) found that special training in analysis, abstraction, and generalization transferred positively to test performances consisting of giving the lesson or moral conveyed by various fables. These and other studies (Hassulrud and Myer, 1958; Ervin, 1960) indicate the possibilities of positive transfer of practice in problem solving with one kind of material to reasoning in other types of problems. They indicate that transfer is achieved by acquiring an understanding of principles, by developing confident, analytical, searching attitudes, and by learning effective procedures.

Table 17.1 presents a summary of results obtained in various transfer of training experiments. Previous experience can affect present learning to a slight or to a great extent depending upon the presence or the absence

TABLE 17.1 AMOUNT OF TRANSFER RESULTING FROM DIFFERENT
TRAINING EXPERIENCES IN EXPERIMENTS ON TRANSFER
OR TRAINING

Amount of transfer reported	Training experience	Transferred to
Maximum transfer (over 50% gains)	Marking words	Other words
	Discrimination of shades of red	Discrimination of other colors
	Mazes	Other mazes
Considerable transfer (25%-50%)	Learning sets on object– equality discrimination	Similar problems
	Estimating areas of geo- metric figures	Similar mazes
	Memorizing techniques	Varied memory tasks
	Mental multiplication	Adding, dividing
	Biology, geometry	Biology and geometry tests
Moderate transfer (10%-25%)	Learning nonsense syllables	Learning prose, poetry
	Poetry	Prose
	Sound intensities	Brightness intensities
	Applying principles of refraction	Hitting underwater targets
Little to negative transfer (under 10%)	Poetry, prose	Dates, syllables
	Estimating line lengths	Similar task
	Cancellation of letters	Cancellation of nouns, verbs
	Card sorting	Reaction time typing
	Computation	Reasoning
	Latin	English vocabulary
	Latin	Spelling
	Biology and geometry	Other subjects

of certain conditions. The higher the degree of similarity between the two tasks, the higher the degree of transfer. Furthermore, if procedures or principles are acquired or understood during the previous training experience, the degree of transfer is likely to be greater than if not. Previous experience, however great, does not automatically insure positive transfer to new learning situations; rather, the extent to which the new is similar to the old or the degree to which the relationships between the two stiuations are understood determines the extent to which previous experience can be a positive factor in new learning.

CONDITIONS OF TRANSFER

Transfer by Similarity. Since the time of the earliest experiments, it has been recognized that the more the two performances involved have in common, the more will training in the first tend to improve the second. The important experiments by Thorndike and Woodworth (1901) led to the formulation by Thorndike of the famous and broadly accepted doctrine of *identical elements.* There might be identical elements in the content of subject matter learned, in attitudes, or in methods of procedure.

Because the term *element,* as commonly used, refers to an unanalyzable or at least very simple constituent of a whole and because transfer may result from a common functional trend or common part-functions in themselves not simple, Woodworth (1938) suggested that it would be more appropriate to use the word *constituent* or *component* in the place of *element.* The mere presence of common components does not assure positive transfer; under some conditions of training, they produce negative transfer. The amount of transfer due to identical features of two functions varies with the locus of identity or the phases of the functions in which identity occurs. Identity in the response phases is conducive to far more positive transfer than identity in the stimulus factors or initial phases. Thus, it is easier to learn to respond to a new situation in an old way, than to develop a new mode of responding to an old situation, for in the latter case the interference from previously formed habits is greater (Duncan, 1953).

Transfer by Principle.   As we move to the level of comprehension, we find that generalizations furnish a ready vehicle for transfer. We have seen that subjects who grasped the principles involved in solving certain types of mechanical puzzles could more easily solve other puzzles to which these same principles applied.

The importance for transfer of generalized experience was early recognized and emphasized by Judd (1908). He believed experience in one situation could be generalized and applied by the learner in many other situations. In an experiment demonstrating his view, he had two groups of boys shoot darts at a target submerged in water. Because of refraction of the light, the target appeared to be in a different position. Before practice, the principle of refraction of light was explained to one group, while the other group received no instruction in this matter. Both groups made similar errors at first and corrected them gradually by trial and error. Then the depth of the target was changed. This time the instructed group saw the application of the principle to their problem and did much better than the group that had not been told about light refraction.

A similar experiment was made more recently by Hendrickson and Schroeder (1941) who had their subjects shoot BB shot at a submerged target with an air rifle. The results were substantially the same, though they found that the theoretical information also aided in learning to hit the target in the initial situation.

Transfer through generalization is not merely a matter of elements trained during practice appearing as actual components of the new functions. The generalization is a form of comprehension which applies beyond the training situation to other situations of the same general class. It should be noted, however, that the mere knowledge of the principle will not insure transfer of training to new situations. Its general applicability must be realized, and the learner must be able to see the possibility of its application to the new situations.

Transfer Through Relationships.   Somewhat akin to the third leg of a triangle is the Gestalt theorists' explanation of transfer as depending upon the transposition of relationships. The analogy of the triangle is useful because none of the three explanations is completely unrelated or detached from each other. The explanation, by way of a pattern of relationships, agrees that similarities in the two situations permit the transfer of training; but it denies that the similarity is one of content in the two situations, holding rather that the patterns of relationships are alike.

It is often claimed that competitive athletics contribute greatly to the successful performance of the American soldier in combat; this statement describes transfer of training from one situation to another. According to the similarity theory, a competitive sport such as football has component parts identical to those performed as a soldier. For instance, both situations require an aggressive attack against the opponent. Both require the ability to carry out direction or instruction. According to the relationship theory, transfer occurs because both activities involve coördinated teamwork of individuals performing related operations. The strategy involved in outthinking and outmaneuvering an opponent would count more than the specific tactics.

Forgus and Schwartz (1960) compared the effectiveness of memorization of specific elements in a verbal task to the defining of an organizing principle underlying the elements. The latter group not only retained the material better but were markedly superior in transfer and problem solving with new material.

Transfer of Attitudes and Ideals.   An important form of generalization through which transfer takes place is the generalization of set in the form of attitudes and ideals. The keynote of the chapter on attitudes and ideals was the importance of developing these generalized controls of conduct to insure socially acceptable forms of behavior in the many and varied situations of life for which specific habit training would be impossible. In that chapter, we considered the widespread influence of these generalized sets. One's reactions to practically any new situation is influenced by attitudes already formed. The bearing on classroom learning of such attitudes as likes, dislikes, respect, antagonism, interest, indifference, punctuality, carelessness, self-confidence, self-repudiation, courtesy, arrogance, pride in work, and fear of failure will be apparent to the most casual observer.

Transfer by Instructional Set.   Attitudes constitute established sets to respond favorably or not to given environmental events. Instructional sets serve similar purposes, except that they are temporarily induced and often specific to the situation. Nevertheless, when the instruction provided is an organizing principle, it has functional similarities. One of the purposes and effects of instructional sets is to facilitate positive transfer. This has been demonstrated by Di Vesta and Blake (1959) and Ervin (1960): positive transfer results where principles are provided, or information is given that the incidents within an experiment are controlled by a principle. A second product of instruction is to speed discrimination of either the relevant stimuli to be attended to or the appropriate responses, which not only facilitates learning but also transfer under conditions of similarity in tasks (Smith, 1952; Lindley, 1959; Stevenson and Moushegian, 1956).

TRANSFER IN SCHOOL SUBJECTS

Of the many studies concerning transfer in school subjects, the most crucial test of their general value was made by Thorndike in 1922 and 1923. Tests of general mental ability were given to 8564 high school pupils in grades nine, ten, and eleven, and after one year of schoolwork, other forms of the same tests were given to discover the intellectual advancement made. By a thoroughgoing analysis of the many different combinations of subjects studied and by a system of weighting the gains to allow for practice effects of taking the tests, for the normal intellectual growth over a year's time, for the fact that pupils with highest initial ability made greatest gains, and also for the fact that the boys gained more than the girls, it was possible to calculate the relative amount contributed by various subjects to the year's gain in the tests. The procedure was to compare the test gains in relation to programs that were alike except for a difference of one subject. If, for example, the programs of two groups equated in terms of initial test scores were alike in that they both included English, history, and geometry but different in that for the fourth subject one group took Latin while the other took chemistry, then it was possible to compare the contributions of Latin and of chemistry to the test gains in the other subjects. The results were most significant. They revealed surprisingly small differences between the various subjects in relation to the test gains and they showed the gains to depend more on initial ability or intelligence than upon any particular subject studied.

A similar study with 5000 pupils was made later (Broyler, *et al.,* 1927). The results agreed for the most part with those of the earlier study. The table below represents the combined results of the two studies and covers data from over 13,000 high school pupils. It shows the subjects listed in rank order according to their computed relative contribution to the gains in the mental ability tests. The scores represent corrected weighted average differences between group VII and each of the others.

They show how much the subjects of the various groups exceeded or fell short of those in group VII.

SUBJECT	RELATIVE EFFECT ON TEST GAINS
1. Algebra, geometry, trigonometry	2.99
2. Civics, economics, psychology, sociology	2.89
3. Chemistry, physics, general science	2.71
4. Arithmetic, bookkeeping	2.60
5. Physical training	0.83
6. Latin, French	0.79
7. English, history, business, drawing	0.00
8. Stenography, cooking, sewing	—0.14
9. Biological sciences, agriculture	—0.15
10. Dramatic art	—0.48

The differences are so slight that there is no convincing evidence of the superiority of any one subject or group of subjects.

ARITHMETIC. Overman (1930) investigated transfer in arithmetic in relation to methods of teaching. His subjects were pupils of fifty-two second grade classes. They were divided into four closely equated groups of 112 each. The training consisted of instruction and practice in addition, with three types of examples involving two-place numbers. Tests were given to determine the extent to which this training transferred to similar addition examples involving two-place and three-place numbers and to examples in subtraction. Group A was shown simply how to do the examples with no attempt to generalize the procedure or to develop comprehension of the underlying principles. In group B, *generalizations* of the procedure were stressed and an effort was made to formulate rules applicable to similar types of examples. With group C, no attempt was made to generalize or formulate rules, but the reasons for the procedures in the specific examples were discussed. In group D, the methods of B and C were combined.

The tests given before and after training showed a considerable amount of transfer for all four groups from the taught to the untaught examples. It varied from 67 percent to 81 percent for the different types of problems. The calculated transfer (on the basis of 100 percent for correct solution of all untaught problems) was 59.6 percent for group A. That generalization greatly facilitated transfer was shown by the fact that group B surpased group A in the untaught examples by 21.5 percent. This difference was statistically significant. Discussions of the underlying principles and reasons for the procedures in the taught examples appeared to contribute little to transfer, for group C surpassed A by only 5.4 percent and the difference was not significant. Group D did about the same as group B, surpassing group A by 20.5 percent. It appeared, therefore, that "rationalization" added nothing to "generalization" (Thorndike, 1924).

CHEMISTRY. A study in the field of high school chemistry showed that students who were given special training in the application of principles derived from the kinetic theory gained more in tests involving the application of other chemical principles than did members of control groups who had the usual instruction. The groups were too small to make the results statistically reliable, but the data indicate that the amount of transfer secured for applying scientific principles in new situations is related to the teaching procedures employed and that it may be increased by means of special training in the application of principles (Babitz, 1939).

GRAMMAR.   The alleged values of formal grammar for developing various types of abilities such as reasoning in other fields were examined by Briggs (1943). The subjects were seventh grade pupils. They were divided into two equivalent groups on the basis of intelligence ratings. One group studied grammar while the other studied composition and language. The before and after tests measured the pupils' ability to see likenesses and differences, to test definitions critically, to apply definitions, to make a rule or definition, and to reason in connection with various matters. With the possible exception of detecting likenesses and differences, the results indicated that there was no gain of any consequence in those aspects of the reasoning processes tested that could be attributed to the study of grammar.

LATIN.   The blasting of the doctrine of formal discipline by experimental evidence discredited the view that Latin is a superior means for "developing the mind." This led to a search for evidence of transfer values to be derived from the study of this language. No one who has studied this problem carefully will deny that the study of Latin has transfer values. What is objected to and what has been disproved is that this subject has a monopoly on transfer values or that it is particularly superior to other subjects in this matter. The question to be faced frankly is whether a high school pupil will receive values commensurate with the time devoted to Latin when other subjects also afford transfer or general values plus a much larger amount of directly useful material.

In a study designed to test the value of first year Latin for developing the ability to read English, several thousand high school pupils were given alternate forms of a reading scale at the beginning, middle, and end of the school year. Pupils taking first year Latin were compared with those who were not studying this subject. It was assumed that if the Latin pupils gained more than the non-Latins in the tests, their superiority could be attributed to the study of Latin. After taking into account differences in initial scores, it was calculated that the Latin pupils for the entire year gained about 1.5 times as much as the non-Latins, but that this superiority was achieved entirely during the first half-year (Thorndike, 1923). Gains in ability to spell words of Latin origin and improvement in English vocabulary occur when the teacher definitely gives such training (Jordan, 1942), otherwise not.

Kirby (1923) compared the grades in first year French of students

who had studied Latin with the grades of students who had not studied
Latin, and found a correlation of .23 between the number of years spent in
studying Latin and grades in French as compared with a correlation of .43
between French grades and intelligence. It appears from this that intelligence had more to do with the French grades than did the previous study
of Latin. When the factor of intelligence was kept constant, a correlation
of .22 was found for French grades and the years spent in the study of
Latin, indicating a slight relationship.

MODERN FOREIGN LANGUAGES. Werner (1930) investigated the influence of the study of modern foreign languages upon the development of
abilities in English. A battery of tests covering punctuation, sentence structure, language and grammar, vocabulary, reading speed, and reading comprehension was given to a large number of high school and college students
at the beginning and at the end of a school year. The gains in the tests made
by the students who during the year studied French, German, or Spanish
were compared with the gains of those who did not study a foreign language.
The results in general indicated that the study of a foreign language did
not always produce an improvement in abilities in English, that such study
contributed to the development of speed and comprehension in reading
that it had a favorable effect on ability in grammar for high school pupils
but not in the case of college freshmen, that it had a negative effect on
improvement in punctuation and the ability to detect faulty sentence
structure, that it had no appreciable effect on the increase of English vocabulary, and that the effect of foreign language study on the development
of abilities in English varied greatly with the degree of mental ability, since
pupils with high grade ability more often profited by such study and the
less gifted individuals more often suffered from the interference produced
by it.

TEACHING FOR TRANSFER

A General Consideration of the Evidence. These and other investigations of the transfer effects of classroom study agree in general with the
laboratory experiments on the fundamental nature and conditions of transfer. They indicate that the training in one school subject transfers to the
study of other subjects or to other activities not directly trained according to
the degree of *similarity* between the trained and untrained activities, according to the extent to which these activities possess *common components,*
and according to the extent to which the learner grasps or recognizes similarities of *relationships.* They have shown that transfer may be secured by
way of *generalizations* in the form of rules and principles when the learner
realizes the applicability of such rules and principles to situations or problems other than those specifically involved in his training. They have shown

also that the ease and extent of transfer increases with the thoroughness of learning, with the intelligence of the learner, and with purposeful effort on the part of the teacher to secure definite transfer values.

They indicate, moreover, that any subject may, if properly taught, have some transfer value, that the differences between subjects in this respect are small, and that no one subject or group of subjects is especially superior in this respect. It appears that the most effective way to secure a desired educational outcome is to train directly for it rather than to expect it to appear as an incidental by-product of other subjects. The evidence from transfer studies supports the modern educational trend toward the teaching of that which is worth learning for its direct values, be those values social, esthetic, recreational, or utilitarian, rather than for any so-called training of the mind.

Teaching for Transfer.   The method of teaching is an important factor in securing transfer. To get transfer, teach for it. Instruction will make little difference in students' lives if they see no connection between events in the classroom and life outside. The similarities in the two must be made clear and the relevant principles and generalizations made explicit.

Some of the ways by which a resourceful teacher can accomplish this are: relating the history lesson to the novel studied in the literature class or to present political problems; relating the geography lesson to travel, to the food on the dinner table, or to the issue of world citizenship; relating the civics lesson to the current town election; relating the elementary science lesson to the family car, the radio, or aviation; relating the foreign language lesson to good English usage; and relating the geometry lesson to finding the range of an enemy target in war or to the building of a house. The essential thing is to help the learner see the many different situations and activities that contain or involve elements or features of the subject he is studying.

The teacher who desires to have the results of his instruction reach beyond the confines of the classroom will underscore the possibilities of transfer through generalization of experience. The principle taught by means of a classroom exercise will be developed to include far more than the specific details of that particular exercise. The learner must see the range of situations to which the principle applies through use of many and varied examples. He must also be shown cases wherein the principle does not apply.

The procedures for developing generalizations were discussed in the chapter on comprehension. They include calling attention to the principle in numerous and varied concrete cases and its isolation by way of contrast through the examination of cases to which it does not apply. Only a few suggestions need to be added here. The good teacher will keep in mind that for greatest transfer, the generalization should be thoroughly mastered and completely understood. Its application in a great variety of situations and problems will need to be pointed out.

The teacher should also consider the important relationship of intelligence to transfer. It is easier for a child of high grade intelligence to generalize than for one less gifted. The brighter child will be quicker to recognize elements of similarity. He will grasp the underlying principle with fewer illustrations. He will show greater facility in drawing from concrete examples the general procedures and methods appropriate for dealing with other cases. For the child of lesser intelligence, therefore, the teacher will need to intensify his effort to secure an understanding of the range of application and usefulness of rules, laws, definitions, methods of procedure, and other generalizations.

SUMMARY

Transfer of training occurs when the results of learning in one situation affect our performance in different situations or when training in one activity affects other forms of activity. The nature and conditions of transfer are of prime importance to education both with regard to what subjects shall be taught and to how they shall be taught.

Prior to the present century, the doctrine of formal discipline dominated educational philosophy and practice. Subjects were taught primarily for their alleged value for training the faculties of the mind, not for their intrinsic worth to the pupil. This doctrine was discredited by controlled experiments made in the early part of this century.

Many experiments on various functions—particularly action, memory, perception, and reasoning—have shown that transfer does take place but that it may be negative as well as positive. These studies have been fruitful in discovering the conditions under which transfer occurs. While the greatest improvement occurs from direct training, transfer takes place through the medium of components common to the activity trained and the activity to which the training is transferred. The greater the similarity, the more will the training of one affect the other.

Transfer also takes place through generalizations developed during training when the learner sees the applicability of a principle, rule, or method of attack to a new situation or problem. Another medium of transfer is found in ideals and attitudes.

The degree of learning is a factor in transfer. As it is increased, the tendency toward negative transference or interference is lessened and the tendency toward positive transfer is increased. There is some evidence that transfer effects are more persistent than the direct results of training.

Studies of transfer in school subjects indicate only small differences between high school subjects in their effect on general mental ability.

Studies of special school subjects indicate that the study of one subject may affect the ability to learn other subjects but that the amount and nature of transfer effects depend upon the intelligence of the pupil and the method of instruction far more than they do upon the subject.

The evidence, in general, points to the conclusion that the most effective way to realize a desired educational outcome is to train directly for it and that no subject merits a place in the curriculum solely on the grounds of its alleged values for mental training. Any subject properly taught has cultural, disciplinary, and transfer values. The direct values, therefore, are to be given the first consideration.

Every subject should be taught so as to secure the maximum spread of learning to situations and activities beyond the classroom. To this end, attention should be called to those aspects of the subject that are common to other subjects and to the various activities in which elements of the subject are employed. Generalizations should be thoroughly taught and the varied possibilities of their use and application pointed out to the learner. In teaching for transfer, we should endeavor to develop attitudes and ideals.

FURTHER READING

Overview

OSGOOD, C. E. 1953. *Method and Theory in Experimental Psychology*. Chapter 12: Serial and transfer phenomena. New York: Oxford, pp. 495-548.

Selected References

MC GEOCH, J. A. and A. L. IRION. 1952. *The Psychology of Human Learning* (rev.). New York: Longmans, Green.

STROUD, J. B. 1946. *Psychology in Education*. New York: Longmans, Green, pp. 555-97.

SWENSON, E. J. 1941. *Retrospective Inhibition: A Review of the Literature*. Minneapolis: Univ. of Minnesota Press.

Original Investigations

GAGNÉ, H. M. and HARRIET FOSTER. 1949. Transfer of training from practice on components in a motor skill. *J. Exper. Psychol.*, 39: 47-68.

HARLOW, H. F. 1949. The formation of learning sets. *Psychol. Rev.*, 56: 51-65.

HENDRICKSON, G. and W. H. SCHROEDER. 1941. Transfer of training in learning to hit a submerged target. *J. of Educ. Psychol.*, 32: 205-13.

MORRISETT, L., JR. and C. I. HOVLAND. 1959. A comparison of three varieties of training in human problem solving. *J. Exper. Psychol.,* 58: 63-72.

MUUS, R. E. 1961. The transfer effect of a learning program in social causality on an understanding of physical causality. *J. Exper. Educ.,* 29: 231-47.

SWENSON, ESTHER, G. L. ANDERSON, and C. L. STACEY. 1949. Learning theory in school situations. *University of Minnesota Studies in Education.* Minneapolis: Univ. of Minnesota Press, p. 103.

General Bibliography

ABOM, M. 1953. The influence of experimentally induced failure on the retention of materials acquired through set and incidental learning. *J. Exp. Psychol.*, 45: 225–31.

ACKERMAN, W. I. and H. LEVIN. 1958. Effects of training in alternative solutions on subsequent problem solving. *J. Educ. Psychol.*, 49: 239–44.

ADAMS, J. A. and R. W. CHAMBERS. 1962. Response to simultaneous stimulation of two sense modalities. *J. Exp. Psychol.*, 63: 198–206.

ADAMSON, R. 1959. Inhibitory set in problem solving as related to reinforcement learning. *J. Exp. Psychol.*, 58: 280–82.

ADORNO, T. W., E. FRENKEL-BRUNSWIK, D. J. LEVINSON, and R. N. SANFORD. 1950. *The Authoritarian Personality*. New York: Harper.

ADRIAN, E. D. 1931. Potential changes in the isolated nervous system of the Dysticus marginalis. *J. Psychol.*, 72: 132–51.

AIKEN, W. M. 1942. *The Story of the Eight-Year Study*. New York: Harper.

ALDERMAN, R. B. 1965. Influence of local fatigue on speed and accuracy in motor learning. *Res. Quart.*, 36: 131–40.

533

ALLEN, C. N. 1931. Individual differences in delayed reactions of children. *Arch. Psychol.*, 19: No. 127.

ALLEN, W. H. 1960. Audio-visual communication. In C. H. Harris (ed.) *Encyclopedia of Educational Research*. New York: Macmillan, 115–30.

——. 1957. Research on film use: student participation. *A-V. Communic. Res.*, 5: 423–50.

ALLPORT, G. W. 1935. *Attitudes. A Handbook of Social Psychology*. C. Murchison (ed.) Worcester, Mass.: Clark Univ. Press, Chapter XVII.

——, and B. KRAMER. 1946. Some roots of prejudice. *J. Psychol.*, 22: 9–39

ALPER, THELMA. 1957. Predicting the direction of selective recall, its relation to ego strength and *N* achievement. *J. Abn. Soc. Psychol.*, 55: 149–65.

ALPERT, AUGUSTA. 1928. The solving of problem situations by preschool children. *Teachers College Contributions to Education. No. 323*. New York: Teachers College, Columbia Univ.

AMMONS, R. B. 1947. Acquisition of motor skill: quantitative analysis and theoretical formulation. *Psych. Review*, 54: 263–81.

——. 1960. Skills. In C. Harris (ed.) *Encyclopedia of Educational Research*. New York: Macmillan, 1282–87.

——, and L. WILLIG. 1956. Acquisition of motor skill: IV. Effects of repeated periods of massed practice. *J. Exp. Psychol.*, 51: 118–26.

ANASTASI, ANNE. 1956. Age changes in adult test performance. *Psychol. Rev.*, 2: 509.

——. 1958. *Differential Psychology*. New York: Macmillan.

——, and F. A. CORDOVA. 1953. Some effects of bilingualism upon the intelligence test performance of Puerto Rican children in New York City. *J. Educ. Psychol.*, 44: 1–19.

——, and J. P. FOLEY. 1950. *Differential Psychology*. New York: Macmillan.

ANDERSON, H. C. 1965. Can first graders learn an advanced problem solving skill? *J. Educ. Psychol.*, 56: 283–94.

ANNETT, J. 1959. Learning a pressure under conditions of immediate and delayed knowledge of results. *Quart. J. Psychol.*, 11: 3–15.

——. 1961. The role of knowledge of results in learning: a survey. *Tech. Rep.* 342–43: NAVTRADEVCEN, Port Washington, N.Y.

ARCHER, E. J. 1962. Concept identification as a function of obviousness of relevant and irrelevant information. *J. Exp. Psychol.*, 63: 616–20.

——. 1953. Retention of serial nonsense syllables as a function of rest interval, responding rate, and meaningfulness. *J. Exp. Psychol.*, 45: 245, 252.

—— and B. J. UNDERWOOD. 1951. Retroactive inhibition of verbal associations as a multiple function of temporal point of interpolation and degree of interpolated learning. *J. Exp. Psychol.*, 42: 283–90.

ARONFREED, J. M., S. A. MESSIC, and J. C. DIGGORY. 1953. Re-examining emotionality and perceptual defense. *J. Personality*, 21: 517–28.

ARROW, B. M. 1958. The influence of consistent and inconsistent guidance on human learning and transfer. *J. Educ. Psychol.*, 49: 80–85.

ARROWOOD, J. A. and D. AMOROSO. 1965. Social comparison and ordinal position. *J. Person. and Soc. Psychol.*, 2: 101–4.

ASCHNER, MARY JANE and C. E. BISH (eds.) 1965. Productive thinking in education. New York: Nat'l. Educ. Assn. and the Carnegie Corporation.

ASH, P. 1950. The relative effectiveness of massed versus spaced film presentation. *Res. Quart.*, 41: 19–30.

AUSUBEL, D. P. 1963. *The Psychology of Meaningful Verbal Learning.* New York: Grune and Stratton.

——. 1960. The use of advance organizers in the learning and retention of meaningful verbal material. *J. Educ. Psychol.*, 51: 267–72.

——, and E. BLAKE, JR. 1958. Proactive inhibition in the forgetting of meaningful school material. *J. Educ. Res.*, 52: 145–49.

——, and D. FITZGERALD. 1962. Organizer, general background and antecedent learning variables in sequential verbal learning. *J. Educ. Psychol.*, 53: 243–49.

—— and D. FITZGERALD. 1961. The role of discriminability in meaningful verbal learning and retention. *J. Educ. Psychol.*, 52: 266–74.

——, S. R. SCHPOONT, and LILLIAN CUKIER. 1957. The influence of intention on the retention of school materials. *J. Educ. Psychol.*, 48: 87–92.

ATKINSON, J. W. 1953. The achievement motive and recall of interrupted and completed tasks. *J. Exp. Psychol.*, 46: 381–90.

BABITZ, M. and N. KEYS. 1939. An experiment in teaching pupils to apply scientific principles. *Science Educ.*, 23: 367–70.

BACHMAN, J. 1961. Specificity vs. generality in learning and performing two large muscle motor tasks. *Res. Quart.*, 32: 3–11.

BAGBY, J. W. 1957. A cross-culture study of perceptual predominance in binocular rivalry. *J. Abn. Soc. Psychol.*, 54: 331–34.

BAHRICK, H. P. 1964. Retention curves: facts or artifacts? *Psychol. Bull.*, 61: 188–94.

BAKER, KATHERINE and R. M. GAGNÉ. 1950. Stimulus pre-differentiation as a factor in transfer of training. *J. Exp. Psychol.*, 40: 439–51.

—— and RUTH WYLIE. 1950. Transfer of verbal training to a motor task. *J. Exp. Psychol.*, 60: 632–38.

BANDURA, A. 1964. Behavioral modification through modeling procedures. In L. Krasner and P. Ullman (eds.) *Research in Behavior Modification.* New York: Rinehart and Winston.

——. 1963. Role of imitation in personality development. *J. Nursery Educ.*, 18: 207, 215.

——. 1966. Social learning theory of identification processes. In D. A. Goslin and D. C. Glass (eds.) *Handbook of Socialization Theory and Research.* Chicago: Rand-McNally.

——. 1962. Social learning through imitation. In M. R. Jones (ed.) *Nebraska Symposium on Motivation*. Lincoln, Nebr.: Univ. of Nebr. Press, pp. 211–69.

——, DOROTHEA ROSS, and SHEILA ROSS. 1963. Imitation of film-mediated aggressive models. *J. Abn. Soc. Psychol.*, 66: 3–11.

——, —— and ——. 1961. Transmission of aggression through imitation of aggressive models. *J. Abn. Soc. Psychol.*, 63: 575–82.

BARKER, R. G., BEATRICE WRIGHT, and MOLLIE GONICK. 1946. Adjustment to physical handicap and illness: a survey of the social psychology of physique and disability. New York: Social Science Research Council, Bull. No. 55.

——, TAMARA DEMBO, and K. LEWIN. 1941. Frustration and regression: studies in topological and vector psychology, II. Univ. of Iowa Studies in Child Welfare, 18: No. 1.

BARKER, R. J., J. S. KOUNIN, and H. F. WRIGHT (Eds.) 1943. *Child Behavior and Development*. New York: McGraw-Hill.

BARLOW, M. C. 1937. Transfer of training in reasoning. *J. Educ. Psychol.*, 28: 122–28.

BARTLETT, F. C. 1950. Incentives. *Brit. J. Psychol.*, 41: 122–28.

——. 1932. Remembering: a study in experimental and social psychology. Cambridge, Eng.: The Univ. Press.

——. 1958. *Thinking*. London: Allen and Unwin.

BARTON, W. A. 1930. Outlining as a study procedure. *Teachers College Contributions to Education. No. 411*. New York: Teachers College, Columbia Univ.

BATTIG, W. F. *et al.* 1957. Effect of verbal pretraining on the acquisition of a complex motor skill. *J. Exper. Psychol.*, 54: 375–76.

BATTY, DOROTHY. 1949. A comparison of individual and paired practices at the pre-primer level. Ed. Thesis, Boston Univ.

BAYLEY, NANCY. 1935. The development of motor ability during the first three years. *Soc. Res. Child. Devel. Monogr.* 1: No. 1.

——. 1955. On the growth of intelligence. *Amer. Psychol.*, 10: 805–18.

——. 1954. Some increasing parent-child similarities during the growth of children. *J. Educ. Psychol.*, 45: 1–21.

—— and ANNA ESPENSCHADE. 1941. Motor development from birth to maturity. *J. Educ. Res.*, 11: 562–72.

BAYTON, J. 1941. The racial stereotypes of Negro college students. *J. Abn. Soc. Psychol.*, 36: 97–102.

BECKHAM, A. S. 1934. A study of race attitudes in Negro children of adolescent age. *J. Abn. Soc. Psychol.*, 29: 18–29.

BEEBE-CENTER, J. 1932. *The Psychology of Pleasantness and Unpleasantness*. Princeton, N.J.: Van Nostrand.

BEECROFT, R. S. 1956. Verbal learning and retention as a function of competing associations. *J. Exper. Psychol.,* 51: 216–21.

BERGEN, C. 1943. Some sources of children's science information. *Teachers College Contributions to Education. No. 881.* New York: Teachers College, Columbia Univ.

BERGER, H. 1929. Uber das elektrenkephalogram des menschen. *Arch. Psychiatr. Nervenkr.,* 87: 527–70.

BERLYNE, D. E. 1967. Arousal and reinforcement. In D. Levine (ed.) *Nebraska Symposium on Motivation.* Lincoln, Nebr.: Univ. Nebr. Press, 1–110.

——. 1960. *Conflict, Arousal and Curiosity.* New York: McGraw-Hill.

——. 1965. *Structure and Direction in Thinking.* New York: Wiley.

BERNARD, J. 1942. The lecture-demonstration vs. the problem solving method of teaching a college science course. *Sci. Educ.,* 26: 121–32.

—— and R. GILBERT. 1941. The specificity of the effect of shock for error in maze learning with human subjects. *J. Exp. Psychol.,* 28: 178–86.

BERNARD, MARY. 1958. Homogeneous groups for reading instruction: upper grade rooms divided for reading lessons. *Chicago Schools J.,* 40: 135–39.

BEVAN, W., BRENDA KATZ, and P. SECORD. 1956. The negro stereotype and perceptual accentuation. *J. Abn. Soc. Psychol.,* 53: 78–83.

—— and K. ZENER. 1952. Some influences of past experience upon the perceptual thresholds of visual form. *Amer. J. Psychol.,* 65: 434–42.

BILODEAU, E. A. 1966. *Acquisitions of Skills.* New York: Academic Press.

——. 1954. Rate recovery in a repetitive motor task as a function of successive rest periods. *J. Exp. Psychol.,* 48: 197–203.

—— and INA BILODEAU. 1961. Motor skills in learning. In P. R. Fransworth (ed.) *Annual Review of Psychology.* Palo Alto, Calif.: Annual Reviews, pp. 243–80.

——, —— and D. A. SCHUMSKY. Some effects of introducing and withdrawing knowledge of results early and late in practice. *J. Educ. Psychol.,* 58: 142–44.

BILODEAU, INA and H. SCHLOSBERG. 1951. Similarity in stimulating conditions as a variable in retroactive inhibition. *J. Exp. Psychol.,* 41: 199–204.

BIRCH, H. C. and H. S. RABINOWITZ. 1951. The negative effect of previous experience on productive thinking. *J. Exp. Psychol.,* 41: 121–25.

BIXBY, LODEMA. 1958. The effectiveness of paired study versus individual study in social studies. Ed. Master's Thesis. Boston Univ.

BLACKBURN, J. M. 1936. Acquisition of a skill: an analysis of learning curves. Great Britain: IHRB Report, No. 73.

BLAKE, R. R. and G. V. RAMSEY (eds.) 1951. *Perception: An Approach to Personality.* New York: Ronald.

BLATT, S. J. and M. I. STEIN. 1959. *Efficiency in problem-solving.* Part I. *J. Psychol.,* 48: 193–206.

BLOOM, B. S. 1964. *Stability and Change in Human Characteristics.* New York: Wiley.

—— (ed.) 1956. *Taxonomy of Educational Objectives.* New York: Longhans.

BLOUGH, D. S. and R. B. MILLWARD. 1965. Learning: operant conditioning and verbal learning. In P. R. Farnsworth (ed.) *Annual Review of Psychology.* Palo Alto, Calif.: Annual Reviews, pp. 63–94.

BOGARDUS, E. S. 1947. Changes in racial distances. *Int. J. Opin. Attitude Res.,* 1: 55–62.

——. 1929. *Immigration and Race Attitudes.* Boston: Heath.

——. 1927. Race friendliness and social distance. *J. Appl. Sociol.,* 11: 272–87.

BOGUSLAVSKY, G. W. and E. R. GUTHRIE. 1941. The recall of completed and interrupted activities: an investigation of Zeigarnik's experiment. *Psychol. Bull.,* 38: 575–76.

BOSTRUM, R. N., J. W. VLANDES, and M. E. ROSENBAUM. 1961. Grades as reinforcing contingencies and attitude changes. *J. Educ. Psychol.,* 52: 112–15.

BOTTOMLY, F. 1961. An experiment with the controlled readers. *J. Educ. Res.,* 54: 265–69.

BOURNE, L. E. 1965. Hypotheses and hypothesis shifts in classification learning. *J. Gen. Psychol.,* 72: 251–61.

BOUSFIELD, W. A., B. H. COHEN and G. A. WHITMARSH. 1958. Associative clustering in the recall of words of different taxonomic frequencies of occurrence. *Psychol. Rep.,* 4: 39–44.

BOVARD, E. W., JR. 1951. Group structure and perception. *J. Abn. Soc. Psychol.,* 46: 398–405.

BRACKBILL, YVONNE. 1958. Extinction of the smiling response in infants as a function of reinforcement schedule. *Child Developm.,* 29: 115–24.

BREAM, H. and L. MESSERSMITH. 1948. An experiment in teaching tumbling with and without motion pictures. *Res. Quart.,* 19: 304–98.

BRENER, R. 1940. An experimental investigation of the memory span. *J. Exp. Psychol.,* 26: 467–82.

BRIDGES, KATHERINE. 1932. Emotional development in early infancy. *Child Developm.,* 3: 324–41.

BRIGGS, G. E. 1957. Retroactive inhibition as a function of the degree of original and interpolated learning. *J. Exp. Psychol.,* 53: 60–67.

—— and W. J. BROGDEN. 1954. The effect of component practice on a lever positioning skill. *J. Exp. Psychol.,* 48: 375–80.

—— and L. K. WATERS. 1958. Training and transfer as a function of component interaction. *J. Exp. Psychol.,* 56: 492–500.

BRIGGS, L. J. 1962. The probable role of teaching machines in classroom practice. *Theory into Practice.* 1: No. 1.

—— and H. B. REED. 1943. The curve of retention for substance material. *J. Exp. Psychol.,* 32: 513–17.

BRISTON, W. H. and D. A. ABRAMSON. 1966. Curriculum planning and development. *Rev. of Educ. Res.*, 36: 339–98.

BRITT, S. H. 1935. Retroactive inhibition: a review of the literature. *Psychol. Bull.* 32: 381–440.

—— and M. E. BUNCH. 1934. Jost's Law and retroactive inhibition. *Amer. J. Psychol.* 46: 299–308.

BROADHEAD, R. and S. DIMOND. 1950. The social studies—thinking. *Rev. of Educ. Res.* 20: 262–63.

BRODIE, A. B., JR. 1964. Attitude toward school and academic achievement. *Pers. and Guid. J.* 43: 375–78.

BRONFENBRENNER, J. 1961. The changing American child: a speculative analysis. *J. Soc. Issues.* 7: 6–18.

BROOKS, N. 1964. *Language and Language Learning: Theory and Practice, 2nd ed.* New York: Harcourt, Brace, & World.

BROWN, F. 1953. Problems presented by the concept of acquired drives. *Current theory and research in motivation: A symposium.* Lincoln, Nebr.: Univ. of Nebraska Press, pp. 1–21.

BROWN, R. W. 1958. *Words and Things.* Glencoe, Ill.: Free Press.

BROWN, W. F. 1954. Motivation differences between high and low scholarship college groups. *J. Educ. Psychol.* 45: 215–23.

BROWNELL, W. A. and CHARLOTTE CHAZEL. 1935. The effects of premature drill in third grade arithmetic. *J. Educ. Res.* 29: 17.

—— and G. HENDRICKSON. 1950. How children learn information, concepts, and generalization. *Nat'l. Soc. Study of Educ.* 49th Yrbk. Chicago: Univ. of Chicago Press. Part I, pp. 92–128.

BROYLER, C. R., E. L. THORNDIKE and ELLA WOODYARD. 1927. A second study of mental discipline in high school studies. *J. Educ. Psychol.* 18: 377–404.

BRUCE, R. W. 1933. Conditions of transfer of training. *J. Exp. Psychol.* 16: 343–61.

BRUNER, J. S. 1961. The act of discovery. *Harvard Educ. Rev.* 31: 21–32.

——. 1964. The course of cognitive growth. *Amer. Psychol.* 19: 1–15.

—— (ed.) 1966. Learning about learning. A conference report. Washington, D.C.: U.S. Dept. of Health, Education, and Welfare.

—— and C. GOODMAN. 1947. Value and need as organizing factors in perception. *J. Abn. Soc. Psychol.* 42: 33–44.

——, JACQUELINE GOODNOW, and G. A. AUSTIN. 1956. *A Study of Thinking.* New York: Wiley.

—— and Q. L. MINTURN. 1955. Perceptual identification and perceptual organization. *J. Gen. Psychol.* 53: 21–28.

BRUNSWIK, E. 1955. Representative design and probabilistic theory in a functional psychology. *Psychol. Rev.* 62: 193–217.

—— and L. POSTMAN. 1947. Emotional selectivity in perception and reaction. *J. Personality.* 16: 69–77.

——, ——, and J. RODRIQUES. 1951. Expectation and the perception of color. *Amer. J. Psychol.* 64: 216–27.

BUCKINGHAM, B. R. and J. MAC LATCHY. 1930. The number abilities of children when they enter grade one. *Twenty-ninth Yearbook of the National Society for the Study of Education.* Part II: 473–549.

BUELL, C. 1951. Motor performance of visually handicapped children. *J. Except. Children.* 17: 69–72.

BUHLER, K. 1930. *The Mental Development of the Children.* New York: Harcourt, Brace, & World.

BUNCH, MARION and FRANCES D. MC TEER. 1932. The influence of punishment during learning upon retroactive inhibition. *J. Exp. Psychol.* 15: 473–95.

—— and K. WIENTAGE. 1933. The relative susceptibility of pleasant, unpleasant, and indifferent material to retroactive inhibition. *J. Gen. Psychol.* 9: 157–78.

BUROS, E. K., JR. (ed.) 1965. *Mental Measurements Yearbooks.* Highland Park, N.J.: Gryphon Press, Editions 1–5 (1941–65).

BURT, H. E. 1941. An experimental study of early childhood memory. *J. Genet. Psychol.* 58: 435–39.

BUSH, R. R. and F. MOSTELLER. 1951. A mathematical model for simple learning. *Psychol. Rev.* 58: 313–23.

——, ——. 1955. *Stochastic Models for Learning.* New York: Wiley.

CADY, HELEN. 1924. On the psychology of testimony. *Amer. J. Psychol.* 35: 110–12.

CAMPBELL, D. T. 1957. Factors relevant to the validity of experiments in social settings. *Psychol. Bull.* 54: 297–312.

—— and J. C. STANLEY. 1963. Experimental and quasi-experimental designs for research in teaching. In N. L. Gage (ed.) *Handbook of Research on Teaching.* Chicago: Rand-McNally, pp. 171–246.

CAPLIN, D. 1937. A special report on retardation of children with impaired hearing in New York City Schools. *Amer. Ann. Deaf.* 82: 234–43.

CAREY, GLORIA. 1958. Sex differences in problem-solving performance as a function of attitude differences. *J. Abn. Soc. Psychol.* 56: 256–60.

CARON, A. J. and M. A. WALLACH. 1957. Recall of interrupted tasks under stress: a phenomenon of memory or learning. *J. Abn. Soc. Psychol.* 55: 372–81.

CARPENTER, C. R. 1963. *Review of research on instructional television.* Waltham, Mass.: Brandeis Univ., Morse Communication Research Center.

—— and L. P. GREENHILL. 1963. *Comparative Research on Methods and Media for Presenting Programmed Courses in Mathematics and English.* University Park, Pa.: The Pennsylvania State Univ. Press.

CARR, H. A. 1930. Teaching and learning. *J. Genet. Psychol.* 37: 189–218.

CASON, H. 1932. The learning and retention of pleasant and unpleasant activities. *Archives of Psychol.* 21: No. 134.

CASTANEDA, A., D. S. PALERMO, and B. R. MC CANDLESS. 1956. Complex learning and performance as a function of anxiety in children and task difficulty. *Child Development.* 27: 327–32.

CHAMBERS, R. M. 1956. Some physiological bases for reinforcing properties of reward injections. *J. Comp. Physiol. Psychol.* 49: 565–68.

CHANDLER, R. E. 1957. The statistical concepts of confidence and significance. *Psychol. Bull.* 54: 429–30.

CHILD, I. L. 1946. Children's preference for goals easy or difficult to attain. *Psychol. Mono.* 60:4.

Children's Bureau. 1953. *Research Relating to Children.* U.S. Dept. of Health, Education, and Welfare. Bull. 2.

CHURCH, R. M. 1963. The varied effects of punishment on behavior. *Psychol. Rev.* 70: 369–402.

CLARK, E. R. 1962. The role of drive (time stress) in complex learning: an emphasis on pre-learning phenomena. *J. Exp. Psychol.* 63: 57–61.

CLARK, K. B. 1962. Segregated schools in New York City. *J. Educ. Soc.* 36: 245–50.

CLARK, V. L. 1960. Effect of mental practice on the development of a certain motor skill. *Res. Quart.* 31: 560–69.

COFER, C. N. 1941. A comparison of logical and verbatim learning of prose passages of different lengths. *Amer. J. Psychol.* 54: 1–20.

COHEN, I. S. 1961. Rigidity and anxiety in a motor response. *Percept. Motor Skills.* 12: 127–30.

COLLINSON, L. 1940. Chronological acceleration and retardation at junior high school level. *Contributions to Education No. 262.* George Peabody College for Teachers.

COMBS, A. W. and C. TAYLOR. 1952. The effect of the perception of mild degrees of threat on performance. *J. Abn. Soc. Psychol.* 47: 420–24.

CONKLIN, J. E. 1957. Effect of controllage on performance of a tracking task. *J. Exp. Psychol.* 53: 261–68.

——. 1959. Linearity of the tracking performance function. *Percept. Motor Skills.* 9: 387–91.

CONWAY, C. B. 1937. The hearing abilities of children in Toronto Public Schools. *Bull. Dept. Educ. Res.* Ontario Coll. Educ. No. 9: 132.

COOK, S. W. and CLAIRE SELLITZ. 1964. A multiple-indicator approach to attitude measurement. *Psychol. Bull.* 62: 36–55.

COOK, W. W. 1941. Some effects of the maintenance of high standards of promotion. *Elem. Sch. J.* 44: 430–37.

COREY, S. M. 1940. Changes in the opinions of female students after one year at a university. *J. Social Psychol.* 11: 341–51.

CORLISS, L. M., MILDRED DOSTER, and GERTRUDE CROMWELL. 1964. Summary analysis of recorded incidence, amount of medical care, and follow-through on organic heart disease in 95,000 pupils. *J. Sch. Health.* 34: 181–84.

CORNER, G. W. 1944. *Ourselves Unborn.* New Haven, Conn.: Yale Univ. Press, p. 188.

COSTER, J. 1958. Attitudes toward school of high school pupils from 3 income levels. *J. Educ. Psychol.* 49: 61–66.

COULSON, P. and H. SILBERMAN. 1960. Effects of three variables in a teaching machine. *J. Educ. Psychol.* 51: 135–43.

COWEN, E. L. 1952. The influence of varying degrees of psychological stress and problem-solving rigidity. *J. Abn. Soc. Psychol.* 47: 512–19.

—— and G. C. THOMPSON. 1951. Problem-solving rigidity and personality structure. *J. Abn. Soc. Psychol.* 46: 165–76.

COXE, W. W. 1923. A controlled experiment to determine the extent to which Latin can function in the spelling of English words. *J. Educ. Res.* 7: 244–50.

——. 1924. Influence of Latin on the spelling of English words. *J. Educ. Res.* 9: 223–33.

COYNE, CATHERINE. 1941. British child evacuees paint American scene for America. *Boston Sunday Herald* (April 6, 1941).

CRATTY, R. J. 1963. Comparisons of verbal-motor performance and learning in serial memory tasks. *Res. Quart.* 34: 431–39.

CRON, G. W. and N. H. PRONKO. 1957. Development of the sense of balance in school children. *J. Educ. Res.* 51: 33–37.

CROSLAND, H. R. 1921. A qualitative analysis of the process of forgetting. *Psychol. Mono.* 29: No. 130.

CROSS, K. PATRICIA, and E. L. GAIER. 1955. Techniques in problem-solving as a predictor of educational achievement. *J. Educ. Psychol.* 46: 193–206.

CROSSMAN, E. R. 1959. A theory of the acquisition of speed-skill. *Ergonomics.,* 2: 153–66.

CULLER, E. A. 1928. The law of effect, IX. *Psychol. Rev.* 45: 206–11.

CURTI, MARGARET. 1950. Child development: concepts. In W. S. Monroe (ed.) *Encyclopedia of Educational Research.* New York: Macmillan.

——. 1938. *Child Psychology.* 2nd ed. New York: Longmans-Green.

DALLENBACH, K. M. 1913. The relation of memory error to time interval. *Psychol. Rev.* 20: 323–37.

DALTON, M. M. 1943. A visual survey of 5000 school children. *J. Educ. Res.* 37: 81–94.

DAMRON, C. 1955. Two and three dimensional slide images used with tachistoscopic training techniques in instructing high school football players in defense. *Res. Quart.* 26: 36–43.

DAVIDSON, H. and G. LANG. 1960. Children's perceptions of their teachers' feelings toward them related to self-perception, school achievement and behavior. *J. Exp. Educ.* 29: 107–18.

DAVIS, A. 1961. *Social Class Influence Upon Learning.* Cambridge, Mass.: Harvard Univ. Press.

——. 1951. Socio-economic status and its influence on children's learning. *Understand the Child.* 20: 10–16.

DAVIS, R. A. 1935. *Psychology of Learning.* New York: McGraw-Hill.

DEARBORN, W. F. and J. ROTHNEY. 1941. *Predicting the Child's Development.* Cambridge, Mass.: *Sci-Art. Pub.*, p. 360.

DE BOER, LOUIS. 1962. Application of screening method for the detection of heart disease in children. *J. Sch. Health.* 32: 41–48.

DEESE, J. 1960. Frequency of usage and number of words in free recall—the role of associations. *Psychol. Rep.* 7: 337–40.

DEMBER, W. N. 1965. The new look in motivation. *Amer. Sci.* 53: 409–27.

DENNIS, W. 1935. A comparison of the rat's first and second explorations of a maze unit. *Amer. J. Psychol.* 47: 488–90.

DENNY, M., M. FRISBEY, and J. WEAVER. 1955. Rotary pursuit performance under alternate conditions of distributed and massed practice. *J. Exp. Psychol.* 49: 48–54.

DE SOTO, C. B., E. B. COLEMAN, and P. L. PUTNAM. 1960. Predictions of sequences of successes and failures. *J. Exp. Psychol.* 59: 41–46.

DEWEY, J. 1910. *How We Think.* Boston: D. C. Heath.

DILLON, E. 1952. A study of the use of music as an aid in teaching swimming. *Res. Quart.* 23: 1–8.

DI VESTA, F. J. and K. BLAKE. 1959. The effects of instructional sets on learning and transfer. *Amer. J. Psychol.* 72: 57–67.

DIXON, J. C. 1957. Development of self-recognition. *J. Genet. Psychol.*, 91: 251–56.

DOANE, B. K. *et al.* 1959. Changes in perceptual function after isolation. *Can. J. Psychol.* 13: 210–19.

DOMINOWSKI, R. L. 1965. Role of memory in concept learning. *Psychol. Bull.* 63: 271–80.

DORE, L. R. and E. R. HILGARD. 1937. Spaced practice and the maturation hypothesis. *J. Psychol.* 27: 303–12.

DOWLING, R. and H. BRAUN. 1957. Retention and meaningfulness of materials. *J. Exp. Psychol.* 54: 213–17.

DRAKE, R. M. 1940. The effect of teaching the vocabulary of algebra. *J. Educ. Res.* 34: 601–10.

DREVDAHL, J. E. 1961. A study of the etiology and development of the creative personality. Washington, D.C.: USOE, pp. 350–71.

DUDYCHA, G. J. 1942. Attitudes toward war. *Psychol. Bull.* 39: 846–58.

——. 1933. The religious beliefs of college students. *J. App. Psychol.* 17: 585–603.

—— and MARTHA DUDYCHA. 1941. Childhood memories: a review of the literature. *Psychol. Bull.* 38: 668–82.

DUNCAN, C. P. 1951. The effects of unequal amounts of practice on motor learning before and after rest. *J. Exp. Psychol.* 42: 257–64.

——. 1959. Recent research on human problem-solving. *Psychol. Bull.* 56: 397–429.

——. 1958. Transfer after training with single vs. multiple tasks. *J. Exp. Psychol.* 55: 63–72.

——. 1953. Transfer of motor learning as a function of degree of first-task learning and inter-task similarity. *J. Exp. Psychol.* 45: 1–11.

—— and B. J. UNDERWOOD. 1953. Retention of transfer in motor learning after 24 hours and 14 months. *J. Exp. Psychol.* 46: 445–52.

DURRELL, D. D. 1940. *Improvement of Basic Reading Abilities*. Yonkers-on-Hudson, N.Y.: World Book Co.

——. 1954. Learning difficulties among children of normal intelligence. *Elem. Sch. J.* 55: 201–8.

—— and SISTER MARY HARRINGTON. 1960. Mental maturity versus perceptual abilities in primary reading. *J. Educ. Psychol.*, p. 50.

DYNES, J. J. 1932. Comparison of two methods of studying history. *J. Exp. Educ.* 1: 42–45.

EAMES, T. H. 1943. The effect of correlation of refractive errors on the distant and near vision of school children. *J. Educ. Res.* 37: 37–542.

——. 1947. The speed of object recognition and of word recognition in groups of passing and failing pupils. *J. Educ. Psychol.* 38: 119–22.

EASLEY, H. 1937. The curve of forgetting and the distribution of practice. *J. Educ. Psychol.* 28: 474–78.

EDGERTON, H. A. and S. H. BRITT. 1944. Sex difference in the science talent test. *Science.* 100: 192–93.

EDMISTON, R. W. and J. G. BENTER. 1949. The relationship between achievement and range of abilities within the group. *J. Educ. Res.* 42: 547–48.

EDWARDS, A. L. and H. B. ENGLISH. 1939. The effect of the immediate test on verbatim and summary retention. *Amer. J. Psychol.* 52: 372–75.

EDWARDS, W. 1956. Reward probability, amount and information as determiners of sequential two-alternative decisions. *J. Exp. Psychol.* 52: 177–88.

EGSTROM, G. E. 1964. Effects of an emphasis on conceptualizing techniques during learning of a gross motor skill. *Res. Quart.,* pp. 472–82.

EIKENBERRY, D. H. 1923. Permanence of high school learning. *J. of Educ. Psychol.* 14: 463–82.

ELKINS, DEBORAH and HILDA TABA. 1966. *Teaching Strategies for the Culturally Disadvantaged.* Chicago: Rand-McNally.

EMMONS, W. H. and C. W. SIMONS. 1956. The non-recall of materials presented during sleep. *Amer. J. of Psychol.* 69: 76–81.

ENTWISLE, DORIS and W. HUGGINS. 1964. Interference in meaningful learning. *J. Educ. Psychol.* 55: 75–78.

ERIKSON, E. 1950. *Childhood and Society.* New York: Norton.

ERVIN, S. M. 1960. Transfer effects of learning a verbal generalization. *Child. Developm.* 31: 537–54.

ESPENSCHADE, ANNA. 1942. Physiological maturity as a factor in the qualification of boys for physical activity. *Res. Quart.,* pp. 113–17.

ESTES, W. K. 1959. The statistical approach to learning theory. In S. Koch (ed.) *Psychology: A Study of Science.* Vol. II, 380–491. New York: McGraw-Hill.

––––. 1944. An experimental study of punishment. *Psychol. Mono.* 57: No. 263.

––––. 1961. Growth and function of mathematical models for learning. In *Current Trends in Psychological Theory.* Pittsburgh: Univ. of Pittsburgh Press, pp. 134–51.

––––. 1956. Learning. *Annual Rev. of Psychol.* 7: 1–38.

––––. 1962. Learning theory. In P. R. Farnsworth (ed.) *Annual Review of Psychology.* Palo Alto, Calif.: Annual Reviews. 13: 107–44.

––––, S. KOCH, K. MAC CORQUODALE, P. E. MEEHL, C. G. MUELLER, W. N. SCHOENFELD, and W. S. VERPLANCK. 1954. *Modern Learning Theory.* New York: Appleton-Century-Crofts.

FABUN, D. 1968. *The Dynamics of Change.* Englewood Cliffs, N.J.: Prentice-Hall.

FALKNER, E. 1960. *Human Development.* Philadelphia: Saunders.

FANTZ, R. L. 1961. The origin of form perception. *Sci. Amer.* 204: 66–72.

FARNSWORTH, P. R. 1937. Changes in attitude toward war during college years. *J. Soc. Psychol.* 8: 274–79.

FARRIS, L. P. Visual defects as factors influencing achievement in reading. *J. Exp. Educ.,* 5: 58–60.

FATTU, N., *et al.* 1955. Partial reinforcement related to free responding in extinction with preschool children. *J. Exp. Educ.* 23: 365–68.

FAY, P. J. 1937. The effects of the knowledge of marks on subsequent achievement of college students. *J. Educ. Psychol.* 28: 548–54.

FEATHER, N. T. 1963. The effect of differential failure on expectation of success, reported anxiety, and response uncertainty. *J. Personality.* 31: 289–312.

FEIFEL, H. and I. LORGE. 1950. Qualitative differences in the vocabulary responses of children. *J. Educ. Psychol.* 41: 1–18.

FELDHUSEN, J. E. and H. J. KLAUSMEIER. 1962. Anxiety, intelligence and achievement in children of low, average, and high intelligence. *Child. Developm.* 33: 403–9.

FERSTER, C. D. and S. M. SAPON. 1958. An application of recent developments in psychology to the teaching of German. *Harvard Educ. Rev.* 28: 58–69.

FESTINGER, L. 1961. The psychological effects of insufficient rewards. *Amer. Psychol.* 16: 1–11.

FINN, J. D. 1960. Automotion and education. In *Technology and the Instructional Process. A. V. Communic. Rev.* Winter: 5–26.

FITTS, P. M. 1964. Skill learning. In A. W. Melton (ed.) *Categories of Human Learning.* New York: Academic Press, pp. 243–85.

———, H. P. BAHRICK, M. E. NOBLE, and G. E. BRIGGS. 1966. *Skilled Performance.* New York: Wiley.

FLANAGAN, J. C. 1951. Units, scores, and norms. In E. F. Lindquist (ed.) *Educational Measurements.* Washington, D.C.: Amer. Council on Educ., pp. 695–763.

FLEISHMAN, E. A. 1957. A comparative study of aptitude patterns in unskilled and skilled psycho-motor performances. *J. Appl. Psychol.* 41: 263–72.

———. 1964. *The Structure and Measurement of Physical Fitness.* Englewood Cliffs, N.J.: Prentice-Hall.

——— and B. FRUCHTER. Factor structure and predictability of successive stages of learning Morse code. *J. Appl. Psychol.* 44: 97–101.

FLÜGEL, J. C. 1925. A quantitative study of feeling and emotion in everyday life. *Brit. J. Psychol.* 15: 318–55.

FORGUS, D. D. and HAZEL MOLITER. 1962. Reinforcement as a function of instructional set. *J. Psychol.* 53: 193–98.

FORGUS, R. H. and R. J. SCHWARTZ. 1957. Efficient retention and transfer as affected by learning method. *J. Psychol.* 43: 135–39.

FORLANO, G. 1936. An experiment in which the delayed and immediate knowledge of results with monetary reward is compared with delayed and immediate knowledge of results. *Teachers College Contributions to Education. No. 688.* New York: Teachers College, Columbia Univ.

———. 1936. School learning with various methods of practice and rewards. *Teachers College Contributions to Education. No. 688.* New York: Teachers College, Columbia Univ.

——— and M. H. HOFFMAN. 1937. Guessing and telling methods in learning words of a foreign language. *J. Educ. Psychol.* 28: 632–36.

FOURACRE, M. H., GLADYS JANN, and ANNA MARTORANA. 1950. Educational abilities and needs of orthopedically handicapped children. *Elem. School J.* Feb.: 331–38.

FOX, MARGARET G. and ETHEL LAMB. 1962. Improvement during a nonpractice period in selected physical education activity. *Res. Quart.* 33: 381–86.

FRANK, J. D. and E. J. LUDVIGH. The retroactive effect of pleasant and unpleasant odors on learning. *Amer. J. Psychol.* 43: 102–8.

FRASER, J. A. 1939. Outcomes of a study excursion. *Teachers College Contributions to Education. No. 778.* New York: Teachers College, Columbia Univ.

FREEBURNE, C. M. 1949. The influence of training in perceptual span and perceptual speed upon reading ability. *J. Educ. Psychol.* 40: 321–51.

FREEDMAN, M. B. 1966. Changes in attitude and values over six decades. In Marie Jahoda and N. Warren (eds.) *Attitudes.* Baltimore, Md.: Penguin Books, pp. 125–35.

FREEMAN, GERALDINE and S. JOHNSON. 1964. Allergic diseases in adolescents: I. *Amer. J. of Diseases in Children.* 26: 549–59.

FREEMAN, J. T. 1954. Set or perceptual defense. *J. Exp. Psychol.* 48: 283–88.

FRENCH, ELIZABETH. 1958. The interaction of achievement motivation and ability in problem-solving success. *J. Abn. Soc. Psychol.* 57: 306–9.

—— and F. H. THOMAS. 1958. The relation of achievement motivation to problem-solving effectiveness. *J. Abn. Soc. Psychol.* 56: 45–48.

FRENKEL-BRUNSWIK, ELSE and JOAN HAVEL. 1953. Prejudice in the interviews of children: attitudes toward minority groups. *Pedag. Sem. and J. Gen. Psychol.* 82: 91–136.

FRIEDMAN, K. 1944. The growth of time concepts. *Soc. Educ.* 8: 29–31.

—— and VIOLA MARTI. 1946. A time comprehension test. *J. Educ. Res.* 39: 62–68.

FRUTCHEY, F. P. 1937. Retention in high school chemistry. *J. Higher Educ.* 8: 217–18; also, *Educ. Res. Bull.,* 1937, 16: 34–37.

FRYMIER, J. R. 1958. Relationship of aural perceptions to cultural situations. *Percept. and Mot. Skills.* 8: 67–70.

GAETH, J. H. and DORIS ALLEN. 1965. Association value for selected trigrams with children. *J. Verb. Learn. and Verb. Behav.* 5: 473–77.

—— and ——. 1966. Effect of similarity upon learning in children. *J. Exp. Child. Psychol.* 4: 381–89.

GAGE, N. L. 1963. *Handbook of Research on Teaching.* Chicago: Rand-McNally.

——. 1963. Paradigms for research on teaching. In N. L. Gage (ed.) *Handbook of Research on Teaching.* Chicago: Rand-McNally, pp. 94–141.

——. 1963. *Readings in Social Psychology Applied to the Classroom.* Boston: Allyn, Bacon.

—— and G. SOUCI. 1951. Social perception and teacher-pupil relationships. *J. of Educ. Psychol.* 42: 145–52.

GAGNÉ, R. M. 1965. *The Conditions of Learning.* New York: Holt, Rinehart, & Winston.

——. 1966. The learning of principles. In H. J. Klausmeier and C. W. Harris (eds.) *Analyses of Concept Learning.* New York: Academic Press.

——. 1964. Problem solving. In A. W. Melton (ed.) *Categories of Human Learning.* New York: Academic Press.

—— and HARRIET FOSTER. 1949. Transfer to a motor skill from practice on a pictured representation. *J. Exp. Psychol.* 39: 342–54.

—— and ——. 1949. Transfer of training from practice on components in a motor skill. *J. Exp. Psychol.* 39: 47–68.

—— and KATHERINE BAKER. 1950. Transfer of discrimination training to a motor task. *J. Exp. Psychol.* 40: 314–28.

——, RUTH WYLIE, and K. E. BAKER. 1950. Transfer of training to a motor skill as a function of variation in rate of response. *J. Exp. Psychol.* 40: 721–32.

GALANTER, E. H. (ed.) 1959. *Automatic Teaching: The State of the Art.* New York: Wiley.

GARRY, R. J. 1963. *The economics of educational television.* Waltham, Mass.: Brandeis Univ., Morse Communication Research Center.

GARRY, R. 1963. *The Psychology of Learning.* New York: Center for Applied Research in Education.

——. 1964. Summary of research on *parlons français.* Boston: Modern Language Project.

—— and ANNA ASCARELLI. 1960. Teaching topographical and special orientation to congenitally blind children. *J. Educ.* No. 2. 143: 1–48.

GATES, A. I. 1917. Recitation as a factor in memorizing. *Archives of Psychol.* 6: No. 40.

GELLERMAN, L. W. 1931. The double alternation problem: II. The behavior of children and human adults in a double alternation temporal maze. *J. Genet. Psychol.* 39: 359–92.

GESELL, A. and LOUISE AMES. 1946. The development of directionality in drawing. *J. Gen. Psychol.* 68: 45–61.

—— and HELEN THOMPSON. 1934. *Infant Behavior: Its Genesis and Growth.* New York: McGraw-Hill.

GETZELS, J. W. 1964. Creative thinking, problem-solving, and instruction. In E. R. Hilgard (ed.) *Theories of Learning and Instruction.* 63rd Yearbook, National Soc. for Study of Educ. Chicago, pp. 240–67.

—— and P. W. JACKSON. 1962. *Creativity and Intelligence: Exploration With Gifted Children.* New York: Wiley.

GIBSON, ELEANOR. 1953. Improvement in perceptual judgments as a function of controlled practice or training. *Psychol. Bull.* 50: 401–31.

—— and J. J. GIBSON. 1934. Retention and the interpolated task. *Amer. J. of Psychol.* 46: 603–10.

GIBSON, J. J. 1959. Perception as a function of stimulation. In S. Koch (ed.) *Psychology: A Study of a Science.* Vol. 1. New York: McGraw-Hill, pp. 456–501.

GILBERT, A. C. F. 1956. Effect of immediacy of knowledge of correctness of response upon learning. *J. Educ. Psychol.* 47: 415–23.

GILBERT, G. M. 1938. The new status of experimental studies on the relationship of feeling to memory. *Psychol. Bull.* 35: 26–35.

——. 1951. Stereotype persistence and change among college students. *J. Abn. Soc. Psychol.* 46: 245–54.

GILLIAND, A. R., MARY MC BATH, and JEANNE PFAFF. 1950. Socio-economic status and race as factors in infant intelligence scores. *Amer. Psychol.* 5: 293.

GLANZER, M. 1958. Curiosity, exploratory drive, and stimulus satisfaction. *Psychol. Bull.* 55: 302–15.

——. 1953. The role of stimulus satisfaction in spontaneous alternation. *J. Exp. Psychol.* 45: 387–93.

—— and R. GLASER. 1961. Techniques for the study of group structure and behavior: II. Empirical studies of the effects of structure in small groups. *Psychol. Bull.* 58: 1–27.

GLASER, R. (ed.) 1962. *Training Research and Education.* Pittsburgh: Univ. of Pittsburgh Press.

GLAZE, J. A. 1928. The association value of nonsense syllables. *J. Genet. Psychol.* 35: 255–67.

GLIXMAN, A. F. 1949. Recall of completed and incompleted activities under varying degrees of stress. *J. Exp. Psychol.* 39: 281–95.

GOLANN, S. E. 1963. Psychological study of creativity. *Psychol. Bull.* 60: 548–65.

GOLLIN, E. S. and A. BARON. 1954. Response consistency in perception and retention. *J. Exp. Psychol.* 47: 259–62.

GOODENOUGH, FLORENCE L. 1935. The development of creative process from early childhood to maturity. *J. Exp. Psychol.* 18: 431–50.

——. 1940. Some special problems of nature-nurture research. *Thirty-ninth Yearbook of the National Society for the Study of Education.* Part I: 367–84.

GOODLAD, J. I. 1954. Room to live and learn: class size and room space as factors in the learning-teaching process. *Childh. Educ.* 30: 355–61.

GOODNOW, JACQUELINE and L. POSTMAN. 1955. Probability learning in a problem solving situation. *J. Exper. Psychol.* 49: 16–21.

GOTKIN, L. and L. GOLDSTEIN. 1962. Programmed instruction for the younger learner: a comparison of two presentation modes in two environments. *Research portfolio*. Center for Programmed Instruction, New York.

GRANT, D. A., H. W. HAKE, and J. P. HORNSETH. 1951. Acquisition and extinction of a verbal conditioned response with differing percentages of reinforcement. *J. Exp. Psychol.* 41: 137–43.

GRAY, S. E. and A. THOMPSON. 1953. The ethnic prejudices of white and negro college students. *J. Abn. Soc. Psychol.* 48: 311–13.

GREEN, D. R. 1964. *Educational Psychology*. Englewood Cliffs, N.J.: Prentice-Hall, pp. 1–31.

GREENE, E. B. 1931. The retention of information learned in college courses. *J. of Educ. Res.* 24: 262–73.

GREENSPOON, J. and R. REDGE. 1957. Stimulus conditions and retroactive inhibition. *J. Exp. Psychol.* 53: 55–59.

GRICE, G. R. 1955. Discrimination reaction time as a function of anxiety and intelligence. *J. Abn. Soc. Psychol.* 50: 71–74.

GROPPER, G. L. 1967. *Teaching via television:* a behavioral view. Waltham, Mass.: Brandeis Univ., Morse Communication Research Center.

GUETZKOW, H. E., L. KELLY, and W. J. MC KEACHIE. 1954. An experimental comparison of recitation, discussion, and tutorial methods in college teaching. *J. Educ. Psychol.* 45: 193–207.

GUILFORD, J. P. 1950. Creativity. *Amer. Psychol.* 5: 444–54.

——. 1934. *Laboratory Studies in Psychology*. New York: Holt, Rinehart & Winston.

——. 1956. The structure of intellect. *Psychol. Bull.* 53: 267–93.

——. 1958. A system of psychomotor abilities. *Amer. J. Psychol.* 71: 164–74.

——. 1959. Three faces of intellect. *Amer. Psychol.* 14: 469–79.

GUNBORG, B. G. 1939. Difficulty of the arithmetic processes. *Elem. School J.* 40: 198.

GYR, J. W. 1966. Computer simulation and psychological theories of perception. *Psychol. Bull.* 65: 174–92.

HAGMAN, E. R. 1932. A study of fears of children of preschool age. *J. Exp. Educ.* 1: 110–30.

HAHN, H. H. and E. L. THORNDIKE. 1914. Some results of practice in addition under school conditions. *J. Educ. Psychol.* 5: 65–84.

HALL, J. F. 1954. Learning as a function of word frequency. *Amer. J. Psychol.* 67: 38–40.

HALLORAN, J. D. 1967. *Attitude Formation and Change*. Leicester, England: Leicester Univ. Press.

HAMBURGER, V. 1955. In H. Waesch (ed.) *Biochemistry of the Developing Nervous System*. New York: Academic Press.

HAMMER, E. F. 1953. Frustration-aggression hypothesis extend to socio-racial areas: comparison of Negro and white children's HTP's. *Psychol. Quart.* 27: 597–607.

HARDING, L. W. and INEZ BRYANT. 1943. An experiment on comparison drill and direct experience in arithmetical learning in a fourth grade. *J. Educ. Res.* 37: 321.

HARLEY, R. K. 1963. Verbalism among blind children. Research Series No. 10. New York: Foundation for the Blind.

HARLOW, H. F. 1949. The formation of learning sets. *Psychol. Rev.* 56: 51–65.

——. 1958. The nature of love. *Amer. Psychol.* 13: 673–85.

——, M. K. HARLOW, R. R. RUEPING, and W. A. MASON. 1960. Performance of infant rhesus monkeys on discrimination learning, delayed response, and discrimination learning sets. *J. Comp. Physiol. Psychol.* 53: 113–21.

HARRIS, C. W. 1960. *Encyclopedia of Educational Research.* New York: Macmillan.

HARRIS, D. B. 1950. How children learn interest, motives, attitudes. *Forty-ninth Yearbook of the National Society for the Study of Education.* Chicago: Univ. of Chicago Press. Part I: 129–82.

HART, R. H. 1959. The effectiveness of an approach to the problem of varying abilities in teaching reading. *J. Educ. Res.* 52: 228–31.

HARTER, G. L. 1930. Overt trial and error in the problem solving of preschool children. *J. Genet. Psychol.* 38: 361–72.

HASELRUD, G. M. and SHIRLEY MEYERS. 1958. The transfer value of given and individually derived principles. *J. Educ. Psychol.* 49: 293–98.

HAVIGHURST, R. J. and F. H. BREESE. 1947. Relation between ability and social status in a midwestern community. III. Primary Mental Abilities. *J. Educ. Psychol.* 38: 241–47.

HAYES, S. P. 1941. Contributions to a psychology of blindness. *Amer. Foundation for the Blind,* p. 296.

——. 1938. What do blind children know? *Tech. Forum.* 11: 22, 32.

HAYNES, H. C. 1936. Teacher intelligence and pupil thinking. *North Carolina Educ.* 2: 306, 346–47.

HEBB, D. O. 1949. *The Organization of Behavior.* New York: Wiley.

HEER, D. M. 1959. The sentiment of white supremacy: an ecological study. *Amer. J. Sociol.* 64: 592–98.

HEIDBREDER, EDNA. 1948. The attainment of concepts. VI. Exploratory experiments on conceptualization at perceptual levels. *J. Psychol.* 26: 193–216.

——. 1928. Problem solving in children and adults. *J. Genet. Psychol.* 35: 522–45.

——. 1927. Reasons used in solving problems. *J. Exp. Psychol.* 10:397–414.

HELMSTADTER, G. C. and D. S. ELLIS. 1952. Rate of manipulative learning as a function of goal-setting techniques. *J. Exp. Psychol.* 43: 125–28.

HENDRICKSON, G. and W. H. SCHROEDER. 1941. Transfer of training in learning to hit a submerged target. *J. of Educ. Psychol.* 32: 205–13.

HENRY, F. M. and G. A. NELSON. 1956. Age difference and interrelationships between skill and learning in gross motor performance of ten- and fifteen-year-old boys. *Res. Quart.* 27: 162–75.

HERNANDEZ-PEON, R., H. SCHERRER, and M. JOUVEN. 1956. Modification of electric activity in cochlear nucleus during "attention" in unanesthetized cats. *Science.* 123: 331–32.

HERON, W. 1961. Cognitive and Physiological Effects of Perceptual Isolation. In P. Solomon (ed.) *Sensory Deprivation.* Cambridge, Mass.: Harvard Univ. Press.

HESS, R. D. 1955. Controlling culture influence in mental testing: an experimental test. *J. Educ. Psychol.* 49: 55–58.

HILDRETH, GERTRUDE. 1942. Puzzle-solving with and without understanding. *J. Educ. Psychol.* 33: 595–604.

——. 1941. The difficulty reduction tendency in perception and problem solving. *J. Educ. Psychol.* 32: 305–13.

HILGARD, E. R. 1949. Distributed practice in motor learning: progressively increasing and decreasing rests. *J. Exp. Psychol.* 39: 169–72.

——. 1951. Methods and procedures in the study of learning. In S. S. Stevens (ed.) *Handbook of Experimental Psychology.* New York: Wiley, pp. 517–67.

——. 1957. *Perception: Introduction to Psychology, 2nd ed.* New York: Harcourt, Brace, & World, pp. 331–89.

—— and G. H. BOWER. 1966. *Theories of Learning, 2nd ed.* Des Moines, Iowa: Meredith Publishing Company.

——, R. P. IRVINE, and J. E. WHIPPLE. 1953. Rote memorization, understanding, and transfer: an extension of Katona's card-trick experiments. *J. Exp. Psychol.* 46: 288–92.

HINDMAN, B. M. 1953. The emotional problems of Negro high school youth which are related to segregation and discrimination in a southern urban community. *J. Educ. Sociol.* 27: 115–27.

HOBSON, J. R. 1947. Sex differences in primary mental abilities. *J. Educ. Res.* 41: 126–33.

HOFFMAN, L. R. and N. F. MAIER. 1961. Quality and acceptance of problem solutions by members of homogeneous and heterogeneous groups. *J. Abn. Soc. Psychol.* 62: 401–7.

HOFFMAN, M. L. and LOUIS HOFFMAN. 1966. *Child Development Research.* New York: Russell Sage Foundation.

HOLADAY, P. W. and G. D. STODDARD. 1933. *Getting Ideas From the Movies.* New York: Macmillan.

HOLLINGSHEAD, A. B. 1949. *Elmtown's Youth: The Impact of Social Class on Adolescents.* New York: Wiley.

HOLMES, P. D., JR. 1959. *Television Research in the Teacher-Learning Process.* Detroit, Mich.: Wayne State Univ., Division of Broadcasting.

HONZIK, MARJORIE. 1957. Developmental studies of parent-child resemblance in intelligence. *Child. Development.* 28: 215–18.

——. 1963. Asex difference in the age of onset of parent-child resemblance in intelligence. *J. Educ. Psychol.* 54: 231–37.

HONZIK, M. P., J. W. MAC FARLANE, and L. ALLEN. 1948. The stability of mental test performance between two and eighteen years. *J. Exp. Educ.* 17: 309–24.

HOOD, H. B. 1949. A preliminary survey of mental abilities of deaf children. *Brit. J. Psychol.* 19: 210–19.

HOVLAND, C. I. 1951. Human learning and retention. In S. S. Stevens (ed.) *Handbook of Experimental Psychology.* New York: Wiley, pp. 613–89.

——. 1938. Experimental studies in rote-learning theory: I. Reminiscence following learning by massed and by distributed practice. *J. Exp. Psychol.* 22: 201–24.

——. 1938. Experimental studies in rote-learning theory: II. Reminiscence with varying speeds of syllable presentation. *J. Exp. Psychol.* 22: 338–53.

——. 1938. Experimental studies in rote-learning theory: III. Distribution of practice with varying speeds of syllable presentation. *J. Exp. Psychol.* 23: 172–90.

——. 1939. Experimental studies in rote-learning theory: IV. Comparison of reminiscence in serial and paired-associate learning. *J. Exp. Psychol.* 24: 466–84.

——. 1939. Experimental studies in rote-learning theory: V. Comparison of distribution of practice in serial and paired-associate learning. *J. Exp. Psychol.* 25: 622–33.

——. 1940. Experimental studies in rote-learning theory: VI: Comparison of retention following learning to the same criterion by massed and distributed practice. *J. Exp. Psychol.* 26: 568–87.

——. 1940. Experimental studies in rote-learning theory: VII. Distribution of practice with varying lengths of list. *J. Exp. Psychol.* 27: 271–84.

——. 1949. Experimental studies in rote-learning theory: VIII. Distributed practice of paired associates with varying rates of presentation. *J. Exp. Psychol.* 39: 714–18.

——, O. J. HARVEY, and M. SHERIF. 1957. Assimilation and content effects in reaction to communication and attitude change. *J. Abn. Soc. Psychol.* 55: 244–52.

HOWELL, M. Use of force-time graphs for performance analysis in facilitating motor learning. *Res. Quart.* 27: 12–21.

HUDGINS, B. B. 1960. Effects of group experience on individual problem solving. *J. Educ. Psychol.* 51: 37–42.

HULL, C. D. 1943. *Principles of Behavior.* New York: Appleton-Century-Crofts.

HULL, C. L. 1952. *A Behavior System: An Introduction to Behavior Theory Concerning the Individual Organism.* New Haven, Conn.: Yale Univ. Press.

———. 1951. *Essentials of Behavior.* New Haven, Conn.: Yale Univ. Press.

HUMPHREY, G. and R. V. COXON. 1963. *The Chemistry of Thinking.* Springfield, Ill.: Charles C Thomas.

HUMPHREYS, L. G. 1939. The effect of random alternation of reinforcement on the acquisition and extinction of conditioned eyelid reactions. *J. Exp. Psychol.* 25: 141–58.

——— and P. L. BOYNTON. 1950. Intelligence and intelligence testing. In W. S. Monroe (ed.) *Encyclopedia of Educational Research.* New York: Macmillan, pp. 600–12.

HUMPHRIES, M. and A. H. SHEPHARD. 1959. Age and training in the development of a perceptual motor skill. *Percept. Motor Skills.* 9: 3–11.

HUNT, J. 1965. Intrinsic motivation and its role in psychological development. In D. Levine (ed.) *Nebraska Symposium on Motivation.* Lincoln, Nebr.: Univ. of Nebr. Press. 13: 189–282.

HUNZIKER, C. W. and H. R. DOUGLASS. 1937. The relative effectiveness of a large unit plan of supervised study and the daily recitation method in the teaching of algebra and geometry. *Math Teacher.* 30: 122–23.

HURLOCK, ELIZABETH. 1925. An evaluation of certain incentives used in school work. *J. Educ. Psychol.* 16: 145–59.

HYMAN, R. 1963. *The Nature of Psychological Inquiry.* Englewood Cliffs, N.J.: Prentice-Hall.

IMUS, H. A. 1936. Visual factors in reading. *Understanding the Child.* 7: 8–15.

INSKO, C. 1965. Verbal reinforcement of attitude in an interview situation. *J. Person. and Soc. Psychol.* 2: 621–23.

IRION, A. L. 1949. Retention as a function of amount of pre-recall warming-up. *Amer. Psychol.* 4: 219–20.

———. 1948. The relation of set to retention. *Psychol. Rev.* 55: 336–41.

JACOBSEN, E. 1932. Electrophysiology of mental activities. *Amer. J. Psychol.* 44: 677–94.

JACOBZINER, H. *et al.* 1963. How well are well children? *Amer. J. Pub. Health.* 53: 1937–52.

JANIS, I., A. LUMSDAINE, and A. I. GLADSTONE. 1951. Effects of preparatory communication on reactions to a subsequent news event. *Public Opinion Quart.* 15: 487–515.

JASPER, H. H. 1937. Electrical signs of cortical activity. *Psychol. Bull.* 34: 411–81.

JEFFREYS, L. A. (ed.) 1951. *Cerebral Mechanisms in Behavior: The Hickson Symposium.* New York: Wiley.

JENKINS, J. G. and K. M. DALLENBACH. 1924. Obliviscence during sleep and waking. *Amer. J. Psychol.* 35: 605–12.

JENKINS, LULU. 1930. A comparative study of motor achievements of children at five, six, and seven years of age. *Teachers College Contributions to Education, No. 44.* New York: Teachers College, Columbia Univ.

JENSEN, M. B. and AGNES LEMAIRE. 1937. Ten experiments on whole and part learning. *J. Educ. Psychol.* 28: 37–54.

JERSILD, A. T. 1954. Emotional development. In L. Carmichael (ed.) *Manual of Child Psychology.* New York: Wiley, pp. 833–901.

—— and F. B. HOLMES. 1935. Children's fears. *Child. Devel. Mono.* No. 20.

——, F. V. MARKEY, and C. L. JERSILD. 1933. Children's fears, dreams, likes, dislikes, pleasant and unpleasant memories. *Child. Devel. Mono.* No. 2.

JOHNSON, LILLIAN. 1933. Similarity of meaning as a factor in retroactive inhibition. *J. Gen. Psychol.* 9: 377–89.

JOHNSON, R. C. and NANCY WATSON. 1962. Individual meaning production as related to amount of verbal learning. *J. Gen. Psychol.* 67: 117–20.

JONES, E. I. 1952. Differential transfer of training between motor tasks of different difficulty: USAF Human Resources Research Center. *Res. Bull.* No. 23: 52–53.

JONES, H. E. 1938. The citizen goes to school. *Nat. Parent Teacher.* 33: No. 4, 8–10.

——. 1954. The environment and mental development. In L. Carmichael (ed.) *Manual of Child Psychology.* New York: Wiley, pp. 631–96.

——. 1959. Intelligence and problem solving–The San Quentin study; and Intelligence and problem solving–Aircrew officers. In J. E. Birren (ed.) *Handbook of Aging and the Individual.* Chicago: Univ. of Chicago Press.

——. 1949. Motor performance and growth: a developmental study of static dynamometric strength. *Univ. Calif. Publ. in Child Devel.,* pp. 1–180.

——, H. S. CONRAD, and M. B. BLANCHARD. 1932. Environmental handicap in mental test performance. *Univ. Calif. Publ. Psychol.* 5: 63–69.

JONES, J. G. 1965. Motor learning without demonstration of physical practice. *Res. Quart.* 36: 270–76.

JONES, J. W. 1963. The visually handicapped child at home and school. Washington, D.C.: USOE Bulletin No. 39.

JORDAN, A. M. 1942. *Educational Psychology.* New York: Holt, Rinehart & Winston.

JOSEPHINA, SISTER. 1959. A study of attitudes in the elementary grades. *J. Educ. Sociol.* 33: 56–60.

JUDD, C. H. 1908. The relation of special training to general intelligence. *Educ. Rev.* 36: 28–42.

JUSTESEN, D. L. and L. E. BOURNE, JR. 1963. A comparison of grouped and paired associates in verbal learning. *J. Gen. Psychol.* 68: 163–68.

KAGAN, J. *et al.* 1958. Personality and IQ change. *J. Abn. Soc. Psychol.* 56: 261–66.

KAMIN, L. J. 1957. Differential changes in mental abilities in old age. *J. Geront.* 12: 66–70.

KAO, DJU-LIH. 1937. Plateaus and the curve of learning in motor skill. *Psychol. Mono.* 49: No. 219, No. 3.

KATES, S. L. and L. YUDIN. 1962. Concept attainment and memory. *J. Educ. Psychol.* 55: 103–9.

KATONA, G. 1954. Economic psychology. *Scientific American.* 191: 35.

———. 1940. *Organizing and Memorizing.* New York: Columbia Univ. Press, p. 319.

KATZ, D., C. MC CLINTOCK, and I. SARNOFF. 1956. The measurement of ego defense as related to attitude change. *J. Personality.* 25: 465–75.

KEAN, J. M. and K. YAMAMOTO. 1965. Grammar signals and assignment of words to parts of speech among young children: an exploration. *J. Verb. Learn. Behav.* 4: 323–36.

KEISLAR, E. 1959. The development of understanding in arithmetic by a teaching machine. *J. Educ. Psychol.* 50: 247–53.

KEISTER, MARY. 1937. The behavior of young children in failure. *Univ. of Iowa Study in Child Welfare.* 14: 27–82.

KELLOGG, W. N., V. B. SCOTT, and I. S. WOLF. 1940. Is movement necessary for learning? An experimental test of the motor theory of conditioning. *J. Comp. Psychol.* 29: 43–74.

KELMAN, H. C. 1958. Compliance, identification, and internalization: three processes of attitude change. *J. Conflict Resol.* 2: 51–60.

KENDALL, P. K. 1966. See Jim read the book. *The Reporter.* 34: 37–38.

KENDLER, H. H. 1947. An investigation of latent learning in a T maze. *J. Comp. Psychol.* 40: 265–70.

——— and TRACY KENDLER. 1961. Effect of verbalization on reversal shifts in children. *Science.* 134: 119–20.

——— and H. C. MENCHER. 1948. The ability of rats to learn the location of food when motivated by thirst–an experimental reply to Leeper. *J. Exp. Psychol.* 38: 82–88.

KEPPEL, G. 1964. Verbal learning in children. *Psychol. Bull.* 1: 63–80.

KERLINGER, F. N. 1964. *Foundations of Behavioral Research.* New York: Holt, Rinehart & Winston.

KERSH, B. 1962. The motivating effect of learning by directed discovery. *J. Educ. Psychol.* 53: 65–71.

KIMBLE, G. A. 1949. An experimental test of a two-factor theory of inhibition. *J. Exp. Psychol.* 39: 15–23.

———. 1961. *Hilgard and Marquis's Conditioning and Learning.* New York: Appleton-Century-Crofts.

—— and E. A. BILODEAU. 1949. Work and rest are variables in motor learning. *J. Exp. Psychol.* 39: 150–57.

—— and B. R. HORENSTEIN. 1948. Reminiscence in motor learning as a function of length of interpolated rest. *J. Exp. Psychol.* 38: 239–44.

—— and R. SHATEL. 1952. The relationship between two kinds of inhibition and the amount of practice. *J. Exp. Psychol.* 44: 355–59.

—— and J. J. WULFF. 1961. The effectiveness of instruction in reading a scale as influenced by the relative amounts of demonstration and problem-solving practice. In A. A. Lumsdaine (ed.) *Student Response in Programmed Instruction: A Symposium.* Washington, D.C.: Nat'l. Acad. Sciences. Chap. 15.

KING, D. J. and G. W. RUSSELL. 1966. A comparison of rote and meaningful learning of connected meaningful material. *J. Verb. Learning and Verb. Behavior.* 5: 478–83.

KINGSLEY, H. L. and MARY CARBONE. 1938. Attitudes of Italian-Americans toward race prejudice. *J. Abn. and Soc. Psychol.* 33: 532–37.

KIRBY, T. J. 1923. Latin as a preparation for French. *School and Society.* 18: 563–69.

KITTELL, J. E. 1957. An experimental study of the effect of external direction during learning on transfer and retention of principles. *J. Educ. Psychol.* 48: 391–405.

KLAPPER, J. 1960. *The effects of mass media.* New York: Oxford.

KLARE, G., E. SHURFORD, and W. NICHOLS. 1957. Relation of style, difficulty, practice, and ability to efficiency of reading and retention. *J. Appl. Psychol.* 41: 222–26.

KLAUSMEIER, H. J. and C. W. HARRIS. 1966. *Analyses of Concept Learning.* New York: Academic Press.

—— and L. J. LOUGHLIN. 1961. Behavior during problem-solving among children of low, average, and high intelligence. *J. Educ. Psychol.* 52: 148–52.

—— and W. WIERSMA. 1964. Relationship of sex, grade level, and locale to performance of high IQ students on divergent thinking tests. *J. Educ. Psychol.* 55: 14–19.

—— and J. F. FELDHUSEN. 1959. Retention in arithmetic among children of low, average, and high IQ at 117 months of age. *J. Educ. Psychol.* 50: 88–92.

KLEINSMITH, L. J., S. KAPLAN, and R. D. TARTE. 1963. The relationship of arousal to short- and long-term verbal recall. *Canad. J. Psychol.* 17: 393–97.

KLINEBERG, O. 1935. *Negro Intelligence and Selective Migration.* New York: Columbia Univ. Press.

KNIGHT, K. 1963. Effect of effort on behavioral rigidity in Luchins Water Jar Test. *J. Abn. Soc. Psychol.* 66: 190–92.

KOCH, S. (ed.) 1959. *Psychology: A Study of a Science: Vol. I-VII.* New York: McGraw-Hill.

KOHLBERG, L. 1964. In M. L. Hoffman and Lois Hoffman (eds.) *Review of Child Development Research*. New York: Russell Sage Foundation, pp. 383–432.

KOHLER, W. 1929. *Gestalt Psychology*. New York: Liveright.

KOONTZ, W. F. 1961. A study of achievement as a function of homogeneous grouping. *J. Exp. Educ.* 30: 249–53.

KORCHIN, S. J. and S. LEVINE. 1957. Anxiety and verbal learning. *J. Abn. Soc. Psychol.* 54: 234–40.

KOUNIN, J. S. and P. V. GUMP. 1961. The comparative influence of punitive and non-punitive teachers upon children's concepts of school misconduct. *J. Educ. Psychol.* 52: 44–49.

KNAPP, C. and W. DIXON. 1952. Learning to juggle: II. A study of whole and part methods. *Res. Quart.* A.A.D.H.E. 23: 398–402.

KRASNER, L. and P. ULLMAN. 1964. *Research in Behavior Modification*. New York: Holt, Rinehart, & Winston.

KRATHWOHL, D. R. *et al.* 1964. *Taxonomy of Educational Objectives: Handbook II, Affective Domain*. New York: McKay.

KRECHEVSKY, I. 1938. A study of the continuity of the problem-solving process. *Psychol. Rev.* 45: 107–33.

KREUGER, W. C. 1929. The effect of overlearning on retention. *J. Exp. Psychol.* 12: 71–78.

——. 1946. Rate of progress as related to difficulty of assignment. *J. Educ. Psychol.* 37: 247–49.

KRULEE, G. K., J. E. PODELL, and P. G. RONCO. 1954. Effect of number of alternatives involved in a particular visual discrimination and the ease of marking such a discrimination. *J. Exp. Psychol.* 48: 75–80.

KUMATA, H. 1956. *An Inventory of Instructional Television Research*. Ann Arbor, Mich.: Educational Television and Radio Center.

L'ABATE, L. 1962. Transfer of learning with differences in associative value and in manifest anxiety. *Amer. J. Psychol.* 75: 251–68.

LAMBERT, W. W., R. L. SOLOMON, and P. D. WATSON. 1949. Reinforcement and extinction as factors in size estimation. *J. Exper. Psychol.* 39: 637–41.

LANA, R. E. 1964. Existing familiarity and order of presentation of persuasive communication. *Psychol. Rep.* 15: 607–10.

LARSON, L. A. 1941. A factor analysis of motor ability variables and tests with tests for college men. *Res. Quart. Amer. Ass. Health Physical Educ.*

LASHLEY, K. S. 1942. An examination of the continuity theory as applied to discrimination learning. *J. Gen. Psychol.* 26: 241–65.

—— and M. WADE. 1946. The Pavlovian theory of generalization. *Psychol. Rev.* 53: 72–87.

LAWRENCE, D. H. 1949. Acquired distinctiveness of cues: I. transfer between discrimination on the basis of familiarity with the stimulus. *J. Exp. Psychol.* 39: 770–84.

———. 1950. Acquired distinctiveness of cues: II. selective association in a constant stimulus situation. *J. Exp. Psychol.,* 40: 175–88.

——— and W. A. MASON. 1955. Systematic behavior during discrimination reversal and change of dimensions. *J. Comp. Physiol. Psychol.* 48: 1–7.

LAZARUS, R. S. and C. W. ERIKSEN. 1952. Effects of failure stress upon skilled performance. *J. Exp. Psychol.* 44: 100–10.

LEAVITT, H. J. and R. A. H. MUELLER. 1951. Some effects of feedback on communications. *Hum. Relations.* 4: 401–10.

——— and H. SCHLOSBERG. 1944. The retention of verbal and motor skills. *J. of Exp. Psychol.* 34: 404–17.

LEE, E. S. 1951. Negro intelligence and selective migration: A Philadelphia test of the Klineberg hypothesis. *Amer. Sociol. Rev.* 16: 222–33.

LEE, J. J. 1943. The crippled. *Nation's School.* 31: 22–23.

LESTER, O. P. 1932. Mental set in relation to retroactive inhibition. *J. Exp. Psychol.* 15: 681–99.

LEVIN, H., J. S. WATSON, and M. FELDMAN. 1964. Writing as pretraining for association learning. *J. Educ. Psychol.* 55: 181–84.

LEVINE, D. (ed.) 1965. *Nebraska Symposium on Motivation.* Lincoln, Nebr.: Univ. of Nebr. Press.

LEVINE, J. and G. MURPHY. 1943. The learning and forgetting of controversial material. *J. Abn. Soc. Psychol.* 38: 507–17.

LEVINE, R., I. CHEIN, and G. MURPHY. 1942. The relation of the intensity of a need to the amount of perceptual distortion. *J. Psychol.* 13: 293–95.

LEWIN, K. 1948. *Resolving Social Conflict.* New York: Harper.

———, R. LIPPITT, and R. WHITE. 1939. Patterns of aggressive behavior in experimentally created "social climates." *J. Soc. Psychol.* 10: 271–99.

LINDLEY, R. H. 1959. Effects of instructions on the transfer of conditioned responses. *J. Exp. Psychol.* 57: 6–8.

LINDQUIST, E. G. 1953. *Design and Analysis of Experiments in Psychology and Education.* Boston: Houghton Mifflin.

LINDSLEY, D. B. 1944. *Electroencephalography.* In J. McV. Hunt (ed.) *Personality and the Behavior Disorders.* New York: Ronald.

———. 1951. Emotion. In S. S. Stevens (ed.) *Handbook of Experimental Psychology.* New York: Ronald.

———. 1957. Psychophysiology and motivation. In M. R. Jones (ed.) *Nebraska Symposium on Motivation.* Lincoln, Nebr.: Univ. of Nebr. Press.

LINDSLEY, O. 1964. In R. Harper (ed.) *The Cognitive Processes: Readings.* Englewood Cliffs, N.J.: Prentice-Hall.

LINDZEY, G. 1953. *Handbook of Social Psychology.* Reading, Mass.: Addison-Wesley.

——— and E. ARONSON. 1968. *Handbook of Social Psychology, 2nd ed.* Reading, Mass.: Addison-Wesley.

LING, B. 1941. Form discrimination as a learning cue in infants. *Comp. Psychol. Mono.,* Serial No. 86.

LOEVINGER, JANE. 1947. A systematic approach to the construction and evaluation of tests of ability. *Psychol. Mono.* 61: No. 4.

LONGWELL, SARAH. 1938. Progressive change in simple action. *Amer. J. Psychol.* 51: 261–82.

LORGE, I. 1936. Irrelevant rewards in animal learning. *J. Comp. Psychol.* 21: 105–28.

——. 1936. The influence of the test upon the nature of mental decline as a function of age. *J. Psychol.* 27: 100–10.

LUBLIN, S. 1965. Reinforcement schedules, scholastic aptitude, autonomy need, and achievement in a programmed course. *J. Educ. Psychol.* 56: 295–301.

LUH, C. W. 1922. The conditions of retention. *Psychol. Mono.* 31: No. 142.

LUMSDAINE, A. A. 1964. Programmed learning and instruction. In E. R. Hilgard (ed.) *Theories of Learning and Instruction.* 63rd Yearbook, Nat'l. Soc. for the Study of Educ. Part I: 371–401.

——. 1963. Instruments and media of instruction. In N. L. Gage (ed.) *Handbook of Research on Teaching.* Chicago: Rand-McNally, pp. 583–682.

——. 1960. Instruments and media of instruction. In N. L. Gage (ed.) *Handbook of Research on Teaching.* Chicago: Rand-McNally, pp. 609–54.

LUNDY, R. M. and L. BERKOWITZ. 1957. Cognitive complexity of an individual and his assimilative projection to attitude change. *J. Abn. Soc. Psychol.* 55: 34–37.

LYON, D. O. 1914. The relation of length of material to the time taken for learning, and the optimum distribution of time. *J. Educ. Psychol.* 5: 1–9, 85–91, 155–63.

MAC CORQUODALE, K. and P. E. MEEHL. 1953. Preliminary suggestions as to a formalization of expectancy theory. *Psychol. Rev.* 60: 55–63.

——. 1949. Cognitive learning in the absence of competition of incentives. *J. Comp. Physiol. Psychol.* 42: 383–90.

MAC KINNON, D. W. 1962. The nature and nurture of creative talent. *Amer. Psychol.* 17: 484–95.

MC ALLISTER, D. E. and D. J. LEWIS. 1951. Facilitation and interference in performance on the modified Mashburn apparatus: II—The effects of varying the amount of interpolated learning. *J. Exp. Psychol.* 41: 356–63.

MC CABE, B. F. 1963. The etiology of deafness. *Volta Rev.* 65: 471–77.

MC CANDLESS, B. R. 1942. Changing relationships between dominance and social acceptability during group democratization. *Amer. J. Orthopsych.* 12: 529–35.

MC CANDLESS, G. and A. CASTANEDA. 1956. Anxiety in children, school achievement, and intelligence. *Child. Developm.* 27: 379–81.

MC CLELLAND, D., *et al.* 1953. *The Achievement Motive.* New York: Appleton-Century-Crofts.

MC CLELLAND, D. C. 1942. Studies in serial verbal discrimination learning: I. Reminiscence with two speeds of pair presentation. *J. Exp. Psychol.* 31: 44–56.

MC CLINTOCK, C. 1958. Personality syndromes and attitude change. *J. Personality.* 26: 479–93.

MC CLOY, C. H. 1935. The influence of chronological age on motor performance. *Res. Quart.* May: 61–64.

MC DOWELL, N. A. 1964. The effectiveness of the controlled reader in developing reading rate, comprehension, and vocabulary as opposed to the regular method of teaching reading. *J. Exp. Psychol.* 32: 363–67.

MC GEOCH, J. A. 1931. The influence of four different interpolated activities upon retroactive inhibition. *J. Exp. Psychol.* 14: 400–13.

———. 1932. The influence of degree of interpolated learning upon retroactive inhibition. *Amer. J. Psychol.* 44: 695–708.

———. 1929. The influence of degree of learning upon retroactive inhibition. *Amer. J. Psychol.* 41: 252–62.

———. 1928. The influence of sex and age upon the ability to report. *Amer. J. Psychol.* 40: 458–66.

———. 1933. Studies in retroactive inhibition: II. Relationships between temporal points of interpolation, length of interval, and amounts of retroactive inhibition. *J. Gen. Psychol.* 9: 44–57.

———. 1936. Studies in retroactive inhibition: VII. Retroactive inhibition as a function of the length and frequency of presentation of the interpolated lists. *J. Exp. Psychol.* 19: 674–93.

———. 1942. *The Psychology of Human Learning.* New York: Longmans, Green.

MC GEOCH, J. A. and A. L. IRION. 1952. *The Psychology of Human Learning* (rev.) New York: Longmans, Green.

——— and W. T. MC DONALD. 1931. Meaningful relation and retroactive inhibition. *Amer. J. Psychol.* 43: 579–88.

——— and GRACE MC GEOCH. 1937. Studies in retroactive inhibition: X. The influence of similarity of meaning between lists of paired associates. *J. Exp. Psychol.* 21: 320–29.

——— and M. E. NOLAN. 1933. Studies in retroactive inhibition: IV. Temporal point of interpolation and degree of retroactive inhibition. *J. Compar. Psychol.* 15: 407–17.

——— and B. J. UNDERWOOD. 1943. Tests of the two-factor theory of retroactive inhibition. *J. Exp. Psychol.* 32: 1–6.

MC GINNIES, E. 1949. Emotionality and perceptual defense. *Psychol. Rev.* 56: 244–51.

MC GINNIS, E. 1929. The acquisition and interference of motor habits in young children. *Genet. Psychol. Mono.* 6: 209–311.

MC GRAW, L. W. 1948. A factor analysis of motor learning. *Res. Quart.* 19: 22–29.

MC KEACHIE, W., D. POLLIE, and J. SPEISMAN. 1955. Relieving anxiety in classroom examinations. *J. Abn. Soc. Psychol.* 50: 93–98.

MC KINNEY, F. 1935. Retroactive inhibition and recognition memory. *J. Exp. Psychol.* 18: 585–98.

MC NEMAR, OLGA. 1955. An attempt to differentiate between individuals with high and low reasoning ability. *Amer. J. Psychol.* 48: 20–36.

MC NEMAR, Q. 1946. Opinion-attitude methodology. *Psychol. Bull.* 37: 289–374.

MC QUEEN, R. and B. CHURN. 1960. The intelligence and educational achievement of a matched sample of white and Negro students. *School and Society.* 92: 327–29.

MACCOBY, ELEANOR, and W. C. WILSON. 1957. Identification and observational learning from films. *J. Abn. Soc. Psychol.* 55: 76–87.

MACCOBY, N. and F. D. SHEFFIELD. 1961. Combining practice with demonstrations in teaching complex sequences. In A. A. Lumsdaine (ed.) *Student Response in Programmed Instruction: A Symposium.* Washington, D.C.: Nat'l Acad. Sciences. Chaps. 3, 5.

MACMEEKEN, A. M. 1939. *The Intelligence of a Representative Group of Scottish Children.* London: Univ. of London Press.

MANDLER, G. and S. SARASON. 1953. The effect of prior experience and subjective failure on the evocation of test anxiety. *J. Person.* 21: 336–41.

—— and SHIRLEY HEINEMANN. 1956. Effect of overtraining of a verbal response on transfer of learning. *J. Exp. Psychol.* 52: 39–46.

MAIER, N. R. F. 1930. Reasoning in humans: I. On direction. *J. Comp. Psychol.* 10: 115–43.

——. 1931. Reasoning in humans: II. The solution of a problem and its appearance in consciousness. *J. Comp. Psychol.* 12: 181–94.

——. 1945. Reasoning in humans: III. The mechanisms of equivalent stimuli and of reasoning. *J. Exp. Psychol.* 35: 349–60.

—— and A. R. SOLEM. 1962. Improving solution by turning choice situations into problems. *Personnel Psychol.* 56: 151–57.

—— and J. B. KLEE. 1945. Studies of abnormal behavior in the rat: XVII. Guidance versus trial and error in the alteration of habits and fixations. *J. Psychol.* 19: 133–63.

——. 1936. Reasoning in children. *J. Comp. Psychol.* 21: 357–66.

MALLER, J. B. 1929. Cooperation and competition: An experimental study in motivation. *Teachers College Contributions to Educ.* No. 384, New York: Teachers College, Columbia Univ.

MALLORY, J. N. 1922. A study of the relation of some physical defects to achievement in the elementary school. *George Peabody College for Teachers Contribution to Educ.* No. 9. Nashville, Tenn.: George Peabody College for Teachers.

MALTZMANN, I. 1960. On the training of originality. *Psychol. Rev.* 67: 229–42.

MANN, J. H. and CAROLE MANN. 1959. The importance of group task in producing group-member personality and behavior changes. *Hum. Relat.* 12: 75–80.

MARQUART, DOROTHY. 1965. Group problem solving. *J. Abn. Soc. Psychol.* 41: 103–13.

MARTIN, A. 1952. Parent's attitudes—children's behavior. *Nat'l Parent Teacher.* 47: 4–6.

MARX, M. H. Motivation. In C. W. Harris (ed.) *Encyclopedia of Educational Research.* New York: Macmillan, pp. 888–901.

MASLOW, A. H. 1943. A theory of human motivation. *Psychol. Rev.* 50: 370–96.

MASSERMAN, J. M. 1943. *Behavior and Neurosis.* Chicago: Univ. Chicago Press.

MATTSON, M. L. 1933. The relation between the complexity of the habit to be acquired and the form of the learning curve in young children. *Genet. Psychol. Mono.* 13: 5–17.

MAYER, B. A. 1935. Negativistic reactions of preschool children on the new revision of the Stanford-Binet. *J. Genet. Psychol.* 46: 311–34.

MEAD, A. R. 1951. What schools can do to improve social attitudes. *Educational Leaders.* 9: 183–87.

MEAD, M. 1927. Group intelligence tests and linguistic disability among Italian children. *Sch. and Soc.* 25: 465–68.

MEAD, MARGARET. 1935. *Sex and Temperament in Three Primitive Societies.* New York: William Morrow & Company, Inc.

MEADOW, A. and S. J. PARNES. 1949. Evaluation of training in creative problem-solving. *J. Appl. Psychol.* 43: 189–94.

MELLIN, G. 1963. The frequency of birth defects. In M. Fishbein (ed.) *Birth Defects.* Philadelphia: Lippincott, pp. 1–37.

MELTON, A. W. 1964. *Categories of Human Learning.* New York: Academic Press.

MELTON, A. W. 1950. Learning. In W. S. Monroe (ed.) *Encyclopedia of Educational Research.* New York: Macmillan, pp. 668–90.

—— and JEAN IRWIN. 1940. The influence of degree of interpolated learning on retroactive inhibition and the over transfer of specific responses. *Amer. J. Psychol.* 53: 173–203.

MELTZER, H. 1930. The present status of experimental studies on the relationship of feeling to memory. *Psychol Rev.* 37: 124–39.

MILLER, G. A., E. GALANTER, and K. H. PRIBRAM. 1960. *Plans and the Structure of Behavior.* New York: Holt.

MILLER, N. E. 1948. Studies of fear as an acquirable drive: I. Fear as motivation and fear reductions as reinforcement in learning of new responses. *J. Exp. Psychol.* 38: 89–101.

MILLER, N. E. 1951. Learnable drives and rewards. In S. S. Stevens (ed.) *Handbook of Exper. Psychol.* New York: Wiley, pp. 435–72.

MILLER, N. E., R. I. SAMPLINER, and P. WOODROW. 1957. Thirst-reducing effects of water by stomach fistula vs. water by mouth measured by both a consummatory and an instrumental response. *J. Comp. Physiol. Psychol.* 50: 1–5.

MILLER, VERA. 1962. Creativity and intelligence in the arts. *Educ.* 82: 488–95.

MILNER, E. A. 1951. A study of the relationship between reading readiness in grade one school children and patterns of parent-child interaction. *Child Develop.* 22: 95–112.

MILTON, G. A. 1959. Sex differences in problem-solving as a function of role appropriateness of the problem content. *Psychol. Reports.* 5: 705–8.

———. 1957. The effects of sex-role identification upon problem-solving skill. *J. Abn. Soc. Psychol.* 55: 208–12.

MINAERT, W. 1950. An analysis of the value of dry-skiing in learning selected skiing skills. *Res. Quart.* 21: 47–52.

MINUCHIN, PATRICIA. 1965. Solving problems cooperatively, a comparison of three classroom groups. *Childh. Educ.* 41: 480–84.

MONROE, W. S. 1950. *Encyclopedia of Educational Research.* New York: Macmillan, pp. 137–207.

MONTAGUE, J. B., JR. 1962. Criticism and difficulties in high-school social status. The sociology of students of different social status. *The Sociol. of Educ.* 19: 271–78.

MONTGOMERY, V. and B. J. UNDERWOOD. 1952. Reminiscence in a manipulative task as a function of work-surface height, present practice, and interpolated rest. *J. Exp. Psychol.* 44: 420–27.

MOOS, R. H. and J. C. SPEISMAN. 1962. Group compatibility and productivity. *J. Abn. Soc. Psychol.* 65: 190–96.

MORGAN, J. J. B. 1945. Value of wrong responses in inductive reasoning. *J. Exp. Psychol.* 35: 141–46.

MORRIS, W. W. 1939. Story remembering among children. *J. Soc. Psychol.* 10: 489–502.

MORRISETT, L. JR. and C. I. HOVLAND. 1959. A comparison of three varieties of training in human problem solving. *J. Exp. Psychol.* 58: 63–72.

MOSHER, H. M. 1952. Subject preference of girls and boys. *School Rev.* 60: 34–38.

MOWRER, O. W. 1952. Motivation. In Calvin Stone (ed.) *Annual Review of Psychol.* Stanford, Calif.: Annual Reviews, Inc., p. 434.

MOWRER, O. H. 1960. *Learning Theory and Behavior.* New York: Wiley.

———. 1950. *Learning Theory and Personality Dynamics.* New York: Ronald.

MUNN, N. L. 1932. Bilateral transfer of learning. *J. Exp. Psychol.* 15: 343–53.

——. 1954. Learning in children. In L. Carmichael (ed.) *Manual of Child Development Psychology*. New York: Wiley, pp. 374–458.

MURDOCK, B. B., JR. 1960. Response factors in learning and transfer. *Amer. J. Psychol.* 73: 355–69.

MURPHY, HELEN. 1943. An evaluation of the effect of specific training in auditory and visual discrimination on beginning reading. Unpubl. Ed. D. dissertation, Boston Univ.

MURRAY, E. J. 1964. *Motivation and Emotion*. Englewood Cliffs, N.J.: Prentice-Hall.

MURRAY, H. A., *et al.* 1938. *Explorations in Personality*. New York: Oxford Press.

MUSCIO, B. 1916. The influence of the form of a question. *Brit. J. Psychol.* 8: 351–89.

MUUS, R. E. 1961. The transfer effect of a learning program in social causality on an understanding of physical causality. *J. Exp. Psychol.* 29: 231–47.

NAKAMURA, C. Y. 1958. Conformity and problem solving. *J. Abn. Soc. Psychol.* 56: 315–20.

NASH, M. 1958. Machine-age Maya. The industrialization of a Guatamalan community. *Amer. Anthrop. Assn.* 60: No. 2.

NASH, P. 1965. *The Educated Man*. New York: Wiley.

NELSON, D. 1958. Effect of slow-motion loopfilms on the learning of golf. *Res. Quart.* 29: 37–44.

NELSON, PEARL. 1957. The acquisition of concepts of light and sound in the intermediate grades. Unpubl. Ed. D. dissertation. Boston Univ.

NEWELL, A. and H. SIMON. 1961. Computer simulation of human thinking. *Science.* 134: 2011–16.

NEWLUN, C. O. 1930. Teaching children to summarize in fifth grade history. *Teachers College Contributions to Education No. 404*. New York: Teachers College, Columbia Univ.

NEWMAN, E. B. 1939. Forgetting of meaningful material during sleep and waking. *Amer. J. Psychol.* 52: 65–71.

NEWMAN, H. H. and F. N. FREEMAN, and K. J. HOLZINGER. 1937. *Twins: A Study of Heredity and Environment*. Chicago: Univ. of Chicago Press.

NEWTON, J. M. and D. D. WICKENS. 1956. Retroactive inhibition as a function of the temperal position of the interpolated learning. *J. Exp. Psychol.* 51: 149–54.

NEWTON, K. R. 1956. Visual recognition thresholds and learning. *Percep. and Motor Skills.* 6: 81–87.

NOBLE, C. E. 1952. The role of stimulus meaning in serial verbal learning. *J. Exp. Psychol.* 43: 437–46.

NOBLE, GLADYS. 1951. High school students report their fears. *J. Educ. Soc.* 25: 97–101.

NOLL, V. H. 1960. Relation of scores on Davis-Eells Games to socio-economic status, intelligence test results, and school achievement. *Educ. & Psychol. Meas.* 20: 119–29.

NOLTE, K. F. 1937. Simplification of vocabulary and comprehension in reading. *Elem Eng. Rev.* 14: 119–24, 146.

OAKES, M. E. 1947. Children's explanations of natural phenomena. *Teachers College Contribution to Education No. 926.* New York: Teachers College, Columbia Univ.

OLDS, J. 1969. The central nervous system and the reinforcement of behavior. *Amer. Psychol.* 24: 114–32.

OLERON, P. 1950. A study of the intelligence of the deaf. *Amer. Ann. Deaf.* 95: 179–95.

OLSON, W. C. 1949. Symptoms in temper outbursts in nursery school children. *Child Developm.*

OSBURN, A. F. 1957. *Principles and Procedures of Creative Thinking.* New York: Scribner.

OSEAS, L. and B. J. UNDERWOOD. 1952. Studies of distributed practice: V. learning and retention of concepts. *J. Exp. Psychol.* 43: 143–48.

OSGOOD, C. E. 1953. *Method and Theory in Experimental Psychology:* Chapter 12—serial and transfer phenomena. New York: Oxford, pp. 495–548; 521–33.

——. 1948. An investigation into the causes of retroactive interference. *J. Exp. Psychol.* 37: 133–54.

OTTO, H. J. *et al.* 1953. *Class Size Factors in Elementary Schools.* Univ. of Texas Press.

OVERTON, R. K. 1958. An effect of high- and low-calcium diets on the maze performance of rats. *J. Comp. Physiol. Psychol.* 51: 697–99.

OXENDINE, R. J. 1965. Effects of progressively changing practice schedules on the learning of a motor skill. *Res. Quart.* 36: 307–15.

PALERMO, D. S. 1956. The relationship of anxiety in children to performance on a complex learning task. *Child Developm.* 27: 332–37.

PARNES, S. J. 1961. Effects of extended effort in creative problem solving. *J. Educ. Psychol.* 52: 117–22.

PAVLOV, I. P. 1927. *Conditioned Reflexes.* London, Oxford Univ. Press.

PEARSON, R. G. and G. T. HAUTY. 1960. Role of postural experiences in proprioceptive perception of verticality. *J. Exp. Psychol.* 59: 425–28.

PECK, R. F. and R. J. HAVIGHURST. 1960. *The Psychology of Character Development.* New York: Wiley.

PERKINS, F. T. 1932. Symmetry in visual recall. *Amer. J. Psychol.* 44: 473–90.

PETERSON, L. R. and MARGARET PETERSON. 1957. The role of context stimuli in verbal learning. *J. Exp. Psychol.* 53: 102–5.

PHILLIPS, B. N. 1956. Effect of cohesion and intelligence on the problem solving efficiency of small face to face groups in cooperative and competitive situations. *J. Educ. Res.* 50: 127–37.

PIAGET, J. 1932. *The Child's Conception of Physical Causality.* New York: Harcourt, Brace.

——. 1954. *The Construction of Reality in the Child.* New York: Basic Books.

——. 1953. How children form mathematical concepts. *Sci. Amer.* 189: 74–79.

——. 1932. *Language and Thought in the Child.* New York: Harcourt Brace.

——. 1950. *The Psychology of Intelligence.* New York: Harcourt, Brace.

PINTNER, R. and J. LEV. 1939. The intelligence of the hard of hearing school child. *J. Gen. Psychol.* 55: 31–48.

PISTOR, F. 1940. How time concepts are acquired by children. *Educ. Methods.* 20: 107–12.

POSTMAN, L. and T. G. ALPER. 1946. Retroactive inhibition as a function of the time of interpolation of the inhibitor between recall and learning. *Amer. J. Psychol.* 59: 439–49.

—— and R. CRUTCHFIELD. 1952. The interaction of need, set and stimulus in a cognitive task. *Amer. J. of Psychol.* 65: 196–218.

—— and J. S. BRUNER. 1949. Multiplicity of set as determinant of perceptual behavior. *J. Exp. Psychol.* 39: 369–77.

—— and ——. 1948. Perception under stress. *Psychol. Rev.* 55: 314–23.

—— and G. MURPHY. 1943. The factor of attitude in associate memory. *J. Exp. Psychol.* 33: 228–38.

—— and L. RAU. 1957. Retention as a function of the method of measurement. *Univ. Calif. Publ. Psychol.* 8: 217–70.

—— and D. A. RILEY. 1957. A critique of Kohler's theory of association. *Psychol. Rev.* 64: 61–72.

POWERS, MARGARET. 1964. Prevalence of deafness in school age children. *Amer. Annals of the Deaf.* 109: 410–17.

PRESCOTT, D. A. 1957. *The Child in the Educative Process.* New York: McGraw-Hill.

PRESSEY, LUELLA. 1927. What are the crucial differences between good and poor students? *Res. Adventures in Univ. Teaching.* Bloomington, Illinois: Public School Publishing Co., pp. 4–10.

PUBOLS, B. 1960. Reminiscence in motor learning as a function of present distribution of practice. *J. Exp. Psychol.* 60: 155–61.

PYLE, W. H. 1919. Transfer and interference on card-distributing. *J. Educ. Psychol.* 110: 107–10.

——. 1928. *The Psychology of Learning,* rev. Baltimore: Warwick and York, pp. 44–45.

RARICK, L. and R. MC KEE. 1949. A study of 20 third grade children exhibiting extreme levels of achievement on tests of motor proficiency. *Res. Quart.* pp. 142–52.

RATHS, L. E., M. HARMEN and S. B. SIMON. 1966. *Values and Teaching.* Columbus, Ohio: Bobbs-Merrill.

RAY, J. J. 1936. The generalizing ability of dull, bright, and superior children. *George Peabody College Contributions to Education, No. 175.* Nashville, Tenn.: George Peabody College for Teachers.

RAY, W. S. 1966. Originality in problem solving as affected by single versus multiple solution training problems. *J. Psychol.* 64: 107–12.

———. 1957. Verbal compared with manipulative solution of an apparatus problem. *Amer. J. Psychol.* 70: 289–90.

REED, H. B. 1935. An experiment on the law of effect in learning the maze by humans. *J. Educ. Psychol.* 26: 695–700.

REISMAN, F. 1962. *The Culturally Deprived Child.* New York: Harper.

REYNOLDS, B. 1951. The effect of learning on the predictability of psychomotor performance. *J. Educ. Psychol.* 42: 162–72.

——— and INA BILODEAU. 1952. Acquisition and retention of three psychomotor tests as a function of distribution of practice during acquisition. *J. Exp. Psychol.* 44: 19–26.

REYNOLDS, J. H. 1966. Cognitive transfer in verbal learning. *J. Educ. Psychol.* 57: 382–88.

RHULE, W. and K. U. SMITH. 1959. Effect of visual pretraining in inverted reading on perceptual motor performance in inverter visual fields. *Percept. Mot. Skills.* 9: 327–31.

RICHARDSON, HELEN. 1932. The growth of adaptive behavior in infants: An experimental study of seven age levels. *Gen. Psychol. Mono.* 12: 195–359.

RIESEN, A. H. 1947. The development of visual perception in man and the chimpanzee. *Science.* 106: 107–8.

RIESTRA, M. A. and C. E. JOHNSON. 1964. Changes in attitudes of elementary pupils toward foreign-speaking people resulting from the study of a foreign language. *J. Exp. Educ.* 33: 65–69.

ROBINSON, E. S. 1927. The similarity factor in retroaction. *Amer. J. Psychol.* 39: 297–312.

——— and C. W. DARROW. 1924. The effect of length of list upon memory for numbers. *Amer. J. Psychol.* 35: 235–43.

——— and W. T. HERON. 1922. Results of variation in length of memorized material. *J. Exp. Psychol.* 5: 428–48.

ROEN, S. R. 1960. Personality and Negro-white intelligence. *J. Abn. Soc. Psychol.* 61: 148–50.

ROETHLISBERGER, F. J. and W. J. DICKSON. 1939. *Management and the Worker.* Cambridge, Mass.: Harvard Univ. Press.

ROGERS, C. 1959. Toward a theory of creativity. In H. A. Anderson (ed.) *Creativity and Its Cultivation.* New York: Harper, pp. 71–82.

ROSENBERG, D. and C. I. HOVLAND. 1960. *Attitude Organization and Change.* New Haven: Yale Univ. Press.

ROSENBLITH, JUDY. 1949. A replication of "Some roots of Prejudice." *J. Abn. Soc. Psychol.* 44: 470–79.

ROSENBLUM, S. 1956. The effects of differential reinforcement and motivation on prediction responses of children. *Child Developm.* 27: 99–108.

ROWLEY, FLORENCE. 1938. Motor coordination in the field of handwriting. Master's thesis, Boston Univ., School of Educ.

ROZENWEIG, S. 1943. An experimental study of "repression" with specific reference to need-persisture and ego-defensive reactions to frustration. *J. Exp. Psychol.* 32: 64–74.

RUNDQUIST, W. N. and VALERIE HUTT. 1961. Verbal concept learning in high school students with pictorial and verbal presentation of stimuli. *J. Educ. Psychol.* 52: 108–11.

RUSSELL, D. and T. SARASON. 1965. Test anxiety, sex, and experimental conditions in relation to anagram solution. *J. Pers. Soc. Psychol.* 1: 493–96.

RUSSELL, D. H. 1960. Concepts. In C. W. Harris (ed.) *Encyclopedia of Educational Research.* New York: Macmillan, pp. 323–39.

——. 1956. *Children's Thinking.* Boston: Ginn.

——. 1960. Higher mental processes. In C. W. Harris (ed.) *Encyclopedia of Educational Research.* New York: Macmillan, pp. 645–61.

RUST, M. M. 1931. The effect of resistance on intelligence scores of young children. *Child Dev. Mono.* New York: Teachers College, Columbia Univ., No. 6.

RYANS, D. G. 1963. *The role of television in an instructional system.* Waltham, Mass.: Brandeis Univ., Morse Communication Research Center.

SAFIER, G. 1964. A study in relationships between the life and earth concepts in children. *J. Genet. Psychol.* 105: 283–94.

SAND, MARGARET C. 1939. The effect of length of list upon retroactive inhibition when degree of learning is controlled. *Archives of Psychol.* 33: No. 238.

SANDIN, A. A. 1942. Social and emotional adjustments of regularly promoted and non-promoted pupils. Ed.D. dissertation, Teachers College, Columbia University.

SARASON, I. G. 1958. Effects on verbal learning of anxiety, reassurance, and meaningfulness of material. *J. Exp. Psychol.* 56: 427–77.

—— et al. 1960. *Anxiety in Elementary School Children.* New York: Wiley.

SATO, T. 1937. The relation between vision and school performance. *Nihon-Gakka Eisei.* 25: 423–24.

SAUGSTAD, P. 1952. Incidental memory and problem solving. *Psychol. Rev.* 59: 221–26.

SCATES, D. E. 1947. Fifty years of measurement and research in education. *J. Educ. Res.* 41: 241–64.

SCHAFER, R. and G. MURPHY. 1943. The role of autism in a visual figure ground relationship. *J. Exp. Psychol.* 32: 335–43.

SCHEIDEL, T. M. 1963. Sex and persuasibility. *Speech Mono.* 30: 353–58.

SCHIFFER, CLARA and ELEANOR HUNT. 1963. Illness among children: Data from U.S. National Health Survey. Washington, D.C.: *U.S. Children's Bureau Publications No. 405.*

SCHLOSBERG, H. 1954. Three dimensions of emotions. *Psychol. Rev.* 61: 81–88.

SCHOELER, H. and G. S. LESSER. 1967. *Teacher Education and the New Media.* Washington, D.C.: AACTE.

SCHOER, L. and S. LOVELL. 1963. Effect of intralist item similarity on paired associate learning by learners of high and low verbal ability. *J. Exp. Psychol.* 54: 249–52.

SCHRAMM, W. 1962. What we know about learning from instructional television. *Educational Television: The Next Ten Years.* Stanford, Calif.: The Institute for Communication Research, Stanford Univ., pp. 52–76.

SCREPEL, MARIE and H. R. LASLETT. 1936. On the loss of knowledge by junior high school pupils over the summer vacation. *J. Educ. Psychol.* 27: 299–303.

SCHRODER, H. M. and J. B. ROTTER. 1953. Rigidity as learned behavior. *J. Exp. Psychol.* 44: 141–50.

SCHULTZ, R. W. 1960. Problem solving behavior and transfer. *Harvard Educ. Rev.* 30: 67–77.

SCHWARTZ, F. O. 1940. Ocular factors in poor readers in the St. Louis public schools. *Amer. J. Ophthalmology.* 23: 535–38.

SCODEL, A. and P. MUSSEN. 1953. Social perceptions of authoritativeness and nonauthoritativeness. *J. Abn. Soc. Psychol.* 48: 181–84.

SCOTT, M. 1954. Learning rate of beginning swimmers. *Res. Quart.* 25: 91–99.

SCOTT, W. A. 1957. Attitude change toward reward of verbal behavior. *J. Abn. Soc. Psychol.* 55: 72–75.

SCOTTISH COUNCIL FOR RESEARCH IN EDUCATION. 1933. *The Intelligence of Scottish Children: A National Survey.* London: Univ. of London Press.

SEAGOE, M. V. 1936. The influence of degree of wholeness on whole-part learning. *J. Exp. Psychol.* 19: 763–68.

SEARS, PAULINE. 1940. Levels of aspiration in academically successful and unsuccessful school children. *J. Abn. Soc. Psychol.* 35: 498–536.

SEARS, R. R. 1937. Initiation of the repression sequence by experienced failure. *J. Exp. Psychol.* 20: 570–80.

SEASHORE, H. G. 1942. Some relationships of fine and gross motor abilities. *Res. Quart.* 13: 259–74.

SECHREST, L. 1963. Implicit reinforcement of responses. *J. Educ. Psychol.* 54: 197–201.

SECORD, P. F. and J. F. MULHARD. 1955. Individual differences in the perception of women's faces. *J. Abn. Soc. Psychol.* 50: 233–43.

SEELS, L. 1951. The relationship between measures of physical growth and gross motor performance. *Res. Quart.* May: 244–50.

SEIDMAN, J. 1955. *Readings in Educational Psychology.* Boston: Houghton-Mifflin, pp. 258–60.

SENDEN, M. VON. 1960. *Space and Sight.* Glencoe, Ill.: Free Press.

SHEFFIELD, F. D. and T. B. ROBY. 1950. Reward value of a non-nutritive sweet taste. *J. Comp. Physiol. Psychol.* 43: 471–81.

SHERMAN, M. 1927. The differentiation of emotional responses in infants. *J. Compar. Psychol.* 7: 265–84, 335–51; 1928, 8: 385–94.

SHIRLEY, MARY. 1931. *The First Two Years.* Minneapolis: Univ. of Minnesota Press.

SHULMAN, L. S. and E. R. KEISLAR. 1966. *Learning by Discovery: A Critical Appraisal.* Chicago: Rand-McNally.

SIAO-SUNG, DJANG. 1937. The role of past experience in the visual apprehension of masked forms. *J. Exp. Psychol.* 20: 29–59.

SIEGEL, L., J. ADAMS, and F. MACOMBER. 1960. Retention of subject matter as a function of large group instructional procedures. *J. Educ. Psychol.* 51: 9–13.

—— and LILA SIEGEL. 1967. A multivariate paradigm for educational research. *Psychol. Bull.* 68: 306–26.

SILLECK, S. B., JR. and C. W. LAPHA. 1937. The relative effectiveness of emphasis upon right and wrong responses in human maze learning. *J. Exp. Psychol.* 20: 195–201.

SILVER, R. J. 1952. Effect of amount of distribution of warming-up activity on retention in motor learning. *J. Exp. Psychol.* 44: 88–95.

SIMS, VERNA M. 1928. The relative influence of two types of motivation on improvement. *J. Educ. Psychol.* 19: 480–84.

SINGER, R. N. 1964. Massed and distributed practice in the acquisition and retention of a new basketball skill. *Res. Quart.* 35: 36–45.

SINHA, A. K. P. and S. N. SINHA. 1960. Intrasensory transfer in learning sequences. *J. Exp. Psychol.* 60: 180–82.

SISSON, E. D. 1939. Retroactive inhibition: serial versus random order presentation of material. *J. Exp. Psychol.* 23: 288–94.

——. 1939. Retroactive inhibition: the temporal position of interpolated activity. *J. Exp. Psychol.* 25: 228–33.

SITGREAVES, ROSEDITH, and H. SOLOMON. 1957. Research methods: status studies and sample surveys. *R. Educ. Res.* 27: 460–70.

SKAGGS, E. B. 1925. Further studies in retroactive inhibition. *Psychol. Mono.* 34: No. 161.

——, S. GROSSMAN, LOUIS KRUEGER, and W. C. F. KRUEGER. 1930. Further studies of the reading-recitation process in learning. *Archives of Psychol.* 18: No. 114.

SKINNER, B. F. 1938. *The Behavior of Organisms.* New York: Appleton-Century.

——. 1953. *Science and Behavior.* New York: Macmillan.

——. 1954. The science of learning and the art of teaching. *Harvard Educ. Rev.* 24: 86–97.

——. 1968. *The Technology of Teaching.* New York: Appleton-Century-Crofts.

——. 1958. Teaching machines. *Science.* 128: 969–77.

SLAMECKA, N. 1962. Retention of connected discourse as a function of duration of interpolated learning. *J. Exp. Psychol.* 63: 480–86.

SMELTZ, J. R. 1956. Retention of learnings in high school chemistry. *Sci. Teacher.* 23: 285–305.

SMITH, E. E. and S. S. KNIGHT. 1959. Effects of feedback on insight and problem solving efficiency in training groups. *J. Appl. Psychol.* 43: 209–11.

SMITH, H. P. and T. R. TATE. 1953. Improvement in reading rate and comprehension of subjects by training with the tachistoscope. *J. Educ. Psychol.* 44: 176–84.

SMITH, L. E. and J. S. HARRISON. 1962. Comparison of the effects of visual, motor, mental, and guided practice upon the speed and accuracy of performing a simple-eye-hand coordination test. *Res. Quart.* 33: 299–308.

SMITH, M. H., JR. 1949. The influence of isolation on memory. *Amer. J. Psychol.* 62: 405–11.

——. 1952. Instructional sets and habit interference. *J. Exp. Psychol.* 44: 267–72.

SMITH, MADORAH. 1926. An investigation of the development of the sentence and the extent of vocabulary in young children. *Univ. of Iowa Stud. Child Welf.* 5: 1–92.

SMITS, S. J. 1964. Reactions of self and others to the obviousness and severity of physical disability. *Dissertation Abstracts.* 25: 1324–25.

SMOCK, C. 1958. Perceptual rigidity and closure phenomenon as a function of manifest anxiety in children. *Child Developm.* 29: 237–47.

SOLBY, C. M. and R. SOMMER. 1957. Perceptual autism in children. *J. Gen. Psychol.* 56: 3–11.

SOLLEY, C. M. and G. MURPHY. 1960. *Development of the Perceptual World.* New York: Basic Books.

SOLLEY, W. H. 1952. The effects of verbal instruction of speed and accuracy upon the learning of a motor skill. *Res. Quart.* 23: 231–40.

SOLOMON, R. L. 1964. Punishment. *Amer. Psychol.* 19: 239–53.

SONES, A. M. and J. B. STROUD. 1940. Review, with special reference to temporal position. *J. Educ. Psychol.* 31: 665–76.

SONTAG, L. W., C. T. BAKER, and V. L. NELSON. 1958. Mental growth and personality development: a longitudinal study. *Mono. Soc. Res. Child Developm.* 23: 1–143.

——, S. I. PYLE, and J. CAPE. 1935. Prenatal conditions and the status of infants at birth. *Amer. J. Diseases of Children.* 50: 337–42.

SPENCE, K. W. 1956. *Behavior Theory and Conditioning.* New Haven: Yale Univ. Press.

——. 1960. *Behavior Theory and Learning: Selected Papers.* Englewood Cliffs, N.J.: Prentice-Hall.

——. 1945. An experimental test of the continuity and noncontinuity theories of discrimination learning. *J. Exp. Psychol.* 35: 253–66.

——. 1951. Theoretical interpretations of learning. In S. S. Stevens (ed.) *Handbook of Experimental Psychology.* New York: Wiley, pp. 690–729.

SPIKER, C. C. 1956. Effects of stimulus similarity on discrimination learning. *J. Exp. Psychol.* 51: 393–95.

——. 1956. A stimulus pretraining and subsequent performance in the delayed reaction experiment. *J. Exp. Psychol.* 52: 107–11.

SPITZ, R. A. 1945. Hospitalism: an inquiry into the genesis of psychiatric conditions of early childhood. *Psychoanalytic Study of the Child.* 1: 53–74.

SPITZER, H. F. 1939. Studies in retention. *J. Educ. Psychol.* 30: 641–56.

SPOERL, DOROTHY. 1951. Some aspects of prejudice as affected by religion and education. *J. Soc. Psychol.* 33: 69–76.

SPRINGER, N. N. 1938. A comparative study of the intelligence of a group of deaf and hearing children. *Amer. Ann. Deaf.* 83: 138–52.

SPRUNT, JULIE and F. W. FINGER. 1949. Auditory deficiency and academic achievement. *J. Speech Hearing Disorders.* 14: 26–32.

STAATS, A. W. and CAROLYN STAATS. 1963. *Complex Human Behavior.* New York: Holt, Rinehart & Winston.

——. 1958. Attitudes established by classical conditioning. *J. Abn. Soc. Psychol.* 57: 37–40.

STACEY, C. I. 1949. The law of effect in the retained situation with meaningful material. *Univ. of Minn. Studies in Educ. No. 2.* Minneapolis: Univ. of Minn. Press.

STANLEY, J. C. 1957. Research methods: experimental design. *Rev. Educ. Res.* 27: 449–59.

STARCH, D. 1927. *Educational Psychology.* New York: Macmillan, pp. 168–69.

START, K. B. 1960. Relationship between intelligence and effects of mental practice on the performance of a motor skill. *Res. Quart.* 31: 210–17.

STEPHENS, J. M. 1956. *Educational Psychology.* New York: Holt, Rinehart, & Winston, pp. 228.

STEVENS, S. S. 1951. Mathematics, measurement, and psychophysics. In *Handbook of Experimental Psychology.* New York: Wiley, pp. 1–49.

STEVENSON, H. and E. STEWART. 1958. A developmental study of racial awareness of young children. *Child Developm.* 29: 399–409.

STEVENSON, H. W. 1961. Developmental mental changes in the effects of reinforcement and nonreinforcement of a single response. *Child Developm.* 32: 1–5.

—— and G. MOUSHEGIAN. 1956. The effects of instruction and degree of training on shifts of discrimination responses. *Amer. J. Psychol.* 69: 281–84.

STICKELL, D. W. 1963. A critical review of the methodology and results of research comparing televised and face-to-face instruction. Unpublished doctoral thesis, The Pennsylvania State University, State College, Pennsylvania.

STOCK, DOROTHY. 1949. An investigation of interrelation between the self concept and feeling directed toward other persons and groups. *J. Consult. Psychol.* 13: 176–80.

STOLUROW, L. M. 1953. *Readings in Learning.* Englewood Cliffs, N.J.: Prentice-Hall.

STORDAHL, K. E. and C. M. CHRISTENSEN. 1956. The effect of study techniques on comprehension and retention. *J. Educ. Res.* 49: 561–70.

STRASSBURGER, R. C. 1950. Resistance to extinction of a conditioned operant as related to drive level at reinforcement. *J. Exp. Psychol.* 40: 473–87.

STRAUSS, A. and K. SCHUESSLER. 1951. Socialization, logical reasoning, and concept development of the child. *Amer. Socio. Review.* 16: 514–23.

STROUD, J. B. 1935. *Educational Psychology.* New York: Macmillan.

——. 1940. Experiments on learning in school situations. *Psychol. Bull.* 37: 777–97.

——. 1946. *Psychology in Education.* London: Longmans, Green, pp. 555–97.

—— and E. F. LINDQUIST. 1932. Sex differences in achievement in the elementary and secondary schools. *J. Educ. Psychol.* 33: 657–67.

—— and RUTH MAUL. 1933. The influence of age upon learning and retention of poetry and nonsense syllables. *J. of Genetic Psychol.* 42: 242–50.

—— and C. W. RIDGEWAY. 1932. The relative efficiency of the whole, part, and progressive part methods when trials are massed. *J. Educ. Psychol.* 23: 632–34.

——. 1942. The role of practice in learning. 41st Yearbook, *Nat'l. Soc. Study Educ.,* Part II: 353–76.

STROUND, J. and L. SCHIER. 1959. Individual difference in memory. *J. Educ. Psychol.* 285–92.

SUPPES, P. 1966. Mathematical concept formation in children. *Amer. Psychol.* 21: 139–50.

SUTHERLAND, JEAN. 1946. The effect of training in perceptual span on rate of reading and rate of perception. *J. Educ. Psychol.* 37: 378–80.

SWENSON, ESTHER. 1941. *Retroactive Inhibition: A Review of the Literature.* Minneapolis: Univ. of Minnesota Press.

——, G. L. ANDERSON, and C. L. STACEY. 1949. Learning theory in school situations. In *University of Minnesota Studies in Education.* Minneapolis: University of Minnesota Press, pp. 9–39.

SYMONDS, P. 1955. Characteristics of the effective teacher based on pupil evaluations. *J. Exp. Educ.* 23: 289, 310.

TAFT, R. and J. COVENTRY. 1958. Neuroticism, extraversion, and the perception of the vertical. *J. Abn. Soc. Psychol.* 58: 139–41.

TAYLOR, JANET. 1958. Anxiety level, stress, and verbal learning. *J. Abn. Soc. Psychol.* 57: 55–60.

——. 1958. The effects of anxiety level and psychological stress on verbal learning. *J. Abn. Soc. Psychol.* 57: 55–60.

—— and JEAN CHAPMAN. 1955. Anxiety and the learning of paired associates. *Amer. J. Psychol.* 68: 67–71.

TENENBAUM, S. 1944. Attitudes of elementary school children toward school, teachers, and classmates. *J. Appl. Psychol.* 134–41.

TERMAN, L. M. and M. A. MERRILL. 1937. *Measuring Intelligence.* Boston: Houghton Mifflin.

THOMPSON, W. C. 1956. A book-centered course versus a machine-centered course in adult reading improvement. *J. Educ. Res.* 49: 437–45.

THORNDIKE, E. L. 1916. *Educational Psychology.* New York: Teachers College, Columbia Univ.

——. 1932. *The Fundamentals of Learning.* New York: Teachers College, Columbia Univ.

——. 1931. *Human Learning.* New York: Appleton-Century.

——. 1933. The influence of irrelevant rewards. *J. Educ. Psychol.* 24: 1–15.

——. 1924. Mental discipline in high school studies. *J. Educ. Psychol.* 15: 98.

—— and R. S. WOODWORTH. 1901. The influence of improvement in one function upon efficiency of other functions. *Psychol. Rev.* 8: 247–61, 384–95, 553–64.

—— et al. 1928. *Adult Learning.* New York: Macmillan, p. 183.

THORNDIKE, R. L. and ELIZABETH HAGEN. 1955. *Measurement and Evaluation in Psychology and Education.* New York: Wiley.

THUNE, L. E. and B. J. UNDERWOOD. 1943. Retroactive inhibition as a function of degree of interpolated learning. *J. Exp. Psychol.* 32: 185–200.

THURLOW, BARBARA. 1960. Analysis of consistencies among intermediate grade teachers in evaluating pupil progress. Unpub. Master's thesis, Boston Univ.

THURSTONE, L. L. 1955. *The Differential Growth of Mental Abilities.* Chapel Hill, N.C.: Univ. of N.C. Psychometric Lab.

TIEDEMAN, D. 1947. A study of retention of classroom learning. *J. Educ. Res.* 41: 516–30.

TILTON, J. W. 1949. Intelligence test scores as indicators of ability to learn. *Educ. Psychol. Meas.* 9: 291–96.

TOLMAN, E. C. 1949. There is more than one kind of learning. *Psychol. Rev.* 56: 144–55.

——. 1949. *Purposive Behavior in Animals and Men.* Berkeley, Calif.: Univ. of California Press, p. 136.

——, C. S. HALL, and E. P. BRETNALL. 1932. A disproof of the law of effect and a substitution of the laws of emphasis, motivation, and disruption. *J. Exp. Psychol.* 15: 601–14.

—— and C. H. HONZIK. 1930. Introduction and removal of reward and maze performance in rats. *Univ. Calif. Publ. Psychol.* 4: 257–75.

——, B. F. RITCHIE, and D. KALISH. 1946. Studies in spatial learning: II. Place learning vs. response learning. *J. Exp. Psychol.* 36: 221–29.

——, ——, and ——. 1947. Studies in spatial learning: IV. The transfer of place learning to other starting paths. *J. Exp. Psychol.* 37: 39–47.

TORKELSON, G. M. (ed.) 1968. *Instructional Materials:* Educational Media and technology. *Rev. of Educ. Res.* 38: 1–195.

TORMEY, T. J. 1934. The effect of drill upon the specific and general comprehension of historical content. *Univ. of Iowa Studies in Educ.* 9: No. 1, 151–81.

TORRANCE, E. P. 1960. Educational achievement of the highly intelligent and highly creative: eight partial replications of the Getzel-Jackson study. Minneapolis: Univ. of Minn. *Bur. of Educ. Res.*

TRAINOR, DORIS and CONSTANCE ROGERS. 1955. Adjustment of non-promoted and regularly promoted children in the same classrooms. Unpub. M.Ed. thesis, Boston Univ.

TRAVIS, R. C. 1939. Length of the practice period and efficiency in motor learning. *J. Exp. Psychol.* 24: 339–45.

TREMBLY, D. 1964. Age curve differences between natural and acquired intellectual characteristics. Paper presented at Amer. Psychol. Assn.

TROWBRIDGE, M. H. and H. CASON. 1932. An experiment study of Thorndike's theory of learning. *J. Gen. Psychol.* 7: 245–88.

TUCKMAN, J. and I. LORGE. 1962. Individual ability as a determinant of group superiority. *Hum. Rel.* 15: 45–51.

TWINING, P. E. 1940. The relative importance of intervening activity and lapse of time in the production of forgetting. *J. Exp. Psychol.* 26: 483–501.

TWINING, W. 1949. Mental and physical practice in learning a motor skill. *Res. Quart.* 20: 432–36.

TYLER, BONNIE. 1958. Expectancy of eventual success as a factor in problem solving behavior. *J. Educ. Psychol.* 49: 166–72.

TYLER, LEONA. 1963. *Tests and Measurements*. Englewood Cliffs, N.J.: Prentice-Hall.

TYLER, R. W. 1933. Permanence of learning. *J. Higher Educ.* 4: 203–4.

ULMER, G. 1939. Teaching geometry to cultivate reflective thinking: An experimental study with 1239 high school pupils. *J. Exp. Educ.* 8: 18–25.

UNDERWOOD, B. J. 1957. Interference and forgetting. *Psychol. Rev.* 64: 49–60.

——. 1951. Studies of distributed practice: III. The influence of stage of practice in serial learning. *J. Exp. Psychol.* 42: 291–95.

——. 1961. Ten years of massed practice on distributed practice. *Psychol. Rev.* 68: 229–47.

——. 1963. Verbal learning in the educative process. *Harvard Educ. Rev.* 34: 362–70.

——, W. N. RUNDQUIST, and R. W. SCHULTZ. 1959. Response learning in paired associate lists as a function of intralist similarity. *J. Exp. Psychol.* 70–78.

—— and J. RICHARDSON. 1956. The influence of meaningfulness, intralist similarity, and serial position on retention. *J. Exp. Psychol.* 52: 119–26.

—— and R. W. SCHULTZ. 1959. Studies of distributed of practice: XIX. The influence of intralist similarity with lists of low meaningfulness. *J. Exp. Psychol.* 106–10.

——. 1960. *Meaningfulness and Verbal Learning*. New York: Lippincott.

——. 1960. Response dominance and rate of learning paired associates. *J. Gen. Psychol.* 62: 153–58.

VAN BERGEIJK, W. A. and E. E. DAVID, JR. 1959. Delayed handwriting. *Percept. Mot. Skills.* 9: 347–59.

VAN DUSEN, F. and H. SCHLOSBERG. 1948. Further study of the retention of verbal and motor skills. *J. Exp. Psychol.* 38: 526–34.

VAN ORMER, E. B. 1932. Retention after intervals of sleep and of waking. *Archives of Psychol.* 21: No. 137.

VAN TILBORG, P. W. 1936. The retention of mental and finger maze habits. *J. Exp. Psychol.* 19: 334–41.

VANDELL, R. A., R. A. DAVIS, and H. A. CLERGSTON. 1943. The function of mental practice in the acquisition of motor skills. *J. Gen. Psychol.* 29: 243–50.

VINACKE, W. E. 1952. *The Psychology of Thinking*. New York: McGraw-Hill.

VOEKS, VIRGINIA. 1950. Formalization and clarification of a theory of learning. *J. Psychol.* 30: 341–62.

WAGNER, MAZIE and EUNICE STRABLE. 1935. Teaching high-school pupils how to study. *Sch. Rev.* 43: 577–89.

WALKER, E. L. 1958. Action decrement and its relation to learning. *Psychol. Rev.* 65: 129–42.

——. 1948. Drive specificity and learning. *J. Exp. Psychol.* 38: 39–49.

WALKER, F. R. 1961. Evaluation of three methods of teaching reading in the seventh grade. *J. Educ. Res.* 54: 56–58.

WALLAS, G. 1926. *The Art of Thought.* New York: Harcourt, Brace.

WARD, L. B. 1937. Reminiscence and rote learning. *Psychol. Mono.* 49: No. 220.

WASSERMAN, H. M. 1951. The effect of motivation and amount of pre-rest practice upon inhibitory potential in motor learning. *J. Exp. Psychol.* 42: 162–72.

WATERS, R. H. and Z. E. PEEL. 1935. Similarity in the form of original and interpolated learning and retroactive inhibition. *Am. J. Psychol.* 47: 477–81.

WATSON, B. 1938. The similarity factor in transfer and inhibition. *J. Educ. Psychol.* 29: 145–57.

WATSON, J. B. 1930. *Behaviorism.* New York: Norton.

WATSON, E. H. and G. H. LOWREY. 1951. *Growth and Development of Children.* Chicago: Yearbook.

WEATHERLY, D. 1963. Maternal response to childhood aggression and subsequent anti-semitism. *J. Abn. Soc. Psychol.* 66: 183–85.

WEAVER, H. E. and E. H. MADDEN. 1949. "Direction" in problem-solving. *J. Psychol.* 27: 331–45.

WECHSLER, D. 1962. Engrams, memory storage, and mnemonic coding. *Amer. Psychol.* 17: 149–53.

——. 1958. *The Measurement and Appraisal of Adult Intelligence.* Baltimore: Williams and Wilkins.

WEINER, B. 1966. Effects of motivation on the availability and retrieval of memory traces. *Psychol. Bull.* 65: 24–37.

WEINER, I. and R. ADER. 1965. Direction of aggression and adaption to free operant avoidance conditioning. *J. Person. Soc. Psychol.* 2: 426–29.

WEINER, M. 1955. Word frequency or motivation in perceptual defense. *J. Abn. Soc. Psychol.* 51: 214–18.

WELCH, L. and L. LONG. 1943. Comparison of reasonability of two age groups. *J. Genet. Psychol.* 62: 63–76.

——. 1940. The higher structural phases of concept formation in children. *J. Psychol.* 9: 59–95.

——. 1942. Methods used by children in solving inductive reasoning problems. *J. Psychol.* 14: 269–75.

WELFORD, A. T. 1951. *Skill and Age: An Experimental Approach.* London: Oxford.

WERNER, O. H. 1930. The influence of the study of modern foreign languages on the development of desirable abilities. *Studies in Modern Language Teaching.* New York: Macmillan, pp. 99–145.

WHITE, M. M. and MARGARET MC LEOD RATLIFF. 1934. The relation of affective tone to the learning and recall of words. *Amer. J. Psychol.* 46: 92–98.

WHITELY, P. L. 1927. The dependence of learning and recall upon prior intellectual activities. *J. Exp. Psychol.* 10: 489–508.

WICKSTROM, R. 1958. Comparative study of methodologies for teaching gymnastics and tumbling stunts. *Res. Quart.* 29: 109–15.

WILDEN, PEGGY. 1956. Comparison of two methods of teaching beginning basketball. *Res. Quart.* 27: 235, 241.

WITTREICH, W. J. and K. B. RADCLIFFE, JR. 1955. The influence of simulated experience upon the perception of the human figure. *J. Abn. Soc. Psychol.* 51: 493–95.

WITTROCK, M. 1963. Effect of certain sets upon complex verbal learning. *J. Educ. Psychol.* 54: 85–88.

WITTROCK, M. C. 1963. Response made in the programming of kinetic molecular theory concepts. *J. Educ. Psychol.* 54: 89–93.

———. 1963. Verbal stimuli in concept formation. *J. Educ. Psychol.* 54: 183–90.

——— and E. R. KEISLER. 1965. Verbal cues in the transfer of concepts. *J. Educ. Psychol.* 56: 16–21.

WOHLWILL, J. F. 1960. Developmental studies of perception. *Psychol. Bull.* 57: 249–88.

———. 1957. The abstraction and conceptualization of form, color and number. *J. Exp. Psychol.* 53: 304–9.

WOLF, THETA. 1938. The effect of praise and competition on the persisting behavior of kindergarten children. *University of Minnesota Institute Child Welfare Monograph Series, No. 15.*

WOOD, DOROTHY. 1961. *Test Construction.* Columbus, Ohio: Bobbs-Merrill.

WOODROW, H. 1927. The effect of type of training upon transference. *J. Educ. Psychol.* 18: 159–72.

WOODWORTH, R. S. 1958. *Dynamics of Behavior.* New York: Holt.

———. 1938. *Experimental Psychology.* New York: Holt.

———. 1940. *Psychology.* Fourth Edition. New York: Holt, p. 441.

WRIGHTSMAN, L. and F. NOBLE. 1965. Reactions to President's assassination and changes in philosophies of human nature. *Psychol. Rep.* 16: 159–62.

WULF, F. 1922. Beiträge zur psychologie der gestalt: VI. Uber die veranderung von vorstellungen (gedachtnis und gestalt). *Psychologische Forschung.* 1: 333–73.

WYER, R., D. WEATHERLEY, and G. TERREL. 1965. Social roles, aggression, and academic achievement. *J. Pers. Soc. Psychol.* 1: 645–49.

YOUNG, O. 1954. Rate of learning in relation to spacing of practice periods in archery and badminton. *Res. Quart.* 25: 231–45.

YOUNG, P. T. 1967. Affective arousal: Some implications. *Amer. Psychol.* 22: 32–40.

———. 1937. A study on the recall of pleasant and unpleasant words. *Amer. J. Psychol.* 49: 581–96.

YUDIN, L. and S. L. KATES. 1963. Concept attainment and adolescent development. *J. Educ. Psychol.* 54: 177–82.

ZANGWILL, O. L. 1938. The problem of retroactive inhibition in relation to recognition. *British J. Psychol.* 28: 229–47.

ZEIGARNIK, B. 1927. On finished and unfinished tasks. *A Source Book of Gestalt Psychology,* W. D. Ellis. New York: Harcourt, Brace, & World, p. 207.

ZELIGS, ROSE. 1951. Nationalities children would choose if they could not be Americans. *J. Gen. Psychol.* 79: 55–68.

——. 1954. Races and nationalities most and least liked by children. *J. Educ. Research.* 48: 1–15.

ZILLIG, MARIA. 1928. Einstellung and Aussage. *Zeitsch. fur Psychol.* 106: 64–66.

ZIMBARDO, P. 1958. Involvement and communication discrepancy as determinants of opinion conformity. *J. Soc. Psychol.* 48: 51–60.

ZIMMERMAN, R. R. 1960. An analysis of discrimination learning capacities in the infant rhesus monkey. *J. Comp. Psychol.* 54: 1–10.

ZINTZ, M. V. 1951. Academic acheivement and social and emotional adjustment of handicapped children. *Elem. School J.* 51: 502–7.

Index

Abom, M., 413
Abstract reasoning, 155–56
Academic preferences, 492
Accessory responses, 346–47
Accuracy, of performance, 349–50, 354–55
Achievement, range of, 271
Ackerman, W. I., 471
Acquisition, 116, 117–18
Action, and repetition, 334, 341–51
Activity, 312
Adams, J., 275
Adams, J. A., 227
Adamson, R., 229
Adaptation, 272
Ader, R., 332
Adjustment, 9
Adorno, T. W., 486, 499
Adrian, E. D., 315
Affect, 317–18, 485
Affective learning, 116, 304–39

Affective toning, 197–98, 414
Age, 116, 129, 131–37
Aided recall, 52
Alderman, R. B., 350
Allen, Doris, 407, 417
Allen, L., 22, 23, 153
Allen, W. H., 221
Allport, G. W., 484, 495
Alper, T. G., 194, 195
Alper, Thelma, 415
Alpert, Augusta, 467
Alpha waves, 315
Alprin, G., 132
Ames, Louise, 125–26
Ammons, R. B., 132, 213, 362–63
Amoroso, D., 502
Amplitude, 49–50
Anastasia, Anne, 22, 144, 258
Anger, 322, 330–32
Annett, J., 249, 396
Annual Review of Psychology, 431